AF873079

MAN AND SOCIETY

Freedom and Liberty

MAN AND SOCIETY
Freedom and Liberty

Edited by

John Phillips Resch
Bowling Green State University

and

John K. Huckaby
Late of Denison University

Charles E. Merrill Publishing Co.
A Bell & Howell Company
Columbus, Ohio

Copyright © 1972 by Charles E. Merrill Publishing Company, Columbus, Ohio. All rights reserved. No part of this book may be reproduced in any form, electronic or mechanical, including photocopy, recording, or any information storage and retrieval system without permission in writing from the publisher.

ISBN: 0-675-09160-8

Library of Congress Catalog Card Number: 71-179455

2 3 4 5 6 7 8—77 76 75 74 73

The reproduction on the cover is *The Curve* by Mary Callery, and is used through the courtesy of The Toledo Museum of Art, Toledo, Ohio.

Printed in the United States of America

For
Carol and our Families

CONTENTS

Part 3 RESPONSE TO INDUSTRIALIZATION [19th Century]

Part 4 REVOLUTION, WAR, AND CONTEMPORARY MAN [20th Century]

Part 5 MAN IN TODAY'S SOCIETY [1945–present]

Part 6 A SHORT STORY: An Allegory Of Man and Freedom

PREFACE

The idea for *Man and Society: Freedom and Liberty* evolved from teaching experiments with the Western civilization courses at Denison University and Bowling Green State University. In the fall of 1968 while John Huckaby and I were teaching at Denison an effort was made to depart from the conventional Western civilization survey course. John, director of the course, conceived the idea of building the course around the theme, freedom. The following semester it was introduced into the curriculum. We hoped to get the students to come to grips with their own concepts of freedom through a perspective of Western history while adding depth to their knowledge and appreciation of Western civilization. Although a few shortcomings appeared in the course, particularly in bibliography, student reactions were favorable. In the fall of 1969 I tried the same approach in my freshman Western civilization class at Bowling Green State University. The students again endorsed the course as refreshing and meaningful in both a personal and historical sense.

That spring John suggested putting together an anthology on freedom. That seemed like the obvious next step since bibliography was a major problem at Denison and Bowling Green. Although numerous readings in Western civilization existed, most selections were too short and unsubstantial to suit our purposes. The majority of the selections were aimed at giving the student a sample of an author's thought and an example of a mode of thinking for a certain period rather than coherently developing a topic. The use of paperbacks and mimeographed exerpts also proved to be costly, and resulted in omissions.

While preparing the readings that summer and reflecting upon our experiences and student evaluations, it became clear that the theme of freedom was too exclusive. The subjects of the selections were expanded to include perceptions of the nature of man, political and social theories, with freedom divided into concepts of liberty and self-actualization. John agreed with the changes in the scope of the anthology and throughout the remainder of the year contributed an enthusiasm and zeal for the project which lightened my burden of editing thousands of pages of Western philosophy, and political and social theories. His sudden death that winter was a loss of an admired colleague, and a generous and dear friend. I hope that this anthology will be part of the memory of John Huckaby's infectious quest for freedom and his commitment to creativity. We both had hoped that the study of man, society, freedom, and liberty would assist the student to see beyond his immediate functional goals, to become deeply involved in a probe of self and society, and to further his understanding of history.

Acknowledgements

The content of this anthology reflects the assistance and suggestions of many people who contributed their efforts to the project. I would like to thank our secretaries, Miss Patricia Bogni, Mrs. Joy Hillis, and Mrs. Phyllis Wulff for putting up with my jumbled corrections and never missing a deadline. I am grateful to the students who were so helpful in evaluating the courses; and, those students, particularly Patricia Kroner and Gail Wessel, who read through the first edition of the selections. I wish to express my appreciation to my former colleagues at Denison University, G. Wallace Chessman, William C. Dennis, Howard R. Holter, Norman H. Pollock, Morton B. Stratton, and David S. Watson for their assistance. My colleagues at Bowling Green State University, Thomas E. Carson, Lawrence J. Daly, and Douglas D. Daye helped to identify selections and improve the historical accuracy of the introductions. The manuscript was substantially improved through the criticisms of J. Russell Major, Alan R. Millett, and John Rothney. Special thanks go to Robert H. Bremner whose wise advice and encouragement has meant so much to me. My wife Carol added her love and support in the difficult task of preparing this anthology.

John Phillips Resch
Bowling Green State University

INTRODUCTION

Histories of Western civilization are largely chronicles of events and personalities. This anthology is an effort to further understand the contours of Western society by documenting the continuity and change in concepts of man, theories of government and social structure, and principles of freedom and liberty which helped to form Western culture. Where possible, each reading is sectioned so that the four topics—man, society, freedom, and liberty—are developed separately. In these selections freedom is interpreted philosophically and theologically as self-actualization, spiritual fulfillment, free choice, and free will. Although liberty is often used interchangeably with freedom, it is defined here as the right of the individual to speak and act in society without restraint. The anthology begins with the medieval perception of man, society, freedom, and liberty which resulted mainly from diverse mixtures of Greek philosophy and Christianity.

Greek philosophers, particularly Aristotle, portrayed man as a rational creature for whom society was a natural part of existence. Aristotle writes that "man is by nature a political animal. And he who is without a state is either a bad man or above humanity" (*Politics,* Book I, chap. 1). The purpose of man's life, as Aristotle sees it, is not to pursue freedom and liberty, but to achieve happiness and pleasure. He observes that although "the mass of mankind are evidently quite slavish in their tastes, preferring a life suitable to beasts . . .," true happiness and pleasure resulted from virtue (*Ethics,* Book I, chap. 5). Since man is not virtuous he has to be trained to act honorably, wisely, and moderately. Aristotle asserts that a just society uses laws to promote virtue and "noble action" (*Politics,* Book III, chap. 9). Aristotle's political and social theories evolve from an examination of the six basic forms of government—royalty and tyranny, aristocracy and oligarchy, constitutional government and democracy. He states that "the true forms of government . . . are those in which the one, or the few or the many, govern with a view to the common interest" (*Politics,* Book III, chaps. 6 and 7). He brands tyranny, oligarchy, and democracy as "perversions" and concludes that the proper structure of society depends upon the size of the state and the quality of its citizens. Christianity, as expressed in the New Testament, sees man as one of God's creatures who was conceived in sin as a legacy of Adam's disobedience to God. Man is also perceived as a dual being with a physical existence and a spiritual life. Being concerned with the spiritual life and salvation the Apostles disregard political theories and instruct Christians to obey all earthly masters while surrendering their souls to God. The New Testament stresses that freedom is spiritual and that it is only partially achieved on earth (1 Peter 2, lines 13-17). The Bible promises everlasting life with absolute freedom in God's Kingdom to persons who live by His commandments.

In the first reading from *The City of God,* St. Augustine develops the apostolic perception of man. Augustine's political and social theories, however, are shaped not only by the Scriptures, but also by the impact of the decaying Roman Empire. He writes that God made man a rational animal who desired happiness which "can come not from himself but only from God." However, individuals are too weak to resist sin which Augustine defines as living by man's rule. The result is a society, The City of Man, full of suffering, pain, and depravity, where the individual futilely struggles to overcome his "evil inclinations." Augustine rejects the Greek idea that society can be molded to extinguish sin and promote virtue; and, he ignores liberty because it was irrelevant to salvation. After placing mankind in an apparently hopeless condition Augustine asserts that man achieves virtue and freedom in heaven, the City of God, by following the Lord's rule. Evil persons are promised "an unending wretchedness that is called 'the second death' . . ." He affirms that God gives man freedom of will to choose the way of sin or the will of God. Augustine's interpretations of the irreconcilable societies of man and God contributes to the dualistic concept of the cosmos which underlay the division of power between the Church and temporal authorities in the Middle Ages. His views of man also reinforce an image of a life of conflict, inner struggles, and a tortuous test for admission into heaven. Finally, Augustine's doctrine of free will, which is included in this selection from *The City of God,* adds a significant dimension to the Christian concept of freedom.

The maturation of medieval society was accompanied by changes in political and social theories, refinement of the principle of free will, and an incipient concept of liberty. That climate of opinion which blended Aristotelian thought with Christian theology is reflected in the selections from *The Policraticus* by John of Salisbury and the works of St. Thomas Aquinas. In contrast to Augustine's pessimism toward the City of Man, John of Salisbury and Aquinas argue that temporal society be made to resemble—although it can never duplicate—God's Kingdom. The duty of the Church and government is to formulate laws approximating God's will, to punish sin, reduce temptation, and promote Christian virtues. At this point the similarity between the theories of John of Salisbury and Aquinas ends. Profound differences arise on the questions of who made the laws, if the laws applied to rulers as well as ruled, and the right of the people to overthrow tyrannical governments. Aquinas's conclusions represent a consensus of political and social thought in the late medieval period. The principles of government, the concept of liberty, and the assumptions of man's character developed by John of Salisbury reveal a dissenting opinion which later found expression in the Enlightenment and revolutionary doctrines.

During the Renaissance the traditional institutions and beliefs of medieval society eroded more quickly. Corruption within the Church, the expansion of capitalism and commerce, the increasing power of temporal authorities, and an enlarging interest in classical literature partially resulted in a drift toward secularism as illustrated in the political thought of Niccolo Machiavelli. Machiavelli envisages man as a dangerous animal needing control. He sees society as a crucible for the struggles for power where concepts of virtue, honor, liberty, and freedom are tools to gain and hold authority. In the selections from *The Prince* Machiavelli disregards the medieval belief that temporal life is a preparation for entrance into God's kingdom and instructs his readers in the art of power politics in a finite world. Man's temporal life is also the concern of St. Thomas More, but from the viewpoint of a Renaissance humanist rather than the vantage of Machiavelli's "Realpolitik." More shares Machiavelli's insight into man's weaknesses—pride, vanity, lust for power. However, More believes that the proper societal structure diminishes those weaknesses and brings out the goodness in man. More's political and social theories, while they are reminiscent of the principles of early Christian communities, contrast to many medieval ideas and practices. In the selections from Book II of *Utopia* More idealizes a state without private property where representatives to the government are elected by the people, and where the laws incorporate Christian morality and observe human dignity. In addition he sees life not in medieval terms of hardship and self denial, but as a pleasure and joy in virtuous fellowship. Perhaps More's most significant contribution is a social philosophy, reprinted in the reading, which stresses the rights of the individual—liberty—as well as the medieval principle of duties.

In the sixteenth century the Reformation theology of Martin Luther and John Calvin generated concepts of freedom and liberty, and theories of government and society, which profoundly altered the religious, social, and governmental patterns of Western civilization. Luther and Calvin believe that daily struggles are not just a test and preparation for heavenly life, but part of the progress toward creating a heaven on earth. In the passages from *Christian Liberty,* Luther asserts that sin and tyranny are overcome by the example of Christians who are spiritually free through faith in God. Luther thinks that eventually goodness extinguishes evil and that a condition of spiritual freedom combined with temporal liberty will be the foundation of society. Calvin dismisses Luther's principles of social passivity and prescribes doctrines of political activism. He asserts that some men have been predestined by God for salvation and that they are responsible for destroying tyranny and wickedness. The doctrine of predestination, developed in the excerpts from Calvin's *Institutes of the Christian Religion,* is a radical departure from Catholic and Lutheran concepts of free will. According to Calvin man does not choose salvation, but is "elected" by God to enter heaven. In a complicated and paradoxical argument, Calvin states that while salvation has already been determined by God, man is still at liberty to shape his society on earth. In fashioning his political and social theories, reprinted in this anthology, Calvin asserts that the elect have no duty to obey tyrannical governments. The elect have the right, indeed the duty, to create a state where church and government work harmoniously to extinguish corruption and ensure Christian morality. These beliefs precipitated challenges to existing governments, particularly in England, social experimentation in Geneva, Switzerland, and contributed to the transformation of European society at the end of the Middle Ages.

During the Enlightenment, the seventeenth through the eighteenth century, new political and social doctrines were used to defend and attack the prevailing culture and governmental structures. Those doctrines contained novel concepts of man, theories of government and society, and principles of liberty which are compared and contrasted in the selections from Thomas Hobbe's *Leviathan,* John Locke's *Second Treatise on Civil Government,* and Jean-Jacques Rousseau's *Social Contract.* Hobbes, Locke, and Rousseau envisage mankind living originally in an abstract "state of nature" where men are mentally and physically equal. They assert that society is formed by a covenant and that governments which violate that social contract are illegitimate.

Despite agreement on elementary assumptions their opinions of man, theories of society, and perceptions of liberty are quite different. Hobbes believes that man is in constant conflict and that he desires an absolutist government to enforce peace and order. Hobbes applies the theory of the social contract to explain and legitimize the creation of an authoritarian society and its restricted liberty. Unlike Hobbes, Locke stresses the compatability of mankind and the existence of inalienable liberties which he calls Natural Rights. Locke makes the classic arguments for government created by a social contract which guarantees control by the people and protection of individual liberties. Their viewpoints contributed to the ideological and political struggles which embroiled England in the seventeenth century. In addition, many of Locke's theories were adapted to the American concept of civil liberties expressed in the Bill of Rights.

Jean-Jacques Rousseau amplifies many of the currents of Enlightenment thought, yet he also has a distinct view toward man, society, and liberty. Rousseau believes that society civilizes man. He argues that individual liberty is ensured when men conform to what he calls the General Will of society. These views, fully developed in the selections from the *Social Contract,* contributed to the attack upon the French monarchy which tried to uphold remnants of medieval society. Many historians have credited Enlightenment thought with preparing the climate of opinion for the 1789 revolution in France.

Rejection and support of the French Revolution form the core of Edmund Burke's *Reflections on the Revolution in France* and Thomas Paine's *Rights of Man.* In advocating privilege and aristocratic government Burke asserts that society is created not to protect vague, abstract liberties, but as a "contrivance of human wisdom to provide for human wants." He writes that civil liberties are not approximations of fictitious Natural Rights, but conditional upon the level of civilization and the character of man. Paine's reply, partly reprinted below, refutes Burke's arguments for an aristocratic government and restricted liberty. Paine eloquently appeals for a republican government which ensures Natural Rights and guarantees full liberty for the individual.

In the nineteenth century, Enlightenment perceptions of man, society and liberty faded before the emergence of an industrial state, and a more complex social and political order. Unlike earlier writers, John Stuart Mill, Herbert Spencer, Karl Marx, and Freidrich Engels believed that the state was a collective tyranny which restricted liberty and repressed freedom. Their concept of freedom was based neither on Christian spirituality nor free will, but on individual fulfillment and self-actualization.

In the sections from *On Liberty,* Mill reveals his view of society as a convenient political and social framework in which each person fully develops his individuality. He argues that freedom depends upon protection from the tyranny of the majority and the pressure by society to conform to its values. From this vantage Mill turns to an analysis of liberty and authority. Mill defines civil liberty as "the nature and limits of power which can be legitimately exercised by society over the individual." In setting up the "limits of power" he writes that "whatever crushed individuality is despotism, by whatever name it may be called and whether it professes to be called enforcing the will of God or the injunctions of men." Yet, Mill also supports the principle that society has the right to interfere with the individual when his behavior is harmful to another person. In the last part of the selection Mill tries to apply his two rules and resolve their contradictions. Despite shortcomings in that effort Mill believes that his principles of liberalism and utilitarianism create the best balance between liberty and authority to encourage freedom.

Herbert Spencer shares Mill's goals but, as the sections from *Social Statics* reveal, he rejects Mill's assumptions about the nature of man and society, and principles of liberty. Spencer considers man an irrational, impulsive, and brutish creature. He believes that society is part of an evolutionary process in which mankind progresses from a lower to a higher form. The only duty of government is to enforce the limits of liberty suitable to the level of civilization. Spencer defines liberty as "equal freedom" which means that each person has the "fullest liberty to exercise his facilities compatible with the possession of the like liberties of every man." Spencer's principles were a foundation for Social Darwinism and a reinforcement of laissez faire economics.

The communist ideology of Marx and Engels reflected and contributed to the social and political upheavals of industrial Europe. Marx and Engels believe that human character is molded by the system of production and distribution. In the selections from *The Communist Manifesto* and *Socialism: Utopian and Scientific,* Marx and Engels develop their dialectic view of social processes, the creed of capitalist oppression, and the doctrine of proletarian revolution. They believe that liberals, Darwinists, and utopian socialists are merely tinkering with capitalism. Those efforts only masked the truth, according to Marx and Engels, that liberty and freedom are impossible until classes are destroyed, private property is abolished, and power is given to the proletariat.

In the twentieth century Nicolai Lenin applied the doctrines of Marx and Engels in the Russian Revolution. Lenin also recast parts of those creeds to fit the struggle for power in Russia. In the *State and Revolution,* which was written on the eve of the 1917 Bolshevik Revolution, Lenin analyzes the relation of revolution and government to freedom and liberty. He states that the end of all revolutions has to be freedom, not the substitution of one authority for another. He argues that freedom is only possible by destroying capitalism and replacing it with communism. As the reading points out, Lenin believes that even communism is ephemeral. The final stage of societal development is the total abolition of the state. Then, he predicts, the individual will experience complete liberty and freedom, and for the first time become his own master.

The revolution in Russia was not the only major upheaval in the first part of the twentieth century to affect the course of Western civilization. Between 1921 and 1939 fascist insurgents took over power in Italy, Germany, and Spain. The fascists, according to Benito Mussolini, rejected humanist and liberal traditions in Western civilization. In *The Political and Social Doctrines of Fascism,* Mussolini asserts that the state is the only "spiritual and moral fact." Fascism substitutes the worship of the state for the worship of God. Mussolini reduces man to an irrational and insignificant creature for whom concepts of liberty and freedom are meaningless.

The appearance of fascism provoked countless studies on the origin and appeal of that secular cult. Historical explanations have stressed the importance of the catastrophic effects of World War I and the emergence of extraordinary political personalities such as Mussolini and Hitler. In *Escape From Freedom,* Eric Fromm adds a social-psychological dimension to the historical accounts. Fromm sees fascism—or totalitarianism as Hanna Arendt later called it—as an aberration nurtured by the modern industrial state. In the first part of the reading Fromm portrays man as a complex biological, psychological, and spiritual being who requires security, liberty, and freedom. He states that industrial society preaches individualism, but extinguishes liberty and freedom by converting men into automatons. The resulting isolation and powerlessness create the psychological and social milieu for fascism in all industrial societies. He warns that the character of the state has to be changed to prevent fascism in the democratic nations. Fromm concludes that a reformed society must provide security, "freedom from" and "freedom to," which he defines as fulfilling the rational powers of the "self."

The military defeat of fascism did not extinguish the conditions which deprived man of his liberty and freedom. Recent society has been tormented with anxiety, doubt, periods of hopelessness and conformity, constant warfare in the hot and cold varieties, and the spectre of nuclear destruction. These conditions have generated diverse views toward man, society, freedom, and liberty. In the reprinted portions of *Existentialism and Humanism* Jean-Paul Sartre focuses on the nature of man and freedom. Sartre rejects preconceived notions of human nature. Man "is what he wills, and as he conceives himself after already existing." He is "nothing else but that which he makes himself." Sartre asserts that questions of morality, spirit, and rationality are irrelevant to the meaning of man and freedom. He dismisses political and social theories because they have nothing to do with becoming a "total being." Society is merely the place where each man unfolds his true self and realizes his freedom.

While Sartre dismisses standards, values, and society in the process of "becoming," Herbert Marcuse and Peter Drucker continue the traditional inquiry into the impact of society upon man's character, the degree of liberty, and the quality of freedom. In the *One Dimensional Man* Marcuse reaffirms many of Fromm's observations and adds that the technocratic society has betrayed its promise of liberty and freedom by becoming another form of totalitarianism. Physical needs are met, but individuality—the self—is largely extinguished. He concludes that human dignity and freedom have to be restored by revolution. He points to the emergence of a new revolutionary class composed of alienated people who are conscious of their servitude. Marcuse states that current violence between the establishment and the new revolutionaries is part of their effort to restore liberty and freedom to society.

Unlike Marcuse, Peter Drucker stresses that society is not a monolithic structure which overwhelms the individual with a smooth and comfortable tyranny. In the parts from *The Age of Discontinuity,* Drucker states that the modern state is pluralistic. The multiplicity of organizations permits the individual greater political liberty and more opportunities for freedom than in previous societies. The greatest challenge facing mankind in achieving liberty and freedom is himself and not the mysterious powers of technology.

This mosaic of Western social and political thought concludes with a short story, "The Long Sheet," by William Sansom. His allegory of man and freedom with its surprising as well as familiar themes captures the transcendent qualities of Western culture. The surrealistic setting for the story symbolizes man's timeless search to understand the meaning of self, society, freedom, and liberty.

Part 1

THE LATE MIDDLE AGES

12th—16th Centuries

MEDIEVAL

St. Augustine

One of the earliest and most influential interpreters of Christianity was Aurelius Augustine (354-430), the Bishop of Hippo and a saint in the Catholic Church. His explanations of God, man, society, and free will contributed to a dualistic concept of the cosmos which underlay the division of power between the Church and temporal authorities in the late Middle Ages. His views also helped to shape the Medieval frame of mind.

Augustine was born of a pagan father and a Christian mother near the ancient city of Hippo Regius, now the Algerian city of Bône. His youth was immersed in sensual pleasures which resulted in a bastard son and a tortured conscience. He tried to escape from his guilt and to find meaning in life through Manicheism, a popular philosophy which saw all life as a conflict between good and evil. Augustine became skeptical of Manicheism and in 386 he turned to Christianity for spiritual fulfillment. In 391 Augustine became a priest and five years later he was appointed the Bishop of Hippo, a position he held the rest of his life. As Bishop, Augustine defended Christianity and attacked heresy through *The Confessions* (written about 400) and *The City of God* (written between 413 and 426).

In *The City of God* Augustine refuted charges that Christianity had caused the collapse of the Roman Empire. He also fashioned an interpretation of God, the character of man, the nature of freedom and society which helped shape medieval thought and social structure. Augustine stated that God was omnipotent and omniscient and that He had created man as a rational animal with a will that was free and a character that was both good and bad. Augustine argued that while man was free—possessed free will—Adam's disobedience of God and his expulsion from the Garden of Eden had led all men to be tempted by evil and enslaved by sin. Man's imperfect reason, pride, and passion for power were the foundation of earthly society which Augustine described as lawless, cruel, and full of suffering, pain, and depravity. That City of Man conflicted with the Heavenly City of God which was filled with beauty, love, and virtue. Because the two cities would never be united man must spend his temporal life preparing to enter Heaven. Augustine believed that men who had faith in God and tried to follow His will would enter the City of God to experience eternal purity, happiness, and absolute freedom.

I.
God, Man And Freedom Of Will

This supreme and true God—with His Word and Holy Spirit which are one with Him—this one omnipotent God is the creator and maker of every soul and of every body. All who find their joy in truth and not in mere shadows derive their happiness from Him. He made man a rational animal, composed of soul and body. He permitted man to sin—but not with impunity—and He pursued him with His mercy. He gave men—both good and bad—their being, as He gave being to the rocks. He let men share generative life in common with the trees, and the life of the senses with the beasts of the fields, but the life of intelligence only with the angels. God is the Author of all measure, form, and order; of all size, number and weight. He is the source of every nature, of whatever sort or condition; of the seed of every form and the form of every seed and the movement of both seeds and forms. He gave to all flesh its beginning, beauty, health, and power of reproduction; the arrangement of its members and the general well-being of a balanced whole. To His irrational creatures He gave memory, perception, and appetite, but to His rational creatures He added a mind with intelligence and will.

He left no part of this creation without its appropriate peace, for in the last and least of all His living things the very entrails are wonderfully ordered—not to mention the beauty of birds' wings, and the flowers of the fields and the leaves of trees. And above the beauty of sky and earth is that of angels and of man. How, then, can anyone believe that it was the will of God to exempt from the laws of His providence the rise and fall of political societies?*

When a man lives 'according to man' and not 'according to God' he is like the Devil. For, even an angel had to live according to God and not according to an angel if he were to remain steadfast in the truth, speaking the truth out of God's grace and not lying out of his own weakness. The same Apostle elsewhere says of man: 'Yet if God's truth has abounded through my lie.'[1] Notice that he says 'my lie' and 'God's truth.' So, then, when a man lives according to truth, he lives not according to himself but according to God. For it was God who said: 'I am the truth.'[2]

When man lives according to himself, that is to say, according to human ways and not according to God's will, then surely he lives according to falsehood. Man himself, of course, is not a lie, since God who is his Author and Creator could not be the Author and Creator of a lie. Rather, man has been so constituted in truth that he was meant to live not according to himself but to Him who made him—that is, he was meant to do the will of God rather than his own. It is a lie not to live as a man was created to live.

Man indeed desires happiness even when he does so live as to make happiness impossible. What could be more of a lie than a desire like that? This is the reason why every sin can be called a lie. For, when we choose to sin, what we want is to get some good or get rid of something bad. The lie is in this, that what is done for our good ends in something bad, or what is done to make things

---

Reprinted from Saint Augustine, *The City of God,* ed. Vernon J. Bourke, (Garden City: Image Books, 1958), Book V, Chap. 11; Book XIV, Chaps. 4, 6, 11, 28; Book XV, Chap. 5; Book XIX, Chaps. 27, 28; Book XXII, Chaps. 22, 24, 30, by permission of the Fathers of the Church, Inc.

*Book V, chap. 11.

[1] Cf. Rom. 3.7.

[2] John 14.6.

better ends by making them worse. Why this paradox, except that the happiness of man can come not from himself but only from God, and that to live according to oneself is to sin, and to sin is to lose God?*

Man's will, then, is all-important. If it is badly directed, the emotions will be perverse; if it is rightly directed, the emotions will be not merely blameless but even praiseworthy. The will is in all of these affections; indeed, they are nothing else but inclinations of the will. For, what are desire and joy but the will in harmony with things we desire? And what are fear and sadness but the will in disagreement with things we abhor?

The consent of the will in the search for what we want is called desire; joy is the name of the will's consent to the enjoyment of what we desire. So, too, fear is aversion from what we do not wish to happen, as sadness is a disagreement of the will with something that happened against our will. Thus, according as the will of a man is attracted or repelled by the variety of things which he either seeks or shuns, so is it changed or converted into one or other of these different emotions.

It is clear, then, that the man who does not live according to man but according to God must be a lover of the good and, therefore, a hater of evil; since no man is wicked by nature but is wicked only by some defect, a man who lives according to God owes it to wicked men that his hatred be perfect, so that, neither hating the man because of his corruption nor loving the corruption because of the man, he should hate the sin but love the sinner. For, once the corruption has been cured, then all that is left should be loved and nothing remains to be hated.†

Take the case of the will. Its choice is truly free only when it is not a slave to sin and vice. God created man with such a free will, but, once that kind of freedom was lost by man's fall from freedom, it could be given back only by Him who had the power to give it. Thus, Truth tells us: 'If therefore the Son makes you free, you will be free indeed.' He might equally have said: 'If, therefore, the Son saves you, you will be saved indeed.' For the same reason that God's Son is our Saviour He is also our Liberator.‡

II.
The Society Of Man And The Society Of God Compared

. . . two societies have issued from two kinds of love. Worldly society has flowered from a selfish love which dared to despise even God, whereas the communion of saints is rooted in a love of God that is ready to trample on self. In a word,

---

*Book XIV, chap. 4.
† Book XIV, chap. 6.
‡ Book XIV, chap. 11.

this latter relies on the Lord, whereas the other boasts that it can get along by itself. The city of man seeks the praise of men, whereas the height of glory for the other is to hear God in the witness of conscience. The one lifts up its head in its own boasting; the other says to God: 'Thou art my glory, thou liftest up my head.'[3]

In the city of the world both the rulers themselves and the people they dominate are dominated by the lust for domination; whereas in the City of God all citizens serve one another in charity, whether they serve by the responsibilities of office or by the duties of obedience. The one city loves its leaders as symbols of its own strength; the other says to its God: 'I love thee, O Lord, my strength.'[4] Hence, even the wise men in the city of man live according to man, and their only goal has been the goods of their bodies or of the mind or of both; though some of them have reached a knowledge of God, 'they did not glorify him as God or give thanks but became vain in their reasonings, and their senseless minds have been darkened. For while professing to be wise (that is to say, while glorying in their own wisdom, under the domination of pride), 'they have become fools, and they have changed the glory of the incorruptible God for an image made like to corruptible man and to birds and four-footed beasts and creeping things' (meaning that they either led their people, or imitated them, in adoring idols shaped like these things), 'and they worshipped and served the creature rather than the Creator who is blessed forever.'[5] In the City of God, on the contrary, there is no merely human wisdom, but there is a piety which worships the true God as He should be worshiped and has as its goal that reward of all holiness whether in the society of saints on earth or in that of angels of heaven, which is 'that God may be all in all.'[6]*

Now, the city of man was first founded by a fratricide who was moved by envy to kill his brother, a man who, in his pilgrimage on earth, was a citizen of the City of God. It need not surprise us, then, that long afterwards, in the founding of that city which was to dominate so many peoples and become the capital of that earthly city with which I am dealing, the copy, so to speak, corresponded to the original—to what the Greeks call the archetype. For, in both cases, we have the same crime. As one of the poets puts it: 'With brother's blood the earliest walls were wet.'[7] For Rome began, as Roman history records, when Remus was killed by Romulus, his brother. However, in this case, both men were citizens of the earthly city. It was the ambition of both of them to have the honor of founding the Roman republic, but that was an honor that could not be shared; it had to belong to one or the other. For, no one who had a passion to glory in domination could be fully the master if his power were diminished by a living co-regent. One of the two wanted to have the whole of the sovereignty; therefore, his associate was removed. Without the crime, his position would have had less power, but more prestige. However, the crime made everything worse than before.

In the case of the brothers Cain and Abel, there was no rivalry in any cupidity for the things of earth, nor was there any envy or temptation to murder arising

---

* Book XIV, chap. 28.

[3] Ps. 3.4.

[4] Ps. 17.2.

[5] Rom. 1.21-25.

[6] 1 Cor. 15.28.

[7] Lucan, *Pharsalia* 1.95.

from a fear of losing the sovereignty if both were ruling together. In this case, Abel had no ambition for domination in the city that his brother was building. The root of the trouble was that diabolical envy which moves evil men to hate those who are good for no other reason than that they are good. Unlike material possessions, goodness is not diminished when it is shared, either momentarily or permanently, with others, but expands and, in fact, the more heartily each of the lovers of goodness enjoys the possession the more does goodness grow. What is more, goodness is not merely a possession that no one can maintain who is unwilling to share it, but it is one that increases the more its possessor loves to share it.

What, then, is revealed in the quarrel between Remus and Romulus is the way in which the city of man is divided against itself, whereas, in the case of Cain and Abel, what we see is the enmity between the two cities, the city of man and the City of God. Thus, we have two wars, that of the wicked at war with the wicked and that of the wicked at war with the good. For, of course, once the good are perfectly good, there can be no war between them. This much is true, however, that while a good man is still on the way to perfection one part of him can be at war with another of his parts; because of this rebellious element, two good men can be at war with each other. The fact is that in everyone 'the flesh lusts against the spirit, and the spirit against the flesh.' [8]

The spiritual longing of one good man can be at war with the fleshly passion of another just as fleshly passion in one man can resist spiritual tendencies in another. And the war here is much like that between good and wicked men. So, too, a good deal like the war of the wicked against the wicked is the rivalry of fleshly desires in two good men, and this will continue until grace wins the ultimate victory of soundness over sickness in both of them.*

The City of God, . . . has a peace of its own, namely, peace with God in this world by faith and in the world to come by vision. Still, any peace we have on earth, whether the peace we share with Babylon or our own peace through faith, is more like a solace for unhappiness than the joy of beatitude. Even our virtue in this life, genuine as it is because it is referred to the true goal of every good, lies more in the pardoning of sins than in any perfection of virtues. Witness the prayer of God's whole City, wandering on earth and calling out to Him through all her members: 'Forgive us our debts as we also forgive our debtors.' [9]

This prayer is effective, not on the lips of those whose faith without works is dead,[10] but only on the lips of men whose faith works through charity.[11] This prayer is necessary for the just because their reason, though submissive to God, has only imperfect mastery over their evil inclinations so long as they live in this world and in a corruptible body that 'is a load upon the soul.' [12] Reason may give commands, but can exercise no control without a struggle. And, in this time of weakness, something will inevitably creep in to make the best of soldiers—whether in victory or still in battle with such foes—offend by some small slip of the tongue, some

* Book XV, chap. 5.

[8] Gal. 5.17.

[9] Matt. 6.12.

[10] Cf. James 2.17.

[11] Cf. Gal. 5.6.

[12] Wisd. 9.15.

passing thought, if not by habitual actions. This explains why we can know no perfect peace so long as there are evil inclinations to master. Those which put up a fight are put down only in perilous conflict; those that are already overcome cannot be kept so if one relaxes, but only at the cost of vigilant control. These are the battles which Scripture sums up in the single phrase: 'The life of man upon earth is a warfare.' [13]

Who, then, save a proud man, will presume that he can live without needing to ask God: 'Forgive us our debts'? Not a great man, you may be sure, but one blown up with the wind of self-reliance—one whom God in His justice resists while He grants His grace to the humble. Hence, it is written: 'God resists the proud, but gives grace to the humble.' [14]

This, then, in this world, is the life of virtue. When God commands, man obeys; when the soul commands, the body obeys; when reason rules, our passions, even when they fight back, must be conquered or resisted; man must beg God's grace to win merit and the remission of his sins and must thank God for the blessings he receives.

But, in that final peace which is the end and purpose of all virtue here on earth, our nature, made whole by immortality and incorruption, will have no vices and experience no rebellion from within or without. There will be no need for reason to govern non-existent evil inclinations. God will hold sway over man, the soul over the body; and the happiness in eternal life and law will make obedience sweet and easy. And in each and all of us this condition will be everlasting, and we shall know it to be so. That is why the peace of such blessedness or the blessedness of such peace is to be our supreme good.

On the other hand, the doom in store for those who are not of the City of God is an unending wretchedness that is called 'the second death,' because neither the soul, cut off from the life of God, nor the body, pounded by perpetual pain, can there be said to live at all. And what will make that second death so hard to bear is that there will be no death to end it.*

III. Human Depravity And Suffering In The Society Of Man

This life of ours—if a life so full of such great ills can properly be called a life—bears witness to the fact that, from its very start, the race of mortal men has been a race condemned. Think, first, of that dreadful abyss of ignorance from which all error flows and so engulfs the sons of Adam in a darksome pool that no one can escape without the toll of toils and tears and fears. Then, take our very love for all those things that prove so vain and poisonous and breed so many heartaches, troubles, griefs, and fears; such insane joys in discord, strife, and war; such wrath

* Book XIX, chaps. 27, 28.

[13] Job 7.1.

[14] James 4.6; 1 Peter 5.5.

and plots of enemies, deceivers, sycophants; such fraud and theft and robbery; such perfidy and pride, envy and ambition, homicide and murder, cruelty and savagery, lawlessness and lust; all the shameless passions of the impure—fornication and adultery, incest and unnatural sins, rape and countless other uncleannesses too nasty to be mentioned; the sins against religion—sacrilege and heresy, blasphemy and perjury; the iniquities against our neighbors—calumnies and cheating, lies and false witness, violence to persons and property; the injustices of the courts and the innumerable other miseries and maladies that fill the world, yet escape attention.

It is true that it is wicked men who do such things, but the source of all such sins is that radical canker in the mind and will that is innate in every son of Adam.[15] For, our infancy proves with what ignorance of the truth man enters upon life, and adolescence makes clear to all the world how full we are of folly and concupiscence. In fact, if anyone were left to live as he pleased and to do what he desired, he would go through practically the whole gamut of lawlessnesses and lust—those which I have just listed and, perhaps, others that I refrained from mentioning.

Yet, for all this blight of ignorance and folly, fallen man has not been left without some ministries of Providence, nor has God, in His anger, shut up His mercies.[16] There are still within the reach of man himself, if only he will pay the price of toil and trouble, the twin resources of law and education. With the one, he can make war on human passion; with the other, he can keep the light of learning lit even in the darkness of our native ignorance.[17] This is the meaning of those many appeals to fear in disciplining the waywardness of growing children. That is why we have tutors and schoolmasters with their ferules and straps and canes, and why, in the training of a child we love, we use the authority of Holy Writ to 'beat his sides . . . lest he grow stubborn'[18]—else he may become too wild ever to be tamed. The point of all such human punishment is to help dispel our ignorance and to bridle our untamed desires—the double birthmark with which we come into this world.

As evidence of this inheritance we have only to recall how difficult it is to remember, how easy to forget; how hard to learn and how easy to be ignorant; how difficult to make an effort and how easy to be lazy. We need go no further to realize to what depths our damaged nature tends to gravitate and what aid it needs to be rescued from its inclinations. We are weighed down in soul and body by sloth and indolence, and disinclined to make an effort because, in fact, this price of effort, even for our good, is a part of the penalty we must pay for sin.

Such, then, are the penalties which must be paid even in childhood and merely for the purpose of learning what our elders want—and this is seldom really useful! But who can describe or even imagine all the later ills that befall mankind? When we are not victims of the lawlessness and lust of wicked men, we have to suffer the miseries that no one in our present condition can escape. Who can be free from fear or grief in a world of mourning and bereavement, of losses and legal

---

[15] *. . . ab illa tamen erroris et perversi amoris radice venientia, cum qua omnis filius Adam nascitur.*

[16] Cf. Ps. 76.10.

[17] *. . . in ipsis sensibus generis humani prohibitio et eruditio contra istas, cum quibus nascimur, tenebras vigilant et contra hos impetus obponuntur.*

[18] Eccli. 30.12.

penalties, of liars and deceivers, of the false imputations, violences and other wickednesses of our neighbors? Think of the tragedies of being robbed or reduced to slavery, of bonds and prison walls, of banishment and torture, of limbs cut off and eyes torn out, of bodies made to minister to an oppressor's lusts, and of all other no less dreadful possibilities.

And think of the dread we have of the countless accidents of nature, of the extremes of heat and cold, of winds and rains and floods, of thunder, lightning and winter storms, of earthquakes, landslides and openings in the earth; of stumbling, shying, biting horses; of poisoned fruits and waters, of pestilential air and animals diseased; of the harmful and often fatal bites of wild animals. Take, for example, the rabies resulting from the bite of a mad dog. Here we have the gentlest and most friendly of all animals making his own master more afraid of a dog than of lions or of dragons, because when a man has been infected by this poison he becomes so raging mad that he frightens his whole family far more than the wildest animals ever could.

Or think of the perils of voyagers at sea and of travelers on land. Even a man taking a walk is liable to the most unsuspected accidents. Here is a man in perfect health returning from downtown to his home; he slips and breaks his leg; the wound festers and he dies. Or take a man sitting down. You would think that no one could be safer, yet Heli, the priest, slipped from a chair and was killed.[19] Or take farmers and all who depend on them. There is the weather to be feared, the soil, the blights that ruin crops. At least, you might think, the fears would vanish when the crops are gathered and are in the barns. Yet I have known cases where a sudden flood has not only driven the men from the fields but has swept the grain from the barns.

Then there are the demons in a thousand forms that fill mankind with dread. Not even innocence is safe from their incursions. No innocence is greater than that of newly baptized children, yet, to give us a lesson in holy diffidence, even they are sometimes attacked by demons. God, who permits this tragedy, could not teach us more emphatically how much the misery of this life is to be moaned and how greatly the blessedness of eternity is to be desired.

Turn, now, to the maladies that afflict our bodies. Not even medical libraries have catalogued all the diseases; in most cases, it takes pain to drive out pain, so that medical care and cures can be as cruel as the complaints themselves.[20] Then there is hunger and thirst. Desperate men have been driven to drink human urine, sometimes their own, and to eat human flesh, and sometimes to kill others in order to eat them—and not always their enemies. There have been mothers driven to desperation by hunger and to the unbelievable monstrosity of devouring their own children.

Even sleep, which we think of as perfect rest, is made restless by dreadful dreams and nightmares so filled with unspeakable phantoms that seem so real that our whole being is filled with fear. And even when we are awake, we are often tortured even more cruelly by delirium induced by some toxic or diseased condition. Worse still are those weird phantasms evoked by malignant demons in the imaginations of perfectly healthy men; even when such men are not seduced by these imaginations to serve the Devil's purposes, the delusions are painfully humiliating.

---

[19] 1 Kings 4.18.

[20] . . . *etiam ipsa adiumenta et medicamenta tormenta sunt.*

From this all but hell of unhappiness here on earth, nothing can save us but the grace of Jesus Christ, who is our Saviour, Lord and God. In fact, the very meaning of the name, Jesus, is Saviour, and when we say 'save' we mean, especially, that He saves us from passing from the misery of this mortal life to a still more miserable condition, which is not so much a life as death. It is true that, even in this life on earth, through the intercession of the saints we have many holy comforts and great remedies. Nevertheless, such favors are not always given to those who ask—lest such favors be mistaken for the real purpose of religion, which is felicity in that other life in which all our ills will be no more. What grace is meant to do is to help good people, not to escape their sufferings, but to bear them with a stout heart, with a fortitude that finds its strength in faith.

To gain such fortitude we need, as even the wisdom of this world assures us, that true philosophy which, as Cicero says,[21] is given by the gods to very few and is a gift greater than any which the gods have given men, or even have the power to give. Here, surely, in this insistence on a true as opposed to any kind of philosophy, we have an admission by our main opponent, the pagan world, of the reality of supernatural grace. And what is more, if it is only to a few that there is given from on high this sole source of solace in the miseries of this life, the pagans should conclude that our human race, taken as a whole, has been condemned to pay mortal misery as a penalty for sin. And if, as they confess, there is no greater gift from God than this, then they should admit that it can be given by no less a divinity than the One than whom, as even the polytheists admit, there is no greater.*

IV.
Blessings From God In The Society Of Man

From all this misery, in which we admire the justice by which God punishes mankind, we must now turn to consider the multitude and munificence of the blessings which God's goodness bestows on the creatures who are ruled by His providence.

First, think of the blessing of fecundity which was bestowed upon man before he fell. God said: 'Be fruitful and multiply and fill the earth.'[22] That blessing did not cease because man sinned, for God willed it to remain in the race even after the race was condemned. Not even the canker of sin, which has involved mankind in the blight of death, was able to take from human seed the miracle of life, nor have human bodies lost that still more mysterious power, woven into their very texture, whereby the seed itself is produced. Thus, in the torrential stream of human history, two currents meet and mix: the current of evil which flows from Adam and that of good which comes from God. The original good includes two quite different things: the procreation of the body and the inbreathing of a soul.

---

* Book XXII, chap. 22.
[21] *De finibus*, 5,21.
[22] Gen. 1.28.

In regard to the principle of human life, God infused into it a capacity for reasoning and intellection. In infancy, this mental capacity seems, as it were, asleep and practically non-existent, but in the course of years it awakens into a life that involves learning and education, skill in grasping the truth and loving the good. This capacity flowers into that wisdom and virtue which enable the soul to battle with the arms of prudence, fortitude, temperance, and justice against error, waywardness, and other inborn weaknesses, and to conquer them with a purpose that is no other than that of reaching the supreme and immutable Good. Even when this Good is not attained, there still remains, rooted in all rational nature, a divinely given capacity for goods so high that this marvel of God's omnipotence is beyond any tongue to express or any mind to comprehend.

And, quite apart from those supernatural arts of living in virtue and of reaching immortal beatitude which nothing but the grace of God which is in Christ can communicate to the sons of promise and heirs of the kingdom, there have been discovered and perfected, by the natural genius of man, innumerable arts and skills which minister not only to the necessities of life but also to human enjoyment. And even in those arts where the purposes may seem superfluous, perilous and pernicious, there is exercised an acuteness of intelligence of so high an order that it reveals how richly endowed our human nature is. For, it has the power of inventing, learning and applying all such arts.

Just think of the progress and perfection which human skill has reached in the astonishing achievements of cloth making, architecture, agriculture and navigation. Or think of the originality and range of what has been done by experts in ceramics, by sculptors and by painters; of the dramas and theatrical spectacles so stupendous that those who have not seen them simply refuse to believe the accounts of those who have. Think even of the contrivances and traps which have been devised for the capturing, killing, or training of wild animals; or, again, of the number of drugs and appliances that medical science has discovered in its zeal for the preservation and restoration of men's health; or, again, of the poisons, weapons, and equipment used in wars, devised by military art for defense against enemy attack; or even of the endless variety of condiments and sauces which culinary art has discovered to minister to the pleasures of the palate.

It was human ingenuity, too, that devised the multitude of signs we use to express and communicate our thoughts—and, especially, speech and writing. The arts of rhetoric and poetry have brought delight to men's spirits by their ornaments of style and varieties of verse; musicians have solaced human ears by their instruments and songs; both theoretical and applied mathematics have made great progress; astronomy has been most ingenious in tracing the movements, and in distinguishing the magnitudes, of the stars. In general, the completeness of scientific knowledge is beyond all words and becomes all the more astonishing when one pursues any single aspect of this immense corpus of information. Last, but not least, is the brilliance of talent displayed by both pagan philosophers and Christian heretics in the defense of error and falsehood. (In saying this, of course, I am thinking only of the nature of the human mind as a glory of this mortal life, not of faith and the way of truth that leads to eternal life.)

Now, the Creator of this noble human nature is the true and supreme God whose providence rules all that He has created, whose power is unlimited, and whose justice is infinite; and, therefore, man could never have fallen into the miseries that he now suffers and is destined to suffer in eternity—excepting only the elect—unless the first man, the father of all the rest, had committed an enormous iniquity.

Turn now from man's mind to his body. It is true that it is no better than the body of a beast as far as dying is concerned and, in life, it is even weaker than that of many of the animals. Nevertheless, the human body is a revelation of the goodness of God and of the providence of the body's Creator. It is a body obviously meant to minister to a rational soul, as you can see from the arrangement of the human organs of sense and of man's other members. This is obvious, too, in man's specific appearance, form, and stature. The bodies of irrational animals are bent toward the ground, whereas man was made to walk erect with his eyes on heaven, as though to remind him to keep his thoughts on things above. And if we need further evidence to show to what kind of a mind the body was meant to minister, we have only to think of the marvelous mobility of the tongue and hands, so perfectly suited for speaking and writing, for the arts, and for the countless other activities of men.

What is more, quite apart from these practical purposes, there is in a man's body such a rhythm, poise, symmetry, and beauty that it is hard to decide whether it was the uses or the beauty of the body that the Creator had most in mind. It is clear that every organ whose function we know adds to the body's beauty, and this beauty would be still more obvious if only we knew the precise proportions by which the parts were fashioned and interrelated. I do not mean merely the surface parts which, no doubt, could be accurately measured by anyone with proper skill. I mean the parts hidden below our skin, the intricate complex of veins and nerves, the inmost elements of the human viscera and vital parts, whose rhythmic relationships have not yet been revealed. Surgeons, of course, have done something in their relatively crude anatomical study of corpses (and in the course of their hardly less inhuman operations on living bodies) to explore the last recesses of the organs they have had to handle in order to learn the best technique in dealing with this or that disorder. But what I have in mind is the rhythm of relationships, the *harmonia,* as the Greeks would say, whereby the whole body, inside and out, can be looked upon as a kind of organ with a music all its own. The beauty of this music no one has yet discovered, because no one has dared look for it. Nevertheless, if this total organic design could only be discerned, even in the seemingly ugly elements of the human viscera, there would be revealed to the soul so ravishing a beauty that no visible shapeliness of form that delights the eye—the mere minister of our mind—could be compared with it.

Of course, some parts of the human body appear to have no other purpose than to add to beauty, as the mamillae on a man's chest or the beard on his face. Certainly, if the beard were meant for protection rather than for beauty, it would have served a better purpose for the weaker sex, whose face remains uncovered. If, then, we argue from the facts, first, that, as everyone admits, not a single visible organ of the body serving a definite function is lacking in beauty, and, second, that there are some parts which have beauty and no apparent function, it follows, I think, that in the creation of the human body God put form before function. After all, function will pass and the time will come when we shall delight solely in the unlibidinous contemplation of one another's beauty, knowing that our joy will be giving glory to the Creator, of whom the Psalmist says: 'Thou hast put on praise and beauty.'[23]

And now, to pass from man to the rest of creation, what beauty for contemplation and what bounties for use God has scattered like largesse for man amid the weariness and miseries of his fallen and penalized lot! What words can describe the myriad beauties of land and sea and sky? Just think of the illimitable abundance and the marvelous loveliness of light, or of the beauty of the sun and moon and stars, of shadowy glades in the woods and of the colors and perfume of flowers, of the songs and plumage of so many varieties of birds, of the innumerable animals of every species that amaze us most when they are smallest in size. For example, the activity of ants and bees seems more stupendous than the sheer immensity of whales. Or take a look at the grandiose spectacle of the open sea, clothing and reclothing itself in dresses of changing shades of green and purple and blue. And what a delight when the ocean breaks into storm and can be enjoyed—at least from the shore where there is no fear of the fury of the waves!

Or think of God's bounty in the never-ending stores of foods that banish hunger; in the variety of flavors which a generous nature provides without calling on the skill of cooks to stimulate our sluggish appetite; in the medicinal value of so many foods, whether we are sick or healthy. We have to thank God, too, for the alternations of day and night, for the solace of soothing breezes, and for the plants and animals that provide the linen and wool for the making of our clothing. No one person could catalogue all of God's bounties. Each of the blessings which I have, as it were, piled up in a heap, contains a multitude of lesser blessings wrapped up within it, and if I were to unfold each of these packages and deal with the blessings in detail I should never end.

And, remember, all these favors taken together are but the fragmentary solace allowed us in a life condemned to misery. What, then, must be the consolations of the blessed, seeing that men on earth enjoy so much of so many and of such marvelous blessings? What good will God not give to those predestined to eternal life, if He gives so much to those who are doomed to death? What joys in the life of beatitude will God not shower on those for whom, in that life of misery, He allowed His only-begotten Son to suffer so many sorrows, even unto death? It was this that St. Paul had in mind when he wrote: 'He who has not spared even His own Son but delivered Him for us all, how can He fail to grant us also all things with Him.' Just imagine how perfectly at peace and how strong will be the human spirit when there will be no passion to play the tyrant or the conqueror, no temptation even to test the spirit's strength. And think of the mind's universal knowledge in that condition where we shall drink, in all felicity and ease, of God's own wisdom at the very source. Think how great, how beautiful, how certain, how unerring, how easily acquired this knowledge then will be. And what a body, too, we shall have, a body utterly subject to our spirit and one so kept alive by spirit that there will be no need of any other food. For, it will be a spiritual body, no longer merely animal, one composed, indeed, of flesh but free from every corruption of the flesh.*

---

* Book XXII, chap. 24.

[23] Ps. 103.1.

V.

The Perfection Of Man, Freedom And Society In The City Of God

Who can measure the happiness of heaven, where no evil at all can touch us, no good will be out of reach; where life is to be one long laud extolling God, who will be all in all; where there will be no weariness to call for rest, no need to call for toil, no place for any energy but praise. Of this I am assured whenever I read or hear the sacred song: 'Blessed are they that dwell in thy house, O Lord: they shall praise thee for ever and ever.' [24] Every fiber and organ of our imperishable body will play its part in the praising of God. On earth these varied organs have each a special function, but, in heaven, function will be swallowed up in felicity, in the perfect certainty of an untroubled everlastingness of joy. Even those muted notes in the diapason of the human organ, which I mentioned earlier, will swell into a great hymn of praise to the supreme Artist who has fashioned us, within and without, in every fiber, and who, by this and every other element of a magnificent and marvelous Order, will ravish our minds with spiritual beauty.[25]

These movements of our bodies will be of such unimaginable beauty that I dare not say more than this: There will be such poise, such grace, such beauty as become a place where nothing unbecoming can be found. Wherever the spirit wills, there, in a flash, will the body be. Nor will the spirit ever will anything unbecoming either to itself or to the body.

In heaven, all glory will be true glory, since no one could ever err in praising too little or too much. True honor will never be denied where due, never be given where undeserved, and, since none but the worthy are permitted there, no one will unworthily ambition glory. Perfect peace will reign, since nothing in ourselves or in any others could disturb this peace. The promised reward of virtue will be the best and the greatest of all possible prizes—the very Giver of virtue Himself, for that is what the Prophet meant: 'I will be your God and you shall be my people.' [26] God will be the source of every satisfaction, more than any heart can rightly crave, more than life and health, food and wealth, glory and honor, peace and every good—so that God, as St. Paul said, 'may be all in all.' [27] He will be the consummation of all our desiring—the object of our unending vision, of our unlessening love, of our unwearying praise. And in this gift of vision, this response of love, this paean of praise, all alike will share, as all will share in everlasting life.

But, now, who can imagine, let alone describe, the ranks upon ranks of rewarded saints, to be graded, undoubtedly, according to their variously merited honor and glory. Yet, there will be no envy of the lower for the higher, as there is no envy of angel for archangel—for this is one of the great blessednesses of this blessed

---

[24] Ps. 83.5.

[25] *Omnes quippe ille . . . qui nunc latent harmoniae corporalis numeri non latebunt . . . rationales mentes in tanti artificis laudem rationabilis pulchritudinis delectatione succendent.*

[26] Lev. 26.12.

[27] 1 Cor. 15.28.

City. The less rewarded will be linked in perfect peace with the more highly favored, but lower could not more long for higher than a finger, in the ordered integration of a body, could want to be an eye. The less endowed will have the high endowment of longing for nothing loftier than their lower gifts.

The souls in bliss will still possess the freedom of will, though sin will have no power to tempt them. They will be more free than ever—so free, in fact, from all delight in sinning as to find, in not sinning, an unfailing source of joy. By the freedom which was given to the first man, who was constituted in rectitude, he could choose either to sin or not to sin; in eternity, freedom is that more potent freedom which makes all sin impossible. Such freedom, of course, is a gift of God, beyond the power of nature to achieve. For, it is one thing to be God, another to be a sharer in the divine nature. God, by His nature, cannot sin, but a mere sharer in His nature must receive from God such immunity from sin. It was proper that, in the process of divine endowment, the first step should be a freedom not to sin, and the last a freedom even from the power to sin. The first gift made merit possible; the second is a part of man's reward. Our nature, when it was free to sin, did sin. It took a greater grace to lead us to that larger liberty which frees us from the very power to sin. Just as the immortality that Adam lost by his sin was, at first, a mere possibility of avoiding death, but, in heaven, becomes the impossibility of death, so free will was, at first, a mere possibility of avoiding sin, but, in heaven, becomes an utter inability to sin.

Our will will be as ineradicably rooted in rectitude and love as in beatitude. It is true that, with Adam's sin, we lost our right to grace and glory, but, with our right, we did not lose our longing to be happy. And, as for freedom, can we think that God himself, who certainly cannot sin, is therefore without freedom? The conclusion is that, in the everlasting City, there will remain in each and all of us an inalienable freedom of the will, emancipating us from every evil and filling us with every good, rejoicing in the inexhaustible beatitude of everlasting happiness, unclouded by the memory of any sin or of sanction suffered, yet with no forgetfulness of our redemption nor any loss of gratitude for our Redeemer.

The memory of our previous miseries will be a matter of purely mental contemplation, with no renewal of any feelings connected with these experiences without the end of all our living, that Kingdom without end, the real goal of our present life.

I am done. With God's help, I have kept my promise. This, I think, is all that I promised to do when I began this huge work. From all who think that I have said either too little or too much, I beg pardon; and those who are satisfied I ask, not to thank me, but to join me in rejoicing and in thanking God. Amen.*

---

* Book XXII, chap. 30.

John of Salisbury

In the Middle Ages earthly life was generally seen as an ephemeral existence where man was confronted with free choice of good or evil. His behavior was believed to lead either to salvation, purgatory, or damnation. The duty of ecclesiastical and secular authorities was to aid man's quest for salvation by promoting virtue, order, and tranquility while constraining man's tendency to sin. John of Salisbury (c. 1115-80) and St. Thomas Aquinas (1225-75) shared these views but disagreed on the relation of the authorities to civil law, the rights of the people to cast out tyrants, and the degree of individual liberty permissible in society.

In the *Policraticus* John of Salisbury, a medieval scholar, argued that although church and state authorities held power as representatives of God they were still servants of the people and subject to civil law. Any authority who broke the law tyrannized society. He concluded that tyrants should be overthrown because virtue existed only where there was liberty. Salisbury recognized that men often concealed ambition under the guise of liberty and used this deception to gain power. He believed, nevertheless, that society must risk a high degree of liberty if man were to become virtuous and free.

I.
The Nature Of Liberty

Liberty means judging everything freely in accordance with one's individual judgment, and does not hesitate to reprove what it sees opposed to good morals. Nothing but virtue is more splendid than liberty, if indeed liberty can ever properly be severed from virtue. For to all right-thinking men it is clear that true liberty issues

Reprinted from John Dickinson, ed. and trans., *The Statesman's Book of John of Salisbury: Policraticus* (New York: Russell and Russell, 1963), pp. 3-9, 33-34, 37-38, 282-83, 292-93, 312, 323-24, 335-38, 367-77, by permission of Appleton-Century-Crofts, Educational Division, Meredith Corporation. Copyright 1927, 1955.

from no other source. Wherefore, since all agree that virtue is the highest good in life, and that it alone can strike off the heavy and hateful yoke of slavery, it has been the opinion of philosophers that men should die, if need arose, for the sake of virtue, which is the only reason for living. But virtue can never be fully attained without liberty, and the absence of liberty proves that virtue in its full perfection is wanting. Therefore a man is free in proportion to the measure of his virtues, and the extent to which he is free determines what his virtues can accomplish; while, on the other hand, it is the vices alone which bring about slavery, and subject a man to persons and things in unmeet obedience; and though slavery of the person may seem at times the more to be pitied, in reality slavery to the vices is ever far the more wretched. And so what is more lovely than liberty? And what more agreeable to a man who has any reverence for virtue? We read that it has been the impelling motive of all good princes; and that none ever trod liberty under foot save the open foes of virtue. The jurists know what good laws were introduced for the sake of liberty, and the testimony of historians has made famous the great deeds done for love of it. Cato drank poison, pierced himself with his sword, and that no delay might prolong life on terms which he deemed ignoble, he thrust in his hand to widen the wound, and poured out his noble blood, that he might not see Caesar reigning. Brutus set on foot civil wars to save the city from slavery; and that seat of empire preferred rather to bear the wretched afflictions of perpetual war than to endure a lord, though of the mildest character. I pass on to the weaker sex. The wives of the Teutons, because of the value they set upon their chastity, besought Marius after his victory that they might be presented as a gift to the Vestal Virgins, promising that they would abstain from all unchastity; and when their prayers were not heeded, on the following night they ended their lives by strangling themselves in order not to become slaves or suffer loss of their chastity. If I wished to recall individual instances of this kind, time would run out before the examples were exhausted. The practice of liberty is a notable thing and displeasing only to those who have the character of slaves.

Things which are done or spoken freely avoid the fault of timidity on the one hand and of rashness on the other, and so long as the straight and narrow path is followed, merit praise and win affection. But when under the pretext of liberty rashness unleashes the violence of its spirit, it properly incurs reproach, although, as a thing more pleasing in the ears of the vulgar than convincing to the mind of the wise man, it often finds in the indulgence of others the safety which it does not owe to its own prudence. Nevertheless, it is the part of a good and wise man to give a free rein to the liberty of others and to accept with patience the words of free speaking, whatever they may be. Nor does he oppose himself to its works so long as these do not involve the casting away of virtue. For since each virtue shines by its own proper light, the merit of tolerance is resplendent with a very special glory.*

* Pp. 323-24.

II.
The Corruption Of Liberty And Man In Church And State

And yet the words of the unjust still prevail, and man, ignorant of the knowledge which belongs to him, and refusing to bear the yoke of the obedience which he owes, aspires to a kind of fictitious liberty, vainly imagining that he can live without fear and do with impunity whatsoever pleases him, and somehow be straightway like unto God; not, however, that he desires to imitate the divine goodness, but rather seeks to incline God to favor his wickedness by granting him immunity from punishment for his evil deeds.

Thus from the root of pride creeps up ambition, to wit the lust of power and glory, so that from hence it draws the strength which prevents it from being trampled down, from hence comes the respect which prevents it from becoming cheap. Now there is none who can help taking joy in liberty, or who does not desire the strength wherewith to preserve it; there is nought which would not be given in exchange therefor if need arose. For slavery is as it were the image of death, and liberty is the assured certainty of life. Therefore it is that wealth is poured out in wooing power; and the more a man lusts after power, the more lavishly he spends for the sake of it. But when such a man does attain to power, he exalts himself into a tyrant, and, spurning equity, does not scruple in the sight of God Himself to oppress and humiliate the equals of his rank and nature. And though it is not given to all men to seize princely or royal power, yet the man who is wholly untainted by tyranny is rare or non-existent. In common speech the tyrant is one who oppresses a whole people by rulership based on force; and yet it is not only over a people as a whole that a man can play the tyrant, but he can do so if he will in even the meanest station. For if not over the whole body of the people, still each man will lord it as far as his power extends. I am not here speaking of men whose hearts are wholly cleansed and who rejoice in continual subjection, declining to be set over any in this life; my task is rather to analyze the life of men in the political state. And whom will you name me among them who does not desire in point of power to be set ahead of at least one other? Who is there who does not wish to have authority over some one? Who is there who treats those subject to him as he would wish to be treated if he were himself a subject? And so when ambition takes root, equity is trampled under foot and injustice advances apace and, giving rise to tyranny, pursues all the means by which the latter grows. He who does not prevail by his own powers, strives to make use of the power of others. It is plain to the sight how many hunters after power, wooers of honors, cleave to the side of the powerful, meddle in the public concerns of the commonwealth, trying to find some way whereby they can lift themselves aloft on one side or the other, whereby they can become more powerful than others, or at least seem more powerful by reason of those with whom they associate. They pour out their patrimony, they set about and perform immense labors; they do not scruple to press with their services and worry with their flatteries those whom they seek to captivate. And so no office is gratuitous, no duke or judge, no centurion or captain of ten, nay, not even a crier or publican is appointed save for a price.

In the sphere of worldly affairs such a situation might be tolerable so long as the point is not reached where the conduct of the public business is subverted by ambition; for whatsoever duties are of a public nature ought to be consecrated to piety and good faith; but still public offices are peculiarly the objects of ambition, and rarely or never fall to the lot of any one gratuitously.*

Though the insolence of the populace or the arbitrary license of rulers can be held in check by the precepts of the law and the divine institutions, yet ambition can never be wholly quelled. For if it does not dare to show itself publicly, yet it gains entrance like a creeping thing, stealthily and by fraud. If it does not force open the gates of the Church by bribes, if they are not unbarred by its own violence or by that of others, it takes refuge in the arts of its own falsehood. It pretends to detest with the whole freedom of the Spirit all things which infringe freedom, all things which violate the statutes and decrees and are contrary to religion. . . . For the man of ambition simulates and dissimulates, and all the while wears the cunning fox under his heart. . . .†

There are many on the contrary who do not dissemble their objective at all, but, in common parlance, blow their own ambitious trumpets and ridicule such people as I have been speaking of, as coward soldiers who do not dare to acknowledge the colors of their profession. These bolder ones, although they are unclean and neither wish to amend their own lives, nor know how to mould the lives of others, yet rush pell-mell with their filthy feet, so to speak, into the very Holy of Holies, bent, if they are permitted, on handling with hands which are not merely unwashed but foul the shew-bread of the Lord and the flesh of the spotless lamb roasted in the fire of the passion on the cross. These are the men who, though they are thought unworthy even to approach the vestibule and gates, yet press straight into the seats of the priesthood, push into the sanctuary, and, repulsing others, make their beds upon the holy altars, so that the priesthood itself seems to have been instituted not for the purpose of affording a model and example to the people but rather to provide an opportunity for such men to live in plenty and in care-free ease. Nor do they regard the office as accountable to the strict judgment of God, but as a comfortable and irresponsible administrative berth. You might suppose that they had all been summoned by the voice of a herald proclaiming in the words of the poet,

"Let the itch take the hindmost." [1]

Hence they contend with the fierceness of the games in the stadium, each panting to keep the others from a bishopric.

In desire, if not in fact, rulers are far more numerous than the number of the ruled. For those who are willing to be ruled are extremely few, and each seeks with all his might to be exempted from subjection to his own proper ruler. Many enjoy such immunity by apostolic or royal privilege, which protects them from having to obey their proper judges or to do justice, or even from being subject to the law of God. I do not criticize the generosity of the Apostolic See, but I do think that these indulgences which it grants are not to the advantage of the

---

* Pp. 282-83.

† P. 312.

[1] Hor., *A. P.*, 417.

Church of God. We read of nothing of the kind among the glorious family of Christ, although there too there was contention among them as to who was to be in authority. But I do not recall that any such exemption was ever granted by the Apostles, although we hear that Paul and Barnabas parted from one another.[2] In that City on High which is our mother we do not believe that there is any matter of contention, and neither should there be here on earth, unless demanded by the most pressing reason. Concerning these men, therefore, (with all due regard for their number and for those who encourage their iniquity), I shall speak what I think, not abating a jot from truth or probability. I say, then, that I indubitably think that these men, who in their overweening pride seek exemptions of this character, would cast off from their necks the yoke of Christ and His Father if they could; nay even, I say more, they do cast off His yoke so far as in them lies, and falsely contradict the divine ordinances.*

III.
The Prevailing Justification Of A Hierarchical Society And The Legitimate Use Of Authority By The Prince

Between a tyrant and a prince there is this single or chief difference, that the latter obeys the law and rules the people by its dictates, accounting himself as but their servant. It is by virtue of the law that he makes good his claim to the foremost and chief place in the management of the affairs of the commonwealth and in the bearing of its burdens; and his elevation over others consists in this, that whereas private men are held responsible only for their private affairs, on the prince fall the burdens of the whole community. Wherefore deservedly there is conferred on him, and gathered together in his hands, the power of all his subjects, to the end that he may be sufficient unto himself in seeking and bringing about the advantage of each individually, and of all; and to the end that the state of the human commonwealth may be ordered in the best possible manner, seeing that each and all are members one of another. Wherein we indeed but follow nature, the best guide of life; for nature has gathered together all the senses of her microcosm or little world, which is man, into the head, and has subjected all the members in obedience to it in such wise that they will all function properly so long as they follow the guidance of the head, and the head remains sane. Therefore the prince stands on a pinnacle which is exalted and made splendid with all the great and high privileges which he deems necessary for himself. And rightly so, because nothing is more advantageous to the people than that the needs of the prince should be fully satisfied; since it is impossible that his will should be found opposed to justice. Therefore, according to the usual definition, the prince is the public power, and a kind of likeness on earth of the divine majesty. Beyond doubt a large share of the divine power is shown to be in princes by the fact that at

---

* Pp. 292-93.

[2] Acts XV, 39.

their nod men bow their necks and for the most part offer up their heads to the axe to be struck off, and, as by a divine impulse, the prince is feared by each of those over whom he is set as an object of fear. And this I do not think could be, except as a result of the will of God. For all power is from the Lord God, and has been with Him always, and is from everlasting. The power which the prince has is therefore from God, for the power of God is never lost, nor severed from Him, but He merely exercises it through a subordinate hand, making all things teach His mercy or justice. "Who, therefore, resists the ruling power, resists the ordinance of God,"[3] in whose hand is the authority of conferring that power, and when He so desires, of withdrawing it again, or diminishing it. For it is not the ruler's own act when his will is turned to cruelty against his subjects, but it is rather the dispensation of God for His good pleasure to punish or chasten them. Thus during the Hunnish persecution, Attila, on being asked by the reverend bishop of a certain city, who he was replied, "I am Attila, the scourge of God." Whereupon it is written that the bishop adored him as representing the divine majesty. "Welcome," he said, "is the minister of God," and "Blessed is he that cometh in the name of the Lord," and with sighs and groans he unfastened the barred doors of the church, and admitted the persecutor through whom he attained straightway to the palm of martyrdom. For he dared not shut out the scourge of God, knowing that His beloved Son was scourged, and that the power of this scourge which had come upon himself was as nought except it came from God. If good men thus regard power as worthy of veneration even when it comes as a plague upon the elect, who should not venerate that power which is instituted by God for the punishment of evil-doers and for the reward of good men, and which is promptest in devotion and obedience to the laws? To quote the words of the Emperor, "it is indeed a saying worthy of the majesty of royalty that the prince acknowledges himself bound by the Laws."[4] For the authority of the prince depends upon the authority of justice and law; and truly it is a greater thing than imperial power for the prince to place his government under the laws, so as to deem himself entitled to do nought which is at variance with the equity of justice.

Princes should not deem that it detracts from their princely dignity to believe that the enactments of their own justice are not to be preferred to the justice of God, whose justice is an everlasting justice, and His law is equity. Now equity, as the learned jurists define it, is a certain fitness of things which compares all things rationally, and seeks to apply like rules of right and wrong to like cases, being impartially disposed toward all persons, and allotting to each that which belongs to him. Of this equity the interpreter is the law, to which the will and intention of equity and justice are known. . . .

All are accordingly bound by the necessity of keeping the law, unless perchance there is any who can be thought to have been given the license of wrong-doing. However, it is said that the prince is absolved from the obligations of the law; but this is not true in the sense that it is lawful for him to do unjust acts, but only in the sense that his character should be such as to cause him to practice equity not through fear of the penalties of the law but through love of justice; and should also be such as to cause him from the same motive to promote the

---

[3] Justin., Cod., I., 14, § 4.

[4] Rom., xiii., 2.

advantage of the commonwealth, and in all things to prefer the good of others before his own private will. Who, indeed, in respect of public matters can properly speak of the will of the prince at all, since therein he may not lawfully have any will of his own apart from that which the law or equity enjoins, or the calculation of the common interest requires? For in these matters his will is to have the force of a judgment; and most properly that which pleases him therein has the force of law, because his decision may not be at variance with the intention of equity. "From thy countenance," says the Lord, "let my judgment go forth, let thine eyes look upon equity";[5] for the uncorrupted judge is one whose decision, from assiduous contemplation of equity, is the very likeness thereof. The prince accordingly is the minister of the common interest and the bond-servant of equity, and he bears the public person in the sense that he punishes the wrongs and injuries of all, and all crimes, with even-handed equity. His rod and staff also, administered with wise moderation, restore irregularities and false departures to the straight path of equity, so that deservedly may the Spirit congratulate the power of the prince with the words, "Thy rod and thy staff, they have comforted me."[6] His shield, too, is strong, but it is a shield for the protection of the weak, and one which wards off powerfully the darts of the wicked from the innocent. Those who derive the greatest advantage from his performance of the duties of his office are those who can do least for themselves, and his power is chiefly exercised against those who desire to do harm. Therefore not without reason he bears a sword, wherewith he sheds blood blamelessly, without becoming thereby a man of blood, and frequently puts men to death without incurring the name or guilt of homicide. . .

Truly the sword of princely power is as the sword of a dove, which contends without gall, smites without wrath, and when it fights, yet conceives no bitterness at all. For as the law pursues guilt without any hatred of persons, so the prince most justly punishes offenders from no motive of wrath but at the behest, and in accordance with the decision, of the passionless law. For although we see that the prince has lictors of his own, we must yet think of him as in reality himself the sole or chief lictor, to whom is granted by the law the privilege of striking by a subordinate hand. If we adopt the opinion of the Stoics, who diligently trace down the reason for particular words, "lictor" means "legis ictor," or "hammer of the law," because the duty of his office is to strike those who the law adjudges shall be struck. Wherefore anciently, when the sword hung over the head of the convicted criminal, the command was wont to be given to the officials by whose hand the judge punishes evil-doers, "Execute the sentence of the law," or "Obey the law," to the end that the misery of the victim might be mitigated by the calm reasonableness of the words.

This sword, then, the prince receives from the hand of the Church, although she herself has no sword of blood at all. Nevertheless she has this sword, but she uses it by the hand of the prince, upon whom she confers the power of bodily coercion, retaining to herself authority over spiritual things in the person of the pontiffs. The prince is, then, as it were, a minister of the priestly power, and one who exercises that side of the sacred offices which seems unworthy of the hands of the priesthood. For every office existing under, and concerned with the execution

---

[5] Ps., xvii, 2.

[6] Ps. xxiii, 4.

of, the sacred laws is really a religious office, but that is inferior which consists in punishing crimes, and which therefore seems to be typified in the person of the hangman.*

Let the whitewashers of rulers now come forward, and let them whisper, or if this is too little, let them trumpet abroad that the prince is not subject to the law, and that whatsoever is his will and pleasure, not merely in establishing law according to the model of equity, but absolutely and free from all restrictions, has the force of law. Let them thus, if they so desire and dare, make of their king, whom they except from the obligations of the law, a very outlaw, and still I will maintain not merely in the teeth of their denials but in the teeth of all the world, that kings are bound by this law. For He who neither deceives nor is deceived says, "By what judgment ye judge, ye shall yourselves be judged."[7] And surely the heaviest judgment that could be passed upon these rulers would be to have their own good measure, pressed down, shaken together, and running over, poured back into their bosoms.†

[Therefore,] it should hold true of the prince, as it should hold true of all men, that no one should seek his own interest but that of others. Yet the measure of the affection with which he should embrace his subjects like brethren in the arms of charity must be kept within the bounds of moderation. For his love of his brethren should not prevent him from correcting their errors with proper medicine; he acknowledges the ties of flesh and blood to the end that he may subdue these to the rule of the spirit. It is the practice of physicians when they cannot heal a disease with poultices and mild medicines to apply stronger remedies such as fire or steel. But they never employ these unless they despair of restoring health by milder means, and so the ruling power when it cannot avail by mild measures to heal the vices of its subjects, rightly resorts, though with grief, to the infliction of sharp punishments, and with pious cruelty vents its rage against wrong-doers to the end that good men may be preserved uninjured. But who was ever strong enough to amputate the members of his own body without grief and pain? Therefore the prince grieves when called upon to inflict the punishment which guilt demands, and yet administers it with reluctant right hand. For the prince has no left hand, and in subjecting to pain the members of the body of which he is the head, he obeys the law in sadness and with groans.‡

IV.
Tyranny And The Right Of The People To Cast Off Tyrants To Restore The Law Of God

Wherein the prince differs from the tyrant has already been set forth above . . ; and the duties of the prince . . . were also carefully explained at that point. Wherefore

---

* Pp. 3-9.
† Pp. 33-34.
‡ Pp. 37-38.
[7] Matt., vii, 2.

it will be easier to make known here, and in fewer words, the opposite characteristics of the tyrant. A tyrant, then, as the philosophers have described him, is one who oppresses the people by rulership based upon force, while he who rules in accordance with the laws is a prince. Law is the gift of god, the model of equity, a standard of justice, a likeness of the divine will, the guardian of well-being, a bond of union and solidarity between peoples, a rule defining duties, a barrier against the vices and the destroyer thereof, a punishment of violence and all wrong-doing. The law is assailed by force or by fraud, and, as it were, either wrecked by the fury of the lion or undermined by the wiles of the serpent. In whatever way this comes to pass, it is plain that it is the grace of God which is being assailed, and that it is God himself who in a sense is challenged to battle. The prince fights for the laws and the liberty of the people; the tyrant thinks nothing done unless he brings the laws to nought and reduces the people to slavery. Hence the prince is a kind of likeness of divinity; and the tyrant, on the contrary, a likeness of the boldness of the Adversary, even of the wickedness of Lucifer, imitating him that sought to build his throne to the north and make himself like unto the Most High,[8] with the exception of His goodness. For had he desired to be like unto Him in goodness, he would never have striven to tear from Him the glory of His power and wisdom. What he more likely did aspire to was to be equal with him in authority to dispense rewards. The prince, as the likeness of the Deity, is to be loved, worshipped and cherished; the tyrant, the likeness of wickedness, is generally to be even killed. The origin of tyranny is iniquity, and springing from a poisonous root, it is a tree which grows and sprouts into a baleful pestilent growth, and to which the axe must by all means be laid. For if iniquity and injustice, banishing charity, had not brought about tyranny, firm concord and perpetual peace would have possessed the peoples of the earth forever, and no one would think of enlarging his boundaries. Then kingdoms would be as friendly and peaceful, according to the authority of the great father Augustine,[9] and would enjoy as undisturbed repose, as the separate families in a well-ordered state, or as different persons in the same family; or perhaps, which is even more credible, there would be no kingdoms at all, since it is clear from the ancient historians that in the beginning these were founded by iniquity as presumptuous encroachments against the Lord, or else were extorted from Him.

It is not only kings who practice tyranny; among private men there are a host of tyrants, since the power which they have, they turn to some forbidden object. Nor let anyone be surprised that I seem to have linked kings with tyrants, since though it is true that a king derives his title from doing right[10] and that which befits a prince, still the name by common abuse comes often to be applied to the tyrant. . . .

Therefore respect for the right and the just is either not sufficiently present or else is wholly wanting from the face of tyrants; and whether they are ecclesiastical or temporal tyrants, they desire for themselves power to do all things, despising what should precede and follow power.*

---

* Pp. 335-38.

[8] Isa., xiv, 12-14.

[9] Aug., *De Civ. Dei.* iv, 15.

[10] Hor., *Ep.*, I, i, 59-60; Isid., *Etym.* ix, 4 (Migne, *P. L.*, tom. lxxxvi, 342).

It would be a long and tedious task if I wished to bring down to our own times the series of gentile tyrants; a man with only one life will hardly be able to recall the list, for it eludes the mind and overpowers the tongue. My opinions on the subject of tyrants are, however, set forth more fully in my little work entitled "Of the Ends of Tyrants,"[11] a brief manual wherein I have carefully sought to avoid the tedium of prolixity and the obscurity of too great compression. But lest the authority of Roman history be held in small account because it has for the most part been written by infidels concerning infidels, let its lesson be confirmed by examples drawn from sacred and Christian history. For it is everywhere obvious that, in the words of Valerius, only that power is secure in the long run which places bounds to its own exercise. And surely nought is so splendid or so magnificent that it does not need to be tempered by moderation. The earliest tyrant whom the divine page brings before us is Nembroth, the mighty hunter before the Lord (who is also called Ninus in some histories, although this does not agree with the proper reckoning of dates); and I have already said above that he was a reprobate. For verily he desired to be lord in his own right and not under God, and it was in his time that the attempt to raise a tower to Heaven was made by frail mortality, destined in their blindness to be overthrown and scattered in confusion. Let us, therefore, advance to him who was set over the people by the divine choice, which deserted him when he gave himself up to a wicked desire of ruling rather than of reigning, and in the end he was so utterly overthrown that in the anguish of his suffering he was compelled to put an end to himself. For a right and wholesome assumption of the royal office is of no avail, or only of very little, if the later life of the ruler is at variance therewith, nor does a judge look wholly to the origin of things, but makes his judgment to depend upon their outcome and ending.

The well-known narrative of the Books of Kings and Chronicles shows, according to the authority of Jerome,[12] that Israel was oppressed by tyrants from the beginning and that Juda had none but wicked kings save only David, Josiah and Ezechiah. Yet I can easily believe that Salomon and perhaps some of the others in Juda recovered when God recalled them to the true way. And I will be readily persuaded that tyrants instead of legitimate princes were rightly deserved by a stiff-necked and stubborn people who always resisted the Holy Spirit, and by their gentile abominations provoked to wrath not Moyses only, the servant of the law, but God Himself, the Lord of the law. For tyrants are demanded, introduced, and raised to power by sin, and are excluded, blotted out, and destroyed by repentance. And even before the time of their kings, as the Book of Judges relates, the children of Israel were time without number in bondage to tyrants, being visited with affliction on many different occasions in accordance with the dispensation of God, and then often, when they cried aloud to the Lord, they were delivered. And when the allotted time of their punishment was fulfilled, they were allowed to cast off the yoke from their necks by the slaughter of their tyrants; nor is blame attached to any of those by whose valor a penitent and humbled people was thus set free, but their memory is preserved in affection by posterity as servants of the Lord. This is clear from the subjoined examples.

---

[11] This work of John of Salisbury is not known to be extant.
[12] *In Ierem*, xxii, 14, Migne, *P. L.*, t, xxiv, 811.

"The people of Israel were in bondage to Eglon the king of Moab for eighteen years; and then they cried aloud to God, who raised up for them a saviour called Aoth, the famous son of Iera, the son of Gemini, who used both hands with the same skill as the right hand. And the children of Israel sent presents to Eglon, the king of Moab, by him; and he made for himself a two-edged sword having in the midst a haft of the length of the palm of the hand, and girded himself therewith beneath his cloak on his right thigh, and presented the gifts to Eglon, the king of Moab. Now Eglon was exceeding fat; and when he had made an end of presenting the gifts, he went away after his companions who had come with him. But he himself turned back from Gilgal where the idols were, and said to the king, 'I have a secret word for thy ear, O king.' And the king commanded silence. And all that were about him having gone forth, Aoth came unto him. And he was sitting alone in a cool upper room. And Aoth said, 'I have a word from God unto thee.' And the king forthwith rose up from his throne. And Aoth put forth his left hand and took the dagger from his right thigh, and thrust it into his belly with such force that the haft also went into the wound after the blade, and the fat closed over it. And he did not draw out the sword, but left it in the body where it had entered. And straightway by nature's secret passages, the excrements of his belly burst forth. But Aoth closed the doors carefully, and fastened them with the bolt and departed by a postern." [13]

And elsewhere, "Sisara, fleeing came to the tent of Jael the wife of Abner Cinei. For there was peace between Jabin the king of Asor and the house of Abner Cinei. Therefore, Jael went forth to meet Sisara and said unto him, 'Come in to me, my lord, come in and fear not.' And he, having entered her tent and been covered by her with a cloak, said to her, 'Give me, I pray thee, a little water because I thirst greatly.' And she opened a skin of milk, and gave him to drink, and covered him. And Sisara said to her, 'Stand before the door of the tent and when any shall come inquiring of thee and shall say "Is there any man here?" thou shalt say, "No, there is none." ' Then Jael, the wife of Abner, took a nail of the tent, and took likewise a hammer. And entering softly and silently, she put the nail upon the temple of his head, and striking it with the hammer, drove it through his brain fast into the ground. And thus passing from sleep into death he fainted away, and died." [14] Did she thereby win the praise or the censure of posterity? "Blessed among women shall be Jael the wife of Abner Cinei," says the Scripture, "and blessed shall she be in her tent. He asked for water, and she gave him milk and offered him butter in a princely dish. She put her left-hand to the nail, and her right-hand to the workmen's hammer, and she smote Sisara, seeking in his head a place for a wound, and piercing his temple forcefully." [15]

Let me prove by another story that it is just for public tyrants to be killed and the people thus set free for the service of God. This story shows that even priests of God repute the killing of tyrants as a pious act, and if it appears to wear the semblance of treachery, they say that it is consecrated to the Lord by a holy mystery. Thus Holofernes fell a victim not to the valor of the enemy but to his own vices by means of a sword in the hands of a woman; and he who had been terrible to strong men was vanquished by luxury and drink, and slain by a woman. Nor

---

[13] Judges iii, 14-24.
[14] Judges iv, 17-21.
[15] Judges v, 24-26.

would the woman have gained access to the tyrant had she not piously dissimulated her hostile intention. For that is not treachery which serves the cause of the faith and fights in behalf of charity. For verily it was due to the woman's faith that she upbraided the priests because they had set a time limit upon the divine mercy by agreeing with the enemy that they would surrender themselves and deliver up the city if the Lord should not come to their aid within five days. Likewise it was because of her charity that she shrank from no perils so long as she might deliver her brethren and the people of the Lord from the enemy. For this is shown by her words as she went forth to save them: "Bring to pass, Lord," she prayed, "that by his own sword his pride may be cut off, and that he may be caught in the net of his own eyes turned upon me, and do Thou destroy him, through the lips of my charity. Grant to me constancy of soul that I may despise him, and fortitude that I may destroy him. For it will be a glorious monument of Thy name when the hand of a woman shall strike him down." [16] "Then she called her maid, and, going down into her house, she took off her hair-cloth from her, and put away the garments of her widowhood, and bathed her body and anointed herself with the finest myrrh, and parted the hair of her head, and placed a mitre upon her head, and clothed herself with garments of gladness, binding sandals upon her feet, and donned her bracelets and lillies and ear-rings and finger-rings, and adorned herself with all her ornaments. And the Lord gave her more beauty because all this toilet was for the sake of virtue and not of lust. And therefore the Lord increased her beauty so that she appeared to the eyes of all men lovely beyond compare." [17] And thus arriving at her destination, and captivating the public enemy, "Judith spake unto Holofernes, saying: 'Receive the words of thy handmaid, for if thou wilt follow them, God will do a perfected work with thee. For Nebugodonosor, the king of the earth, liveth, and thy virtue liveth, which is in thee for the correction of all erring souls, since not men alone, but also the beasts of the field serve him through thee, and obey him. For the strength and industry of thy mind is heralded abroad to all the nations, and it has been told to the whole age that thou alone art mighty and good in all his kingdom, and thy discipline is preached to all nations.' " [18] And in addition she said, "I will come and tell all things to thee, so that I may bring thee through the midst of Jerusalem, and thou shalt have all the people of Israel as sheep that have no shepherd; and not a single dog shall bark against thee, because these things are told to me by the providence of God." [19] What more insidious scheme, I ask you, could have been devised, what could have been said that would have been more seductive than this bestowal of mystic counsel? And so Holofernes said: "There is not another such woman upon the earth in look, in beauty, or in the sense of her words." [20] For his heart was sorely smitten and burned with desire of her. Then he said, "Drink now and lay thee down for jollity since thou hast found favor in my sight." [21] But she who had not come to wanton, used a borrowed wantonness as the instrument of her devotion and courage. And his cruelty she first lulled asleep by her blandishments,

---

[16] Judith ix, 12-15.
[17] Judith x, 2-4.
[18] Judith xi, 4-6.
[19] Judith xi, 15-16.
[20] Judith xi, 19.
[21] Judith xii, 17.

and then with the weapons of affection she slew him to deliver her people. Therefore she struck Holofernes upon the neck, and cut off his head, and handed it to her maid that it might be placed in a wallet to be carried back into the city which had been saved by the hand of a woman.

The histories teach, however, that none should undertake the death of a tyrant who is bound to him by an oath or by the obligation of fealty. For we read that Sedechias, because he disregarded the sacred obligation of fealty, was led into captivity; and that in the case of another of the kings of Juda whose name escapes my memory, his eyes were plucked out because, falling into faithlessness, he did not keep before his sight God, to whom the oath is taken; since sureties for good behavior are justly given even to a tyrant.

But as for the use of poison, although I see it sometimes wrongfully adopted by infidels, I do not read that it is ever permitted by any law. Not that I do not believe that tyrants ought to be removed from our midst, but it should be done without loss of religion and honor. For David, the best of all kings that I have read of, and who, save in the incident of Urias Etheus, walked blamelessly in all things, although he had to endure the most grievous tyrant, and although he often had an opportunity of destroying him, yet preferred to spare him, trusting in the mercy of God, within whose power it was to set him free without sin. He therefore determined to abide in patience until the tyrant should either suffer a change of heart and be visited by God with return of charity, or else should fall in battle, or otherwise meet his end by the just judgment of God. How great was his patience can be discerned from the fact that when he had cut off the edge of Saul's robe in the cave, and again when, having entered the camp by night, he rebuked the negligence of the sentinels, in both cases he compelled the king to confess that David was acting the juster part. And surely the method of destroying tyrants which is the most useful and the safest, is for those who are oppressed to take refuge humbly in the protection of God's mercy, and lifting up undefiled hands to the Lord, to pray devoutly that the scourge wherewith they are afflicted may be turned aside from them. For the sins of transgressors are the strength of tyrants. Wherefore Achior, the captain of all the children of Amon, gave this most wholesome counsel to Holofernes: "Inquire diligently, my lord," said he, "whether there be any iniquity of the people in the sight of their God, and then let us go up to them, because their God will abandon them and deliver them to thee, and they shall be subdued beneath the yoke of thy power. But if there be no offence of this people in the sight of their God, we shall not be able to withstand them, because their God will defend them, and we shall be exposed to the reproach and scorn of all the earth." [22]

Thus the end of tyrants is confusion, leading to destruction if they persist in malice, to pardon if they return into the way of righteousness. For there is prepared a great fire wherewith to consume the scourge after the Father has employed it for the correction of His children. And it is written, "Acab has humbled himself before my face; therefore will I not bring evil in his days." [23] But Jezebel, who persisted in cruelty, paid the penalty therefor in the merited cruelty of her end, giving her blood to be lapped up by dogs in the place where dogs had lapped up the blood of innocent Naboth. But if the blood of innocent Naboth was thus

---

[22] Judith v, 5, 24-25.

[23] I Kings xxi, 29.

required at her hands, will not the blood of so many other innocent victims also be required? Her unrighteousness coveted the vineyard of a just man, and as the price thereof she lost her rights to a whole kingdom. Thus wickedness is always punished by the Lord; but sometimes it is His own, and at others it is a human hand, which He employs as a weapon wherewith to administer punishment to the unrighteous.

Pharao oppressed the people of God, and God scourged him, as we read in Exodus, with the most grievous plagues. That these may be briefly kept in mind with greater accuracy, I insert a metrical list of them:

> First a blood-red flood and second a slimy plague of frogs.
> Then the miserable louse and afterward the fly more harmful than the louse.
> Fifth the destruction of cattle, sixth the swelling of boils;
> Next followed hail, after that the locust with destructive tooth;
> For the ninth, the sun was veiled in darkness, the last destroyed the first-born.

I am not interested in the question of the authorship of these lines, but solely in the point that they include in the briefest compass all the plagues of Egypt in the time of Pharao. But in spite of them all, his anger was not turned aside from the people of God, but after their departure he pursued them with his chariots and horsemen, with whom he was drowned in the sea. For the Lord employed the waters as a wall of protection for the people, and as a weapon of offence for the overthrow of the tyrant. Again during the reign of Ezechias, Salmanasar oppressed the people of God, and the king, taking refuge in prayer, opposed the shield of the divine protection against the threats of the tyrant. Wherefore the Lord comforted him through the mouth of the prophet, saying: "He shall not enter into this city, nor shoot an arrow into it, neither shall he come before it with shield, nor cast a trench around it. He shall return by the way that he came, and he shall not enter into this city, saith the Lord. And I will defend this city and will save it for mine own sake and for the sake of my servant David." [24] And it was done accordingly on that very night. For there came an angel of the Lord and smote in the camp of the Assyrians an hundred and eighty-five thousand; and when the king had risen at dawn, he saw all the bodies of the dead, and he departed and went away. And Sennacherib, the king of the Assyrians, returned and dwelt at Nineve. And while he was worshipping in the temple of Nesarach his God, his sons Adramelech and Sarasar struck him dead with a sword, and escaped into the land of the Armenians; and Eseradon his son reigned in his stead. And let it cause no wonder if the king of whom we have been speaking is called by different names in different histories, because according to the Hebrew tradition, as Jerome tells, he had five names. For he was called Salmanasar and Sennacherib and Phul and Teglad Phalasar and Sargon. For if we do not hold that he thus had a number of names, then the authority of the historians will be weakened because of their differences and contradictions. In this instance therefore the Lord employed first the sword of the angel against the army of the wicked king, and afterwards against the king himself He used the hands of his own sons.

[24] II Kings xix, 32-34.

Nature herself is at times struck with amazement at the vengeance of the Most High, and is subservient in marvellous fashion to the laws of her Creator when provoked by the wickedness of men. Hence it is that Nabugodonosor, becoming swollen with pride against the Lord, was required for seven years to live the life of a beast, and then repenting, was turned again into a man and restored to his kingdom and fortune, although afterwards he deserved to be once more deprived of them by a most miserable death.*

* Pp. 367-77.

St. Thomas Aquinas

Thomas Aquinas (1225-75), a Dominican Friar, Scholastic, and a saint in the Catholic Church, was born in Italy. He was educated at the Benedictine Monastery of Monte Cassino, the University of Naples, and the University of Paris where in 1253 he joined the theological faculty. The remainder of Aquinas's life was spent as a teacher and scholar. More than John of Salisbury, Aquinas stressed that obedience to superiors was a supreme virtue and a necessity for an orderly society. Subjects should be submissive to authorities because they ruled by the grace of God and reflected His pleasure and wrath. People should endure tyranny and even cruelty as part of God's righteous punishment. Aquinas's principles reflected and reinforced existing medieval society, while the doctrines expressed by John of Salisbury shed light on the issues in the 1688 English Revolution and the French Revolution of 1789.[1]

I.
The Nature Of Man And the Existence Of Freedom—Free Choice

Without doubt it must be said that man has free choice. Faith demands that we hold this position, since without free choice one could not merit or demerit, or be justly rewarded or punished. There are clear indications of this if one considers

---

[1] John Dickinson, *The Statesman's Book of John of Salisbury: Policraticus* (New York: Russell & Russell, 1963), p. xi.

Reprinted from Saint Thomas Aquinas, *De Veritate*, Question 24, "On Free Choice," from *Selected Writings of St. Thomas Aquinas*, ed. Robert P. Goodwin (Indianapolis: Bobbs-Merrill Company, 1965), pp. 121-28, 132-37, 140-43, 145-47, 149; Saint Thomas Aquinas, *The Summa Theologica*, trans. Father of the English Dominican Province (London: Thomas Baker, 1915), Part I-II, Q. 97; Part II-II, Q. 104; Saint Thomas Aquinas, *De Regimine Principum*, "On Kingship," trans. Gerald B. Phelan (Toronto: The Pontifical Institute of Medieval Studies, 1949), pp. 3-29, by permission. The selection from the *Selected Writings of St. Thomas Aquinas* is copyright © 1965 by The Bobbs-Merrill Company, Inc.

the occasions when man appears to choose one thing freely and reject another. Finally, reason, too, demands that we hold this position.

Men act and are moved by a judgment of reason, for they deliberate about courses of action. All brute animals, however, act and are moved by a natural judgment. This is evident when you consider that all the members of a species act in a similar way, as, for example, swallows all build their nests in the same way. It is also evident from the fact that their judgment is determined to one course of action and not open to all, as bees are skilled in producing nothing but honeycombs. The case is similar for other animals.

Hence, it is clear to anyone who considers the matter rightly that the way in which motion and action are attributed to inanimate things of nature is the same as the way in which the judging of actions is attributed to brute animals. Just as heavy and light things do not move themselves such that they would be the causes of their own motion, so too brutes do not judge of their own judgments, but follow the judgment imprinted upon them by God. And since they do not cause their choice, they do not have freedom of choice.

Man, however, judging about his actions through his power of reason, can judge concerning his choice insofar as he can know the nature of the end and of the means to the end, and, likewise, the relation and order of the one to the other. Man, therefore, is his own cause, not only in moving but also in judging. Hence he has free choice, as one is speaking of the free judgments as to whether to act or not. . . .

Indeed to judge of one's own judgment belongs only to reason, which reflects upon its own act and knows the relations of things of which it judges and through which it judges. The root of all liberty, therefore, is found in reason. Hence, according as something is related to reason, so is it related to free choice.

Now reason is found fully and perfectly only in man, and so free choice is found fully in him alone.

Brutes, however, have a certain semblance of reason, insofar as they participate in a certain natural prudence, in accordance with the way an inferior nature in some way attains what belongs to a superior one. This similitude consists in their having an orderly judgment about certain things. This judgment, however, arises out of a natural estimation, and not from any deliberation, since they are ignorant of the rationale of their judgments. Because their judgment is of this kind, it does not extend to all things as does the judgment of reason, but only to certain determinate things.

Likewise, they possess something similar to free choice inasmuch as they are able to do or not do one and the same thing in accordance with their judgment. Therefore they possess something close to a certain conditioned liberty. If they judge that they should act, they can act; if they do not so judge, they can abstain from acting.

Since their judgment is determined to one thing, it follows that their appetite and action are likewise determined to one thing. Accordingly, . . . they naturally judge according to such sights or passions. By necessity they are moved by the sight of something or by an aroused passion toward it to flee or pursue that thing, as a sheep necessarily becomes afraid and flees at the sight of a wolf, or as a dog, because of an aroused passion of anger, must bark and pursue something in order to do it harm.

Man, however, is not moved necessarily by things appearing to him or by aroused passions, since he can either accept or reject them. Therefore, man has free choice, but brutes do not.

That God has free choice is evident from the fact that He has for His will an end which He naturally wills, that is, His own goodness. He wills all other things as ordered to this end, but, speaking absolutely, He does not will them necessarily. . . .

Now the faculty of free choice presupposes two things, namely, a nature and a cognitive power. The way nature is found in God is different from the way it is in men and angels. For divine nature is uncreated, and is its own act of existing and its own goodness. Hence, there cannot be any deficiency in it as regards the act of existing or goodness. Human and angelic nature, however, is created and arises out of nothing. Hence, considered in itself, it can be defective. Accordingly God's free choice can in no way be turned to evil, whereas the free choice of men and angels, considered in what is natural to it, can be turned to evil. Cognition as found in man is different from cognition as found in God and in angels. For man's cognition is obscure, arriving at a knowledge of truth in a discursive way. Hence, he is subject to doubt and to difficulties of discerning and judging. . . . But in God, and in angels in their own way, there is a simple vision of truth without any discursiveness or inquiry; neither doubt nor difficulty in discerning or in judging occurs in them. Therefore, both God and angels choose readily, but man suffers difficulty in choosing because of his uncertainty and doubt.*

II.
Freedom For Good Or Evil

The free choice of a creature cannot be naturally confirmed in goodness because its nature does not possess the character of the perfect and absolutely good, but of a certain particular good. Through grace, however, free choice is united to the absolute and perfect good, namely, God. Hence, if the union is perfect so that God Himself is the total cause of the action of free choice, a defection to evil is not possible. This indeed happens to some creatures, especially the blessed. This is evident as follows.

The will naturally tends to good as its object. That it sometimes tends to evil happens only because the evil is proposed to it under the aspect of goodness. For evil is involuntary. . . . Hence, there can be no sin in a movement of the will, that is, the will cannot desire evil, unless there pre-exists a defect in the cognitive power, through which the evil is proposed to the will as a good.

This defect in reason can occur in two ways: either by reason itself or through something extrinsic to reason.

It can occur in reason itself because, although it naturally and immutably possesses a faultless knowledge of good in general, both the good which is an end and the

* *De Veritate*, pp. 121-27.

good which is a means, it does not possess such knowledge of the good in particular. Concerning this it can err, as when it judges something to be an end which is not an end, or something to be useful for an end which indeed is not useful thus. Because of this the will naturally desires the good that is an end—namely, happiness in general—and similarly the good that is a means, for everyone naturally desires what is useful to him. The will sins, however, in seeking this or that end, or in choosing this or that useful thing.

On the other hand, reason is deficient through something extrinsic to it, when an act of reason is hampered by inferior powers which are moved intensely to something. Consequently reason does not clearly and firmly propose its judgment about the good to the will. For example, when someone has judged rightly about preserving chastity, he might very well choose contrary to chastity through an ardent desire for the pleasurable. . . .

Now both of these defects are totally lacking in the blessed, because of their union with God. For those who see the divine essence know that God Himself is the end to whom the greatest love is due. They know also all those things in particular, both those things united to Him and those things distinct from Him, since they know God not only in Himself but also insofar as He is the reason for all other things. Through the clarity of this knowledge their minds will be so strengthened that no motion of the inferior powers can arise except according to the rule of reason. Therefore, just as now we immutably desire the good in general, so the minds of the blessed immutably desire in particular the appropriate good.*

[F]ree choice does have a remedy for renouncing sin. For he who is impelled by passion judges rightly concerning the end which is, as it were, a principle of those things which can be done. . . .

Hence, just as a man, through the true judgment that he has of the principle, can of himself reject any erroneous conclusions he may suffer, so too he can of himself reject every impetus of passion by being rightly disposed regarding the end. . . .

Similarly, free choice has a remedy against the inclination of habit. For no one habit corrupts all the potencies of the soul. Hence, despite the corruption of one potency by habit, there remains some rectitude in the other powers. Accordingly, man is induced to consider and to do those things opposed to that habit. For example, if someone's concupiscible power is corrupted by a habit of lust, he is incited by the irascible power to pursue something arduous, and the exercise of the irascible power removes the debilitating effects of lust. . . .

Furthermore, free choice has a remedy against the third, namely, the false judgment of reason in its choice of something particular. For whatever man accepts, he accepts, as it were, rationally—that is, through inquiry and comparison. Hence when reason errs about something, that error can be removed by contrary arguments, no matter what the source of the error might be. Accordingly, man is able to withdraw and desist from sin. . . .

[However] if man is impelled necessarily either to good or to evil, he cannot

* *De Veritate,* pp. 135-36.

then choose freely. The unacceptability of this can be proved by experience, by the doctrines of philosophers, and by the divine authorities.*

Catholic faith . . . follows a middle course, preserving freedom of choice without rejecting the necessity of grace.

As evidence for this it must be understood that since free choice is a certain power constituted under reason and over the consequent action, something is beyond the power of free choice in two ways. First, something exceeds the efficacy of the consequent action, which occurs at the command of free choice. Thus to fly is not within man's power of free choice, because it exceeds the ability of man's motor power. Second, something is beyond the power of free choice because of the fact that the act of reason does not extend to it. Since the act of free choice is an election following counsel—that is, the deliberation of reason—it follows that free choice cannot extend itself to what evades the deliberation of reason, like those things which occur without forethought.

In the first way, therefore, neither sin nor the avoidance of sin exceeds the power of free choice; for sin is accomplished in the will itself, through consent alone before the execution of the act, although the sin is completed by an exterior act in the execution of the motor power. Consequently, free choice is not impeded from sin or its avoidance because of a defect of the motor powers. It is sometimes impeded from executing the act, as when someone wills to kill, fornicate, or steal, but nevertheless cannot do so.

According to the second way, however, sin and the avoidance of sin can exceed the power of free choice, since some sins occur suddenly and take a person by surprise. They thus escape the election of free choice, although a person could freely choose to do or avoid them if he directed his attention or effort to them.

Now something can occur by surprise in us in two ways. First, from the impetus of passion; for example, a movement of anger or concupiscence sometimes prevents the deliberation of reason. Such a movement, tending to something illicit thanks to our corrupt nature, is a venial sin.

Therefore, following upon the state of corrupt nature, it is not in the power of free choice to avoid all sins of this kind because they escape its act, although it can impede any one of these movements if it tries. However, it is impossible for a man to strive continually to avoid movements of this type, because of the mind's various preoccupations and because of the necessity for peace. . . .†

From all the above, therefore, it is evident that we do not deny free choice, since we say that free choice is capable of avoiding or committing any sin taken singly; nor do we deny the necessity of grace, since we say that man cannot avoid all venial sin, although he can avoid individual ones. This is true even of the man who has grace, before that grace is perfected in the state of glory, because of the defect of our being.‡

---

* *De Veritate*, pp. 141-43.
† *De Veritate*, pp. 146-47.
‡ *De Veritate*, p. 149.

III.
The Strengths And Weaknesses Of Various Forms Of Government

All law proceeds from the reason and will of the lawgiver: the divine and natural laws from the reasonable will of God, the human law from the will of man regulated by reason.*

Just as the actions of natural things proceed from natural powers, so do human actions proceed from the human will. In natural things it behooved the higher to move the lower to their actions by the excellence of the natural power bestowed on them by God; and so in human affairs also the higher must move the lower by their will in virtue of a divinely established authority. Now to move by reason and will is to command. Wherefore just as in virtue of the divinely established natural order the lower natural things need to be subject to the movement of the higher, so too in human affairs, in virtue of the order of natural and divine law, inferiors are bound to obey their superiors.†

As stated above, he who obeys is moved by the command of the person he obeys, just as natural things are moved by their motive causes. Now just as God is the first mover of all things that are moved naturally, so too is He the first mover of all wills, as shown above. Therefore just as all natural things are subject to the divine motion by a natural necessity, so too all wills, by a kind of necessity of justice, are bound to obey the divine command.‡

Faith in Christ is the origin and cause of justice, according to Romans iii. 22: "The justice of God by faith of Jesus Christ"; wherefore faith in Christ does not void the order of justice, but strengthens it. Now the order of justice requires that subjects obey their superiors, else the stability of human affairs would cease. Hence faith in Christ does not excuse the faithful from the obligation of obeying secular princes.§

Now obedience to a superior is due in accordance with the divinely established order of things, as shown above, and therefore it is a good, since good consists in mode, species, and order, as Augustine states. Again, this act has a special aspect of praiseworthiness by reason of its object. For while subjects have many obligations toward their superiors, this one, that they are bound to obey their commands, stands out as special among the rest. Wherefore obedience is a special virtue, and its specific object is a command tacit or express; because the superior's will, however it become known, is a tacit precept, and a man's obedience seems to be all the more prompt forasmuch as by obeying he forestalls the express command as soon as he understands his superior's will.||

In all things which are ordered toward an end wherein this or that course may be adopted, some directive principle is needed through which the due end may be reached by the most direct route. A ship, for example, which moves in different directions according to the impulse of the changing winds would never reach its

---

* *Summa,* Part I-II, Q. 97, Art. 3.
† *Summa,* Part II-II, Q. 104, Art. 1.
‡ *Summa,* Q. 104, Art. 4.
§ *Summa,* Q. 104, Art. 6.
|| *Summa,* Q. 104, Art. 2.

destination were it not brought to port by the skill of the pilot. Now, man has an end to which his whole life and all his actions are ordered; for man is an intelligent agent, and it is clearly the part of an intelligent agent to act in view of an end. Men also adopt different methods in proceeding toward their proposed end, as the diversity of men's pursuits and actions clearly indicates. Consequently man needs some directive principle to guide him toward his end.

To be sure, the light of reason is placed by nature in every man, to guide him in his acts toward his end. Wherefore, if man were intended to live alone, as many animals do, he would require no other guide to his end. Each man would be a king unto himself, under God, the highest King, inasmuch as he would direct himself in his acts by the light of reason given him from on high. Yet it is natural for man, more than for any other animal, to be a social and political animal, to live in a group.

This is clearly a necessity of man's nature. For all other animals, nature has prepared food, hair as a covering, teeth, horns, claws as means of defense, or at least speed in flight, while man alone was made without any natural provisions for these things. Instead of all these, man was endowed with reason, by the use of which he could procure all these things for himself by the work of his hands. Now, one man alone is not able to procure them all for himself, for one man could not sufficiently provide for life unassisted. It is therefore natural that man should live in the society of many.

Moreover, all other animals are able to discern, by inborn skill, what is useful and what is injurious, even as the sheep naturally regards the wolf as his enemy. Some animals also recognize by natural skill certain medicinal herbs and other things necessary for their life. Man, on the contrary, has a natural knowledge of the things which are essential for his life only in a general fashion, inasmuch as he is able to attain knowledge of the particular things necessary for human life by reasoning from natural principles. But it is not possible for one man to arrive at a knowledge of all these things by his own individual reason. It is therefore necessary for man to live in a multitude so that each one may assist his fellows, and different men may be occupied in seeking, by their reason, to make different discoveries—one, for example, in medicine, one in this and another in that.

This point is further and most plainly evidenced by the fact that the use of speech is a prerogative proper to man. By this means, one man is able fully to express his conceptions to others. Other animals, it is true, express their feelings to one another in a general way, as a dog may express anger by barking and other animals give vent to other feelings in various fashions. But man communicates with his kind more completely than any other animal known to be gregarious, such as the crane, the ant, or the bee.—With this in mind, Solomon says: "It is better that there be two than one; for they have the advantage of their company."

If, then, it is natural for man to live in the society of many, it is necessary that there exist among men some means by which the group may be governed. For where there are many men together and each one is looking after his own interest, the multitude would be broken up and scattered unless there were also an agency to take care of what appertains to the common weal. In like manner, the body of a man or any other animal would disintegrate unless there were a general ruling force within the body which watches over the common good of all members.—With this in mind, Solomon says: "Where there is no governor, the people shall fall."

Indeed it is reasonable that this should happen, for what is proper and what is common are not identical. Things differ by what is proper to each; they are united by what they have in common. But diversity of effects is due to diversity of causes. Consequently, there must exist something which impels toward the common good of the many, over and above that which impels toward the particular good of each individual. Wherefore also in all things that are ordained toward one end, one thing is found to rule the rest. Thus in the corporeal universe, by the first body, i.e., the celestial body, the other bodies are regulated according to the order of divine providence; and all bodies are ruled by a rational creature. So, too, in the individual man, the soul rules the body; and among the parts of the soul, the irascible and the concupiscible parts are ruled by reason. Likewise, among the members of a body, one, such as the heart or the head, is the principal and moves all the others. Therefore in every multitude there must be some governing power.

Now it happens in certain things which are ordained toward an end that one may proceed in a right way and also in a wrong way. So, too, in the government of a multitude there is a distinction between right and wrong. A thing is rightly directed when it is led toward a befitting end, wrongly when it is led toward an unbefitting end. Now the end which befits a multitude of free men is different from that which befits a multitude of slaves, for the free man is one who exists for his own sake, while the slave, as such, exists for the sake of another. If, therefore, a multitude of free men is ordered by the ruler toward the common good of the multitude, that rulership will be right and just, as is suitable to free men. If, on the other hand, a rulership aims, not at the common good of the multitude, but at the private good of the ruler, it will be an unjust and perverted rulership. The Lord, therefore, threatens such rulers, saying by the mouth of Ezechiel: "Woe to the shepherds that feed themselves (seeking, that is, their own interest): should not the flocks be fed by the shepherd?" Shepherds indeed should seek the good of their flocks, and every ruler, the good of the multitude subject to him.

If an unjust government is carried on by one man alone, who seeks his own benefit from his rule and not the good of the multitude subject to him, such a ruler is called a "tyrant"—a word derived from "strength"—because he oppresses by might instead of ruling by justice. Thus among the ancients all powerful men were called tyrants. If an unjust government is carried on, not by one but by several, and if they be few, it is called an "oligarchy," that is, the rule of a few. This occurs when a few, who differ from the tyrant only by the fact that they are more than one, oppress the people by means of their wealth. If, finally, the bad government is carried on by the multitude, it is called a "democracy," i.e., control by the populace, which comes about when the plebeian people by force of numbers oppress the rich. In this way the whole people will be as one tyrant.

In like manner we must divide just governments. If the government is administered by many, it is given the name common to all forms of government, viz., "polity," as for instance when a group of warriors exercise dominion over a city or province. If it is administered by a few men of virtue, this kind of government is called an "aristocracy," i.e., noble governance, or governance by noble men, who for this reason are called the "Optimates." And if a just government is in the hands of one man alone, he is properly called a "king." Wherefore the Lord says by the mouth of Ezechiel: "My servant, David, shall be king over them and all of them shall have one shepherd."

From this it is clearly shown that the idea of king implies that he be one man who is chief and that he be a shepherd seeking the common good of the multitude and not his own.

Now since man must live in a group, because he is not sufficient unto himself to procure the necessities of life were he to remain solitary, it follows that a society will be the more perfect the more it is sufficient unto itself to procure the necessities of life. There is, to some extent, sufficiency for life in one family of one household, namely, in so far as pertains to the natural acts of nourishment and the begetting of offspring and other things of this kind. Self-sufficiency exists, furthermore, in one street with regard to those things which belong to the trade of one guild. In a city, which is the perfect community, it exists with regard to all the necessities of life. Still more self-sufficiency is found in a province because of the need of fighting together and of mutual help against enemies. Hence the man ruling a perfect community, i.e., a city or a province, is antonomastically called the king. The ruler of a household is called father, not king, although he bears a certain resemblance to the king, for which reason kings are sometimes called the fathers of their peoples.

It is plain, therefore, from what has been said, that a king is one who rules the people of one city or province, and rules them for the common good. Wherefore Solomon says: "The king ruleth over all the land subject to him."

Having set forth these preliminary points we must now inquire what is better for a province or a city: whether to be ruled by one man or by many.

This question may be considered first from the viewpoint of the purpose of government. The aim of any ruler should be directed toward securing the welfare of that which he undertakes to rule. The duty of the pilot, for instance, is to preserve his ship amidst the perils of the sea and to bring it unharmed to the port of safety. Now the welfare and safety of a multitude formed into a society lies in the preservation of its unity, which is called peace. If this is removed, the benefit of social life is lost and, moreover, the multitude in its disagreement becomes a burden to itself. The chief concern of the ruler of a multitude, therefore, is to procure the unity of peace. It is not even legitimate for him to deliberate whether he shall establish peace in the multitude subject to him, just as a physician does not deliberate whether he shall heal the sick man encharged to him, for no one should deliberate about an end which he is obliged to seek, but only about the means to attain that end. Wherefore the Apostle, having commended the unity of the faithful people says: "Be ye careful to keep the unity of the spirit in the bond of peace." Thus, the more efficacious a government is in keeping the unity of peace, the more useful it will be. For we call that more useful which leads more directly to the end. Now it is manifest that what is itself one can more efficaciously bring about unity than several—just as the most efficacious cause of heat is that which is by its nature hot. Therefore the rule of one man is more useful than the rule of many.

Furthermore, it is evident that several persons could by no means preserve the stability of the community if they totally disagreed. For union is necessary among them if they are to rule at all; several men, for instance, could not pull a ship in one direction unless joined together in some fashion. Now several are said to be united according as they come closer to being one. So one man rules better than several who come near being one.

Again, whatever is in accord with nature is best, for in all things nature does what is best. Now every natural governance is governance by one. In the multitude of bodily members there is one which is the principal mover, namely, the heart; and among the powers of the soul one power presides as chief, namely, the reason. Among bees there is one king bee, and in the whole universe there is One God, Maker and Ruler of all things. And there is a reason for this. Every multitude is derived from unity. Wherefore, if artificial things are an imitation of natural things and a work of art is better according as it attains a closer likeness to what is in nature, it follows that it is best for a human multitude to be ruled by one person.

This is also evident from experience. For provinces or cities which are not ruled by one person are torn with dissensions and tossed about without peace, so that the complaint seems to be fulfilled which the Lord uttered through the Prophet: "Many pastors have destroyed my vineyard." On the other hand, provinces and cities which are ruled under one king enjoy peace, flourish in justice, and delight in prosperity. Hence, the Lord by His prophets promises to His people as a great reward that He will give them one head and that "one Prince will be in the midst of them."

Just as the government of a king is the best, so the government of a tyrant is the worst.

For democracy stands in contrary opposition to polity, since both are governments carried on by many persons, as is clear from what has already been said; while oligarchy is the opposite of aristocracy, since both are governments carried on by a few persons; and kingship is the opposite of tyranny, since both are carried on by one person. Now, as has been shown above, monarchy is the best government. If, therefore, "it is the contrary of the best that is worst," it follows that tyranny is the worst kind of government.

Further, a united force is more efficacious in producing its effect than a force which is scattered or divided. Many persons together can pull a load which could not be pulled by each one taking his part separately and acting individually. Therefore, just as it is more useful for a force operating for a good to be more united, in order that it may work good more effectively, so a force operating for evil is more harmful when it is one than when it is divided. Now, the power of one who rules unjustly works to the detriment of the multitude, in that he diverts the common good of the multitude to his own benefit. Therefore, for the same reason that, in a just government, the government is better in proportion as the ruling power is one—thus monarchy is better than aristocracy, and aristocracy better than polity—so the contrary will be true of an unjust government, namely, that the ruling power will be more harmful in proportion as it is more unitary. Consequently, tyranny is more harmful than oligarchy and oligarchy more harmful than democracy.

Moreover, a government becomes unjust by the fact that the ruler, paying no heed to the common good, seeks his own private good. Wherefore the further he departs from the common good the more unjust will his government be. But there is a greater departure from the common good in an oligarchy, in which the advantage of a few is sought, than in a democracy, in which the advantage of many is sought; and there is a still greater departure from the common good in a tyranny, where the advantage of only one man is sought. For a large number is closer to the totality than a small number, and a small number than only one. Thus, the government of a tyrant is the most unjust.

The same conclusion is made clear to those who consider the order of divine providence, which disposes everything in the best way. In all things, good ensues from one perfect cause, i.e., from the totality of the conditions favorable to the production of the effect, while evil results from any one partial defect. There is beauty in a body when all its members are fittingly disposed; ugliness, on the other hand, arises when any one member is not fittingly disposed. Thus ugliness results in different ways from many causes, beauty in one way from one perfect cause. It is thus with all good and evil things, as if God so provided that good, arising from one cause, be stronger, and evil, arising from many causes, be weaker. It is expedient therefore that a just government be that of one man only in order that it may be stronger; however, if the government should turn away from justice, it is more expedient that it be a government by many, so that it may be weaker and the many may mutually hinder one another. Among unjust governments, therefore, democracy is the most tolerable, but the worst is tyranny.

This same conclusion is also apparent if one considers the evils which come from tyrants. Since a tyrant, despising the common good, seeks his private interest, it follows that he will oppress his subjects in different ways according as he is dominated by different passions to acquire certain goods. The one who is enthralled by the passion of cupidity seizes the goods of his subjects; whence Solomon says: "A just king setteth up the land; a covetous man shall destroy it." If he is dominated by the passion of anger, he sheds blood for nothing; whence it is said by Ezechiel: "Her princes in the midst of her are like wolves ravening the prey to shed blood." Therefore this kind of government is to be avoided as the Wise man admonishes: "Keep thee far from the man who has the power to kill," because, forsooth, he kills not for justice' sake but by his power, for the lust of his will. Thus there can be no safety. Everything is uncertain when there is a departure from justice. Nobody will be able firmly to state: This thing is such and such, when it depends upon the will of another, not to say upon his caprice. Nor does the tyrant merely oppress his subjects in corporal things but he also hinders their spiritual good. Those who seek more to use than to be of use to their subjects prevent all progress, suspecting all excellence in their subjects to be prejudicial to their own evil domination. For tyrants hold the good in greater suspicion than the wicked, and to them the valor of others is always fraught with danger.

So the above-mentioned tyrants strive to prevent those of their subjects who have become virtuous from acquiring valor and high spirit in order that they may not want to cast off their iniquitous domination. They also see to it that there be no friendly relations among these so that they may not enjoy the benefits resulting from being on good terms with one another, for as long as one has no confidence in the other, no plot will be set up against the tyrant's domination. Wherefore they sow discords among the people, foster any that have arisen, and forbid anything which furthers society and co-operation among men, such as marriage, company at table, and anything of like character, through which familiarity and confidence are engendered among men. They moreover strive to prevent their subjects from becoming powerful and rich since, suspecting these to be as wicked as themselves, they fear their power and wealth; for the subjects might become harmful to them even as they are accustomed to use power and wealth to harm others. Whence in the Book of Job it is said of the tyrant: "The sound of dread is always in his ears, and when there is peace (that is, when there is no one to harm him) he always suspects treason."

It thus results that when rulers, who ought to induce their subjects to virtue, are wickedly jealous of the virtue of their subjects and hinder it as much as they can, few virtuous men are found under the rule of tyrants. For, according to Aristotle's sentence, brave men are found where brave men are honored. And as Cicero says: "Those who are despised by everybody are disheartened and flourish but little." It is also natural that men brought up in fear should become mean of spirit and discouraged in the face of any strenuous and manly task. This is shown by experience in provinces that have long been under tyrants. Hence the Apostle says to the Colossians: "Fathers, provoke not your children to indignation, lest they be discouraged."

So, considering these evil effects of tyranny, King Solomon says: "When the wicked reign, men are ruined," because, forsooth, through the wickedness of tyrants, subjects fall away from the perfection of virtue. And again he says: "When the wicked shall bear rule the people shall mourn, as though led into slavery." And again: "When the wicked rise up men shall hide themselves," that they may escape the cruelty of the tyrant. It is no wonder, for a man governing without reason, according to the lust of his soul, in no way differs from the beast. Whence Solomon says: "As a roaring lion and a hungry bear, so is a wicked prince over the poor people." Therefore men hide from tyrants as from cruel beasts, and it seems that to be subject to a tyrant is the same thing as to lie prostrate beneath a raging beast.

Because both the best and the worst government are latent in monarchy, i.e. in the rule of one man, the royal dignity is rendered hateful to many people on account of the wickedness of tyrants. Some men, indeed, whilst they desire to be ruled by a king, fall under the cruelty of tyrants, and not a few rulers exercise tyranny under the cloak of royal dignity.

A clear example of this is found in the Roman Republic. When the kings had been driven out by the Roman people, because they could not bear the royal, or rather tyrannical, arrogance, they instituted consuls and other magistrates by whom they began to be ruled and guided. They changed the kingdom into an aristocracy, and, as Sallust relates: "The Roman city, once liberty was won, waxed incredibly strong and great in a remarkably short time." For it frequently happens that men living under a king strive more sluggishly for the common good, inasmuch as they consider that what they devote to the common good they do not confer upon themselves but upon another, under whose power they see the common goods to be. But when they see that the common good is not under the power of one man, they do not attend to it as if it belonged to another, but each one attends to it as if it were his own.

Experience thus teaches that one city administered by rulers, changing annually, is sometimes able to do more than some kings having, perchance, two or three cities; and small services exacted by kings weigh more heavily than great burdens imposed by the community of citizens. This held good in the history of the Roman

Republic. The plebs were enrolled in the army and were paid wages for military service. Then when the common treasury was failing, private riches came forth for public uses, to such an extent that not even the senators retained any gold for themselves save one ring and the one *bulla* (the insignia of their dignity).

On the other hand, when the Romans were worn out by continual dissensions taking on the proportion of civil wars, and when by these wars the freedom for which they had greatly striven was snatched from their hands, they began to find themselves under the power of emperors who, from the beginning, were unwilling to be called kings, for the royal name was hateful to the Romans. Some emperors, it is true, faithfully cared for the common good in a kingly manner, and by their zeal the commonwealth was increased and preserved. But most of them became tyrants toward their subjects while indolent and vacillating before their enemies, and brought the Roman commonwealth to naught.

A similar process took place, also, among the Hebrew people. At first, while they were ruled by judges, they were ravished by their enemies on every hand, for each one "did what was good in his sight." Yet when, at their own pressing, God gave them kings, they departed from the worship of the one God and were finally led into bondage, on account of the wickedness of their kings.

Danger thus lurks on either side. Either men are held by the fear of a tyrant and they miss the opportunity of having that very best government which is kingship, or they want a king and the kingly power turns into tyrannical wickedness.

When a choice is to be made between two things, from both of which danger impends, surely that one should be chosen from which the lesser evil follows. Now, lesser evil follows from the corruption of a monarchy (which is tyranny) than from the corruption of an aristocracy.

Group government [polyarchy] most frequently breeds dissension. This dissension runs counter to the good of peace, which is the principal social good. A tyrant, on the other hand, does not destroy this good; rather he obstructs one or the other individual interest of his subjects—unless, of course, there be an excess of tyranny and the tyrant rages against the whole community. Monarchy is therefore to be preferred to polyarchy, although either form of government might become dangerous.

Further, that from which great dangers may follow more frequently is, it would seem, the more to be avoided. Now, considerable dangers to the multitude follow more frequently from polyarchy than from monarchy. There is a greater chance that, where there are many rulers, one of them will abandon the intention of the common good than that it will be abandoned when there is but one ruler. When any one among several rulers turns aside from the pursuit of the common good, danger of internal strife threatens the group because, when the chiefs quarrel, dissension will follow in the people. When, on the other hand, one man is in command, he more often keeps to governing for the sake of the common good. Should he not do so, it does not immediately follow that he also proceeds to the total oppression of his subjects. This, of course, would be the excess of tyranny and the worst wickedness in government, as has been shown above. The dangers, then, arising from a polyarchy are more to be guarded against than those arising from a monarchy.

Moreover, in point of fact, a polyarchy deviates into tyranny not less but perhaps more frequently than a monarchy. When, on account of there being many rulers, dissensions arise in such a government, it often happens that the power of one preponderates and he then usurps the government of the multitude for himself. This indeed may be clearly seen from history. There has hardly ever been a polyarchy that did not end in tyranny. The best illustration of this fact is the history of the Roman Republic. It was for a long time administered by the magistrates, but then animosities, dissensions, and civil wars arose, and it fell into the power of the most cruel tyrants. In general, if one carefully considers what has happened in the past and what is happening in the present, he will discover that more men have held tyrannical sway in lands previously ruled by many rulers than in those ruled by one.

The strongest objection why monarchy, although it is "the best form of government," is not agreeable to the people is that, in fact, it may deviate into tyranny. Yet tyranny is wont to occur not less but more frequently on the basis of a polyarchy than on the basis of a monarchy. It follows that it is, in any case, more expedient to live under one king than under the rule of several men.

Therefore, since the rule of one man, which is the best, is to be preferred, and since it may happen that it be changed into a tyranny, which is the worst (all this is clear from what has been said), a scheme should be carefully worked out which would prevent the multitude ruled by a king from falling into the hands of a tyrant.

First, it is necessary that the man who is raised up to be king by those whom it concerns should be of such condition that it is improbable that he should become a tyrant. Wherefore Daniel, commending the providence of God with respect to the institution of the king says: "The Lord hath sought him a man according to his own heart, and the Lord hath appointed him to be prince over his people." Then, once the king is established, the government of the kingdom must be so arranged that opportunity to tyrannize is removed. At the same time his power should be so tempered that he cannot easily fall into tyranny. How these things may be done we must consider in what follows.

IV.
Tyranny And The Right Of The People To Cast Off Tyrants

Finally, provision must be made for facing the situation should the king stray into tyranny.

Indeed, if there be not an excess of tyranny it is more expedient to tolerate the milder tyranny for a while than, by acting against the tyrant, to become involved in many perils more grievous than the tyranny itself. For it may happen that those who act against the tyrant are unable to prevail and the tyrant then will rage the more. But should one be able to prevail against the tyrant, from this fact itself very grave dissensions among the people frequently ensue: the multitude may be broken up into factions either during their revolt against the tyrant or in process of the organization of the government, after the tyrant has been overthrown. Moreover, it sometimes happens that while the multitude is driving out the tyrant by the help of some man, the latter, having received the power, thereupon seizes the tyranny. Then, fearing to suffer from another what he did to his predecessor, he oppresses his subjects with an even more grievous slavery. This is wont to happen in tyranny, namely, that the second becomes more grievous than the one preceding, inasmuch as, without abandoning the previous oppressions, he himself thinks up fresh ones from the malice of his heart. Whence in Syracuse, at a time when everyone desired the death of Dionysius, a certain old woman kept constantly praying that he might be unharmed and that he might survive her. When the tyrant learned this he asked why she did it. Then she said: "When I was a girl we had a harsh tyrant and I wished for his death: when he was killed, there succeeded him one who was a little harsher. I was very eager to see the end of his dominion also, and we began to have a third ruler still more harsh—that was you. So if you should be taken away, a worse would succeed in your place."

If the excess of tyranny is unbearable, some have been of the opinion that it would be an act of virtue for strong men to slay the tyrant and to expose themselves to the danger of death in order to set the multitude free. An example of this occurs even in the Old Testament, for a certain Aioth slew Eglon, King of Moab, who was oppressing the people of God under harsh slavery, thrusting a dagger into his thigh; and he was made a judge of the people.

But this opinion is not in accord with apostolic teaching. For Peter admonishes us to be reverently subject to our masters, not only to the good and gentle but also the forward: "For if one who suffers unjustly bear his trouble for conscience' sake, this is grace." Wherefore, when many emperors of the Romans tyrannically persecuted the faith of Christ, a great number both of the nobility and the common people were converted to the faith and were praised for patiently bearing death for Christ. They did not resist although they were armed, and this is plainly manifested in the case of the holy Theban legion. Aioth, then, must be considered rather as having slain a foe than assassinated a ruler, however tyrannical, of the people. Hence in the Old Testament we also read that they who killed Joas, the King of Juda, who had fallen away from the worship of God, were slain and their children spared according to the precept of the law.

Should private persons attempt on their own private presumption to kill the rulers, even though tyrants, this would be dangerous for the multitude as well as for their rulers. This is because the wicked usually expose themselves to dangers of this kind more than the good, for the rule of a king, no less than that of a tyrant, is burdensome to them, since, according to the words of Solomon: "A wise king scattereth the wicked." Consequently, by presumption of this kind, danger to the people from the loss of a good king would be more probable than relief through the removal of a tyrant.

Furthermore, it seems that to proceed against the cruelty of tyrants is an action to be undertaken, not through the private presumption of a few, but rather by public authority.

If to provide itself with a king belongs to the right of a given multitude, it is not unjust that the king be deposed or have his power restricted by that same multitude if, becoming a tyrant, he abuses the royal power. It must not be thought that such a multitude is acting unfaithfully in deposing the tyrant, even though it had previously subjected itself to him in perpetuity, because he himself has deserved that the covenant with his subjects should not be kept, since, in ruling the multitude, he did not act faithfully as the office of a king demands. Thus did the Romans, who had accepted Tarquin the Proud as their king, cast him out from the kingship on account of his tyranny and the tyranny of his sons; and they set up in their place a lesser power, namely, the consular power. Similarly Domitian, who had succeeded those most moderate emperors, Vespasian, his father, and Titus, his brother, was slain by the Roman senate when he exercised tyranny, and all his wicked deeds were justly and profitably declared null and void by a decree of the senate. Thus it came about that Blessed John the Evangelist, the beloved disciple of God, who had been exiled to the island of Patmos by that very Domitian, was sent back to Ephesus by a decree of the senate.

If, on the other hand, it pertains to the right of a higher authority to provide a king for a certain multitude, a remedy against the wickedness of a tyrant is to be looked for from him. Thus when Archelaus, who had already begun to reign in Judaea in the place of Herod, his father, was imitating his father's wickedness, a complaint against him having been laid before Caesar Augustus by the Jews, his power was at first diminished by depriving him of his title of king and by dividing one-half of his kingdom between his two brothers. Later, since he was not restrained from tyranny even by this means, Tiberius Caesar sent him into exile to Lugdunum, a city in Gaul.

Should no human aid whatsoever against a tyrant be forthcoming, recourse must be had to God, the King of all, Who is a helper in due time in tribulation. For it lies in his power to turn the cruel heart of the tyrant to mildness. According to Solomon: "The heart of the king is in the hand of the Lord, withersoever He will He shall turn it." He it was who turned into mildness the cruelty of King Assuerus, who was preparing death for the Jews. He it was who so filled the cruel king Nabuchodonosor with piety that he became a proclaimer of the divine power. "Therefore," he said, "I, Nabuchodonosor do now praise and magnify and glorify the King of Heaven; because all His works are true and His ways judgments, and they that walk in pride He is able to abase." Those tryants, however, whom He deems unworthy of conversion He is able to put out of the way or to degrade, according to the words of the Wise Man: "God hath overturned the thrones of proud princes and hath set up the meek in their stead." He it was who, seeing the affliction of his people in Egypt and hearing their cry, hurled Pharaoh, a tyrant over God's people, with all his army into the sea. He it was who not only banished from his kingly throne the above-mentioned Nabuchodonosor because of his former pride, but also cast him from the fellowship of men and changed him into the likeness of a beast. Indeed, his hand is not shortened that He cannot free his people from tyrants. For by Isaias He promised to give his people rest from their labors and lashings and harsh slavery in which they had formerly served; and by Ezechiel He says: "I will deliver my flock from their mouth," i.e., from the mouth of shepherds who feed themselves.

But to deserve to secure this benefit from God, the people must desist from sin, for it is by divine permission that wicked men receive power to rule as a punishment for sin, as the Lord says by the Prophet Osee: "I will give thee a king in my wrath," and it is said in Job that he "maketh a man that is a hypocrite to reign for the sins of the people." Sin must therefore be done away with in order that the scourge of tyrants may cease.*

---

* *De Regimine Principum,* pp. 3-29.

THE RENAISSANCE

Niccolo Machiavelli

During the Renaissance belief in man's free will and evil tendencies continued, but significant changes occurred in the conception of society. A revival of commerce, the spread of the spirit and practice of capitalism, the rise of new towns, and the expansion of secular government had slowly eroded medieval social and political doctrines. Niccolo Machiavelli (1469–1527) was a spokesman for "Realpolitik" (political realism) which emerged during this period.

Niccolo Machiavelli was born into old but not wealthy nobility. He had served his native Florence as a minor clerk in the chancery and as a diplomat. During his political career Machiavelli practiced and observed the intrigue which affected republican Florence and other principalities of Italy. In 1512 the Florentine republic was overthrown by the Medici family and Machiavelli was dismissed from office. Being suspected of treason he was tortured, imprisoned, and then banished from Florence. These experiences with secular and ecclesiastical power struggles provided the embittered exile with the foundation for his histories, views of man, society, and the principles of statecraft. He rejected the Augustinian dualism of a City of Man and a City of God and disregarded the Christian spiritual world. Unlike John of Salisbury and St. Thomas Aquinas, Machiavelli showed little interest in using society, government, and law as means for man's moral improvement. Machiavelli concentrated on temporal life and the practical problems of power, authority, and order among predatory men.

The Discourses (1514) revealed Machiavelli's cynical attitude toward his fellow man: "How easily men are corrupted and in nature become transformed, however good they may be and however well brought up . . ." (I.42.1). Thus, he continued, when considering regulation for the state it must "be taken for granted that all men are wicked and that they will always give vent to the malignity that is in their minds when the opportunity offers" (I.3.1.). In *The Prince* (1513) Machiavelli put aside morality to prescribe the principles of "Realpolitik." He argued that concepts of virtue did not apply to man in society and that the only rules which were applicable were those which provided ways amd means to obtain and hold power. Rejecting the medieval doctrine that the prince ruled by God's grace, Machiavelli asserted that the prince held authority by cunning, ability to parry enemies, and skillful use of allies. With the application of these principles the concept of liberty assumed a new dimension. Man's liberty was not bounded by virtue or law but by political expediency.

I.
Types Of Kingdoms And The Difficulties Of Holding Power

[All governments can be divided into two kinds, republic and monarchy.] I will leave out all discussion on republics, inasmuch as in another place I have written of them at length, and will address myself only to principalities. In doing so I will keep to the order indicated above, and discuss how such principalities are to be ruled and preserved.

I say at once there are fewer difficulties in holding hereditary states, and those long accustomed to the family of their prince, than new ones; for it is sufficient only not to transgress the customs of his ancestors, and to deal prudently with circumstances as they arise, for a prince of average powers to maintain himself in his state, unless he be deprived of it by some extraordinary and excessive force; and if he should be so deprived of it, whenever anything sinister happens to the usurper, he will regain it. . . . For the hereditary prince has less cause and less necessity to offend; hence it happens that he will be more loved; and unless extraordinary vices cause him to be hated, it is reasonable to expect that his subjects will be naturally well disposed towards him; and in the antiquity and duration of his rule the memories and motives that make for change are lost.*

But the difficulties occur in a new principality. And firstly, if it be not entirely new, but is, as it were, a member of a state which, taken collectively, may be called composite, the changes arise chiefly from an inherent difficulty which there is in all new principalities; for men change their rulers willingly, hoping to better themselves, and this hope induces them to take up arms against him who rules: wherein they are deceived, because they afterwards find by experience they have gone from bad to worse. This follows also on another natural and common necessity, which always causes a new prince to burthen those who have submitted to him with his soldiery and with infinite other hardships which he must put upon his new acquisition.

In this way you have enemies in all those whom you have injured in seizing that principality, and you are not able to keep those friends who put you there because of your not being able to satisfy them in the way they expected, and you cannot take strong measures against them, feeling bound to them. For, although one may be very strong in armed forces, yet in entering a province one has always need of the goodwill of the natives.

Reprinted from Niccolo Machiavelli, *The Prince* (London: J. M. Dent & Sons, 1908), pp. 11-12, 15-22, 39-41, 45-49, 53-54, 67, 71-73, 77-82, 85-88, 97-99, 107-9, 111-12, 115-18, 121-23, 127-30, 133-37, 141-45, 149-52, 177-82, 197, 203-7.

* Pp. 11-12.

It is very true that, after acquiring rebellious provinces a second time, they are not so lightly lost afterwards, because the prince, with little reluctance, takes the opportunity of the rebellion to punish the delinquents, to clear out the suspects, and to strengthen himself in the weakest places. . . .

Now I say that those dominions which, when acquired, are added to an ancient state by him who acquires them, are either of the same country and language, or they are not. When they are, it is easier to hold them, especially when they have not been accustomed to self-government; and to hold them securely it is enough to have destroyed the family of the prince who was ruling them; because the two peoples, preserving in other things the old conditions, and not being unlike in customs, will live quietly together. . . .

He who has annexed them, if he wishes to hold them, has only to bear in mind two considerations: the one, that the family of their former lord is extinguished; the other, that neither their laws nor their taxes are altered, so that in a very short time they will become entirely one body with the old principality.

But when states are acquired in a country differing in language, customs, or laws, there are difficulties, and good fortune and great energy are needed to hold them, and one of the greatest and most real helps would be that he who has acquired them should go and reside there. This would make his position more secure and durable, . . .

Because, if one is on the spot, disorders are seen as they spring up, and one can quickly remedy them; but if one is not at hand, they are heard of only when they are great, and then one can no longer remedy them. Besides this, the country is not pillaged by your officials; the subjects are satisfied by prompt recourse to the prince; thus, wishing to be good, they have more cause to love him, and wishing to be otherwise, to fear him. He who would attack that state from the outside must have the utmost caution; as long as the prince resides there it can only be wrested from him with the greatest difficulty.

The other and better course is to send colonies to one or two places, which may be as keys to that state, for it is necessary either to do this or else to keep there a great number of cavalry and infantry. A prince does not spend much on colonies, for with little or no expense he can send them out and keep them there, and he offends a minority only of the citizens from whom he takes lands and houses to give them to the new inhabitants; and those whom he offends, remaining poor and scattered, are never able to injure him; whilst the rest being uninjured are easily kept quiet, and at the same time are anxious not to err for fear it should happen to them as it has to those who have been despoiled. In conclusion, I say that these colonies are not costly, they are more faithful, they injure less, and the injured, as has been said, being poor and scattered, cannot hurt. Upon this one has to remark that men ought either to be well treated or crushed, because they can avenge themselves of lighter injuries, of more serious ones they cannot; therefore the injury that is to be done to a man ought to be of such a kind that one does not stand in fear of revenge.

But in maintaining armed men there in place of colonies one spends much more, having to consume on the garrison all the income from the state, so that the acquisition turns into a loss, and many more are exasperated, because the whole state is injured; through the shifting of the garrison up and down all become acquainted with hardship, and all become hostile, and they are enemies who, whilst beaten on their own ground, are yet able to do hurt. For every reason, therefore, such guards are as useless as a colony is useful.

Again, the prince who holds a country differing in the above respects ought to make himself the head and defender of his less powerful neighbours, and to weaken the more powerful amongst them, taking care that no foreigner as powerful as himself shall, by any accident, get a footing there; for it will always happen that such a one will be introduced by those who are discontented, either through excess of ambition or through fear, as one has seen already. . . .

And the usual course of affairs is that, as soon as a powerful foreigner enters a country, all the subject states are drawn to him, moved by the hatred which they feel against the ruling power. So that in respect to these subject states he has not to take any trouble to gain them over to himself, for the whole of them quickly rally to the state which he has acquired there. He has only to take care that they do not get hold of too much power and too much authority, and then with his own forces, and with their goodwill, he can easily keep down the more powerful of them, so as to remain entirely master in the country. And he who does not properly manage this business will soon lose what he has acquired, and whilst he does hold it he will have endless difficulties and troubles. . . . all prudent princes, who have to regard not only present troubles, but also future ones, for which they must prepare with every energy, [ought to anticipate troubles] because, when foreseen, it is easy to remedy them; but if you wait until they approach, the medicine is no longer in time because the malady has become incurable; for it happens in this, as the physicians say it happens in hectic fever, that in the beginning of the malady it is easy to cure but difficult to detect, but in the course of time, not having been either detected nor treated in the beginning, it becomes easy to detect but difficult to cure. Thus it happens in affairs of state, for when the evils that arise have been foreseen (which it is only given to a wise man to see), they can be quickly redressed, but when, through not having been foreseen, they have been permitted to grow in a way that every one can see them, there is no longer a remedy.*

II.
How Once Independent States Must Be Governed After Conquest

Whenever those states which have been acquired as stated have been accustomed to live under their own laws and in freedom, there are three courses for those who wish to hold them: the first is to ruin them, the next is to reside there in person, the third is to permit them to live under their own laws, drawing a tribute, and establishing within it an oligarchy which will keep it friendly to you. Because such a government, being created by the prince, knows that it cannot stand without his friendship and interest, and does its utmost to support him; and therefore he

* Pp. 15-22.

who would keep a city accustomed to freedom will hold it more easily by the means of its own citizens than in any other way.

So to hold it they were compelled to dismantle many cities in the country, for in truth there is no safe way to retain them otherwise than by ruining them. And he who becomes master of a city accustomed to freedom and does not destroy it, may expect to be destroyed by it, for in rebellion it has always the watchword of liberty and its ancient privileges as a rallying point, which neither time nor benefits will ever cause it to forget. And whatever you may do or provide against, they never forget that name or their privileges unless they are disunited or dispersed, but at every chance they immediately rally to them. . . .

But when cities or countries are accustomed to live under a prince, and his family is exterminated, they, being on the one hand accustomed to obey and on the other hand not having the old prince, cannot agree in making one from amongst themselves, and they do not know how to govern themselves. For this reason they are very slow to take up arms, and a prince can gain them to himself and secure them much more easily. But in republics there is more vitality, greater hatred, and more desire for vengeance, which will never permit them to allow the memory of their former liberty to rest; so that the safest way is to destroy them or to reside there.*

III.
How A Prince Should Rule A State Acquired By Force, Fortune Or Intrigue

A wise man ought always to follow the paths beaten by great men, and to imitate those who have been supreme, so that if his ability does not equal theirs, at least it will savour of it. Let him act like the clever archers who, designing to hit the mark which yet appears too far distant, and knowing the limits to which the strength of their bow attains, take aim much higher than the mark, not to reach by their strength or arrow to so great a height, but to be able with the aid of so high an aim to hit the mark they wish to reach.

I say, therefore, that in entirely new principalities, where there is a new prince, more or less difficulty is found in keeping them, accordingly as there is more or less ability in him who has acquired the state. Now, as the fact of becoming a prince from a private station presupposes either ability or fortune, it is clear that one or other of these two things will mitigate in some degree many difficulties. Nevertheless, he who has relied least on fortune is established the strongest. Further, it facilitates matters when the prince, having no other state, is compelled to reside there in person. . . .

Those who by valorous ways become princes, like these men, acquire a principality with difficulty, but they keep it with ease. The difficulties they have in acquiring

---

* Pp. 39-41.

it arise in part from the new rules and methods which they are forced to introduce to establish their government and its security. And it ought to be remembered that there is nothing more difficult to take in hand, more perilous to conduct, or more uncertain in its success, than to take the lead in the introduction of a new order of things. Because the innovator has for enemies all those who have done well under the old conditions, and lukewarm defenders in those who may do well under the new. This coolness arises partly from fear of the opponents, who have the laws on their side, and partly from the incredulity of men, who do not readily believe in new things until they have had a long experience of them. Thus it happens that whenever those who are hostile have the opportunity to attack they do it like partisans, whilst the others defend lukewarmly, in such wise that the prince is endangered along with them.

It is necessary, therefore, if we desire to discuss this matter thoroughly, to inquire whether these innovators can rely on themselves or have to depend on others: that is to say, whether, to consummate their enterprise, have they to use prayers or can they use force? In the first instance they always succeed badly, and never compass anything; but when they can rely on themselves and use force, then they are rarely endangered. Hence it is that all armed prophets have conquered, and the unarmed ones have been destroyed. Besides the reasons mentioned, the nature of the people is variable, and whilst it is easy to persuade them, it is difficult to fix them in that persuasion. And thus it is necessary to take such measures that, when they believe no longer, it may be possible to make them believe by force.*

Those who solely by good fortune become princes from being private citizens have little trouble in rising, but much in keeping atop; they have not any difficulties on the way up, because they fly, but they have many when they reach the summit. Such are those to whom some state is given either for money or by the favour of him who bestows it; . . . [They] stand simply upon the goodwill and the fortune of him who has elevated them—two most inconstant and unstable things. Neither have they the knowledge requisite for the position; because, unless they are men of great worth and ability, it is not reasonable to expect that they should know how to command, having always lived in a private condition; besides, they cannot hold it because they have not forces which they can keep friendly and faithful.

States that rise unexpectedly, then, like all other things in nature which are born and grow rapidly, cannot have their foundations and correspondencies fixed in such a way that the first storm will not overthrow them; unless, as is said, those who unexpectedly become princes are men of so much ability that they know they have to be prepared at once to hold that which fortune has thrown into their laps, and that those foundations, which others have laid *before* they became princes, they must lay *afterwards*.†

Although a prince may rise from a private station in two ways, neither of which can be entirely attributed to fortune or genius, yet it is manifest to me that I must not be silent on them, although one could be more copiously treated when I discuss republics. These methods are when, either by some wicked or nefarious ways,

---

* Pp. 45-49.

† Pp. 53-54.

one ascends to the principality, or when by the favour of his fellow-citizens a private person becomes the prince of his country.*

Some may wonder how it can happen that Agathocles,[1] and his like, after infinite treacheries and cruelties, should live for long secure in his country, and defend himself from external enemies, and never be conspired against by his own citizens, seeing that many others, by means of cruelty, have never been able even in peaceful times to hold the state, still less in the doubtful times of war. I believe that this follows from severities being badly or properly used. Those may be called properly used, if of evil it is lawful to speak well, that are applied at one blow and are necessary to one's security, and that are not persisted in afterwards unless they can be turned to the advantage of the subjects. The badly employed are those which, notwithstanding they may be few in the commencement, multiply with time rather than decrease. Those who practise the first system are able, by aid of God or man, to mitigate in some degree their rule, as Agathocles did. It is impossible for those who follow the other to maintain themselves.

Hence it is to be remarked that, in seizing a state, the usurper ought to examine closely into all those injuries which it is necessary for him to inflict, and to do them all at one stroke so as not to have to repeat them daily; and thus by not unsettling men he will be able to reassure them, and win them to himself by benefits. He who does otherwise, either from timidity or evil advice, is always compelled to keep the knife in his hand; neither can he rely on his subjects, nor can they attach themselves to him, owing to their continued and repeated wrongs. For injuries ought to be done all at one time, so that, being tasted less, they offend less; benefits ought to be given little by little, so that the flavour of them may last longer.

And above all things, a prince ought to live amongst his people in such a way that no unexpected circumstances, whether of good or evil, shall make him change; because if the necessity for this comes in troubled times, you are too late for harsh measures; and mild ones will not help you, for they will be considered as forced from you, and no one will be under any obligation to you for them.†

IV.
How A Prince Should Rule A Country Acquired By The Support Of Its Citizens

But coming to the other point—where a leading citizen becomes the prince of his country, not by wickedness or any intolerable violence, but by the favour of his fellow citizens—this may be called a civil principality: nor is genius or fortune altogether necessary to attain to it, but rather a happy shrewdness. I say then that such a principality is obtained either by the favour of the people or by the favour

---

* P. 67.
† Pp. 71-73.
[1] *Agathocles.* A Sicilian military leader and tyrant, 361-289 B.C.

of the nobles. Because in all cities these two distinct parties are found, and from this it arises that the people do not wish to be ruled nor oppressed by the nobles, and the nobles wish to rule and oppress the people; and from these two opposite desires there arises in cities one of three results, either a principality, self-government, or anarchy.

A principality is created either by the people or by the nobles, accordingly as one or other of them has the opportunity; for the nobles, seeing they cannot withstand the people, begin to cry up the reputation of one of themselves, and they make him a prince, so that under his shadow they can give vent to their ambitions. The people, finding they cannot resist the nobles, also cry up the reputation of one of themselves, and make him a prince so as to be defended by his authority. He who obtains sovereignty by the assistance of the nobles maintains himself with more difficulty than he who comes to it by the aid of the people, because the former finds himself with many around him who consider themselves his equal, and because of this he can neither rule nor manage them to his liking. But he who reaches sovereignty by popular favour finds himself alone, and has none around him, or few, who are not prepared to obey him.

Besides this, one cannot by fair dealing, and without injury to others, satisfy the nobles, but you can satisfy the people, for their object is more righteous than that of the nobles, the latter wishing to oppress, whilst the former only desire not to be oppressed. It is to be added also that a prince can never secure himself against a hostile people, because of their being too many, whilst from the nobles he can secure himself, as they are few in number. The worst that a prince may expect from a hostile people is to be abandoned by them; but from hostile nobles he has not only to fear abandonment, but also that they will rise against him; for they, being in these affairs more far-seeing and astute, always come forward in time to save themselves, and to obtain favours from him whom they expect to prevail. Further, the prince is compelled to live always with the same people, but he can do well without the same nobles, being able to make and unmake them daily, and to give or take away authority when it pleases him.

Therefore, to make this point clearer, I say that the nobles ought to be looked at mainly in two ways: that is to say, they either shape their course in such a way as binds them entirely to your fortune, or they do not. Those who so bind themselves, and are not rapacious, ought to be honoured and loved; those who do not bind themselves may be dealt with in two ways; they may fail to do this through pusillanimity and a natural want of courage, in which case you ought to make use of them, especially of those who are of good counsel; and thus, whilst in prosperity you honour yourself, in adversity you have not to fear them. But when for their own ambitious ends they shun binding themselves, it is a token that they are giving more thought to themselves than to you, and a prince ought to guard against such, and to fear them as if they were open enemies, because in adversity they always help to ruin him.

Therefore, one who becomes a prince through the favour of the people ought to keep them friendly, and this he can easily do seeing they only ask not to be oppressed by him. But one who, in opposition to the people, becomes a prince by the favour of the nobles, ought, above everything, to seek to win the people over to himself, and this he may easily do if he takes them under his protection. Because men, when they receive good from him of whom they were expecting evil, are bound more closely to their benefactor; thus the people quickly become more devoted to him than if he had been raised to the principality by their favours; and the prince can win their affections in many ways, but as these vary according to the circumstances one cannot give fixed rules, so I omit them; but, I repeat, it is necessary for a prince to have the people friendly, otherwise he has no security in adversity. . . .

But granted a prince who has established himself as above, who can command, and is a man of courage, undismayed in adversity, who does not fail in other qualifications, and who, by his resolution and energy, keeps the whole people encouraged—such a one will never find himself deceived in them, and it will be shown that he has laid his foundations well.

These principalities are liable to danger when they are passing from the civil to the absolute order of government, for such princes either rule personally or through magistrates. In the latter case their government is weaker and more insecure, because it rests entirely on the goodwill of those citizens who are raised to the magistracy, and who, especially in troubled times, can destroy the government with great ease, either by intrigue or open defiance; and the prince has not the chance amid tumults to exercise absolute authority, because the citizens and subjects, accustomed to receive orders from magistrates, are not of a mind to obey him amid these confusions, and there will always be in doubtful times a scarcity of men whom he can trust. For such a prince cannot rely upon what he observes in quiet times, when citizens have need of the state, because then every one agrees with him; they all promise, and when death is far distant they all wish to die for him; but in troubled times, when the state has need of its citizens, then he finds but few. And so much the more is this experiment dangerous, inasmuch as it can only be tried once. Therefore a wise prince ought to adopt such a course that his citizens will always in every sort and kind of circumstance have need of the state and of him, and then he will always find them faithful.*

V.
How To Measure The Strength Of All Monarchies

It is necessary to consider another point in examining the character of these principalities: that is, whether a prince has such power that, in case of need, he can support himself with his own resources, or whether he has always need of the assistance of others. And so to make this quite clear I say that I consider those are able to support themselves by their own resources who can, either by abundance of men or money, raise a sufficient army to join battle against any one who comes to attack them; and I consider those always to have need of others who cannot show themselves against the enemy in the field, but are forced to defend themselves by sheltering behind walls. The first case has been discussed, but we will speak of it again should it recur. In the second case one can say nothing except to encourage such princes to provision and fortify their towns, and not on any account to defend the country. And whoever shall fortify his town well, and shall have managed

* Pp. 77-82.

the other concerns of his subjects in the way stated above, and to be often repeated, will never be attacked without great caution, for men are always adverse to enterprises where difficulties can be seen, and it will be seen not to be an easy thing to attack one who has his town well fortified, and is not hated by his people. . . .

Therefore, a prince who has a strong city, and has not made himself odious, will not be attacked, or if any one should attack he will only be driven off with disgrace; again, because that the affairs of this world are so changeable, it is almost impossible to keep an army a whole year in the field without being interfered with. And whoever should reply: if the people have property outside the city, and see it burnt, they will not remain patient, and the long siege and self-interest will make them forget their prince; to this I answer that a powerful and courageous prince will overcome all such difficulties by giving at one time hope to his subjects that the evil will not be for long, at another time fear of the cruelty of the enemy, then preserving himself adroitly from those subjects who seem to him to be too bold.

Further, the enemy would naturally on his arrival at once burn and ruin the country at the time when the spirits of the people are still hot and ready for the defence; and, therefore, so much the less ought the prince to hesitate; because after a time, when spirits have cooled, the damage is already done, the ills are incurred, and there is no longer any remedy; and therefore they are so much the more ready to unite with their prince, he appearing to be under obligations to them now that their houses have been burnt and their possessions ruined in his defence. For it is the nature of men to be bound by the benefits they confer as much as by those they receive. Therefore, if everything is well considered, it will not be difficult for a wise prince to keep the minds of his citizens steadfast from first to last, when he does not fail to support and defend them.*

VI.
Military Power; The Value Of Mercinary, Auxiliary And Citizen Troops; And, The Duties Of The Prince

Having discoursed particularly on the characteristics of such principalities as in the beginning I proposed to discuss, and having considered in some degree the causes of their being good or bad, and having shown the methods by which many have sought to acquire them and to hold them, it now remains for me to discuss generally the means of offence and defence which belong to each of them.

We have seen above how necessary it is for a prince to have his foundations well laid, otherwise it follows of necessity he will go to ruin. The chief foundations of all states, new as well as old or composite, are good laws and good arms; and as there cannot be good laws where the state is not well armed, it follows that where they are well armed they have good laws. I shall leave the laws out of the discussion and shall speak of the arms.

---

* Pp. 85-88.

I say, therefore, that the arms with which a prince defends his state are either his own or they are mercenaries, auxiliaries, or mixed. Mercenaries and auxiliaries are useless and dangerous; and if one holds his state based on these arms, he will stand neither firm nor safe; for they are disunited, ambitious and without discipline, unfaithful, valiant before friends, cowardly before enemies; they have neither the fear of God nor fidelity to men, and destruction is deferred only so long as the attack is; for in peace one is robbed by them, and in war by the enemy. The fact is, they have no other attraction or reason for keeping the field than a trifle of stipend, which is not sufficient to make them willing to die for you. They are ready enough to be your soldiers whilst you do not make war, but if war comes they take themselves off or run from the foe; . . .

I wish to demonstrate further the infelicity of these arms. The mercenary captains are either capable men or they are not; if they are, you cannot trust them, because they always aspire to their own greatness, either by oppressing you, who are their master, or others contrary to your intentions; but if the captain is not skilful, you are ruined in the usual way.

And if it be urged that whoever is armed will act in the same way, whether mercenary or not, I reply that when arms have to be resorted to, either by a prince or a republic, then the prince ought to go in person and perform the duty of captain; the republic has to send its citizens, and when one is sent who does not turn out satisfactorily, it ought to recall him, and when one is worthy, to hold him by the laws so that he does not leave the command. And experience has shown princes and republics, single-handed, making the greatest progress, and mercenaries doing nothing except damage; . . .*

Auxiliaries, which are the other useless arm, are employed when a prince is called in with his forces to aid and defend, . . . These arms may be useful and good in themselves, but for him who calls them in they are always disadvantageous; for losing, one is undone, and winning, one is their captive.

Therefore, let him who has no desire to conquer make use of these arms, for they are much more hazardous than mercenaries, because with them the ruin is ready made; they are all united, all yield obedience to others; but with mercenaries, when they have conquered, more time and better opportunities are needed to injure you; they are not all of one community, they are found and paid by you, and a third party, which you have made their head, is not able all at once to assume enough authority to injure you. In conclusion, in mercenaries dastardy is most dangerous; in auxiliaries, valour. The wise prince, therefore, has always avoided these arms and turned to his own; and has been willing rather to lose with them than to conquer with others, not deeming that a real victory which is gained with the arms of others.†

I conclude, therefore, that no principality is secure without having its own forces; on the contrary, it is entirely dependent on good fortune, not having the valour which in adversity would defend it. And it has always been the opinion and judgment of wise men that nothing can be so uncertain or unstable as fame or power not founded on its own strength.‡

---

* Pp. 97-99.
† Pp. 107-9.
‡ Pp. 111-12.

A prince ought to have no other aim or thought, nor select anything else for his study, than war and its rules and discipline; for this is the sole art that belongs to him who rules, and it is of such force that it not only upholds those who are born princes, but it often enables men to rise from a private station to that rank. And, on the contrary, it is seen that when princes have thought more of ease than of arms they have lost their states. And the first cause of your losing it is to neglect this art; and what enables you to acquire a state is to be master of the art. . . .

For among other evils which being unarmed brings you, it causes you to be despised, and this is one of those ignominies against which a prince ought to guard himself, as is shown later on. Because there is nothing proportionate between the armed and the unarmed; and it is not reasonable that he who is armed should yield obedience willingly to him who is unarmed, or that the unarmed man should be secure among armed servants. Because, there being in the one disdain and in the other suspicion, it is not possible for them to work well together. And therefore a prince who does not understand the art of war, over and above the other misfortunes already mentioned, cannot be respected by his soldiers, nor can he rely on them. He ought never, therefore, to have out of his thoughts this subject of war, and in peace he should addict himself more to its exercise than in war; this he can do in two ways, the one by action, the other by study.

As regards action, he ought above all things to keep his men well organised and drilled, to follow incessantly the chase, by which he accustoms his body to hardships, and learns something of the nature of localities, and gets to find out how the mountains rise, how the valleys open out, how the plains lie, and to understand the nature of rivers and marshes, and in all this to take the greatest care. Which knowledge is useful in two ways. Firstly, he learns to know his country, and is better able to undertake its defence; afterwards, by means of the knowledge and observation of that locality, he understands with ease any other which it may be necessary for him to study hereafter; because the hills, valleys, and plains, and rivers and marshes that are, for instance, in Tuscany, have a certain resemblance to those of other countries, so that with a knowledge of the aspect of one country one can easily arrive at a knowledge of others. And the prince that lacks this skill lacks the essential which it is desirable that a captain should possess, for it teaches him to surprise his enemy, to select quarters, to lead armies, to array the battle, to besiege towns to advantage.

Philopoemen, Prince of the Acheans, among other praises which writers have bestowed on him, is commended because in time of peace he never had anything in his mind but the rules of war; and when he was in the country with friends, he often stopped and reasoned with them: "If the enemy should be upon that hill, and we should find ourselves here with our army, with whom would be the advantage? How should one best advance to meet him, keeping the ranks? If we should wish to retreat, how ought we to set about it? If they should retreat, how ought we to pursue?" And he would set forth to them, as he went, all the chances that could befall an army; he would listen to their opinion and state his, confirming it with reasons, so that by these continual discussions there could never arise, in time of war, any unexpected circumstances that he could not deal with.

But to exercise the intellect the prince should read histories, and study there the actions of illustrious men, to see how they have borne themselves in war, to examine the causes of their victories and defeat, so as to avoid the latter and imitate the former; and above all do as an illustrious man did, who took as an exemplar one who had been praised and famous before him, and whose achievements and deeds he always kept in his mind, as it is said Alexander the Great imitated Achilles, Caesar Alexander, Scipio Cyrus. And whoever reads the life of Cyrus, written by Xenophon, will recognise afterwards in the life of Scipio how that imitation was his glory, and how in chastity, affability, humanity, and liberality Scipio conformed to those things which have been written of Cyrus by Xenophon. A wise prince ought to observe some such rules, and never in peaceful times stand idle, but increase his resources with industry in such a way that they may be available to him in adversity, so that if fortune changes it may find him prepared to resist her blows.*

VII.
Characteristics A Prince Should Adopt To Sustain Power And Authority—The Lion And The Fox

It remains now to see what ought to be the rules of conduct for a prince towards subject and friends. And as I know that many have written on this point, I expect I shall be considered presumptuous in mentioning it again, especially as in discussing it I shall depart from the methods of other people. But, it being my intention to write a thing which shall be useful to him who apprehends it, it appears to me more appropriate to follow up the real truth of a matter than the imagination of it; for many have pictured republics and principalities which in fact have never been known or seen, because how one lives is so far distant from how one ought to live, that he who neglects what is done for what ought to be done, sooner effects his ruin than his preservation; for a man who wishes to act entirely up to his professions of virtue soon meets with what destroys him among so much that is evil.

Hence it is necessary for a prince wishing to hold his own to know how to do wrong, and to make use of it or not according to necessity. Therefore, putting on one side imaginary things concerning a prince, and discussing those which are real, I say that all men when they are spoken of, and chiefly princes for being more highly placed, are remarkable for some of those qualities which bring them either blame or praise; and thus it is that one is reputed liberal, another miserly, . . . one is reputed generous, one rapacious; one cruel, one compassionate; one faithless, another faithful; one effeminate and cowardly, another bold and brave; one affable, another haughty; one lascivious, another chaste; one sincere, another cunning; one hard, another easy; one grave, another frivolous; one religious, another unbelieving, and the like. And I know that every one will confess that it would be most praiseworthy in a prince to exhibit all the above qualities that are considered good; but because they can neither be entirely possessed nor observed, for human

* Pp. 115-18.

conditions do not permit it, it is necessary for him to be sufficiently prudent that he may know how to avoid the reproach of those vices which would lose him his state; and also to keep himself, if it be possible, from those which would not lose him it; but this not being possible, he may with less hesitation abandon himself to them. And again, he need not make himself uneasy at incurring a reproach for those vices without which the state can only be saved with difficulty, for if everything is considered carefully, it will be found that something which looks like virtue, if followed, would be his ruin; whilst something else, which looks like vice, yet followed brings him security and prosperity.*

Commencing then with the first of the above-named characteristics, I say that it would be well to be reputed liberal. Nevertheless, liberality exercised in a way that does not bring you the reputation for it, injures you; for if one exercises it honestly and as it should be exercised, it may not become known, and you will not avoid the reproach of its opposite. Therefore, any one wishing to maintain among men the name of liberal is obliged to avoid no attribute of magnificence; so that a prince thus inclined will consume in such acts all his property, and will be compelled in the end, if he wish to maintain the name of liberal, to unduly weigh down his people, and tax them, and do everything he can to get money. This will soon make him odious to his subjects, and becoming poor he will be little valued by any one; thus, with his liberality, having offended many and rewarded few, he is affected by the very first trouble and imperilled by whatever may be the first danger; recognising this himself, and wishing to draw back from it, he runs at once into the reproach of being miserly.

Therefore, a prince, not being able to exercise this virtue of liberality in such a way that it is recognised, except to his cost, if he is wise he ought not to fear the reputation of being mean, for in time he will come to be more considered than if liberal, seeing that with his economy his revenues are enough, that he can defend himself against all attacks, and is able to engage in enterprises without burdening his people; thus it comes to pass that he exercises liberality towards all from whom he does not take, who are numberless, and meanness towards those to whom he does not give, who are few. . . .

A prince, therefore, provided that he has not to rob his subjects, that he can defend himself, that he does not become poor and abject, that he is not forced to become rapacious, ought to hold of little account a reputation for being mean, for it is one of those vices which will enable him to govern.

And if any one should say: Caesar obtained empire by liberality, and many others have reached the highest positions by having been liberal, and by being considered so, I answer: Either you are a prince in fact, or in a way to become one. In the first case this liberality is dangerous, in the second it is very necessary to be considered liberal; and Caesar was one of those who wished to become pre-eminent in Rome; but if he had survived after becoming so, and had not moderated his expenses, he would have destroyed his government. And if any one should reply: Many have been princes, and have done great things with armies, who have been considered very liberal, I reply: Either a prince spends that which is his own or his subjects' or else that of others. In the first case he ought to be sparing, in the second he ought not to neglect any opportunity for liberality.

---

* Pp. 121-23.

And to the prince who goes forth with his army, supporting it by pillage, sack, and extortion, handling that which belongs to others, this liberality is necessary, otherwise he would not be followed by soldiers. And of that which is neither yours nor your subjects' you can be a ready giver, as were Cyrus, Caesar, and Alexander; because it does not take away your reputation if you squander that of others, but adds to it; it is only squandering your own that injures you.

And there is nothing wastes so rapidly as liberality, for even whilst you exercise it you lose the power to do so, and so become either poor or despised, or else, in avoiding poverty, rapacious and hated. And a prince should guard himself, above all things, against being despised and hated; and liberality leads you to both. Therefore it is wiser to have a reputation for meanness which brings reproach without hatred, than to be compelled through seeking a reputation for liberality to incur a name for rapacity which begets reproach with hatred.*

Coming now to the other qualities mentioned above, I say that every prince ought to desire to be considered clement and not cruel. Nevertheless he ought to take care not to misuse this clemency. . . .

Therefore a prince, so long as he keeps his subjects united and loyal, ought not to mind the reproach of cruelty; because with a few examples he will be more merciful than those who, through too much mercy, allow disorders to arise, from which follow murder or robbery; for these are wont to injure the whole people, whilst those executions which originate with a prince offend the individual only. . . .

And of all princes, it is impossible for the new prince to avoid the imputation of cruelty, owing to new states being full of dangers. . . . he ought to be slow to believe and to act, nor should he himself show fear, but proceed in a temperate manner with prudence and humanity, so that too much confidence may not make him incautious and too much distrust render him intolerable.

Upon this a question arises: whether it be better to be loved than feared or feared than loved? It may be answered that one should wish to be both, but, because it is difficult to unite them in one person, it is much safer to be feared than loved, when, of the two, either must be dispensed with. Because this is to be asserted in general of men, that they are ungrateful, fickle, false, cowards, covetous, and as long as you succeed they are yours entirely; they will offer you their blood, poverty, life, and children, as is said above, when the need is far distant; but when it approaches they turn against you. And that prince who, relying entirely on their promises, has neglected other precautions, is ruined; because friendships that are obtained by payments, and not by greatness or nobility of mind, may indeed be earned, but they are not secured, and in time of need cannot be relied upon; and men have less scruple in offending one who is beloved than one who is feared, for love is preserved by the link of obligation which, owing to the baseness of men, is broken at every opportunity for their advantage; but fear preserves you by a dread of punishment which never fails.

Nevertheless a prince ought to inspire fear in such a way that, if he does not win love, he avoids hatred; because he can endure very well being feared whilst he is not hated, which will always be as long as he abstains from the property of his citizens and subjects and from their women. But when it is necessary for him to proceed against the life of some one, he must do it on proper justification

---

* Pp. 127-30.

and for manifest cause, but above all things he must keep his hands off the property of others, because men more quickly forget the death of their father than the loss of their patrimony. Besides, pretexts for taking away the property are never wanting; for he who has once begun to live by robbery will always find pretexts for seizing what belongs to others; but reasons for taking life, on the contrary, are more difficult to find and sooner lapse. But when a prince is with his army, and has under control a multitude of soldiers, then it is quite necessary for him to disregard the reputation of cruelty, for without it he would never hold his army united or disposed to its duties. . . .

Returning to the question of being feared or loved, I come to the conclusion that, men loving according to their own will and fearing according to that of the prince, a wise prince should establish himself on that which is in his own control and not in that of others; he must endeavour only to avoid hatred, as is noted.*

Every one admits how praiseworthy it is in a prince to keep faith, and to live with integrity and not with craft. Nevertheless our experience has been that those princes who have done great things have held good faith of little account, and have known how to circumvent the intellect of men by craft, and in the end have overcome those who have relied on their word. You must know there are two ways of contesting, the one by the law, the other by force; the first method is proper to men, the second to beasts; but because the first is frequently not sufficient, it is necessary to have recourse to the second. Therefore it is necessary for a prince to understand how to avail himself of the beast and the man. . . .

A prince, therefore, being compelled knowingly to adopt the beast, ought to choose the fox and the lion; because the lion cannot defend himself against snares and the fox cannot defend himself against wolves. Therefore, it is necessary to be a fox to discover the snares and a lion to terrify the wolves. Those who rely simply on the lion do not understand what they are about. Therefore a wise lord cannot, nor ought he to, keep faith when such observance may be turned against him, and when the reasons that caused him to pledge it exist no longer. If men were entirely good this precept would not hold, but because they are bad, and will not keep faith with you, you too are not bound to observe it with them. Nor will there ever be wanting to a prince legitimate reasons to excuse this non-observance. Of this endless modern examples could be given, showing how many treaties and engagements have been made void and of no effect through the faithlessness of princes; and he who has known best how to employ the fox has succeeded best.

But it is necessary to know well how to disguise this characteristic, and to be a great pretender and dissembler; and men are so simple, and so subject to present necessities, that he who seeks to deceive will always find some one who will allow himself to be deceived.

Therefore it is unnecessary for a prince to have all the good qualities I have enumerated, but it is very necessary to appear to have them. And I shall dare to say this also, that to have them and always to observe them is injurious, and that to appear to have them is useful; to appear merciful, faithful, humane, religious, upright, and to be so, but with a mind so framed that should you require not to be so, you may be able and know how to change to the opposite.

---

* Pp. 133-37.

And you have to understand this, that a prince, especially a new one, cannot observe all those things for which men are esteemed, being often forced, in order to maintain the state, to act contrary to fidelity, friendship, humanity, and religion. Therefore it is necessary for him to have a mind ready to turn itself accordingly as the winds and variations of fortune force it, yet, as I have said above, not to diverge from the good if he can avoid doing so, but, if compelled, then to know how to set about it.

For this reason a prince ought to take care that he never lets anything slip from his lips that is not replete with the above-named five qualities, that he may appear to him who sees and hears him altogether merciful, faithful, humane, upright, and religious. There is nothing more necessary to appear to have than this last quality, inasmuch as men judge generally more by the eye than by the hand, because it belongs to everybody to see you, to few to come in touch with you. Every one sees what you appear to be, few really know what you are, and those few dare not oppose themselves to the opinion of the many, who have the majesty of the state to defend them; and in the actions of all men, and especially of princes, which it is not prudent to challenge, one judges by the result.

For that reason, let a prince have the credit of conquering and holding his state, the means will always be considered honest, and he will be praised by everybody; because the vulgar are always taken by what a thing seems to be and by what comes of it; and in the world there are only the vulgar, for the few find a place there only when the many have no ground to rest on.

One prince of the present time, whom it is not well to name, never preaches anything else but peace and good faith, and to both he is most hostile, and either, if he had kept it, would have deprived him of reputation and kingdom many a time.*

Now, concerning the characteristics of which mention is made above, I have spoken of the more important ones, the others I wish to discuss briefly under this generality, that the prince must consider, as has been in part said before, how to avoid those things which will make him hated or contemptible; and as often as he shall have succeeded he will have fulfilled his part, and he need not fear any danger in other reproaches.

It makes him hated above all things, as I have said, to be rapacious, and to be a violator of the property and women of his subjects, from both of which he must abstain. And when neither their property nor honour is touched, the majority of men live content, and he has only to contend with the ambition of a few, whom he can curb with ease in many ways.

It makes him contemptible to be considered fickle, frivolous, effeminate, mean-spirited, irresolute, from all of which a prince should guard himself as from a rock; and he should endeavour to show in his actions greatness, courage, gravity, and fortitude; and in his private dealings with his subjects let him show that his judgments are irrevocable, and maintain himself in such reputation that no one can hope either to deceive him or to get round him.

That prince is highly esteemed who conveys this impression of himself, and he who is highly esteemed is not easily conspired against; for, provided it is well known that he is an excellent man and revered by his people, he can only be

---

* Pp. 141-45.

attacked with difficulty. For this reason a prince ought to have two fears, one from within, on account of his subjects, the other from without, on account of external powers. From the latter he is defended by being well armed and having good allies, and if he is well armed he will have good friends, and affairs will always remain quiet within when they are quiet without, unless they should have been already disturbed by conspiracy; and even should affairs outside be disturbed, if he has carried out his preparations and has lived as I have said, as long as he does not despair, he will resist every attack, . . .

But concerning his subjects, when affairs outside are disturbed he has only to fear that they will conspire secretly, from which a prince can easily secure himself by avoiding being hated and despised, and by keeping the people satisfied with him, which it is most necessary for him to accomplish, as I said above at length. And one of the most efficacious remedies that a prince can have against conspiracies is not to be hated and despised by the people, for he who conspires against a prince always expects to please them by his removal; but when the conspirator can only look forward to offending them, he will not have the courage to take such a course, for the difficulties that confront a conspirator are infinite. And as experience shows, many have been the conspiracies, but few have been successful; because he who conspires cannot act alone, nor can he take a companion except from those whom he believes to be malcontents, and as soon as you have opened your mind to a malcontent you have given him the material with which to content himself, for by denouncing you he can look for every advantage; so that, seeing the gain from this course to be assured, and seeing the other to be doubtful and full of dangers, he must be a very rare friend, or a thoroughly obstinate enemy of the prince, to keep faith with you.

And, to reduce the matter into a small compass, I say that, on the side of the conspirator, there is nothing but fear, jealousy, prospect of punishment to terrify him; but on the side of the prince there is the majesty of the principality, the laws, the protection of friends and the state to defend him; so that, adding to all these things the popular goodwill, it is impossible that any one should be so rash as to conspire. For whereas in general the conspirator has to fear before the execution of his plot, in this case he has also to fear the sequel to the crime; because on account of it he has the people for an enemy, and thus cannot hope for any escape.*

VIII.
How A Prince Acquires Prestige

Nothing makes a prince so much esteemed as great enterprises and setting a fine example. . . .

Again, it much assists a prince to set unusual examples in internal affairs, similar to those which are related of Messer Bernabo da Milano, who, when he had the opportunity, by any one in civil life doing some extraordinary thing, either good

* Pp. 149-52.

or bad, would take some method of rewarding or punishing him, which would be much spoken about. And a prince ought, above all things, always to endeavour in every action to gain for himself the reputation of being a great and remarkable man.

A prince is also respected when he is either a true friend or a downright enemy; that is to say, when, without any reservation, he declares himself in favour of one party against the other; which course will always be more advantageous than standing neutral; because if two of your powerful neighbours come to blows, they are of such a character that, if one of them conquers, you have either to fear him or not. In either case it will always be more advantageous for you to declare yourself and to make war strenuously; because, in the first case, if you do not declare yourself, you will invariably fall a prey to the conqueror, to the pleasure and satisfaction of him who has been conquered, and you will have no reasons to offer, nor anything to protect or to shelter you. Because he who conquers does not want doubtful friends who will not aid him in the time of trial; and he who loses will not harbour you because you did not willingly, sword in hand, court his fate. . . .

Thus it will always happen that he who is not your friend will demand your neutrality, whilst he who is your friend will entreat you to declare yourself with arms. And irresolute princes, to avoid present dangers, generally follow the neutral path, and are generally ruined. But when a prince declares himself gallantly in favour of one side, if the party with whom he allies himself conquers, although the victor may be powerful and may have him at his mercy, yet he is indebted to him, and there is established a bond of amity; and men are never so shameless as to become a monument of ingratitude by oppressing you. Victories after all are never so complete that the victor must not show some regard, especially to justice. But if he with whom you ally yourself loses, you may be sheltered by him, and whilst he is able he may aid you, and you become companions in a fortune that may rise again.

In the second case, when those who fight are of such a character that you have no anxiety as to who may conquer, so much the more is it greater prudence to be allied, because you assist at the destruction of one by the aid of another who, if he had been wise, would have saved him; and conquering, as it is impossible that he should not with your assistance, he remains at your discretion. And here it is to be noted that a prince ought to take care never to make an alliance with one more powerful than himself for the purpose of attacking others, unless necessity compels him, as is said above; because if he conquers you are at his discretion, and princes ought to avoid as much as possible being at the discretion of any one. . . .

Never let any Government imagine that it can choose perfectly safe courses; rather let it expect to have to take very doubtful ones, because it is found in ordinary affairs that one never seeks to avoid one trouble without running into another; but prudence consists in knowing how to distinguish the character of troubles, and for choice to take the lesser evil.

A prince ought also to show himself a patron of ability, and to honour the proficient in every art. At the same time he should encourage his citizens to practise their callings peaceably, both in commerce and agriculture, and in every other following, so that the one should not be deterred from improving his possessions for fear lest they be taken away from him or another from opening up trade for fear of taxes; but the prince ought to offer rewards to whoever wishes to do these things and designs in any way to honour his city or state.

Further, he ought to entertain the people with festivals and spectacles at convenient seasons of the year; and as every city is divided into guilds or into societies, he ought to hold such bodies in esteem, and associate with them sometimes, and show himself an example of courtesy and liberality; nevertheless, always maintaining the majesty of his rank, for this he must never consent to abate in anything.*

IX.
Summary: The Role Of Fortune And Free Will

The previous suggestions, carefully observed, will enable a new prince to appear well established, and render him at once more secure and fixed in the state than if he had been long seated there. For the actions of a new prince are more narrowly observed than those of an hereditary one, and when they are seen to be able they gain more men and bind far tighter than ancient blood; because men are attracted more by the present than by the past, and when they find the present good they enjoy it and seek no further; they will also make the utmost defence for a prince if he fails them not in other things. Thus it will be a double glory to him to have established a new principality, and adorned and strengthened it with good laws, good arms, good allies, and with a good example; so will it be a double disgrace to him who, born a prince, shall lose his state by want of wisdom.†

It is not unknown to me how many men have had, and still have, the opinion that the affairs of the world are in such wise governed by fortune and by God that men with their wisdom cannot direct them and that no one can even help them; and because of this they would have us believe that it is not necessary to labour much in affairs, but to let chance govern them. This opinion has been more credited in our times because of the great changes in affairs which have been seen, and may still be seen, every day, beyond all human conjecture. Sometimes pondering over this, I am in some degree inclined to their opinion. Nevertheless, not to extinguish our free will, I hold it to be true that fortune is the arbiter of one half of our actions, but that she still leaves us to direct the other half, or perhaps a little less.

I compare her to one of those raging rivers, which when in flood overflows the plains, sweeping away trees and buildings, bearing away the soil from place to place; everything flies before it, all yield to its violence, without being able in any way to withstand it; and yet, though its nature be such, it does not follow therefore that men, when the weather becomes fair, shall not make provision, both with defences and barriers, in such a manner that, rising again, the waters may pass away by canal, and their force be neither so unrestrained nor so dangerous. So it happens with fortune, who shows her power where valour has not prepared

* Pp. 177-82.

† P. 197.

to resist her, and thither she turns her forces where she knows that barriers and defences have not been raised to constrain her.

And if you will consider Italy, which is the seat of these changes, and which has given to them their impulse, you will see it to be an open country without barriers and without any defence. For if it had been defended by proper valour, as are Germany, Spain, and France, either this invasion would not have made the great changes it has made or it would not have come at all. And this I consider enough to say concerning resistance to fortune in general.

But confining myself more to the particular, I say that a prince may be seen happy to-day and ruined to-morrow without having shown any change of disposition or character. This, I believe, arises firstly from causes that have already been discussed at length, namely, that the prince who relies entirely upon fortune is lost when it changes. I believe also that he will be successful who directs his actions according to the spirit of the times, and that he whose actions do not accord with the times will not be successful. Because men are seen, in affairs that lead to the end which every man has before him, namely, glory and riches, to get there by various methods; one with caution, another with haste; one by force, another by skill; one by patience, another by its opposite; and each one succeeds in reaching the goal by a different method. One can also see of two cautious men the one attain his end, the other fail; and similarly, two men by different observances are equally successful, the one being cautious, the other impetuous; all this arises from nothing else than whether or not they conform in their methods to the spirit of the times. This follows from what I have said, that two men working differently bring about the same effect, and of two working similarly, one attains his object and the other does not.

Changes in estate also issue from this, for if, to one who governs himself with caution and patience, times and affairs converge in such a way that his administration is successful, his fortune is made; but if times and affairs change, he is ruined if he does not change his course of action. But a man is not often found sufficiently circumspect to know how to accommodate himself to the change, both because he cannot deviate from what nature inclines him to, and also because, having always prospered by acting in one way, he cannot be persuaded that it is well to leave it; and, therefore, the cautious man, when it is time to turn adventurous, does not know how to do it, hence he is ruined; but had he changed his conduct with the times fortune would not have changed. . . .

I conclude therefore that, fortune being changeful and mankind steadfast in their ways, so long as the two are in agreement men are successful, but unsuccessful when they fall out. For my part I consider that it is better to be adventurous than cautious, because fortune is a woman, and if you wish to keep her under it is necessary to beat and ill-use her; and it is seen that she allows herself to be mastered by the adventurous rather than by those who go to work more coldly. She is, therefore, always, woman-like, a lover of young men, because they are less cautious, more violent, and with more audacity command her.*

---

* Pp. 203-7.

Thomas More

The Renaissance was characterized not only by the emergence of "Realpolitik" but also by a humanistic view toward man and society. Humanist philosophy of man was probably best described by Giovanni Pico (1463–94) in his *Oration on the Dignity of Man.* Pico stated that man was born with free will and that each man could forge a life of dignity and self-fulfillment. Sir Thomas More (1478–1535), Chancellor of England and later a saint in the Catholic Church, blended the humanist optimism toward the potential goodness of man with pietism in his *Utopia* (1515-16).

In Book I of *Utopia* More exposed the greed, pride, and lust for power which permeated England and resulted in social turmoil. In Book II—sections reprinted below—More fantasied the existence of a society where virtue, ethics, and duty were given the force of law. He described a cooperative community without private property where tyranny was repressed by a political system of representation, checks, and balances. More prescribed a framework of liberty which permitted the individual to develop his mind and satisfy his needs within a social structure of morality and order. His devotion to social virtue based on reason and religion left significant impressions on other humanists such as Erasmus of Rotterdam (1469–1536). More's convictions also led to his execution by order of Henry VIII for refusing to exchange his beliefs for political expediency.

I.
A Description Of The Utopian Countryside And Cities

The island of Utopia in the middle, where it is broadest, is two hundred miles broad, and holds almost at the same breadth over a great part of it, but grows narrower toward both ends. Its figure is not unlike a crescent; between its horns

Reprinted from Thomas More, *Utopia* (London: Joseph Rickerby, 1838), pp. 77-96, 109-36, 143-51, 190-96.

the sea comes in eleven miles broad, and spreads itself into a great bay, which is [encircled] with land [with a boundary] of about five hundred miles, and is well secured from winds. There is no great current in the bay, and the whole coast is, as it were, one continued harbour, which gives all that live in the island great convenience for mutual commerce, but the entry into the bay, what by rocks on one hand, and shallows on the other, is very dangerous. In the middle of it there is one single rock which appears above water, and so is not dangerous: on the top of it there is a tower built, in which a garrison is kept. The other rocks lie under water, and are very dangerous. The channel is known only to the natives; so that if any stranger should enter into the bay, without one of their pilots, he would run a great danger of shipwreck; for even they themselves could not pass it safe, if some marks that are on their coast did not direct their way; and if these should be but a little shifted, any fleet that might come against them, how great soever it were, would be certainly lost. On the other side of the island there are likewise many harbours; and the coast is so fortified, both by nature and art, that a small number of men can hinder the descent of a great army. But they report (and there remain good marks of it to make it credible) that this was no island at first, but a part of the continent. Utopus that conquered it . . . and brought the rude and uncivilized inhabitants into such a good government, and to that measure of politeness that they do now far excel all the rest of mankind. Having soon subdued them, he designed to separate them from the continent, and to bring the sea quite about them; and in order to that, he made a deep channel to be digged, fifteen miles long. He not only forced the inhabitants to work at it, but likewise his own soldiers, that the natives might not think he treated them like slaves; and, having set vast numbers of men to work, he brought it to a speedy conclusion, beyond all men's expectations. By this their neighbours, who laughed at the folly of the undertaking at first, were struck with admiration and terror, when they saw it brought to perfection.

There are fifty-four cities in the island, all large and well-built. The manners, customs, and laws of all their cities are the same, and they are all contrived as near in the same manner as the ground on which they stand will allow; the nearest lie at least twenty-four miles distance from one another, and the most remote are not so far distant but that a man can go on foot in one day from it to that which lies next it. Every city sends three of their wisest senators once a year to Amaurot, for consulting about their common concerns; for that is the chief town of the island, being situated near the centre of it, so that it is the most convenient place for their assemblies. Every city has so much ground set off for its jurisdiction that there is twenty miles of soil round it, assigned to it; and where the towns lie wider, they have much more ground. No town desires to enlarge their bounds; for they consider themselves rather as tenants than landlords of their soil.

They have built over all the country, farmhouses for husbandmen, which are well-contrived, and are furnished with all things necessary for country labour. Inhabitants are sent by turns from the cities to dwell in them; no country family has fewer than forty men and women in it, besides two slaves. There is a master and a mistress set over every family; and over thirty families there is a magistrate settled. Every year, twenty of this family come back to the town, after they have stayed out two years in the country; and, in their room, there are other twenty sent from the town, that they may learn country work from those that have been already one year in the country, which they must teach those that come to them the next year from the town. By this means such as dwell in those country farms are never ignorant of agriculture, and so commit no errors in it, which might otherwise be fatal to them, and bring them under a scarcity of corn. But, though there is every year such a shifting of the husbandmen, that none may be forced against his mind to follow that hard course of life too long, yet many among them take such pleasure in it, that they desire leave to continue many years in it. These husbandmen labour the ground, breed cattle, hew wood, and convey it to the towns, either by land or water, as is most convenient. They breed an infinite multitude of chickens in a very curious manner; for the hens do not sit and hatch them, but they lay vast numbers of eggs in a gentle and equal heat, in which they are hatched; and they are no sooner out of the shell, and able to stir about, but they seem to consider those that feed them as their mothers, and follow them as other chickens do the hen that hatched them. They breed very few horses, but those they have are full of mettle, and are kept only for exercising their youth in the art of sitting and riding of them; for they do not put them to any work, either of ploughing or carriage, in which they employ oxen; for, though horses are stronger, yet they find oxen can hold out longer; and, as they are not subject to so many diseases, so they are kept upon a less charge, and with less trouble; and when they are so worn out that they are no more fit for labour, they are good meat at last. They sow no corn but that which is to be their bread; for they drink either wine, cider, or perry, and often water,—sometimes pure, and sometimes boiled with honey or liquorice, with which they abound. And, though they know exactly well how much corn will serve every town, and all that tract of country which belongs to it, yet they sow much more, and breed more cattle than are necessary for their consumption; and they give that overplus of which they make no use to their neighbours. When they want anything in the country which it does not produce, they fetch that from the town, without carrying anything in exchange for it; and the magistrates of the town take care to see it given them; for they meet generally in the town once a month, upon a festival day. When the time of harvest comes, the magistrates in the country send to those in the towns, and let them know how many hands they will need for reaping the harvest; and the number they call for being sent to them, they commonly dispatch it all in one day.

He that knows one of their towns knows them all, they are so like one another, except where the situation makes some difference. I shall therefore describe one of them, and it is no matter which; but none is so proper as Amaurot; for, as none is more eminent, all the rest yielding in precedence to this, because it is the seat of their supreme council, so there was none of them better known to me, I having lived for five years altogether in it. . . .

The town is [surrounded by] a high and thick wall, in which there are many towers and forts; there is also a broad and deep dry ditch, set thick with thorns, cast round three sides of the town, and the river is instead of a ditch on the fourth side. The streets are made very convenient for all carriages, and are well sheltered from the winds. Their buildings are good, and are so uniform that a whole side of a street looks like one house. The streets are twenty feet broad; there lie gardens behind all their houses; these are large, but inclosed with buildings that on all hands face the streets; so that every house has both a door to the street, and a back-door to the garden; their doors have all two leaves, which as they are easily opened, so they shut of their own accord; and, there being no property among them, every man may freely enter into any house whatsoever. At every ten years' end they shift their houses by lots. They cultivate their gardens with great care, so that they have both vines, fruits, herbs, and flowers in them; and all is well ordered and so finely kept, that I never saw gardens anywhere that were both so fruitful as theirs are. And this humour of ordering their gardens so well, is not only kept up by the pleasure they find in it, but also by an emulation between the inhabitants of the several streets, who vie with one another in this matter; and there is, indeed, nothing belonging to the whole town that is both more useful and more pleasant.*

II.
Civil Government And The Law

Thirty families choose every year a magistrate, who was called anciently the Syphogrant, but is now called the Philarch; and over every ten syphogrants, with the families subject to them, there is another magistrate, who was anciently called the Tranibore, but of late the Archphilarch. All the syphogrants, who are in number two hundred, choose the Prince out of a list of four, whom the people of the four divisions of the city name to them, but they take an oath before they proceed to an election that they will choose him whom they think [best fit] for the office; they give their voices secretly, so that it is not known for whom everyone gives his suffrage. The prince [rules] for life, unless he is removed upon suspicion of some design to enslave the people. The tranibors are newly chosen every year, but they are for the most part still continued. All their other magistrates are only annual.

The tranibors meet every third day, and oftener if need be, and consult with the prince, either concerning the affairs of the state in general, or such private differences as may arise sometimes among the people; though that falls out but seldom. There are always two syphogrants called into the council-chamber, and these are changed every day. It is a fundamental rule of their government, that no conclusion can be made in anything that relates to the public, till it has been first debated three several days in their council. It is death, for any to meet and consult concerning the state, unless it be either in their ordinary council, or in the assembly of the whole body of the people.

These things have been so provided among them, that the prince and the tranibors may not conspire together to change the government, and enslave the people; and, therefore, when anything of great importance is set on foot, it is sent to the syphogrants, who, after they have communicated it with the families that belong to their divisions, and have considered it among themselves, make report to the senate; and upon great occasions, the matter is referred to the council of

---

* Pp. 77-84.

the whole island. One rule observed in their council is, never to debate a thing on the same day in which it is first proposed; for that is always referred to the next meeting, that so men may not [act] rashly, and in the heat of discourse engage themselves too soon, which may bias them so much that, instead of considering the good of the public, they will rather study to maintain their own notions; and, by a perverse and preposterous sort of shame, hazard their country, rather than endanger their own reputation, or venture the being suspected to have wanted foresight in the expedients that they proposed at first. And, therefore, to prevent this they take care that they may rather be deliberate than sudden in their motions.*

Their law does not determine the punishment for [serious] crimes; but that is left to the senate, to temper it according to the circumstances of the fact. Husbands have power to correct their wives, and parents to correct their children, unless the fault is so great, that a public punishment is thought necessary for the striking terror into others. For the most part, slavery is the punishment even of the greatest crimes; for as that is no less terrible to the criminals themselves than death, so they think the preserving them in a state of servitude is more for the interest of the commonwealth, than the killing them outright; since as their labour is a greater benefit to the public than their death could be, so the sight of their misery is a more lasting terror to other men, than that which would be given by their death. If their slaves rebel, and will not bear their yoke, and submit to the labour that is enjoined them, they are treated as wild beasts that cannot be kept in order, neither by a prison, nor by their chains, and are at last put to death. But those who bear their punishment patiently, and are so much wrought on by that pressure that lies so hard on them, that it appears that they are really more troubled for the crimes they have committed than for the miseries they suffer, are not out of hope, but that at last either the prince will by his prerogative, or the people will by their intercession restore them again to their liberty, or at least very much mitigate their slavery. He that tempts a married woman to adultery, is no less severely punished than he that commits it; for they reckon that a laid and studied design of committing any crime, is equal to the fact itself; since its not taking effect does not make the person that did all that in him lay in order to it, a whit the less guilty.

They take great pleasure in fools, and as it is thought a base and unbecoming thing to use them ill, so they do not think it amiss for people to divert themselves with their folly. And they think this is a great advantage to the fools themselves; for if men were so sullen and severe, as not at all to please themselves with their ridiculous behaviour and foolish sayings, which is all that they can do to recommend themselves to others, it could not be expected that they would be so well looked to, nor so tenderly used as they must otherwise be. If any man should reproach another for his being misshaped or imperfect in any part of his body, it would not at all be thought a reflection on the person that was so [afflicted], but it would be accounted a very unworthy thing for him that had [ridiculed] another with that which he could not help. It is thought a sign of a sluggish and sordid mind, not to preserve carefully one's natural beauty, but it is likewise an infamous thing among them to use paint or [cosmetics]. And they all see that no beauty recommends a wife so much to her husband, as the [virtue] of her life, and her obedience;

* Pp. 85-87.

for as some few are catched and held only by beauty, so all people are held by the other excellencies which charm all the world.

As they fright[en] men from committing crimes by punishments, so they invite them to the love of virtue by public honours. Therefore they erect statues in honour to the memories of such worthy men as have deserved well of their country, and set these in their market-places, both to perpetuate the remembrance of their actions, and to be an incitement to their posterity to follow their example.

If any man aspires to any office he is sure never to [get] it: they live all easily together, for none of the magistrates are either insolent or cruel to the people; but they affect rather to be called fathers, and, by being really so, they well deserve that name; and the people pay them all the marks of honour the more freely because none are exacted of them. The prince himself has no distinction, either of garments or of a crown; but is only known by a sheaf of corn that is carried before him,—as the high-priest is also known by a wax light that is carried before him.

They have but few laws, and such is their constitution that they need not many. They do very much condemn other nations whose laws, together with the commentaries on them, swell up to so many volumes; for they think it an unreasonable thing to oblige men to obey a body of laws that are both of such a bulk and so dark that they cannot be read or understood by every one of the subjects.

They have no lawyers among them, for they consider them as a sort of people whose profession it is to disguise matters as well as to [twist] laws; and, therefore, they think it is much better that every man should plead his own cause, and trust it to the judge, as well as in other places the client does it to a counsellor. By this means they both cut off many delays and find out truth more certainly; for, after the parties have laid open the merits of their cause, without those artifices which lawyers are apt to suggest, the judge examines the whole matter, and supports the simplicity of such well-meaning persons whom otherwise crafty men would be sure to run down; and thus they avoid those evils which appear very remarkably among all those nations that labour under a vast load of laws. Every one of them is skilled in their law, for as it is a very short study, so the plainest meaning of which words are capable is always the sense of their laws. And they argue thus: all laws are promulgated for this end, that every man may know his duty; and, therefore, the plainest and most obvious sense of the words is that which must be put on them; since a more refined exposition cannot be easily comprehended, and laws become thereby useless to the greater part of mankind who need most the direction of them: for to them it is all one not to make a law at all, and to couch it in such terms that, without a quick apprehension and much study, a man cannot find out the true meaning of it; and [most] of mankind are both so dull and so much employed in their several trades, that they have neither the leisure nor the capacity requisite for such an inquiry.*

* Pp. 146-51.

III.
The Utopian Social Order

Agriculture is . . . so universally understood among them all, that no person, either man or woman, is ignorant of it; from their childhood they are instructed in it, partly by what they learn at school, and partly by practice, they being led out often into the fields about the town, where they not only see others at work, but are likewise exercised in it themselves.

Besides agriculture, which is so common to them all, every man has some peculiar trade to which he applies himself, such as the manufacture of wool, or flax, masonry, smiths' work, or carpenters' work; for there is no other sort of trade that is in great esteem among them.

All the island over they wear the same sort of clothes, without any other distinction except that which is necessary for marking the difference between the two sexes, and the married and unmarried. The fashion never alters; and, as it is not [displeasing], nor uneasy, so it is fitted for their climate, and calculated both for their summers and winters. Every family makes their own clothes; but all among them, women as well as men, learn one or other of the trades formerly mentioned. Women, for the most part, deal in wool and flax, which suit better with their feebleness, leaving the other ruder trades to the men. Generally the same trade passes down from father to son, inclinations often following descent; but if any man's genius lies another way, he is [moved] into a family that deals in the trade to which he is inclined; and when that is to be done, care is taken, not only by his father but by the magistrate, that he may be put to a discreet and good man. And if, after a man has learned one trade, he desires to acquire another, that is also allowed, and is managed in the same manner as the former. When he has learned both, he follows that which he likes best, unless the public has more occasion for the other.

The chief, and almost the only business of the syphogrants is, to take care that no man may live idle, but that every one may follow his trade diligently. Yet they do not wear themselves out with perpetual toil from morning to night, as if they were beasts of burden, which as it is indeed a heavy slavery, so it is the common course of life of all tradesmen everywhere, except among the Utopians; but they, dividing the day and night into twenty-four hours, appoint six of these for work, three of them are before dinner; and after that they dine, and interrupt their labour for two hours, and then they go to work again for other three hours, and after that they sup, and at eight o'clock, counting from noon, they go to bed, and sleep eight hours; and for their other hours, besides those of work, and those that go for eating and sleeping, they are left to every man's discretion: yet they are not to abuse that interval to luxury and idleness, but must employ it in some proper exercise, according to their various inclinations, which is for the most part reading.

It is ordinary to have public lectures every morning before day-break; to which none are obliged to go but those that are marked out for literature; yet a great many, both men and women of all ranks, go to hear lectures of one sort or another, according to the variety of their inclinations. But if others that are not made for contemplation choose rather to employ themselves at that time in their trade, as many of them do, they are not hindered, but are commended rather as men that take care to serve their country. After supper, they spend an hour in some diversion; in summer it is in their gardens, and in winter it is in the halls where they eat; and they entertain themselves in them, either with music or discourse. They do not so much as know dice, or such like foolish and mischievous games. They have two sorts of games not unlike our chess; the one is between several numbers, by which one number, as it were, consumes another; the other resembles a battle between the vices and the virtues, in which the enmity in the vices among themselves, and their agreement against virtue is not unpleasantly represented; together with the special oppositions between the particular virtues and vices; as also the methods by which vice does either openly assault or secretly undermine virtue, and virtue, on the other hand, resists it, and the means by which either side obtains the victory.

But this matter of the time set off for labour is to be narrowly examined, otherwise you may, perhaps, imagine that, since there are only six hours appointed for work, they may fall under a scarcity of necessary provisions. But it is so far from being true, that this time is not sufficient for supplying them with a plenty of all things, that are either necessary or convenient, that it is rather too much; and this you will easily apprehend, if you consider how great a part of all other nations is quite idle. First, women generally do little, who are the half of mankind; and if some few women are diligent their husbands are idle. Then consider the great company of the idle priests, and of those that are called religious men; add to these all the rich men, chiefly those that have estates in lands, who are called noblemen and gentlemen, together with their families, made up of idle persons that do nothing but go swaggering about. Reckon in with these all those strong and lusty beggars that go about pretending some disease in excuse for their begging; and upon the whole account you will find that the number of those by whose labours mankind are supplied, is much less than you did perhaps imagine. Then consider how few of those that work are employed in labours that men do really need; for we who measure all things by money, give occasions to many trades that are both vain and superfluous, and that serve only to support riot and luxury. For if those who are at work were employed only in such things as the conveniences of life require, there would be such an abundance of them, and by that means the prices of them would so sink, that tradesmen could not be maintained by their gains; if all those who labour about useless things were set to more profitable trades; and if all that number that languish out their life in sloth and idleness, of whom every one consumes as much as any two of the men that are at work do, were forced to labour, you may easily imagine that a small proportion of time would serve for doing all that is either necessary, profitable, or pleasant to mankind, pleasure being still kept within its due bounds, which appears very plainly in Utopia, for there, in a great city, and in all the territory that lies round it, you can scarce find five hundred, either men or women, that by their age and strength are capable of labour, that are not engaged in it; even the syphogrants themselves, though the law excuses them, yet do not excuse themselves, that so by their examples they may excite the industry of the rest of the people; the like exemption is allowed to those who, being recommended to the people by the priests, are by the secret suffrages of the syphogrants privileged from labour, that they may apply themselves wholly to study; and if any of these fall short of those hopes that he seemed to give at first, he is obliged to go to work. And sometimes a mechanic that does so employ his leisure hours that he makes a considerable advancement in learning is eased from being a tradesman, and ranked among their learned men. Out of these they choose their ambassadors, their priests, their tranibors, and the prince himself. . . .

And thus from the great numbers among them that are neither [forced] to be idle, nor to be employed in any fruitless labour; you may easily make the estimate, how much good work may be done in those few hours in which they are obliged to labour. But besides all that has been already said, this is to be considered, that those needful arts which are among them are managed with less labour than anywhere else. The building, or the repairing of houses among us, employs many hands, because often a thriftless heir [lets] a house that his father built to fall into decay, so that his successor must, at a great cost, repair that which he might have kept up with a small charge: and often it falls out, that the same house which one built at a vast expense, is neglected by another that thinks he has a more delicate sense of such things, and he [letting] it to fall to ruin, builds another at no less charge. But among the Utopians, all things are so regulated, that men do very seldom build upon any new piece of ground; and they are not only very quick in repairing their houses, but show their foresight in preventing their decay, so that their buildings are preserved very long, with very little labour: and thus the craftsmen to whom that care belongs, are often without any employment, except it be the hewing of timber, and the squaring of stones, that so the materials may be in readiness for raising a building very suddenly when there is any occasion for it.

As for their clothes, observe how little work goes for them. While they are at labour, they are clothed with leather and skins, cast carelessly about them, which will last seven years; and when they appear in public, they put on an upper garment, which hides the other, and these are all of one colour, and that is the natural colour of the wool: and as they need less woollen cloth than is used anywhere else, so that which they do need is much less costly. They use linen cloth more: but that is prepared with less labour, and they value cloth only by the whiteness of the linen, or the cleanness of the wool, without much regard to the fineness of the thread; and whereas in other places, four or five upper garments of woollen cloth, and of different colours, and as many vests of silk will scarce serve one man; and those that are nicer, think ten too few: every man there is contented with one, which very oft serves him two years. Nor is there anything that can tempt a man to desire more; for if he had them, he would neither be the warmer, nor would he make one jot the better appearance for it.

And thus since they are all employed in some useful labour, and since they content themselves with fewer things, it falls out that there is a great abundance of all things among them; so that often, for want of other work, if there is any need of mending their highways at any time, you will see marvellous numbers of people brought out to work at them; and when there is no occasion of any public work, the hours of working are lessened by public proclamation, for the magistrates do not engage the people into any needless labour, since by their constitution they aim chiefly at this, that except in so far as public necessity requires it, all the people may have as much free time for themselves as may be necessary for the improvement of their minds, for in this they think the happiness of life consists.

But it is now time to explain to you [their courtship and marriage customs].*

Their women are not married before eighteen, nor their men before two-and-twenty; and if any of them [are caught in] forbidden embraces before their marriage, they are severely punished, and the privilege of marriage is denied them, unless there is a special warrant obtained for it afterwards from the prince. Such disorders cast a great reproach upon the master and mistress of the family in which they fall out; for it is supposed they have been wanting to their duty. The reason of punishing this so severely is, because they think that if they were not strictly restrained from all vagrant appetites, very few would engage in a married state, in which men venture the quiet of their whole life, being restricted to one person; besides many other inconveniences that do accompany it. In the way of choosing of their wives, they use a method that would appear to us very absurd and ridiculous, but is constantly observed among them, and accounted a wise and good rule. Before marriage, some grave matron presents the bride naked, whether she is a virgin or a widow, to the bridegroom; and after that, some grave man presents the bridegroom naked to the bride. We indeed both laughed at this, and condemned it as a very indecent thing. But they, on the other hand, wondered at the folly of the men of all other nations, who if they are but to buy a horse of a small value, are so cautious, that they will see every part of him, and take off both his saddle, and all his other tackle, that there may be no secret ulcer hid under any of them; and that yet in the choice of a wife, on which depends the happiness or unhappiness of the rest of his life, a man should venture upon trust, and only see about a hand-breadth of the face, all the rest of the body being covered, under which there may lie hid that which may be contagious, as well as loathesome. All men are not so wise, that they choose a woman only for her good qualities; and even wise men consider the body as that which adds not a little to the mind. And it is certain, there may be some such deformity covered with one's clothes, as may totally alienate a man from his wife when it is too late to part with her; for if such a thing is discovered after marriage, a man has no remedy but patience: so they think it is reasonable, that there should be a good provision made against such mischievous frauds.

There was so much the more reason in making a regulation in this matter, because they are the only people of those parts that do neither allow of polygamy, nor of divorces, except in the case of adultery, or insufferable perverseness: for in these cases the senate dissolves the marriage, and grants the injured person leave to marry again; but the guilty are made infamous, and are never allowed the privilege of a second marriage. None are [forced] to put away their wives against their wills, because of any great calamity that may have fallen on their person; for they look on it as the height of cruelty and treachery to abandon either of the married persons, when they need most the tender care of their consort; and that chiefly in the case of old age, which as it carries many diseases along with it, so it is a disease of itself. But it falls often out, that when a married couple do not agree well together, they by mutual consent separate, and find out other persons with whom they hope they may live more happily. Yet this is not done without obtaining leave of the senate, which never admits of a divorce, but upon

*Pp. 89-96.

a strict inquiry made, both by the senators and their wives, into the grounds upon which it proceeds; and even when they are satisfied concerning the reasons of it, they go on but slowly, for they reckon that too great easiness in granting leave for new marriages, would very much shake the kindness of married persons. They punish severely those that defile the marriage bed. If both parties are married, they are divorced, and the injured persons may marry one another, or whom they please; but the adulterer and the adulteress are condemned to slavery. Yet if either of the injured persons cannot shake off the love of the married person, they may live with them still in that state, but they must follow them to that labour to which the slaves are condemned; and sometimes the repentance of the condemned person, together with the unshaken kindness of the innocent and injured person, has prevailed so far with the prince, that he has taken off the sentence: but those that relapse after they are once pardoned, are punished with death.*

IV.
Man And Materialism

[T]hey have an incredible treasure; but they do not keep it as a treasure, but in such a manner as I am almost afraid to tell it, least you think it so extravagant, that you can hardly believe it; which I have the more reason to apprehend from others, because if I had not seen it myself, I could not have been easily persuaded to have believed it upon any man's report.

It is certain, that all things appear so far incredible to us as they differ from our own customs; but one who can judge aright will not wonder to find that, since their other constitutions differ so much from ours, their value of gold and silver should be measured, not by our standard, but by one that is very different from it; for, since they have no use for money among themselves, but keep it for an accident, that though, as it may possibly fall out, it may have great intervals, they value it no farther than it deserves, or may be useful to them. So that it is plain that they must prefer iron either to gold or silver; for men can no more live without iron than without fire or water; but nature has marked out no use for the other metals with which we may not very well dispense. The folly of man has enhanced the value of gold and silver because of their scarcity; whereas, on the contrary, they reason, that Nature, as an indulgent parent, has given us all the best things very freely and in great abundance, such as are water and earth, but has laid up and hid from us the things that are vain and useless.

If those metals were laid up in any tower among them, it would give jealousy of the prince and senate, according to that foolish mistrust into which the rabble are apt to fall, as if they intended to cheat the people and make advantages to themselves by it; or, if they should work it into vessels, or any sort of plate, they fear that the people might grow too fond of it, and so be unwilling to let the plate be run down, if a war made it necessary to pay their soldiers with it. Therefore,

* Pp. 143-46.

to prevent all these inconveniences, they have fallen upon an expedient which, as it agrees with their other policy, so is very different from ours, and will scarcely gain belief among us, who value gold so much, and lay it up so carefully; for, whereas they eat and drink out of vessels of earth, or glass, that, though they look very pretty, yet are of very slight materials, they make their chamber-pots and close-stools of gold and silver; and that not only in their public halls, but in their private houses. Of the same metals they likewise make chains and fetters for their slaves; and, as a badge of infamy, they hang an earring of gold to some, and make others wear a chain or a coronet of gold; and thus they take care by all manner of ways, that gold and silver may be of no esteem among them. And from hence it is, that, whereas other nations part with their gold and their silver as unwillingly as if one tore out their bowels, those of Utopia would look on their giving in all their gold or silver, when there was any use for it, but as the parting with a trifle, or as we would estimate the loss of a penny. They find pearls on their coast, and diamonds and carbuncles on their rocks; they do not look after them, but, if they find any by chance, they polish them, and therewith adorn their children, who are delighted with and glory in them during their childhood; but, when they grow to years, and see that none but children use such baubles, they of their own accord, without being bid by their parents, lay them aside, and would be as much ashamed to use them afterwards, as children among us, when they come to years are of their nuts, puppets, and other toys.

I never saw a clearer instance of the different impressions that different customs make on people than I observed in the ambassadors of the Anemolians, who came to Amaurot when I was there. And, because they came to treat of affairs of great consequence, the deputies from several towns had met to wait for their coming. The ambassadors of the nations that lie near Utopia, knowing their customs, and that fine clothes are of no esteem among them, that silk is despised, and gold is a badge of infamy, used to come very modestly clothed; but the Anemolians that lay more remote, and so had little commerce with them, when they understood that they were coarsely clothed, and all in the same manner, they took it for granted that they had none of those fine things among them of which they made no use; and they, being a vain-glorious, rather than a wise people, resolved to set themselves out with so much pomp, that they should look like gods, and so strike the eyes of the poor Utopians with their splendour. Thus, three ambassadors made their entry with an hundred attendants that were all clad in garments of different colours, and the greater part in silk; the ambassadors themselves, who were of the nobility of their country, were in cloth of gold, and adorned with massy chains, ear-rings, and rings of gold; their caps were covered with bracelets set full of pearls and other gems. In a word, they were set out with all those things that, among the Utopians, were either the badges of slavery, the marks of infamy, or children's rattles. It was not unpleasant to see, on the one side, how they looked big, when they compared their rich habits with the plain clothes of the Utopians, who were come out in great numbers to see them make their entry. And, on the other side, to observe how much they were mistaken in the impression on which they hoped this pomp would have made on them; it appeared so ridiculous a show to all that had never stirred out of their country, and so had not seen the customs of other nations; that, though they paid some reverence to those that were the most meanly clad, as if they had been the ambassadors, yet when they saw the ambassadors themselves, so full of gold chains, they looked upon them as slaves, and made them no reverence at all. You might have seen their children, who were grown up to that bigness that they had thrown away their jewels, call to their mothers, and push them gently, and cry out, 'See that great fool that wears pearls and gems, as if he were yet a child!' And their mothers answered them in good earnest, 'Hold your peace! this is, I believe, one of the ambassador's fools!' Others censured the fashion of their chains, and observed that they were of no use, for they were too slight to bind their slaves, who could easily break them; and they saw them hang so loose about them, that they reckoned they could easily throw them away, and so get from them. But, after the ambassadors had staid a day among them, and saw so vast a quantity of gold in their houses, which was as much despised by them as it was esteemed in other nations, and that there was more gold and silver in the chains and fetters of one slave than all their ornaments amounted to, their plumes fell, and they were ashamed of all that glory for which they had formerly valued themselves, and so laid it aside: to which they were the more determined when, upon their engaging into some free discourse with the Utopians, they discovered their sense of such things, and their other customs.*

V.
The Utopian Philosophy Of Man And Society

The Utopians wonder how any man should be so much taken with the glaring, doubtful lustre of a jewel or stone, that can look up to a star, or to the sun itself: or how any should value himself because his cloth is made of a finer thread; for, how fine soever that thread may be, it was once no better than the fleece of a sheep, and that sheep was a sheep still for all its wearing it. They wonder much to hear that gold, which in itself is so useless a thing, should be everywhere so much esteemed that even man, for whom it was made, and by whom it has its value, should yet be thought of less value than it is; so that a man of lead, who has no more sense than a log of wood, and is as bad as he is foolish, should have many wise and good men serving him, only because he has a great heap of that metal; and if it should so happen that by some accident, or trick of law, which does sometimes produce as great changes as chance itself, all this wealth should pass from the master to the meanest varlet of his whole family, he himself would very soon become one of his servants, as if he were a thing that belonged to his wealth, and so were bound to follow its fortune. But they do much more admire and detest their folly who, when they see a rich man, though they neither owe him anything, nor are in any sort obnoxious to him, yet merely because he is rich, they give him little less than divine honours; even though they know him to be so covetous and base-minded that, notwithstanding all his wealth, he will not part with one farthing of it to them as long as he lives.

---

* Pp. 109-14.

These and such like notions have [been accepted by the people], partly from their education, being bred in a country whose customs and constitutions are very opposite to all such foolish maxims; and partly from their learning and studies. For, though there are but few in any town that are excused from labour so that they may give themselves wholly to their studies, these being only such persons as discover from their childhood an extraordinary capacity and disposition for letters, yet their children and a great part of the nation, both men and women, are taught to spend those hours in which they are not obliged to work in reading; and this they do their whole life long.

They have all their learning in their own tongue; which is both a copious and pleasant language, and in which a man can fully express his mind: it runs over a great tract of many countries, but it is not equally pure in all places; they have never so much as heard of the names of any of those philosophers that are so famous in these parts of the world before we went among them; and yet they had made the same discoveries that the Greeks had done, both in music, logic, arithmetic, and geometry. But as they are equal to the ancient philosophers almost in all things, so they far exceed our modern logicians, for they have never yet fallen upon the barbarous niceties that our youth are forced to learn in those trifling logical schools that are among us; and they are so far from minding chimeras and fantastical images made in the mind, that none of them could comprehend what we meant when we talked to them of a man in the abstract as common to all men in particular, (so that though we spoke of him as a thing that we could point at with our fingers, yet none of them could perceive him,) and yet distinct from every one, as if he were some monstrous colossus or giant. Yet for all this ignorance of these empty notions, they knew astronomy, and all the motions of the orbs exactly; and they have many instruments, well contrived and divided, by which they do very accurately compute the course and positions of the sun, moon, and stars. But for fraudulent prophecy by the stars and by their oppositions or conjunctions, it has not so much as entered into their thoughts. They have a particular sagacity, founded on much observation, of judging of the weather, by which they know when they may look for rain, wind, or other alterations in the air. But as to the philosophy of those things, and the causes of the saltness of the sea, and of its ebbing and flowing, and of the origin and nature both of the heavens and the earth, they dispute of them, partly as our ancient philosophers have done, and partly upon some new hypothesis, in which, as they differ from them, so they do not in all things agree among themselves.

As for moral philosophy, they have the same disputes among them that we have here: they examine what things are properly good, both for the body and the mind; and whether any outward thing can be calculated truly good, or if that term belongs only to the endowments of the mind. They inquire likewise into the nature of virtue and pleasure; but their chief dispute is concerning the happiness of a man, and wherein it consists, whether in some one thing, or in a great many? They seem indeed more inclinable to that opinion that places, if not the whole, yet the chief part of a man's happiness in pleasure; and which may seem more strange, they make use of arguments even from religion, notwithstanding its severity and roughness, for the support of that opinion that is so indulgent to pleasure; for they never dispute concerning happiness without fetching some arguments from the principles of religion, as well as from natural reason, since without the former, they reckon that all our enquiries after happiness must be but conjectural and defective.

Those principles of their religion are, that the soul of man is immortal, and that God of his goodness has designed that it should be happy; and that he has therefore appointed rewards for good and virtuous actions, and punishments for vice, to be distributed after this life. And though these principles of religion are conveyed down among them by tradition, they think that even reason itself determines a man to believe and acknowledge them: and they freely confess, that if these were taken away, no man would be so insensible, as not to seek after pleasure by all manner of ways, lawful or unlawful; using only this caution, that a lesser pleasure might not stand in the way of a greater, and that no pleasure ought to be pursued that should draw a great deal of pain after it; for they think it the maddest thing in the world to pursue virtue, that is a sour and difficult thing: and not only to renounce the pleasures of life, but willingly to undergo much pain and trouble, if a man has no prospect of a reward. And what reward can there be for one that has passed his whole life, not only without pleasure, but in pain, if there is nothing to be expected after death? Yet they do not place happiness in all sorts of pleasures, but only in those that in themselves are good and honest: for whereas there is a party among them that places happiness in bare virtue, others think that our natures are conducted by virtue to happiness, as that which is the chief good of man. They define virtue thus, that it is a living according to nature, and think that we are made by God for that end. They do believe that a man does then follow the dictates of nature, when he pursues or avoids things according to the direction of reason: they say, that the first dictate of reason is, the kindling in us a love and reverence for the Divine Majesty, to whom we owe both all that we have, and all that we can ever hope for. In the next place, reason directs us to keep our minds as free of passion, and as cheerful as we can; and that we should consider ourselves as bound by the ties of good nature and humanity, to use our utmost endeavours to help forward the happiness of all other persons; for there was never any man that was such a morose and severe pursuer of virtue, and such an enemy to pleasure, that though he set hard rules to men to undergo much pain, many watchings, and other rigours, yet did not at the same time advise them to do all they could in order to the relieving and easing such people as were miserable; and did not represent it as a mark of a laudable temper, that it was gentle and good natured: and they infer from thence, that if a man ought to advance the welfare and comfort of the rest of mankind, there being no virtue more proper and peculiar to our nature, than to ease the miseries of others, to free them from trouble and anxiety in furnishing them with the comforts of life, that consist in pleasure; nature does much more vigorously lead him to do all this for himself. A life of pleasure is either a real evil, and in that case we ought not only not to assist others in their pursuit of it, but on the contrary, to keep them from it all we can, as from that which is hurtful and deadly to them; or if it is a good thing, so that we not only may, but ought to help others to it, why then ought not a man to begin with himself? Since no man can be more bound to look after the good of another, than after his own; for nature cannot direct us to be good and kind to others, and yet at the same time to be unmerciful and cruel to ourselves. Thus as they define virtue to be a living according to nature, so they reckon that nature sets all people on to seek after pleasure as the end of all they do.

They do also observe, that in order to [pursue] supporting the pleasures of life, nature inclines us to enter into society; for there is no man so much raised above the rest of mankind, that he should be the only favourite of nature, which on the contrary seems to have levelled all those together that belong to the same species. Upon this they infer that no man ought to seek his own conveniences so eagerly, that thereby he should prejudice others; and therefore they think that not only all agreements between private persons ought to be observed, but likewise that all those laws ought to be kept, which either a good prince has published in due form, or to which a people, that is neither oppressed with tyranny nor circumvented by fraud, has consented, for distributing those conveniences of life which afford us all our pleasures.

They think it is an evidence of true wisdom for a man to pursue his own advantages, as far as the laws allow it. They account it piety to prefer the public good to one's private concerns; but they think it unjust for a man to seek for his own pleasure, by snatching another man's pleasures from him. And on the contrary, they think it a sign of a gentle and good soul, for a man to dispense with his own advantage for the good of others; and that by so doing, a good man finds as much pleasure one way as he parts with another; for as he may expect the like from others when he may come to need it, so if that should fail him, yet the sense of a good action, and the reflections that one makes on the love and gratitude of those whom he has so obliged, give the mind more pleasure than the body could have found in that from which it had restrained itself. They are also persuaded that God will make up the loss of those small pleasures with a vast and endless joy, of which religion does easily convince a good soul.

Thus upon an inquiry into the whole matter, they reckon that all our actions, and even all our virtues, terminate in pleasure as in our chief end and greatest happiness: and they call every motion or state, either of body or mind, in which nature teaches us to delight, a pleasure. And thus they cautiously limit pleasure, only to those appetites to which nature leads us; for they reckon that nature leads us only to those delights to which reason as well as sense carries us, and by which we neither injure any other person, nor let go greater pleasures for it, and which do not draw troubles on us after them: but they look upon those delights which men, by a foolish, though common mistake, call pleasure, as if they could change the nature of things as well as the use of words, as things that not only do not advance our happiness, but do rather obstruct it very much, because they do so entirely possess the minds of those that once go into them with a false notion of pleasure, that there is no room left for truer and purer pleasures.

There are many things that in themselves have nothing that it is truly delighting: on the contrary, they have a good deal of bitterness in them; and yet by our perverse appetites after forbidden objects, are not only ranked among the pleasures, but are made even the greatest designs of life. Among those who pursue these sophisticated pleasures, they reckon those whom I mentioned before, who think themselves really the better for having fine clothes; in which they think they are doubly mistaken, both in the opinion that they have of their clothes, and in the opinion that they have of themselves; for if you consider the use of clothes, why should a fine thread be thought better than a coarse one? And yet that sort of men, as if they had some real advantages beyond others, and did not owe it wholly to their mistakes, look big, and seem to fancy themselves to be the more valuable on that account, and imagine that a respect is due to them for the sake of a rich garment, to which they would not have pretended if they had been more meanly clothed; and they resent it as an affront if that respect is not paid them. It is also a great folly to be taken with these outward marks of respect which signify nothing; for what true or real pleasure can one find in this, that another man stand bare, or makes legs to him? Will the bending another man's thighs give you any ease? And will his head's being bare cure the madness of yours? And yet it is wonderful to see how this false notion of pleasure bewitches many who delight themselves with the fancy of their nobility, and are pleased with this conceit, that they are descended from ancestors who have been held for some successions rich, and that they have had great possessions; for this is all that makes nobility at present. Yet they do not think themselves a whit the less noble, though their immediate parents have left none of this wealth to them; or though they themselves have squandered it all away.

The Utopians have no better opinion of those who are much taken with gems and precious stones, and who account it a degree of happiness next to a divine one if they can purchase one that is very extraordinary; especially if it be of that sort of stones that is then in greatest request: for the same sort is not at all times of the same value with all sorts of people; nor will men buy it unless it be dismounted and taken out of the gold; and then the jeweller is made to give good security, and required solemnly to swear that the stone is true, that by such an exact caution a false one may not be bought instead of a true. Whereas, if you were to examine it, your eye could find no difference between that which is counterfeit and that which is true; so that they are all one to you as much as if you were blind. And can it be thought that they who heap up an useless mass of wealth, not for any use that it is to bring them, but merely to please themselves with the contemplation of it, enjoy any true pleasure in it? The delight they find is only a false shadow of joy. Those are no better whose error is somewhat different from the former, and who hide it out of their fear of losing it; for what other name can fit the hiding it in the earth, or rather the restoring it to it again, it being thus cut off from being useful either to its owner or to the rest of mankind? And yet the owner, having hid it carefully is glad, because he thinks he is now sure of it. And in case one should come to steal it, the owner, though he might live perhaps ten years after that, would all that while after the theft, of which he knew nothing, find no difference between his having it or losing it, for both ways it was equally useless to him.

Among those foolish pursuers of pleasure they reckon all those that delight in hunting, or birding, or gaming; of whose madness they have only heard, for they have no such things among them. But they have asked us, what sort of pleasure it is that men can find in throwing the dice? For, if there were any pleasure in it, they think the doing it so often should give one a surfeit of it. And what pleasure can one find in hearing the barking and howling of dogs, which seem rather odious than pleasant sounds? Nor can they comprehend the pleasure of seeing dogs run after a hare, more than of seeing one dog run after another; for you have the same entertainment to the eye on both these occasions, if the seeing them run is that which gives the pleasure, since that is the same in both cases; but if the pleasure lies in seeing the hare killed and torn by the dogs, this ought rather to stir pity, when a weak, harmless, and fearful hare is devoured by a strong, fierce, and cruel dog. Therefore all this business of hunting is, among the Utopians, turned over to their butchers; and those are all slaves, as was formerly said; and they look on hunting as one of the basest parts of a butcher's work; for they account it both more profitable and more decent to kill those beasts that are more necessary and useful to mankind; whereas the killing and tearing of so small and miserable an animal, which a huntsman proposes to himself, can only attract him with the false show of pleasure; for it is of so little use to him. They look on the desire of the bloodshed even of beasts as a mark of a mind that is already corrupted with cruelty, or that at least by the frequent returns of so brutal a pleasure must degenerate into it.

Thus though the rabble of mankind look upon these, and all other things of this kind, which are indeed innumerable, as pleasures, the Utopians on the contrary observing, that there is nothing in the nature of them that is truly pleasant, conclude that they are not to be reckoned among pleasures; for though these things may create some tickling in the senses, (which seems to be a true notion of pleasure,) yet they reckon that this does not arise from the thing itself, but from a depraved custom, which may so vitiate a man's taste, that bitter things may pass for sweet; as women with child think pitch or tallow tastes sweeter than honey: but as a man's sense when corrupted, either by a disease or some ill habit, does not change the nature of other things, so neither can it change the nature of pleasure.

They reckon up several sorts of these pleasures, which they call true ones: some belong to the body, and others to the mind. The pleasures of the mind lie in *knowledge,* and in that delight which the contemplation of truth carries with it; to which they add the joyful reflections on a well-spent life, and the assured hopes of a future happiness. They divide the pleasures of the body into two sorts; the one is that which gives our senses some real delight, and is performed either by the recruiting of nature, and supplying those parts on which the internal heat of life feeds, and that is done by eating or drinking; or when nature is eased of any surcharge that oppresses, it, as when we empty our guts, beget children, or free any of the parts of our body from aches or heats by friction. There is another kind of this sort of pleasure, that neither gives us anything that our bodies require, nor frees us from anything with which we are overcharged; and yet it excites our senses by a secret unseen virtue, and by a generous impression, it so tickles and affects them, that it turns them inwardly upon themselves, and this is the pleasure begot by music. Another sort of bodily pleasure is that which consists in a quiet and good constitution of body, by which there is an entire healthiness spread over all the parts of the body, not allayed with any disease. This, when it is free from all mixture of pain, gives an inward pleasure of itself, even though it should not be excited by any external and delighting object; and although this pleasure does not so vigorously affect the sense, nor act so strongly upon it, yet as it is the greatest of all pleasures, so almost all the Utopians reckon it the foundation and basis of all the other joys of life, since this alone makes one's state of life to be easy and desirable; and when this is wanting, a man is really capable of no other pleasure. They look upon indolence and freedom from pain, if it does not rise from a perfect health, to be a state of stupidity rather than of pleasure. There has been a controversy in this matter very [thoroughly discussed] among them, whether a firm and entire health could be called a pleasure or not? Some have thought that there was no pleasure, but that which was excited by some sensible motion in the body. But this opinion has been long ago run down among them, so that now they do almost all agree in this, that health is the greatest of all bodily pleasures; and that as there is a pain in sickness, which is as opposite in its nature to pleasure as sickness itself is to health, so they hold that health carries a pleasure along with it: and if any should say, that sickness is not really a pain, but that it only carries a pain along with it, they look upon that as a fetch of subtlety that does not much alter the matter. So they think it is all one, whether it be said that health is in itself a pleasure, or that it begets a pleasure, as fire gives heat; so it be granted, that all those whose health is [complete], have a true pleasure in it: and they reason thus—what is the pleasure of eating, but that a man's health which had been weakened, does with the assistance of food, drive away hunger, and so recruiting itself, recovers its former vigour? And being thus refreshed, it finds a pleasure in that conflict: and if the conflict is pleasure, the victory must yet breed a greater pleasure, except we will fancy that it becomes stupid as soon as it has obtained that which it pursued, and so does neither know nor rejoice in its own welfare. If it is said, that health cannot be felt, they absolutely deny that; for what man is in health, that does not perceive it when he is awake? Is there any man that is so dull and stupid, as not to acknowledge that he feels a delight in health? And what is delight, but another name for pleasure?

But of all pleasures, they esteem those to be the most valuable that lie in the mind; and the chief of these are those that arise out of true virtue, and the witness of a good conscience. They account health the chief pleasure that belongs to the body, for they think that the pleasure of eating and drinking, and all the other delights of the body are only so far desirable, as they give or maintain health. But they are not pleasant in themselves otherwise than as they resist those impressions that our natural infirmity is still making upon us: and as a wise man desires rather to avoid diseases than to take physic, and to be freed from pain rather than to find ease by remedies, so it were a more desirable state not to need this sort of pleasure, than to be obliged to indulge it. And if any man imagines that there is a real happiness in this pleasure, he must then confess that he would be the happiest of all men, if he were to lead his life in a perpetual hunger, thirst, and itching, and by consequence in perpetual eating, drinking, and scratching himself, which any one may easily see would be not only a base but a miserable state of life. These are indeed the lowest of pleasures, and the least pure; for we can never relish them, but when they are mixed with the contrary pains. The pain of hunger must give us the pleasure of eating, and here the pain out-balances the pleasure: and as the pain is more vehement, so it lasts much longer; for as it is upon us before the pleasure comes, so it does not cease, but with the pleasure that extinguishes it, and that goes off with it; so that they think none of those pleasures are to be valued, but as they are necessary. Yet they rejoice in them, and with due gratitude acknowledge the tenderness of the great Author of nature, who has planted in us appetites, by which those things that are necessary for our preservation are likewise made pleasant to us. For how miserable a thing would life be, if those daily diseases of hunger and thirst were to be carried off by such bitter drugs, as we must use for those diseases that return seldomer upon us? And thus these pleasant, as well as proper gifts of nature, do maintain the strength and the sprightliness of our bodies.

They do also entertain themselves with the other delights that they let in at their eyes, their ears, and their nostrils, as the pleasant relishes and seasonings of life, which nature seems to have marked out peculiarly for man; since no other sort of animal contemplates the figure and beauty of the universe, nor is delighted with smells, but as they distinguish meats by them, nor do they apprehend the concords or discords of sounds; yet in all pleasures whatsoever, they observe this temper, that a lesser joy may not hinder a greater, and that pleasure may never breed pain, which they think does always follow dishonest pleasures. But they think it a madness for a man to wear out the beauty of his face, or the force of his natural strength, and to corrupt the sprightliness of his body by sloth and laziness, or to waste his body by fasting, and so to weaken the strength of his constitution, and reject the other delights of life; unless by renouncing his own satisfaction, he can either serve the public, or promote the happiness of others, from which he expects a greater recompense from God. So that they look on such a course of life as a mark of a mind, that is both cruel to itself, and ungrateful to the Author of nature, as if we would not be beholden to him for his favours, and therefore would reject all his blessings, and should afflict himself for the empty shadow of virtue; or for no better end than to render himself capable to bear those misfortunes which possibly will never happen.

This is their notion of virtue and pleasure; they think that no man's reason can carry him to a truer idea of them, unless some discovery from heaven should inspire one with sublimer notions. I have not now the leisure to examine all this, whether they think right or wrong in this matter; nor do I judge it necessary, for I have only undertaken to give you an account of their constitution, but not to defend everything that is among them. I am sure, that whatsoever may be said of their notions, there is not in the whole world, either a better people, or a happier government. Their bodies are vigorous and lively; and though they are but of a middle stature, and though they have neither the fruitfullest soil, nor the purest air in the world, yet they do so fortify themselves by their temperate course of life against the unhealthiness of their air, and by their industry they do so cultivate their soil, that there is nowhere to be seen a greater increase, both of corn and cattle: nor are there any where healthier men to be found, and freer from diseases than among them; for one may see there, not only such things put in practice, that husbandmen do commonly for manuring and improving an ill soil, but in some places a whole wood is plucked up by the roots, as well as whole ones planted in other places, where there were formerly none. In doing of this, the chief consideration they have is of carriage, that their timber may be either near their towns, or lie upon the sea, or some river, so that it may be floated to them; for it is a harder work to carry wood at any distance over land, than corn. The people are industrious, apt to learn, as well as cheerful and pleasant; and none can endure more labour, when it is necessary, than they; but except in that case, they love their ease.*

VI.
Summary

Thus have I described to you as particularly as I could the constitution of that commonwealth, which I do not only think to be the best in the world, but to

* Pp. 114-36.

be, indeed, the only commonwealth that truly deserves that name. In all other places it is visible that whereas people talk of a commonwealth, every man only seeks his own wealth; but there, where no man has any property, all men do zealously pursue the good of the public; and, indeed, it is no wonder to see men act so differently, for in other commonwealths every man knows that, unless he provides for himself, how flourishing soever the commonwealth may be, he must die of hunger; so that he sees the necessity of preferring his own concerns to the public. But in Utopia, where every man has a right to everything, they do all know that if care is taken to keep the public stores full, no private man can want anything; for among them there is no unequal distribution, so that no man is poor, nor in any necessity; and though no man has anything yet they are all rich; for what can make a man so rich as to lead a serene and cheerful life, free from anxieties; neither apprehending want himself, nor vexed with the endless complaints of his wife? He is not afraid of the misery of his children, nor is he contriving how to raise a portion for his daughters, but is secure in this, that both he and his wife, his children and grandchildren, to as many generations as he can fancy, will all live both plentifully and happily, since among them there is no less care taken of those who were once engaged in labour, but grow afterwards unable to follow it, than there is elsewhere for these that continue still at it. I would gladly hear any man compare the justice that is among them, with that which is among all other nations; among whom, may I perish, if I see anything that looks either like justice or equity. For what justice is there in this, that a nobleman, a goldsmith, or a banker, or any other man that either does nothing at all, or at best is employed in things that are of no use to the public, should live in great luxury and splendour upon that which is so ill-acquired, and a mean man, a carter, a smith, or a ploughman, that works harder even than the beasts themselves, and is employed in labours that are so necessary that no commonwealth could hold out a year to an end without them, can yet be able to earn so poor a livelihood out of it, and must lead so miserable a life in it, that the beasts' condition is much better than theirs? For, as the beasts do not work so constantly, so they feed almost as well, and more pleasantly, and have no anxiety about that which is to come; whereas these men are depressed by a barren and fruitless employment, and are tormented with the apprehensions of want in their old age; since that which they get by their daily labour does but maintain them at present, and is consumed as fast as it comes in; so that there is no overplus left them which they can lay up for old age.

Is not that government both unjust and ungrateful that is so prodigal of its favours to those that are called gentlemen, or goldsmiths, or such others that are idle, or live either by flattery, or by contriving the arts of vain pleasure; and, on the other hand, takes no care of those of a meaner sort, such as ploughmen, colliers, and smiths, without whom it could not subsist; but, after the public has been served by them, and that they come to be oppressed with age, sickness, and want, all their labours and the good that they have done are forgotten, and all the recompence given them is, that they are left to die in great misery; and the richer sort are often endeavouring to bring the hire of labourers lower, not only by their fraudulent practices, but by the laws which they procure to be made to that effect; so that, though it is a thing most unjust in itself to give such small rewards to those who deserve so well of the public, yet they have given these hardships the name and colour of justice, by procuring laws to be made for regulating it.

Therefore I must say that, as I hope for mercy, I can have no other notion of all the other governments that I see or know, than that they are a conspiracy of the richer sort, who, on pretence of managing the public, do only pursue their private ends, and devise all the ways and arts that they can find out; first, that they may, without danger, preserve all that they have so ill acquired, and then, that they may engage the poorer sort to toil and labour for them at as low rates as is possible, and oppress them as much as they please; and if they can but prevail to get these contrivances established by the show of public authority, which is considered as the representative of the whole people, then they are accounted laws; and yet these wicked men, after they have by a most insatiable covetousness divided that among themselves with which all the rest might have been well supplied, are far from that happiness that is enjoyed among the Utopians; for the use, as well as the desire of money being extinguished, there is much anxiety and great occasions of mischief cut off with it. And who does not see that frauds, thefts, robberies, quarrels, tumults, contentions, seditions, murders, treacheries, and witchcrafts, that are indeed rather punished than restrained by the severities of law, would all fall off if money were not any more valued by the world? Men's fears, solicitudes, cares, labours, and watchings would all perish in the same moment that the value of money did sink. Even poverty itself, for the relief of which money seems most necessary, would fall, if there were no money in the world. . . .

Pride is that infernal serpent that creeps into the breasts of mortals, and possesses them too much to be easily drawn out; and therefore I am glad that the Utopians have fallen upon this form of government, in which I wish that all the world could be so wise as to imitate them; for they have indeed laid down such a scheme and foundation of policy that, as men live happy under it, so it is like to be of great continuance: for, they having rooted out of the minds of their people all the seeds, both of ambition and faction, there is no danger of any commotion at home; which alone has been the ruin of many states that seemed otherwise to be well secured; but as long as they live in peace at home, and are governed by such good laws, the envy of all their neighbouring princes, who have often attempted their ruin, but in vain, will never be able to put their state into any commotion or disorder.*

* Pp. 190-96.

THE REFORMATION

Martin Luther

During the Reformation the theological and civil doctrines of Martin Luther (1483–1546) and John Calvin (1509–64) contributed to the dissolution of medieval society and the creation of new perceptions of freedom, liberty, man, and his relation to society. Martin Luther was born of former peasant stock in Eastern Germany. His father had been able to improve his class by accumulating wealth through copper mining and to provide his son with an excellent education. In 1505 Luther graduated from Erfurt University with a master's degree. According to popular accounts he was returning to Erfurt in 1506 to study law when he was caught in a thunderstorm and nearly killed by lightning. In a moment of panic, Luther vowed to join the priesthood should his life be spared. The following year he was ordained at the Augustinian monastery at Erfurt.

Luther hoped to find solace from the spiritual uneasiness which had tormented him since his youth. He feared damnation and was vexed by feelings of insignificance and powerlessness. Suffering from repeated periods of depression Luther probed his mind and soul for an answer to the gripping question: "How can I be saved?" Catholic doctrine and liturgy gave him little satisfaction. Increasingly Luther turned to the Bible to find salvation. Blending mysticism and scholarship, Luther concluded that salvation could not occur through rituals and "works" but from "faith alone."

The quiet development of these religious views was shattered in 1517 when Luther posted his ninety-five theses opposing the sale of indulgences (remissions of sins) and challenging the power of the priests to grant absolution through the sacrament of penance. The controversy was intensified by papal attempts to suppress Luther and his followers. In 1520 Luther wrote three tracts clarifying and strengthening his views. In *The Address to the German Nobility* Luther denied that the Church had secular authority and called for reform of ecclesiastical corruption. In *The Babylonian Captivity of the Church* he asserted that sacraments or "works" were not a substitute for salvation by faith.

Christian Liberty contained Luther's statement of evangelical theology and doctrines regarding the character of man, the nature of freedom and liberty, and the proper relation of man to society. Luther's concept of an inner spiritual and outer physical man was similar to the medieval image, but he insisted that human perfection resulted only from faith in God and not in good works. He accepted the Augustinian dualism of the society of flesh (man) and the society of spirit (God), but he rejected the medieval view that man would never realize heaven on earth. Luther argued that man was progressing toward eventual union of the temporal and spiritual kingdoms. Until that union was completed, however, man must live a spiritual life where the "Christian is a perfectly free lord of all, subject to none" and a secular life where he "is a perfectly dutiful servant of all, subject to all."

I.
Man And Spiritual Freedom

Many people have considered Christian faith an easy thing, and not a few have given it a place among the virtues. They do this because they have not experienced it and have never tasted the great strength there is in faith. It is impossible to write well about it or to understand what has been written about it unless one has at one time or another experienced the courage which faith gives a man when trials oppress him. But he who has had even a faint taste of it can never write, speak, meditate, or hear enough concerning it. It is a living "spring of water welling up to eternal life," as Christ calls it in John 4 [:14].

As for me, although I have no wealth of faith to boast of and know how scant my supply is, I nevertheless hope that I have attained to a little faith, even though I have been assailed by great and various temptations; and I hope that I can discuss it, if not more elegantly, certainly more to the point, than those literalists and subtile disputants have previously done, who have not even understood what they have written.

To make the way smoother for the unlearned—for only them do I serve—I shall set down the following two propositions concerning the freedom and the bondage of the spirit:

A Christian is a perfectly free lord of all, subject to none.

A Christian is a perfectly dutiful servant of all, subject to all.

These two theses seem to contradict each other. If, however, they should be found to fit together they would serve our purpose beautifully. Both are Paul's own statements, who says in I Cor. 9 [:19], "For though I am free from all men, I have made myself a slave to all," and in Rom. 13 [:8], "Owe no one anything, except to love one another." Love by its very nature is ready to serve and be subject to him who is loved. So Christ, although he was Lord of all, was "born of woman, born under the law" [Gal. 4:4], and therefore was at the same time a free man and a servant, "in the form of God" and "of a servant" [Phil. 2:6-7].

Let us start, however, with something more remote from our subject, but more obvious. Man has a twofold nature, a spiritual and a bodily one. According to

---

Reprinted from Martin Luther, *Christian Liberty,* ed. Harold J. Grimm (Philadelphia: Fortress Press, 1957), pp. 6-24, 26-29, 32-34, by permission of the publisher.

the spiritual nature, which men refer to as the soul, he is called a spiritual, inner, or new man. According to the bodily nature, which men refer to as flesh, he is called a carnal, outward, or old man, of whom the Apostle writes in II Cor. 4 [:16], "Though our outer nature is wasting away, our inner nature is being renewed every day." Because of this diversity of nature the Scriptures assert contradictory things concerning the same man, since these two men in the same man contradict each other, "for the desires of the flesh are against the Spirit, and the desires of the Spirit are against the flesh," according to Gal. 5 [:17].

First, let us consider the inner man to see how a righteous, free, and pious Christian, that is, a spiritual, new, and inner man, becomes what he is. It is evident that no external thing has any influence in producing Christian righteousness or freedom, or in producing unrighteousness or servitude. A simple argument will furnish the proof of this statement. What can it profit the soul if the body is well, free, and active, and eats, drinks, and does as it pleases? For in these respects even the most godless slaves of vice may prosper. On the other hand, how will poor health or imprisonment or hunger or thirst or any other external misfortune harm the soul? Even the most godly men, and those who are free because of clear consciences, are afflicted with these things. None of these things touch either the freedom or the servitude of the soul. It does not help the soul if the body is adorned with the sacred robes of priests or dwells in sacred places or is occupied with sacred duties or prays, fasts, abstains from certain kinds of food, or does any work that can be done by the body and in the body. The righteousness and the freedom of the soul require something far different since the things which have been mentioned could be done by any wicked person. Such works produce nothing but hypocrites. On the other hand, it will not harm the soul if the body is clothed in secular dress, dwells in unconsecrated places, eats and drinks as others do, does not pray aloud, and neglects to do all the above-mentioned things which hypocrites can do.

Furthermore, to put aside all kinds of works, even contemplation, meditation, and all that the soul can do, does not help. One thing, and only one thing, is necessary for Christian life, righteousness, and freedom. That one thing is the most holy Word of God, the gospel of Christ, as Christ says, John 11 [:25], "I am the resurrection and the life; he who believes in me, though he die, yet shall he live"; and John 8 [:36], "So if the Son makes you free, you will be free indeed"; and Matt. 4 [:4], "Man shall not live by bread alone, but by every word that proceeds from the mouth of God." Let us then consider it certain and firmly established that the soul can do without anything except the Word of God and that where the Word of God is missing there is no help at all for the soul. If it has the Word of God it is rich and lacks nothing since it is the Word of life, truth, light, peace, righteousness, salvation, joy, liberty, wisdom, power, grace, glory, and of every incalculable blessing. This is why the prophet in the entire Psalm [119] and in many other places yearns and sighs for the Word of God and uses so many names to describe it.

On the other hand, there is no more terrible disaster with which the wrath of God can afflict men than a famine of the hearing of his Word, as he says in Amos [8:11]. Likewise there is no greater mercy than when he sends forth his Word, as we read in Psalm 107 [:20]: "He sent forth his word, and healed them, and delivered them from destruction." Nor was Christ sent into the world for any other ministry except that of the Word. Moreover, the entire spiritual estate—all the apostles, bishops, and priests—has been called and instituted only for the ministry of the Word.

You may ask, "What then is the Word of God, and how shall it be used, since there are so many words of God?" I answer: The Apostle explains this in Romans 1. The Word is the gospel of God concerning his Son, who was made flesh, suffered, rose from the dead, and was glorified through the Spirit who sanctifies. To preach Christ means to feed the soul, make it righteous, set it free, and save it, provided it believes the preaching. Faith alone is the saving and efficacious use of the Word of God, according to Rom. 10[:9]: "If you confess with your lips that Jesus is Lord and believe in your heart that God raised him from the dead, you will be saved." Furthermore, "Christ is the end of the law, that every one who has faith may be justified" [Rom. 10:4]. Again, in Rom. 1 [:17], "He who through faith is righteous shall live." The Word of God cannot be received and cherished by any works whatever but only by faith. Therefore it is clear that, as the soul needs only the Word of God for its life and righteousness, so it is justified by faith alone and not any works; for if it could be justified by anything else, it would not need the Word, and consequently it would not need faith.

This faith cannot exist in connection with works—that is to say, if you at the same time claim to be justified by works, whatever their character—for that would be the same as "limping with two different opinions" [I Kings 18:21], as worshiping Baal and kissing one's own hand [Job 31:27-28], which, as Job says, is a very great iniquity. Therefore the moment you begin to have faith you learn that all things in you are altogether blameworthy, sinful, and damnable, as the Apostle says in Rom. 3 [:23], "Since all have sinned and fall short of the glory of God," and, "None is righteous, no, not one; . . . all have turned aside, together they have gone wrong" (Rom. 3:10-12). When you have learned this you will know that you need Christ, who suffered and rose again for you so that, if you believe in him, you may through this faith become a new man in so far as your sins are forgiven and you are justified by the merits of another, namely, of Christ alone.

Since, therefore, this faith can rule only in the inner man, as Rom. 10 [:10] says, "For man believes with his heart and so is justified," and since faith alone justifies, it is clear that the inner man cannot be justified, freed, or saved by any outer work or action at all, and that these works, whatever their character, have nothing to do with this inner man. On the other hand, only ungodliness and unbelief of heart, and no outer work, make him guilty and a damnable servant of sin. Wherefore it ought to be the first concern of every Christian to lay aside all confidence in works and increasingly to strengthen faith alone and through faith to grow in the knowledge, not of works, but of Christ Jesus, who suffered and rose for him, as Peter teaches in the last chapter of his first Epistle (I Pet. 5:10). No other work makes a Christian. Thus when the Jews asked Christ, as related in John 6 [:28], what they must do "to be doing the work of God," he brushed aside the multitude of works which he saw they did in great profusion and suggested one work, saying, "This is the work of God, that you believe in him whom he has sent" [John 6:29]); "for on him has God the Father set his seal" [John 6:27].

Therefore true faith in Christ is a treasure beyond comparison which brings with it complete salvation and saves man from every evil, as Christ says in the last chapter of Mark [16:16]: "He who believes and is baptized will be saved; but he who does not believe will be condemned." Isaiah contemplated this treasure and foretold it in chapter 10: "The Lord will make a small and consuming word upon the land, and it will overflow with righteousness" [Cf. Isa. 10:22]. This is as though he said, "Faith, which is a small and perfect fulfilment of the law, will fill believers with so great a righteousness that they will need nothing more to become righteous." So Paul says, Rom. 10 [:10], "For man believes with his heart and so is justified."

Should you ask how it happens that faith alone justifies and offers us such a treasure of great benefits without works in view of the fact that so many works, ceremonies, and laws are prescribed in the Scriptures, I answer: First of all, remember what has been said, namely, that faith alone, without works, justifies, frees, and saves; we shall make this clearer later on. Here we must point out that the entire Scripture of God is divided into two parts: commandments and promises. Although the commandments teach things that are good, the things taught are not done as soon as they are taught, for the commandments show us what we ought to do but do not give us the power to do it. They are intended to teach man to know himself, that through them he may recognize his inability to do good and may despair of his own ability. That is why they are called the Old Testament and constitute the Old Testament. For example, the commandment, "You shall not covet" [Exod. 20:17], is a command which proves us all to be sinners, for no one can avoid coveting no matter how much he may struggle against it. Therefore, in order not to covet and to fulfil the commandment, a man is compelled to despair of himself, to seek the help which he does not find in himself elsewhere and from someone else, as stated in Hosea [13:9]: "Destruction is your own, O Israel: your help is only in me." As we fare with respect to one commandment, so we fare with all, for it is equally impossible for us to keep any one of them.

Now when a man has learned through the commandments to recognize his helplessness and is distressed about how he might satisfy the law—since the law must be fulfilled so that not a jot or tittle shall be lost, otherwise man will be condemned without hope—then, being truly humbled and reduced to nothing in his own eyes, he finds in himself nothing whereby he may be justified and saved. Here the second part of Scripture comes to our aid, namely, the promises of God which declare the glory of God, saying, "If you wish to fulfil the law and not covet, as the law demands, come, believe in Christ in whom grace, righteousness, peace, liberty, and all things are promised you. If you believe, you shall have all things; if you do not believe, you shall lack all things." That which is impossible for you to accomplish by trying to fulfil all the works of the law—many and useless as they all are—you will accomplish quickly and easily through faith. God our Father has made all things depend on faith so that whoever has faith will have everything, and whoever does not have faith will have nothing. "For God has consigned all men to disobedience, that he may have mercy upon all," as it is stated in Rom. 11 [:32]. Thus the promises of God give what the commandments of God demand and fulfil what the law prescribes so that all things may be God's alone, both the commandments and the fulfilling of the commandments. He alone commands, he alone fulfils. Therefore the promises of God belong to the New Testament. Indeed, they are the New Testament.

Since these promises of God are holy, true, righteous, free, and peaceful words, full of goodness, the soul which clings to them with a firm faith will be so closely united with them and altogether absorbed by them that it not only will share in all their power but will be saturated and intoxicated by them. If a touch of Christ healed, how much more will this most tender spiritual touch, this absorbing of the Word, communicate to the soul all things that belong to the Word. This, then, is how through faith alone without works the soul is justified by the Word of God, sanctified, made true, peaceful, and free, filled with every blessing and truly made a child of God, as John 1 [:12] says: "But to all who . . . believed in his name, he gave power to become children of God."

From what has been said it is easy to see from what source faith derives such great power and why a good work or all good works together cannot equal it. No good work can rely upon the Word of God or live in the soul, for faith alone and the Word of God rule in the soul. Just as the heated iron glows like fire because of the union of fire with it, so the Word imparts its qualities to the soul. It is clear, then, that a Christian has all that he needs in faith and needs no works to justify him; and if he has no need of works, he has no need of the law; and if he has no need of the law, surely he is free from the law. It is true that "the law is not laid down for the just" [I Tim. 1:9]. This is that Christian liberty, our faith, which does not induce us to live in idleness or wickedness but makes the law and works unnecessary for any man's righteousness and salvation.

This is the first power of faith. Let us now examine also the second. It is a further function of faith that it honors him whom it trusts with the most reverent and highest regard since it considers him truthful and trustworthy. There is no other honor equal to the estimate of truthfulness and righteousness with which we honor him whom we trust. Could we ascribe to a man anything greater than truthfulness and righteousness and perfect goodness? On the other hand, there is no way in which we can show greater contempt for a man than to regard him as false and wicked and to be suspicious of him, as we do when we do not trust him. So when the soul firmly trusts God's promises, it regards him as truthful and righteous. Nothing more excellent than this can be ascribed to God. The very highest worship of God is this that we ascribe to him truthfulness, righteousness, and whatever else should be ascribed to one who is trusted. When this is done, the soul consents to his will. Then it hallows his name and allows itself to be treated according to God's good pleasure for, clinging to God's promises, it does not doubt that he who is true, just, and wise will do, dispose, and provide all things well.

Is not such a soul most obedient to God in all things by this faith? What commandment is there that such obedience has not completely fulfilled? What more complete fulfilment is there than obedience in all things? This obedience, however, is not rendered by works, but by faith alone. On the other hand, what greater rebellion against God, what greater wickedness, what greater contempt of God is there than not believing his promise? For what is this but to make God a liar or to doubt that he is truthful?—that is, to ascribe truthfulness to one's self but lying and vanity to God? Does not a man who does this deny God and set himself up as an idol in his heart? Then of what good are works done in such wickedness, even if they were the works of angels and apostles? Therefore God has rightly included all things, not under anger or lust, but under unbelief, so that they who imagine that they are fulfilling the law by doing the works of chastity and mercy required by the law (civil and human virtues) might not be saved. They are included under the sin of unbelief and must either seek mercy or be justly condemned.

When, however, God sees that we consider him truthful and by the faith of our heart pay him the great honor which is due him, he does us that great honor of considering us truthful and righteous for the sake of our faith. Faith works truth and righteousness by giving God what belongs to him. Therefore God in turn glorifies our righteousness. It is true and just that God is truthful and just, and to consider and confess him to be so is the same as being truthful and just. Accordingly he says in I Sam. 2 [:30], "Those who honor me I will honor, and those who despise me shall be lightly esteemed." So Paul says in Rom. 4 [:3] that Abraham's faith "was reckoned to him as righteousness" because by it he gave glory most perfectly to God, and that for the same reason our faith shall be reckoned to us as righteousness if we believe.

The third incomparable benefit of faith is that it unites the soul with Christ as a bride is united with her bridegroom. By this mystery, as the Apostle teaches, Christ and the soul become one flesh [Eph. 5:31-32]. And if they are one flesh and there is between them a true marriage—indeed the most perfect of all marriages, since human marriages are but poor examples of this one true marriage—it follows that everything they have they hold in common, the good as well as the evil. Accordingly the believing soul can boast of and glory in whatever Christ has as though it were its own, and whatever the soul has Christ claims as his own. Let us compare these and we shall see inestimable benefits. Christ is full of grace, life, and salvation. The soul is full of sins, death, and damnation. Now let faith come between them and sins, death, and damnation will be Christ's, while grace, life, and salvation will be the soul's; for if Christ is a bridegroom, he must take upon himself the things which are his bride's and bestow upon her the things that are his. If he gives her his body and very self, how shall he not give her all that is his? And if he takes the body of the bride, how shall he not take all that is hers?

Here we have a most pleasing vision not only of communion but of a blessed struggle and victory and salvation and redemption. Christ is God and man in one person. He has neither sinned nor died, and is not condemned, and he cannot sin, die, or be condemned; his righteousness, life, and salvation are unconquerable, eternal, omnipotent. By the wedding ring of faith he shares in the sins, death, and pains of hell which are his bride's. As a matter of fact, he makes them his own and acts as if they were his own and as if he himself had sinned; he suffered, died, and descended into hell that he might overcome them all. Now since it was such a one who did all this, and death and hell could not swallow him up, these were necessarily swallowed up by him in a mighty duel; for his righteousness is greater than the sins of all men, his life stronger than death, his salvation more invincible than hell. Thus the believing soul by means of the pledge of its faith is free in Christ, its bridegroom, free from all sins, secure against death and hell, and is endowed with the eternal righteousness, life, and salvation of Christ its bridegroom. So he takes to himself a glorious bride, "without spot or wrinkle, cleansing her by the washing of water with the word" [Cf. Eph. 5:26-27] of life, that is, by faith in the Word of life, righteousness, and salvation. In this way he marries her in faith, steadfast love, and in mercies, righteousness, and justice, as Hos. 2 [:19-20] says.

Who then can fully appreciate what this royal marriage means? Who can understand the riches of the glory of this grace? Here this rich and divine bridegroom Christ marries this poor, wicked harlot, redeems her from all her evil, and adorns her with all his goodness. Her sins cannot now destroy her, since they are laid upon Christ and swallowed up by him. And she has that righteousness in Christ, her husband, of which she may boast as of her own and which she can confidently display alongside her sins in the face of death and hell and say, "If I have sinned, yet my Christ, in whom I believe, has not sinned, and all his is mine and all mine is his," as the bride in the Song of Solomon [2:16] says, "My beloved is mine and I am his." This is what Paul means when he says in I Cor. 15 [:57], "Thanks be to God, who gives us the victory through our Lord Jesus Christ," that is, the victory over sin and death, as he also says there, "The sting of death is sin, and the power of sin is the law" [I Cor. 15:56].

From this you once more see that much is ascribed to faith, namely, that it alone can fulfil the law and justify without works. You see that the First Commandment, which says, "You shall worship one God," is fulfilled by faith alone. Though you were nothing but good works from the soles of your feet to the crown of your head, you would still not be righteous or worship God or fulfil the First Commandment, since God cannot be worshiped unless you ascribe to him the glory of truthfulness and all goodness which is due him. This cannot be done by works but only by the faith of the heart. Not by the doing of works but by believing do we glorify God and acknowledge that he is truthful. Therefore faith alone is the righteousness of a Christian and the fulfilling of all the commandments, for he who fulfils the First Commandment has no difficulty in fulfilling all the rest.

But works, being inanimate things, cannot glorify God, although they can, if faith is present, be done to the glory of God. Here, however, we are not inquiring what works and what kind of works are done, but who it is that does them, who glorifies God and brings forth the works. This is done by faith which dwells in the heart and is the source and substance of all our righteousness. Therefore it is a blind and dangerous doctrine which teaches that the commandments must be fulfilled by works. The commandments must be fulfilled before any works can be done, and the works proceed from the fulfilment of the commandments [Rom. 13:10], as we shall hear.

That we may examine more profoundly that grace which our inner man has in Christ, we must realize that in the Old Testament God consecrated to himself all the first-born males. The birthright was highly prized for it involved a twofold honor, that of priesthood and that of kingship. The first-born brother was priest and lord over all the others and a type of Christ, the true and only first-born of God the Father and the Virgin Mary and true king and priest, but not after the fashion of the flesh and the world, for his kingdom is not of this world [John 18:36]. He reigns in heavenly and spiritual things and consecrates them—things such as righteousness, truth, wisdom, peace, salvation, etc. This does not mean that all things on earth and in hell are not also subject to him—otherwise how could he protect and save us from them?—but that his kingdom consists neither in them nor of them. Nor does his priesthood consist in the outer splendor of robes and postures like those of the human priesthood of Aaron and our present-day church; but it consists of spiritual things through which he by an invisible service intercedes for us in heaven before God, there offers himself as a sacrifice, and does all things a priest should do, as Paul describes him under the type of Melchizedek in the Epistle to the Hebrews [Heb. 6-7]. Nor does he only pray and intercede for us but he teaches us inwardly through the living instruction of his Spirit, thus performing the two real functions of a priest, of which the prayers and the preaching of human priests are visible types.

Now just as Christ by his birthright obtained these two prerogatives, so he imparts them to and shares them with everyone who believes in him according to the law of the above-mentioned marriage, according to which the wife owns whatever belongs to the husband. Hence all of us who believe in Christ are priests and kings in Christ, as I Pet. 2 [:9] says: "You are a chosen race, God's own people, a royal priesthood, a priestly kingdom, that you may declare the wonderful deeds of him who called you out of darkness into his marvelous light."

The nature of this priesthood and kingship is something like this: First, with respect to the kingship, every Christian is by faith so exalted above all things that, by virtue of a spiritual power, he is lord of all things without exception, so that nothing can do him any harm. As a matter of fact, all things are made subject to him and are compelled to serve him in obtaining salvation. Accordingly Paul says in Rom. 8 [:28], "All things work together for good for the elect," and in I Cor. 3 [:21-23], "All things are yours whether . . . life or death or the present or the future, all are yours; and you are Christ's. . . ." This is not to say that every Christian is placed over all things to have and control them by physical power—a madness with which some churchmen are afflicted—for such power belongs to kings, princes, and other men on earth. Our ordinary experience in life shows us that we are subjected to all, suffer many things, and even die. As a matter of fact, the more Christian a man is, the more evils, sufferings, and deaths he must endure, as we see in Christ the first-born prince himself, and in all his brethren, the saints. The power of which we speak is spiritual. It rules in the midst of enemies and is powerful in the midst of oppression. This means nothing else than that "power is made perfect in weakness" [II Cor. 12:9] and that in all things I can find profit toward salvation [Rom. 8:28], so that the cross and death itself are compelled to serve me and to work together with me for my salvation. This is a splendid privilege and hard to attain, a truly omnipotent power, a spiritual dominion in which there is nothing so good and nothing so evil but that it shall work together for good to me, if only I believe. Yes, since faith alone suffices for salvation, I need nothing except faith exercising the power and dominion of its own liberty. Lo, this is the inestimable power and liberty of Christians.

Not only are we the freest of kings, we are also priests forever, which is far more excellent than being kings, for as priests we are worthy to appear before God to pray for others and to teach one another divine things. These are the functions of priests, and they cannot be granted to any unbeliever. Thus Christ has made it possible for us, provided we believe in him, to be not only his brethren, co-heirs, and fellow-kings, but also his fellow-priests. Therefore we may boldly come into the presence of God in the spirit of faith [Heb. 10:19, 22] and cry "Abba, Father!" pray for one another, and do all things which we see done and foreshadowed in the outer and visible works of priests.

He, however, who does not believe is not served by anything. On the contrary, nothing works for his good, but he himself is a servant of all, and all things turn out badly for him because he wickedly uses them to his own advantage and not to the glory of God. So he is no priest but a wicked man whose prayer becomes sin and who never comes into the presence of God because God does not hear sinners [John 9:31]. Who then can comprehend the lofty dignity of the Christian? By virtue of his royal power he rules over all things, death, life, and sin, and through his priestly glory is omnipotent with God because he does the things which God asks and desires, as it is written, "He will fulfil the desire of those who fear him; he also will hear their cry and save them" [Cf. Phil. 4:13]. To this glory a man attains, certainly not by any works of his, but by faith alone.

From this anyone can clearly see how a Christian is free from all things and over all things so that he needs no works to make him righteous and save him, since faith alone abundantly confers all these things. Should he grow so foolish, however, as to presume to become righteous, free, saved, and a Christian by means of some good work, he would instantly lose faith and all its benefits, a foolishness aptly illustrated in the fable of the dog who runs along a stream with a piece of meat in his mouth and, deceived by the reflection of the meat in the water, opens his mouth to snap at it and so loses both the meat and the reflection.[1]

You will ask, "If all who are in the church are priests, how do these whom we now call priests differ from laymen?" I answer: Injustice is done those words "priest," "cleric," "spiritual," "ecclesiastic," when they are transferred from all Christians to those few who are now by a mischievous usage called "ecclesiastics." Holy Scripture makes no distinction between them, although it gives the name "ministers," "servants," "stewards" to those who are now proudly called popes, bishops, and lords and who should according to the ministry of the Word serve others and teach them the faith of Christ and the freedom of believers. Although we are all equally priests, we cannot all publicly minister and teach. We ought not do so even if we could. Paul writes accordingly in I Cor. 4 [1], "This is how one should regard us, as servants of Christ and stewards of the mysteries of God."

That stewardship, however, has now been developed into so great a display of power and so terrible a tyranny that no heathen empire or other earthly power can be compared with it, just as if laymen were not also Christians. Through this perversion the knowledge of Christian grace, faith, liberty, and of Christ himself has altogether perished, and its place has been taken by an unbearable bondage of human works and laws until we have become, as the Lamentations of Jeremiah [1] say, servants of the vilest men on earth who abuse our misfortune to serve only their base and shameless will.

To return to our purpose, I believe that it has now become clear that it is not enough or in any sense Christian to preach the works, life, and words of Christ as historical facts, as if the knowledge of these would suffice for the conduct of life; yet this is the fashion among those who must today be regarded as our best preachers. Far less is it sufficient or Christian to say nothing at all about Christ and to teach instead the laws of men and the decrees of the fathers. Now there are not a few who preach Christ and read about him that they may move men's affections to sympathy with Christ, to anger against the Jews, and such childish and effeminate nonsense. Rather ought Christ to be preached to the end that faith in him may be established that he may not only be Christ, but be Christ for you

[1] Luther was fond of Aesop's Fables, of which this is one.

and me, and that what is said of him and is denoted in his name may be effectual in us. Such faith is produced and preserved in us by preaching why Christ came, what he brought and best owed, what benefit it is to us to accept him. This is done when that Christian liberty which he bestows is rightly taught and we are told in what way we Christians are all kings and priests and therefore lords of all and may firmly believe that whatever we have done is pleasing and acceptable in the sight of God, as I have already said.

What man is there whose heart, upon hearing these things, will not rejoice to its depth, and when receiving such comfort will not grow tender so that he will love Christ as he never could by means of any laws or works? Who would have the power to harm or frighten such a heart? If the knowledge of sin or the fear of death should break in upon it, it is ready to hope in the Lord. It does not grow afraid when it hears tidings of evil. It is not disturbed when it sees its enemies. This is so because it believes that the righteousness of Christ is its own and that its sin is not its own, but Christ's, and that all sin is swallowed up by the righteousness of Christ. This, as has been said above, is a necessary consequence on account of faith in Christ. So the heart learns to scoff at death and sin and to say with the Apostle, "O death, where is thy victory? O death, where is thy sting? The sting of death is sin, and the power of sin is the law. But thanks be to God, who gives us the victory through our Lord Jesus Christ" [I Cor. 15:55-57]. Death is swallowed up not only in the victory of Christ but also by our victory, because through faith his victory has become ours and in that faith we also are conquerors.

Let this suffice concerning the inner man, his liberty, and the source of his liberty, the righteousness of faith. He needs neither laws nor good works but, on the contrary, is injured by them if he believes that he is justified by them.

II.
Spiritual Freedom, Physical Liberty And The Law

Now let us turn to the second part, the outer man. Here we shall answer all those who, offended by the word "faith" and by all that has been said, now ask, "If faith does all things and is alone sufficient unto righteousness, why then are good works commanded? We will take our ease and do no works and be content with faith." I answer: not so, you wicked men, not so. That would indeed be proper if we were wholly inner and perfectly spiritual men. But such we shall be only at the last day, the day of the resurrection of the dead. As long as we live in the flesh we only begin to make some progress in that which shall be perfected in the future life. For this reason the Apostle in Rom. 8 [:23] calls all that we attain in this life "the first fruits of the Spirit" because we shall indeed receive the greater portion, even the fulness of the Spirit, in the future. This is the place to assert that which was said above, namely, that a Christian is the servant of all and made subject to all. Insofar as he is free he does no works, but insofar as he is a servant he does all kinds of works. How this is possible we shall see.

Although, as I have said, a man is abundantly and sufficiently justified by faith inwardly, in his spirit, and so has all that he needs, except insofar as this faith and these riches must grow from day to day even to the future life; yet he remains in this mortal life on earth. In this life he must control his own body and have dealings with men. Here the works begin; here a man cannot enjoy leisure; here he must indeed take care to discipline his body by fastings, watchings, labors, and other reasonable discipline and to subject it to the Spirit so that it will obey and conform to the inner man and faith and not revolt against faith and hinder the inner man, as it is the nature of the body to do if it is not held in check. The inner man, who by faith is created in the image of God, is both joyful and happy because of Christ in whom so many benefits are conferred upon him; and therefore it is his one occupation to serve God joyfully and without thought of gain, in love that is not constrained.

While he is doing this, behold, he meets a contrary will in his own flesh which strives to serve the world and seeks its own advantage. This the spirit of faith cannot tolerate, but with joyful Zeal it attempts to put the body under control and hold it in check, as Paul says in Rom. 7 [:22-23], "For I delight in the law of God, in my inmost self, but I see in my members another law at war with the law of my mind and making me captive to the law of sin," and in another place, "But I pommel my body and subdue it, lest after preaching to others I myself should be disqualified" [I Cor. 9:27], and in Galatians [5:24], "And those who belong to Christ Jesus have crucified the flesh with its passions and desires."

In doing these works, however, we must not think that a man is justified before God by them, for faith, which alone is righteousness before God, cannot endure that erroneous opinion. We must, however, realize that these works reduce the body to subjection and purify it of its evil lusts, and our whole purpose is to be directed only toward the driving out of lusts. Since by faith the soul is cleansed and made to love God, it desires that all things, and especially its own body, shall be purified so that all things may join with it in loving and praising God. Hence a man cannot be idle, for the need of his body drives him and he is compelled to do many good works to reduce it to subjection. Nevertheless the works themselves do not justify him before God, but he does the works out of spontaneous love in obedience to God and considers nothing except the approval of God, whom he would most scrupulously obey in all things. . . .

The following statements are therefore true: "Good works do not make a good man, but a good man does good works; evil works do not make a wicked man, but a wicked man does evil works."*

From this it is easy to know how far good works are to be rejected or not, and by what standard all the teachings of men concerning works are to be interpreted. If works are sought after as a means to righteousness, are burdened with this perverse leviathan,[2] and are done under the false impression that through them one is justified, they are made necessary and freedom and faith are destroyed; and this addition to them makes them no longer good but truly damnable works. They are not free, and they blaspheme the grace of God since to justify and to

* Pp. 6-24.

[2] Probably a reminiscence of Leviathan, the twisting serpent, in Isa. 27:1.

save by faith belongs to the grace of God alone. What the works have no power to do they nevertheless—by a godless presumption through this folly of ours—pretend to do and thus violently force themselves into the office and glory of grace. We do not, therefore, reject good works; on the contrary, we cherish and teach them as much as possible. We do not condemn them for their own sake but on account of this godless addition to them and the perverse idea that righteousness is to be sought through them; for that makes them appear good outwardly, when in truth they are not good. They deceive men and lead them to deceive one another like ravening wolves in sheep's clothing [Matt. 7:15].

But this leviathan, or perverse notion concerning works, is unconquerable where sincere faith is wanting. Those work-saints cannot get rid of it unless faith, its destroyer, comes and rules in their hearts. Nature of itself cannot drive it out or even recognize it, but rather regards it as a mark of the most holy will. If the influence of custom is added and confirms this perverseness of nature, as wicked teachers have caused it to do, it becomes an incurable evil and leads astray and destroys countless men beyond all hope of restoration. Therefore, although it is good to preach and write about penitence, confession, and satisfaction, our teaching is unquestionably deceitful and diabolical if we stop with that and do not go on to teach about faith.

Christ, like his forerunner John, not only said, "Repent" [Matt. 3:2; 4:17], but added the word of faith, saying, "The kingdom of heaven is at hand." We are not to preach only one of these words of God, but both; we are to bring forth out of our treasure things new and old, the voice of the law as well as the word of grace [Matt. 13:52]. We must bring forth the voice of the law that men may be made to fear and come to a knowledge of their sins and so be converted to repentance and a better life. But we must not stop with that, for that would only amount to wounding and not binding up, smiting and not healing, killing and not making alive, leading down into hell and not bringing back again, humbling and not exalting. Therefore we must also preach the word of grace and the promise of forgiveness by which faith is taught and aroused. Without this word of grace the works of the law, contrition, penitence, and all the rest are done and taught in vain.

Preachers of repentance and grace remain even to our day, but they do not explain God's law and promise that a man might learn from them the source of repentance and grace. Repentance proceeds from the law of God, but faith or grace from the promise of God, as Rom. 10 [:17] says: "So faith comes from what is heard, and what is heard comes by the preaching of Christ." Accordingly man is consoled and exalted by faith in the divine promise after he has been humbled and led to a knowledge of himself by the threats and the fear of the divine law. So we read in Psalm 30 [:5]: "Weeping may tarry for the night, but joy comes with the morning."

Let this suffice concerning works in general and at the same time concerning the works which a Christian does for himself. Lastly, we shall also speak of the things which he does toward his neighbor. A man does not live for himself alone in this mortal body to work for it alone, but he lives also for all men on earth; rather, he lives only for others and not for himself. To this end he brings his body into subjection that he may the more sincerely and freely serve others, as

Paul says in Rom. 14 [:7-8], "None of us lives to himself, and none of us dies to himself. If we live, we live to the Lord, and if we die, we die to the Lord." He cannot ever in this life be idle and without works toward his neighbors, for he will necessarily speak, deal with, and exchange views with men, as Christ also, being made in the likeness of men [Phil. 2:7], was found in form as a man and conversed with men, as Baruch 3 [:38] says.

Man, however, needs none of these things for his righteousness and salvation. Therefore he should be guided in all his works by this thought and contemplate this one thing alone, that he may serve and benefit others in all that he does, considering nothing except the need and the advantage of his neighbor. Accordingly the Apostle commands us to work with our hands so that we may give to the needy, although he might have said that we should work to support ourselves. He says, however, "that he may be able to give to those in need" [Eph. 4:28]. This is what makes caring for the body a Christian work, that through its health and comfort we may be able to work, to acquire, and lay by funds with which to aid those who are in need, that in this way the strong member may serve the weaker, and we may be sons of God, each caring for and working for the other, bearing one another's burdens and so fulfilling the law of Christ [Gal. 6:2]. This is a truly Christian life. Here faith is truly active through love [Gal. 5:6], that is, it finds expression in works of the freest service, cheerfully and lovingly done, with which a man willingly serves another without hope of reward; and for himself he is satisfied with the fullness and wealth of his faith.

Accordingly Paul, after teaching the Philippians how rich they were made through faith in Christ, in which they obtained all things, thereafter teaches them, saying, "So if there is any encouragement in Christ, any incentive of love, any participation in the Spirit, any affection and sympathy, complete my joy by being of the same mind, having the same love, being in full accord and of one mind. Do nothing from selfishness or conceit, but in humility count others better than yourselves. Let each of you look not only to his own interests, but also to the interests of others" [Phil. 2:1-4]. Here we see clearly that the Apostle has prescribed this rule for the life of Christians, namely, that we should devote all our works to the welfare of others, since each has such abundant riches in his faith that all his other works and his whole life are a surplus with which he can by voluntary benevolence serve and do good to his neighbor.*

Of the same nature are the precepts which Paul gives in Rom. 13 [:1-7], namely, that Christians should be subject to the governing authorities and be ready to do every good work, not that they shall in this way be justified, since they already are righteous through faith, but that in the liberty of the Spirit they shall by so doing serve others and the authorities themselves and obey their will freely and out of love. The works of all colleges,[3] monasteries, and priests should be of this nature. Each one should do the works of his profession and station, not that by them he may strive after righteousness, but that through them he may keep his body under control, be an example to others who also need to keep their bodies under control, and finally that by such works he may submit his will to that of others in the freedom of love. But very great care must always be exercised so

---

* Pp. 26-29.

[3] The word "college" here denotes a corporation of clergy supported by a foundation and performing certain religious services.

that no man in a false confidence imagines that by such works he will be justified or acquire merit or be saved; for this is the work of faith alone, as I have repeatedly said.

Anyone knowing this could easily and without danger find his way through those numberless mandates and precepts of pope, bishops, monasteries, churches, princes, and magistrates upon which some ignorant pastors insist as if they were necessary to righteousness and salvation, calling them "precepts of the church," although they are nothing of the kind. For a Christian, as a free man, will say, "I will fast, pray, do this and that as men command, not because it is necessary to my righteousness or salvation; but that I may show due respect to the pope, the bishop, the community, a magistrate, or my neighbor, and give them an example. I will do and suffer all things, just as Christ did and suffered far more for me, although he needed nothing of it all for himself, and was made under the law for my sake, although he was not under the law." Although tyrants do violence or injustice in making their demands, yet it will do no harm as long as they demand nothing contrary to God.

From what has been said, everyone can pass a safe judgment on all works and laws and make a trustworthy distinction between them and know who are the blind and ignorant pastors and who are the good and true. Any work that is not done solely for the purpose of keeping the body under control or of serving one's neighbor, as long as he asks nothing contrary to God, is not good or Christian. For this reason I greatly fear that few or no colleges, monasteries, altars, and offices of the church are really Christian in our day—nor the special fasts and prayers on certain saints' days. I fear, I say, that in all these we seek only our profit, thinking that through them our sins are purged away and that we find salvation in them. In this way Christian liberty perishes altogether. This is a consequence of our ignorance of Christian faith and liberty.

This ignorance and suppression of liberty very many blind pastors take pains to encourage. They stir up and urge on their people in these practices by praising such works, puffing them up with their indulgences, and never teaching faith. If, however, you wish to pray, fast, or establish a foundation in the church, I advise you to be careful not to do it in order to obtain some benefit, whether temporal or eternal, for you would do injury to your faith which alone offers you all things. Your one care should be that faith may grow, whether it is trained by works or sufferings. Make your gifts freely and for no consideration, so that others may profit by them and fare well because of you and your goodness. In this way you shall be truly good and Christian. Of what benefit to you are the good works which you do not need for keeping your body under control? Your faith is sufficient for you, through which God has given you all things.

See, according to this rule the good things we have from God should flow from one to the other and be common to all, so that everyone should "put on" his neighbor and so conduct himself toward him as if he himself were in the other's place. From Christ the good things have flowed and are flowing into us. He has so "put on" us and acted for us as if he had been what we are. From us they flow on to those who have need of them so that I should lay before God my faith and my righteousness that they may cover and intercede for the sins of my neighbor which I take upon myself and so labor and serve in them as if they were my very own. That is what Christ did for us. This is true love and the genuine rule of a Christian life. Love is true and genuine where there is true and genuine faith. Hence the Apostle says of love in I Cor. 13 [:5] that "it does not seek its own."

We conclude, therefore, that a Christian lives not in himself, but in Christ and in his neighbor. Otherwise he is not a Christian. He lives in Christ through faith, in his neighbor through love. By faith he is caught up beyond himself into God. By love he descends beneath himself into his neighbor. Yet he always remains in God and in his love, as Christ says in John 1 [:51], "Truly, truly, I say to you, you will see heaven opened, and the angels of God ascending and descending upon the Son of man."

Enough now of freedom. As you see, it is a spiritual and true freedom and makes our hearts free from all sins, laws and commands, as Paul says, I Tim. 1 [:9], "The law is not laid down for the just." It is more excellent than all other liberty, which is external, as heaven is more excellent than earth. May Christ give us this liberty both to understand and to preserve. Amen.*

---

* Pp. 32-34.

John Calvin

Born in the French town of Noyon, John Calvin (1509–64) was trained for the priesthood and law but rejected both professions to pursue humanism. In 1532 he experienced a "revelation," left his cloistered academic life, and joined the protest against corruption within the Catholic Church. In 1536 after moving to Basel, Switzerland, Calvin wrote the *Institutes of the Christian Religion* which contained his doctrines on man, society, freedom, and liberty. Calvin's most radical principles rejected the medieval and Lutheran belief that man had free will. Calvin asserted that God determined all events and that man, born in sin and corruption, was predestined either to salvation or damnation. He argued that those who were predestined to be saved had a responsibility to follow God's will and create a society resembling God's Kingdom by joining government and church to suppress corruption. These activist doctrines led to social experiments in Geneva, Switzerland, efforts by Calvinists to reform English society, and the migration of thousands of Puritans to America to create a godly community modeled after Calvin's principles, and contributed to the transformation of European society at the end of the Middle Ages.

I.
The Nature Of God

To represent God as a Creator only for a moment, who entirely finished all his work at once, were frigid and jejune [barren]; and in this it behoves us especially

---

Reprinted from John Calvin, *Institutes of the Christian Religion,* ed. Benjamin B. Warfield, trans. John Allen (Philadelphia: Presbyterian Board of Christian Education, 1936), Vols. I & II, Book I; chaps. 15, 16; Book II, chap. 2; Book III, chaps. 12, 19; Book IV, chaps. 11, 12, 20, by permission of the publisher.

to differ from the heathen, that the presence of the Divine power may appear to us no less in the perpetual state of the world than in its first origin. . . .

When it has learned that he is the Creator of all things, it should immediately conclude that he is also their perpetual governor and preserver; and that not by a certain universal motion, actuating the whole machine of the world, and all its respective parts, but by a particular providence sustaining, nourishing, and providing for every thing which he has made. . . .* we assert, that not only the heaven and the earth, and inanimate creatures, but also the deliberations and volitions of men, are so governed by his providence, as to be directed to the end appointed by it. What then? you will say; does nothing happen fortuitously or contingently?

For if all success be the benediction of God, and calamity and adversity his malediction, there is no room left in human affairs for fortune or chance.

Let us suppose, for example, that a merchant, having entered a wood in the company of honest men, imprudently wanders from his companions, and, pursuing a wrong course, falls into the hands of robbers, and is murdered. His death was not only foreseen by God, but also decreed by him. For it is said, not that he has foreseen to what limits the life of every man would extend, but that he "hath appointed bounds which he cannot pass." Yet, as far as our minds are capable of comprehending, all these circumstances appear fortuitous. What opinion shall a Christian form on this case? He will consider all the circumstances of such a death as in their nature fortuitous; yet he will not doubt that the providence of God presided, and directed fortune to that end. The same reasoning will apply to future contingencies. All future things being uncertain to us, we hold them in suspense, as though they might happen either one way or another. Yet this remains a fixed principle in our hearts, that there will be no event which God has not ordained. . . .

What God decrees, must necessarily come to pass.†

II.
The Nature Of Man And Free Will

We must now treat of the creation of man, not only because he exhibits the most noble and remarkable specimen of the Divine justice, wisdom, and goodness, among all the works of God, but because, as we observed in the beginning, we cannot attain to a clear and solid knowledge of God, without a mutual acquaintance with ourselves. . . .

That man consists of soul and body, ought not to be controverted. By the "soul" I understand an immortal, yet created essence, which is the nobler part of him. Sometimes it is called a "spirit;" . . .‡

God has furnished the soul of man, therefore, with a mind capable of discerning good from evil, and just from unjust; and of discovering, by the light of reason,

* Book I, chap. 16, pp. 217-18.
† Book I, chap. 16, pp. 228-30.
‡ Book I, chap. 15, pp. 202-3.

what ought to be pursued or avoided; whence the philosophers called this directing faculty *το ηγεμονικον*, the principal or governing part. To this he has annexed the will, on which depends the choice. The primitive condition of man was ennobled with those eminent faculties; he possessed reason, understanding, prudence, and judgment, not only for the government of his life on earth, but to enable him to ascend even to God and eternal felicity. To these was added choice, to direct the appetites, and regulate all the organic motions; so that the will should be entirely conformed to the government of reason. In this integrity man was endued with free will, by which, if he had chosen, he might have obtained eternal life. For here it would be unreasonable to introduce the question respecting the secret predestination of God, because we are not discussing what might possibly have happened or not, but what was the real nature of man. Adam, therefore, could have stood if he would, since he fell merely by his own will; but because his will was flexible to either side, and he was not endued with constancy to persevere, therefore he so easily fell. Yet his choice of good and evil was free; and not only so, but his mind and will were possessed of consummate rectitude, and all his organic parts were rightly disposed to obedience, till, destroying himself, he corrupted all his excellencies. Hence proceeded the darkness which overspread the minds of the philosophers, because they sought for a complete edifice among ruins, and for beautiful order in the midst of confusion. They held this principle, that man would not be a rational animal, unless he were endued with a free choice of good or evil; they conceived also that otherwise all difference between virtue and vice would be destroyed, unless man regulated his life according to his own inclination. Thus far it had been well, if there had been no change in man, of which as they were ignorant, it is not to be wondered at if they confound heaven and earth together. But those who profess themselves to be disciples of Christ, and yet seek for free will in man, now lost and overwhelmed in spiritual ruin, in striking out a middle path between the opinions of the philosophers and the doctrine of heaven, are evidently deceived, so that they touch neither heaven nor earth. But these things will be better introduced in the proper place. At present be it only remembered, that man, at his first creation, was very different from all his posterity, who, deriving their original from him in his corrupted state, have contracted an hereditary defilement. For all the parts of his soul were formed with the utmost rectitude; he enjoyed soundness of mind, and a will free to the choice of good. If any object, that he was placed in a dangerous situation on account of the imbecility of this faculty, I reply, that the station in which he was placed was sufficient, to deprive him of all excuse. For it would have been unreasonable that God should be confined to this condition, to make man so as to be altogether incapable either of choosing or of committing any sin. It is true that such a nature would have been more excellent; but to expostulate with God as though he had been under any obligation to bestow this upon man, were unreasonable and unjust in the extreme; since it was at his choice to bestow as little as he pleased. But why he did not sustain him with the power of perseverance, remains concealed in his mind; but it is our duty to restrain our investigations within the limits of sobriety. He had received the power, indeed, if he chose to exert it; but he had not the will to use that power; for the consequence of this will would have been perseverance. Yet there is no excuse for him; he received so much, that he was the voluntary procurer of his own destruction; but God was under no necessity to give him any other than an indifferent and mutable will, that from his fall he might educe matter for his own glory.*

Therefore, since the image of God is the uncorrupted excellence of human nature, which shone in Adam before his defection, but was afterwards so corrupted, and almost obliterated, that nothing remains from the ruin but what is confused, mutilated, and defiled,—it is now partly visible in the elect, inasmuch as they are regenerated by the Spirit, but it will obtain its full glory in heaven.†

Since we have seen that the domination of sin, from the time of its subjugation of the first man, not only extends over the whole race, but also exclusively possesses every soul, it now remains to be more closely investigated, whether we are despoiled of all freedom, and, if any particle of it yet remain, how far its power extends.‡

Now it must be carefully observed that Christian liberty is . . . a spiritual thing; all the virtue of which consists in appeasing terrified consciences before God, whether they are disquieted and solicitous concerning the remission of their sins or are anxious to know if their works, which are imperfect and contaminated by the defilements of the flesh, be acceptable to God; or are tormented concerning the use of things that are indifferent. Wherefore they are guilty of perverting its meaning who either make it the pretext of their irregular appetites, that they may abuse the Divine blessings to the purposes of sensuality, or who suppose that there is no liberty but what is used before men, and therefore in the exercise of it totally disregard their weak brethren. The former of these sins is the more common in the present age. There is scarcely anyone whom his wealth permits to be sumptuous, who is not delighted with luxurious splendor in his entertainments, in his dress, and in his buildings; who does not desire a pre-eminence in every species of luxury; who does not strangely flatter himself on his elegance. And all these things are defended under the pretext of Christian liberty. They allege that they are things indifferent; this I admit provided they be indifferently used. But where they are too ardently coveted, proudly boasted, or luxuriously lavished, these things, of themselves otherwise indifferent, are completely polluted by such vices. This passage of Paul makes an excellent distinction respecting things which are indifferent: "Unto the pure all things are pure; but unto them that are defiled and unbelieving is nothing pure; but even their mind and conscience are defiled." [1] For why are curses denounced on rich men, who "receive their consolation," who are "satiated," who "now laugh," who "lie on beds of ivory," who "join field to field," who "have the harp, and the lyre, and the tabret, and wine in their feasts"? [2] Ivory and gold, and riches of all kinds, are certainly blessings of Divine Providence, not only permitted, but expressly designed for the use of men; nor are we anywhere prohibited to laugh or to be satiated with food, or to annex new possessions to those already enjoyed by ourselves or by our ancestors, or to be delighted with musical harmony, or to drink wine. This indeed is true; but amidst an abundance of all things, to be immersed in sensual delights, to inebriate the heart and mind with present pleasures, and perpetually to grasp at new ones—these things are very remote from a legitimate use of the Divine blessings. Let them banish, therefore,

---

* Book I, chap. 15, p. 214.

† Book I, chap. 15, p. 210.

‡ Book II, chap. 2, p. 279.

[1] Titus 1:15.

[2] Luke 6:24-25. Amos 6:1f. Isaiah 5:8f.

immoderate cupidity, excessive profusion, vanity, and arrogance; that with a pure conscience they may make a proper use of the gifts of God. When their hearts shall be formed to this sobriety, they will have a rule for the legitimate enjoyment of them. On the contrary, without this moderation even common and ordinary pleasures are chargeable with excess. For it is truly observed that a proud heart frequently dwells under coarse and ragged garments, and that simplicity and humility are sometimes concealed under purple and fine linen. Let all men, in their respective stations, whether of poverty, of competence, or of splendor, live in the remembrance of this truth that God confers his blessings on them for the support of life, not for luxury; and let them consider this as the law of Christian liberty that they learn the lesson which Paul had learned, when he said, "I have learned, in whatsoever state I am, therewith to be content. I know both how to be abased, and I know how to abound: everywhere and in all things I am instructed both to be full and to be hungry, both to abound and to suffer need."

Many persons err likewise in this respect that, as if their liberty would not be perfectly secure unless witnessed by men, they make an indiscriminate and imprudent use of it—a disorderly practice which occasions frequent offense to their weak brethren. There are some to be found, in the present day, who imagine their liberty would be abridged if they were not to enter on the enjoyment of it by eating animal food on Friday. Their eating is not the subject of my reprehension; but their minds require to be divested of this false notion; for they ought to consider that they obtain no advantage from their liberty before men, but with God; and that it consists in abstinence as well as in use. If they apprehend it to be immaterial in God's view whether they eat animal food or eggs, whether their garments be scarlet or black, it is quite sufficient. The conscience to which the benefit of this liberty was due is now emancipated. Therefore, though they abstain from flesh and wear but one color during all the rest of their lives, this is no diminution of their freedom. Nay, because they are free, they therefore abstain with a free conscience.*

III.
Man, Society, Civil Liberty And The Necessity Of Government

Now, since the consciences of believers, being privileged with the liberty which we have described, have been delivered by the favor of Christ from all necessary obligation to the observance of those things in which the Lord has been pleased they should be left free, we conclude that they are exempt from all human authority. . . .

[However] as soon as a word is mentioned concerning the abrogation of human establishments, great tumults are excited, partly by seditious persons, partly by cavillers, as though all obedience of men were at once subverted and destroyed.

To prevent anyone from falling into this error, let us therefore consider, in the first place, that man is under two kinds of government—one spiritual, by which

* Book III, chap. 19, pp. 83-85.

the conscience is formed to piety and the service of God; the other political, by which a man is instructed in the duties of humanity and civility, which are to be observed in an intercourse with mankind. They are generally, and not improperly, denominated the spiritual and the temporal jurisdiction, indicating that the former species of government pertains to the life of the soul, and that the latter relates to the concerns of the present state, not only to the provision of food and clothing, but to the enactment of laws to regulate a man's life among his neighbors by the rules of holiness, integrity, and sobriety. For the former has its seat in the interior of the mind, whilst the latter only directs the external conduct: one may be termed a spiritual kingdom, and the other a political one.*

Having already stated that man is the subject of two kinds of government . . . we are . . . to say something . . . which relates to civil justice and the regulation of the external conduct. For, though the nature of this argument seems to have no connection with the spiritual doctrine of faith . . . the sequel will show that I have sufficient reason for connecting them together, and, indeed, that necessity obliges me to it, especially since, on the one hand, infatuated and barbarous men madly endeavor to subvert this ordinance established by God, and, on the other hand, the flatterers of princes, extolling their power beyond all just bounds, hesitate not to oppose it to the authority of God himself. Unless both these errors be resisted, the purity of the faith will be destroyed. Besides, it is of no small importance for us to know what benevolent provision God has made for mankind in this instance, that we may be stimulated by a greater degree of pious zeal to testify our gratitude. In the first place, before we enter on the subject itself, it is necessary for us to recur to the distinction which we have already established, lest we fall into an error very common in the world, and injudiciously confound together these two things the nature of which is altogether different. For some men, when they hear that the Gospel promises a liberty which acknowledges no king or magistrate among them, but submits to Christ alone, think they can enjoy no advantage of their liberty while they see any power exalted above them. They imagine, therefore, that nothing will prosper unless the whole world be modeled in a new form, without any tribunals or laws, or magistrates, or anything of a similar kind which they consider injurious to their liberty. But he who knows how to distinguish between the body and the soul, between this present transitory life and the future eternal one, will find no difficulty in understanding that the spiritual kingdom of Christ and civil government are things very different and remote from each other.

Yet this distinction does not lead us to consider the whole system of civil government as a polluted thing which has nothing to do with Christian men. Some fanatics who are pleased with nothing but liberty, or rather licentiousness without any restraint, do indeed boast and vociferate, That since we are dead with Christ to the elements of this world and, being translated into the kingdom of God, sit among the celestials, it is a degradation to us and far beneath our dignity to be occupied with those secular and impure cares which relate to things altogether uninteresting to a Christian man. Of what use, they ask, are laws without judgments and tribunals? But what have judgments to do with a Christian man? And if it be unlawful to kill, of what use are laws and judgments to us? But as we have just suggested that this kind of government is distinct from that spiritual and internal reign of

* Book III, chap. 19, pp. 89-90.

Christ, so it ought to be known that they are in no respect at variance with each other. For that spiritual reign, even now upon earth, commences within us some preludes of the heavenly kingdom, and in this mortal and transitory life affords us some prelibations of immortal and incorruptible blessedness; but this civil government is designed, as long as we live in this world, to cherish and support the external worship of God, to preserve the pure doctrine of religion, to defend the constitution of the Church, to regulate our lives in a manner requisite for the society of men, to form our manners to civil justice, to promote our concord with each other, and to establish general peace and tranquility—all of which I confess to be superfluous if the kingdom of God, as it now exists in us, extinguishes the present life. But if it is the will of God that while we are aspiring toward our true country, we be pilgrims on the earth, and if such aids are necessary to our pilgrimage, they who take them from man deprive him of his human nature. They plead that there should be so much perfection in the Church of God that its order would suffice to supply the place of all laws; but they foolishly imagine a perfection which can never be found in any community of men. For since the insolence of the wicked is so great, and their iniquity so obstinate, that it can scarcely be restrained by all the severity of the laws, what may we expect they would do if they found themselves at liberty to perpetuate crimes with impunity whose outrages even the arm of power cannot altogether prevent?

But for speaking of the exercise of civil polity, there will be another place more suitable. At present we only wish it to be understood that to entertain a thought of its extermination is inhuman barbarism; it is equally as necessary to mankind as bread and water, light and air, and far more excellent. For it not only tends to secure the accommodations arising from all these things, that men may breathe, eat, drink, and be sustained in life, though it comprehends all these things while it causes them to live together, yet I say this is not its only tendency; its objects also are that idolatry, sacrileges against the name of God, blasphemies against his truth, and other offenses against religion may not openly appear and be disseminated among the people; that the public tranquility may not be disturbed; that every person may enjoy his property without molestation; that men may transact their business together without fraud or injustice; that integrity and modesty may be cultivated among them; in short, that there may be a public form of religion among Christians, and that humanity may be maintained among men. Nor let anyone think it strange that I now refer to human polity the charge of the due maintenance of religion, which I may appear to have placed beyond the jurisdiction of men. For I do not allow men to make laws respecting religion and the worship of God now any more than I did before, though I approve of civil government which provides that the true religion contained in the law of God be not violated and polluted by public blasphemies with impunity.*

* Book IV, Chap. 20, pp. 770-73.

IV.
The Structure Of Civil Government, The Role Of The Magistrate, And Liberty

But the perspicuity [understanding] of order will assist the readers to attain a clearer understanding of what sentiments ought to be entertained respecting the whole system of civil administration, if we enter on a discussion of each branch of it. These are three: The magistrate, who is the guardian and conservator of the laws; the laws according to which he governs; the people, who are governed by the laws and obey the magistrate. Let us, therefore, examine, first, the function of a magistrate, whether it be a legitimate calling and approved by God, the nature of the duty, and the extent of the power; secondly, by what laws Christian government ought to be regulated; and lastly, what advantage the people derive from the laws, and what obedience they owe to the magistrate.

The Lord has not only testified that the function of magistrates has his approbation and acceptance, but has eminently commended it to us, by dignifying it with the most honorable titles. We will mention a few of them. When all who sustain the magistracy are called "gods," it ought not to be considered as an appellation of trivial importance, for it implies that they have their command from God, that they are invested with his authority; and are altogether his representatives, and act as his vicegerents.[3]

. . . This consideration ought continually to occupy the magistrates themselves, since it is calculated to furnish them with a powerful stimulus by which they may be excited to their duty, and to afford them peculiar consolation by which the difficulties of their office, which certainly are many and arduous, may be alleviated. For what an ardent pursuit of integrity, prudence, clemency, moderation, and innocence ought they to prescribe to themselves who are conscious of having been constituted ministers of the Divine justice! With what confidence will they admit iniquity to their tribunal, which they understand to be the throne of the living God? With what audacity will they pronounce an unjust sentence with that mouth which they know to be the destined organ of Divine truth? With what conscience will they subscribe to impious decrees with that hand which they know to be appointed to register the edicts of God? In short, if they remember that they are the vicegerents of God, it behooves them to watch with all care, earnestness, and diligence, that in their administration they may exhibit to men an image, as it were, of the providence, care, goodness, benevolence, and justice of God. And they must constantly bear this in mind that if in all cases "he be cursed that doeth the work of the Lord deceitfully,"[4] a far heavier curse awaits those who act fraudulently in a righteous calling. Therefore, when Moses and Jehoshaphat wished to exhort their judges to the discharge of their duty, they had nothing to suggest more efficacious than the principle which we have already mentioned. Moses says, "Judge righteously between every man and his brother, and the stranger that is with him. For the judgment is God's."[5] Jehoshaphat says, "Take heed what ye

---

[3] Psalm 82:1,6.
[4] Jer. 47:10.
[5] Deut. 1:16-17.

do; for ye judge not for man, but for the Lord, who is with you in the judgment. Wherefore now let the fear of the Lord be upon you: take heed and do it; for there is no iniquity with the Lord our God."[6] And in another place it is said, "God standeth in the congregation of the mighty: he judgeth among the gods";[7] that they may be animated to their duty when they understand that they are delegated by God, to whom they must one day render an account of their administration. And this admonition is entitled to have considerable weight with them; for if they fail in their duty, they not only injure men by criminally distressing them, but even offend God by polluting his sacred judgments. On the other hand, it opens a source of peculiar consolation to them to reflect that they are not employed in profane things, or occupations unsuitable to a servant of God, but in a most sacred function, inasmuch as they execute a Divine commission.

Those who are not restrained by so many testimonies of Scripture, but still dare to stigmatize this sacred ministry as a thing incompatible with religion and Christian piety, do they not offer an insult to God himself, who cannot but be involved in the reproach cast upon his ministry? And in fact they do not reject magistrates, but they reject God, "that he should not reign over them."[8]

And for private men, who have no authority to deliberate on the regulation of any public affairs, it would surely be a vain occupation to dispute which would be the best form of government in the place where they live. Besides, this could not be simply determined, as an abstract question, without great impropriety, since the principle to guide the decision must depend on circumstances. And even if we compare the different forms together, without their circumstances, their advantages are so nearly equal that it will not be easy to discover of which the utility preponderates. . . .

Those who would wish to introduce anarchy . . . betray not only their ignorance but their diabolical pride, in boasting of perfection of which not the smallest particle can be discovered in them. . . .

. . . no government can be happily constituted unless its first object be the promotion of piety, and that all laws are preposterous which neglect the claims of God and merely provide for the interests of men. Therefore, as religion holds the first place among all the philosophers, and as this has always been regarded by the universal consent of all nations, Christian princes and magistrates ought to be ashamed of their indolence if they do not make it the object of their most serious care. We have already shown that this duty is particularly enjoined upon them by God; for it is reasonable that they should employ their utmost efforts in asserting and defending the honor of Him whose vicegerents they are and by whose favor they govern. And the principal commendations given in the Scripture to the good kings are for having restored the worship of God when it had been corrupted or abolished, or for having devoted their attention to religion, that it might flourish in purity and safety under their reigns. . . . These things evince the folly of those who would wish magistrates to neglect all thoughts of God, and to confine themselves entirely to the administration of justice among men, as though God appointed governors in his name to decide secular controversies,

---

[6] II Chron. 19:6-7.
[7] Psalm 82:1.
[8] I Sam. 8:7.

and disregarded that which is of far greater importance—the pure worship of himself according to the rule of his law. . . .

We see, therefore, that they are constituted the protectors and vindicators of the public innocence, modesty, probity, and tranquility, whose sole object it ought to be to promote the common peace and security of all. But as they cannot do this unless they defend good men from the injuries of the wicked and aid the oppressed by their relief and protection, they are likewise armed with power for the suppression of crimes, and the severe punishment of malefactors whose wickedness disturbs the public peace. For experience fully verifies the observation of Solon: "That all states are supported by reward and punishment; and that when these two things are removed, all the discipline of human societies is broken and destroyed." For the minds of many lose their regard for equity and justice unless virtue be rewarded with due honor; nor can the violence of the wicked be restrained unless crimes are followed by severe punishments. And these two parts are included in the injunction of the prophet to kings and other governors to "execute judgment and righteousness." [9] "Righteousness" means the care, patronage, defense, vindication, and liberation of the innocent; "judgment" imports the repression of the audacity, the coercion of the violence, and the punishment of the crime of the impious.

But here, it seems, arises an important and difficult question. If by the law of God all Christians are forbidden to kill,[10] and the prophet predicts respecting the Church that "they shall not hurt nor destroy in all my holy mountain, saith the Lord," [11] how can it be compatible with piety for magistrates to shed blood? But if we understand that in the infliction of punishments the magistrate does not act at all from himself, but merely executes the judgments of God, we shall not be embarrassed with this scruple. The law of the Lord commands, "Thou shalt not kill"; but that homicide may not go unpunished, the legislator himself puts the sword into the hands of his ministers, to be used against all homicides.[12] *To hurt* and *to destroy* are incompatible with the character of the godly; but to avenge the afflictions of the righteous at the command of God is neither *to hurt* nor *to destroy.* Therefore it is easy to conclude that in this respect magistrates are not subject to the common law, by which, though the Lord binds the hands of men, he does not bind his own justice, which he exercises by the hands of magistrates. So, when a prince forbids all his subjects to strike or wound anyone, he does not prohibit his officers from executing that justice which is particularly committed to them. I sincerely wish that this consideration were constantly in our recollection, that nothing is done here by the temerity of men, but everything by the authority of God, who commands it, and under whose guidance we never err from the right way. . . .

Now, as it is sometimes necessary for kings and nations to take up arms for the infliction of such public vengeance, the same reason will lead us to infer the lawfulness of wars which are undertaken for this end. For if they have been entrusted with power to preserve the tranquility of their own territories, to suppress the

[9] Jer. 22:3.
[10] Exod. 20:13.
[11] Isaiah 11:9; 65:25.
[12] Gen. 9:6. Exod. 21:12.

seditious tumults of disturbers, to succor the victims of oppression, and to punish crimes—can they exert this power for a better purpose than to repel the violence of him who disturbs both the private repose of individuals and the general tranquility of the nation, who excites insurrections and perpetrates acts of oppression, cruelty, and every species of crime? If they ought to be the guardians and defenders of the laws, it is incumbent upon them to defeat the efforts of all by whose injustice the discipline of the laws is corrupted. And if they justly punish those robbers whose injuries have only extended to a few persons, shall they suffer a whole district to be plundered and devastated with impunity? For there is no difference whether he who in a hostile manner invades, disturbs, and plunders the territory of another to which he has no right be a king or one of the meanest of mankind: all persons of this description are equally to be considered as robbers, and ought to be punished as such. It is the dictate both of natural equity and of the nature of the office, therefore, that princes are armed, not only to restrain the crimes of private individuals by judicial punishments, but also to defend the territories committed to their charge by going to war against any hostile aggression; and the Holy Spirit, in many passages of Scripture, declares such wars to be lawful. . . .

But here all magistrates ought to be very cautious, that they follow not in any respect the impulse of their passions. On the contrary, if punishments are to be inflicted, they ought not to be precipitated with anger, exasperated with hatred, or inflamed with implacable severity; they ought, as Augustine says, "to commiserate our common nature even in him whom they punish for his crime." Or, if arms are to be resorted to against an enemy, that is, an armed robber, they ought not to seize a trivial occasion, nor even to take it when presented, unless they are driven to it by extreme necessity. For, if it be our duty to exceed what was required by that heathen writer who maintained that the evident object of war ought to be the restoration of peace, certainly we ought to make every other attempt before we have recourse to the decision of arms. In short, in both cases they must not suffer themselves to be carried away by any private motive, but be wholly guided by public spirit; otherwise they grossly abuse their power, which is given them, not for their own particular advantage, but for the benefit and service of others.*

V.
The Duty Of The People Toward The Magistrates

The first duty of subjects toward their magistrates is to entertain the most honorable sentiments of their function, which they know to be a jurisdiction delegated to them from God, and on that account to esteem and reverence them as God's ministers and vicegerents. For there are some persons to be found who show themselves very obedient to their magistrates and have not the least wish that there were

* Book IV, chap. 20, pp. 773-86.

no magistrates for them to obey, because they know them to be so necessary to the public good, but who, nevertheless, consider the magistrates themselves as no other than necessary evils. . . .

Hence follows another duty—that, with minds disposed to honor and reverence magistrates, subjects approve their obedience to them in submitting to their edicts, in paying taxes, in discharging public duties, and bearing burdens which relate to the common defense, and in fulfilling all their other commands. Paul says to the Romans, "Let every soul be subject unto the higher powers. Whosoever resisteth the power, resisteth the ordinance of God." [13] He writes to Titus, "Put them in mind to be subject to principalities and powers, to obey magistrates, to be ready to every good work." [14] Peter exhorts, "Submit yourselves to every ordinance of man for the Lord's sake; whether it be to the king, as supreme; or unto governors, as unto them that are sent by him for the punishment of evildoers, and for the praise of them that do well." [15] Moreover, that subjects may testify that theirs is not a hypocritical but a sincere and cordial submission, Paul teaches that they ought to pray to God for the safety and prosperity of those under whose government they live. "I exhort," he says, "that supplications, prayers, intercessions, and giving of thanks be made for all men; for kings, and for all that are in authority; that we may lead a quiet and peaceable life in all godliness and honesty." [16] Here let no man deceive himself. For as it is impossible to resist the magistrate without at the same time resisting God himself, though an unarmed magistrate may seem to be despised with impunity, yet God is armed to inflict exemplary vengeance on the contempt offered to himself. Under this obedience I also include the moderation which private persons ought to prescribe to themselves in relation to public affairs, that they do not, without being called upon, intermeddle with affairs of state or rashly intrude themselves into the office of magistrates, or undertake anything of a public nature. If there be anything in the public administration which requires to be corrected, let them not raise any tumults or take the business into their own hands, which ought to be all bound in this respect, but let them refer it to the cognizance of the magistrate, who is alone authorized to regulate the concerns of the public. I mean that they ought to attempt nothing without being commanded; for when they have the command of a governor, then they also are invested with public authority. For, as we are accustomed to call the counsellors of a prince "his eyes and ears," so they may not unaptly be called "his hands" whom he has commissioned to execute his commands.

Now, as we have hitherto described a magistrate who truly answers to his title—who is the father of his country and, as the poet calls him, the pastor of his people, the guardian of peace, the protector of justice, the avenger of innocence; he would justly be deemed insane who disapproved of such a government. But, as it has happened, in almost all ages, that some princes, regardless of everything to which they ought to have directed their attention and provision, give themselves up to their pleasures in indolent exemption from every care; others, absorbed in their own interest, expose to sale all laws, privileges, rights, and judgments; others

---

[13] Rom. 13:1-2.
[14] Titus 3:1.
[15] I Peter 2:13-14.
[16] I Tim. 2:1-2.

plunder the public wealth which they afterwards lavish in mad prodigality; others commit flagrant outrages, pillaging houses, violating virgins and matrons, and murdering infants; many persons cannot be persuaded that such ought to be acknowledged as princes whom, as far as possible, they ought to obey. For in such enormities and actions so completely incompatible, not only with the office of a magistrate, but with the duty of every man, they discover no appearance of the image of God, which ought to be conspicuous in a magistrate; while they perceive no vestige of that minister of God who is "not a terror to good works, but to the evil," who is sent "for the punishment of evildoers, and for the praise of them that do well"; nor recognize that governor whose dignity and authority the Scripture recommends to us. And certainly the minds of men have always been naturally disposed to hate and execrate tyrants as much as to love and reverence legitimate kings.

But, if we direct our attention to the word of God, it will carry us much farther: even to submit to the government, not only of those princes who discharge their duty to us with becoming integrity and fidelity, but of all who possess the sovereignty, even though they perform none of the duties of their function. For, though the Lord testifies that the magistrate is an eminent gift of his liberality to preserve the safety of men, and prescribes to magistrates themselves the extent of their duty, yet he at the same time declares that whatever be their characters, they have their government only from him; that those who govern for the public good are true specimens and mirrors of his beneficence; and that those who rule in an unjust and tyrannical manner are raised up by him to punish the iniquity of the people; that all equally possess that sacred majesty with which he has invested legitimate authority. I will not proceed any further till I have subjoined a few testimonies in proof of this point. It is unnecessary, however, to labor much to evince an impious king to be a judgment of God's wrath upon the world, as I have no expectation that anyone will deny it; and in this we say no more of a king than of any other robber who plunders our property, or adulterer who violates our bed, or assassin who attempts to murder us; since the Scripture enumerates all these calamities among the curses inflicted by God. But let us rather insist on the proof of that which the minds of men do not so easily admit—that a man of the worst character, and most undeserving of all honor, who holds the sovereign power, really possesses that eminent and Divine authority which the Lord has given by his word to the ministers of his justice and judgment; and, therefore, that he ought to be regarded by his subjects, as far as pertains to public obedience, with the same reverence and esteem which they would show to the best of kings, if such a one were granted to them.*

. . . If we have this constantly present to our eyes and impressed upon our hearts, that the most iniquitous kings are placed on their thrones by the same decree by which the authority of all kings is established, those seditious thoughts will never enter our minds that a king is to be treated according to his merits, and that it is not reasonable for us to be subject to a king who does not on his part perform toward us those duties which his office requires.†

---

* Book IV. chap. 20, pp. 795-99.

† Book IV, chap. 20, p. 801.

. . . yet the Lord equally executed his work when he broke the sanguinary scepters of insolent kings and overturned tyrannical governments. Let princes hear and fear. But, in the meanwhile, it behooves us to use the greatest caution, that we do not despise or violate that authority of magistrates which is entitled to the greatest veneration, which God has established by the most solemn commands, even though it reside in those who are most unworthy of it, and who, as far as in them lies, pollute it by their iniquity. . . .

But in the obedience which we have shown to be due to the authority of governors, it is always necessary to make one exception, and that is entitled to our first attention—that it do not seduce us from obedience to him to whose will the desires of all kings ought to be subject, to whose decrees all their commands ought to yield, to whose majesty all their scepters ought to submit. And, indeed, how preposterous it would be for us, with a view to satisfy men, to incur the displeasure of him on whose account we yield obedience to men! The Lord, therefore, is the King of kings; who, when he has opened his sacred mouth, is to be heard alone, above all, for all, and before all; in the next place, we are subject to those men who preside over us, but no otherwise than in him. If they command anything against him, it ought not to have the least attention, nor, in this case, ought we to pay any regard to all that dignity attached to magistrates, to which no injury is done when it is subjected to the unrivaled and supreme power of God. On this principle Daniel denied that he had committed any crime against the king in disobeying his impious decree;[17] because the king had exceeded the limits of his office, and had not only done an injury to men, but, by raising his arm against God, had degraded his own authority. . . .

But since this edict has been proclaimed by that celestial herald, Peter, "We ought to obey God rather than men,"[18]—let us console ourselves with this thought, that we truly perform the obedience which God requires of us when we suffer anything rather than deviate from piety. And that our hearts may not fail us, Paul stimulates us with another consideration—that Christ has redeemed us at the immense price which our redemption cost him, that we may not be submissive to the corrupt desires of men, much less be slaves to their impiety.[19]*

VI.
The Proper Role Of The Church In Society And The Relation Of The Church To Individual Liberty

For as no city or town can exist without a magistracy and civil polity, so the Church of God, as I have already stated, but am now obliged to repeat, stands in need of a certain spiritual polity; which, however, is entirely distinct from civil polity,

---

* Book IV, chap. 20, pp. 804-6.

[17] Dan. 6:22.

[18] Acts 5:29.

[19] I Cor. 7:23.

and is so far from obstructing or weakening it, that, on the contrary, it highly conduces to its assistance and advancement. This power of jurisdiction, therefore, will, in short, be no other than an order instituted for the preservation of the spiritual polity. For this end, there were from the beginning judiciaries appointed in the Churches, to take cognizance of manners, to pass censures on vices, and to preside over the use of the keys in excommunication.*

. . . the Church has no power of the sword to punish or to coerce, no authority to compel, no prisons, fines, or other punishments, like those inflicted by the civil magistrate. Besides, the object of this power is, not that he who has transgressed may be punished against his will but that he may profess his repentance by a voluntary submission to chastisement. The difference therefore is very great; because the Church does not assume to itself what belongs to the magistrate, nor can the magistrate execute that which is executed by the Church. This will be better understood by an example. Is any man intoxicated? In a well regulated city he will be punished by imprisonment. Has he committed fornication? He will receive the same or a severer punishment. With this, the laws, the magistrate, and the civil judgment, will all be satisfied; though it may happen that he will give no sign of repentance, but will rather murmur and repine against his punishment. Will the Church stop here? Such persons cannot be admitted to the sacred supper without doing an injury to Christ and to his holy institution. And reason requires, that he who has offended the Church with an evil example, should remove, by a solemn declaration of repentance, the offence which he has excited. The argument adduced by those who espouse a contrary opinion, is of no force. They say, that Christ assigned this office to the Church, when there was no magistrate to execute it. But it frequently happens that the magistrate is too negligent, and sometimes that he even deserves to be chastised himself. . . . Besides, the same argument might be extended to the whole ministry of the word. Now, then, according to them, pastors must no longer censure notorious crimes; they must cease to chide, to reprove, to rebuke; for there are Christian magistrates, whose duty it is to correct such offences by the civil sword. But as it is the duty of the magistrate, by punishment and corporeal coercion, to purge the Church from offences, so it behoves the minister of the word, on his part, to relieve the magistrate by preventing the multiplication of offenders. Their respective operations ought to be so connected as to be an assistance, and not an obstruction to each other.†

The discipline of the Church . . . depends chiefly on the power of the keys, and the spiritual jurisdiction. To make this more easily understood, let us divide the Church into two principal orders—the clergy and the people. I use the word *clergy* as the common, though improper, appellation of those who execute the public ministry in the Church. We shall, first, speak of the common discipline to which all ought to be subject; and in the next place we shall proceed to the clergy, who, beside this common discipline, have a discipline peculiar to themselves. But as some have such a hatred of discipline, as to abhor the very name, they should attend to the following consideration: That if no society, and even no house, though containing only a small family, can be preserved in a proper state without discipline, this is far more necessary in the Church, the state of which ought to be the most

---

* Book IV, chap. 11, p. 483.
† Book IV, chap. 11, pp. 487-88.

orderly of all. As the saving doctrine of Christ is the soul of the Church, so discipline forms the ligaments which connect the members together, and keep each in its proper place. Whoever, therefore, either desire the abolition of all discipline, or obstruct its restoration, whether they act from design or inadvertency, they certainly promote the entire dissolution of the Church. For what will be the consequence, if every man be at liberty to follow his own inclinations? But such would be the case, unless the preaching of the doctrine were accompanied with private admonitions, reproofs, and other means to enforce the doctrine, and prevent it from being altogether ineffectual. Discipline, therefore, serves as a bridle to curb and restrain the refractory, who resist the doctrine of Christ; or as a spur to stimulate the inactive; and sometimes as a father's rod, with which those who have grievously fallen may be chastised in mercy, and with the gentleness of the Spirit of Christ. Now, when we see the approach of certain beginnings of a dreadful desolation in the Church, since there is no solicitude or means to keep the people in obedience to our Lord, necessity itself proclaims the want of a remedy; and this is the only remedy which has been commanded by Christ, or which has ever been adopted among believers. . . .

The first foundation of discipline consists in the use of private admonitions; that is to say, that if any one be guilty of a voluntary omission of duty, or conduct himself in an insolent manner, or discover a want of virtue in his life, or commit any act deserving of reprehension, he should suffer himself to be admonished; and that every one should study to admonish his brother, whenever occasion shall require; but that pastors and presbyters, beyond all others, should be vigilant in the discharge of this duty, being called by their office, not only to preach to the congregation, but also to admonish and exhort in private houses, if in any instances their public instructions may not have been sufficiently efficacious; as Paul inculcates, when he says, that he "taught publicly and from house to house," and protests himself to be "pure from the blood of all men," having "ceased not to warn every one night and day with tears." [20] For the doctrine then obtains its full authority, and produces its due effect, when the minister not only declares to all the people together what is their duty to Christ, but has the right and means of enforcing it upon them whom he observes to be inattentive, or not obedient to the doctrine. If any one either obstinately reject such admonitions, or manifest his contempt of them by persisting in his misconduct; after he shall have been admonished a second time in the presence of witnesses, Christ directs him to be summoned before the tribunal of the Church, that is, the assembly of the elders, and there to be more severely admonished by the public authority, that if he reverence the Church, he may submit and obey; but if this do not overcome him, and he still persevere in his iniquity, our Lord then commands him, as a despiser of the Church, to be excluded from the society of believers.[21]

It is also necessary to make another distinction between different sins; some are smaller delinquencies, others are flagitious or enormous crimes. For the correction of atrocious crimes, it is not sufficient to employ admonition or reproof; recourse must be had to a severer remedy; as Paul shows, when he does not content himself with censuring the incestuous Corinthian, but pronounces sentence of excommu-

[20] Acts 20:20, 26, 31.
[21] Matt. 18:15-17.

nication immediately on being certified of his crime. Now, then, we begin to have a clearer perception how the spiritual jurisdiction of the Church, which corrects sins according to the word of the Lord, is a most excellent preservative of health, foundation of order, and bond of unity. Therefore when the Church excludes from its society all who are known to be guilty of adultery, fornication, theft, robbery, sedition, perjury, false witness, and other similar crimes, together with obstinate persons, who, after having been admonished even of smaller faults, condemn God and his judgment,—it usurps no unreasonable authority, but only exercises the jurisdiction which God has given it. And that no one may despise this judgment of the Church, or consider it as of little importance that he is condemned by the voice of the faithful, God has testified that it is no other than a declaration of his sentence, and that what they do on earth shall be ratified in heaven. For they have the word of the Lord, to condemn the perverse; they have the word, to receive the penitent into favour. Persons who believe that the Church could not subsist without this bond of discipline, are mistaken in their opinion, unless we could safely dispense with that remedy which the Lord foresaw would be necessary for us; and how very necessary it is, will be better discovered from its various use.

Now, there are three ends proposed by the Church in those corrections, and in excommunication. The first is, that those who lead scandalous and flagitious lives, may not, to the dishonour of God, be numbered among Christians; as if his holy Church were a conspiracy of wicked and abandoned men. For as the Church is the body of Christ, it cannot be contaminated with such foul and putrid members without some ignominy being reflected upon the Head. That nothing may exist in the Church, therefore, from which any disgrace may be thrown upon his venerable name, it is necessary to expel from his family all those from whose turpitude infamy would redound to the profession of Christianity. Here it is also necessary to have particular regard to the Lord's supper, that it may not be profaned by a promiscuous administration. For it is certain that he who is intrusted with the dispensation of it, if he knowingly and intentionally admit an unworthy person, whom he might justly reject, is as guilty of sacrilege as if he were to give the Lord's body to dogs.

The second end is, that the good may not be corrupted, as is often the case, by constant association with the wicked. For, such is our propensity to error, nothing is more easy than for evil examples to seduce us from rectitude of conduct. . . .

The third end is, that those who are censured or excommunicated, confounded with the shame of their turpitude, may be led to repentance. Thus it is even conducive to their own benefit for their iniquity to be punished, that the stroke of the rod may arouse to a confession of their guilt, those who would only be rendered more obstinate by indulgence. . . .

Having stated these ends, it remains for us to examine how the Church exercises this branch of discipline, which consists in jurisdiction. In the first place, let us keep in view the distinction before mentioned, that some sins are public, and others private, or more concealed. Public sins are those which are not only known to one or two witnesses, but are committed openly, and to the scandal of the whole Church. By private sins, I mean, not such as are entirely unknown to men, like those of hypocrites,—for these never come under the cognizance of the Church,—but those of an intermediate class, which are not without the knowledge of some witnesses, and yet are not public. The first sort requires not the adoption of the gradual measures enumerated by Christ; but it is the duty of the Church, on the occurrence of any notorious scandal, immediately to summon the offender, and to punish him in proportion to his crime. Sins of the second class, according to the rule of Christ, are not to be brought before the Church, unless they are attended with contumacy, in rejecting private admonition. When they are submitted to the cognizance of the Church, then attention is to be paid to the other distinction, between smaller delinquencies and more atrocious crimes. For slighter offences require not the exertion of extreme severity; it is sufficient to administer verbal castigation, and that with paternal gentleness, not calculated to exasperate or confound the offender, but to bring him to himself, that his correction may be an occasion of joy rather than of sorrow. But it is proper that flagitious crimes should receive severer punishment; for it is not enough for him who has grievously offended the Church by the bad example of an atrocious crime, merely to receive verbal castigation; he ought to be deprived of the communion of the Lord's supper for a time, till he shall have given satisfactory evidence of repentance. For Paul not only employs verbal reproof against the Corinthian transgressor, but excludes him from the Church, and blames the Corinthians for having tolerated him so long. This order was retained in the ancient and purer Church, while any legitimate government continued. For if any one had perpetrated a crime which was productive of offence, he was commanded, in the first place, to abstain from the Lord's supper, and, in the next place, to humble himself before God, and to testify his repentance before the Church. There were, likewise, certain solemn rites which it was customary to enjoin upon those who had fallen, as signs of their repentance. When the sinner had performed these for the satisfaction of the Church, he was then, by imposition of hands, readmitted to the communion. . . .

From this discipline none were exempted; so that princes and plebeians yielded the same submission to it; and that with the greatest propriety, since it is evidently the discipline of Christ, to whom it is reasonable that all the sceptres and diadems of kings should be subject.*

Therefore, if we would obey the call of Christ, let us dismiss all arrogance and carelessness from our minds. The former arises from a foolish persuasion of our own righteousness, when a man supposes himself to be possessed of any thing, the merit of which can recommend him to God; the latter may exist without any consideration of works. For multitudes of sinners, inebriated with criminal pleasures, and forgetful of the Divine judgment, are in a state, as it were, of lethargic insensibility, so that they never aspire after the mercy which is offered to them. But it is equally necessary for us to shake off such stupidity, and to reject all confidence in ourselves, in order that, being freed from every incumbrance, we may hasten to Christ all destitute and hungry, to be filled with his blessings. For we shall never have sufficient confidence in him, unless we entirely lose all confidence in ourselves; we shall never find sufficient encouragement in him, unless we are previously dejected in ourselves; we shall never enjoy sufficient consolation in him, unless we are utterly disconsolate in ourselves. We are prepared, therefore, to seek and obtain the grace of God, discarding at the same time all confidence in ourselves, and relying solely on the assurance of his mercy, "when," as Augustine says,

* Book IV, chap. 12, pp. 503-9.

"forgetting our own merits, we embrace the free gifts of Christ; because if he sought merits in us, we should not come to his free gifts." . . .

But not to dwell any longer on this, we may lay it down as a brief, but general and certain maxim, that he is prepared for a participation of the benefits of Divine mercy, who has wholly divested himself, I will not say of his righteousness, which is a mere nullity, but of the vain and airy phantom of righteousness; for as far as any man is satisfied with himself, so far he raises an impediment to the exercise of the grace of God.*

* Book III, chap. 12, pp. 830-31.

Part 2

THE ENLIGHTENMENT

17th and 18th Centuries

ABSOLUTISM AND CONSTITUTIONALISM

Thomas Hobbes and John Locke

During the Enlightenment political theorists were influenced by mathematical proof of the existence of universal laws which controlled the movement of matter. Theorists reasoned that if laws directed the physical world there must also be universal principles governing man and society. To complete this analogy Enlightenment intellectuals constructed a hypothetical state of nature where man lived without government and was bound only by natural laws, natural rights, and human instincts. Because this natural state was precarious man created society to serve his needs and protect his rights. The theorists concluded that society was artificial—not the work of God—and the result of an agreement or contract. Despite agreement on these broad principles there were diverse interpretations, partly due to political and social circumstances, among Enlightenment intellectuals of the true character of man, the meaning of liberty, and the function of government.

Thomas Hobbes (1588–1679) and John Locke (1632–1704) were deeply affected by seventeenth-century scientific discoveries and nearly a century of English political turmoil caused by the struggle for power between Stuart Monarchs, Puritans, and Parliament. These experiences contributed to their profoundly contrasting views toward the nature of man, the forms of society, and purposes of civil government. In the *Leviathan* (1651) Hobbes argued that because men were in constant conflict the purpose of society was to provide peace and security. In joining society man surrendered his natural rights for the protection of an absolute sovereign. In contrast to Hobbes, Locke, in *The Second Treatise of Government* (1690), stated that man joined society to protect his natural rights of life, liberty, and estate. In joining society man consented to make civil government the trustee of natural rights and to give the sovereign power to protect those rights and promote the common good. From these two vantage points—one viewing society as a means of controlling aggression and the other seeing government as a means of assuring natural rights—Hobbes and Locke developed conflicting dimensions of liberty and systems of government.

Thomas Hobbes

I.
Introduction

Nature, the art whereby God has made and governs the world, is by the *art* of man, as in many other things, so in this also imitated—that it can make an artificial animal. For seeing life is but a motion of limbs, the beginning whereof is in some principal part within, why may we not say that all *automata* (engines that move themselves by springs and wheels as does a watch) have an artificial life? For what is the *heart* but a *spring,* and the *nerves* but so many *strings,* and the *joints* but so many *wheels* giving motion to the whole body such as was intended by the artificer? *Art* goes yet further, imitating that rational and most excellent work of nature, *man.* For by art is created that great LEVIATHAN called a COMMONWEALTH or STATE—in Latin, CIVITAS—which is but an artificial man, though of greater stature and strength than the natural, for whose protection and defense it was intended; and in which the *sovereignty* is an artificial *soul,* as giving life and motion to the whole body; the *magistrates* and other *officers* of judicature and execution, artificial *joints; reward* and *punishment,* by which, fastened to the seat of the sovereignty, every joint and member is moved to perform his duty, are the *nerves,* that do the same in the body natural; the *wealth* and *riches* of all the particular members are the *strength; salus populi,* the *people's safety,* its *business; counselors,* by whom all things needful for it to know are suggested unto it, are the *memory; equity* and *laws,* an artificial *reason* and *will; concord, health; sedition, sickness;* and *civil war, death.* Lastly, the *pacts* and *covenants* by which the parts of this body politic were at first made, set together, and united resemble that *fiat,* or the *let us make man,* pronounced by God in the creation.*

II.
The Condition Of Man In A State Of Nature Before Society

Nature has made men so equal in the faculties of the body and mind as that, though there be found one man sometimes manifestly stronger in body or of quicker mind than another, yet, when all is reckoned together, the difference between man and man is not so considerable as that one man can thereupon claim to himself any benefit to which another may not pretend as well as he. For as to the strength of body, the weakest has strength enough to kill the strongest, either by secret

---

* P. 23.

Reprinted from Thomas Hobbes, *Leviathan,* copyright © 1958, by The Liberal Arts Press, Inc., pp. 23, 104-13, 118-19, 131-32, 139-50, 170-78, by permission of the Liberal Arts Press Division of The Bobbs-Merrill Company, Inc.

machination or by confederacy with others that are in the same danger with himself.

And as to the faculties of the mind, setting aside the arts grounded upon words, and especially that skill of proceeding upon general and infallible rules called science—which very few have and but in few things, as being not a native faculty born with us, nor attained, as prudence, while we look after somewhat else—I find yet a greater equality among men than that of strength. For prudence is but experience, which equal time equally bestows on all men in those things they equally apply themselves unto. That which may perhaps make such equality incredible is but a vain conceit of one's own wisdom, which almost all men think they have in a greater degree than the vulgar—that is, than all men but themselves and a few others whom, by fame or for concurring with themselves, they approve. For such is the nature of men that howsoever they may acknowledge many others to be more witty or more eloquent or more learned, yet they will hardly believe there be many so wise as themselves; for they see their own wit at hand and other men's at a distance. But this proves rather that men are in that point equal than unequal. For there is not ordinarily a greater sign of the equal distribution of anything than that every man is contented with his share.

From this equality of ability arises equality of hope in the attaining of our ends. And therefore if any two men desire the same thing, which nevertheless they cannot both enjoy, they become enemies; and in the way to their end, which is principally their own conservation, and sometimes their delectation only, endeavor to destroy or subdue one another. And from hence it comes to pass that where an invader has no more to fear than another man's single power, if one plant, sow, build, or possess a convenient seat, others may probably be expected to come prepared with forces united to dispossess and deprive him, not only of the fruit of his labor, but also of his life or liberty. And the invader again is in the like danger of another. . . .

So that in the nature of man we find three principal causes of quarrel; first, competition; secondly, diffidence; thirdly, glory.

The first makes men invade for gain, the second for safety, and the third for reputation. The first use violence to make themselves masters of other men's persons, wives, children, and cattle; the second, to defend them; the third, for trifles, as a word, a smile, a different opinion, and any other sign of undervalue, either direct in their persons or by reflection in their kindred, their friends, their nation, their profession, or their name.

Hereby it is manifest that, during the time men live without a common power to keep them all in awe, they are in that condition which is called war, and such a war as is of every man against every man. For WAR consists not in battle only, or the act of fighting, but in a tract of time wherein the will to contend by battle is sufficiently known; and therefore the notion of *time* is to be considered in the nature of war as it is in the nature of weather. For as the nature of foul weather lies not in a shower or two of rain but in an inclination thereto of many days together, so the nature of war consists not in actual fighting but in the known disposition thereto during all the time there is no assurance to the contrary. All other time is PEACE.

Whatsoever, therefore, is consequent to a time of war where every man is enemy to every man, the same is consequent to the time wherein men live without other security than what their own strength and their own invention shall furnish them withal. In such condition there is no place for industry, because the fruit thereof is uncertain: and consequently no culture of the earth; no navigation nor use of the commodities that may be imported by sea; no commodious building; no instruments of moving and removing such things as require much force; no knowledge of the face of the earth; no account of time; no arts; no letters; no society; and, which is worst of all, continual fear and danger of violent death; and the life of man solitary, poor, nasty, brutish, and short.

It may seem strange to some man that has not well weighed these things that nature should thus dissociate and render men apt to invade and destroy one another; and he may therefore, not trusting to this inference made from the passions, desire perhaps to have the same confirmed by experience. Let him therefore consider with himself—when taking a journey he arms himself and seeks to go well accompanied, when going to sleep he locks his doors, when even in his house he locks his chests, and this when he knows there be laws and public officers, armed, to revenge all injuries shall be done him—what opinion he has of his fellow subjects when he rides armed, of his fellow citizens when he locks his doors, and of his children and servants when he locks his chests. Does he not there as much accuse mankind by his actions as I do by my words? But neither of us accuse man's nature in it. The desires and other passions of man are in themselves no sin. No more are the actions that proceed from those passions till they know a law that forbids them, which, till laws be made, they cannot know, nor can any law be made till they have agreed upon the person that shall make it. . . .

To this war of every man against every man, this also is consequent: that nothing can be unjust. The notions of right and wrong, justice and injustice, have there no place. Where there is no common power, there is no law; where no law, no injustice. Force and fraud are in war the two cardinal virtues. Justice and injustice are none of the faculties neither of the body nor mind. If they were, they might be in a man that were alone in the world, as well as his senses and passions. They are qualities that relate to men in society, not in solitude. It is consequent also to the same condition that there be no propriety, no dominion, no *mine* and *thine* distinct; but only that to be every man's that he can get, and for so long as he can keep it. And thus much for the ill condition which man by mere nature is actually placed in, though with a possibility to come out of it consisting partly in the passions, partly in his reason.

The passions that incline men to peace are fear of death, desire of such things as are necessary to commodious living, and a hope by their industry to obtain them. And reason suggests convenient articles of peace, upon which men may be drawn to agreement. These articles are they which otherwise are called the Laws of Nature. . . .*

---

* Pp. 104-9.

III.
The Laws Of Nature, Liberty And The Social Contract

The RIGHT OF NATURE, which writers commonly call *jus naturale,* is the liberty each man has to use his own power, as he will himself, for the preservation of his own nature—that is to say, of his own life—and consequently of doing anything which, in his own judgment and reason, he shall conceive to be the aptest means thereunto.

By LIBERTY is understood, according to the proper signification of the word, the absence of external impediments; which impediments may oft take away part of a man's power to do what he would, but cannot hinder him from using the power left him according as his judgment and reason shall dictate to him.

A LAW OF NATURE, *lex naturalis,* is a precept or general rule, found out by reason, by which a man is forbidden to do that which is destructive of his life or takes away the means of preserving the same and to omit that by which he thinks it may be best preserved. For though they that speak of this subject use to confound *jus* and *lex, right* and *law,* yet they ought to be distinguished; because RIGHT consists in liberty to do or to forbear, whereas LAW determines and binds to one of them; so that law and right differ as much as obligation and liberty, which in one and the same matter are inconsistent. And because the condition of man, as has been declared in the precedent chapter, is a condition of war of every one against every one—in which case everyone is governed by his own reason and there is nothing he can make use of that may not be a help unto him in preserving his life against his enemies—it follows that in such a condition every man has a right to everything, even to one another's body. And therefore, as long as this natural right of every man to everything endures, there can be no security to any man, how strong or wise soever he be, of living out the time which nature ordinarily allows men to live. And consequently it is a precept or general rule of reason *that every man ought to endeavor peace, as far as he has hope of obtaining it; and when he cannot obtain it, that he may seek and use all helps and advantages of war.* The first branch of which rule contains the first and fundamental law of nature, which is *to seek peace and follow it.* The second, the sum of the right of nature, which is, *by all means we can to defend ourselves.*

From this fundamental law of nature, by which men are commanded to endeavor peace, is derived this second law: *that a man be willing, when others are so too, as far forth as for peace and defense of himself he shall think it necessary, to lay down this right to all things, and be contented with so much liberty against other men as he would allow other men against himself.* For as long as every man holds this right of doing anything he likes, so long are all men in the condition of war. But if other men will not lay down their right as well as he, then there is no reason for anyone to divest himself of his, for that were to expose himself to prey, which no man is bound to, rather than to dispose himself to peace. This is that law of the gospel: *whatsoever you require that others should do to you, that do ye to them.* And that law of all men, *quod tibi fieri non vis, alteri ne feceris.*[1]

[1] [Matt. 7:12; Luke 6:31. The Latin expresses the same rule negatively: "What you would not have done to you, do not do to others."]

To *lay down* a man's *right* to anything is to *divest* himself of the *liberty* of hindering another of the benefit of his own right to the same. . . .

The mutual transferring of right is that which men call CONTRACT.

There is difference between transferring of right to the thing and transferring, or tradition—that is, delivery—of the thing itself. For the thing may be delivered together with the translation of the right, as in buying and selling with ready money or exchange of goods or lands, and it may be delivered some time after.

Again, one of the contractors may deliver the thing contracted for on his part and leave the other to perform his part at some determinate time after and in the meantime be trusted and then the contract on his part is called PACT or COVENANT; or both parts may contract now to perform hereafter, in which cases he that is to perform in time to come, being trusted, his performance is called *keeping of promise* or faith, and the failing of performance, if it be voluntary, *violation of faith.**

The force of words being, as I have formerly noted, too weak to hold men to the performance of their covenants, there are in man's nature but two imaginable helps to strengthen it. And those are either a fear of the consequence of breaking their word, or a glory or pride in appearing not to need to break it. This latter is a generosity too rarely found to be presumed on, especially in the pursuers of wealth, command, or sensual pleasure—which are the greatest part of mankind. The passion to be reckoned upon is fear, whereof there be two very general objects: one, the power of spirits invisible; the other, the power of those men they shall therein offend. Of these two, though the former be the greater power, yet the fear of the latter is commonly the greater fear. The fear of the former is in every man his own religion, which has place in the nature of man before civil society. The latter has not so, at least not place enough to keep men to their promises, because in the condition of mere nature the inequality of power is not discerned but by the event of battle. So that before the time of civil society, or in the interruption thereof by war, there is nothing can strengthen a covenant of peace agreed on against the temptations of avarice, ambition, lust, or other strong desire but the fear of that invisible power, which they everyone worship as God and fear as a revenger of their perfidy. All therefore that can be done between two men not subject to civil power is to put one another to swear by the God he fears . . . *swearing* or OATH is a *form of speech, added to a promise, by which he that promises signifies that, unless he perform, he renounces the mercy of his God, or calls to him for vengeance on himself.* Such was the heathen form, *Let Jupiter kill me else, as I kill this beast.* So is our form, *I shall do thus and thus, so help me God.* And this, with the rites and ceremonies which everyone uses in his own religion, that the fear of breaking faith might be the greater.

By this it appears that an oath taken according to any other form or rite than his that swears is in vain and no oath, and that there is no swearing by anything which the swearer thinks not God. For though men have sometimes used to swear by their kings, for fear or flattery, yet they would have it thereby understood they attributed to them divine honor. And that swearing unnecessarily by God is but profaning of his name; and swearing by other things, as men do in common discourse, is not swearing but an impious custom gotten by too much vehemence of talking.

---

* Pp. 109-13.

It appears also that the oath adds nothing to the obligation. For a covenant, if lawful, binds in the sight of God without the oath as much as with it; if unlawful, binds not at all, though it be confirmed with an oath.*

The laws of nature are immutable and eternal, for injustice, ingratitude, arrogance, pride, iniquity, acception of persons, and the rest can never be made lawful. For it can never be that war shall preserve life and peace destroy it.

The same laws, because they oblige, only to a desire and endeavor—I mean an unfeigned and constant endeavor—are easy to be observed. For in that they require nothing but endeavor, he that endeavors their performance fulfills them; and he that fulfills the law is just.

And the science of them is the true and only moral philosophy. For moral philosophy is nothing else but the science of what is *good* and *evil* in the conversation and society of mankind. *Good* and *evil* are names that signify our appetites and aversions, which in different tempers, customs, and doctrines of men are different; and divers men differ not only in their judgment on the senses of what is pleasant and unpleasant to the taste, smell, hearing, touch, and sight but also of what is conformable or disagreeable to reason in the actions of common life. Nay, the same man in divers times differs from himself, and one time praises—that is, calls good—what another time he dispraises and calls evil; from whence arise disputes, controversies, and at last war. And therefore so long as a man is in the condition of mere nature, which is a condition of war, private appetite is the measure of good and evil; and consequently all men agree on this: that peace is good, and therefore also the way or means of peace, which, as I have showed before, are *justice, gratitude, modesty, equity, mercy,* and the rest of the laws of nature, are good—that is to say, *moral virtues*—and their contrary *vices* evil. Now the science of virtue and vice is moral philosophy; and therefore the true doctrine of the laws of nature is the true moral philosophy. But the writers of moral philosophy, though they acknowledge the same virtues and vices, yet, not seeing wherein consisted their goodness nor that they come to be praised as the means of peaceable, sociable, and comfortable living, place them in a mediocrity of passions; as if not the cause but the degree of daring made fortitude, or not the cause but the quantity of a gift made liberality.

These dictates of reason men used to call by the name of laws, but improperly, for they are but conclusions or theorems concerning what conduces to the conservation and defense of themselves, whereas law, properly, is the word of him that by right has command over others. But yet if we consider the same theorems as delivered in the word of God, that by right commands all things, then are they properly called laws.†

---

* Pp. 118-19.

† Pp. 131-32.

IV.

The Necessity Of Civil Government; The Nature Of The Commonwealth; And, The Power Of The Sovereign

The final cause, end, or design of men, who naturally love liberty and dominion over others, in the introduction of that restraint upon themselves in which we see them live in commonwealths is the foresight of their own preservation, and of a more contented life thereby—that is to say, of getting themselves out from that miserable condition of war which is necessarily consequent to the natural passions of men when there is no visible power to keep them in awe and tie them by fear of punishment to the performance of their covenants and observation of those laws of nature set down in the fourteenth and fifteenth chapters.

For the laws of nature—as *justice, equity, modesty, mercy,* and, in sum, *doing to others as we would be done to*—of themselves, without the terror of some power to cause them to be observed, are contrary to our natural passions, that carry us to partiality, pride, revenge, and the like. And covenants without the sword are but words, and of no strength to secure a man at all. Therefore, notwithstanding the laws of nature (which everyone has then kept when he has the will to keep them, when he can do it safely), if there be no power erected, or not great enough for our security, every man will—and may lawfully—rely on his own strength and art for caution against all other men. And in all places where men have lived by small families, to rob and spoil one another has been a trade, and so far from being reputed against the law of nature that the greater spoils they gained, the greater was their honor; and men observed no other laws therein but the laws of honor—that is, to abstain from cruelty, leaving to men their lives and instruments of husbandry. And as small families did then, so now do cities and kingdoms, which are but greater families, for their own security enlarge their dominions upon all pretenses of danger and fear of invasion or assistance that may be given to invaders, and endeavor as much as they can to subdue or weaken their neighbors by open force and secret arts, for want of other caution, justly; and are remembered for it in after ages with honor.

Nor is it the joining together of a small number of men that gives them this security, because in small numbers small additions on the one side or the other make the advantage of strength so great as is sufficient to carry the victory, and therefore gives encouragement to an invasion. The multitude sufficient to confide in for our security is not determined by any certain number but by comparison with the enemy we fear, and is then sufficient when the odds of the enemy is not of so visible and conspicuous moment to determine the event of war as to move him to attempt.

And be there never so great a multitude, yet if their actions be directed according to their particular judgments and particular appetites, they can expect thereby no defense nor protection, neither against a common enemy nor against the injuries of one another. For being distracted in opinions concerning the best use and application of their strength, they do not help but hinder one another, and reduce their strength by mutual opposition to nothing; whereby they are easily not only subdued by a very few that agree together, but also, when there is no common enemy, they make war upon each other for their particular interest. For if we could suppose a great multitude of men to consent in the observation of justice and other laws of nature without a common power to keep them all in awe, we might as well suppose all mankind to do the same; and then there neither would be, nor need to be, any civil government or commonwealth at all, because there would be peace without subjection.

Nor is it enough for the security which men desire should last all the time of their life that they be governed and directed by one judgment for a limited time, as in one battle or one war. For though they obtain a victory by their unanimous endeavor against a foreign enemy, yet afterwards, when either they have no common enemy or he that by one part is held for an enemy is by another part held for a friend, they must needs, by the difference of their interests, dissolve and fall again into a war among themselves. . . .

The only way to erect such a common power as may be able to defend them from the invasion of foreigners and the injuries of one another, and thereby to secure them in such sort as that by their own industry and by the fruits of the earth they may nourish themselves and live contentedly, is to confer all their power and strength upon one man, or upon one assembly of men that may reduce all their wills, by plurality of voices, unto one will; which is as much as to say, to appoint one man or assembly of men to bear their person, and everyone to own and acknowledge himself to be author of whatsoever he that so bears their person shall act or cause to be acted in those things which concern the common peace and safety, and therein to submit their wills every one to his will, and their judgments to his judgment. This is more than consent or concord; it is a real unity of them all in one and the same person, made by covenant of every man with every man, in such manner as if every man should say to every man, *I authorize and give up my right of governing myself to this man, or to this assembly of men, on this condition, that you give up your right to him and authorize all his actions in like manner.* This done, the multitude so united in one person is called a COMMONWEALTH, in Latin CIVITAS. This is the generation of that great LEVIATHAN (or rather, to speak more reverently, of that *mortal god*) to which we owe, under the *immortal God,* our peace and defense. For by this authority, given him by every particular man in the commonwealth, he has the use of so much power and strength conferred on him that, by terror thereof, he is enabled to form the wills of them all to peace at home and mutual aid against their enemies abroad. And in him consists the essence of the commonwealth, which, to define it, is *one person, of whose acts a great multitude, by mutual covenants one with another, have made themselves every one the author, to the end he may use the strength and means of them all as he shall think expedient for their peace and common defense.* And he that carries this person is called SOVEREIGN and said to have *sovereign power;* and everyone besides, his SUBJECT.

The attaining to this sovereign power is by two ways. One, by natural force, as when a man makes his children to submit themselves and their children to his government, as being able to destroy them if they refuse, or by war subdues his enemies to his will, giving them their lives on that condition. The other is when men agree among themselves to submit to some man or assembly of men voluntarily, on confidence to be protected by him against all others. This latter may be called a political commonwealth, or commonwealth by *institution,* and the former a commonwealth by *acquisition.* And first I shall speak of a commonwealth by institution.

A *commonwealth* is said to be *instituted* when a *multitude* of men do agree and *covenant, every one with every one,* that to whatsoever *man* or *assembly of men* shall be given by the major part the *right* to *present* the person of them all—that is to say, to be their *representative*—every one, as well he that *voted for it* as he that *voted against it,* shall *authorize* all the actions and judgments of that man or assembly of men in the same manner as if they were his own, to the end to live peaceably among themselves and be protected against other men.

From this institution of a commonwealth are derived all the *rights* and *faculties* of him or them on whom the sovereign power is conferred by the consent of the people assembled. First, because they covenant, it is to be understood they are not obliged by former covenant to anything repugnant hereunto. And consequently they that have already instituted a commonwealth, being thereby bound by covenant to own the actions and judgments of one, cannot lawfully make a new covenant among themselves to be obedient to any other, in anything whatsoever, without his permission. And therefore, they that are subjects to a monarch cannot without his leave cast off monarchy and return to the confusion of a disunited multitude, nor transfer their person from him that bears it to another man or other assembly of men; for they are bound, every man to every man, to own and be reputed author of all that he that already is their sovereign shall do and judge fit to be done; so that any one man dissenting, all the rest should break their covenant made to that man, which is injustice; and they have also every man given the sovereignty to him that bears their person, and therefore if they depose him they take from him that which is his own, and so again it is injustice. Besides, if he that attempts to depose his sovereign be killed or punished by him for such attempt, he is author of his own punishment, as being by the institution author of all his sovereign shall do; and because it is injustice for a man to do anything for which he may be punished by his own authority, he is also upon that title unjust. And whereas some men have pretended for their disobedience to their sovereign a new covenant, made not with men but with God, this also is unjust; for there is no covenant with God but by mediation of somebody that represents God's person, which none does but God's lieutenant, who has the sovereignty under God. But this pretense of covenant with God is so evident a lie, even in the pretenders' own consciences, that it is not only an act of an unjust but also of a vile and unmanly disposition.

Secondly, because the right of bearing the person of them all is given to him they make sovereign by covenant only of one to another and not of him to any of them, there can happen no breach of covenant on the part of the sovereign; and consequently none of his subjects, by any pretense of forfeiture, can be freed from his subjection. That he which is made sovereign makes no covenant with his subjects beforehand is manifest, because either he must make it with the whole multitude, as one party to the covenant, or he must make a several covenant with every man. With the whole, as one party, it is impossible because as yet they are not one person; and if he make so many several covenants as there be men, those covenants after he has the sovereignty are void because what act soever can be pretended by any one of them for breach thereof is the act both of himself and of all the rest, because done in the person and by the right of every one of them in particular. Besides, if any one or more of them pretend a breach of the covenant made by the sovereign at his institution, and others, or one other of his subjects, or himself alone, pretend there was no such breach, there is in this case no judge to decide the controversy; it returns therefore to the sword again, and every man recovers the right of protecting himself by his own strength, contrary to the design they had in the institution. It is therefore in vain to grant sovereignty by way of precedent covenant. The opinion that any monarch receives his power by covenant—that is to say, on condition—proceeds from want of understanding this easy truth: that covenants, being but words and breath, have no force to oblige, contain, constrain, or protect any man but what it has from the public sword—that is, from the untied hands of that man or assembly of men that has the sovereignty, and whose actions are avouched by them all and performed by the strength of them all in him united. But when an assembly of men is made sovereign, then no man imagines any such covenant to have passed in the institution; for no man is so dull as to say, for example, the people of Rome made a covenant with the Romans to hold the sovereignty on such or such conditions, which not performed, the Romans might lawfully depose the Roman people. That men see not the reason to be alike in a monarchy and in a popular government proceeds from the ambition of some that are kinder to the government of an assembly, whereof they may hope to participate, than of monarchy, which they despair to enjoy.

Thirdly, because the major part has by consenting voices declared a sovereign, he that dissented must now consent with the rest—that is, be contented to avow all the actions he shall do—or else justly be destroyed by the rest. For if he voluntarily entered into the congregation of them that were assembled, he sufficiently declared thereby his will, and therefore tacitly covenanted, to stand to what the major part should ordain; and therefore, if he refuse to stand thereto or make protestation against any of their decrees, he does contrary to his covenant, and therefore unjustly. And whether he be of the congregation or not, and whether his consent be asked or not, he must either submit to their decrees or be left in the condition of war he was in before, wherein he might without injustice be destroyed by any man whatsoever.

Fourthly, because every subject is by this institution author of all the actions and judgments of the sovereign instituted, it follows that whatsoever he does, it can be no injury to any of his subjects; nor ought he to be by any of them accused of injustice. For he that does anything by authority from another does therein no injury to him by whose authority he acts; but by this institution of a commonwealth, every particular man is author of all the sovereign does; and consequently he that complains of injury from his sovereign complains of that whereof he himself is author, and therefore ought not to accuse any man but himself—no, nor himself of injury, because to do injury to one's self is impossible. It is true that they that have sovereign power may commit iniquity, but not injustice or injury in the proper signification.

Fifthly, and consequently to that which was said last, no man that has sovereign power can justly be put to death or otherwise in any manner by his subjects punished. For seeing every subject is author of the actions of his sovereign, he punishes another for the actions committed by himself.

And because the end of this institution is the peace and defense of them all, and whosoever has right to the end has right to the means, it belongs of right to whatsoever man or assembly that has the sovereignty to be judge both of the means of peace and defense and also of the hindrances and disturbances of the same, and to do whatsoever he shall think necessary to be done, both beforehand, for the preserving of peace and security by prevention of discord at home and hostility from abroad, and, when peace and security are lost, for the recovery of the same. And therefore,

Sixthly, it is annexed to the sovereignty to be judge of what opinions and doctrines are averse and what conducing to peace, and consequently on what occasions, how far, and what men are to be trusted withal in speaking to multitudes of people, and who shall examine the doctrines of all books before they be published. For the actions of men proceed from their opinions, and in the well-governing of opinions consists the well-governing of men's actions, in order to their peace and concord. And though in matter of doctrine nothing ought to be regarded but the truth, yet this is not repugnant to regulating the same by peace. For doctrine repugnant to peace can no more be true than peace and concord can be against the law of nature. It is true that in a commonwealth, where by the negligence or unskillfulness of governors and teachers false doctrines are by time generally received, the contrary truths may be generally offensive. Yet the most sudden and rough bustling in of a new truth that can be does never break the peace but only sometimes awake the war. For those men that are so remissly governed that they dare take up arms to defend or introduce an opinion are still in war, and their condition not peace but only a cessation of arms for fear of one another, and they live, as it were, in the precincts of battle continually. It belongs therefore to him that has the sovereign power to be judge or constitute all judges of opinions and doctrines as a thing necessary to peace, thereby to prevent discord and civil war.

Seventhly is annexed to the sovereignty the whole power of prescribing the rules whereby every man may know what goods he may enjoy and what actions he may do without being molested by any of his fellow subjects; and this is it men call *propriety*. For before constitution of sovereign power, as has already been shown, all men had right to all things, which necessarily causes war; and therefore this propriety, being necessary to peace and depending on sovereign power, is the act of that power in order to the public peace. These rules of propriety, or *meum* and *tuum*,[2] and of *good, evil, lawful,* and *unlawful* in the actions of subjects, are the civil laws—that is to say, the laws of each commonwealth in particular—though the name of civil law be now restrained to the ancient civil laws of the city of Rome, which being the head of a great part of the world, her laws at that time were in these parts the civil law.

Eighthly is annexed to the sovereignty the right of judicature—that is to say, of hearing and deciding all controversies which may arise concerning law, either civil or natural, or concerning fact. For without the decision of controversies, there is no protection of one subject against the injuries of another; the laws concerning *meum* and *tuum* are in vain; and to every man remains, from the natural and necessary appetite of his own conservation, the right of protecting himself by his private strength, which is the condition of war and contrary to the end for which every commonwealth is instituted.

Ninthly is annexed to the sovereignty the right of making war and peace with other nations and commonwealths—that is to say, of judging when it is for the public good, and how great forces are to be assembled, armed, and paid for that

[2] [Mine and thine.]

end, and to levy money upon the subjects to defray the expenses thereof. For the power by which the people are to be defended consists in their armies, and the strength of an army in the union of their strength under one command, which command the sovereign instituted therefore has; because the command of the *militia,* without other institution, makes him that has it sovereign. And therefore whosoever is made general of an army, he that has the sovereign power is always generalissimo.

Tenthly is annexed to the sovereignty the choosing of all counselors, ministers, magistrates, and officers, both in peace and war. For seeing the sovereign is charged with the end, which is the common peace and defense, he is understood to have power to use such means as he shall think most fit for his discharge.

Eleventhly, to the sovereign is committed the power of rewarding with riches or honor, and of punishing with corporal or pecuniary punishment or with ignominy, every subject according to the law he has formerly made; or if there be no law made, according as he shall judge most to conduce to the encouraging of men to serve the commonwealth or deterring of them from doing disservice to the same.

Lastly, considering what value men are naturally apt to set upon themselves, what respect they look for from others, and how little they value other men—from whence continually arise among them emulation, quarrels, factions, and at last war, to the destroying of one another and diminution of their strength against a common enemy—it is necessary that there be laws of honor and a public rate of the worth of such men as have deserved or are able to deserve well of the commonwealth, and that there be force in the hands of some or other to put those laws in execution. But it has already been shown that not only the whole *militia* or forces of the commonwealth, but also the judicature of all controversies is annexed to the sovereignty. To the sovereign therefore it belongs also to give titles of honor, and to appoint what order of place and dignity each man shall hold, and what signs of respect, in public or private meetings, they shall give to one another.

These are the rights which make the essence of sovereignty, and which are the marks whereby a man may discern in what man or assembly of men the sovereign power is placed and resides. For these are incommunicable and inseparable.*

V.
Liberty And The Individual Within The State

Liberty, or freedom, signifies properly the absence of opposition—by opposition I mean external impediments of motion—and may be applied no less to irrational and inanimate creatures than to rational. For whatsoever is so tied or environed as it cannot move but within a certain space, which space is determined by the opposition of some external body, we say it has not liberty to go farther. And so of all living creatures while they are imprisoned or restrained with walls or chains, and of the water while it is kept in by banks or vessels that otherwise would spread itself into a larger space, we use to say they are not at liberty to move in such manner as without those external impediments they would. But when

* Pp. 139-50.

the impediment of motion is in the constitution of the thing itself, we use not to say it wants the liberty but the power to move—as when a stone lies still or a man is fastened to his bed by sickness.

And according to this proper and generally received meaning of the word, a FREEMAN *is he that in those things which by his strength and wit he is able to do is not hindered to do what he has a will to.* But when the words *free* and *liberty* are applied to anything but *bodies,* they are abused, for that which is not subject to motion is not subject to impediment; and therefore, when it is said, for example, the way is free, no liberty of the way is signified but of those that walk in it without stop. And when we say a gift is free, there is not meant any liberty of the gift but of the giver, that was not bound by any law or covenant to give it. So when we *speak freely,* it is not the liberty of voice or pronunciation but of the man, whom no law has obliged to speak otherwise than he did. Lastly, from the use of the word *free will,* no liberty can be inferred of the will, desire, or inclination but the liberty of the man, which consists in this: that he finds no stop in doing what he has the will, desire, or inclination to do.

Fear and liberty are consistent, as when a man throws his goods into the sea for *fear* the ship should sink, he does it nevertheless very willingly, and may refuse to do it if he will: it is therefore the action of one that was *free;* so a man sometimes pays his debt only for *fear* of imprisonment, which, because nobody hindered him from detaining, was the action of a man at *liberty.* And generally all actions which men do in commonwealths for *fear* of the law are actions which the doers had *liberty* to omit.

Liberty and *necessity* are consistent, as in the water that has not only *liberty* but a *necessity* of descending by the channel; so likewise in the actions which men voluntarily do, which, because they proceed from their will, proceed from *liberty,* and yet—because every act of man's will and every desire and inclination proceeds from some cause, and that from another cause, in a continual chain whose first link is in the hand of God, the first of all causes—proceed from *necessity.* So that to him that could see the connection of those causes the *necessity* of all men's voluntary actions would appear manifest. And therefore God, that sees and disposes all things, sees also that the *liberty* of man in doing what he will is accompanied with the *necessity* of doing that which God will, and no more nor less. For though men may do many things which God does not command, nor is therefore author of them, yet they can have no passion nor appetite to anything of which appetite God's will is not the cause. And did not his will assure the *necessity* of man's will, and consequently of all that on man's will depends, the *liberty* of men would be a contradiction and impediment to the omnipotence and *liberty* of God. And this shall suffice, as to the matter in hand, of that natural *liberty* which only is properly called *liberty.*

But as men, for the attaining of peace and conservation of themselves thereby, have made an artificial man, which we call a commonwealth, so also have they made artificial chains, called *civil laws,* which they themselves, by mutual covenants, have fastened at one end to the lips of that man or assembly to whom they have given the sovereign power, and at the other end to their own ears. These bonds, in their own nature but weak, may nevertheless be made to hold by the danger, though not by the difficulty, of breaking them.

In relation to these bonds only it is that I am to speak now of the *liberty* of *subjects.* For seeing there is no commonwealth in the world wherein there be rules enough set down for the regulating of all the actions and words of men, as being a thing impossible, it follows necessarily that in all kinds of actions by the laws pretermitted men have the liberty of doing what their own reasons shall suggest for the most profitable to themselves. For if we take liberty in the proper sense for corporal liberty—that is to say, freedom from chains and prison—it were very absurd for men to clamor as they do for the liberty they so manifestly enjoy. Again, if we take liberty for an exemption from laws, it is no less absurd for men to demand as they do that liberty by which all other men may be masters of their lives. And yet, as absurd as it is, this is it they demand, not knowing that the laws are of no power to protect them without a sword in the hands of a man or men to cause those laws to be put in execution. The liberty of a subject lies, therefore, only in those things which, in regulating their actions, the sovereign has pretermitted: such as is the liberty to buy and sell and otherwise contract with one another; to choose their own abode, their own diet, their own trade of life, and institute their children as they themselves think fit; and the like.

Nevertheless we are not to understand that by such liberty the sovereign power of life and death is either abolished or limited. For it has been already shown that nothing the sovereign representative can do to a subject, on what pretense soever, can properly be called injustice or injury, because every subject is author of every act the sovereign does, so that he never wants right to anything otherwise than as he himself is the subject of God and bound thereby to observe the laws of nature. . . .

And the same holds also in a sovereign prince that puts to death an innocent subject. For though the action be against the law of nature as being contrary to equity. . . .

The liberty whereof there is so frequent and honorable mention in the histories and philosophy of the ancient Greeks and Romans, and in the writings and discourse of those that from them have received all their learning in the politics, is not the liberty of particular men but the liberty of the commonwealth—which is the same with that which every man then should have if there were no civil laws nor commonwealth at all. And the effects of it also be the same. For as among masterless men there is perpetual war of every man against his neighbor—no inheritance to transmit to the son nor to expect from the father, no propriety of goods or lands, no security, but a full and absolute liberty in every particular man—so in states and commonwealths not dependent on one another every commonwealth, not every man, has an absolute liberty to do what it shall judge—that is to say, what that man or assembly that represents it shall judge—most conducing to their benefit. But withal they live in the condition of a perpetual war and upon the confines of battle, with their frontiers armed and cannons planted against their neighbors round about. The Athenians and Romans were free—that is, free commonwealths; not that any particular men had the liberty to resist their own representative, but that their representative had the liberty to resist or invade other people. There is written on the turrets of the city of Lucca in great characters at this day the word LIBERTAS, yet no man can thence infer that a particular man has more liberty or immunity from the service of the commonwealth there than in Constantinople.

Whether a commonwealth be monarchical or popular, the freedom is still the same.

But it is an easy thing for men to be deceived by the specious name of liberty and, for want of judgment to distinguish, mistake that for their private inheritance and birthright which is the right of the public only. And when the same error is confirmed by the authority of men in reputation for their writings on this subject, it is no wonder if it produce sedition and change of government. In these western parts of the world, we are made to receive our opinions concerning the institution and rights of commonwealths from Aristotle, Cicero, and other men, Greeks and Romans that, living under popular states, derived those rights not from the principles of nature but transcribed them into their books out of the practice of their own commonwealths which were popular—as the grammarians describe the rules of language out of the practice of the time, or the rules of poetry out of the poems of Homer and Virgil. And because the Athenians were taught, to keep them from desire of changing their government, that they were freemen and all that lived under monarchy were slaves, therefore Aristotle puts it down in his *Politics* (lib. 6. cap. 2): *In democracy,* LIBERTY *is to be supposed; for it is commonly held that no man is* FREE *in any other government.* And as Aristotle, so Cicero and other writers have grounded their civil doctrine on the opinions of the Romans, who were taught to hate monarchy at first by them that, having deposed their sovereign, shared among them the sovereignty of Rome, and afterwards by their successors. And by reading of these Greek and Latin authors, men from their childhood have gotten a habit, under a false show of liberty, of favoring tumults and of licentious controlling the actions of their sovereigns and again of controlling those controllers, with the effusion of so much blood as I think I may truly say there was never anything so dearly bought as these western parts have bought the learning of the Greek and Latin tongues.

To come now to the particulars of the true liberty of a subject—that is to say, what are the things which, though commanded by the sovereign, he may nevertheless without injustice refuse to do—we are to consider what rights we pass away when we make a commonwealth, or, which is all one, what liberty we deny ourselves by owning all the actions, without exception, of the man or assembly we make our sovereign. For in the act of our *submission* consists both our *obligation* and our *liberty,* which must therefore be inferred by arguments taken from thence, there being no obligation on any man which arises not from some act of his own, for all men equally are by nature free. And because such arguments must either be drawn from the express words, *I authorize all his actions,* or from the intention of him that submits himself to his power, which intention is to be understood by the end for which he so submits, the obligation and liberty of the subject is to be derived either from those words or others equivalent, or else from the end of the institution of sovereignty—namely, the peace of the subjects within themselves and their defense against a common enemy.

First, therefore, seeing sovereignty by institution is by covenant of every one to every one, and sovereignty by acquisition by covenants of the vanquished to the victor or child to the parent, it is manifest that every subject has liberty in all those things the right whereof cannot by covenant be transferred. I have shown before in the fourteenth chapter that covenants not to defend a man's own body are void. Therefore, if the sovereign command a man, though justly condemned, to kill, wound, or maim himself, or not to resist those that assault him, or to abstain from the use of food, air, medicine, or any other thing without which he cannot live, yet has that man the liberty to disobey.

If a man be interrogated by the sovereign or his authority concerning a crime done by himself, he is not bound, without assurance of pardon, to confess it; because no man, as I have shown in the same chapter, can be obliged by covenant to accuse himself.

Again, the consent of a subject to sovereign power is contained in these words: *I authorize, or take upon me, all his actions;* in which there is no restriction at all of his own former natural liberty, for by allowing him to *kill me* I am not bound to kill myself when he commands me. It is one thing to say: *kill me, or my fellow, if you please;* another thing to say, *I will kill myself, or my fellow.* It follows therefore, that—

No man is bound by the words themselves either to kill himself or any other man, and consequently that the obligation a man may sometimes have, upon the command of the sovereign, to execute any dangerous or dishonorable office depends not on the words of our submission but on the intention, which is to be understood by the end thereof. When, therefore, our refusal to obey frustrates the end for which the sovereignty was ordained, then there is no liberty to refuse; otherwise there is.

Upon this ground, a man that is commanded as a soldier to fight against the enemy, though his sovereign have right enough to punish his refusal with death, may nevertheless in many cases refuse, without injustice—as when he substitutes a sufficient soldier in his place, for in this case he deserts not the service of the commonwealth. And there is allowance to be made for natural timorousness, not only to women, of whom no such dangerous duty is expected, but also to men of feminine courage. When armies fight, there is on one side or both a running away; yet when they do it not out of treachery but fear, they are not esteemed to do it unjustly but dishonorably. For the same reason, to avoid battle is not injustice but cowardice. But he that enrolls himself a soldier, or takes impressed money, takes away the excuse of a timorous nature, and is obliged not only to go to the battle but also not to run from it without his captain's leave. And when the defense of the commonwealth requires at once the help of all that are able to bear arms, everyone is obliged; because otherwise the institution of the commonwealth, which they have not the purpose or courage to preserve, was in vain.

To resist the sword of the commonwealth in defense of another man, guilty or innocent, no man has liberty; because such liberty takes away from the sovereign the means of protecting us, and is therefore destructive of the very essence of government. But in case a great many men together have already resisted the sovereign power unjustly, or committed some capital crime for which every one of them expects death, whether have they not the liberty then to join together and assist and defend one another? Certainly they have, for they but defend their lives, which the guilty man may as well do as the innocent. There was indeed injustice in the first breach of their duty; their bearing of arms subsequent to it, though it be to maintain what they have done, is no new unjust act. And if it be only to defend their persons, it is not unjust at all. But the offer of pardon takes from them to whom it is offered the plea of self-defense, and makes their perseverance in assisting or defending the rest unlawful.

As for other liberties, they depend on the silence of the law. In cases where the sovereign has prescribed no rule, there the subject has the liberty to do or forbear according to his own discretion. And therefore such liberty is in some places more and in some less, and in some times more, in other times less, according as they that have the sovereignty shall think most convenient.*

John Locke

I.
Man In The State Of Nature: Political Power, Liberty, Freedom And The Laws Of Nature

To understand political power [correctly] we must consider what state all men are naturally in, and that is a state of perfect freedom to order their actions and dispose of their possessions and persons as they think fit, within the bounds of the law of nature, without asking leave or depending upon the will of any other man.

A state also of equality, wherein all the power and jurisdiction is reciprocal, no one having more than another; there being nothing more evident than that creatures of the same species and rank, promiscuously born to all the same advantages of nature and the use of the same faculties, should also be equal one amongst another without subordination or subjection. . . .

But though this be a state of liberty, yet it is not a state of license; though man in that state have an uncontrollable liberty to dispose of his person or possessions, yet he has not liberty to destroy himself, or so much as any creature in his possession, but where some nobler use than its bare preservation calls for it. The state of nature has a law of nature to govern it, which obliges every one; and reason, which is that law, teaches all mankind who will but consult it that, being all equal and independent, no one ought to harm another in his life, health, liberty, or possessions; for men being all the workmanship of one omnipotent and infinitely wise Maker—all the servants of one sovereign master, sent into the world by his order, and about his business—they are his property whose workmanship they are, made to last during his, not one another's pleasure; and being furnished with like faculties, sharing all in one community of nature, there cannot be supposed any such subordination among us that may authorize us to destroy another, as if we were made for one another's uses as the inferior ranks of creatures are for ours. Every one, as he is bound to preserve himself and not to quit his station wilfully, so by the like reason, when his own preservation comes not in competition, ought he, as much as he can, to preserve the rest of mankind, and may not, unless it be to do justice to an offender, take away or impair the life or what

* Pp. 170-78.

Reprinted from John Locke, *Two Treatises on Civil Government: An Essay Concerning The True Original, Extent, And End Of Civil Government* (London: George Routledge and Sons, 1887), chaps. 2, 3, 4, 6, 8, 9, 11, 13, and 19.

tends to the preservation of the life, the liberty, health, limb, or goods of another.

And that all men may be restrained from invading others' rights and from doing hurt to one another, and the law of nature be observed, which wills the peace and preservation of all mankind, the execution of the law of nature is, in that state, put into every man's hands, whereby everyone has a right to punish the transgressors of that law to such a degree as may hinder its violation; for the law of nature would, as all other laws that concern men in this world, be in vain if there were nobody that in that state of nature had a power to execute that law and thereby preserve the innocent and restrain offenders. And if anyone in the state of nature may punish another for any evil he has done, everyone may do so; for in that state of perfect equality, where naturally there is no superiority or jurisdiction of one over another, what any may do in prosecution of that law, everyone must needs have a right to do.

And thus in the state of nature one man comes by a power over another; but yet no absolute or arbitrary power to use a criminal, when he has got him in his hands, according to the passionate heats or boundless extravagance of his own will; but only to retribute to him, so far as calm reason and conscience dictate, what is proportionate to his transgression, which is so much as may serve for reparation and restraint; for these two are the only reasons why one man may lawfully do harm to another, which is that we call punishment. In transgressing the law of nature, the offender declares himself to live by another rule than that of reason and common equity, which is that measure God has set to the actions of men for their mutual security; and so he becomes dangerous to mankind, the tie which is to secure them from injury and violence being slighted and broken by him. Which being a trespass against the whole species and the peace and safety of it provided for by the law of nature, every man upon this score, by the right he has to preserve mankind in general, may restrain, or, where it is necessary, destroy things noxious to them, and so may bring such evil on any one who has transgressed that law, as may make him repent the doing of it and thereby deter him, and by his example others, from doing the like mischief. And in this case, and upon this ground, every man has a right to punish the offender and be executioner of the law of nature.*

[However] he who attempts to get another man into his absolute power does thereby put himself into a state of war with him, it being to be understood as a declaration of a design upon his life; for I have reason to conclude that he who would get me into his power without my consent would use me as he pleased when he got me there, and destroy me, too, when he had a fancy to it; for nobody can desire to have me in his absolute power unless it be to compel me by force to that which is against the right of my freedom, i.e., make me a slave. To be free from such force is the only security of my preservation; and reason bids me look on him as an enemy to my preservation who would take away that freedom which is the fence to it; so that he who makes an attempt to enslave me thereby puts himself into a state of war with me. He that, in the state of nature, would take away the freedom that belongs to any one in that state must necessarily be supposed to have a design to take away everything else, that freedom being the foundation of all the rest; as he that, in the state of society, would take away

---

* Pp. 192-95.

the freedom belonging to those of that society or commonwealth must be supposed to design to take away from them everything else, and so be looked on as in a state of war.*

The natural liberty of man [therefore] is to be free from any superior power on earth, and not to be under the will or legislative authority of man, but to have only the law of nature for his rule. The liberty of man in society is to be under no other legislative power but that established by consent in the commonwealth, nor under the dominion of any will or restraint of any law but what that legislative shall enact according to the trust put in it. Freedom then is not . . . "a liberty for every one to do what he lists, to live as he pleases, and not to be tied by any laws"; but freedom of men under government is to have a standing rule to live by, common to every one of that society and made by the legislative power erected in it, a liberty to follow my own will in all things where the rule prescribes not, and not to be subject to the inconstant, uncertain, unknown, arbitrary will of another man; as freedom of nature is to be under no other restraint but the law of nature.

This freedom from absolute, arbitrary power is so necessary to, and closely joined with, a man's preservation that he cannot part with it but by what forfeits his preservation and life together; for a man not having the power of his own life cannot by compact or his own consent enslave himself to any one, nor put himself under the absolute arbitrary power of another to take away his life when he pleases. Nobody can give more power than he has himself; and he that cannot take away his own life cannot give another power over it.†

Though I have said above that all men by nature are equal, I cannot be supposed to understand all sorts of equality. Age or virtue may give men a just precedence; excellence of parts and merit may place others above the common level; birth may subject some, and alliance or benefits others, to pay an observance to those whom nature, gratitude, or other respects may have made it due; and yet all this consists with the equality which all men are in, in respect of jurisdiction or dominion one over another, which was the equality I there spoke of as proper to the business in hand, being that equal right that every man has to his natural freedom, without being subjected to the will or authority of any other man.

Children, I confess, are not born in this state of equality, though they are born to it. Their parents have a sort of rule and jurisdiction over them when they come into the world, and for some time after, but it is but a temporary one. The bonds of this subjection are like the swaddling clothes they are wrapped up in and supported by in the weakness of their infancy; age and reason, as they grow up, loosen them, till at length they drop quite off and leave a man at his own free disposal. . . .

The power, then, that parents have over their children arises from that duty which is incumbent on them—to take care of their offspring during the imperfect state of childhood. To inform the mind and govern the actions of their yet ignorant nonage till reason shall take its place and ease them of that trouble is what the children want and the parents are bound to; for God, having given man an understanding to direct his actions, has allowed him a freedom of will and liberty of acting as properly belonging thereunto, within the bounds of that law he is under.

* P. 200.
† P. 202.

But while he is in an estate wherein he has not understanding of his own to direct his will, he is not to have any will of his own to follow; he that understands for him must will for him, too; he must prescribe to his will and regulate his actions; but when he comes to the estate that made his father a freeman, the son is a freeman, too.

This holds in all the laws a man is under, whether natural or civil. Is a man under the law of nature? What made him free of that law? What gave him a free disposing of his property, according to his own will, within the compass of that law? I answer, a state of maturity wherein he might be supposed capable to know that law, that so he might keep his actions within the bounds of it. When he has acquired that state, he is presumed to know how far that law is to be his guide, and how far he may make use of his freedom, and so comes to have it; till then somebody else must guide him who is presumed to know how far the law allows a liberty. If such a state of reason, such an age of discretion, made him free, the same shall make his son free, too. Is a man under the law of England? What made him free of that law, that is, to have the liberty to dispose of his actions and possessions according to his own will, within the permission of that law? A capacity of knowing that law; which is supposed by that law at the age of twenty-one, and in some cases sooner. If this made the father free, it shall make the son free, too. Till then we see the law allows the son to have no will, but he is to be guided by the will of his father or guardian who is to understand for him. And if the father die and fail to substitute a deputy in his trust, if he has not provided a tutor to govern his son during his minority, during his want of understanding the law takes care to do it. Some other must govern him and be a will to him, till he has attained to a state of freedom and his understanding be fit to take the government of his will. But after that the father and son are equally free as much as tutor and pupil after nonage [childhood]; equally subjects of the same law together, without any dominion left in the father over the life, liberty, or estate of his son, whether they be only in the state and under the law of nature, or under the positive laws of an established government.*

[Therefore] every man's children, being by nature as free as himself or any of his ancestors ever were, may, while they are in that freedom, choose what society they will join themselves to, what commonwealth they will put themselves under. But if they will enjoy the inheritance of their ancestors, they must take it on the same terms their ancestors had it and submit to all the conditions annexed to such a possession.†

Thus we are born free as we are born rational, not that we have actually the exercise of either; age that brings one brings with it the other, too. And thus we see how natural freedom and subjection to parents may consist together and are both founded on the same principle. A child is free by his father's title, by his father's understanding which is to govern him till he has it of his own. The freedom of a man at years of discretion and the subjection of a child to his parents while yet short of that age are so consistent and so distinguishable that the most blinded contenders for monarchy by 'right of fatherhood' cannot miss this difference; the most obstinate cannot but allow their consistency.‡

---

* Pp. 217-20.
† P. 227.
‡ P. 221.

II.
The Social Contract

Men being, as has been said, by nature all free, equal, and independent, no one can be put out of this estate and subjected to the political power of another without his own consent. The only way whereby any one divests himself of his natural liberty and puts on the bonds of civil society is by agreeing with other men to join and unite into a community for their comfortable, safe, and peaceable living one amongst another, in a secure enjoyment of their properties and a greater security against any that are not of it. This any number of men may do, because it injures not the freedom of the rest; they are left as they were in the liberty of the state of nature. When any number of men have so consented to make one community or government, they are thereby presently incorporated and make one body politic wherein the majority have a right to act and conclude the rest.

For when any number of men have, by the consent of every individual, made a community, they have thereby made that community one body, with a power to act as one body, which is only by the will and determination of the majority; . . .

And therefore we see that in assemblies impowered to act by positive laws, where no number is set by that positive law which impowers them, the act of the majority passes for the act of the whole and, of course, determines, as having by the law of nature and reason the power of the whole.

And thus every man, by consenting with others to make one body politic under one government, puts himself under an obligation to every one of that society to submit to the determination of the majority and to be concluded by it; or else this original compact, whereby he with others incorporates into one society, would signify nothing, and be no compact, if he be left free and under no other ties than he was in before in the state of nature. For what appearance would there be of any compact? . . .

For if the consent of the majority shall not in reason be received as the act of the whole and conclude every individual, nothing but the consent of every individual can make anything to be the act of the whole; but such a consent is next to impossible ever to be had if we consider the infirmities of health and avocations of business which in a number, though much less than that of a commonwealth, will necessarily keep many away from the public assembly [and] the variety of opinions and contrariety of interests which unavoidably happen in all collections of men.*

[Now] every man being, as has been shown naturally free, and nothing being able to put him into subjection to any earthly power but only his own consent, it is to be considered what shall be understood to be a sufficient declaration of a man's consent to make him subject to the laws of any government. There is a common distinction of an express and a tacit consent which will concern our present case. Nobody doubts but an express consent of any man entering into any society makes him a perfect member of that society, a subject of that government. The difficulty is, what ought to be looked upon as a tacit consent, and how far

---

* Pp. 240-42.

it binds—i.e., how far any one shall be looked upon to have consented and thereby submitted to any government, where he has made no expressions of it at all. And to this I say that every man that has any possessions or enjoyment of any part of the dominions of any government does thereby give his tacit consent and is as far forth obliged to obedience to the laws of that government, during such enjoyment, as anyone under it; whether this his possession be of land to him and his heirs for ever, or a lodging only for a week, or whether it be barely traveling freely on the highway; and, in effect, it reaches as far as the very being of anyone within the territories of that government.

To understand this the better, it is fit to consider that every man, when he at first incorporates himself into any commonwealth, he, by his uniting himself thereunto, annexes also, and submits to the community, those possessions which he has or shall acquire that do not already belong to any other government; for it would be a direct contradiction for any one to enter into society with others for the securing and regulating of property, and yet to suppose his land, whose property is to be regulated by the laws of the society, should be exempt from the jurisdiction of that government to which he himself, the proprietor of the land, is a subject. By the same act, therefore, whereby any one unites his person, which was before free, to any commonwealth, by the same he unites his possessions which were before free to it also; and they become, both of them, person and possession, subject to the government and dominion of that commonwealth as long as it has a being. Whoever, therefore, from thenceforth by inheritance, purchase, permission; or otherwise, enjoys any part of the land so annexed to, and under the government of that commonwealth, must take it with the condition it is under—that is, of submitting to the government of the commonwealth under whose jurisdiction it is as far forth as any subject of it. . . .

[However] whenever the owner, who has given nothing but such a tacit consent to the government, will, by donation, sale, or otherwise, quit the said possession, he is at liberty to go and incorporate himself into any other commonwealth, or to agree with others to begin a new one *in vacuis locis,* in any part of the world they can find free and unpossessed. Whereas he that has once, by actual agreement and any express declaration, given his consent to be of any commonwealth is perpetually and indispensably obliged to be and remain unalterably a subject to it, and can never be again in the liberty of the state of nature, unless by any calamity the government he was under comes to be dissolved, or else, by some public act, cuts him off from being any longer a member of it.

But submitting to the laws of any country, living quietly and enjoying privileges and protection under them, makes not a man a member of that society; this is only a local protection and homage due to and from all those who, not being in a state of war, come within the territories belonging to any government, to all parts whereof the force of its laws extends. But this no more makes a man a member of that society, a perpetual subject of that commonwealth, than it would make a man a subject to another in whose family he found it convenient to abide for some time, though, while he continued in it, he were obliged to comply with the laws and submit to the government he found there. And thus we see that foreigners, by living all their lives under another government and enjoying the privileges and protection of it, though they are bound, even in conscience, to submit to its administration as far forth as any denizen, yet do not thereby come to be subjects or members of that commonwealth. Nothing can make any man so but his actually entering into it by positive engagement and express promise and compact. That is that which I think concerning the beginning of political societies and that consent which makes any one a member of any commonwealth.*

III.
Why Man Forms A Society; The Purposes And Power Of Civil Government; And, The Liberty To Alter Or Abolish Government

If man in the state of nature be so free, as has been said, if he be absolute lord of his own person and possessions, equal to the greatest, and subject to nobody, why will he part with his freedom, why will he give up his empire and subject himself to the dominion and control of any other power? To which it is obvious to answer that though in the state of nature he has such a right, yet the enjoyment of it is very uncertain and constantly exposed to the invasion of others; for all being kings as much as he, every man his equal, and the greater part no strict observers of equity and justice, the enjoyment of the property he has in this state is very unsafe, very unsecure. This makes him willing to quit a condition which, however free, is full of fears and continual dangers; and it is not without reason that he seeks out and is willing to join in society with others who are already united, or have a mind to unite, for the mutual preservation of their lives, liberties, and estates, which I call by the general name 'property.'

The great and chief end, therefore, of men's uniting into commonwealths and putting themselves under government is the preservation of their property. To which in the state of nature there are many things wanting:

First, there wants an established, settled, known law, received and allowed by common consent to be the standard of right and wrong and the common measure to decide all controversies between them; for though the law of nature be plain and intelligible to all rational creatures, yet men, being biased by their interest as well as ignorant for want of studying it, are not apt to allow of it as a law binding to them in the application of it to their particular cases.

Secondly, in the state of nature there wants a known and indifferent judge with authority to determine all differences according to the established law; for every one in that state being both judge and executioner of the law of nature, men being partial to themselves, passion and revenge is very apt to carry them too far and with too much heat in their own cases, as well as negligence and unconcernedness to make them too remiss in other men's.

Thirdly, in the state of nature there often wants power to back and support the sentence when right, and to give it due execution. They who by any injustice offend will seldom fail, where they are able, by force, to make good their injustice;

* Pp. 253-56.

such resistance many times makes the punishment dangerous and frequently destructive to those who attempt it.

Thus mankind, notwithstanding all the privileges of the state of nature, being but in an ill condition while they remain in it, are quickly driven into society. Hence it comes to pass that we seldom find any number of men live any time together in this state. The inconveniences that they are therein exposed to by the irregular and uncertain exercise of the power every man has of punishing the transgressions of others make them take sanctuary under the established laws of government and therein seek the preservation of their property. It is this makes them so willingly give up every one his single power of punishing, to be exercised by such alone as shall be appointed to it amongst them; and by such rules as the community, or those authorized by them to that purpose, shall agree on. And in this we have the original right of both the legislative and executive power, as well as of the governments and societies themselves.

For in the state of nature, to omit the liberty he has of innocent delights, a man has two powers:

The first is to do whatsoever he thinks fit for the preservation of himself and others within the permission of the law of nature, by which law, common to them all, he and all the rest of mankind are one community, make up one society, distinct from all other creatures. And, were it not for the corruption and viciousness of degenerate men, there would be no need of any other, no necessity that men should separate from this great and natural community and by positive agreements combine into smaller and divided associations.

The other power a man has in the state of nature is the power to punish the crimes committed against that law. Both these he gives up when he joins in a private, if I may so call it, or particular politic society and incorporates into any commonwealth separate from the rest of mankind.

The first power . . . doing whatsoever he thought fit for the preservation of himself and the rest of mankind, he gives up to be regulated by laws made by the society, so far forth as the preservation of himself and the rest of that society shall require; which laws of the society in many things confine the liberty he had by the law of nature.

Secondly, the power of punishing he wholly gives up, and engages his natural force—which he might before employ in the execution of the law of nature by his own single authority, as he thought fit—to assist the executive power of the society, as the law thereof shall require; for being now in a new state, wherein he is to enjoy many conveniences from the labor, assistance, and society of others in the same community as well as protection from its whole strength, he is to part also with as much of his natural liberty, in providing for himself, as the good, prosperity, and safety of the society shall require, which is not only necessary, but just, since the other members of the society do the like.

But though men when they enter into society give up the equality, liberty, and executive power they had in the state of nature into the hands of the society, to be so far disposed of by the legislative as the good of the society shall require, yet it being only with an intention in every one the better to preserve himself, his liberty and property—for no rational creature can be supposed to change his condition with an intention to be worse—the power of the society, or legislative constituted by them, can never be supposed to extend farther than the common good, but is obliged to secure every one's property [life, liberty and estate] by providing against those three defects above-mentioned that made the state of nature so unsafe and uneasy. And so whoever has the legislative or supreme power of any commonwealth is bound to govern by established standing laws, promulgated and known to the people, and not by extemporary decrees; by indifferent and upright judges who are to decide controversies by those laws; and to employ the force of the community at home only in the execution of such laws, or abroad to prevent or redress foreign injuries, and secure the community from inroads and invasion. And all this to be directed to no other end but the peace, safety, and public good of the people.*

Though the legislative, whether placed in one or more [Houses], whether it be always in being, or only by intervals, though it be the supreme power in every commonwealth; yet:

First, it is not, nor can possibly be, absolutely arbitrary over the lives and fortunes of the people; for it being but the joint power of every member of the society given up to that person or assembly which is legislator, it can be no more than those persons had in a state of nature before they entered into society and gave up to the community; for nobody can transfer to another more power than he has in himself, and nobody has an absolute arbitrary power over himself or over any other, to destroy his own life or take away the life or property of another. A man, as has been proved, cannot subject himself to the arbitrary power of another; and having in the state of nature no arbitrary power over the life, liberty, or possession of another, but only so much as the law of nature gave him for the preservation of himself and the rest of mankind, this is all he does or can give up to the commonwealth, and by it to the legislative power, so that the legislative can have no more than this. Their power, in the utmost bounds of it, is limited to the public good of the society. It is a power that has no other end but preservation, and therefore can never have a right to destroy, enslave, or designedly to impoverish the subjects. The obligations of the law of nature cease not in society but only in many cases are drawn closer and have by human laws known penalties annexed to them to enforce their observation. Thus the law of nature stands as an eternal rule to all men, legislators as well as others. The rules that they make for other men's actions must, as well as their own and other men's actions, be conformable to the law of nature—i.e., to the will of God, of which that is a declaration—and the fundamental law of nature being the preservation of mankind, no human sanction can be good or valid against it.

Secondly, the legislative or supreme authority cannot assume to itself a power to rule by extemporary, arbitrary decrees, but is bound to dispense justice and to decide the rights of the subject by promulgated, standing laws, and known authorized judges.†

. . . For all the power the government has, being only for the good of the society, as it ought not to be arbitrary and at pleasure, so it ought to be exercised by established and promulgated laws; that both the people may know their duty and be safe and secure within the limits of the law; and the rulers, too, kept within their bounds, and not be tempted by the power they have in their hands to employ

* Pp. 256-59.
† Pp. 261-262.

it to such purposes and by such measures as they would not have known, and own not willingly.

Thirdly, the supreme power cannot take from any man part of his property [Life, Liberty and Estate] without his own consent; for the preservation of property being the end of government and that for which men enter into society, it necessarily supposes and requires that the people should have property; without which they must be supposed to lose that, by entering into society, which was the end for which they entered into it—too gross an absurdity for any man to own. Men, therefore, in society having property, they have such right to the goods which by the law of the community are theirs, that nobody has a right to take their substance or any part of it from them without their own consent; without this, they have no property at all, for I have truly no property in that which another can by right take from me when he pleases, against my consent. Hence it is a mistake to think that the supreme or legislative power of any commonwealth can do what it will and dispose of the estates of the subject arbitrarily, or take any part of them at pleasure. This is not much to be feared in governments where the legislative consists, wholly or in part, in assemblies which are variable, whose members, upon the dissolution of the assembly, are subjects under the common laws of their country, equally with the rest. But in governments where the legislative is in one lasting assembly, always in being, or in one man, as in absolute monarchies, there is danger still that they will think themselves to have a distinct interest from the rest of the community, and so will be apt to increase their own riches and power by taking what they think fit from the people; for a man's property is not at all secure, though there be good and equitable laws to set the bounds of it between him and his fellow subjects, if he who commands those subjects have power to take from any private man what part he pleases of his property and use and dispose of it as he thinks good. . . .

It is true, governments cannot be supported without great charge, and it is fit every one who enjoys his share of the protection should pay out of his estate his proportion for the maintenance of it. But still it must be with his own consent—i.e., the consent of the majority, giving it either by themselves or their representatives chosen by them. For if any one shall claim a power to lay and levy taxes on the people, by his own authority and without such consent of the people, he thereby invades the fundamental law of property and subverts the end of government; for what property have I in that which another may by right take, when he pleases, to himself?

Fourthly, the legislative cannot transfer the power of making laws to any other hands; for it being but a delegated power from the people, they who have it cannot pass it over to others. The people alone can appoint the form of the commonwealth, which is by constituting the legislative and appointing in whose hands that shall be. And when the people have said, we will submit to rules and be governed by laws made by such men, and in such forms, nobody else can say other men shall make laws for them; nor can the people be bound by any laws but such as are enacted by those whom they have chosen and authorized to make laws for them. The power of the legislative, being derived from the people by a positive voluntary grant and institution, can be no other than what that positive grant conveyed, which being only to make laws, and not to make legislators, the legislative can have no power to transfer their authority of making laws and place it in other hands.

These are the bounds which the trust that is put in them by the society and the law of God and nature have set to the legislative power of every commonwealth, in all forms of government:

First, they are to govern by promulgated established laws, not to be varied in particular cases, but to have one rule for rich and poor, for the favorite at court and the countryman at plough.

Secondly, these laws also ought to be designed for no other end ultimately but the good of the people.

Thirdly, they must not raise taxes on the property of the people without the consent of the people, given by themselves or their deputies. And this property concerns only such governments where the legislative is always in being, or at least where the people have not reserved any part of the legislative to deputies to be from time to time chosen by themselves.

Fourthly, the legislative neither must nor can transfer the power of making laws to anybody else, or place it anywhere but where the people have.*

Though in a constituted commonwealth, standing upon its own basis and acting according to its own nature, that is, acting for the preservation of the community, there can be but one supreme power which is the legislative, to which all the rest are and must be subordinate, yet, the legislative being only a fiduciary power to act for certain ends, there remains still in the people a supreme power to remove or alter the legislative when they find the legislative act contrary to the trust reposed in them; for all power given with trust for the attaining an end being limited by that end; whenever that end is manifestly neglected or opposed, the trust must necessarily be forfeited and the power devolve into the hands of those that gave it, who may place it anew where they shall think best for their safety and security. And thus the community perpetually retains a supreme power of saving themselves from the attempts and designs of anybody, even of their legislators whenever they shall be so foolish or so wicked as to lay and carry on designs against the liberties and properties of the subject; for no man or society of men having a power to deliver up their preservation, or consequently the means of it, to the absolute will and arbitrary dominion of another, whenever any one shall go about to bring them into such a slavish condition, they will always have a right to preserve what they have not a power to part with, and to rid themselves of those who invade this fundamental, sacred, and unalterable law of self-preservation for which they entered into society. And thus the community may be said in this respect to be always the supreme power, but not as considered under any form of government, because this power of the people can never take place till the government be dissolved.†

---

* Pp. 264-67.

† Pp. 269-70.

IV.
The Dissolution Of Government

He that will with any clearness speak of the dissolution of government ought in the first place to distinguish between the dissolution of the society and the dissolution of the government. That which makes the community and brings men out of the loose state of nature into one politic society is the agreement which everybody has with the rest to incorporate and act as one body, and so be one distinct commonwealth. The usual and almost only way whereby this union is dissolved is the inroad of foreign force making a conquest upon them; for in that case, not being able to maintain and support themselves as one entire and independent body, the union belonging to that body which consisted therein must necessarily cease, and so every one return to the state he was in before, with a liberty to shift for himself and provide for his own safety, as he thinks fit, in some other society. Whenever the society is dissolved, it is certain the government of that society cannot remain. Thus conquerors' swords often cut up governments by the roots and mangle societies to pieces, separating the subdued or scattered multitude from the protection of and dependence on that society which ought to have preserved them from violence. The world is too well instructed in, and too forward to allow of, this way of dissolving of governments to need any more to be said of it; and there wants not much argument to prove that where the society is dissolved, the government cannot remain—that being as impossible as for the frame of a house to subsist when the materials of it are scattered and dissipated by a whirlwind, or jumbled into a confused heap by an earthquake.

Besides this overturning from without, governments are dissolved from within.

First, when the legislative is altered. Civil society being a state of peace amongst those who are of it, from whom the state of war is excluded by the umpirage which they have provided in their legislative for the ending all differences that may arise amongst any of them, it is in their legislative that the members of a commonwealth are united and combined together into one coherent living body. This is the soul that gives form, life, and unity to the commonwealth; from hence the several members have their mutual influence, sympathy, and connection; and, therefore, when the legislative is broken or dissolved, dissolution and death follows; for the essence and union of the society consisting in having one will, the legislative, when once established by the majority, has the declaring and, as it were, keeping of that will. The constitution of the legislative is the first and fundamental act of society, whereby provision is made for the continuation of their union under the direction of persons and bonds of laws made by persons authorized thereunto by the consent and appointment of the people, without which no one man or number of men amongst them can have authority of making laws that shall be binding to the rest. When any one or more shall take upon them to make laws, whom the people have not appointed so to do, they make laws without authority, which the people are not therefore bound to obey; by which means they come again to be out of subjection and may constitute to themselves a new legislative as they think best, being in full liberty to resist the force of those who without authority would impose anything upon them. Everyone is at the disposure of his own will when those who had by the delegation of the society the declaring of the public will are excluded from it, and others usurp the place who have no such authority or delegation.*

There is one way more whereby such a government may be dissolved, and that is when he who has the supreme executive power neglects and abandons that charge, so that the laws already made can no longer be put in execution. This is demonstratively to reduce all to anarchy, and so effectually to dissolve the government; for laws not being made for themselves, but to be by their execution the bonds of the society, to keep every part of the body politic in its due place and function, when that totally ceases, the government visibly ceases, and the people become a confused multitude, without order or connection. Where there is no longer the administration of justice for the securing of men's rights, nor any remaining power within the community to direct the force to provide for the necessities of the public, there certainly is no government left. Where the laws cannot be executed, it is all one as if there were no laws; and a government without laws is, I suppose, a mystery in politics, inconceivable to human capacity and inconsistent with human society.

In these and the like cases, when the government is dissolved, the people are at liberty to provide for themselves by erecting a new legislative, differing from the other by the change of persons or form, or both, as they shall find it most for their safety and good; for the society can never by the fault of another lose the native and original right it has to preserve itself, which can only be done by a settled legislative, and a fair and impartial execution of the laws made by it. But the state of mankind is not so miserable that they are not capable of using this remedy till it be too late to look for any. To tell people they may provide for themselves by erecting a new legislative, when by oppression, artifice, or being delivered over to a foreign power, their old one is gone, is only to tell them they may expect relief when it is too late and the evil is past cure. This is in effect no more than to bid them first be slaves, and then to take care of their liberty; and when their chains are on, tell them they may act like freemen. This, if barely so, is rather mockery than relief; and men can never be secure from tyranny if there be no means to escape it till they are perfectly under it; and therefore it is that they have not only a right to get out of it, but to prevent it.

There is, therefore, another way whereby governments are dissolved, and that is when the legislative or the prince, either of them, act contrary to their trust.

First, the legislative acts against the trust reposed in them when they endeavor to invade the property of the subject, and to make themselves or any part of the community masters or arbitrary disposers of the lives, liberties, or fortunes of the people.

The reason why men enter into society is the preservation of their property [Life, Liberty and Estate]; and the end why they choose and authorize a legislative is that there may be laws made and rules set as guards and fences to the properties of all the members of the society to limit the power and moderate the dominion of every part and member of the society; for since it can never be supposed to

* Pp. 301-3.

be the will of the society that the legislative should have a power to destroy that which every one designs to secure by entering into society, and for which the people submitted themselves to legislators of their own making. Whenever the legislators endeavor to take away and destroy the property of the people, or to reduce them to slavery under arbitrary power, they put themselves into a state of war with the people who are thereupon absolved from any further obedience, and are left to the common refuge which God has provided for all men against force and violence. Whensoever, therefore, the legislative shall transgress this fundamental rule of society, and either by ambition, fear, folly, or corruption, endeavor to grasp themselves, or put into the hands of any other, an absolute power over the lives, liberties, and estates of the people, by this breach of trust they forfeit the power the people had put into their hands for quite contrary ends, and it devolves to the people, who have a right to resume their original liberty and, by the establishment of a new legislative, such as they shall think fit, provide for their own safety and security, which is the end for which they are in society. What I have said here concerning the legislative in general holds true also concerning the supreme executor, who having a double trust put in him—both to have a part in the legislative and the supreme execution of the law—acts against both when he goes about to set up his own arbitrary will as the law of the society. He acts also contrary to his trust when he either employs the force, treasure, and offices of the society to corrupt the representatives and gain them to his purposes, or openly pre-engages the electors and prescribes to their choice such whom he has by solicitations, threats, promises, or otherwise won to his designs, and employs them to bring in such who have promised beforehand what to vote and what to enact. Thus to regulate candidates and electors, and new-model the ways of election, what is it but to cut up the government by the roots, and poison the very fountain of public security? For the people, having reserved to themselves the choice of their representatives, as the fence to their properties, could do it for no other end but that they might always be freely chosen, and, so chosen, freely act and advise as the necessity of the commonwealth and the public good should upon examination and mature debate be judged to require. This those who give their votes before they hear the debate and have weighed the reasons on all sides are not capable of doing. To prepare such an assembly as this, and endeavor to set up the declared abettors of his own will for the true representatives of the people and the lawmakers of the society, is certainly as great a breach of trust and as perfect a declaration of a design to subvert the government as is possible to be met with. To which if one shall add rewards and punishments visibly employed to the same end, and all the arts of perverted law made use of to take off and destroy all that stand in the way of such a design, and will not comply and consent to betray the liberties of their country, it will be past doubt what is doing. What power they ought to have in the society who thus employ it contrary to the trust that went along with it in its first institution is easy to determine; and one cannot but see that he who has once attempted any such thing as this cannot any longer be trusted.

To this perhaps it will be said that, the people being ignorant and always discontented, to lay the foundation of government in the unsteady opinion and uncertain humor of the people is to expose it to certain ruin; and no government will be able long to subsist if the people may set up a new legislative whenever they take offense at the old one. To this I answer: Quite the contrary. People are not so easily got out of their old forms as some are apt to suggest. They are hardly to be prevailed with to amend the acknowledged faults in the frame they have been accustomed to. And if there be any original defects, or adventitious ones introduced by time or corruption, it is not an easy thing to get them changed, even when all the world sees there is an opportunity for it. This slowness and aversion in the people to quit their old constitutions has in the many revolutions which have been seen in this kingdom, in this and former ages, still kept us to, or after some interval of fruitless attempts still brought us back again to, our old legislative of king, lords, and commons; and whatever provocations have made the crown be taken from some of our princes' heads, they never carried the people so far as to place it in another line.

But it will be said this hypothesis lays a ferment for frequent rebellion. To which I answer:

First, no more than any other hypothesis; for when the people are made miserable, and find themselves exposed to the ill-usage of arbitrary power, cry up their governors as much as you will for sons of Jupiter, let them be sacred or divine, descended or authorized from heaven, give them out for whom or what you please, the same will happen. The people generally ill-treated, and contrary to right, will be ready upon any occasion to ease themselves of a burden that sits heavy upon them. They will wish and seek for the opportunity, which in the change, weakness, and accidents of human affairs seldom delays long to offer itself. He must have lived but a little while in the world who has not seen examples of this in his time, and he must have read very little who cannot produce examples of it in all sorts of governments in the world.

Secondly, I answer, such revolutions happen not upon every little mismanagement in public affairs. Great mistakes in the ruling part, many wrong and inconvenient laws, and all the slips of human frailty will be born by the people without mutiny or murmur. But if a long train of abuses, prevarications, and artifices, all tending the same way, make the design visible to the people, and they cannot but feel what they lie under and see whither they are going, it is not to be wondered that they should then rouse themselves and endeavor to put the rule into such hands which may secure to them the ends for which government was at first erected, and without which ancient names and specious forms are so far from being better that they are much worse than the state of nature or pure anarchy—the inconveniences being all as great and as near, but the remedy farther off and more difficult.

Thirdly, I answer that this doctrine of a power in the people of providing for their safety anew by a new legislative, when their legislators have acted contrary to their trust by invading their property, is the best fence against rebellion, and the probablest means to hinder it; for rebellion being an opposition, not to persons, but authority which is founded only in the constitutions and laws of the government, those, whoever they be, who by force break through, and by force justify their violation of them, are truly and properly rebels; for when men, by entering into society and civil government, have excluded force and introduced laws for the preservation of property, peace, and unity amongst themselves, those who set up force again in opposition to the laws do *rebellare*—that is, bring back again the state of war—and are properly rebels; which they who are in power, by the pretense they have to authority, the temptation of force they have in their hands, and the flattery of those about them, being likeliest to do, the properest way to prevent the evil is to show them the danger and injustice of it who are under the greatest temptation to run into it.

In both the forementioned cases, when either the legislative is changed or the legislators act contrary to the end for which they were constituted, those who are guilty are guilty of rebellion; for if any one by force takes away the established legislative of any society, and the laws of them made pursuant to their trust, he thereby takes away the umpirage which every one had consented to for a peaceable decision of all their controversies, and a bar to the state of war amongst them. They who remove or change the legislative take away this decisive power which nobody can have but by the appointment and consent of the people, and so destroying the authority which the people did, and nobody else can, set up, and introducing a power which the people has not authorized, they actually introduce a state of war which is that of force without authority; and thus by removing the legislative established by the society—in whose decisions the people acquiesced and united as to that of their own will—they unite the knot and expose the people anew to the state of war. And if those who by force take away the legislative are rebels, the legislators themselves, as has been shown, can be no less esteemed so, when they who were set up for the protection and preservation of the people, their liberties and properties, shall by force invade and endeavor to take them away; and so they putting themselves into a state of war with those who made them the protectors and guardians of their peace, are properly, and with the greatest aggravation, *rebellantes,* rebels.

But if they who say "it lays a foundation for rebellion" mean that it may occasion civil wars or intestine broils, to tell the people they are absolved from obedience when illegal attempts are made upon their liberties or properties, and may oppose the unlawful violence of those who were their magistrates when they invade their properties contrary to the trust put in them, and that therefore this doctrine is not to be allowed, being so destructive to the peace of the world; they may as well say, upon the same ground, that honest men may not oppose robbers or pirates because this may occasion disorder or bloodshed. If any mischief come in such cases, it is not to be charged upon him who defends his own right, but on him that invades his neighbor's. If the innocent honest man must quietly quit all he has, for peace's sake, to him who will lay violent hands upon it, I desire it may be considered what a kind of peace there will be in the world, which consists only in violence and rapine, and which is to be maintained only for the benefit of robbers and oppressors. Who would not think it an admirable peace betwixt the mighty and the mean when the lamb without resistance yielded his throat to be torn by the imperious wolf. . . .

The end of government is the good of mankind. And which is best for mankind? That the people should be always exposed to the boundless will of tyranny, or that the rulers should be sometimes liable to be opposed when they grow exorbitant in the use of their power and employ it for the destruction and not the preservation of the properties of their people?

Nor let any one say that mischief can arise from hence, as often as it shall please a busy head or turbulent spirit to desire the alteration of the government. It is true such men may stir whenever they please, but it will be only to their own just ruin and perdition; for till the mischief be grown general, and the ill designs of the rulers become visible, or their attempts sensible to the greater part, the people, who are more disposed to suffer than right themselves by resistance, are not apt to stir. The examples of particular injustice or oppression of here and there an unfortunate man moves them not. But if they universally have a persuasion grounded upon manifest evidence that designs are carrying on against their liberties, and the general course and tendency of things cannot but give them strong suspicions of the evil intention of their governors, who is to be blamed for it? Who can help it if they who might avoid it bring themselves into this suspicion? Are the people to be blamed if they have the sense of rational creatures and can think of things no otherwise than as they find and feel them? And is it not rather their fault who put things into such a posture that they would not have them thought to be as they are? I grant that the pride, ambition, and turbulence of private men have sometimes caused great disorders in commonwealths, and factions have been fatal to states and kingdoms. But whether the mischief has oftener begun in the people's wantonness and a desire to cast off the lawful authority of their rulers, or in the rulers' insolence and endeavors to get and exercise an arbitrary power over their people—whether oppression or disobedience gave the first rise to the disorder, I leave it to impartial history to determine. This I am sure: whoever, either ruler, or subject, by force goes about to invade the rights of either prince or people and lays the foundation for overturning the constitution and frame of any just government is highly guilty of the greatest crime I think a man is capable of—being to answer for all those mischiefs of blood, rapine, and desolation, which the breaking to pieces of governments bring on a country. And he who does it is justly to be esteemed the common enemy and pest of mankind, and is to be treated accordingly.

That subjects or foreigners attempting by force on the properties of any people may be resisted with force, is agreed on all hands. But that magistrates doing the same thing may be resisted has of late been denied; as if those who had the greatest privileges and advantages by the law had thereby a power to break those laws by which alone they were set in a better place than their brethren; whereas their offense is thereby the greater, both as being ungrateful for the greater share they have by the law, and breaking also that trust which is put into their hands by their brethren.

Whosoever uses force without right, as every one does in society who does it without law, puts himself into a state of war with those against whom he so uses it; and in that state all former ties are canceled, all other rights cease, and every one has a right to defend himself and to resist the aggressor.*

Here, it is like, the common question will be made: Who shall be judge whether the prince or legislative act contrary to their trust? This, perhaps, ill-affected and factious men may spread amongst the people, when the prince only makes use of his due prerogative. To this I reply: The people shall be judge; for who shall be judge whether his trustee or deputy acts well and according to the trust reposed in him but he who deputes him and must, by having deputed him, have still a power to discard him when he fails in his trust? If this be reasonable in particular cases of private men, why should it be otherwise in that of the greatest moment where the welfare of millions is concerned, and also where the evil, if not prevented, is greater and the redress very difficult, dear, and dangerous? . . .

---

* Pp. 305-12.

If a controversy arise betwixt a prince and some of the people in a matter where the law is silent or doubtful, and the thing be of great consequence, I should think the proper umpire in such a case should be the body of the people; for in cases where the prince has a trust reposed in him and is dispensed from the common ordinary rules of the law, there, if any men find themselves aggrieved and think the prince acts contrary to or beyond that trust, who so proper to judge as the body of the people (who, at first, lodged that trust in him) how far they meant it should extend? But if the prince, or whoever they be in the administration, decline that way of determination, the appeal then lies nowhere but to heaven; force between either persons who have no known superior on earth, or which permits no appeal to a judge on earth, being properly a state of war wherein the appeal lies only to heaven; and in that state the injured party must judge for himself when he will think fit to make use of that appeal and put himself upon it.

To conclude, the power that every individual gave the society when he entered into it can never revert to the individuals again as long as the society lasts, but will always remain in the community, because without this there can be no community, no commonwealth, which is contrary to the original agreement; so also when the society has placed the legislative in any assembly of men, to continue in them and their successors with direction and authority for providing such successors, the legislative can never revert to the people while that government lasts, because having provided a legislative with power to continue for ever, they have given up their political power to the legislative and cannot resume it. But if they have set limits to the duration of their legislative and made this supreme power in any person or assembly only temporary, or else when by the miscarriages of those in authority it is forfeited, upon the forfeiture, or at the determination of the time set, it reverts to the society, and the people have a right to act as supreme and continue the legislative in themselves, or erect a new form, or under the old form place it in new hands, as they think good.*

---

* Pp. 318-20.

Jean-Jacques Rousseau

In 1741 Jean-Jacques Rousseau (1712–78) settled in Paris, penniless and unknown. As an essayist and a composer of operas and ballets, Rousseau eventually joined the circle of fashionable philosophers such as Diderot and Voltaire. Among these intellectuals Rousseau's mind turned from the arts to an inquiry of man and society which he developed in *Arts and Science* (1750), *Origin of Inequality Among Men* (1753), and *Emile,* a novel published in 1762. *The Social Contract* (1762) altered and refined his earlier views and became an outstanding contribution to Enlightenment thought on the nature of man, society, and liberty.

Rousseau believed that man was born free in a state of nature and could choose to remain in nature or join society. He pointed out that man was uncivilized in nature where he behaved instinctively while in society man's conduct was governed by justice, his mind enlarged, and his sentiments "ennobled and whole spirit so elevated. . . ." Unlike either Hobbes or Locke, Rousseau envisaged a society where each man gave himself to all and where the whole of society was greater than the sum of its parts. "Each one of us puts into the community his person and all his powers under the supreme direction of the general will and as a body, we incorporate every member as an indivisible part of the whole." Rousseau argued that in joining society and creating the general will man gave up his inferior natural liberties for pure and virtuous civil liberty. He believed that through the continuation of the general will "the true principles of political right," freedom, and liberty would flourish.

I.
Freedom And Liberty In The "State Of Nature" And Artificial Society

Man is born free; and everywhere he is in chains. One thinks himself the master of others, and still remains a greater slave than they. How did this change come

Reprinted from Jean-Jacques Rousseau, *The Social Contract,* trans. G.D.H. Cole (London: J. M. Dent & Sons, 1913), pp. 5-6, 8-10, 13-25, 28-38, 40-45, 47, 49-53, 73-78, 90-91, 123.

about? I do not know. What can make it legitimate? That question I think I can answer.

If I took into account only force, and the effects derived from it, I should say: "As long as a people is compelled to obey, and obeys, it does well; as soon as it can shake off the yoke, and shakes it off, it does still better; for, regaining its liberty by the same right as took it away, either it is justified in resuming it, or there was no justification for those who took it away." But the social order is a sacred right which is the basis of all other rights. Nevertheless, this right does not come from nature, and must therefore be founded on conventions. Before coming to that, I have to prove what I have just asserted.

The most ancient of all societies, and the only one that is natural, is the family: and even so the children remain attached to the father only so long as they need him for their preservation. As soon as this need ceases, the natural bond is dissolved. The children, released from the obedience they owed to the father, and the father, released from the care he owed his children, return equally to independence. If they remain united, they continue so no longer naturally, but voluntarily; and the family itself is then maintained only by convention.

This common liberty results from the nature of man. His first law is to provide for his own preservation, his first cares are those which he owes to himself; and, as soon as he reaches years of discretion, he is the sole judge of the proper means of preserving himself, and consequently becomes his own master.

The family then may be called the first model of political societies: the ruler corresponds to the father, and the people to the children; and all, being born free and equal, alienate their liberty only for their own advantage. The whole difference is that, in the family, the love of the father for his children repays him for the care he takes of them, while, in the State, the pleasure of commanding takes the place of the love which the chief cannot have for the peoples under him.*

The strongest is never strong enough to be always the master, unless he transforms strength into right, and obedience into duty. Hence the right of the strongest, which, though to all seeming meant ironically, is really laid down as a fundamental principle. But are we never to have an explanation of this phrase? Force is a physical power, and I fail to see what moral effect it can have. To yield to force is an act of necessity, not of will—at the most, an act of prudence. In what sense can it be a duty?

Suppose for a moment that this so-called "right" exists. I maintain that the sole result is a mass of inexplicable nonsense. For, if force creates right, the effect changes with the cause: every force that is greater than the first succeeds to its right. As soon as it is possible to disobey with impunity, disobedience is legitimate; and, the strongest being always in the right, the only thing that matters is to act so as to become the strongest. But what kind of right is that which perishes when force fails? If we must obey perforce, there is no need to obey because we ought; and if we are not forced to obey, we are under no obligation to do so. Clearly, the word "right" adds nothing to force: in this connection, it means absolutely nothing.

Obey the powers that be. If this means yield to force, it is a good precept, but superfluous: I can answer for its never being violated. All power comes from

---

* Pp. 5-6.

God, I admit; but so does all sickness: does that mean that we are forbidden to call in the doctor? A brigand surprises me at the edge of a wood: must I not merely surrender my purse on compulsion; but, even if I could withhold it, am I in conscience bound to give it up? For certainly the pistol he holds is also a power. . . .

Since no man has a natural authority over his fellow, and force creates no right, we must conclude that conventions form the basis of all legitimate authority among men.

If an individual, says Grotius, can alienate his liberty and make himself the slave of a master, why could not a whole people do the same and make itself subject to a king? There are in this passage plenty of ambiguous words which would need explaining; but let us confine ourselves to the word *alienate.* To alienate is to give or to sell. Now, a man who becomes the slave of another does not give himself; he sells himself at the least for his subsistence: but for what does a people sell itself? A king is so far from furnishing his subjects with their subsistence that he gets his own only from them; and, according to Rabelais, kings do not live on nothing. Do subjects then give their persons on condition that the king takes their goods also? I fail to see what they have left to preserve.

It will be said that the despot assures his subjects civil tranquillity. Granted; but what do they gain, if the wars his ambition brings down upon them, his insatiable avidity, and the vexatious conduct of his ministers press harder on them than their own dissensions would have done? What do they gain, if the very tranquillity they enjoy is one of their miseries? Tranquillity is found also in dungeons; but is that enough to make them desirable places to live in? The Greeks imprisoned in the cave of the Cyclops lived there very tranquilly, while they were awaiting their turn to be devoured.

To say that a man gives himself gratuitously, is to say what is absurd and inconceivable, such an act is null and illegitimate, from the mere fact that he who does it is out of his mind. To say the same of a whole people is to suppose a people of madmen; and madness creates no right.

Even if each man could alienate himself, he could not alienate his children: they are born men and free; their liberty belongs to them, and no one but they has the right to dispose of it. Before they come to years of discretion, the father can, in their name, lay down conditions for their preservation and well-being, but he cannot give them irrevocably and without conditions: such a gift is contrary to the ends of nature, and exceeds the rights of paternity. It would therefore be necessary, in order to legitimise an arbitrary government, that in every generation the people should be in a position to accept or reject it; but, were this so, the government would be no longer arbitrary.

To renounce liberty is to renounce being a man, to surrender the rights of humanity and even its duties. For him who renounces everything no indemnity is possible. Such a renunciation is incompatible with man's nature; to remove all liberty from his will is to remove all morality from his acts. Finally, it is an empty and contradictory convention that sets up, on the one side, absolute authority, and, on the other, unlimited obedience. Is it not clear that we can be under no obligation to a person from whom we have the right to exact everything? Does not this condition alone, in the absence of equivalence or exchange, in itself involve the nullity of the act? For what right can my slave have against me, when all that he has belongs to me, and, his right being mine, this right of mine against myself is a phrase devoid of meaning?*

So, from whatever aspect we regard the question, the right of slavery is null and void, not only as being illegitimate, but also because it is absurd and meaningless. The words *slave* and *right* contradict each other, and are mutually exclusive. It will always be equally foolish for a man to say to a man or to a people: "I make with you a convention wholly at your expense and wholly to my advantage; I shall keep it as long as I like, and you will keep it as long as I like."

Even if I granted all that I have been refuting, the friends of despotism would be no better off. There will always be a great difference between subduing a multitude and ruling a society. Even if scattered individuals were successively enslaved by one man, however numerous they might be, I still see no more than a master and his slaves, and certainly not a people and its ruler; I see what may be termed an aggregation, but not an association; there is as yet neither public good nor body politic. The man in question, even if he has enslaved half the world, is still only an individual; his interest, apart from that of others, is still a purely private interest. If this same man comes to die, his empire, after him, remains scattered and without unity, as an oak falls and dissolves into a heap of ashes when the fire has consumed it.

A people, says Grotius, can give itself to a king. Then, according to Grotius, a people is a people before it gives itself. The gift is itself a civil act, and implies public deliberation. It would be better, before examining the act by which a people gives itself to a king, to examine that by which it has become a people; for this act, being necessarily prior to the other, is the true foundation of society.

Indeed, if there were no prior convention, where, unless the election were unanimous, would be the obligation on the minority to submit to the choice of the majority? How have a hundred men who wish for a master the right to vote on behalf of ten who do not? The law of majority voting is itself something established by convention, and presupposes unanimity on one occasion at least.†

II.
The Social Contract

I suppose men to have reached the point at which the obstacles in the way of their preservation in the state of nature show their power of resistance to be greater than the resources at the disposal of each individual for his maintenance in that state. That primitive condition can then subsist no longer; and the human race would perish unless it changed its manner of existence.

But, as men cannot engender new forces, but only unite and direct existing ones, they have no other means of preserving themselves than the formation, by aggregation, of a sum of forces great enough to overcome the resistance. These they have to bring into play by means of a single motive power, and cause to act in concert.

* Pp. 8-10.
† Pp. 13-14.

This sum of forces can arise only where several persons come together: but, as the force and liberty of each man are the chief instruments of his self-preservation, how can he pledge them without harming his own interests, and neglecting the care he owes to himself? This difficulty, in its bearing on my present subject, may be stated in the following terms—

"The problem is to find a form of association which will defend and protect with the whole common force the person and goods of each associate, and in which each, while uniting himself with all, may still obey himself alone, and remain as free as before." This is the fundamental problem of which the *Social Contract* provides the solution.

The clauses of this contract are so determined by the nature of the act that the slightest modification would make them vain and ineffective; so that, although they have perhaps never been formally set forth, they are everywhere the same and everywhere tacitly admitted and recognised, until, on the violation of the social compact, each regains his original rights and resumes his natural liberty, while losing the conventional liberty in favour of which he renounced it.

These clauses, properly understood, may be reduced to one—the total alienation of each associate, together with all his rights, to the whole community; for, in the first place, as each gives himself absolutely, the conditions are the same for all; and, this being so, no one has any interest in making them burdensome to others.

Moreover, the alienation being without reserve, the union is as perfect as it can be, and no associate has anything more to demand: for, if the individuals retained certain rights, as there would be no common superior to decide between them and the public, each, being on one point his own judge, would ask to be so on all; the state of nature would thus continue, and the association would necessarily become inoperative or tyrannical.

Finally, each man, in giving himself to all, gives himself to nobody; and as there is no associate over whom he does not acquire the same right as he yields others over himself, he gains an equivalent for everything he loses, and an increase of force for the preservation of what he has.

If then we discard from the social compact what is not of its essence, we shall find that it reduces itself to the following terms—

"Each of us puts his person and all his power in common under the supreme direction of the general will, and, in our corporate capacity, we receive each member as an indivisible part of the whole."

At once, in place of the individual personality of each contracting party, this act of association creates a moral and collective body, composed of as many members as the assembly contains votes, and receiving from this act its unity, its common identity, its life and its will. This public person, so formed by the union of all other persons, formerly took the name of *city,* and now takes that of *Republic* or *body politic;* it is called by its members *State* when passive, *Sovereign* when active, and *Power* when compared with others like itself. Those who are associated in it take collectively the name of *people,* and severally are called *citizens,* as sharing in the sovereign power, and *subjects,* as being under the laws of the State. But these terms are often confused and taken one for another: it is enough to know how to distinguish them when they are being used with precision. . . .

. . . the Sovereign, being formed wholly of the individuals who compose it, neither has nor can have any interest contrary to theirs; and consequently the sovereign power need give no guarantee to its subjects, because it is impossible for the body to wish to hurt all its members. We shall also see later on that it cannot hurt any in particular. The Sovereign, merely by virtue of what it is, is always what it should be.

This, however, is not the case with the relation of the subjects to the Sovereign, which, despite the common interest, would have no security that they would fulfil their undertakings, unless it found means to assure itself of their fidelity.

In fact, each individual, as a man, may have a particular will contrary or dissimilar to the general will which he has as a citizen. His particular interest may speak to him quite differently from the common interest: his absolute and naturally independent existence may make him look upon what he owes to the common cause as a gratuitous contribution, the loss of which will do less harm to others than the payment of it is burdensome to himself; and, regarding the moral person which constitutes the State as a *persona ficta,* because not a man, he may wish to enjoy the rights of citizenship without being ready to fulfil the duties of a subject. The continuance of such an injustice could not but prove the undoing of the body politic.

In order then that the social compact may not be an empty formula, it tacitly includes the undertaking, which alone can give force to the rest, that whoever refuses to obey the general will shall be compelled to do so by the whole body. This means nothing less than that he will be forced to be free; for this is the condition which, by giving each citizen to his country, secures him against all personal dependence. In this lies the key to the working of the political machine; this alone legitimises civil undertakings, which, without it, would be absurd, tyrannical, and liable to the most frightful abuses.*

III.
The Benefits Of Civil Society

The passage from the state of nature to the civil state produces a very remarkable change in man, by substituting justice for instinct in his conduct, and giving his actions the morality they had formerly lacked. Then only, when the voice of duty takes the place of physical impulses and right of appetite, does man, who so far had considered only himself, find that he is forced to act on different principles, and to consult his reason before listening to his inclinations. Although, in this state, he deprives himself of some advantages which he got from nature, he gains in return others so great, his faculties are so stimulated and developed, his ideas so extended, his feelings so ennobled, and his whole soul so uplifted, that, did not the abuses of this new condition often degrade him below that which he left, he would be bound to bless continually the happy moment which took him from it for ever, and, instead of a stupid and unimaginative animal, made him an intelligent being and a man.

---

* Pp. 14-18.

Let us draw up the whole account in terms easily commensurable. What man loses by the social contract is his natural liberty and an unlimited right to everything he tries to get and succeeds in getting; what he gains is civil liberty and the proprietorship of all he possesses. If we are to avoid mistake in weighing one against the other, we must clearly distinguish natural liberty, which is bounded only by the strength of the individual, from civil liberty, which is limited by the general will; and possession, which is merely the effect of force or the right of the first occupier, from property, which can be founded only on a positive title.

We might, over and above all this, add, to what man acquires in the civil state, moral liberty, which alone makes him truly master of himself; for the mere impulse of appetite is slavery, while obedience to a law which we prescribe to ourselves is liberty. . . .

Each member of the community gives himself to it, at the moment of its foundation, just as he is, with all the resources at his command, including the goods he possesses. This act does not make possession, in changing hands, change its nature, and become property in the hands of the Sovereign; but, as the forces of the city are incomparably greater than those of an individual, public possession is also, in fact, stronger and more irrevocable, without being any more legitimate, at any rate from the point of view of foreigners. For the State, in relation to its members, is master of all their goods by the social contract, which, within the State, is the basis of all rights; but, in relation to other powers, it is so only by the right of the first occupier, which it holds from its members.

The right of the first occupier, though more real than the right of the strongest, becomes a real right only when the right of property has already been established. Every man has naturally a right to everything he needs; but the positive act which makes him proprietor of one thing excludes him from everything else. Having his share, he ought to keep to it, and can have no further right against the community. This is why the right of the first occupier, which in the state of nature is so weak, claims the respect of every man in civil society. In this right we are respecting not so much what belongs to another as what does not belong to ourselves.

In general, to establish the right of the first occupier over a plot of ground, the following conditions are necessary: first, the land must not yet be inhabited; secondly, a man must occupy only the amount he needs for his subsistence; and, in the third place, possession must be taken, not by an empty ceremony, but by labour and cultivation, the only sign of proprietorship that should be respected by others, in default of a legal title.

In granting the right of first occupancy to necessity and labour, are we not really stretching it as far as it can go? Is it possible to leave such a right unlimited? Is it to be enough to set foot on a plot of common ground, in order to be able to call yourself at once the master of it? Is it to be enough that a man has the strength to expel others for a moment, in order to establish his right to prevent them from ever returning? How can a man or a people seize an immense territory and keep it from the rest of the world except by a punishable usurpation, since all others are being robbed, by such an act, of the place of habitation and the means of subsistence which nature gave them in common? . . .

We can imagine how the lands of individuals, where they were contiguous and came to be united, became the public territory, and how the right of Sovereignty, extending from the subjects over the lands they held, became at once real and personal. The possessors were thus made more dependent, and the forces at their command used to guarantee their fidelity. The advantage of this does not seem to have been felt by ancient monarchs, who called themselves King of the Persians, Scythians, or Macedonians, and seemed to regard themselves more as rulers of men than as masters of a country. Those of the present day more cleverly call themselves Kings of France, Spain, England, etc.: thus holding the land, they are quite confident of holding the inhabitants.

The peculiar fact about this alienation is that, in taking over the goods of individuals, the community, so far from despoiling them, only assures them legitimate possession, and changes usurpation into a true right and enjoyment into proprietorship. Thus the possessors, being regarded as depositaries of the public good, and having their rights respected by all the members of the State and maintained against foreign aggression by all its forces, have, by a cession which benefits both the public and still more themselves, acquired, so to speak, all that they gave up. This paradox may easily be explained by the distinction between the rights which the Sovereign and the proprietor have over the same estate, as we shall see later on.

It may also happen that men begin to unite one with another before they possess anything, and that, subsequently occupying a tract of country which is enough for all, they enjoy it in common, or share it out among themselves, either equally or according to a scale fixed by the Sovereign. However the acquisition be made, the right which each individual has to his own estate is always subordinate to the right which the community has over all: without this, there would be neither stability in the social tie, nor real force in the exercise of Sovereignty.

I shall end this chapter and this book by remarking on a fact on which the whole social system should rest: *i.e.* that, instead of destroying natural inequality, the fundamental compact substitutes, for such physical inequality as nature may have set up between men, an equality that is moral and legitimate, and that men, who may be unequal in strength or intelligence, become every one equal by convention and legal right.[1] *

IV.
The Nature Of Civil Society, The General Will, And Law

The first and most important deduction from the principles we have so far laid down is that the general will alone can direct the State according to the object for which it was instituted, *i.e.* the common good: for if the clashing of particular interests made the establishment of societies necessary, the agreement of these very interests made it possible. The common element in these different interests is what forms the social tie; and, were there no point of agreement between them all, no society could exist. It is solely on the basis of this common interest that every society should be governed.

---

* Pp. 18-22.

[1] Under bad governments, this equality is only apparent and illusory: it serves only to keep the pauper in his poverty and the rich man in the position he has usurped. In fact, laws are always of use to those who possess and harmful to those who have nothing: from which it follows that the social state is advantageous to men only when all have something and none too much.

I hold then that Sovereignty, being nothing less than the exercise of the general will, can never be alienated, and that the Sovereign, who is no less than a collective being, cannot be represented except by himself: the power indeed may be transmitted, but not the will.

In reality, if it is not impossible for a particular will to agree on some point with the general will, it is at least impossible for the agreement to be lasting and constant; for the particular will tends, by its very nature, to partiality, while the general will tends to equality. It is even more impossible to have any guarantee of this agreement; for even if it should always exist, it would be the effect not of art, but of chance. The Sovereign may indeed say: "I now will actually what this man wills, or at least what he says he wills"; but it cannot say: "What he wills tomorrow, I too shall will" because it is absurd for the will to bind itself for the future, nor is it incumbent on any will to consent to anything that is not for the good of the being who wills. If then the people promises simply to obey, by that very act it dissolves itself and loses what makes it a people; the moment a master exists, there is no longer a Sovereign, and from that moment the body politic has ceased to exist.

This does not mean that the commands of the rulers cannot pass for general wills, so long as the Sovereign, being free to oppose them, offers no opposition. In such a case, universal silence is taken to imply the consent of the people. . . .

Sovereignty, for the same reason as makes it inalienable, is indivisible; for will either is, or is not, general; it is the will either of the body of the people, or only of a part of it. In the first case, the will, when declared, is an act of Sovereignty and constitutes law: in the second, it is merely a particular will, or act of magistracy—at the most a decree.

But our political theorists, unable to divide Sovereignty in principle, divide it according to its object: into force and will; into legislative power and executive power; into rights of taxation, justice and war; into internal administration and power of foreign treaty. Sometimes they confuse all these sections, and sometimes they distinguish them; they turn the Sovereign into a fantastic being composed of several connected pieces: it is as if they were making man of several bodies, one with eyes, one with arms, another with feet, and each with nothing besides. We are told that the jugglers of Japan dismember a child before the eyes of the spectators; then they throw all the members into the air one after another, and the child falls down alive and whole. The conjuring tricks of our political theorists are very like that; they first dismember the body politic by an illusion worthy of a fair, and then join it together again we know not how.

This error is due to a lack of exact notions concerning the Sovereign authority, and to taking for parts of it what are only emanations from it. Thus, for example, the acts of declaring war and making peace have been regarded as acts of Sovereignty; but this is not the case, as these acts do not constitute law, but merely the application of a law, a particular act which decides how the law applies, as we shall see clearly when the idea attached to the word *law* has been defined.

If we examined the other divisions in the same manner, we should find that, whenever Sovereignty seems to be divided, there is an illusion: the rights which are taken as being part of Sovereignty are really all subordinate, and always imply supreme wills of which they only sanction the execution. . . .

It follows from what has gone before that the general will is always right and tends to the public advantage; but it does not follow that the deliberations of the people are always equally correct. Our will is always for our own good, but we do not always see what that is; the people is never corrupted, but it is often deceived, and on such occasions only does it seem to will what is bad.

There is often a great deal of difference between the will of all and the general will; the latter considers only the common interest, while the former takes private interest into account, and is no more than a sum of particular wills.*

It should be seen from the foregoing that what makes the will general is less the number of voters than the common interest uniting them; for, under this system, each necessarily submits to the conditions he imposes on others: and this admirable agreement between interest and justice gives to the common deliberations an equitable character which at once vanishes when any particular question is discussed, in the absence of a common interest to unite and identify the ruling of the judge with that of the party.

From whatever side we approach our principle, we reach the same conclusion, that the social compact sets up among the citizens an equality of such a kind, that they all bind themselves to observe the same conditions and should therefore all enjoy the same rights. Thus, from the very nature of the compact, every act of Sovereignty, *i.e.* every authentic act of the general will, binds or favours all the citizens equally; so that the Sovereign recognises only the body of the nation, and draws no distinctions between those of whom it is made up. What, then, strictly speaking, is an act of Sovereignty? It is not a convention between a superior and an inferior, but a convention between the body and each of its members. It is legitimate, because based on the social contract, and equitable, because common to all; useful, because it can have no other object than the general good, and stable, because guaranteed by the public force and the supreme power. So long as the subjects have to submit only to conventions of this sort, they obey no-one but their own will; and to ask how far the respective rights of the Sovereign and the citizens extend, is to ask up to what point the latter can enter into undertakings with themselves, each with all, and all with each.

We can see from this that the sovereign power, absolute, sacred and inviolable as it is, does not and cannot exceed the limits of general conventions, and that every man may dispose at will of such goods and liberty as these conventions leave him; so that the Sovereign never has a right to lay more charges on one subject than on another, because, in that case, the question becomes particular, and ceases to be within its competency.

When these distinctions have once been admitted, it is seen to be so untrue that there is, in the social contract, any real renunciation on the part of the individuals, that the position in which they find themselves as a result of the contract is really preferable to that in which they were before. Instead of a renunciation, they have made an advantageous exchange: instead of an uncertain and precarious way of living they have got one that is better and more secure; instead of natural independence they have got liberty, instead of the power to harm others security for themselves, and instead of their strength, which others might overcome, a right which social union makes invincible. Their very life, which they have devoted to

* Pp. 22-25.

the State, is by it constantly protected; and when they risk it in the State's defence, what more are they doing than giving back what they have received from it? What are they doing that they would not do more often and with greater danger in the state of nature, in which they would inevitably have to fight battles at the peril of their lives in defence of that which is the means of their preservation? All have indeed to fight when their country needs them; but then no one has ever to fight for himself. Do we not gain something by running, on behalf of what gives us our security, only some of the risks we should have to run for ourselves, as soon as we lost it?

The question is often asked how individuals, having no right to dispose of their own lives, can transfer to the Sovereign a right which they do not possess. The difficulty of answering this question seems to me to lie in its being wrongly stated. Every man has a right to risk his own life in order to preserve it. Has it ever been said that a man who throws himself out of the window to escape from a fire is guilty of suicide? Has such a crime ever been laid to the charge of him who perishes in a storm because, when he went on board, he knew of the danger?

The social treaty has for its end the preservation of the contracting parties. He who wills the end wills the means also, and the means must involve some risks, and even some losses. He who wishes to preserve his life at others' expense should also, when it is necessary, be ready to give it up for their sake. Furthermore, the citizen is no longer the judge of the dangers to which the law desires him to expose himself; and when the prince says to him: "It is expedient for the State that you should die," he ought to die, because it is only on that condition that he has been living in security up to the present, and because his life is no longer a mere bounty of nature, but a gift made conditionally by the State.

The death-penalty inflicted upon criminals may be looked on in much the same light: it is in order that we may not fall victims to an assassin that we consent to die if we ourselves turn assassins. In this treaty, so far from disposing of our own lives, we think only of securing them, and it is not to be assumed that any of the parties then expects to get hanged.

Again, every malefactor, by attacking social rights, becomes on forfeit a rebel and a traitor to his country; by violating its laws he ceases to be a member of it; he even makes war upon it. In such a case the preservation of the State is inconsistent with his own, and one or the other must perish; in putting the guilty to death, we slay not so much the citizen as an enemy. The trial and the judgment are the proofs that he has broken the social treaty, and is in consequence no longer a member of the State. Since, then, he has recognised himself to be such by living there, he must be removed by exile as a violator of the compact, or by death as a public enemy; for such an enemy is not a moral person, but merely a man; and in such a case the right of war is to kill the vanquished.

But, it will be said, the condemnation of a criminal is a particular act. I admit it: but such condemnation is not a function of the Sovereign; it is a right the Sovereign can confer without being able itself to exert it. All my ideas are consistent, but I cannot expound them all at once.

We may add that frequent punishments are always a sign of weakness or remissness on the part of the government. There is not a single ill-doer who could not be turned to some good. The State has no right to put to death, even for the sake of making an example, any one whom it can leave alive without danger.

The right of pardoning or exempting the guilty from a penalty imposed by the law and pronounced by the judge belongs only to the authority which is superior to both judge and law, *i.e.* the Sovereign; even its right in this matter is far from clear, and the cases for exercising it are extremely rare. In a well-governed State, there are few punishments, not because there are many pardons, but because criminals are rare; it is when a State is in decay that the multitude of crimes is a guarantee of impunity. . . .

Humanly speaking, in default of natural sanctions, the laws of justice are ineffective among men: they merely make for the good of the wicked and the undoing of the just, when the just man observes them towards everybody and nobody observes them towards him. Conventions and laws are therefore needed to join rights to duties and refer justice to its object. In the state of nature, where everything is common, I owe nothing to him whom I have promised nothing; I recognise as belonging to others only what is of no use to me. In the state of society all rights are fixed by law, and the case becomes different.

But what, after all, is a law? As long as we remain satisfied with attaching purely metaphysical ideas to the word, we shall go on arguing without arriving at an understanding; and when we have defined a law of nature, we shall be no nearer the definition of a law of the State.

I have already said that there can be no general will directed to a particular object. Such an object must be either within or outside the State. If outside, a will which is alien to it cannot be, in relation to it, general; if within, it is part of the State, and in that case there arises a relation between whole and part which makes them two separate beings, of which the part is one, and the whole minus the part the other. But the whole minus a part cannot be the whole; and while this relation persists, there can be no whole, but only two unequal parts; and it follows that the will of one is no longer in any respect general in relation to the other.

But when the whole people decrees for the whole people, it is considering only itself; and if a relation is then formed, it is between two aspects of the entire object, without there being any division of the whole. In that case the matter about which the decree is made is, like the decreeing will, general. This act is what I call a law.

When I say that the object of laws is always general, I mean that law considers subjects *en masse* and actions in the abstract, and never a particular person or action. Thus the law may indeed decree that there shall be privileges, but cannot confer them on anybody by name. It may set up several classes of citizens, and even lay down the qualifications for membership of these classes, but it cannot nominate such and such persons as belonging to them; it may establish a monarchical government and hereditary succession, but it cannot choose a king, or nominate a royal family. In a word, no function which has a particular object belongs to the legislative power.

On this view, we at once see that it can no longer be asked whose business it is to make laws, since they are acts of the general will; nor whether the prince is above the law, since he is a member of the State; nor whether the law can be unjust, since no one is unjust to himself; nor how we can be both free and subject to the laws, since they are but registers of our wills.

We see further that, as the law unites universality of will with universality of object, what a man, whoever he be, commands of his own motion cannot be a law; and even what the Sovereign commands with regard to a particular matter is no nearer being a law, but is a decree, an act, not of sovereignty, but of magistracy.*

Laws are, properly speaking, only the conditions of civil association. The people, being subject to the laws, ought to be their author. The conditions of the society ought to be regulated solely by those who come together to form it. But how are they to regulate them? Is it to be by common agreement, by a sudden inspiration? Has the body politic an organ to declare its will? Who can give it the foresight to formulate and announce its acts in advance? Or how is it to announce them in the hour of need? How can a blind multitude, which often does not know what it wills, because it rarely knows what is good for it, carry out for itself so great and difficult an enterprise as a system of legislation? Of itself the people wills always the good, but of itself it by no means always sees it. The general will is always in the right, but the judgment which guides it is not always enlightened. It must be got to see objects as they are, and sometimes as they ought to appear to it; it must be shown the good road it is in search of, secured from the seductive influences of indiviudal wills, taught to see times and spaces as a series, and made to weigh the attractions of present and sensible advantages against the danger of distant and hidden evils. The individuals see the good they reject; the public wills the good it does not see. All stand equally in need of guidance. The former must be compelled to bring their wills into conformity with their reason; the latter must be taught to know what it wills. If that is done, public enlightenment leads to the union of understanding and will in the social body: the parts are made to work exactly together, and the whole is raised to its highest power. This makes a legislator necessary. . . .

The legislator is the engineer who invents the machine, the prince merely the mechanic who sets it up and makes it go. "At the birth of societies," says Montesquieu, "the rulers of Republics establish institutions, and afterwards the institutions mould the rulers."

He who dares to undertake the making of a people's institutions ought to feel himself capable, so to speak, of changing human nature, of transforming each individual, who is by himself a complete and solitary whole, into part of a greater whole from which he in a manner receives his life and being; of altering man's constitution for the purpose of strengthening it; and of substituting a partial and moral existence for the physical and independent existence nature has conferred on us all. He must, in a word, take away from man his own resources and give him instead new ones alien to him, and incapable of being made use of without the help of other men. The more completely these natural resources are annihilated, the greater and the more lasting are those which he acquires, and the more stable and perfect the new institutions; so that if each citizen is nothing and can do nothing without the rest, and the resources acquired by the whole are equal or superior to the aggregate of the resources of all the individuals, it may be said that legislation is at the highest possible point of perfection.

The legislator occupies in every respect an extraordinary position in the State. If he should do so by reason of his genius, he does so no less by reason of his

* Pp. 28-33.

office, which is neither magistracy, nor Sovereignty. This office, which sets up the Republic, nowhere enters into its constitution; it is an individual and superior function, which has nothing in common with human empire; for if he who holds command over men ought not to have command over the laws, he who has command over the laws ought not any more to have it over men; or else his laws would be the ministers of his passions and would often merely serve to perpetuate his injustices: his private aims would inevitably mar the sanctity of his work. . . .

He, therefore, who draws up the laws has, or should have, no right of legislation, and the people cannot, even if it wishes, deprive itself of this incommunicable right, because, according to the fundamental compact, only the general will can bind the individuals, and there can be no assurance that a particular will is in conformity with the general will, until it has been put to the free vote of the people. This I have said already; but it is worth while to repeat it.

Thus in the task of legislation we find together two things which appear to be incompatible: an enterprise too difficult for human powers, and, for its execution, an authority that is no authority. . . .

This is what has, in all ages, compelled the fathers of nations to have recourse to divine intervention and credit the gods with their own wisdom, in order that the peoples, submitting to the laws of the State as to those of nature, and recognising the same power in the formation of the city as in that of man, might obey freely, and bear with docility the yoke of the public happiness.

This sublime reason, far above the range of the common herd, is that whose decisions the legislator puts into the mouth of the immortals, in order to constrain by divine authority those whom human prudence could not move. But it is not anybody who can make the gods speak, or get himself believed when he proclaims himself their interpreter. The great soul of the legislator is the only miracle that can prove his mission. Any man may grave tablets of stone, or buy an oracle, or feign secret intercourse with some divinity, or train a bird to whisper in his ear, or find other vulgar ways of imposing on the people. He whose knowledge goes no further may perhaps gather round him a band of fools; but he will never found an empire, and his extravangances will quickly perish with him. Idle tricks form a passing tie; only wisdom can make it lasting.*

V.
The Type Of People Fit To Receive Laws And The Model Society

What people, then, is a fit subject for legislation? One which, already bound by some unity of origin, interest, or convention, has never yet felt the real yoke of law; one that has neither customs nor superstitions deeply ingrained, one which

* Pp. 34-38.

stands in no fear of being overwhelmed by sudden invasion; one which, without entering into its neighbours' quarrels, can resist each of them single-handed, or get the help of one to repel another; one in which every member may be known by every other, and there is no need to lay on any man burdens too heavy for a man to bear; one which can do without other peoples, and without which all others can do; one which is neither rich nor poor, but self-sufficient; and, lastly, one which unites the consistency of an ancient people with the docility of a new one. Legislation is made difficult less by what it is necessary to build up than by what has to be destroyed; and what makes success so rare is the impossibility of finding natural simplicity together with social requirements. All these conditions are indeed rarely found united, and therefore few States have good constitutions.*

As nature has set bounds to the stature of a well-made man, and, outside those limits, makes nothing but giants or dwarfs, similarly, for the constitution of a State to be at its best, it is possible to fix limits that will make it neither too large for good government, nor too small for self-maintenance. In every body politic there is a *maximum* strength which it cannot exceed and which it only loses by increasing in size. Every extension of the social tie means its relaxation; and, generally speaking, a small State is stronger in proportion than a great one.

A thousand arguments could be advanced in favour of this principle. First, long distances make administration more difficult, just as a weight becomes heavier at the end of a longer lever. Administration therefore becomes more and more burdensome as the distance grows greater; for, in the first place, each city has its own, which is paid for by the people: each district its own, still paid for by the people: then comes each province, and then the great governments, satrapies, and vice-royalties, always costing more the higher you go, and always at the expense of the unfortunate people. Last of all comes the supreme administration, which eclipses all the rest. All these overcharges are a continual drain upon the subjects; so far from being better governed by all these different orders, they are worse governed than if there were only a single authority over them. In the meantime, there scarce remain resources enough to meet emergencies; and, when recourse must be had to these, the State is always on the eve of destruction.

This is not all; not only has the government less vigour and promptitude for securing the observance of the laws, preventing nuisances, correcting abuses, and guarding against seditious undertakings begun in distant places; the people has less affection for its rulers, whom it never sees, for its country, which, to its eyes, seems like the world, and for its fellow-citizens, most of whom are unknown to it. The same laws cannot suit so many diverse provinces with different customs, situated in the most various climates, and incapable of enduring a uniform government. Different laws lead only to trouble and confusion among peoples which, living under the same rulers and in constant communication one with another, intermingle and intermarry, and, coming under the sway of new customs, never know if they can call their very patrimony their own. Talent is buried, virtue unknown and vice unpunished, among such a multitude of men who do not know one another, gathered together in one place at the seat of the central administration. The leaders, overwhelmed with business, see nothing for themselves; the State is governed by clerks. Finally, the measures which have to be taken to maintain the general authority, which all these distant officials wish to escape or to impose

---

* Pp. 44-45.

upon, absorb all the energy of the public, so that there is none left for the happiness of the people. There is hardly enough to defend it when need arises, and thus a body which is too big for its constitution gives way and falls crushed under its own weight.

Again, the State must assure itself a safe foundation, if it is to have stability, and to be able to resist the shocks it cannot help experiencing, as well as the efforts it will be forced to make for its maintenance; for all peoples have a kind of centrifugal force that makes them continually act one against another, and tend to aggrandise themselves at their neighbours' expense, like the vortices of Descartes. Thus the weak run the risk of being soon swallowed up; and it is almost impossible for any one to preserve itself except by putting itself in a state of equilibrium with all, so that the pressure is on all sides practically equal.

It may therefore be seen that there are reasons for expansion and reasons for contraction; and it is no small part of the statesman's skill to hit between them the mean that is most favourable to the preservation of the State. It may be said that the reason for expansion, being merely external and relative, ought to be subordinate to the reasons for contraction, which are internal and absolute. A strong and healthy constitution is the first thing to look for; and it is better to count on the vigour which comes of good government than on the resources a great territory furnishes.

It may be added that there have been known States so constituted that the necessity of making conquests entered into their very constitution, and that, in order to maintain themselves, they were forced to expand ceaselessly. It may be that they congratulated themselves greatly on this fortunate necessity, which none the less indicated to them, along with the limits of their greatness, the inevitable moment of their fall.*

What makes the constitution of a State really solid and lasting is the due observance of what is proper, so that the natural relations are always in agreement with the laws on every point, and law only serves, so to speak, to assure, accompany and rectify them. But if the legislator mistakes his object and adopts a principle other than circumstances naturally direct; if his principle makes for servitude while they make for liberty, or if it makes for riches, while they make for populousness, or if it makes for peace, while they make for conquest—the laws will insensibly lose their influence, the constitution will alter, and the State will have no rest from trouble till it is either destroyed or changed, and nature has resumed her invincible sway.†

VI.
The Characteristics Of The State

What then is government? An intermediate body set up between the subjects and the Sovereign, to secure their mutual correspondence, charged with the execution of the laws and the maintenance of liberty, both civil and political.

* Pp. 40-42.
† P. 47.

The members of this body are called magistrates or *kings*, that is to say *governors*, and the whole body bears the name *prince.* Thus those who hold that the act, by which a people puts itself under a prince, is not a contract, are certainly right. It is simply and solely a commission, an employment, in which the rulers, mere officials of the Sovereign, exercise in their own name the power of which it makes them depositaries. This power it can limit, modify or recover at pleasure; for the alienation of such a right is incompatible with the nature of the social body, and contrary to the end of association.

I call then *government*, or supreme administration, the legitimate exercise of the executive power, and prince or magistrate the man or the body entrusted with that administration. . . .

Suppose the State is composed of ten thousand citizens. The Sovereign can only be considered collectively and as a body; but each member, as being a subject, is regarded as an individual: thus the Sovereign is to the subject as ten thousand to one, *i.e.* each member of the State has as his share only a ten-thousandth part of the sovereign authority, although he is wholly under its control. If the people numbers a hundred thousand, the condition of the subject undergoes no change, and each equally is under the whole authority of the laws, while his vote, being reduced to one hundred thousandth part, has ten times less influence in drawing them up. The subject therefore remaining always a unit, the relation between him and the Sovereign increases with the number of the citizens. From this it follows that, the larger the State, the less the liberty. . . .

On the other hand, as the growth of the State gives the depositaries of the public authority more temptations and chances of abusing their power, the greater the force with which the government ought to be endowed for keeping the people in hand, the greater too should be the force at the disposal of the Sovereign for keeping the government in hand. I am speaking, not of absolute force, but of the relative force of the different parts of the State. . . .

The government is on a small scale what the body politic which includes it is on a great one. It is a moral person endowed with certain faculties, active like the Sovereign and passive like the State, and capable of being resolved into other similar relations. This accordingly gives rise to a new proportion, within which there is yet another, according to the arrangement of the magistracies, till an indivisible middle term is reached, *i.e.* a single ruler or supreme magistrate, who may be represented, in the midst of this progression, as the unity between the fractional and the ordinal series.

Without encumbering ourselves with this multiplication of terms, let us rest content with regarding government as a new body within the State, distinct from the people and the Sovereign, and intermediate between them.

There is between these two bodies this essential difference, that the State exists by itself, and the government only through the Sovereign. Thus the dominant will of the prince is, or should be, nothing but the general will or the law; his force is only the public force concentrated in his hands, and, as soon as he tries to base any absolute and independent act on his own authority, the tie that binds the whole together begins to be loosened. If finally the prince should come to have a particular will more active than the will of the Sovereign, and should employ the public force in his hands in obedience to this particular will, there would be, so to speak, two Sovereigns, one rightful and the other actual, the social union would evaporate instantly, and the body politic would be dissolved.*

VII.
The Degeneration And Death Of The State; And, The Continuation Of The General Will

The question "What absolutely is the best government?" is unanswerable as well as indeterminate; or rather, there are as many good answers as there are possible combinations in the absolute and relative situations of all nations.

But if it is asked by what sign we may know that a given people is well or ill governed, that is another matter, and the question, being one of fact, admits of an answer.

It is not, however, answered, because every-one wants to answer it in his own way. Subjects extol public tranquillity, citizens individual liberty; the one class prefers security of possessions, the other that of person; the one regards as the best government that which is most severe, the other maintains that the mildest is the best; the one wants crimes punished, the other wants them prevented; the one wants the State to be feared by its neighbours, the other prefers that it should be ignored; the one is content if money circulates, the other demands that the people shall have bread. Even if an agreement were come to on these and similar points, should we have got any further? As moral qualities do not admit of exact measurement, agreement about the mark does not mean agreement about the valuation.

For my part, I am continually astonished that a mark so simple is not recognised, or that men are of so bad faith as not to admit it. What is the end of political association? The preservation and prosperity of its members. And what is the surest mark of their preservation and prosperity? Their numbers and population. Seek then nowhere else this mark that is in dispute. The rest being equal, the government under which, without external aids, without naturalisation or colonies, the citizens increase and multiply most, is beyond question the best. The government under which a people wanes and diminishes is the worst. Calculators, it is left for you to count, to measure, to compare. . . .

There are two general courses by which government degenerates: *i.e.* when it undergoes contraction, or when the State is dissolved.

Government undergoes contraction when it passes from the many to the few, that is, from democracy to aristocracy, and from aristocracy to royalty. To do so is its natural propensity. If it took the backward course from the few to the many it could be said that it was relaxed; by this inverse sequence is impossible.

Indeed, governments never change their form except when their energy is exhausted and leaves them too weak to keep what they have. If a government at

* Pp. 49-53.

once extended its sphere and relaxed its stringency, its force would become absolutely nil, and it would persist still less. It is therefore necessary to wind up the spring and tighten the hold as it gives way: or else the State it sustains will come to grief.

The dissolution of the State may come about in either of two ways.

First, when the prince ceases to administer the State in accordance with the laws, and usurps the Sovereign power. A remarkable change then occurs: not the government, but the State, undergoes contraction; I mean that the great State is dissolved, and another is formed within it, composed solely of the members of the government, which becomes for the rest of the people merely master and tyrant. So that the moment the government usurps the Sovereignty, the social compact is broken, and all private citizens recover by right their natural liberty, and are forced, but not bound, to obey.

The same thing happens when the members of the government severally usurp the power they should exercise only as a body; this is as great an infraction of the laws, and results in even greater disorders. There are then, so to speak, as many princes as there are magistrates, and the State, no less divided than the government, either perishes or changes its form.

When the State is dissolved, the abuse of government, whatever it is, bears the common name of *anarchy.* To distinguish, democracy degenerates into *ochlocracy,* and aristocracy into *oligarchy;* and I would add that royalty degenerates into *tyranny;* but this last word is ambiguous and needs explanation . . . The tyrant is he who thrusts himself in contrary to the laws to govern in accordance with the laws; the despot is he who sets himself above the laws themselves. Thus the tyrant cannot be a despot, but the despot is always a tyrant.

Such is the natural and inevitable tendency of the best constituted governments. If Sparta and Rome perished, what State can hope to endure for ever? If we would set up a long-lived form of government, let us not even dream of making it eternal. If we are to succeed, we must not attempt the impossible, or flatter ourselves that we are endowing the work of man with a stability of which human conditions do not permit.

The body politic, as well as the human body, begins to die as soon as it is born, and carries in itself the causes of its destruction. But both may have a constitution that is more or less robust and suited to preserve them a longer or a shorter time. The constitution of man is the work of nature; that of the State the work of art. It is not in men's power to prolong their own lives; but it is for them to prolong as much as possible the life of the State, by giving it the best possible constitution. The best constituted State will have an end; but it will end later than any other, unless some unforeseen accident brings about its untimely destruction.

The life-principle of the body politic lies in the sovereign authority. The legislative power is the heart of the State; the executive power is its brain, which causes the movement of all the parts. The brain may become paralysed and the individual still live. A man may remain an imbecile and live; but as soon as the heart ceases to perform its functions, the animal is dead.

The State subsists by means not of the laws, but of the legislative power. Yesterday's law is not binding to-day; but silence is taken for tacit consent, and the

Sovereign is held to confirm incessantly the laws it does not abrogate as it might. All that it has once declared itself to will it wills always, unless it revokes its declaration.

Why then is so much respect paid to old laws? For this very reason. We must believe that nothing but the excellence of old acts of will can have preserved them so long: if the Sovereign had not recognised them as throughout salutary, it would have revoked them a thousand times. This is why, so far from growing weak, the laws continually gain new strength in any well constituted State; the precedent of antiquity makes them daily more venerable: while wherever the laws grow weak as they become old, this proves that there is no longer a legislative power, and that the State is dead.*

As long as several men in assembly regard themselves as a single body, they have only a single will which is concerned with their common preservation and general well-being. In this case, all the springs of the State are vigorous and simple and its rules clear and luminous; there are no embroilments or conflicts of interests; the common good is everywhere clearly apparent, and only good sense is needed to perceive it. Peace, unity and equality are the enemies of political subtleties. Men who are upright and simple are difficult to deceive because of their simplicity; lures and ingenious pretexts fail to impose upon them, and they are not even subtle enough to be dupes. When, among the happiest people in the world, bands of peasants are seen regulating affairs of State under an oak, and always acting wisely, can we help scorning the ingenious methods of other nations, which make themselves illustrious and wretched with so much art and mystery?

A State so governed needs very few laws; and, as it becomes necessary to issue new ones, the necessity is universally seen. The first man to propose them merely says what all have already felt, and there is no question of factions or intrigues or eloquence in order to secure the passage into law of what every one has already decided to do, as soon as he is sure that the rest will act with him.

But when the social bond begins to be relaxed and the State to grow weak, when particular interests begin to make themselves felt and the smaller societies to exercise an influence over the larger, the common interest changes and finds opponents: opinion is no longer unanimous; the general will ceases to be the will of all; contradictory views and debates arise; and the best advice is not taken without question.

Finally, when the State, on the eve of ruin, maintains only a vain, illusory and formal existence, when in every heart the social bond is broken, and the meanest interest brazenly lays hold of the sacred name of "public good," the general will becomes mute: all men, guided by secret motives, no more give their views as citizens than if the State had never been; and iniquitous decrees directed solely to private interest get passed under the name of laws.

Does it follow from this that the general will is exterminated or corrupted? Not at all: it is always constant, unalterable and pure; but it is subordinated to other wills which encroach upon its sphere.†

Now that I have laid down the true principles of political right, and tried to give

---

* Pp. 73-78.
† Pp. 90-91.

the State a basis of its own to rest on, I ought next to strengthen it by its external relations, which would include the law of nations, commerce, the right of war and conquest, public right, leagues, negotiations, treaties, etc. But all this forms a new subject that is far too vast for my narrow scope. I ought throughout to have kept to a more limited sphere.*

* P. 123.

AGE OF REVOLUTION

Edmund Burke and Thomas Paine

The manifestos of the American and French Revolutions were largely based on the Enlightenment theories of natural law and natural rights. Those revolutionary doctrines shared a perception of man as basically good and rational. However, these doctrines and their catalytic political effects did not go unchallenged. The most prominent and enduring critic was Edmund Burke (1729-97), a son of an Irish lawyer and member of Parliament. In *Reflections on the Revolution in France* (1790) Burke, while admitting that society was created by contract, rejected as pious abstractions the existence of natural rights and laws. He recoiled from the French Revolution as a foolish attempt to conform society to "airy" ideas and predicted that anarchy, chaos, and tyranny would result. Burke argued that rather than overturning the state, society should be permitted to grow and evolve naturally.

Burke's appraisal of man, society, liberty, and the French Revolution was answered directly by Thomas Paine (1737–1809), pamphleteer and author of *Common Sense.* Born in England of poor Quaker parents, Paine migrated to Philadelphia in 1774 where he soon became involved with the revolutionary movement as a popularizer of Enlightenment theories and republicanism. In 1789, Paine left the United States to join French revolutionaries. In *The Rights of Man* (1791–92) Paine eloquently synthesized Lockean philosophy and revolutionary doctrines to refute Edmund Burke's arguments and defend radical beliefs in man, liberty, and society.

Edmund Burke

I.
Introduction

It may not be unnecessary to inform the Reader, that the following Reflections had their origin in a correspondence between the Author and a very young gentleman

Reprinted from Edmund Burke, *Reflections on the Revolution in France* (New York: Macmillan and Company, 1890), pp. 2, 7-9, 23-24, 28, 36-43, 64-69, 107-8, 189-94, 278-80.

at Paris, who did him the honour of desiring his opinion upon the important transactions, which then, and ever since, have so much occupied the attention of all men. An answer was written some time in the month of October 1789; but it was kept back upon prudential considerations. That letter is alluded to in the beginning of the following sheets. It has been since forwarded to the person to whom it was addressed. The reasons for the delay in sending it were assigned in a short letter to the same gentleman. This produced on his part a new and pressing application for the Author's sentiments.

The Author began a second and more full discussion on the subject. This he had some thoughts of publishing early in the last spring; but the matter gaining upon him, he found that what he had undertaken not only far exceeded the measure of a letter, but that its importance required rather a more detailed consideration than at that time he had any leisure to bestow upon it. However, having thrown down his first thoughts in the form of a letter, and indeed when he sat down to write, having intended it for a private letter, he found it difficult to change the form of address, when his sentiments had grown into a greater extent, and had received another direction. A different plan, he is sensible, might be more favourable to a commodious division and distribution of his matter.*

II.
The Rights Of Man In Civil Society

Far am I from denying in theory; full as far is my heart from withholding in practice (if I were of power to give or to withhold) the *real* rights of men. In denying their false claims of right, I do not mean to injure those which are real, and are such as their pretended rights would totally destroy. If civil society be made for the advantage of man, all the advantages for which it is made become his right. It is an institution of beneficence; and law itself is only beneficence acting by a rule. Men have a right to live by that rule; they have a right to justice; as between their fellows, whether their fellows are in politic function or in ordinary occupation. They have a right to the fruits of their industry; and to the means of making their industry fruitful. They have a right to the acquisitions of their parents; to the nourishment and improvement of their offspring; to instruction in life, and to consolation in death. Whatever each man can separately do, without trespassing upon others, he has a right to do for himself; and he has a right to a fair portion of all which society, with all its combinations of skill and force, can do in his favour. In this partnership all men have equal rights; but not to equal things. He that has but five shillings in the partnership, has as good a right to it, as he that has five hundred pound has to his larger proportion. But he has not a right to an equal dividend in the product of the joint stock; and as to the share of power, authority, and direction which each individual ought to have in the management of the state, that I must deny to be amongst the direct original rights of man

* P. 2.

in civil society; for I have in my contemplation the civil social man, and no other. It is a thing to be settled by convention.

If civil society be the offspring of convention, that convention must be its law. That convention must limit and modify all the descriptions of constitution which are formed under it. Every sort of legislative, judicial, or executory power are its creatures. They can have no being in any other state of things; and how can any man claim, under the conventions of civil society, rights which do not so much as suppose its existence? Rights which are absolutely repugnant to it? One of the first motives to civil society, and which becomes one of its fundamental rules, is, *that no man should be judge in his own cause.* By this each person has at once divested himself of the first fundamental right of uncovenanted man, that is, to judge for himself, and to assert his own cause. He abdicates all right to be his own governor. He inclusively, in a great measure, abandons the right of self-defence, the first law of nature. Men cannot enjoy the rights of an uncivil and of a civil state together. That he may obtain justice he gives up his right of determining what it is in points the most essential to him. That he may secure some liberty, he makes a surrender in trust of the whole of it.

Government is not made in virtue of natural rights, which may and do exist in total independence of it; and exist in much greater clearness, and in a much greater degree of abstract perfection: but their abstract perfection is their practical defect. By having a right to every thing they want every thing. Government is a contrivance of human wisdom to provide for human *wants.* Men have a right that these wants should be provided for by this wisdom. Among these wants is to be reckoned the want, out of civil society, of a sufficient restraint upon their passions. Society requires not only that the passions of individuals should be subjected, but that even in the mass and body as well as in the individuals, the inclinations of men should frequently be thwarted, their will controlled, and their passions brought into subjection. This can only be done *by a power out of themselves;* and not, in the exercise of its function, subject to that will and to those passions which it is its office to bridle and subdue. In this sense the restraints on men, as well as their liberties, are to be reckoned among their rights. But as the liberties and the restrictions vary with times and circumstances, and admit of infinite modifications, they cannot be settled upon any abstract rule; and nothing is so foolish as to discuss them upon that principle.

The moment you abate any thing from the full rights of men, each to govern himself, and suffer any artificial positive limitation upon those rights, from that moment the whole organization of government becomes a consideration of convenience. This it is which makes the constitution of a state, and the due distribution of its powers, a matter of the most delicate and complicated skill. It requires a deep knowledge of human nature and human necessities, and of the things which facilitate or obstruct the various ends which are to be pursued by the mechanism of civil institutions. The state is to have recruits to its strength, and remedies to its distempers. What is the use of discussing a man's abstract right to food or to medicine? The question is upon the method of procuring and administering them. In that deliberation I shall always advise to call in the aid of the farmer and the physician, rather than the professor of metaphysics.

The science of constructing a commonwealth, or renovating it, or reforming it, is, like every other experimental science, not to be taught *à priori.* Nor is it a short experience that can instruct us in that practical science; because the real effects of moral causes are not always immediate; but that which in the first instance is prejudicial may be excellent in its remoter operation; and its excellence may arise even from the ill effects it produces in the beginning. The reverse also happens; and very plausible schemes, with very pleasing commencements, have often shameful and lamentable conclusions. In states there are often some obscure and almost latent causes, things which appear at first view of little moment, on which a very great part of its prosperity or adversity may most essentially depend. The science of government being therefore so practical in itself, and intended for such practical purposes, a matter which requires experience, and even more experience than any person can gain in his whole life, however sagacious and observing he may be, it is with infinite caution than any man ought to venture upon pulling down an edifice which has answered in any tolerable degree for ages the common purposes of society, or on building it up again, without having models and patterns of approved utility before his eyes.

These metaphysic rights entering into common life, like rays of light which pierce into a dense medium, are, by the laws of nature, refracted from their straight line. Indeed in the gross and complicated mass of human passions and concerns, the primitive rights of men undergo such a variety of refractions and reflections, that it becomes absurd to talk of them as if they continued in the simplicity of their original direction. The nature of man is intricate; the objects of society are of the greatest possible complexity; and therefore no simple disposition or direction of power can be suitable either to man's nature, or to the quality of his affairs. When I hear the simplicity of contrivance aimed at and boasted of in any new political constitutions, I am at no loss to decide that the artificers are grossly ignorant of their trade, or totally negligent of their duty. The simple governments are fundamentally defective, to say no worse of them. If you were to contemplate society in but one point of view, all these simple modes of polity are infinitely captivating. In effect each would answer its single end much more perfectly than the more complex is able to attain all its complex purposes. But it is better that the whole should be imperfectly and anomalously answered, than that, while some parts are provided for with great exactness, others might be totally neglected, or perhaps materially injured, by the over-care of a favourite member.

The pretended rights of these theorists are all extremes; and in proportion as they are metaphysically true, they are morally and politically false. The rights of men are in a sort of *middle,* incapable of definition, but not impossible to be discerned. The rights of men in governments are their advantages; and these are often in balances between differences of good; in compromises sometimes between good and evil, and sometimes, between evil and evil. Political reason is a computing principle; adding, subtracting, multiplying, and dividing, morally and not metaphysically or mathematically, true moral denominations.

By these theorists the right of the people is almost always sophistically confounded with their power. The body of the community, whenever it can come to act, can meet with no effectual resistance; but till power and right are the same, the whole body of them has no right inconsistent with virtue, and the first of all virtues, prudence. Men have no right to what is not reasonable, and to what is not for their benefit.*

---

* Pp. 64–69.

III.
The Nature Of Freedom And Liberty: The French Revolution And The English Constitution Compared

I flatter myself that I love a manly, moral, regulated liberty as well as any gentleman of that society, be he who he will; and perhaps I have given as good proofs of my attachment to that cause, in the whole course of my public conduct. I think I envy liberty as little as they do, to any other nation. But I cannot stand forward, and give praise or blame to any thing which relates to human actions, and human concerns, on a simple view of the object, as it stands stripped of every relation, in all the nakedness and solitude of metaphysical abstraction. Circumstances (which with some gentlemen pass for nothing) give in reality to every political principle its distinguishing colour, and discriminating effect. The circumstances are what render every civil and political scheme beneficial or noxious to mankind. Abstractedly speaking, government, as well as liberty, is good; yet could I, in common sense, ten years ago, have felicitated France on her enjoyment of a government (for she then had a government) without enquiry what the nature of that government was, or how it was administered? Can I now congratulate the same nation upon its freedom? Is it because liberty in the abstract may be classed amongst the blessings of mankind, that I am seriously to felicitate a madman, who has escaped from the protecting restraint and wholesome darkness of his cell, on his restoration to the enjoyment of light and liberty? Am I to congratulate an highwayman and murderer, who has broke prison, upon the recovery of his natural rights? This would be to act over again the scene of the criminals condemned to the gallies, and their heroic deliverer, the metaphysic Knight of the Sorrowful Countenance.

When I see the spirit of liberty in action, I see a strong principle at work; and this, for a while, is all I can possibly know of it. The wild *gas*, the fixed air is plainly broke loose: but we ought to suspend our judgment until the first effervescence is a little subsided, till the liquor is cleared, and until we see something deeper than the agitation of a troubled and frothy surface. I must be tolerably sure, before I venture publicly to congratulate men upon a blessing, that they have really received one. Flattery corrupts both the receiver and the giver; and adulation is not of more service to the people than to kings. I should therefore suspend my congratulations on the new liberty of France, until I was informed how it had been combined with government; with public force; with the discipline and obedience of armies; with the collection of an effective and well-distributed revenue; with morality and religion; with the solidity of property; with peace and order; with civil and social manners. All these (in their way) are good things too; and, without them, liberty is not a benefit whilst it lasts, and is not likely to continue long. The effect of liberty to individuals is, that they may do what they please: We ought to see what it will please them to do, before we risque congratulations, which may be soon turned into complaints. Prudence would dictate this in the case of separate insulated private men; but liberty, when men act in bodies, is *power*. Considerate people, before they declare themselves, will observe the use which is made of *power;* and particularly of so trying a thing as *new* power in *new* persons, of whose principles, tempers, and dispositions, they have little or no experience, and in situations where those who appear the most stirring in the scene may possibly not be the real movers.*

It is far from impossible to reconcile, if we do not suffer ourselves to be entangled in the mazes of metaphysic sophistry, the use both of a fixed rule and an occasional deviation; the sacredness of an hereditary principle of succession in our government, with a power of change in its application in cases of extreme emergency. Even in that extremity (if we take the measure of our rights by our exercise of them at the Revolution) the change is to be confined to the peccant part only; to the part which produced the necessary deviation; and even then it is to be effected without a decomposition of the whole civil and political mass, for the purpose of originating a new civil order out of the first elements of society.

A state without the means of some change is without the means of its conservation. Without such means it might even risque the loss of that part of the constitution which it wished the most religiously to preserve. The two principles of conservation and correction operated strongly at the two critical periods of the Restoration and Revolution [of 1688], when England found itself without a king. At both those periods the nation had lost the bond of union in their antient edifice; they did not, however, dissolve the whole fabric. On the contrary, in both cases they regenerated the deficient part of the old constitution through the parts which were not impaired. They kept these old parts exactly as they were, that the part recovered might be suited to them. They acted by the ancient organized states in the shape of their old organization, and not by the organic *moleculae* of a disbanded people. At no time, perhaps, did the sovereign legislature manifest a more tender regard to that fundamental principle of British constitutional policy, than at the time of the Revolution, when it deviated from the direct line of hereditary succession. The crown was carried somewhat out of the line in which it had before moved; but the new line was derived from the same stock. It was still a line of hereditary descent; still an hereditary descent in the same blood, though an hereditary descent qualified with protestantism. When the legislature altered the direction, but kept the principle, they shewed that they held it inviolable.†

The people of England will not ape the fashions they have never tried; nor go back to those which they have found mischievous on trial. They look upon the legal hereditary succession of their crown as among their rights, not as among their wrongs; as a benefit, not as a grievance; as a security for their liberty, not as a badge of servitude. They look on the frame of their commonwealth, *such as it stands,* to be of inestimable value; and they conceive the undisturbed succession of the crown to be a pledge of the stability and perpetuity of all the other members of our constitution.‡

You will observe, that from Magna Charta to the Declaration of Right, it has been the uniform policy of our constitution to claim and assert our liberties, as an *entailed inheritance* derived to us from our forefathers, and to be transmitted to our posterity; as an estate specially belonging to the people of this kingdom without any reference whatever to any other more general or prior right. By this means our constitution preserves an unity in so great a diversity of its parts. We have an inheritable crown; an inheritable peerage; and an house of commons and a

---

* Pp. 7-9.
† Pp. 23-24.
‡ P. 28.

people inheriting privileges, franchises, and liberties, from a long line of ancestors.

This policy appears to me to be the result of profound reflection; or rather the happy effect of following nature, which is wisdom without reflection, and above it. A spirit of innovation is generally the result of a selfish temper and confined views. People will not look forward to posterity, who never look backward to their ancestors. Besides, the people of England well know, that the idea of inheritance furnishes a sure principle of conservation, and a sure principle of transmission; without at all excluding a principle of improvement. It leaves acquisition free; but it secures what it acquires. Whatever advantages are obtained by a state proceeding on these maxims, are locked fast as in a sort of family settlement; grasped as in a kind of mortmain for ever. By a constitutional policy, working after the pattern of nature, we receive, we hold, we transmit our government and our privileges, in the same manner in which we enjoy and transmit our property and our lives. The institutions of policy, the goods of fortune, the gifts of Providence, are handed down, to us and from us, in the same course and order. Our political system is placed in a just correspondence and symmetry with the order of the world, and with the mode of existence decreed to a permanent body composed of transitory parts; wherein, by the disposition of a stupendous wisdom, moulding together the great mysterious incorporation of the human race, the whole, at one time, is never old, or middle-aged, or young, but in a condition of unchangeable constancy, moves on through the varied tenour of perpetual decay, fall, renovation, and progression. Thus, by preserving the method of nature in the conduct of the state, in what we improve we are never wholly new; in what we retain we are never wholly obsolete. By adhering in this manner and on those principles to our forefathers, we are guided not by the superstition of antiquarians, but by the spirit of philosophic analogy. In this choice of inheritance we have given to our frame of polity the image of a relation in blood; binding up the constitution of our country with our dearest domestic ties; adopting our fundamental laws into the bosom of our family affections; keeping inseparable, and cherishing with the warmth of all their combined and mutually reflected charities, our state, our hearths, our sepulchres, and our altars.

Through the same plan of a conformity to nature in our artificial institutions, and by calling in the aid of her unerring and powerful instincts, to fortify the fallible and feeble contrivances of our reason, we have derived several other, and those no small benefits, from considering our liberties in the light of an inheritance. Always acting as if in the presence of canonized forefathers, the spirit of freedom, leading in itself to misrule and excess, is tempered with an awful gravity. This idea of a liberal descent inspires us with a sense of habitual native dignity, which prevents that upstart insolence almost inevitably adhering to and disgracing those who are the first acquirers of any distinction. By this means our liberty becomes a noble freedom. It carries an imposing and majestic aspect. It has a pedigree and illustrating ancestors. It has its bearings and its ensigns armorial. It has its gallery of portraits; its monumental inscriptions; its records, evidences, and titles. We procure reverence to our civil institutions on the principle upon which nature teaches us to revere individual men; on account of their age; and on account of those from whom they are descended. All your sophisters cannot produce any thing better adapted to preserve a rational and manly freedom than the course that we have pursued, who have chosen our nature rather than our speculations, our breasts rather than our inventions, for the great conservatories and magazines of our rights and privileges.

You might, if you pleased, have profited of our example, and have given to your recovered freedom a correspondent dignity. Your privileges, though discontinued, were not lost to memory. Your constitution, it is true, whilst you were out of possession, suffered waste and dilapidation; but you possessed in some parts the walls, and in all the foundations of a noble and venerable castle. You might have repaired those walls; you might have built on those old foundations. Your constitution was suspended before it was perfected; but you had the elements of a constitution very nearly as good as could be wished. In your old states you possessed that variety of parts corresponding with the various descriptions of which your community was happily composed; you had all that combination, and all that opposition of interests, you had that action and counteraction which, in the natural and in the political world, from the reciprocal struggle of discordant powers, draws out the harmony of the universe. These opposed and conflicting interests, which you considered as so great a blemish in your old and in our present constitution, interpose a salutary check to all precipitate resolutions; They render deliberation a matter not of choice, but of necessity; they make all change a subject of *compromise,* which naturally begets moderation; they produce *temperaments,* preventing the sore evil of harsh, crude, unqualified reformations; and rendering all the headlong exertions of arbitrary power, in the few or in the many, for ever impracticable. Through that diversity of members and interests, general liberty had as many securities as there were separate views in the several orders; whilst by pressing down the whole by the weight of a real monarchy, the separate parts would have been prevented from warping and starting from their allotted places.

You had all these advantages in your ancient states; but you chose to act as if you had never been moulded into civil society, and had every thing to begin anew. You began ill, because you began by despising every thing that belonged to you. You set up your trade without a capital. If the last generations of your country appeared without much lustre in your eyes, you might have passed them by, and derived your claims from a more early race of ancestors. Under a pious predilection for those ancestors, your imaginations would have realized in them a standard of virtue and wisdom, beyond the vulgar practice of the hour: and you would have risen with the example to whose imitation you aspired. Respecting your forefathers, you would have been taught to respect yourselves. You would not have chosen to consider the French as a people of yesterday, as a nation of low-born servile wretches until the emancipating year of 1789. In order to furnish, at the expence of your honour, an excuse to your apologists here for several enormities of yours, you would not have been content to be represented as a gang of . . . slaves, suddenly broke loose from the house of bondage, and therefore to be pardoned for your abuse of the liberty to which you were not accustomed and ill fitted. Would it not, my worthy friend, have been wiser to have you thought, what I, for one, always thought you, a generous and gallant nation, long misled to your disadvantage by your high and romantic sentiments of fidelity, honour, and loyalty; that events had been unfavourable to you, but that you were not enslaved through any illiberal or servile disposition; that in your most devoted submission, you were actuated by a principle of public spirit, and that it was your country you worshipped, in the person of your king? Had you made it to be understood, that in the delusion of this amiable error you had gone further than your wise ancestors; that you were resolved to resume your ancient privileges, whilst you preserved the spirit of your ancient and your recent loyalty and honour; or, if diffident of yourselves, and not clearly discerning the almost obliterated constitution of your ancestors, you had looked to your neighbours in this land, who had kept alive the ancient principles and models of the old common law of Europe meliorated and adapted to its present state—by following wise examples you would have given new examples of wisdom to the world. You would have rendered the cause of liberty venerable in the eyes of every worthy mind in every nation. You would have shamed despotism from the earth, by shewing that freedom was not only reconcileable, but as, when well disciplined it is, auxiliary to law. You would have had an unoppressive but a productive revenue. You would have had a flourishing commerce to feed it. You would have had a free constitution; a potent monarchy; a disciplined army; a reformed and venerated clergy; a mitigated but spirited nobility, to lead your virtue, not to overlay it; you would have had a liberal order of commons, to emulate and to recruit that nobility; you would have had a protected, satisfied, laborious, and obedient people, taught to seek and to recognize the happiness that is to be found by virtue in all conditions; in which consists the true moral equality of mankind, and not in that monstrous fiction, which, by inspiring false ideas and vain expectations into men destined to travel in the obscure walk of laborious life, serves only to aggravate and imbitter that real inequality, which it never can remove; and which the order of civil life establishes as much for the benefit of those whom it must leave in an humble state, as those whom it is able to exalt to a condition more splendid, but not more happy. You had a smooth and easy career of felicity and glory laid open to you, beyond any thing recorded in the history of the world; but you have shewn that difficulty is good for man.

Compute your gains: see what is got by those extravagant and presumptuous speculations which have taught your leaders to despise all their predecessors, and all their contemporaries, and even to despise themselves, until the moment in which they became truly despicable. By following those false lights, France has bought undignified calamities at a higher price than any nation has purchased the most unequivocal blessings! France has bought poverty by crime! France has not sacrificed her virtue to her interest; but she has abandoned her interest, that she might prostitute her virtue. All other nations have begun the fabric of a new government, or the reformation of an old, by establishing originally, or by enforcing with greater exactness some rites or other of religion. All other people have laid the foundations of civil freedom in severer manners, and a system of a more austere and masculine morality. France, when she let loose the reins of regal authority, doubled the licence, of a ferocious dissoluteness in manners, and of an insolent irreligion in opinions and practices; and has extended through all ranks of life, as if she were communicating some privilege, or laying open some secluded benefit, all the unhappy corruptions that usually were the disease of wealth and power. This is one of the new principles of equality in France.

France, by the perfidy of her leaders, has utterly disgraced the tone of lenient council in the cabinets of princes, and disarmed it of its most potent topics. She has sanctified the dark suspicious maxims of tyrannous distrust; and taught kings to tremble at (what will hereafter be called) the delusive plausibilities, of moral politicians. Sovereigns will consider those who advise them to place an unlimited confidence in their people, as subverters of their thrones; as traitors who aim at their destruction, by leading their easy good-nature, under specious pretences, to admit combinations of bold and faithless men into a participation of their power. This alone (if there were nothing else) is an irreparable calamity to you and to mankind. Remember that your parliament of Paris told your king, that in calling the states together, he had nothing to fear but the prodigal excess of their zeal in providing for the support of the throne. It is right that these men should hide their heads. It is right that they should bear their part in the ruin which their counsel has brought on their sovereign and their country. Such sanguine declarations tend to lull authority asleep; to encourage it rashly to engage in perilous adventures of untried policy; to neglect those provisions, preparations, and precautions, which distinguish benevolence from imbecillity; and without which no man can answer for the salutary effect of any abstract plan of government or of freedom. For want of these, they have seen the medicine of the state corrupted into its poison. They have seen the French rebel against a mild and lawful monarch, with more fury, outrage, and insult, than ever any people has been known to rise against the most illegal usurper, or the most sanguinary tyrant. Their resistance was made to concession; their revolt was from protection; their blow was aimed at an hand holding out graces, favours, and immunities.

This was unnatural. The rest is in order. They have found their punishment in their success. Laws overturned; tribunals subverted; industry without vigour; commerce expiring; the revenue unpaid, yet the people impoverished; a church pillaged, and a state not relieved; civil and military anarchy made the constitution of the kingdom; every thing human and divine sacrificed to the idol of public credit, and national bankruptcy the consequence; and to crown all, the paper securities of new, precarious, tottering power, the discredited paper securities of impoverished fraud, and beggared rapine, held out as a currency for the support of an empire, in lieu of the two great recognized species that represent the lasting conventional credit of mankind, which disappeared and hid themselves in the earth from whence they came, when the principle of property, whose creatures and representatives they are, was systematically subverted.

Were all these dreadful things necessary? Were they the inevitable results of the desperate struggle of determined patriots, compelled to wade through blood and tumult, to the quiet shore of a tranquil and prosperous liberty? No! nothing like it. The fresh ruins of France, which shock our feelings wherever we can turn our eyes, are not the devastation of civil war; they are the sad but instructive monuments of rash and ignorant counsel in time of profound peace. They are the display of inconsiderate and presumptuous, because unresisted and irresistible authority. The persons who have thus squandered away the precious treasure of their crimes, the persons who have made this prodigal and wild waste of public evils (the last stake reserved for the ultimate ransom of the state) have met in their progress with little, or rather with no opposition at all. Their whole march was more like a triumphal procession than the progress of a war. Their pioneers have gone before them, and demolished and laid every thing level at their feet. Not one drop of *their* blood have they shed in the cause of the country they have ruined. They have made no sacrifices to their projects of greater consequence than their shoe-buckles, whilst they were imprisoning their king, murdering their fellow citizens, and bathing in tears, and plunging in poverty and distress, thousands of worthy men and worthy families. Their cruelty has not even been the base result of fear. It has been the effect of their sense of perfect safety, in authorizing treasons, robberies, rapes, assassinations, slaughters, and burnings throughout their harrassed land.*

IV.
Evolution Versus Revolution To Reform The State

Society is indeed a contract. Subordinate contracts for objects of mere occasional interest may be dissolved at pleasure—but the state ought not to be considered as nothing better than a partnership agreement in a trade of pepper and coffee, callico or tobacco, or some other such low concern, to be taken up for a little temporary interest, and to be dissolved by the fancy of the parties. It is to be looked on with other reverence; because it is not a partnership in things subservient only to the gross animal existence of a temporary and perishable nature. It is a partnership in all science; a partnership in all art; a partnership in every virtue, and in all perfection. As the ends of such a partnership cannot be obtained in many generations, it becomes a partnership not only between those who are living, but between those who are living, those who are dead, and those who are to be born. Each contract of each particular state is but a clause in the great primaeval contract of eternal society, linking the lower with the higher natures, connecting the visible and invisible world, according to a fixed compact sanctioned by the inviolable oath which holds all physical and all moral natures, each in their appointed place. This law is not subject to the will of those, who by an obligation above them, and infinitely superior, are bound to submit their will to that law. The municipal corporations of that universal kingdom are not morally at liberty at their pleasure, and on their speculations of a contingent improvement, wholly to separate and tear asunder the bands of their subordinate community, and to dissolve it into an unsocial, uncivil, unconnected chaos of elementary principles. It is the first and supreme necessity only, a necessity that is not chosen but chooses, a necessity paramount to deliberation, that admits no discussion, and demands no evidence, which alone can justify a resort to anarchy. This necessity is no exception to the rule; because this necessity itself is a part too of that moral and physical disposition of things to which man must be obedient by consent or force; but if that which is only submission to necessity should be made the object of choice, the law is broken, nature is disobeyed, and the rebellious are outlawed, cast forth, and exiled, from this world of reason, and order, and peace, and virtue, and fruitful penitence, into the antagonist world of madness, discord, vice, confusion, and unavailing sorrow.†

---

* Pp. 36-43.
† Pp. 107-8.

At once to preserve and to reform society is quite another thing. When the useful parts of an old establishment are kept, and what is superadded is to be fitted to what is retained, a vigorous mind, steady persevering attention, various powers of comparison and combination, and the resources of an understanding fruitful in expedients are to be exercised; they are to be exercised in a continued conflict with the combined force of opposite vices; with the obstinacy that rejects all improvement, and the levity that is fatigued and disgusted with every thing of which it is in possession. But you may object—"A process of this kind is slow. It is not fit for an assembly, which glories in performing in a few months the work of ages. Such a mode of reforming, possibly might take up many years." Without question it might; and it ought. It is one of the excellencies of a method in which time is amongst the assistants, that its operation is slow, and in some cases almost imperceptible. If circumspection and caution are a part of wisdom, when we work only upon inanimate matter, surely they become a part of duty too, when the subject of our demolition and construction is not brick and timber, but sentient beings, by the sudden alteration of whose state, condition, and habits, multitudes may be rendered miserable. But it seems as if it were the prevalent opinion in Paris, that an unfeeling heart, and an undoubting confidence, are the sole qualifications for a perfect legislator. Far different are my ideas of that high office. The true lawgiver ought to have an heart full of sensibility. He ought to love and respect his kind, and to fear himself. It may be allowed to his temperament to catch his ultimate object with an intuitive glance; but his movements towards it ought to be deliberate. Political arrangement, as it is a work for social ends, is to be only wrought by social means. There mind must conspire with mind. Time is required to produce that union of minds which alone can produce all the good we aim at. Our patience will achieve more than our force. If I might venture to appeal to what is so much out of fashion in Paris, I mean to experience, I should tell you, that in my course I have known, and, according to my measure, have co-operated with great men; and I have never yet seen any plan which has not been mended by the observations of those who were much inferior in understanding to the person who took the lead in the business. By a slow but well-sustained progress, the effect of each step is watched; the good or ill success of the first, gives light to us in the second; and so, from light to light, we are conducted with safety through the whole series. We see, that the parts of the system do not clash. The evils latent in the most promising contrivances are provided for as they arise. One advantage is as little as possible sacrificed to another. We compensate, we reconcile, we balance. We are enabled to unite into a consistent whole the various anomalies and contending principles that are found in the minds and affairs of men. From hence arises, not an excellence in simplicity, but one far superior, an excellence in composition. Where the great interests of mankind are concerned through a long succession of generations, that succession ought to be admitted into some share in the councils which are so deeply to affect them. If justice requires this, the work itself requires the aid of more minds than one age can furnish. It is from this view of things that the best legislators have been often satisfied with the establishment of some sure, solid, and ruling principle in government; a power like that which some of the philosophers have called a plastic nature; and having fixed the principle, they have left it afterwards to its own operation.

To proceed in this manner, that is, to proceed with a presiding principle, and a prolific energy, is with me the criterion of profound wisdom. What your politicians think the marks of a bold, hardy genius, are only proofs of a deplorable want of ability. By their violent haste, and their defiance of the process of nature, they are delivered over blindly to every projector and adventurer, to every alchymist and empiric. They despair of turning to account any thing that is common. Diet is nothing in their system of remedy. The worst of it is, that this their despair of curing common distempers by regular methods, arises not only from defect of comprehension, but, I fear, from some malignity of disposition. Your legislators seem to have taken their opinions of all professions, ranks, and offices, from the declamations and buffooneries of satirists; who would themselves be astonished if they were held to the letter of their own descriptions. By listening only to these, your leaders regard all things only on the side of their vices and faults, and view those vices and faults under every colour of exaggeration. It is undoubtedly true, though it may seem paradoxical; but in general, those who are habitually employed in finding and displaying faults, are unqualified for the work of refoımation: because their minds are not only unfurnished with patterns of the fair and good, but by habit they come to take no delight in the contemplation of those things. By hating vices too much, they come to love men too little. It is therefore not wonderful, that they should be indisposed and unable to serve them. From hence arises the complexional disposition of some of your guides to pull every thing in pieces. At this malicious game they display the whole of their *quadrimanous* activity. As to the rest, the paradoxes of eloquent writers, brought forth purely as a sport of fancy, to try their talents, to rouze attention, and excite surprize, are taken up by these gentlemen, not in the spirit of the original authors, as means of cultivating their taste and improving their style. These paradoxes become with them serious grounds of action, upon which they proceed in regulating the most important concerns of the state. . . .

Old establishments are tried by their effects. If the people are happy, united, wealthy, and powerful, we presume the rest. We conclude that to be good from whence good is derived. In old establishments various correctives have been found for their aberrations from theory. Indeed they are the results of various necessities and expediencies. They are not often constructed after any theory; theories are rather drawn from them. In them we often see the end best obtained, where the means seem not perfectly reconcileable to what we may fancy was the original scheme. The means taught by experience may be better suited to political ends than those contrived in the original project. They again re-act upon the primitive constitution, and sometimes improve the design itself from which they seem to have departed. I think all this might be curiously exemplified in the British constitution. At worst, the errors and deviations of every kind in reckoning are found and computed, and the ship proceeds in her course. This is the case of old establishments; but in a new and merely theoretic system, it is expected that every contrivance shall appear, on the face of it, to answer its end; especially where the projectors are no way embarrassed with an endeavour to accommodate the new building to an old one, either in the walls or on the foundations.*

* Pp. 189-94.

V.
Conclusion

I wish my countrymen to recommend to our neighbours the example of the British constitution, than to take models from them for the improvement of our own. In the former they have got an invaluable treasure. They are not, I think, without some causes of apprehension and complaint; but these they do not owe to their constitution, but to their own conduct. I think our happy situation owing to our constitution; but owing to the whole of it, and not to any part singly; owing in a great measure to what we have left standing in our several reviews and reformations, as well as to what we have altered or superadded. Our people will find employment enough for a truly patriotic, free, and independent spirit, in guarding what they possess, from violation. I would not exclude alteration neither; but even when I changed, it should be to preserve. I should be led to my remedy by a great grievance. In what I did, I should follow the example of our ancestors. I would make the reparation as nearly as possible in the style of the building. A politic caution, a guarded circumspection, a moral rather than a complexional timidity were among the ruling principles of our forefathers in their most decided conduct. Not being illuminated with the light of which the gentlemen of France tell us they have got so abundant a share, they acted under a strong impression of the ignorance and fallibility of mankind. He that had made them thus fallible, rewarded them for having in their conduct attended to their nature. Let us imitate their caution, if we wish to deserve their fortune, or to retain their bequests. Let us add, if we please, but let us preserve what they have left; and, standing on the firm ground of the British constitution, let us be satisfied to admire rather than attempt to follow in their desperate flights the aeïonauts of France.

I have told you candidly my sentiments. I think they are not likely to alter yours. I do not know that they ought. You are young; you cannot guide, but must follow the fortune of your country. But hereafter they may be of some use to you, in some future form which your commonwealth may take. In the present it can hardly remain; but before its final settlement it may be obliged to pass, as one of our poets says, "through great varieties of untried being," and in all its transmigrations to be purified by fire and blood.

I have little to recommend my opinions, but long observation and much impartiality. They come from one who has been no tool of power, no flatterer of greatness; and who in his last acts does not wish to belye the tenour of his life.They come from one, almost the whole of whose public exertion has been a struggle for the liberty of others; from one in whose breast no anger durable or vehement has ever been kindled, but by what he considered as tyranny; and who snatches from his share in the endeavours which are used by good men to discredit opulent oppression, the hours he has employed on your affairs; and who in so doing persuades himself he has not departed from his usual office: they come from one who desires honours, distinctions, and emoluments, but little; and who expects them not at all; who has no contempt for fame, and no fear of obloquy; who shuns contention, though he will hazard an opinion: from one who wishes to preserve consistency; but who would preserve consistency by varying his means to secure the unity of his end; and, when the equipoise of the vessel in which he sails, may be endangered by overloading it upon one side, is desirous of carrying the small weight of his reasons to that which may preserve its equipoise.*

Thomas Paine

I.
An Opening Reply To Edmund Burke

Every age and generation must be as free to act for itself *in all cases* as the ages and generation which preceded it. The vanity and presumption of governing beyond the grave, is the most ridiculous and insolent of all tyrannies. Man has no property in man; neither has any generation a property in the generations which are to follow. . . . Every generation is, and must be, competent to all the purposes which its occasions require. It is the living, and not the dead, that are to be accommodated. When man ceases to be, his power and his wants cease with him; and having no longer any participation in the concerns of this world, he has no longer any authority in directing who shall be its governors, or how its Government shall be organized, or how administered. That which a whole Nation chooses to do, it has a right to do. Mr. Burke says, No. Where then *does* the right exist? I am contending for the rights of the *living,* and against their being willed away, and controlled and contracted for, by the manuscript assumed authority of the dead; and Mr. Burke is contending for the authority of the dead over the rights and freedom of the living. There was a time when kings disposed of their crowns by will upon their death-beds, and consigned the people, like beasts of the field, to whatever successor they appointed. This is now so exploded as scarcely to be remembered, and so monstrous as hardly to be believed. But the Parliamentary clauses upon which Mr. Burke builds his political church, are of the same nature.

The laws of every country must be analogous to some common principle. In England, no parent or master, nor all the authority of Parliament, omnipotent as it has called itself, can bind or controul the personal freedom even of an individual beyond the age of twenty-one years. On what ground of right, then, could the Parliament of 1688, or any other Parliament, bind all posterity for ever?

Those who have quitted the world, and those who are not yet arrived in it, are as remote from each other, as the utmost stretch of moral imagination can conceive. What possible obligation, then, can exist between them; what rule or principle can be laid down, that two nonentities, the one out of existence, and

---

* Pp. 278-80.

Reprinted from Thomas Paine, *The Rights of Man* (London: J. M. Dent and Sons, 1915), pp. 12-16, 40-47, 94-98, 130-35, 157-60, 170-73, 176-78, 181-82, 210-11.

the other not in, and who never can meet in this world, that the one should controul the other to the end of time?

A greater absurdity cannot present itself to the understanding of man, than what Mr. Burke offers to his readers. He tells them, and he tells the world to come, that a certain body of men, who existed a hundred years ago, made a law; and that there does not now exist in the Nation, nor ever will, nor ever can, a power to alter it. Under how many subtleties, or absurdities, has the divine right to govern been imposed on the credulity of mankind!

From what, or from whence, does Mr. Burke prove the right of any human power to bind posterity for ever? He has produced his clauses; but he must produce also his proofs that such a right existed, and show how it existed. If it ever existed, it must now exist; for whatever appertains to the nature of man, cannot be annihilated by man. It is the nature of man to die, and he will continue to die as long as he continues to be born. But Mr. Burke has set up a sort of political Adam, in whom all posterity are bound for ever; he must therefore prove that his Adam possessed such a power, or such a right.

The weaker any cord is, the less it will bear to be stretched and the worse is the policy to stretch it, unless it is intended to break it. Had a person contemplated the overthrow of Mr. Burke's positions, he would have proceeded as Mr. Burke has done. He would have magnified the authorities, on purpose to have called the *right* of them into question; and the instant the question of right was started, the authorities must have been given up.

It requires but a very small glance of thought to perceive, that although laws made in one generation often continue in force through succeeding generations, yet they continue to derive their force from the consent of the living. A law not repealed continues in force, not because it *cannot* be repealed, but because it is *not* repealed; and the non-repealing passes for consent.

But Mr. Burke's clauses have not even this qualification in their favor. They become null, by attempting to become immortal. The nature of them precludes consent. They destroy the right which they *might* have, by grounding it on a right which they *cannot* have. Immortal power is not a human right, and therefore cannot be a right of Parliament.

The circumstances of the world are continually changing, and the opinions of men change also; and as Government is for the living, and not for the dead, it is the living only that has any right in it. That which may be thought right and found convenient in one age, may be thought wrong and found inconvenient in another. In such cases, who is to decide, the living, or the dead?*

I have now to follow Mr. Burke through a pathless wilderness of rhapsodies, and a sort of descant [melody] upon Governments, in which he asserts whatever he pleases, on the presumption of its being believed, without offering either evidence or reasons for so doing. . . . Does Mr. Burke mean to deny that *man* has any rights? If he does, then he must mean that there are no such things as rights any where, and that he has none himself; for who is there in the world but man? But if Mr. Burke means to admit that man has rights, the question then will be, what are those rights, and how came man by them originally?

---

* Pp. 12-16.

The error of those who reason by precedents drawn from antiquity, respecting the rights of man, is that they do not go far enough into antiquity. They do not go the whole way. They stop in some of the intermediate stages of an hundred or a thousand years, and produce what was then done as a rule for the present day. This is no authority at all. If we travel still further into antiquity, we shall find a directly contrary opinion and practise prevailing; and, if antiquity is to be authority, a thousand such authorities may be produced, successively contradicting each other; but if we proceed on, we shall at last come out right; we shall come to the time when man came from the hand of his Maker.*

II.
The Origin Of Man And The Existence Of Natural And Civil Rights; The Character Of Man And The Proper Limits Of Government

What was he then? Man. Man was his high and only title, and a higher cannot be given him. . . .

We have now arrived at the origin of man, and at the origin of his rights. As to the manner in which the world has been governed from that day to this, it is no further any concern of ours than to make a proper use of the errors or the improvements which the history of it presents. Those who lived a hundred or a thousand years ago, were then moderns as we are now. They had *their* ancients, and those ancients had others, and we also shall be ancients in our turn. If the mere name of antiquity is to govern in the affairs of life, the people who are to live an hundred or a thousand years hence, may as well take us for a precedent, as we make a precedent of those who lived an hundred or a thousand years ago. The fact is, that portions of antiquity, by proving every thing, establish nothing. It is authority against authority all the way, till we come to the divine origin of the rights of man, at the Creation. Here our inquiries find a resting-place, and our reason finds a home. If a dispute about the rights of man had arisen at a distance of an hundred years from the Creation, it is to this source of authority they must have referred, and it is to the same source of authority that we must now refer.

Though I mean not to touch upon any sectarian principle of religion, yet it may be worth observing, that the genealogy of Christ is traced to Adam. Why then not trace the rights of man to creation of man? I will answer the question. Because there have been upstart Governments, thrusting themselves between, and presumptuously working to *unmake* man.

If any generation of men ever possessed the right of dictating the mode by which the world should be governed for ever, it was the first generation that existed; and if that generation did it not, no succeeding generation can show any authority

* Pp. 40-41.

for doing it, nor can set any up. The illuminating and divine principle of the equal rights of man (for it has its origin from the Maker of man), relates not only to the living individuals, but to generations of men succeeding each other. Every generation is equal in rights to the generations which preceded it, by the same rule that every individual is born equal in rights with his contemporary.

Every history of the Creation, and every traditionary account, whether from the lettered or unlettered world, however they may vary in their opinion or belief of certain particulars, all agree in establishing one point, *the unity of man;* by which I mean that men are all of *one degree,* and consequently that all men are born equal, and with equal natural rights, in the same manner as if posterity had been continued by *creation* instead of *generation,* the latter being only the mode by which the former is carried forward; and consequently, every child born into the world must be considered as deriving its existence from God. The world is as new to him as it was to the first man that existed, and his natural right in it is of the same kind. . . .

It is also to be observed, that all the religions known in the world are founded, so far as they relate to man, on the *unity of man,* as being all of one degree. Whether in heaven or in hell, or in whatever state man may be supposed to exist hereafter, the good and the bad are the only distinctions. Nay, even the laws of Governments are obliged to slide into this principle, by making degrees to consist in crimes and not in persons.

It is one of the greatest of all truths, and of the highest advantage to cultivate. By considering man in this light, and by instructing him to consider himself in this light, it places him in a close connection with all his duties, whether to his Creator or to the creation, of which he is a part; and it is only when he forgets his origin, or, to use a more fashionable phrase, his *birth and family,* that he becomes dissolute. It is not among the least of the evils of the present existing Governments in all parts of Europe, that man, considered as man, is thrown back to a vast distance from his Maker, and the artificial chasm filled up by a succession of barriers, or a sort of turnpike gates, through which he has to pass. I will quote Mr. Burke's catalogue of barriers that he has set up between man and his Maker. Putting himself in the character of a herald, he says—"*We fear God—we look with awe to kings—with affection to Parliaments—with duty to magistrates—with reverence to priests, and with respect to nobility.*" Mr. Burke has forgotten to put in "*chivalry.*" He has also forgotten to put in Peter.

The duty of man is not a wilderness of turnpike gates, through which he is to pass by tickets from one to the other. It is plain and simple, and consists but of two points. His duty to God, which every man must feel; and with respect to his neighbor, to do as he would be done by. If those to whom power is delegated do well, they will be respected; if not, they will be despised; and with regard to those to whom no power is delegated, but who assume it, the rational world can know nothing of them. . . .

We have now to consider the civil rights of man, and to show how the one originates from the other. Man did not enter into society to become *worse* than he was before, nor to have fewer rights than he had before, but to have those rights better secured. His natural rights are the foundation of all his civil rights. But in order to pursue this distinction with more precision, it is necessary to make the different qualities of natural and civil rights.

A few words will explain this. Natural rights are those which appertain to man in right of his existence. Of this kind are all the intellectual rights, or rights of the mind, and also all those rights of acting as an individual for his own comfort and happiness, which are not injurious to the natural rights of others. Civil rights are those which appertain to man in right of his being a member of society. Every civil right has for its foundation some natural right pre-existing in the individual, but to the enjoyment of which his individual power is not, in all cases, sufficiently competent. Of this kind are all those which relate to security and protection.

From this short review, it will be easy to distinguish between that class of natural rights which man retains after entering into society, and those which he throws into the common stock as a member of society.

The natural rights which he retains, are all those in which the *power* to execute is as perfect in the individual as the right itself. Among this class, as is before mentioned, are all the intellectual rights, or rights of the mind: consequently, religion is one of those rights. The natural rights which are not retained, are all those in which, though the right is perfect in the individual, the power to execute them is defective. They answer not his purpose. A man, by natural right, has a right to judge in his own cause; and so far as the right of the mind is concerned, he never surrenders it: but what availeth it him to judge, if he has not power to redress? He therefore deposits his right in the common stock of society, and takes the arm of society, of which he is a part, in preference and in addition to his own. Society *grants* him nothing. Every man is proprietor in society, and draws on the capital as a matter of right.

From these premises, two or three certain conclusions will follow.

First, That every civil right grows out of a natural right; or, in other words, is a natural right exchanged.

Secondly, That civil power, properly considered as such, is made up of the aggregate of that class of the natural rights of man, which becomes defective in the individual in point of power, and answers not his purpose, but when collected to a focus, becomes competent to the purpose of every one.

*Thirdly, That the power produced from the aggregate of natural rights, imperfect in power in the individual, cannot be applied to invade the natural rights which are retained in the individual, and in which the power to execute is as perfect as the right itself.**

Nature [has] created him [man] for social life, she fitted him for the station she intended. In all cases she made his natural wants greater than his individual powers. No one man is capable, without the aid of society, of supplying his own wants; and those wants acting upon every individual, impel the whole of them into society, as naturally as gravitation acts to a center.

But she has gone further. She has not only forced man into society, by a diversity of wants, which the reciprocal aid of each other can supply, but she has implanted in him a system of social affections, which, though not necessary to his existence, are essential to his happiness. There is no period in life when this love for society ceases to act. It begins and ends with our being.

If we examine, with attention, into the composition and constitution of man, the diversity of his wants, and the diversity of talents in different men for reciprocally accommodating the wants of each other, his propensity to society, and consequently

---

* Pp. 41-45.

to preserve the advantages resulting from it, we shall easily discover that a great part of what is called Government is mere imposition.

Government is no farther necessary than to supply the few cases to which society and civilization are not conveniently competent; and instances are not wanting to show, that every thing which Government can usefully add thereto, has been performed by the common consent of society, without Government. . . . There is a natural aptness in man, and more so in society, because it embraces a greater variety of abilities and resources, to accommodate itself to whatever situation it is in. The instant formal Government is abolished, society begins to act. A general association takes place, and common interest produces common security.

So far is it from being true, as has been pretended, that the abolition of any formal Government is the dissolution of society, that it acts by a contrary impulse, and brings the latter the closer together. All that part of its organization which it had committed to its Government, devolves again upon itself, and acts through its medium. When men, as well from natural instinct, as from reciprocal benefits, have habituated themselves to social and civilized life, there is always enough of its principles in practise to carry them through any changes they may find necessary or convenient to make in their Government. In short, man is so naturally a creature of society, that it is almost impossible to put him out of it.

Formal Government makes but a small part of civilized life; and when even the best that human wisdom can devise is established, it is a thing more in name and idea, than in fact. It is to the great and fundamental principles of society and civilization—to the common usage universally consented to, and mutually and reciprocally maintained—to the unceasing circulation of interest, which, passing through its million channels, invigorates the whole mass of civilized man—it is to these things, infinitely more than to any thing which even the best instituted Government can perform, that the safety and prosperity of the individual and of the whole depends.

The more perfect civilization is, the less occasion has it for Government, because the more does it regulate its own affairs, and govern itself; but so contrary is the practise of old Governments to the reason of the case, that the expenses of them increase in the proportion they ought to diminish. It is but few general laws that civilized life requires, and those of such common usefulness, that whether they are enforced by the forms of Government or not, the effect will be nearly the same. If we consider what the principles are that first condense men into society, and what the motives that regulate their mutual intercourse afterwards, we shall find, by the time we arrive at what is called Government, that nearly the whole of the business is performed by the natural operation of the parts upon each other.

Man, with respect to all those matters, is more a creature of consistency than he is aware, or that Governments would wish him to believe. All the great laws of society are laws of nature. Those of trade and commerce, whether with respect to the intercourse of individuals, or of nations, are laws of mutual and reciprocal interest. They are followed and obeyed because it is the interest of the parties so to do, and not on account of any formal laws their Governments may impose or interpose.*

* Pp. 157-60.

III.
The Nature Of Governments And The Deficiencies Of A Monarchy

We have now, in a few words, traced man from a natural individual to a member of society, and shown, or endeavored to show, the quality of the natural rights retained, those which are exchanged for civil rights ["and the quantity of government proper for man"]. Let us now apply those principles to Governments.

In casting our eyes over the world, it is extremely easy to distinguish the Governments which have arisen out of society, or out of the social compact, from those which have not; but to place this in a clearer light than what a single glance may afford, it will be proper to take a review of the several sources from which Governments have arisen and on which they have been founded.

They may be all comprehended under three heads.

First, *Superstition.*

Secondly, *Power.*

Thirdly, *The common interest of society and the common rights of man.*

The first was a Government of Priestcraft, the second of Conquerors, and the third of Reason.

When a set of artful men pretended, through the medium of oracles, to hold intercourse with the Deity, as familiarly as they now march up the back-stairs in European Courts, the world was completely under the Government of superstition. The oracles were consulted, and whatever they were made to say became the law; and this sort of Government lasted as long as this sort of superstition lasted.

After these a race of conquerors arose, whose Government, like that of William the Conqueror, was founded in power, and the sword assumed the name of a sceptre. Governments thus established last as long as the power to support them lasts; but that they might avail themselves of every engine in their favour, they united fraud to force, and set up an idol which they called *Divine Right,* and which, in imitation of the Pope, who affects to be spiritual and temporal, and in contradiction to the Founder of the Christian religion, twisted itself afterwards into an idol of another shape, called *Church and State.* The key of St. Peter and the key of the Treasury.

When I contemplate the natural dignity of man; when I feel (for Nature has not been kind enough to me to blunt my feelings) for the honor and happiness of its character, I become irritated at the attempt to govern mankind by force and fraud, as if they were all knaves and fools, and can scarcely avoid disgust at those who are thus imposed upon.

We have now to review the Governments which arise out of society, in contradistinction to those which arose out of superstition and conquest.

It has been thought a considerable advance toward establishing the principles of freedom, to say, that Government is a compact between those who govern and those who are governed: but this cannot be true, because it is putting the effect before the cause; for as a man must have existed before Governments existed, there necessarily was a time when Goverments did not exist, and consequently there could originally exist no Governments to form such a compact with.

The fact therefore must be, that the *individuals themselves,* each in his own personal and sovereign right, *entered into a compact with each other* to produce a Government: and this is the only mode in which Governments have a right to arise, and the only principle on which they have a right to exist.*

REASON and Ignorance, the opposites of each other, influence the great bulk of mankind. If either of these can be rendered sufficiently extensive in a country, the machinery of Government goes easily on. Reason obeys itself; and Ignorance submits to whatever is dictated to it.

The two modes of Government which prevail in the world, are, *First,* Government by election and representation:

Secondly, Government by hereditary succession.

The former is generally known by the name of republic; the latter by that of monarchy and aristocracy.

Those two distinct and opposite forms, erect themselves on the two distinct and opposite bases of Reason and Ignorance.

As the exercise of Government requires talents and abilities, and as talents and abilities cannot have hereditary descent, it is evident that hereditary succession requires a belief from man, to which his reason cannot subscribe, and which can only be established upon his ignorance; and the more ignorant any country is, the better it is fitted for this species of Government.

On the contrary, Government in a well constituted republic, requires no belief from man beyond what his reason can give.

He sees the *rationale* of the whole system, its origin and its operation; and as it is best supported when best understood, the human faculties act with boldness, and acquire, under this form of Government, a gigantic manliness.

As, therefore, each of those forms acts on a different base, the one moving freely by the aid of reason, the other by ignorance; we have next to consider, what it is that gives motion to that species of Government which is called mixed Government, or, as it is sometimes ludicrously styled, a Government of *this, that,* and *t'other.*

The moving power of this species of Government, is of necessity, corruption. However imperfect election and representation may be in mixed Governments, they still give exercise to a greater portion of reason than is convenient to the hereditary part; and therefore it becomes necessary to buy the reason up.

A mixed Government is an imperfect everything, cementing and soldering the discordant parts together by corruption, to act as a whole. Mr. Burke appears highly disgusted, that France, since she had resolved on a revolution, did not adopt what he calls, *"A British Constitution,"* and the regretful manner in which he expresses himself on this occasion, implies a suspicion, that the British Constitution needed something to keep its defects in countenance.

In mixed Governments there is no responsibility: the parts cover each other till responsibility is lost; and the corruption which moves the machine, contrives at the same time its own escape. When it is laid down as a maxim, that *a king can do no wrong,* it places him in a state of similar security with that of idiots and

---

* Pp. 45-47.

persons insane, and responsibility is out of the question with respect to himself.

It then descends upon the minister, who shelters himself under a majority in Parliament, which, by places, pensions, and corruption, he can always command; and that majority justifies itself by the same authority with which it protects the minister. In this rotary motion, responsibility is thrown off from the parts, and from the whole.

When there is a part in a Government which can do no wrong, it implies that it does nothing; and is only the machine of another power, by whose advice and direction it acts.

What is supposed to be the king in mixed Governments is the cabinet; and as the cabinet is always a part of the Parliament, and the members justifying in one character what they advise and act in another, a mixed Government becomes a continual enigma; entailing upon a country, by the quantity of corruption necessary to solder the parts, the expense of supporting all the forms of Government at once, and finally resolving itself into a Government by committee; in which the advisers, the actors, the approvers, the justifiers, the persons responsible, and the persons not responsible, are the same persons.

By this pantomimical contrivance, and change of scene and character, the parts help each other out in matters which neither of them singly would assume to act.

When money is to be obtained, the mass of variety apparently dissolves, and a profusion of parliamentary praises passes between the parts. Each admires with astonishment, the wisdom, the liberality, the disinterestedness of the other; and all of them breathe a pitying sigh at the burdens of the nation.

When men are spoken of as kings and subjects, or when Government is mentioned under the distinct or combined heads of Monarchy, Aristocracy, and Democracy, what is it that *reasoning* man is to understand by the terms? If there really existed in the world two or more distinct and separate *elements* of human power, we should then see the several origins to which those terms would descriptively apply; but as there is but one species of man, there can be but one element of human power, and that element is man himself. Monarchy, Aristocracy, and Democracy, are but creatures of imagination; and a thousand such may be contrived, as well as three.

From the Revolutions of America and France, and the symptoms that have appeared in other countries, it is evident that the opinion of the world is changed with respect to systems of Government, and that Revolutions are not within the compass of political calculations.

The progress of time and circumstances, which men assign to the accomplishment of great changes, is too mechanical to measure the force of the mind, and the rapidity of reflection, by which revolutions are generated. All the old Governments have received a shock from those that already appear, and which were once more improbable, and are a greater subject of wonder, than a general Revolution in Europe would be now. . . .

When we survey the wretched condition of man under the monarchical and hereditary systems of Government, dragged from his home by one power, or driven by another, and impoverished by taxes more than by enemies, it becomes evident that those systems are bad, and that a general Revolution in the principle and construction of Governments is necessary.

What is Government more than the management of the affairs of a Nation?

It is not, and from its nature cannot be, the property of any particular man or family, but of the whole community, at whose expense it is supported; and though by force or contrivance it has been usurped into an inheritance, the usurpation cannot alter the right of things. Sovereignty, as a matter of right, appertains to the Nation only, and not to any individual, and a Nation has at all times an inherent indefeasible right to abolish any form of Government it finds inconvenient, and establish such as accords with its interest, disposition, and happiness.

What were formerly called Revolutions, were little more than a change of persons, or an alteration of local circumstances. They rose and fell like things of course, and had nothing in their existence or their fate that could influence beyond the spot that produced them. But what we now see in the world, from the Revolutions of America and France, is a renovation of the natural order of things, a system of principles as universal as truth and the existence of man, and combining moral with political happiness and national prosperity.

"I. *Men are born and always continue free and equal in respect to their rights. Civil distinctions, therefore, can be founded only on public utility.*

"II. *The end of all political associations is the preservation of the natural and imprescriptible rights of man; and these rights are liberty, property, security, and resistance of oppression.*

"III. *The Nation is essentially the source of all Sovereignty; nor can any individual or any body of men, be entitled to any authority which is not expressly derived from it.*"

In these principles, there is nothing to throw a Nation into confusion by inflaming ambition. They are calculated to call forth wisdom and abilities, and to exercise them for the public good, and not for the emolument or aggrandizement of particular descriptions of men or families. Monarchial sovereignty, the enemy of mankind, and the source of misery, is abolished; and sovereignty itself is restored to its natural and original place, the Nation. Were this the case throughout Europe, the cause of wars would be taken away.*

It [also] shows, that man, were he not corrupted by Governments, is naturally the friend of man, and that human nature is not of itself vicious. That spirit of jealousy and ferocity, which the Governments of the two countries inspired, and which they rendered subservient to the purpose of taxation, is now yielding to the dictates of reason, interest and humanity.†

IV.
The Wisdom Of Representative Government

Having thus glanced at a few of the defects of the old, or hereditary system of Government, let us compare it with the new, or representative system.

The representative system takes society and civilization for its basis; nature, reason, and experience for its guide.

Experience, in all ages, and in all countries, has demonstrated, that it is impossible to control Nature in her distribution of mental powers. She gives them as she pleases. Whatever is the rule by which she, apparently to us, scatters them among

---

* Pp. 130-35.
† Pp. 210-11.

mankind, that rule remains a secret to man. It would be as ridiculous to attempt to fix the hereditaryship of human beauty, as of wisdom. Whatever wisdom constituently is, it is like a seedless plant; it may be reared when it appears, but it cannot be voluntarily produced. There is always a sufficiency somewhere in the general mass of society for all purposes; but with respect to the parts of society, it is continually changing its place. It rises in one to-day, in another to-morrow, and has most probably visited in rotation every family of the earth, and again withdrawn.

As this is the order of nature, the order of Government must necessarily follow it, or Government will, as we see it does, degenerate into ignorance. The hereditary system, therefore, is as repugnant to human wisdom, as to human rights, and is as absurd, as it is unjust.

As the republic of letters brings forward the best literary productions, by giving to genius a fair and universal chance; so the representative system of Government is calculated to produce the wisest laws, by collecting wisdom where it can be found. I smile to myself when I contemplate the ridiculous insignificance into which literature and all the sciences would sink, were they made hereditary; and I carry the same idea into Governments. An hereditary governor is as inconsistent as an hereditary author. I know not whether Homer or Euclid had sons; but I will venture an opinion, that if they had, and had left their works unfinished, those sons could not have completed them.

Do we need a stronger evidence of the absurdity of hereditary Government, than is seen in the descendants of those men, in any line of life, who once were famous? Is there scarcely an instance in which there is not a total reverse of character? It appears as if the tide of mental faculties flowed as far as it could in certain channels, and then forsook its course, and arose in others. How irrational then is the hereditary system which establishes channels of power, in company with which wisdom refuses to flow! By continuing this absurdity, man is perpetually in contradiction with himself; he accepts, for a king, or a chief magistrate, or a legislator, a person whom he would not elect for a constable.

It appears to general observation, that revolutions create genius and talents; but those events do no more than bring them forward. There is existing in man, a mass of sense lying in a dormant state, and which, unless something excites it to action, will descend with him, in that condition, to the grave. As it is to the advantage of society that the whole of its faculties should be employed, the construction of Government ought to be such as to bring forward, by a quiet and regular operation, all that extent of capacity which never fails to appear in revolutions.

This cannot take place in the insipid state of hereditary Government, not only because it prevents, but because it operates to benumb. When the mind of a nation is bowed down by any political superstition in its Government, such as hereditary succession is, it loses a considerable portion of its powers on all other subjects and objects. Hereditary succession requires the same obedience to ignorance, as to wisdom; and when once the mind can bring itself to pay this indiscriminate reverence, it descends below the stature of mental manhood. It is fit to be great only in little things. It acts a treachery upon itself, and suffocates the sensations that urge to detection. . . . Had the system of representation been then understood, as it now is, there is no reason to believe that those forms of Government, now called monarchical and aristocratical, would ever have taken place. It was the want of some method to consolidate the parts of society, after it became too populous, and too extensive for the simple democratical form, and also the lax and solitary condition of shepherds and herdsmen in other parts of the world, that afforded opportunities to those unnatural modes of Government to begin.*

As to the aristocratical form, it has the same vices and defects with the monarchical, except that the chance of abilities is better from the proportion of numbers, but there is still no security for the right use and application of them.

Referring, then, to the original simple Democracy, it affords the true data from which Government on a large scale can begin. It is incapable of extension, not from its principle, but from the inconvenience of its form; and Monarchy and Aristocracy, from their incapacity. Retaining, then, Democracy as the ground, and rejecting the corrupt systems of Monarchy and Aristocracy, the representative system naturally presents itself; remedying at once the defects of the simple Democracy as to form, and the incapacity of the other two with respect to knowledge.

Simple Democracy was society governing itself without the aid of secondary means. By ingrafting representation upon Democracy, we arrive at a system of Government capable of embracing and confederating all the various interests and every extent of territory and population; and that also with advantages as much superior to hereditary Government, as the republic of letters is to hereditary literature.

It is on this system that the American Government is founded. It is representation ingrafted upon Democracy. It has fixed the form by a scale parallel in all cases to the extent of the principle. What Athens was in miniature, America will be in magnitude. The one was the wonder of the ancient world; the other is becoming the admiration and model of the present. It is the easiest of all the forms of Government to be understood, and the most eligible in practise; and excludes at once the ignorance and insecurity of the hereditary mode, and the inconvenience of the simple Democracy.

It is impossible to conceive a system of Government capable of acting over such an extent of territory, and such a circle of interests, as is immediately produced by the operation of representation. France, great and popular as it is, is but a spot in the capaciousness of the system. It adapts itself to all possible cases. It is preferable to simple Democracy even in small territories. Athens, by representation, would have outrivalled her own Democracy.

That which is called Government, or rather that which we ought to conceive Government to be, is no more than some common center, in which all the parts of society unite. This cannot be accomplished by any method so conducive to the various interest of the community, as by the representative system. It concentrates the knowledge necessary to the interests of the parts, and of the whole. It places Government in a state of constant maturity. It is, as has been already observed, never young, never old. It is subject neither to nonage, nor dotage. It is never in the cradle, nor on crutches. It admits not of a separation between knowledge and power, and is superior, as Government always ought to be, to all the accidents of individual man, and is therefore superior to what is called Monarchy.

A Nation is not a body, the figure of which is to be represented by the human body; but is like a body contained within a circle, having a common center, in which every radius meets; and that center is formed by representation. To connect

* Pp. 170–73.

representation with what is called Monarchy is eccentric Government. Representation is of itself the delegated Monarchy of a Nation, and cannot debase itself by dividing it with another.*

In the representative system, the reason for everything must publicly appear. Every man is a proprietor in Government and considers it a necessary part of his business to understand. It concerns his interest, because it affects his property. He examines the cost, and compares it with the advantages; and above all, he does not adopt the slavish custom of following what in other Governments are called LEADERS.

It can only be by blinding the understanding of man, and making him believe that Government is some wonderful mysterious thing, that excessive revenues are obtained. Monarchy is well calculated to ensure this end. It is the popery of Government; a thing kept up to amuse the ignorant, and quiet them into paying taxes.

The Government of a free country, properly speaking, is not in the persons, but in the laws. The enacting of those requires no great expense; and when they are administered, the whole of civil government is performed—the rest is all court contrivance.†

V.
Conclusion: The French Constitution, Liberty And The Rights Of Man

The representatives of the people of France, *formed into a* National Assembly, considering that ignorance, neglect, or contempt of human rights, are the sole causes of public misfortunes and corruptions of Government, have resolved to set forth in a solemn declaration, these natural, imprescriptible, and unalienable rights: that this declaration, being constantly present to the minds of the members of the body social, they may be ever kept attentive to their rights and their duties: that the acts of the legislative and executive powers of Government, being capable of being every moment compared with the end of political institutions, may be more respected: and also, that the future claims of the citizens, being directed by simple and incontestible principles, may always tend to the maintenance of the Constitution, and the general happiness.

"For these reasons the National Assembly doth recognize and declare, in the presence of the Supreme Being, and with the hope of His blessing and favor, the following *sacred* rights of men and of citizens:

"I. Men are born, and always continue, free, and equal in respect of their rights. Civil distinctions, therefore, can be founded only on public utility.

"II. The end of all political associations, is, the preservation of the natural and imprescriptible rights of man; and these rights are liberty, property, security, and resistance of oppression.

---

* Pp. 176-78.
† Pp. 181-82.

"III. The nation is essentially the source of all sovereignty; nor can an individual, or any body of men, be entitled to any authority which is not expressly derived from it.

"IV. Political liberty consists in the power of doing whatever does not injure another. The exercise of the natural rights of every man has no other limits than those which are necessary to secure to every *other* man the free exercise of the same rights; and these limits are determinable only by the law.

"V. The law ought to prohibit only actions hurtful to society. What is not prohibited by the law, should not be hindered; nor should any one be compelled to that which the law does not require.

"VI. The law is an expression of the will of the community. All citizens have a right to concur, either personally, or by their representatives, in its formation. It should be the same to all, whether it protects or punishes; and all being equal in its sight, are equally eligible to all honors, places, and employments, according to their different abilities, without any other distinction than that created by their virtues and talents.

"VII. No man should be accused, arrested, or held in confinement, except in cases determined by the law, and according to the forms which it has prescribed. All who promote, solicit, execute, or cause to be executed, arbitrary orders, ought to be punished; and every citizen called upon or apprehended by virtue of the law, ought immediately to obey, and renders himself culpable by resistance.

"VIII. The law ought to impose no other penalties but such as are absolutely and evidently necessary: and no one ought to be punished, but in virtue of a law promulgated before the offense, and legally applied.

"IX. Every man being presumed innocent till he has been convicted, whenever his detention becomes indispensable, all rigor to him, more than is necessary to secure his person, ought to be provided against by the law.

"X. No man ought to be molested on account of his opinions, not even on account of his *religious* opinions, provided his avowal of them does not disturb the public order established by the law.

"XI. The unrestrained communication of thoughts and opinions being one of the most precious rights of man, every citizen may speak, write, and publish freely, provided he is responsible for the abuse of this liberty in cases determined by the law.

"XII. A public force being necessary to give security to the rights of men and of citizens, that force is instituted for the benefit of the community, and not for the particular benefit of the persons with whom it is intrusted.

"XIII. A common contribution being necessary for the support of the public force, and for defraying the other expenses of Government, it ought to be divided equally among the members of the community, according to their abilities.

"XIV. Every citizen has a right, either by himself or his representative, to a free voice in determining the necessity of public contributions, the appropriation of them, and their amount, mode of assessment, and duration.

"XV. Every community has a right to demand of all its agents, an account of their conduct.

"XVI. Every community in which a separation of powers and a security of rights is not provided for, wants a constitution.

XVII. The rights to property being inviolable and sacred, no one ought to be deprived of it, except in cases of evident public necessity, legally ascertained, and on condition of a previous just indemnity."

The three first articles are the basis of liberty, as well individual as national; nor can any country be called free, whose Government does not take its beginning from the principles they contain, and continue to preserve them pure; and the whole of the Declaration of Rights is of more value to the world, and will do more good, than all the laws and statutes that have yet been promulgated.

In the declaratory exordium which prefaces the Declaration of Rights, we see the solemn and majestic spectacle of a Nation opening its commission, under the auspices of its Creator, to establish a Government; a scene so new, and so transcendently unequalled by any thing in the European world, that the name of a revolution is diminutive of its character, and it rises into a REGENERATION OF MAN. What are the present Governments of Europe, but a scene of iniquity and oppression? What is that of England; Do not its own inhabitants say, It is a market where every man has his price, and where corruption is common traffic, at the expense of a deluded people? No wonder, then, that the French Revolution is traduced. Had it confined itself merely to the destruction of flagrant despotism, perhaps Mr. Burke and some others had been silent. Their cry now is, "It is gone too far": that is, it has gone too far for them. It stares corruption in the face, and the venal tribe are all alarmed. Their fear discovers itself in their outrage, and they are but publishing the groans of a wounded vice. But from such opposition, the French Revolution, instead of suffering, receives an homage. The more it is struck, the more sparks it will emit; and the fear is, it will not be struck enough. It has nothing to dread from attacks: Truth has given it an establishment; and Time will record it with a name as lasting as his own.

Having now traced the progress of the French Revolution through most of its principal stages . . . and its establishment by the Declaration of Rights, I will close the subject with the energetic apostrophe of M. de Lafayette—MAY THIS GREAT MONUMENT, RAISED TO LIBERTY, SERVE AS A LESSON TO THE OPPRESSOR, AND AN EXAMPLE TO THE OPPRESSED!*

---

* Pp. 94-98.

Part 3

RESPONSE TO INDUSTRIALIZATION

19th Century

LIBERALISM

John Stuart Mill

In the nineteenth century, John Stuart Mill's (1806–73) liberal doctrines attempted to come to grips with the overpowering social, economic, and political changes which were threatening man's freedom and liberty. Mill's perceptions of man and society were largely shaped by his father, James Mill, who trained his son as a Utilitarian—"the greatest good for the greatest number"—and rationalist. Mill was also influenced by his wife who introduced him to romanticism which stressed transcendental and emotional human qualities. In his popular essay, "On Liberty" (1859) Mill blended Utilitarian and romantic strains to create a classic analysis of the dilemma of authority versus liberty.

Mill viewed society as a collective tyranny which repressed the individual. He argued that the individual had to be protected from the tyranny of the majority and also "against the tendency of society to impose, by other means than civil penalties, its own ideas and practices as rules of conduct on those who dissent from them. . . ." While citing the duty of government to correct societal inequities, liberalism cautioned against the dangers of excessive authority. Mill concluded that the state should be the framework in which each person fully developed his individuality. These principles diminished, but did not dispel the role of the state. He believed that society had a right to interfere with an individual when his behavior was harmful to another person, but that right of interference had to be limited by civil liberties which protected the individual. The result was a continuing struggle between liberty and authority which Mill saw as "the most conspicuous feature of history."

I.
The Struggle Between Liberty And Authority; And, The Tyranny Of The Majority

The subject of this essay is not the so-called "liberty of the will," so unfortunately opposed to the misnamed doctrine of philosophical necessity; but civil, or social liberty: the nature and limits of the power which can be legitimately exercised by society over the individual. A question seldom stated, and hardly ever discussed in general terms, but which profoundly influences the practical controversies of the age by its latent presence, and is likely soon to make itself recognized as the vital question of the future. It is so far from being new that, in a certain sense, it has divided mankind almost from the remotest ages; but in the stage of progress into which the more civilized portions of the species have now entered, it presents itself under new conditions and requires a different and more fundamental treatment.

The struggle between liberty and authority is the most conspicuous feature in the portions of history with which we are earliest familiar, particularly in that of Greece, Rome, and England. But in old times this contest was between subjects, or some classes of subjects, and the government. By liberty was meant protection against the tyranny of the political rulers. The rulers were conceived (except in some of the popular governments of Greece) as in a necessarily antagonistic position to the people whom they ruled. They consisted of a governing One, or a governing tribe or caste, who derived their authority from inheritance or conquest, who, at all events, did not hold it at the pleasure of the governed, and whose supremacy men did not venture, perhaps did not desire, to contest, whatever precautions might be taken against its oppressive exercise. Their power was regarded as necessary, but also as highly dangerous; as a weapon which they would attempt to use against their subjects, no less than against external enemies. To prevent the weaker members of the community from being preyed upon by innumerable vultures, it was needful that there should be an animal of prey stronger than the rest, commissioned to keep them down. But as the king of the vultures would be no less bent upon preying on the flock than any of the minor harpies, it was indispensable to be in a perpetual attitude of defense against his beak and claws. The aim, therefore, of patriots was to set limits to the power which the ruler should be suffered to exercise over the community; and this limitation was what they meant by liberty. It was attempted in two ways. First, by obtaining a recognition of certain immunities, called political liberties or rights, which it was to be regarded as a breach of duty in the ruler to infringe, and which if he did infringe, specific resistance or general rebellion was held to be justifiable. A second, and generally a later, expedient was the establishment of constitutional checks by which the consent of the community, or of a body of some sort, supposed to represent its interests, was made a necessary condition to some of the more important acts of the governing power. To the first of these modes of limitation, the ruling power, in most European countries, was compelled, more or less, to submit. It was not so with the second; and, to attain this, or, when already in some degree possessed, to attain it more

Reprinted from John Stuart Mill, *On Liberty* (Boston: Ticknor and Fields, 1863), pp. 7-15, 22-24, 27-29, 31-36, 101-13, 121-25, 130-32, 144-61, 223.

completely, became everywhere the principal object of the lovers of liberty. And so long as mankind were content to combat one enemy by another, and to be ruled by a master on condition of being guaranteed more or less efficaciously against his tyranny, they did not carry their aspirations beyond this point.

A time, however, came, in the progress of human affairs, when men ceased to think it a necessity of nature that their governors should be an independent power opposed in interest to themselves. It appeared to them much better that the various magistrates of the state should be their tenants or delegates, revocable at their pleasure. In that way alone, it seemed, could they have complete security that the powers of government would never be abused to their disadvantage. By degrees this new demand for elective and temporary rulers became the prominent object of the exertions of the popular party wherever any such party existed, and superseded, to a considerable extent, the previous efforts to limit the power of rulers. As the struggle proceeded for making the ruling power emanate from the periodical choice of the ruled, some persons began to think that too much importance had been attached to the limitation of the power itself. *That* (it might seem) was a resource against rulers whose interests were habitually opposed to those of the people. What was now wanted was that the rulers should be identified with the people, that their interest and will should be the interest and will of the Nation. The Nation did not need to be protected against its own will. There was no fear of its tyrannizing over itself. Let the rulers be effectually responsible to it, promptly removable by it, and it could afford to trust them with power of which it could itself dictate the use to be made. Their power was but the Nation's own power, concentrated and in a form convenient for exercise. This mode of thought, or rather perhaps of feeling, was common among the last generation of European liberalism, in the Continental section of which it still apparently predominates. Those who admit any limit to what a government may do, except in the case of such governments as they think ought not to exist, stand out as brilliant exceptions among the political thinkers of the Continent. A similar tone of sentiment might by this time have been prevalent in our own country if the circumstances which for a time encouraged it had continued unaltered.

But, in political and philosophical theories as well as in persons, success discloses faults and infirmities which failure might have concealed from observation. The notion that the people have no need to limit their power over themselves might seem axiomatic, when popular government was a thing only dreamed about, or read of as having existed at some distant period of the past. Neither was that notion necessarily disturbed by such temporary aberrations as those of the French Revolution, the worst of which were the work of a usurping few, and which, in any case, belonged, not to the permanent working of popular institutions, but to a sudden and convulsive outbreak against monarchical and aristocratic despotism. In time, however, a democratic republic came to occupy a large portion of the earth's surface and made itself felt as one of the most powerful members of the community of nations; and elective and responsible government became subject to the observations and criticisms which wait upon a great existing fact. It was now perceived that such phrases as "self-government," and "the power of the people over themselves," do not express the true state of the case. The "people" who exercise the power are not always the same people with those over whom it is exercised; and the "self-government" spoken of is not the government of each by himself, but of each by all the rest. The will of the people, moreover, practically means the will of the most numerous or the most active *part* of the people—the majority, or those who succeed in making themselves accepted as the majority; the people, consequently, *may* desire to oppress a part of their number, and precautions are as much needed against this as against any other abuse of power. The limitation, therefore, of the power of government over individuals loses none of its importance when the holders of power are regularly accountable to the community, that is, to the strongest party therein. This view of things, recommending itself equally to the intelligence of thinkers and to the inclination of those important classes in European society to whose real or supposed interests democracy is adverse, has had no difficulty in establishing itself; and in political speculations "the tyranny of the majority" is now generally included among the evils against which society requires to be on its guard.

Like other tyrannies, the tyranny of the majority was at first, and is still vulgarly, held in dread, chiefly as operating through the acts of the public authorities. But reflecting persons perceived that when society is itself the tyrant—society collectively over the separate individuals who compose it—its means of tyrannizing are not restricted to the acts which it may do by the hands of its political functionaries. Society can and does execute its own mandates; and if it issues wrong mandates instead of right, or any mandates at all in things with which it ought not to meddle, it practices a social tyranny more formidable than many kinds of political oppression, since, though not usually upheld by such extreme penalties, it leaves fewer means of escape, penetrating much more deeply into the details of life, and enslaving the soul itself. Protection, therefore, against the tyranny of the magistrate is not enough; there needs protection also against the tyranny of the prevailing opinion and feeling, against the tendency of society to impose, by other means than civil penalties, its own ideas and practices as rules of conduct on those who dissent from them; to fetter the development and, if possible, prevent the formation of any individuality not in harmony with its ways, and compel all characters to fashion themselves upon the model of its own. There is a limit to the legitimate interference of collective opinion with individual independence; and to find that limit, and maintain it against encroachment, is as indispensable to a good condition of human affairs as protection against political despotism.

But though this proposition is not likely to be contested in general terms, the practical question where to place the limit—how to make the fitting adjustment between individual independence and social control—is a subject on which nearly everything remains to be done.*

II.
The Nature Of Liberty

The object of this essay is to assert one very simple principle, as entitled to govern absolutely the dealings of society with the individual in the way of compulsion

* Pp. 7-15.

and control, whether the means used be physical force in the form of legal penalties or the moral coercion of public opinion. That principle is that the sole end for which mankind are warranted, individually or collectively, in interfering with the liberty of action of any of their number is self-protection. That the only purpose for which power can be rightfully exercised over any member of a civilized community, against his will, is to prevent harm to others. His own good, either physical or moral, is not a sufficient warrant. He cannot rightfully be compelled to do or forbear because it will be better for him to do so, because it will make him happier, because, in the opinions of others, to do so would be wise or even right. There are good reasons for remonstrating with him, or reasoning with him, or persuading him, or entreating him, but not for compelling him or visiting him with any evil in case he do otherwise. To justify that, the conduct from which it is desired to deter him must be calculated to produce evil to someone else. The only part of the conduct of anyone for which he is amenable to society is that which concerns others. In the part which merely concerns himself, his independence is, of right, absolute. Over himself, over his own body and mind, the individual is sovereign.

It is, perhaps, hardly necessary to say that this doctrine is meant to apply only to human beings in the maturity of their faculties. We are not speaking of children or of young persons below the age which the law may fix as that of manhood or womanhood. Those who are still in a state to require being taken care of by others must be protected against their own actions as well as against external injury.*

. . . This, then, is the appropriate region of human liberty. It comprises, first, the inward domain of consciousness, demanding liberty of conscience in the most comprehensive sense, liberty of thought and feeling, absolute freedom of opinion and sentiment on all subjects, practical or speculative, scientific, moral, or theological. The liberty of expressing and publishing opinions may seem to fall under a different principle, since it belongs to that part of the conduct of an individual which concerns other people, but, being almost of as much importance as the liberty of thought itself and resting in great part on the same reasons, is practically inseparable from it. Secondly, the principle requires liberty of tastes and pursuits, of framing the plan of our life to suit our own character, of doing as we like, subject to such consequences as may follow, without impediment from our fellow creatures, so long as what we do does not harm them, even though they should think our conduct foolish, perverse, or wrong. Thirdly, from this liberty of each individual follows the liberty, within the same limits, of combination among individuals; freedom to unite for any purpose not involving harm to others: the persons combining being supposed to be of full age and not forced or deceived.

No society in which these liberties are not, on the whole, respected is free, whatever may be its form of government; and none is completely free in which they do not exist absolute and unqualified. The only freedom which deserves the name is that of pursuing our own good in our own way, so long as we do not attempt to deprive others of theirs or impede their efforts to obtain it. Each is the proper guardian of his own health, whether bodily *or* mental and spiritual. Mankind are greater gainers by suffering each other to live as seems good to themselves than by compelling each to live as seems good to the rest.†

---

* Pp. 22-24.

† Pp. 27-29.

It will be convenient for the argument if, instead of at once entering upon the general thesis, we confine ourselves in the first instance to a single branch of it on which the principle here stated is, if not fully, yet to a certain point, recognized by the current opinions. This one branch is the Liberty of Thought, from which it is impossible to separate the cognate liberty of speaking and of writing.*

III.
"The Liberty Of Thought And Discussion"

The time, it is to be hoped, is gone by when any defense would be necessary of the "liberty of the press" as one of the securities against corrupt or tyrannical government. No argument, we may suppose, can now be needed against permitting a legislature or an executive, not identified in interest with the people, to prescribe opinions to them and determine what doctrines or what arguments they shall be allowed to hear. This aspect of the question, besides, has been so often and so triumphantly enforced by preceding writers that it needs not be specially insisted on in this place. Though the law of England, on the subject of the press, is as servile to this day as it was in the time of the Tudors, there is little danger of its being actually put in force against political discussion except during some temporary panic when fear of insurrection drives ministers and judges from their propriety; and, speaking generally, it is not, in constitutional countries, to be apprehended that the government, whether completely responsible to the people or not, will often attempt to control the expression of opinion, except when in doing so it makes itself the organ of the general intolerance of the public. Let us suppose, therefore, that the government is entirely at one with the people, and never thinks of exerting any power of coercion unless in agreement with what it conceives to be their voice. But I deny the right of the people to exercise such coercion, either by themselves or by their government. The power itself is illegitimate. The best government has no more title to it than the worst. It is as noxious, or more noxious, when exerted in accordance with public opinion than when in opposition to it. If all mankind minus one were of one opinion, mankind would be no more justified in silencing that one person than he, if he had the power, would be justified in silencing mankind. Were an opinion a personal possession of no value except to the owner, if to be obstructed in the enjoyment of it were simply a private injury, it would make some difference whether the injury was inflicted only on a few persons or on many. But the peculiar evil of silencing the expression of an opinion is that it is robbing the human race, posterity as well as the existing generation—those who dissent from the opinion, still more than those who hold it. If the opinion is right, they are deprived of the opportunity of exchanging error for truth; if wrong, they lose, what is almost as great a benefit, the clearer perception and livelier impression of truth produced by its collision with error.†

* Pp. 31-32.

† Pp. 33-36.

We have [to] recognize the necessity to the mental well-being of mankind (on which all their other well-being depends) of freedom of opinion, and freedom of the expression of opinion, on four distinct grounds, which we will now briefly summarize:

First, if any opinion is compelled to silence, that opinion may, for aught we can certainly know, be true. To deny this is to assume our own infallibility.

Secondly, though the silenced opinion be an error, it may, and very commonly does, contain a portion of truth; and since the general or prevailing opinion on any subject is rarely or never the whole truth, it is only by the collision of adverse opinions that the remainder of the truth has any chance of being supplied.

Thirdly, even if the received opinion be not only true, but the whole truth; unless it is suffered to be, and actually is, vigorously and earnestly contested, it will, by most of those who receive it, be held in the manner of a prejudice, with little comprehension or feeling of its rational grounds. And not only this, but, fourthly, the meaning of the doctrine itself will be in danger of being lost or enfeebled, and deprived of its vital effect on the character and conduct: the dogma becoming a mere formal profession, inefficacious for good, but cumbering the ground and preventing the growth of any real and heartfelt conviction from reason or personal experience.

Before quitting the subject of freedom of opinion, it is fit to take some notice of those who say that the free expression of all opinions should be permitted on condition that the manner be temperate, and do not pass the bounds of fair discussion. Much might be said on the impossibility of fixing where these supposed bounds are to be placed; for if the test be offense to those whose opinions are attacked, I think experience testifies that this offense is given whenever the attack is telling and powerful, and that every opponent who pushes them hard, and whom they find it difficult to answer, appears to them, if he shows any strong feeling on the subject, an intemperate opponent. But this, though an important consideration in a practical point of view, merges in a more fundamental objection. Undoubtedly, the manner of asserting an opinion, even though it be a true one, may be very objectionable and may justly incur severe censure. But the principal offenses of the kind are such as it is mostly impossible, unless by accidental self-betrayal, to bring home to conviction. The gravest of them is, to argue sophistically, to suppress facts or arguments, to misstate the elements of the case, or misrepresent the opposite opinion. But all this, even to the most aggravated degree, is so continually done in perfect good faith by persons who are not considered, and in many other respects may not deserve to be considered, ignorant or incompetent, that it is rarely possible, on adequate grounds, conscientiously to stamp the misrepresentation as morally culpable, and still less could law presume to interfere with this kind of controversial misconduct. With regard to what is commonly meant by intemperate discussion, namely invective, sarcasm, personality, and the like, the denunciation of these weapons would deserve more sympathy if it were ever proposed to interdict them equally to both sides; but it is only desired to restrain the employment of them against the prevailing opinion; against the unprevailing they may not only be used without general disapproval, but will be likely to obtain for him who uses them the praise of honest zeal and righteous indignation. Yet whatever mischief arises from their use is greatest when they are employed against the comparatively defenseless; and whatever unfair advantage can be derived by any opinion from this mode of asserting it accrues almost exclusively to received opinions. The worst offense of this kind which can be committed by a polemic is to stigmatize those who hold the contrary opinion as bad and immoral men. To calumny of this sort, those who hold any unpopular opinion are peculiarly exposed, because they are in general few and uninfluential, and nobody but themselves feels much interested in seeing justice done them; but this weapon is, from the nature of the case, denied to those who attack a prevailing opinion: they can neither use it with safety to themselves, nor, if they could, would it do anything but recoil on their own cause. In general, opinions contrary to those commonly received can only obtain a hearing by studied moderation of language and the most cautious avoidance of unnecessary offense, from which they hardly ever deviate even in a slight degree without losing ground, while unmeasured vituperation employed on the side of the prevailing opinion really does deter people from professing contrary opinions and from listening to those who profess them. For the interest, therefore, of truth and justice it is far more important to restrain this employment of vituperative language than the other; and, for example, if it were necessary to choose, there would be much more need to discourage offensive attacks on infidelity than on religion. It is, however, obvious that law and authority have no business with restraining either, while opinion ought, in every instance, to determine its verdict by the circumstances of the individual case—condemning everyone, on whichever side of the argument he places himself, in whose mode of advocacy either want of candor, or malignity, bigotry, or intolerance of feeling manifest themselves; but not inferring these vices from the side which a person takes, though it be the contrary side of the question to our own; and giving merited honor to everyone, whatever opinion he may hold, who has calmness to see and honesty to state what his opponents and their opinions really are, exaggerating nothing to their discredit, keeping nothing back which tells, or can be supposed to tell, in their favor. This is the real morality of public discussion; and if often violated, I am happy to think that there are many controversialists who to a great extent observe it, and a still greater number who conscientiously strive towards it.*

IV.
The Liberty Of An Individual To Act Upon His Own Opinions

Such being the reasons which make it imperative that human beings should be free to form opinions and to express their opinions without reserve; and such the baneful consequences to the intellectual, and through that to the moral nature of man, unless this liberty is either conceded or asserted in spite of prohibition; let us next examine whether the same reasons do not require that men should be

* Pp. 101-6.

free to act upon their opinions—to carry these out in their lives without hindrance, either physical or moral, from their fellow men, so long as it is at their own risk and peril. This last proviso is of course indispensable. No one pretends that actions should be as free as opinions. On the contrary, even opinions lose their immunity when the circumstances in which they are expressed are such as to constitute their expression a positive instigation to some mischievous act. An opinion that corn dealers are starvers of the poor, or that private property is robbery, ought to be unmolested when simply circulated through the press, but may justly incur punishment when delivered orally to an excited mob assembled before the house of a corn dealer, or when handed about among the same mob in the form of a placard. Acts, of whatever kind, which without justifiable cause do harm to others may be, and in the more important cases absolutely require to be, controlled by the unfavorable sentiments, and, when needful, by the active interference of mankind. The liberty of the individual must be thus far limited; he must not make himself a nuisance to other people. But if he refrains from molesting others in what concerns them, and merely acts according to his own inclination and judgment in things which concern himself, the same reasons which show that opinion should be free prove also that he should be allowed, without molestation, to carry his opinions into practice at his own cost. That mankind are not infallible; that their truths, for the most part, are only half-truths; that unity of opinion, unless resulting from the fullest, and freest comparison of opposite opinions, is not desirable, and diversity not an evil, but a good, until mankind are much more capable than at present of recognizing all sides of the truth, are principles applicable to men's modes of action not less than to their opinions. As it is useful that while mankind are imperfect there should be different opinions, so it is that there should be different experiments of living; that free scope should be given to varieties of character, short of injury to others; and that the worth of different modes of life should be proved practically, when anyone thinks fit to try them. It is desirable, in short, that in things which do not primarily concern others individuality should assert itself. Where not the person's own character but the traditions or customs of other people are the rule of conduct, there is wanting one of the principal ingredients of human happiness, and quite the chief ingredient of individual and social progress.

In maintaining this priciple, the greatest difficulty to be encountered does not lie in the appreciation of means toward an acknowledged end, but in the indifference of persons in general to the end itself. It it were felt that the free development of individuality is one of the leading essentials of well-being; that it is not only a co-ordinate element with all that is designated by the terms civilization, instruction, education, culture, but is itself a necessary part and condition of all those things, there would be no danger that liberty should be undervalued, and the adjustment of the boundaries between it and social control would present no extraordinary difficulty. But the evil is that individual spontaneity is hardly recognized by the common modes of thinking as having any intrinsic worth, or deserving any regard on its own account. The majority, being satisfied with the ways of mankind as they now are (for it is they who make them what they are), cannot comprehend why those ways should not be good enough for everybody; and what is more, spontaneity forms no part of the ideal of the majority of moral and social reformers, but is rather looked on with jealousy, as a troublesome and perhaps rebellious obstruction to the general acceptance of what these reformers, in their own judgment, think would be best for mankind. . . .

No one's idea of excellence in conduct is that people should do absolutely nothing but copy one another. No one would assert that people ought not to put into their mode of life, and into the conduct of their concerns, any impress whatever of their own judgment or of their own individual character. On the other hand, it would be absurd to pretend that people ought to live as if nothing whatever had been known in the world before they came into it; as if experience had as yet done nothing toward showing that one mode of existence, or of conduct, is preferable to another. Nobody denies that people should be so taught and trained in youth as to know and benefit by the ascertained results of human experience. But it is the privilege and proper condition of a human being, arrived at the maturity of his faculties, to use and interpret experience in his own way. It is for him to find out what part of recorded experience is properly applicable to his own circumstances and character. The traditions and customs of other people are, to a certain extent, evidence of what their experience has taught *them*—presumptive evidence, and as such, have a claim to his deference: but, in the first place, their experience may be too narrow, or they may have not interpreted it rightly. Secondly, their interpretation of experience may be correct, but unsuitable to him. Customs are made for customary circumstances and customary characters; and his circumstances or his character may be uncustomary. Thirdly, though the customs be both good as customs and suitable to him, yet to conform to custom merely *as* custom does not educate or develop in him any of the qualities which are the distinctive endowment of a human being. The human faculties of perception, judgment, discriminative feeling, mental activity, and even moral preference are exercised only in making a choice. He who does anything because it is the custom makes no choice. He gains no practice either in discerning or in desiring what is best. The mental and moral, like the muscular, powers are improved only by being used. The faculties are called into no exercise by doing a thing merely because others do it, no more than by believing a thing only because others believe it. If the grounds of an opinion are not conclusive to the person's own reason, his reason cannot be strengthened, but is likely to be weakened, by his adopting it: and if the inducements to an act are not such as are consentaneous to his own feelings and character (where affection, or the rights of others, are not concerned), it is so much done toward rendering his feelings and character inert and torpid instead of active and energetic.*

It is not by wearing down into uniformity all that is individual in themselves, but by cultivating it and calling it forth, within the limits imposed by the rights and interests of others, that human beings become a noble and beautiful object of contemplation; and as the works partake the character of those who do them, by the same process human life also becomes rich, diversified, and animating, furnishing more abundant aliment to high thoughts and elevating feelings, and strengthening the tie which binds every individual to the race, by making the race infinitely better worth belonging to. In proportion to the development of his individuality, each person becomes more valuable to himself, and is, therefore, capable of being more valuable to others. There is a greater fullness of life about his own existence, and when there is more life in the units there is more in the mass which

* Pp. 107-13.

is composed of them. As much compression as is necessary to prevent the stronger specimens of human nature from encroaching on the rights of others cannot be dispensed with; but for this there is ample compensation even in the point of view of human development. The means of development which the individual loses by being prevented from gratifying his inclinations to the injury of others are chiefly obtained at the expense of the development of other people. And even to himself there is a full equivalent in the better development of the social part of his nature, rendered possible by the restraint put upon the selfish part. To be held to rigid rules of justice for the sake of others develops the feelings and capacities which have the good of others for their object. But to be restrained in things not affecting their good, by their mere displeasure, develops nothing valuable except such force of character as may unfold itself in resisting the restraint. If acquiesced in, it dulls and blunts the whole nature. To give any fair play to the nature of each, it is essential that different persons should be allowed to lead different lives. In proportion as this latitude has been exercised in any age has that age been noteworthy to posterity. Even despotism does not produce its worst effects so long as individuality exists under it; and whatever crushes individuality is despotism, by whatever name it may be called and whether it professes to be enforcing the will of God or the injunctions of men.

Having said that the individuality is the same thing with development, and that it is only the cultivation of individuality which produces, or can produce, well-developed human beings, I might here close the argument; for what more or better can be said of any condition of human affairs than that it brings human beings themselves nearer to the best thing they can be? Or what worse can be said of any obstruction to good than that it prevents this? Doubtless, however, these considerations will not suffice to convince those who most need convincing; and it is necessary further to show that these developed human beings are of some use to the undeveloped—to point out to those who do not desire liberty, and would not avail themselves of it, that they may be in some intelligible manner rewarded for allowing other people to make use of it without hindrance.

In the first place, then, I would suggest that they might possibly learn something from them. It will not be denied by anybody that originality is a valuable element in human affairs. There is always need of persons not only to discover new truths and point out when what were once truths are true no longer, but also to commence new practices and set the example of more enlightened conduct and better taste and sense in human life. This cannot well be gainsaid by anybody who does not believe that the world has already attained perfection in all its ways and practices. It is true that this benefit is not capable of being rendered by everybody alike; there are but few persons, in comparison with the whole of mankind, whose experiments, if adopted by others, would be likely to be any improvement on established practice. But these few are the salt of the earth; without them, human life would become a stagnant pool. Not only is it they who introduce good things which did not before exist; it is they who keep the life in those which already exist. If there were nothing new to be done, would human intellect cease to be necessary? Would it be a reason why those who do the old things should forget why they are done, and do them like cattle, not like human beings? There is only too great a tendency in the best beliefs and practices to degenerate into the mechanical; and unless there were a succession of persons whose ever-recurring originality prevents the grounds of those beliefs and practices from becoming merely traditional, such dead matter would not resist the smallest shock from anything really alive, and there would be no reason why civilization should not die out, as in the Byzantine Empire. Persons of genius, it is true, are, and are always likely to be, a small minority; but in order to have them, it is necessary to preserve the soil in which they grow. Genius can only breathe freely in an *atmosphere* of freedom. Persons of genius are, *ex vi termini,* more individual than any other people—less capable, consequently, of fitting themselves, without hurtful compression, into any of the small number of molds which society provides in order to save its members the trouble of forming their own character.*

I have said that it is important to give the freest scope possible to uncustomary things, in order that it may in time appear which of these are fit to be converted into customs. But independence of action and disregard of custom are not solely deserving of encouragement for the chance they afford that better modes of action, and customs more worthy of general adoption, may be struck out; nor is it only persons of decided mental superiority who have a just claim to carry on their lives in their own way. There is no reason that all human existence should be constructed on some one or some small number of patterns. If a person possesses any tolerable amount of common sense and experience, his own mode of laying out his existence is the best, not because it is the best in itself, but because it is his own mode. Human beings are not like sheep; and even sheep are not undistinguishably alike. A man cannot get a coat or a pair of boots to fit him unless they are either made to his measure or he has a whole warehouseful to choose from; and is it easier to fit him with a life than with a coat, or are human beings more like one another in their whole physical and spiritual conformation than in the shape of their feet? If it were only that people have diversities of taste, that is reason enough for not attempting to shape them all after one model. But different persons also require different conditions for their spiritual development; and can no more exist healthily in the same moral than all the variety of plants can in the same physical, atmosphere and climate. The same things which are helps to one person toward the cultivation of his higher nature are hindrances to another. The same mode of life is a healthy excitement to one, keeping all his faculties of action and enjoyment in their best order, while to another it is a distracting burden which suspends or crushes all internal life. Such are the differences among human beings in their sources of pleasure, their susceptibilities of pain, and the operation on them of different physical and moral agencies that, unless there is a corresponding diversity in their modes of life, they neither obtain their fair share of happiness, nor grow up to the mental, moral, and aesthetic stature of which their nature is capable. Why then should tolerance, as far as the public sentiment is concerned, extend only to tastes and modes of life which extort acquiescence by the multitude of their adherents? Nowhere (except in some monastic institutions) is diversity of taste entirely unrecognized; a person may, without blame, either like or dislike rowing, or smoking, or music, or athletic exercises, or chess, or cards, or study, because both those who like each of these things and those who

* Pp. 121-25.

dislike them are too numerous to be put down. But the man, and still more the woman, who can be accused either of doing "what nobody does," or of not doing "what everybody does," is the subject of as much depreciatory remark as if he or she had committed some grave moral delinquency. Persons require to possess a title, or some other badge of rank, or of the consideration of people of rank, to be able to indulge somewhat in the luxury of doing as they like without detriment to their estimation. To indulge somewhat, I repeat: for whoever allow themselves much of that indulgence incur the risk of something worse than disparaging speeches—they are in peril of a commission *de lunatico* and of having their property taken from them and given to their relations.*

V.
"The Limit To The Authority Of Society Over The Individual"

What, then, is the rightful limit to the sovereignty of the individual over himself? Where does the authority of society begin? How much of human life should be assigned to individuality, and how much to society?

Each will receive its proper share if each has that which more particularly concerns it. To individuality should belong the part of life in which it is chiefly the individual that is interested; to society, the part which chiefly interests society.

Though society is not founded on a contract, and though no good purpose is answered by inventing a contract in order to deduce social obligations from it, everyone who receives the protection of society owes a return for the benefit, and the fact of living in society renders it indispensable that each should be bound to observe a certain line of conduct toward the rest. This conduct consists, first, in not injuring the interests of one another, or rather certain interests which, either by express legal provision or by tacit understanding, ought to be considered as rights; and secondly, in each person's bearing his share (to be fixed on some equitable principle) of the labors and sacrifices incurred for defending the society or its members from injury and molestation. These conditions society is justified in enforcing at all costs to those who endeavor to withhold fulfillment. Nor is this all that society may do. The acts of an individual may be hurtful to others or wanting in due consideration for their welfare, without going to the length of violating any of their constituted rights. The offender may then be justly punished by opinion, though not by law. As soon as any part of a person's conduct affects prejudicially the interests of others, society has jurisdiction over it, and the question whether the general welfare will or will not be promoted by interfering with it becomes open to discussion. But there is no room for entertaining any such question when a person's conduct affects the interests of no persons besides himself, or

* Pp. 130-32.

needs not affect them unless they like (all the persons concerned being of full age and the ordinary amount of understanding). In all such cases, there should be perfect freedom, legal and social, to do the action and stand the consequences.

It would be a great misunderstanding of this doctrine to suppose that it is one of selfish indifference which pretends that human beings have no business with each other's conduct in life, and that they should not concern themselves about the well-doing or well-being of one another, unless their own interest is involved. Instead of any diminution, there is need of a great increase of disinterested exertion to promote the good of others. But disinterested benevolence can find other instruments to persuade people to their good than whips and scourges, either of the literal or the metaphorical sort. I am the last person to undervalue the self-regarding virtues; they are only second in importance, if even second, to the social. It is equally the business of education to cultivate both. But even education works by conviction and persuasion as well as by compulsion, and it is by the former only that, when the period of education is passed, the self-regarding virtues should be inculcated. Human beings owe to each other help to distinguish the better from the worse, and encouragement to choose the former and avoid the latter. They should be forever stimulating each other to increased exercise of their higher faculties and increased direction of their feelings and aims toward wise instead of foolish, elevating instead of degrading, objects and contemplations. But neither one person, nor any number of persons, is warranted in saying to another human creature of ripe years that he shall not do with his life for his own benefit what he chooses to do with it. He is the person most interested in his own well-being: the interest which any other person, except in cases of strong personal attachment, can have in it is trifling compared with that which he himself has; the interest which society has in him individually (except as to his conduct to others) is fractional and altogether indirect, while with respect to his own feelings and circumstances the most ordinary man or woman has means of knowledge immeasurably surpassing those that can be possessed by anyone else. The interference of society to overrule his judgment and purposes in what only regards himself must be grounded on general presumptions which may be altogether wrong and, even if right, are as likely as not to be misapplied to individual cases, by persons no better acquainted with the circumstances of such cases than those are who look at them merely from without. In this department, therefore, of human affairs, individuality has its proper field of action. In the conduct of human beings toward one another it is necessary that general rules should for the most part be observed in order that people may know what they have to expect; but in each person's own concerns his individual spontaneity is entitled to free exercise. Considerations to aid his judgment, exhortations to strengthen his will may be offered to him, even obtruded on him, by others; but he himself is the final judge. All errors which he is likely to commit against advice and warning are far outweighed by the evil of allowing others to constrain him to what they deem his good. . . .

We have a right, also, in various ways, to act upon our unfavorable opinion of anyone, not to the oppression of his individuality, but in the exercise of ours. We are not bound, for example, to seek his society; we have a right to avoid it (though not to parade the avoidance), for we have a right to choose the society most acceptable to us. We have a right, and it may be our duty, to caution others against him if we think his example or conversation likely to have a pernicious effect on those with whom he associates. We may give others a preference over him in optional good offices, except those which tend to his improvement. In these various modes a person may suffer very severe penalties at the hands of others for faults which directly concern only himself; but he suffers these penalties only in so far as they are the natural and, as it were, the spontaneous consequences of the faults themselves, not because they are purposely inflicted on him for the sake of punishment. A person who shows rashness, obstinacy, self-conceit—who cannot live within moderate means; who cannot restrain himself from hurtful indulgence; who pursues animal pleasures at the expense of those of feeling and intellect—must expect to be lowered in the opinion of others, and to have a less share of their favorable sentiments; but of this he has no right to complain unless he has merited their favor by special excellence in his social relations and has thus established a title to their good offices, which is not affected by his demerits toward himself.

What I contend for is that the inconveniences which are strictly inseparable from the unfavorable judgment of others are the only ones to which a person should ever be subjected for that portion of his conduct and character which concerns his own good, but which does not affect the interest of others in their relations with him. Acts injurious to others require a totally different treatment. Encroachment on their rights; infliction on them of any loss or damage not justified by his own rights; falsehood or duplicity in dealing with them; unfair or ungenerous use of advantages over them; even selfish abstinence from defending them against injury—these are fit objects of moral reprobation and, in grave cases, of moral retribution and punishment. And not only these acts, but the dispositions which lead to them, are properly immoral and fit subjects of disapprobation which may rise to abhorrence. Cruelty of disposition: malice and ill-nature: that most antisocial and odious of all passions, envy: dissimulation and insincerity, irascibility on insufficient cause, and resentment disproportioned to the provocation; the love of domineering over others; the desire to engross more than one's share of advantages (the *pleonexia* of the Greeks); the pride which derives gratification from the abasement of others; the egotism which thinks self and its concerns more important than everything else, and decides all doubtful questions in its own favor—these are moral vices and constitute a bad and odious moral character; unlike the self-regarding faults previously mentioned, which are not properly immoralities and, to whatever pitch they may be carried, do not constitute wickedness. They may be proofs of any amount of folly or want of personal dignity and self-respect, but they are only a subject of moral reprobation when they involve a breach of duty to others, for whose sake the individual is bound to have care for himself. What are called duties to ourselves are not socially obligatory unless circumstances render them at the same time duties to others. The term duty to oneself, when it means anything more than prudence, means self-respect or self-development, and for none of these is anyone accountable to his fellow creatures, because for none of them is it for the good of mankind that he be held accountable to them.

The distinction between the loss of consideration which a person may rightly incur by defect of prudence or of personal dignity, and the reprobation which is due to him for an offense against the rights of others, is not a merely nominal distinction. It makes a vast difference both in our feelings and in our conduct toward him whether he displeases us in things in which we think we have a right to control him or in things in which we know that we have not. If he displeases us, we may express our distaste, and we may stand aloof from a person as well as from a thing that displeases us; but we shall not therefore feel called on to make his life uncomfortable. We shall reflect that he already bears, or will bear, the whole penalty of his error; if he spoils his life by mismanagement, we shall not, for that reason, desire to spoil it still further: instead of wishing to punish him, we shall rather endeavor to alleviate his punishment by showing him how he may avoid or cure the evils his conduct tends to bring upon him. He may be to us an object of pity, perhaps of dislike, but not of anger or resentment; we shall not treat him like an enemy of society; the worst we shall think ourselves justified in doing is leaving him to himself, if we do not interfere benevolently by showing interest or concern for him. It is far otherwise if he has infringed the rules necessary for the protection of his fellow creatures, individually or collectively. The evil consequences of his acts do not then fall on himself, but on others; and society, as the protector of all its members, must retaliate on him, must inflict pain on him for the express purpose of punishment, and must take care that it be sufficiently severe. In the one case, he is an offender at our bar, and we are called on not only to sit in judgment on him, but, in one shape or another, to execute our own sentence; in the other case, it is not our part to inflict any suffering on him, except what may incidentally follow from our using the same liberty in the regulation of our own affairs which we allow to him in his.

The distinction here pointed out between the part of a person's life which concerns only himself and that which concerns others, many persons will refuse to admit. How (it may be asked) can any part of the conduct of a member of society be a matter of indifference to the other members? No person is an entirely isolated being; it is impossible for a person to do anything seriously or permanently hurtful to himself without mischief reaching at least to his near connections, and often far beyond them. If he injures his property, he does harm to those who directly or indirectly derived support from it, and usually diminishes, by a greater or less amount, the general resources of the community. If he deteriorates his bodily or mental faculties, he not only brings evil upon all who depended on him for any portion of their happiness, but disqualifies himself for rendering the services which he owes to his fellow creatures generally, perhaps becomes a burden on their affection or benevolence; and if such conduct were very frequent hardly any offense that is committed would detract more from the general sum of good. Finally, if by his vices or follies a person does no direct harm to others, he is nevertheless (it may be said) injurious by his example, and ought to be compelled to control himself for the sake of those whom the sight or knowledge of his conduct might corrupt or mislead.

And even (it will be added) if the consequences of misconduct could be confined to the vicious or thoughtless individual, ought society to abandon to their own guidance those who are manifestly unfit for it? If protection against themselves is confessedly due to children and persons under age, is not society equally bound to afford it to persons of mature years who are equally incapable of self-government? If gambling, or drunkenness, or incontinence, or idleness, or uncleanliness are as injurious to happiness, and as great a hindrance to improvement, as many or most of the acts prohibited by law, why (it may be asked) should not law, so far as is consistent with practicability and social convenience, endeavor to repress these also? And as a supplement to the unavoidable imperfections of law, ought not opinion at least to organize a powerful police against these vices and visit rigidly with social penalties those who are known to practice them? There is no question here (it may be said) about restricting individuality, or impeding the trial of new and original experiments in living. The only things it is sought to prevent are things which have been tried and condemned from the beginning of the world until now—things which experience has shown not to be useful or suitable to any person's individuality. There must be some length of time and amount of experience after which a moral or prudential truth may be regarded as established; and it is merely desired to prevent generation after generation from falling over the same precipice which has been fatal to their predecessors.

I fully admit that the mischief which a person does to himself may seriously affect, both through their sympathies and their interests, those nearly connected with him and, in a minor degree, society at large. When, by conduct of this sort, a person is led to violate a distinct and assignable obligation to any other person or persons, the case is taken out of the self-regarding class and becomes amenable to moral disapprobation in the proper sense of the term. If, for example, a man, through intemperance or extravagance, becomes unable to pay his debts, or, having undertaken the moral responsibility of a family, becomes from the same cause incapable of supporting or educating them, he is deservedly reprobated and might be justly punished; but it is for the breach of duty to his family or creditors, not for the extravagance. If the resources which ought to have been devoted to them had been diverted from them for the most prudent investment, the moral culpability would have been the same. George Barnwell murdered his uncle to get money for his mistress, but if he had done it to set himself up in business, he would equally have been hanged. Again, in the frequent case of a man who causes grief to his family by addiction to bad habits, he deserves reproach for his unkindness or ingratitude; but so he may for cultivating habits not in themselves vicious, if they are painful to those with whom he passes his life, or who from personal ties are dependent on him for their comfort. Whoever fails in the consideration generally due to the interests and feelings of others, not being compelled by some more imperative duty, or justified by allowable self-preference, is a subject of moral disapprobation for that failure, but not for the cause of it, nor for the errors, merely personal to himself, which may have remotely led to it. In like manner, when a person disables himself, by conduct purely self-regarding, from the performance of some definite duty incumbent on him to the public, he is guilty of a social offense. No person ought to be punished simply for being drunk; but a soldier or a policeman should be punished for being drunk on duty. Whenever, in short, there is a definite damage, or a definite risk of damage, either to an individual or to the public, the case is taken out of the province of liberty and placed in that of morality or law.

But with regard to the merely contingent or, as it may be called, constructive injury which a person causes to society by conduct which neither violates any specific duty to the public, nor occasions perceptible hurt to any assignable individual except himself, the inconvenience is one which society can afford to bear, for the sake of the greater good of human freedom. If grown persons are to be punished for not taking proper care of themselves, I would rather it were for their own sake than under pretense of preventing them from impairing their capacity or rendering to society benefits which society does not pretend it has a right to exact. But I cannot consent to argue the point as if society had no means of bringing its weaker members up to its ordinary standard of rational conduct, except waiting till they do something irrational, and then punishing them, legally or morally, for it. Society has had absolute power over them during all the early portion of their existence; it has had the whole period of childhood and nonage in which to try whether it could make them capable of rational conduct in life. The existing generation is master both of the training and the entire circumstances of the generation to come; it cannot indeed make them perfectly wise and good, because it is itself so lamentably deficient in goodness and wisdom; and its best efforts are not always, in individual cases, its most successful ones; but it is perfectly well able to make the rising generation, as a whole, as good as, and a little better than, itself. If society lets any considerable number of its members grow up mere children, incapable of being acted on by rational consideration of distant motives, society has itself to blame for the consequences. Armed not only with all the powers of education, but with the ascendancy which the authority of a received opinion always exercises over the minds who are least fitted to judge for themselves, and aided by the *natural* penalties which cannot be prevented from falling on those who incur the distaste or the contempt of those who know them—let not society pretend that it needs, besides all this, the power to issue commands and enforce obedience in the personal concerns of individuals in which, on all principles of justice and policy, the decision ought to rest with those who are to abide the consequences. Nor is there anything which tends more to discredit and frustrate the better means of influencing conduct than a resort to the worse. If there be among those whom it is attempted to coerce into prudence or temperance any of the material of which vigorous and independent characters are made, they will infallibly rebel against the yoke. No such person will ever feel that others have a right to control him in his concerns, such as they have to prevent him from injuring them in theirs; and it easily comes to be considered a mark of spirit and courage to fly in the face of such usurped authority and do with ostentation the exact opposite of what it enjoins, as in the fashion of grossness which succeeded, in the time of Charles II, to the fanatical moral intolerance of the Puritans. With respect to what is said of the necessity of protecting society from the bad example set to others by the vicious or the self-indulgent, it is true that bad example may have a pernicious effect, especially the example of doing wrong to others with impunity to the wrong-doer. But we are now speaking of conduct which, while it does no wrong to others, is supposed to do great harm to the agent himself; and I do not see how those who believe this can think otherwise than that the example, on the whole, must be more salutary than hurtful, since, if it displays the misconduct, it displays also the painful or degrading consequences which, if the conduct is justly censured, must be supposed to be in all or most cases attendant on it.*

* Pp. 144-61.

. . . The worth of a State, in the long run, is the worth of the individuals composing it; and a State which postpones the interests of *their* mental expansion and elevation to a little more of administrative skill, or of that semblance of it which practice gives in the details of business; a State which dwarfs its men, in order that they may be more docile instruments in its hands even for beneficial purposes—will find that with small men no great thing can really be accomplished; and that the perfection of machinery to which it has sacrificed everything will in the end avail it nothing, for want of the vital power which, in order that the machine might work more smoothly, it has preferred to banish.*

* P. 223.

SOCIAL DARWINISM

Herbert Spencer

Herbert Spencer was the most important popularizer of what became known as Social Darwinism. Spencer was born in Derby, England, the son of a nonconformist schoolteacher. Although he was a poor student, Spencer showed an aptitude for science and a keen interest in evolutionary doctrines. While working as an editor for the *Economist* from 1848 to 1852, Spencer transformed evolutionary principles into a social philosophy.

In *Social Statics* (1850) Spencer equated human existence to processes within the animal kingdom. He viewed man as irrational with "vicious propensities." Improvement in man's character occurred only through a gradual and often brutal process of natural selection. Spencer saw little use for society except as a crucible where man fought his struggle for the survival of the fittest. He asserted that the struggle required that each man have the "fullest liberty to exercise his facilities compatible with the possession of the like liberty of every man." Spencer believed that his doctrine of liberty and society based on "equal freedom" rather than Mill's "fallacious" principles of individuality, pleasure, and pain ensured the natural process of societal improvements and human advancement.

I.
Freedom And Liberty—The Fallacy Of The Principle Of Pleasure And Pain; And The Meaning Of Equal Freedom

If men have like claims to that freedom which is needful for the exercise of their faculties, then must the freedom of each be bounded by the similar freedoms of all. When, in the pursuit of their respective ends, two individuals clash, the movements of the one remain free only in so far as they do not interfere with the

Reprinted from Herbert Spencer, *Social Statics* (New York: D. Appleton and Co., 1910), pp. 36-42, 44-45, 55, 109-12, 114-15, 117, 121-28, 131, 133, 137-38, 146-49, 156-57, 173-75, 201-2, 204-7.

like movements of the other. This sphere of existence into which we are thrown, not affording room for the unrestrained activity of all, and yet all possessing in virtue of their constitutions similar claims to such unrestrained activity, there is no course but to apportion the unavoidable restraint equally. Wherefore we arrive at the general proposition, that every man may claim the fullest liberty to exercise his faculties compatible with the possession of like liberty by every other man.

Upon a partial consideration this statement of the law will perhaps seem open to criticism. It may be thought better to limit the right of each to exercise his faculties, by the proviso that he shall not *hurt* any one else—shall not inflict *pain* on any one else. But although at first sight satisfactory, this expression of the law allows of erroneous deductions. It is true that men, who fulfil those conditions to greatest happiness . . ., cannot exercise their faculties to the aggrieving of one another. It is not, however, that each avoids giving pain by refraining from the full exercise of his faculties; but it is that the faculties of each are such that the full exercise of them offends no one. And herein lies the difference. The giving of pain may have two causes. Either the abnormally-constituted man may do something displeasing to the normal feelings of his neighbours, in which case he acts wrongly; or the behaviour of the normally-constituted man may irritate the abnormal feelings of his neighbours, in which case it is not his behaviour that is wrong, but their characters that are so. Under such circumstances the due exercise of his faculties is right, although it gives pain; and the remedy for the evil lies in the modification of those abnormal feelings to which pain is given.

To elucidate this distinction let us take a few illustrations. An honest man discovers some friend, of whom he had previously thought well, to be a rogue. He has certain high instincts to which roguery is repugnant; and, allowing free play to these, he drops the acquaintanceship of this unworthy one. Now, though in doing so he gives pain, it does not follow that he transgresses the law. The evil must be ascribed, not to an undue exercise of faculties by him, but to the immorality of the man who suffers. Again, a Protestant in a Roman Catholic country refuses to uncover his head on the passing of the host. In so obeying the promptings of certain sentiments, he annoys the spectators; and were the above modified expression of the law correct, would be blameable. The fault, however, is not with him, but with those who are offended. It is not that he is culpable in thus testifying to his belief, but it is that they ought not to have so tyrannical an intolerance of other opinions than their own. Or again, a son, to the great displeasure of his father and family, marries one who, though in all respects admirable, is dowerless. In thus obeying the dictates of his nature, he may entail considerable distress of mind on his relatives; but it does not follow that his conduct is bad; it follows, rather, that the feelings which his conduct has wounded are bad.

Hence we see that in hourly-occurring cases like these, to limit the exercise of faculties by the necessity of not giving pain to others, would be to stop the proper exercise of faculties in some persons, for the purpose of allowing the improper exercise of faculties in the rest. Moreover, the observance of such a rule does not, in reality, prevent pain. For though he who is restrained by it avoids inflicting suffering on his fellows, he does so at the expense of suffering to himself. The evil must be borne by some one, and the question is by whom. Shall the Protestant, by showing reverence for what he does not revere, tell a virtual lie, and thus do violence to his conscientious feeling that he may avoid vexing the intolerant spirit of his Catholic neighbours? or shall he give the rein to his own healthy sincerity and independence, and offend their unhealthy bigotry? Shall the honest man repress those sentiments that make him honest, lest the exhibition of them should give pain to a rogue? or shall he respect his own nobler feelings, and hurt the other's baser ones? Between these alternatives no one can well pause. And here indeed we get down to the root of the matter. For be it remembered the universal law of life is, that the exercise or gratification of faculties strengthens them; while, contrariwise, the curbing or inflicting pain on them, entails a diminution of their power. And hence it follows that when the action of a normal faculty is checked, to prevent pain being given to the abnormal faculties of others, those abnormal faculties remain as active as they were, and the normal one becomes weaker or abnormal. Whereas under converse circumstances the normal one remains strong, and the abnormal ones are weakened, or made more normal. In the one case the pain is detrimental, because it retards the approximation to that form of human nature under which the faculties of each may be fully exercised without displeasure to the like faculties of all. In the other case the pain is beneficial, because it aids the approximation to that form. Thus, that first expression of the law which arises immediately from the conditions to social existence, turns out to be the true one: any such modification of it as the above, necessitating conduct that is in many cases mischievous.

And yet, on the other hand, when to express the law by saying that every man has full liberty to exercise his faculties, provided always he does not trench upon the similar liberty of any other, we commit ourselves to an imperfection of an opposite character; and we find that there are many cases in which the above modified expression answers better. Various ways exist in which the faculties may be exercised to the aggrieving of other persons, without the law of equal freedom being overstepped. A man may behave unamiably, may use harsh language, may annoy by disgusting habits; and whoso thus offends the normal feelings of his fellows, manifestly diminishes happiness. If we say that every one is free to exercise his faculties so long only as he does not inflict pain upon any one else, we forbid all such conduct. Whereas if we simply limit the liberty of each by the like liberties of all, we do not forbid it; seeing that he who exercises his faculties in this way, does not hinder others from exercising theirs in the same way, and to the same extent. How then are we to escape from this difficulty? Neither statement of the law quite fulfils our requirement, and yet we must choose one of them. Which must it be, and why?

It must be the original one, and for a very good reason. Limiting the liberty of each by the like liberties of all, excludes a wide range of improper actions, but does not exclude certain other improper ones. Limiting the liberty of each by the necessity of not giving pain to the rest, excludes the whole of these improper actions, but excludes along with them many others that are proper. The one does not cut off enough; the other cuts off too much. The one is negatively erroneous; the other is positively so. Evidently, then, we must adopt the negatively erroneous one, seeing that its shortcomings may be made good by a supplementary law. . . .

Yet another objection will probably be started. By full liberty to exercise the faculties, is meant full liberty to do all that the faculties prompt, or, in other words, to do all that the individual wills; and it may be said that if the individual is free to do all that he wills, provided he does not trespass upon certain specified claims of others, then he is free to do things which are injurious to himself—is free to get drunk, for instance. To this it must in the first place be replied, as above, that while the law now laid down forbids a certain class of actions as immoral, it does not recognize all kinds of immorality—that the restriction it puts on the free exercise of faculties, though the chief, is not the sole restriction, and must be received without prejudice to further ones. Of the need for such further ones, the difficulty here raised furnishes a second instance.

Mark now, however, that these supplementary restrictions are of inferior authority to the original law. Instead of being, like it, capable of scientific development, they can be unfolded only into superior forms of expediency. The limit put to each man's freedom by the like freedom of every other man, is a limit almost always possible of ascertainment; for the respective amounts of freedom men assume can usually be compared, and the equality or inequality of those amounts recognized. But when we set about drawing practical deductions from the propositions that a man is not at liberty to do things injurious to himself, and that he is not at liberty (except in cases like those lately cited) to do what may give unhappiness to his neighbours, we find ourselves involved in complicated estimates of pleasures and pains, to the obvious peril of our conclusions. For example, though it is manifest that to get drunk is an injurious exercise of faculties, it is by no means manifest how much work is proper for us, and when work becomes detrimental; it is by no means manifest where lies the line between due and undue intellectual activity; it is by no means manifest what amount of advantage will justify a man in submitting to unsuitable climate and mode of life; and yet in each of these cases happiness is at stake, and the wrong course is wrong for the same reason that drunkenness is so. Even were it possible to say of each private action whether the resulting gratification did or did not preponderate over the resulting suffering, there would still present itself this second difficulty, that we cannot in all cases distinguish suffering which is detrimental, from suffering which is beneficial. While we are as yet imperfectly adapted to our conditions, pain must inevitably arise from the repression of faculties that are too active, and from the overtasking of those that are not equal to their duties; and, as being needful to the development of the ultimate man, such pain cannot be held damnatory of the actions causing it. Thus, referring again to the instances just cited, it is evident that the ability to work is needful for the production of the greatest happiness; but the acquirement of this ability by the uncivilized man is so distressing, that only severe discipline will force him to it. The degree of intelligence which our existing mode of life necessitates, cannot be arrived at without ages of wearisome application, and perhaps cannot get organized in the race without a partial and temporary sacrifice of bodily health. Here, then, are cases in which men's liberties must not be limited by the necessity of not inflicting pain on themselves; seeing that it cannot be so limited without a suspension of our approach to greatest happiness. Similarly, we saw that there are cases in which, for the same reason, men's liberties must not be limited by the necessity of not inflicting pain on others. And the fact now to be noticed is, that we possess no certain way of distinguishing the two groups of cases thus exemplified, from those cases in which the doing what diminishes happiness, either in ourselves or others, is both immediately and ultimately detrimental, and therefore wrong. As both of these supplementary limitations involve the term *happiness,* and as happiness is for the present capable only of a generic and not of a specific definition, they do not admit of scientific development.*

Of this difficulty nothing can be said, save that it seems due to the impossibility of making the perfect law recognize an imperfect state. As matters stand, however, we must deal with it as best we may. There is clearly no alternative but to declare man's freedom to exercise his faculties. There is clearly no alternative but to declare the several limitations of that freedom needful for the achievement of greatest happiness. And there is clearly no alternative but to develop the first and chief of these limitations separately; seeing that a development of the others is at present impossible. Against the consequence of neglecting these secondary limitations, we must guard ourselves as well as we can: supplying the place of scientific deductions by such inferences as observation and experience enable us to make.

Finally, however, there is satisfaction in the thought, that no such imperfection as this can vitiate any of the conclusions we are now about to draw. Liberty of action being the first essential to exercise of faculties, and therefore the first essential to happiness; and the liberty of each limited by the like liberties of all, being the form which this first essential assumes when applied to many instead of one; it follows that this liberty of each, limited by the like liberties of all, is the rule in conformity with which society must be organized. Freedom being the pre-requisite to normal life in the individual, equal freedom becomes the pre-requisite to normal life in society. And if this law of equal freedom is the *primary* law of right relationship between man and man, then no desire to get fulfilled a *secondary* law can warrant us in breaking it.†

Thus are we brought by several routes to the same conclusion. Whether we reason our way from those fixed conditions under which alone greatest happiness can be realized—whether we draw our inferences from man's constitution, considering him as a congeries of faculties—or whether we listen to the monitions of a certain mental agency, which seems to have the function of guiding us in this matter; we are alike taught, as the law of right social relationships, that—*Every man has freedom to do all that he wills, provided he infringes not the equal freedom of any other man.* Though further qualifications of the liberty of action thus asserted are necessary, yet we have seen that in the just regulation of a community no further qualifications of it can be recognized. Such further qualifications must remain for private and individual application. We must therefore adopt this law of equal freedom in its entirety, as the law on which a correct system of equity is to be based.‡

---

* Pp. 36-42.

† Pp. 44-45.

‡ P. 55.

II.
The Limitation Of State Duties And Powers; The Nature Of Man; And, The Evolution Of Liberty

. . . let us inquire whether it is not the fact that in assuming any office besides its essential one, the State begins to lose the power of fulfilling its essential one. So long as our joint-stock protection-society confines itself to guaranteeing the rights of its members, it is pretty certain to be co-extensive with the nation; for while such an organization is needed at all, most men will sacrifice something to secure its guardianship. But let an additional duty be assigned to it, and there will immediately arise more or less schism. Observe how the matter stands between the government and the dissentient citizen. Says the citizen:—

"What is it that you, as the ruling agency, have been appointed for? Is it not to maintain the rights of those who employ you; or, in other words, to guarantee to each the fullest freedom for the exercise of his faculties compatible with the equal freedom of all others?"

"It has been so decided."

"And it has been also decided that you are justified in diminishing this freedom only to such an extent as may be needful for preserving the remainder, has it not?"

"That is evidently a corollary."

"Exactly. And now let me ask what is this property, this money, of which, in the shape of taxes, you are demanding from me an additional amount for a further purpose? Is it not that which enables me to get food, clothing, shelter, recreation, or, to repeat the original expression—that on which I depend for the exercise of most of my faculties?"

"It is."

"Therefore to decrease my property is to decrease my freedom to exercise my faculties, is it not?"

"Clearly."

"Then this new impost of yours will practically decrease my freedom to exercise my faculties?"

"Yes."

"Well, do you not now perceive the contradiction? Instead of acting the part of a protector you are acting the part of an aggressor. What you were appointed to guarantee me and others, you are now taking away. To see that the liberty of each man to pursue the objects of his desires is unrestricted, save by the like liberty of all, is your special function. To diminish this liberty by means of taxes, or civil restraints, more than is needful for performing such function, is wrong, because adverse to the function itself. Now your new impost does so diminish this liberty more than is needful, and is consequently unjustifiable."

It will perhaps be urged, however, that the evil done by a government, when it thus oversteps its original duty, is only an apparent one; seeing that although it diminishes men's spheres of action in one direction, it adds to them in another. All such supplementary functions, an objector may say, subserve in some way or other the wants of society; that is, they facilitate the satisfaction of men's desires;

that is, they afford to men greater freedom for the exercise of their faculties. For if you argue that taking away a man's property diminishes his freedom to exercise his faculties, because it diminishes his *means* of exercising them, then you must in fairness admit that, by procuring for him certain of the objects he desires, or by taking away the obstacles that lie between him and those objects, or by otherwise helping him to his ends, the State is increasing his power to exercise his faculties, and hence is practically increasing his freedom.

To all which the answer is, that cutting away men's opportunities on one side, to add to them on another, is at best accompanied by a loss. Let us remember that the force by which a society, through its government, works out certain results, is not increased by administrative mechanisms, but that part of it escapes in friction. Government evidently cannot *create* any facilities for the exercise of faculties; all it can do is to re-distribute them. Set down the amount of power to satisfy his wants, which it takes from a citizen in extra taxes; deduct the serious waste occurring under official manipulations; and the remainder, transformed into some new shape, is all that can be returned to him. The transaction is consequently a losing one. So that while, in attempting to serve the public by undertaking supplementary functions, a government fails in its duty towards all who dissent; it does not really compensate for this by additional advantages afforded to the rest; to whom it merely gives with one hand, less than it takes away with the other.

But in truth the transaction is a yet more detrimental one than it thus appears, for even the gift is a delusion. The expediency-philosophy, of which this general State-superintendence is a practical expression, embodies the belief that government ought not only to guarantee men the unmolested pursuit of happiness, but should provide the happiness for them. Now no scheme could be more self-defeating. Man, . . . consists of a congeries of faculties qualifying him for surrounding conditions. Each of these faculties, if normally developed, yields to him, when exercised, a gratification constituting part of his happiness. . . .

To do anything for him by some artificial agency, is to supersede certain of his powers—is to leave them unexercised, and therefore to diminish his happiness.

"But men are *not* complete; they are *not* healthily developed, they have *not* capacities in harmony with their wants; and therefore, as matters stand, a government does *not* by its interpositions pre-occupy offices which there are faculties to fill." Very true; but next to being what we ought to be, the most desirable thing is that we should become what we ought to be as fast as possible. We have to lose the characteristics which fitted us for our original state, and to gain those which will fit us for our present state; and the question to be asked, respecting these mechanical remedies for our deficiencies, is—do they facilitate the change? A moment's thought will convince us that they retard it. Demand and supply is the law of life as well as the law of trade. Would you draw out and increase some feeble sentiment? Then you must set it to do, as well as it can, the work required of it. It must be kept ever active, ever strained, ever inconvenienced by its incompetence. Under this treatment it will, in the slow course of generations, attain to efficiency; and what was once its impossible task will become the source of a healthy, pleasurable, and desired excitement. But let a State-instrumentality be thrust between such faculty and its work, and the process of adaptation is at once suspended. The embryo agency now superseded by some commission—some board and staff of officers, straightway dwindles; for power is as inevitably lost by inactivity as it is gained by activity. Hence, humanity no longer goes on moulding itself into harmony with the natural requirements of the social state; but begins, instead, to assume a form fitting these artificial requirements. And thus, as before said, not only does a government reverse its function by taking away more property than is needful for protective purposes, but even what it gives, in return for the excess so taken, is in essence a loss.

There is indeed one faculty, or rather combination of faculties, for whose shortcomings the State, as far as in it lies, may advantageously compensate—that, namely, by which society is made possible. It is clear that any being whose constitution is to be moulded into fitness for new conditions of existence, must be placed under those conditions. This granted, it follows that as man has been, and is still, deficient in those feelings which prevent the recurring antagonisms of individuals and their consequent disunion, some artificial agency is required by which their union may be maintained. Only by the process of adaptation itself, can be produced that character which makes social equilibrium spontaneous. And hence, while this process is going on, an instrumentality must be employed, firstly, to bind men into the social state, and secondly to check all conduct endangering the existence of that state. Such an instrumentality we have in a government.

And now mark that whether we consider government from this point of view, or from that previously occupied, our conclusions respecting it are in essence identical. For when government fulfils the function here assigned it, of retaining men in the circumstances to which they are to be adapted, it fulfils the function which we on other grounds assigned it—that of protector. To administer justice,—to mount guard over men's rights,—is simply to render society possible. And seeing that the two definitions are thus at root the same, we shall be prepared for the fact that, in whichever way we specify its duty, the State cannot exceed that duty without defeating itself. For, if regarded as a protector, we find that the moment it does anything more than protect, it becomes an aggressor instead of a protector; and, if regarded as a help to adaptation, we find that when it does anything more than sustain the social state, it retards adaptation instead of hastening it.

To the assertion that the boundary line of State-duty as above drawn is at the wrong place, the obvious rejoinder is—show us where it should be drawn. This appeal the expediency-philosophers have never yet been able to answer. Their alleged definitions are no definitions at all. As was proved at the outset, to say that government ought to do that which is "expedient," or to do that which will tend to produce the "greatest happiness," or to do that which will subserve the "general good," is to say just nothing; for there are countless disagreements respecting the natures of these desiderata. A definition of which the terms are indefinite is an absurdity. Whilst the practical interpretation of "expediency" remains a matter of opinion, to say that a government should do that which is "expedient," is to say that it should do, what we think it should do!

Still then our demand is—a definition. Between the two extremes of its possible action, where lies the proper limitation? Shall it extend its interference to the fixing of creeds, as in the old times; or to overlooking modes of manufacture, farming operations, and domestic affairs, as it once did; or to commerce, as of late—to popular education, as now—to public health, as already—to dress, as in China—to literature, as in Austria—to charity, to manners, to amusements? If not to all of them, to which of them?*

Between the one extreme of entire non-interference, and the other extreme in which every citizen is to be transformed into a grown-up baby, there lie innumerable stopping places; and he who would have the State do more than protect, is required to say where he means to draw the line, and to give us reasons why it must be just there and nowhere else.†

[But] let a people believe in government-omnipotence, and they will be pretty certain to get up revolutions to achieve impossibilities. Between their exorbitant ideas of what the State ought to do for them on the one side, and its miserable performances on the other, there will surely be generated feelings extremely inimical to social order.‡

III.
The Inequity Of State Justice

Our system of jurisprudence takes a very one-sided view of the reciprocal claims of State and subject. It is stringent enough in enforcing the claim of the State against the subject; but as to the correlative claim of the subject against the State it is comparatively careless. That it recognizes the title of the tax-payer to protection is true; but it is also true that it does this but partially. From certain infringements of rights, classed as criminal, it is ready to defend every complainant; but against others, not so classed, it leaves every one to defend himself. The most trifling injury, if inflicted in a specified manner, is cognizable by the magistrate, and redress may be obtained for nothing; but if otherwise inflicted, the injury, no matter how serious, must be passively borne, unless the sufferer has plenty of money and a sufficiency of daring. Let a man have his hat knocked over his eyes, and the law will zealously espouse his cause—will mulct his assailant in a fine and costs, and will do this without charge. But if, instead of having been bonneted he has been wrongfully imprisoned, he is politely referred to a solicitor, with the information that the offence committed against him is actionable: which means, that if rich he may play double or quits with Fate; and that if poor he must go without even this chance of compensation. Against picking of pockets, as ordinarily practised, the ruling power grants its lieges gratuitous protection; but pockets may be picked in various indirect ways, and it will idly look on unless costly means are taken to interest it. It will rush to the defence of one who has been deprived of a few turnips by a half-starved tramp; but as to the estate on which these turnips grew, that may be stolen without risk, so long as the despoiled owner is left friendless and penniless. Some complaints need only to be whispered, and the State forthwith plays the parts of constable, lawyer, judge, and gaoler; while to others it turns

* Pp. 121-28.
† P. 131.
‡ P. 133.

a deaf ear unless they are made through its bribed hangers-on. Now it is the injured man's champion; and now it throws down its weapons and seats itself as umpire, while oppressor and oppressed run a tilt at each other.

That men should sit down as apathetically as they do under the present corrupt administration of justice, is not a little remarkable. That we, with all our jealousy of abuses, with all our opportunities of canvassing, blaming, and amending the acts of the legislature, with all our readiness to organize and agitate, with the Anti-Corn-Law, Slavery-Abolition, and Catholic-Emancipation victories fresh in remembrance—that we, the independent, self-ruling English, should daily behold the abominations of our judicial system, and yet do nothing to rectify them, is really quite incomprehensible. It is not as though the facts were disputed; all men are agreed upon them. The dangers of law are proverbial. The names of its officers are used as synonyms for trickery and greediness. The decisions of its courts are typical of chance. In all companies you hear but one opinion; and each person confirms it by a fresh illustration. Now you are informed of £300 having been expended in the recovery of forty shillings' worth of property; and again of a cause that was lost because an affirmation could not be received in place of an oath. A right-hand neighbour can tell you of a judge who allowed an indictment to be objected to, on the plea that the words, "in the year of our Lord," were not inserted before the date; and another to your left narrates how a thief lately tried for stealing a guinea-pig was acquitted, because a guinea-pig was shown to be a kind of rat, and a rat could not be property. At one moment the story is of a poor man whose rich enemy has deliberately ruined him by tempting him into litigation; and at the next it is of a child who has been kept in prison for six weeks, in default of sureties for her appearance as witness against one who had assaulted her. This gentleman has been cheated out of half his property, but dared not attempt to recover it for fear of losing more; while his less prudent companion can parallel the experience of him who said that he had only twice been on the verge of ruin—once when he had lost a law-suit, and once when he had gained one. On all sides you are told of trickery and oppression, and revenge, committed in the name of justice; of wrongs endured for want of money wherewith to purchase redress; of rights unclaimed because contention with the powerful usurper was useless; of chancery-suits that outlasted the lives of the suitors; of fortunes swallowed up in settling a title; of estates lost by an informality. And then comes a catalogue of victims—of those who had trusted and been deceived; grayheaded men whose hardly-earned savings went to fatten the attorney; threadbare and hollow-cheeked insolvents who lost all in the attempt to get their due; some who had been reduced to subsist on the charity of friends; others who had died the death of a pauper; with not a few whose anxieties had produced insanity, or who in their desperation had committed suicide. Yet, while all echo one another's exclamations of disgust, these iniquities continue unchecked!

There are not wanting, however, men who defend this state of things—who actually argue that government should perform but imperfectly what they allow to be its special function. While, on the one hand, they admit that administration of justice is the vital necessity of civilized life, they maintain, on the other, that justice may be administered too well!*

---

* Pp. 109-12.

But, after all, it is not the setting up of this or that system of jurisprudence which causes the intercourse of men with one another to be equitable or otherwise. The matter lies deeper. As with forms of government, so with forms of law, it is the national character that decides. The power of an apparatus primarily depends, not on the ingenuity of its design, but on the strength of its materials. Be his plan never so well devised, yet if our engineer has not considered whether the respective parts of his structure will bear the strains to be put upon them, we must call him a bungler. Similarly with the institution-maker. If the people with whom he has to deal are not of the requisite quality, no cleverness in his contrivance will avail anything. Let us not forget that institutions are *made* of men, and that frame them together as we may, it is their nature which must finally determine whether the institutions can stand. These social forms which we regard as all-potent, are things of quite secondary importance. What mattered it that the Roman plebeians were endowed with certain privileges, when the patricians prevented them from exercising those privileges by ill-treatment carried even to the death? What mattered it that our statute-book contained equitable provisions, and that officers were appointed to enforce them, when there needed a Magna Charta to demand that justice should neither be sold, denied, nor delayed? What matters it even now, that all men are declared equal before the law, when magistrates are swayed by class-sympathies, and treat a gentleman more leniently than an artizan? If we think that we can rectify the relationships of men at will, we deceive ourselves.*

But must not this imply that government is of no use whatever? Not at all. Although unable to alter the sum total of injustice to be supported, it can still alter its *distribution.* And this is what it really does. By its aid, men to a considerable extent equalize the evil they have to bear—spread it out more uniformly over the whole community, and over the life of each citizen. Entire freedom to exercise the faculties, interrupted by entire deprivations of it, and marred by the perpetual danger of these deprivations, is exchanged for a freedom on which the restrictions are constant but partial. Instead of those losses of life, of limb, or of the means of subsistence, which, under a state of anarchy, all are liable to, and many suffer, a political organization commits universal aggressions of a comparatively mild type. Wrongs that were before occasional but crushing, are now unceasing but bearable. The system is one of mutual insurance against moral disasters. Just as men, while they cannot prevent fires and shipwrecks, can yet guarantee one another against ruin from these, by bearing them in common, and distributing the injuries entailed over long periods of time; so, although by uniting together for judicial purposes men cannot diminish the amount of injustice to be borne, they can, and do, insure themselves against its otherwise fatal results.†

---

* Pp. 114-15.
† P. 117.

IV.
The Proper Role Of The State In Promoting And Protecting Equal Freedom And Liberty—Commerce, Public Welfare, Education, Public Health As Illustrations

In putting a veto upon any commercial intercourse, or in putting obstacles in the way of any such intercourse, a government trenches upon men's liberties of action; and by so doing directly reverses its function. To secure for each man the fullest freedom to exercise his faculties compatible with the like freedom of all others, we find to be the State's duty. Now trade-prohibitions and trade-restrictions not only do not secure this freedom, but they take it away. So that in enforcing them the State is transformed from a maintainer of rights into a violator of rights. If it be criminal in a civil power commissioned to shield us from murder to turn murderer itself; if it be criminal in it to play the thief, though set to keep off thieves; then must it be criminal in it to deprive men, in any way, of liberty to pursue the objects they desire, when it was appointed to insure them that liberty.

We saw that as unjust institutions derive their viciousness from moral defects in the people living under them, they must be *uniformly* pervaded by that viciousness—that as social laws, creeds, and arrangements consist merely of solidified character, the same character will be shown in *all* the social laws, creeds, and arrangements which co-exist; and, further, that any process of amelioration will affect them simultaneously. We saw that tyranny in forms of government, tyranny in the conduct of lord to serf, tyranny in religious organizations and discipline, tyranny in the marital relationship, and tyranny in the treatment of children, regularly flourish together and regularly decrease at like rates. In the same category we must now put—tyranny in commercial laws. Sinking those minor irregularities which pervade all Nature's processes, we shall find that from the days when exportation was a capital crime, down to our own free-trade era, there has been a constant ratio kept between the stringency of mercantile restraints and the stringency of other restraints, as there has also between the increase of commercial liberty and the increase of general liberty.*

[The same principle holds true for public welfare and poor laws] whether the sufferings of the unfortunate shall be soothed in obedience to the gentle whisperings of benevolence, or whether fear of the harsh threats of law shall be the motive for relieving them, is indeed a question of no small importance. In deciding how misery is best alleviated, we have to consider, not only what is done for the afflicted, but what is the reactive effect upon those who do it. The relationship that springs up between benefactor and beneficiary is, for this present state of the world, a refining one. The emotion accompanying every generous act adds an atom to the fabric of the ideal man. As no cruel thing can be done without character being thrust a degree back towards barbarism, so no kind thing can be done without character being moved a degree forward towards perfection. Doubly efficacious, therefore, are all assuagings of distress instigated by sympathy; for not only do

* Pp. 137-38.

they remedy the particular evils to be met, but they help to mould humanity into a form by which such evils will one day be precluded.

Far otherwise is it with law-enforced plans of relief. These exercise just the opposite influence. "The quality of mercy (or pity) is not strained," says the poet. But a poor-law tries to make men pitiful by force. "It droppeth as the gentle rain from heaven," continues the poet. By a poor-law it is wrung from the unwilling. "It blesses him that gives, and him that takes," adds the poet. A poor-law makes it curse both; the one with discontent and recklessness, the other with complainings and often-renewed bitterness.

This turning of balm into poison must have been remarked by the most careless. Watch a ratepayer when the collector's name is announced. You shall observe no kindling of the eye at some thought of happiness to be conferred—no relaxing of the mouth as though selfish cares had for the moment been forgotten—no softening of the voice to tell of compassionate emotion: no, none of these; but rather will you see contracted features, a clouded brow, a sudden disappearance of what habitual kindliness of expression there may be. The tax-payer is glanced over half in fear and half in vexation; there are grumblings about the short time that has elapsed since the last rate. The purse comes slowly from the pocket; and after the collector, who is treated with bare civility, has made his exit, some little time passes before the usual equanimity is regained. Is there anything in this to remind us of the virtue which is "twice blessed?" Note, again, how this act-of-parliament charity perpetually supersedes men's better sentiments. Here is a respectable citizen with enough and to spare: a man of some feeling; liberal, if there is need; generous even; if his pity is excited. A beggar knocks at his door; or he is accosted in his walk by some way-worn tramp. What does he do? Does he listen, investigate, and, if proper, assist? No; he commonly cuts short the tale with—"I have nothing for you, my good man; you must go to your parish." And then he shuts the door, or walks on, as the case may be, with evident unconcern. Thus does the consciousness that there exists a legal provision for the indigent, act as an opiate to the yearnings of sympathy. Had there been no ready-made excuse, the behaviour would probably have been different. Commiseration, pleading for at least an inquiry into the case, would most likely have prevailed; and, in place of an application to the board of guardians, ending in a pittance coldly handed across the paytable to be thanklessly received, might have commenced a relationship good for both parties—a generosity humanizing to the one, and a succour made doubly valuable to the other by a few words of consolation and encouragement, followed, it may be, by a lift into some self-supporting position.

In truth there could hardly be found a more efficient device for decreasing fellow-feeling, than this system of State-almsgiving. Being kind by proxy!—could anything be more blighting to the finer instincts? Here is an institution through which, for a few shillings periodically paid, the citizen may compound for all kindness owing from him to his poorer brothers. Is he troubled with twinges of conscience? here is an anodyne for him, to be had by subscribing so much in the pound on his rental. Is he indifferent as to the welfare of others? why then in return for punctual payment of rates he shall have absolution for hardness of heart. Look: here is the advertisement. "Gentlemen's benevolence done for them, in the most business-like manner, and on the lowest terms. Charity doled out by a patent apparatus, warranted to save all soiling of fingers and offence to the nose. Good works undertaken by contract. Infallible remedies for self-reproach always on hand. Tender feelings kept easy at per annum."

Thus we have the gentle, softening, elevating intercourse that should be habitually taking place between rich and poor, superseded by a cold, hard lifeless mechanism, bound together by dry parchment acts and regulations—managed by commissioners, boards, clerks, and collectors, who perform their respective functions as tasks—and kept going by money forcibly taken from all classes indiscriminately. In place of the music breathed by feelings attuned to kind deeds, we have the harsh creaking and jarring of a thing that cannot stir without creating discord—a thing whose every act, from the gathering of its funds to their final distribution, is prolific of grumblings, discontent, anger—a thing that breeds squabbles about authority, disputes as to claims, brow-beatings, jealousies, litigations, corruption, trickery, lying, ingratitude—a thing that supplants, and therefore makes dormant, men's nobler feelings, while it stimulates their baser ones.

And now mark how we find illustrated in detail the truth elsewhere expressed in the abstract, that whenever a government oversteps its duty—the maintaining of men's rights—it inevitably retards the process of adaptation. For what faculty is it whose work a poor-law so officiously undertakes? Sympathy. The very faculty above all others needing to be exercised. The faculty which distinguishes the social man from the savage. The faculty which originates the idea of justice and makes men regardful of one another's claims. Of this faculty poor-laws partially supply the place. By doing which they diminish the demands made upon it, limit its exercise, check its development, and therefore retard the process of adaptation.*

In the same way that our definition of State-duty forbids the State to administer religion or charity, so likewise does it forbid the State to administer education. Inasmuch as the taking away, by Government, of more of a man's property than is needful for maintaining his rights, is an infringement of his rights, and therefore a reversal of the Government's function towards him; and inasmuch as the taking away of his property to educate his own or other people's children is not needful for the maintaining of his rights; the taking away of his property for such a purpose is wrong.

Should it be said that the rights of the children are involved, and that State-interposition is required to maintain these, the reply is that no cause for such interposition can be shown until the children's rights have been violated, and that their rights are not violated by a neglect of their education. For, as repeatedly explained, what we call rights are merely arbitrary subdivisions of the general liberty to exercise the faculties; and that only can be called an infringement of rights which actually diminishes this liberty—cuts off a previously existing power to pursue the objects of desire. Now the parent who is careless of a child's education does not do this. The liberty to exercise the faculties is left intact. Omitting instruction in no way takes from a child's freedom to do whatsoever it wills in the best way it can; and this freedom is all that equity demands. Every aggression, be it remembered—every infraction of rights, is necessarily *active;* whilst every neglect, carelessness, omission, is as necessarily *passive.* Consequently, however wrong the nonperformance of a parental duty may be, it does not amount to a breach of the law of equal freedom, and cannot therefore be taken cognizance of by the State.

---

* Pp. 146-49.

Were there no direct disproof of the frequently-alleged right to education at the hands of the State, the absurdities in which it entangles its assertors would sufficiently show its invalidity. Conceding for a moment that the Government is bound to educate a man's children, then, what kind of logic will demonstrate that it is not bound to feed and clothe them? If there should be an act-of-parliament provision for the development of their minds, why should there not be an act-of-parliament provision for the development of their bodies? The reasoning which is held to establish the right to intellectual food will equally well establish the right to material food: nay, will do more—will prove that children should be altogether cared for by Government. For if the benefit, importance, or necessity, of education, be assigned as a sufficient reason why Government should educate, then may the benefit, importance, or necessity, of food, clothing, shelter, and warmth be assigned as a sufficient reason why Government should administer these also. So that the alleged right cannot be established without annulling all parental responsibility whatever.*

[As far as the improvement of man is concerned] the fact is, that scarcely any connexion exists between morality and the discipline of ordinary teaching. Mere culture of the intellect (and education as usually conducted amounts to little more) is hardly operative upon conduct. Creeds pasted upon the mind, good principles learnt by rote, lessons in right and wrong, will not eradicate vicious propensities; though people, in spite of their experience as parents and as citizens, persist in hoping they will. Intellect is not a power but an instrument—not a thing which itself moves and works, but a thing which is moved and worked by forces behind it. To say that men are ruled by reason, is as irrational as to say that men are ruled by their eyes. Reason *is* an eye—the eye through which the desires see their way to gratification. And educating it only makes it a better eye—gives it a vision more accurate and more comprehensive—does not at all alter the desires subserved by it. However far-seeing you make it, the passions will still determine the directions in which it shall be turned—the objects on which it shall dwell. Just those ends which the instincts or sentiments propose, will the intellect be employed to accomplish: culture of it having done nothing but increase the ability to accomplish them. Probably some will urge that enlightening men enables them to discern the penalties which naturally attach to wrong-doing; and in a certain sense this is true. But it is only superficially true. Though they may learn that the grosser crimes commonly bring retribution in one shape or other, they will not learn that the subtler ones do. Their sins will merely be made more Machiavellian. If, as Coleridge says, "a knave is a fool with a circumbendibus," then, by instructing the knave, you do but make the circumbendibus a wider one. Did much knowledge and piercing intelligence suffice to make men good, then Bacon should have been honest, and Napoleon should have been just. Where the character is defective, intellect, no matter how high, fails to regulate rightly, because predominant desires falsify its estimates. Nay, even a distinct foresight of evil consequences will not restrain when strong passions are at work. How else does it happen that men will get drunk, though they *know* drunkenness will entail on them suffering and disgrace, and (as with the poor) even starvation? How else is it that medical students, who *know* the diseases brought on by dissolute living better than other young men, are just

* Pp. 156-57.

as reckless, and even more reckless? How else is it that the London thief, who has been at the treadmill a dozen times, will steal again as soon as he is at liberty?

It is, indeed, strange that with the facts of daily life before them in the street, in the counting-house, and in the family, thinking men should still expect education to cure crime. If armies of teachers, regarded with a certain superstitious reverence, have been unable to purify society in all these eighteen centuries, it is hardly likely that other armies of teachers, not so regarded, will be able to do it. If natural persuasion, backed by supernatural authority, will not induce men to do as they would be done by, it is hardly likely that natural persuasion alone will induce them. If hopes of eternal happiness and terrors of eternal damnation fail to make human beings virtuous, it is hardly likely that the commendations and reproofs of the schoolmaster will succeed.

There is, in fact, a quite sufficient reason for failure—no less a reason than the impossibility of the task. The expectation that crime may presently be cured, whether by State-education, or the silent system, or the separate system, or any other system, is one of those Utopianisms fallen into by people who pride themselves on being practical. Crime is incurable, save by that gradual process of adaptation to the social state which humanity is undergoing. Crime is the continual breaking out of the old unadapted nature—the index of a character unfitted to its conditions; and only as fast as the unfitness diminishes can crime diminish. Reforming men's conduct without reforming their natures is impossible; and to expect that their natures may be reformed, otherwise than by the forces which are slowly civilizing us, is visionary. Schemes of discipline or culture are of use only in proportion as they organically alter the national character, and the extent to which they do this is by no means great. It is not by humanly-devised agencies, good as these may be in their way, but it is by the never-ceasing action of circumstances upon men—by the constant pressure of their new conditions upon them—that the required change is mainly effected.

Meanwhile it may be remarked, that whatever moral benefit *can* be effected by education, must be effected by an education which is emotional rather than intellectual. If, in place of making a child *understand* that this thing is right and the other wrong, you make it *feel* that they are so—if you make virtue *loved* and vice *loathed*—if you arouse a noble *desire,* and make torpid an inferior one—if you bring into life a previously dormant *sentiment*—if you cause a sympathetic *impulse* to get the better of one that is selfish—if, in short, you produce a state of mind to which proper behaviour is *natural, spontaneous, instinctive,* you do some good. But no drilling in catechisms, no teaching of moral codes, can effect this. Only by repeatedly awakening the appropriate *emotions* can character be changed. Mere ideas received by the intellect, meeting no response from within, are quite inoperative upon conduct, and are quickly forgotten after entering into life.

Perhaps it will be said that a discipline like this now described as the only efficient one, might be undertaken by the State. No doubt it might. But from all legislative attempts at emotional education may Heaven defend us!*

[Finally, the principle of equal freedom condemns interference not only in commerce, public welfare, and education, but also public health.] The theory which Boards of Health and the like imply, is not only inconsistent with our definition

* Pp. 173-75.

of State-duty, but is open to strictures similar to those made in analogous cases. If, by saying "that it is the duty of the State to adopt measures for protecting the health of its subjects," it is meant (as *is* meant by the majority of the medical profession) that the State should interpose between quacks and those who patronize them, or between the druggist and the artizan who wants a remedy for his cold—if it is meant that to guard people against empirical treatment, the State should forbid all unlicensed persons from prescribing; then the reply is, that to do so is directly to violate the moral law. Men's rights are infringed by these as much as by all other, trade-interferences. The invalid is at liberty to buy medicine and advice from whomsoever he pleases; the unlicensed practitioner is at liberty to sell these to whosoever will buy. On no pretext can a barrier be set up between the two, without the law of equal freedom being broken; and least of all may the Government, whose office it is to uphold that law, become a transgressor of it.

Moreover this doctrine, that it is the duty of the State to protect the health of its subjects, cannot be established, for the same reason that its kindred doctrines cannot namely, the impossibility of saying how far the alleged duty shall be carried. Health depends on the fulfilment of numerous conditions—can be "protected" only by insuring that fulfilment. If, therefore, it is the duty of the State to protect the health of its subjects, it is its duty to see that all the conditions to health are fulfilled by them. The legislature must prescribe so many meals a day for each individual; fix the quantities and qualities of food for men, women and children; state the proportion of fluids, when to be taken, and of what kind; specify the amount of exercise, and define its character; describe the clothing to be employed; determine the hours of sleep; and to enforce these regulations it must employ officials to oversee every one's domestic arrangements. If, on the other hand, a universal supervision of private conduct is not meant, then there comes the question—Where, between this and no supervision at all, lies the boundary up to which supervision is a duty?*

Inconvenience, suffering, and death, are the penalties attached by Nature to ignorance, as well as to incompetence—are also the means of remedying these. Partly by weeding out those of lowest development, and partly by subjecting those who remain to the never-ceasing discipline of experience, Nature secures the growth of a race of men who shall both understand the conditions of existence, and be able to act up to them. It is impossible in any degree to suspend this discipline by stepping in between ignorance and its consequences, without, to a corresponding degree, suspending the progress. If to be ignorant were as safe as to be wise, no one would become wise. And all measures which tend to put ignorance upon a par with wisdom, inevitably check the growth of wisdom. Acts of Parliament to save silly people from the evils which putting faith in empirics may entail on them, do this, and are therefore bad. It is best to let the foolish man suffer the penalty of his foolishness. For the pain—he must bear it as well as he can: for the experience—he must treasure it up, and act more rationally in future. To others as well as to himself will his case be a warning. And by multiplication of such warnings, there cannot fail to be generated a caution corresponding to the danger to be shunned.

A sad population of imbeciles would our schemers fill the world with, could

* Pp. 201-2.

their plans last. A sorry kind of human constitution would they make for us—a constitution continually going wrong, and needing to be set right again—a constitution ever tending to self-destruction. Why the whole effort of Nature is to get rid of such—to clear the world of them, and make room for better. Mark how the diseased are dealt with. Consumptive patients, with lungs incompetent to perform the duties of lungs, people with digestive organs that will not take up enough nutriment, people with defective hearts which break down under effort, people with any constitutional flaw preventing due fulfilment of the conditions of life, are continually dying out, and leaving behind those fit for the climate, food, and habits to which they are born. Even the less-imperfectly organized who, under ordinary circumstances, manage to live with comfort, are still the first to be carried off by adverse influences; and only such as are robust enough to resist these—that is, only such as are tolerably well adapted to both the usual and incidental necessities of existence, remain. And thus is the race kept free from vitiation. Of course this statement is in substance a truism; for no other arrangement of things is conceivable. But it is a truism to which most men pay little regard. And if they commonly overlook its application to body, still less do they note its bearing upon mind. Yet it is equally true here. Nature just as much insists on fitness between mental character and circumstances, as between physical character and circumstances; and radical defects are as much causes of death in the one case as in the other. He on whom his own stupidity, or vice, or idleness, entails loss of life, must, in the generalizations of philosophy, be classed with the victims of weak viscera or malformed limbs. In his case, as in the others, there exists a fatal non-adaptation; and it matters not in the abstract whether it be a moral, an intellectual, or a corporeal one. Beings thus imperfect are Nature's failures, and are recalled by her when found to be such. Along with the rest they are put upon trial. If they are sufficiently complete to live, they *do* live, and it is well they should live. If they are not sufficiently complete to live, they die, and it is best they should die. And however irregular the action of this law may appear—however it may seem that much chaff is left behind which should be winnowed out, and that much grain is taken away which should be left behind; yet due consideration must satisfy every one that the *average* effect is to purify society from those who are, *in some respect or other, essentially faulty.*

Of course, in so far as the severity of this process is mitigated by the spontaneous sympathy of men for one another, it is proper that it should be mitigated: albeit there is unquestionably harm done when sympathy is shown, without any regard to ultimate results. But the drawbacks hence arising are nothing like commensurate with the benefits otherwise conferred. Only when this sympathy prompts to a breach of equity—only when it originates an interference forbidden by the law of equal freedom—only when, by so doing it suspends in some particular department of life the relationship between constitution and conditions, does it work pure evil. Then, however, it defeats its own end. It favours the multiplication of those fitted for existence, and, by consequence, hinders the multiplication of those best fitted for existence—leaving, as it does, less room for them. It tends to fill the world with those to whom life will bring most pain, and tends to keep out of it those to whom life will bring most pleasure. It inflicts positive misery, and prevents positive happiness.*

* Pp. 204-7.

MARXISM

Karl Marx and Friedrich Engels

One does not need to read history to be aware that Marxist thought is the purported ideological framework for the structure of societies and concepts of man and freedom for nearly half the world's population. Yet, it would be shortsighted to imagine that the views of Karl Marx (1818–83), Friedrich Engels (1820–95), and Nicolai Lenin (1870–1924) have remained pure. The doctrines of Marx and Engels and the vision of Lenin, while creating a catalyst for revolution and an inspiration to many persons to better man's condition, have indeed been twisted and submerged by the very forces they helped to create.

Marx and his followers saw man as an economic animal whose character was shaped by the material-economic system in which he lived. They envisaged society as a process of class antagonisms which emerged in the nineteenth century as warfare between the bourgeoisie and proletariat. In the *Communist Manifesto* (1848) Marx and Engels called for the overthrow of the capitalists and the creation of a classless society in which "the free development of each is the condition for the free development of all."

Engels further refined Marxist doctrines in *Socialism: Utopian and Scientific* (1892). Engels rejected contract theory as a bourgeois rationalization for capitalist domination. He explained the "scientific" premises and the "indelible" process of social change which made socialism inevitable. Engels also displayed optimism toward social progress and man's potential goodness which inspired a generation of idealists and political activists. He asserted that through communism each man can become his own master, develop his individuality fully, and enjoy complete freedom.

Marx and Engels

I.
Bourgeois And Proletarian Societies

A spectre is haunting Europe—the spectre of communism. All the powers of old Europe have entered into a holy alliance to exorcise this spectre: Pope and Czar, Metternich and Guizot, French Radicals and German police-spies.

Where is the party in opposition that has not been decried as communistic by its opponents in power? Where the opposition that has not hurled the branding reproach of communism, against the more advanced opposition parties, as well as against its reactionary adversaries?

Two things result from this fact.

I. Communism is already acknowledged by all European Powers to be itself a Power.

II. It is high time that Communists should openly, in the face of the whole world, publish their views, their aims, their tendencies, and meet this nursery tale of the Spectre of Communism with a Manifesto of the party itself.

To this end, Communists of various nationalities have assembled in London, and sketched the following Manifesto, to be published in the English, French, German, Italian, Flemish, and Danish languages.

The history of all hitherto existing society is the history of class struggles.

Freeman and slave, patrician and plebeian, lord and serf, guild-master and journeyman, in a word, oppressor and oppressed, stood in constant opposition to one another, carried on an uninterrupted, now hidden, now open fight, a fight that each time ended, either in a revolutionary reconstitution of society at large, or in the common ruin of the contending classes.

In the earlier epochs of history, we find almost everywhere a complicated arrangement of society into various orders, a manifold gradation of social rank. In ancient Rome we have patricians, knights, plebeians, slaves; in the middle ages, feudal lords, vassals, guild-masters, journeymen, apprentices, serfs; in almost all of these classes, again, subordinate gradations.

The modern bourgeois society that has sprouted from the ruins of feudal society has not done away with class antagonisms. It has but established new classes, new conditions of oppression, new forms of struggle in place of the old ones.

Our epoch, the epoch of the bourgeoisie, possesses, however, this distinctive feature: it has simplified the class antagonisms. Society as a whole is more and more splitting up into two great hostile camps, into two great classes directly facing each other: Bourgeoisie and Proletariat.

From the serfs of the middle ages sprang the chartered burghers of the earliest towns. From these burgesses the first elements of the bourgeoisie were developed.

The discovery of America, the rounding of the Cape, opened up fresh ground

---

Reprinted from Karl Marx and Friedrich Engels, *The Communist Manifesto* (Chicago: Charles H. Kerr, 1888), pp. 11-42, 57-58.

for the rising bourgeoisie. The East-Indian and Chinese markets, the colonization of America, trade with the colonies, the increase in the means of exchange and in commodities generally, gave to commerce, to navigation, to industry, an impulse never before known, and, thereby, a rapid development to the revolutionary element in the tottering feudal society.

The feudal system of industry, under which industrial production was monopolized by closed guilds, now no longer sufficed for the growing wants of the new markets. The manufacturing system took its place. The guild-masters were pushed to one side by the manufacturing middle class; division of labor between the different corporate guilds vanished in the face of division of labor in each single workshop.

Meantime the markets kept ever growing, the demand ever rising. Even manufacture no longer sufficed. Thereupon, steam and machinery revolutionized industrial production. The place of manufacture was taken by the giant, modern industry, the place of the industrial middle class, by industrial millionaires, the leaders of whole industrial armies, the modern bourgeois.

Modern industry has established the world market, for which the discovery of America paved the way. This market has given an immense development to commerce, to navigation, to communication by land. This development has, in its turn, reacted on the extension of industry; and in proportion as industry, commerce, navigation, railways extended, in the same proportion the bourgeoisie developed, increased its capital, and pushed into the background every class handed down from the middle ages.

We see, therefore, how the modern bourgeoisie is itself the product of a long development, of a series of revolutions in the modes of production and exchange.

Each step in the development of the bourgeoisie was accompanied by a corresponding political advance of that class. An oppressed class under the sway of the feudal nobility, an armed and self-governing association in the medieval commune. At first, an independent urban republic (as in Italy and Germany) or a taxable "third estate" of the monarchy (as in France), afterwards, in the period of manufacture proper, serving either the semi-feudal or the absolute monarchy as a counterpoise against the nobility, and, in fact, cornerstone of the great monarchies in general, the bourgeoisie has at last, since the establishment of Modern Industry and of the world market, conquered for itself, in the modern representative State, exclusive political sway. The executive of the modern State is but a committee for managing the common affairs of the whole bourgeoisie.

The bourgeoisie, historically, has played a most revolutionary part.

The bourgeoisie, wherever it has got the upper hand, has put an end to all feudal, patriarchal, idyllic relations. It has pitilessly torn asunder the motley feudal ties that bound man to his "natural superiors," and has left remaining no other nexus between man and man than naked self-interest, than callous "cash payment." It has drowned the most heavenly ecstasies of religious fervor, of chivalrous enthusiasm, of philistine sentimentalism, in the icy water of egotistical calculation. It has resolved personal worth into exchange value, and in place of the numberless indefeasible chartered freedoms, has set up that single, unconscionable freedom—Free Trade. In a word, for exploitation, veiled by religious and political illusions, it has substituted naked, shameless, direct, brutal exploitation.

The bourgeoisie has stripped of its halo every occupation hitherto honored and looked up to with reverent awe. It has converted the physician, the lawyer, the priest, the poet, and the man of science into its paid wage-laborers.

The bourgeoisie has torn away from the family its sentimental veil and has reduced the family relation to a mere money relation.

The bourgeoisie has disclosed how it came to pass that the brutal display of vigor in the Middle Ages, which reactionaries so much admire, found its fitting complement in the most slothful indolence. It has been the first to show what man's activity can bring about. It has accomplished wonders far surpassing Egyptian pyramids, Roman aqueducts, and Gothic cathedrals. It has conducted expeditions that put in the shade all former Exoduses of nations and crusades.

The bourgeoisie cannot exist without constantly revolutionizing the instruments of production, and thereby the relations of production, and with them all social relations. Conservation of the old modes of production in unaltered form, was, on the contrary, the first condition to existence for all earlier industrial classes. Constant revolutionizing of production, uninterrupted disturbance of all social conditions, everlasting uncertainty and agitation distinguish the bourgeois epoch from all earlier ones. All fixed, fast-frozen relations, with their train of ancient and venerable prejudices and opinions are swept away, all newly formed ones become antiquated before they can ossify. All that is solid melts into air, all that is holy is profaned, and man is at last compelled to face with sober senses, his real conditions of life, and his relations with his kind.

The need of a constantly expanding market for its products chases the bourgeoisie over the whole face of the globe. It must nestle everywhere, settle everywhere, establish connections everywhere.

The bourgeoisie has through its exploitation of the world market given a cosmopolitan character to production and consumption in every country. To the great chagrin of reactionists, it has drawn from under the feet of industry the national ground on which it stood. All old, established national industries have been destroyed or are daily being destroyed. They are dislodged by new industries, whose introduction becomes a life and death question for all civilized nations, industries that no longer work with indigenous raw material, but raw material drawn from the remotest regions, industries whose products are consumed, not only at home, but in every quarter of the globe. In place of the old wants, satisfied by the productions of the country, we find new wants, requiring for their satisfaction the products of distant lands and climes. In place of the old local and national seclusion and self-sufficiency, we have intercourse in every direction, a universal interdependence of nations. And as in material, so also in intellectual production. The intellectual creations of individual nations become common property. National one-sidedness and narrow-mindedness become more and more impossible, and from the numerous national and local literatures, there arises a world literature.

The bourgeoisie, by the rapid improvement of all instruments of production, by the immensely facilitated means of communication, draws all, even the most barbarian, nations into civilization. The cheap prices of its commodities are the heavy artillery with which it batters down all Chinese walls, with which it forces the barbarians' intensely obstinate hatred of foreigners to capitulate. It compels all nations, on pain of extinction, to adopt the bourgeois mode of production; it compels them to introduce what it calls civilization into their midst, *i.e.*, to become bourgeois themselves. In one word, it creates a world after its own image.

The bourgeoisie has subjected the country to the rule of the towns. It has created enormous cities, greatly increased the urban population as compared with the rural, and thus rescued a considerable part of the population from the idiocy of rural life. Just as it has made the country dependent on the towns, so it has made barbarian and semi-barbarian countries dependent on the civilized ones, nations of peasants on nations of bourgeoisie, the East on the West. More and more the bourgeoisie continues to do away with the scattered state of population, means of production, and property. It has agglomerated population, centralized means of production, and concentrated property in a few hands. The necessary consequence of this was political centralization. Independent, or but loosely connected, provinces with separate interests, laws, governments and systems of taxation, became lumped together into one nation, with one government, one code of laws, one national class-interest, one frontier and one customs-tariff.

The bourgeoisie, during its rule of scarcely one hundred years, has created more massive and more colossal productive forces than have all preceding generations together. The subjection of Nature's forces to man and machinery; the application of chemistry to industry and agriculture; [the development of] steam-navigation, railways and electric telegraphs; the clearing of whole continents for cultivation; the canalization of rivers and the conjuring of whole populations out of the ground—what earlier century had even a presentiment that such productive forces slumbered in the lap of social labor?

We see then: the means of production and exchange, on whose foundation the bourgeoisie built itself up, were generated in feudal society. At a certain stage in the development of these means of production and exchange, the conditions under which feudal society produced and exchanged, the feudal organization of agriculture and manufacturing industry, in one word, the feudal relations of property became no longer compatible with the already developed productive forces; they became so many fetters. They had to be burst asunder. They were burst asunder.

Into their place stepped free competition, accompanied by a social and political constitution adapted to it and by the economical and political sway of the bourgeois class.

A similar movement is going on before our own eyes. Modern bourgeois society with its relations of production, exchange and property, a society that has conjured up such gigantic means of production and exchange, is like the sorcerer, who is no longer able to control the powers of the nether world whom he has called up by his spells. For many decades the history of industry and commerce has been but the history of the revolt of modern productive forces against modern conditions of production, against the property relations that are the conditions for the existence of the bourgeoisie and of its rule. It is enough to mention the commercial crises that by their periodic return put on its trial, each time more threateningly, the existence of the entire bourgeois society. In these crises a great part not only of the existing products, but also of the previously created productive forces are periodically destroyed. In these crises there breaks out an epidemic that in all earlier epochs would have seemed an absurdity—the epidemic of overproduction. Society suddenly finds itself put back into a state of momentary barbarism. It appears as if a famine or a universal war of devastation had cut off the supply of every means of subsistence. Industry and commerce seem to be destroyed. And why? Because there is too much civilization, too much means of subsistence, too much industry, too much commerce. The productive forces at the disposal of society no longer tend to further the development of the conditions of bourgeois property. On the contrary, they have become too powerful for these conditions, by which they are fettered, and so soon as they overcome these fetters, they bring disorder into the whole of bourgeois society, endanger the existence of bourgeois property. The conditions of bourgeois society are too narrow to encompass the wealth created by them. And how does the bourgeoisie get over these crises? On the one hand by enforced destruction of a mass of productive forces; on the other, by the conquest of new markets, and by the more thorough exploitation of the old ones. That is to say, by paving the way for more extensive and more destructive crises, and by diminishing the means whereby crises are prevented.

The weapons with which the bourgeoisie brought feudalism to the ground are now turned against the bourgeoisie itself.

But not only has the bourgeoisie forged the weapons that bring death to itself; it has also called into existence the men who are to wield those weapons—the modern working class—the proletariat.

In proportion as the bourgeoisie, *i.e.*, capital, develops, in the same proportion the proletariat, the modern working class, develops—a class of laborers, who live only so long as they find work, and who find work only so long as their labor increases capital. These laborers, who must sell themselves piecemeal, are a commodity, like every other article of commerce, and are consequently exposed to all the vicissitudes of competition, to all the fluctuations of the market.

Owing to the extensive use of machinery and to the division of labor, work for the proletarians has lost all individual character, and, consequently, all charm for the workman. He becomes an appendage of the machine, and it is only the simplest, most monotonous, and most easily acquired knack that is required of him. Hence, the cost of production of a workman is restricted, almost entirely, to the means of subsistence that he requires for his maintenance and for the propagation of his race. But the price of a commodity, and therefore also of labor, is equal to its cost of production. In proportion, therefore, as the repulsiveness of the work increases, the wage decreases. Nay more, to the extent that the use of machinery and the division of labor increases, to the same extent the burden of toil also increases, whether by the prolongation of working hours, the increase of the work exacted in a given time or the increased speed of the machinery, etc.

Modern industry has converted the little workshop of the patriarchal master into the great factory of the industrial capitalist. Masses of laborers crowded into the factory are organized like soldiers. As privates of the industrial army they are placed under the command of a perfect hierarchy of officers and sergeants. Not only are they slaves of the bourgeois class and the bourgeois State; they are daily and hourly enslaved by the machine, by the supervisor, and, above all, by the individual bourgeois manufacturer himself. The more openly this despotism proclaims gain to be its end and aim, the more petty, the more hateful and the more embittering it is.

The less the skill and exertion of strength involved in manual labor (in other words, the more modern industry becomes developed), the more the labor of men is replaced by that of women. Differences of age and sex have no longer any distinctive social validity for the working class. All are instruments of labor, more or less expensive to use, according to their age and sex.

No sooner is the exploitation of the laborer by the manufacturer, so far, at an end, that he receives his wages in cash, than he is set upon by the other portions of the bourgeoisie, the landlord, the shopkeeper, the pawnbroker, etc.

The lower strata of the Middle class—small tradespeople, shopkeepers, retired tradesmen, handicraftsmen and peasants—all these sink gradually into the proletariat, partly because their diminutive capital does not suffice for the scale on which Modern Industry is carried on and is swamped in the competition with the large capitalists, partly because their specialized skill is rendered worthless by new methods of production. Thus, the proletariat is recruited from all classes of the population.

The proletariat goes through various stages of development. With its birth begins its struggle with the bourgeoisie. At first the contest is carried on by individual laborers, then by the workers of a factory, then by the laborers of one trade in one locality, against the individual bourgeois who directly exploits them. They direct their attacks not against the bourgeois conditions of production, but against the instruments of production themselves; they destroy imported wares that compete with their labor, they smash to pieces machinery, they set factories ablaze, they seek to restore by force the vanished status of the workman of the Middle Ages.

At this stage the laborers still form an incoherent mass scattered over the whole country, and divided by their mutual competition. If they unite anywhere to form more compact bodies, this is not yet the consequence of their own active union, but of the union of the bourgeoisie, which, in order to attain its own political ends, is compelled to set the whole proletariat in motion, and is moreover yet, for a time, able to do so. At this stage, therefore, the proletarians do not fight their enemies, but the enemies of their enemies, the remnants of absolute monarchy, the landowners, the non-industrial bourgeois, the petty bourgeoisie. Thus the whole historical movement is concentrated in the hands of the bourgeoisie; every victory so obtained is a victory for the bourgeoisie.

But with the development of industry the proletariat not only increases in number; it becomes concentrated in greater masses, its strength grows, and it becomes more aware of that strength. The various interests and conditions of life within the ranks of the proletariat are more and more equalized, in proportion as machinery obliterates all distinctions of labor, and nearly everywhere reduces wages to the same low level. The growing competition among the bourgeoisie and the resulting commercial crises, make the wages of the workers ever more fluctuating. The unceasing improvement of machinery, ever more rapidly developing, makes their livelihood more and more precarious. The collisions between individual workmen and individual bourgeois take more and more the character of collisions between two classes. Thereupon the workers begin to form combinations (Trade Unions) against the bourgeois; they join together in order to keep up the rate of wages; they form permanent associations in order to make provision beforehand for these occasional revolts. Here and there the contest breaks out into riots.

Now and then the workers are victorious, but only for a time. The real fruit of their battles lies, not in the immediate result, but in the ever-expanding union of the workers. This union is helped on by the improved means of communication that are created by modern industry and that place the workers of different localities in contact with one another. It was just this contact that was needed to centralize the numerous local struggles, all of the same character, into one national struggle between classes. But every class struggle is a political struggle. And that union, which took the burghers of the Middle Ages, with their miserable highways, centuries to acquire, the modern proletarians, thanks to railways, achieve in a few years.

This organization of the proletarians into a class, and consequently into a political party, is continually being upset again by the competition between the workers themselves. But it continually re-emerges, stronger, firmer, mightier. It compels legislative recognition of particular interests of the workers, by taking advantage of the divisions among the bourgeoisie itself. Thus the ten-hours' bill in England was carried.

The sum of these collisions between the classes of the old society further, in many ways, the development of the proletariat. The bourgeoisie finds itself involved in a constant battle. At first with the aristocracy; later, with those portions of the bourgeoisie itself, whose interests have become antagonistic to the progress of industry; at all times, with the bourgeoisie of foreign countries. In all these battles it sees itself compelled to appeal to the proletariat, to ask for its help, and thus, to drag it into the political arena. The bourgeoisie itself, therefore, supplies the proletariat with its own elements of political and general education, in other words, it furnishes the proletariat with weapons for fighting the bourgeoisie.

Further, as we have already seen, entire sections of the ruling classes are, by the advance of industry, precipitated into the proletariat, or are at least threatened in their conditions of existence. These also supply the proletariat with fresh elements of enlightenment and progress.

Finally, in times when the class struggle nears the decisive hour, the process of dissolution going on within the ruling class (in fact, within the whole range of old society) assumes such a violent, glaring character, that a small section of the ruling class cuts itself adrift, and joins the revolutionary class, the class that holds the future in its hands. Just as, therefore, at an earlier period, a section of the nobility went over to the bourgeoisie, so now a portion of the bourgeoisie goes over to the proletariat, and in particular, a portion of the bourgeois ideologists, who have raised themselves to the level of comprehending theoretically the historical movement as a whole.

Of all the classes that stand face to face with the bourgeoisie today, the proletariat alone is a really revolutionary class. The other classes decay and finally disappear in the face of modern industry; the proletariat is its special and essential product.

The lower middle class, the small manufacturer, the shopkeeper, the artisan, the peasant—all these fight against the bourgeoisie, to save from extinction their existence as fractions of the middle class. They are therefore not revolutionary, but conservative. Nay more, they are reactionary, for they try to roll back the wheel of history. If by chance they are revolutionary, they are so only in view of their impending transfer into the proletariat, they thus defend not their present, but their future interests, they desert their own standpoint to place themselves at that of the proletariat.

The "dangerous class," the social scum, that passively rotting mass thrown off by the lowest layers of the old society, may, here and there, be swept into the movement by a proletarian revolution; its conditions of life, however, prepare it far more for the part of a bribed tool of reactionary intrigue.

For the proletariat, the conditions of the old society are already virtually swamped.

The proletarian is without property; his relation to his wife and children has no longer anything in common with the bourgeois family relations; modern industrial labor, modern subjection to capital, the same in England as in France, in America as in Germany, has stripped him of every trace of national character. Law, morality, religion, are to him so many bourgeois prejudices, behind which lurk in ambush just as many bourgeois interests.

All the preceding classes that got the upper hand sought to fortify their already acquired status by subjecting society at large to their conditions of appropriation. The proletarians cannot become masters of the productive forces of society, except by abolishing their own previous mode of appropriation, and thereby also every other previous mode of appropriation. They have nothing of their own to secure and to fortify; their mission is to destroy all previous securities for, and insurances of, individual property.

All previous historical movements were movements of minorities, or in the interest of minorities. The proletarian movement is the self-conscious, independent movement of the immense majority, in the interest of the immense majority. The proletariat, the lowest stratum of our present society, cannot stir, cannot raise itself, without the whole overlying strata of official society being sprung into the air.

Though not in substance, yet in form, the struggle of the proletariat with the bourgeoisie is at first a national struggle. The proletariat of each country must, of course, first of all settle matters with its own bourgeoisie.

In depicting the most general phases of the development of the proletariat, we traced the more or less veiled civil war raging within existing society, up to the point where that war breaks out into open revolution, and where the violent overthrow of the bourgeoisie lays the foundation for the sway of the proletariat.

Hitherto, every form of society has been based, as we have already seen, on the antagonism between oppressing and oppressed classes. But in order to oppress a class, certain conditions must be assured to it under which it can, at least, continue its slavish existence. The serf, in the period of serfdom, raised himself to membership in the commune, just as the petty bourgeois, under the yoke of feudal absolutism, managed to develop into a bourgeois. The modern laborer, on the contrary, instead of rising with the progress of industry, sinks deeper and deeper below the conditions of existence of his own class. He becomes a pauper, and pauperism develops more rapidly than population and wealth. And here it becomes evident that the bourgeoisie is unfit any longer to be the ruling class in society and to impose on society its own conditions of existence as an overriding law. It is unfit to rule because it is incompetent to assure an existence to its slave within his slavery, because it cannot help letting him sink into such a state that it has to feed him, instead of being fed by him. Society can no longer live under this bourgeoisie. In other words, its existence is no longer compatible with society.

The essential condition for the existence, and for the sway of the bourgeois class is the formation and augmentation of capital; the condition for capital is wage labor. Wage labor rests exclusively on competition between the laborers. The advance of industry, that the bourgeoisie involuntarily promotes, replaces the isolation of the laborers, due to competition, by their revolutionary combination, due to association. The development of Modern Industry, therefore, cuts from under its feet the very foundation on which the bourgeoisie produces and appropriates products. What the bourgeoisie, therefore, produces, above all, is its own gravediggers. Its fall and the victory of the proletariat are equally inevitable.

II.
The Proletariat And Communism—
Property And Liberty

In what relation do the Communists stand to the proletarians as a whole?

The Communists do not form a separate party opposed to other working-class parties.

They have no interests separate and apart from those of the proletariat as a whole.

They do not set up any sectarian principles of their own, by which to shape and mold the proletarian movement.

The Communists are distinguished from the other working-class parties by this only: 1. In the national struggles of the proletarians of the different countries, they point out and bring to the fore the common interests of the entire proletariat, independent of all nationality. 2. In the various stages of development through which the struggle of the working class against the bourgeoisie has to pass, they always and everywhere represent the interests of the movement as a whole.

The Communists, therefore, are on the one hand, in the sphere of practice, the most advanced and resolute section of the working-class parties of every country, that section which pushes forward all others; and on the other hand, in the realm of theory, they have over the great mass of the proletariat the advantage of clearly understanding the line of march, the conditions, and the ultimate general results of the proletarian movement.

The immediate aim of the Communists is the same as that of all the other proletarian parties: the formation of the proletariat into a class; the overthrow of the bourgeois supremacy; and the conquest of political power by the proletariat.

The theoretical conclusions of the Communists are in no way based on ideas or principles that have been invented or discovered by this or that would-be universal reformer.

They merely express, in general terms, actual relations springing from an existing class struggle, from a historical movement going on under our very eyes. The abolition of existing property relations is not at all a distinctive feature of Communism.

All property relations in the past have continually been subject to historical change resulting from the change in historical conditions.

The French Revolution, for example, abolished feudal property in favor of bourgeois property.

The distinguishing feature of Communism is not the abolition of property generally, but the abolition of bourgeois property. But modern bourgeois private property is the final and most complete expression of the system of producing and appropriating products, that is based on class antagonisms, on the exploitation of the many by the few.

In this sense, the theory of the Communists may be summed up in the single sentence: the abolition of private property.

We Communists have been reproached with the desire of abolishing the right of personally acquiring property as the fruit of a man's own labor, the property that is alleged to be the foundation of all personal freedom, activity and independence.

Hard-won, self-acquired, self-earned property! Do you mean the property of the petty artisan and of the small peasant, a form of property that preceded the bourgeois form? There is no need to abolish that: the development of industry has to a great extent already destroyed it and is still destroying it daily.

Or do you mean modern bourgeois private property?

But does wage labor create any property for the laborer? Not a bit. It creates capital, *i.e.*, that kind of property which exploits wage labor, and which cannot increase except upon condition of begetting a new supply of wage labor for fresh exploitation. Property, in its present form, is based on the antagonism of capital and wage labor. Let us examine both sides of this antagonism.

To be a capitalist, is to have not only a purely personal, but also a social status in production. Capital is a collective product, and only by the united action of many members, nay, in the last resort, only by the united action of all members of society, can it be set in motion.

Capital is, therefore, not a personal but a social power.

When, therefore, capital is converted into common property, into the property of all members of society, personal property is not thereby transformed into social property. It is only the social character of the property that is changed. It loses its class character.

Let us now take wage labor.

The average price of wage labor is the minimum wage, *i.e.*, that quantity of the means of subsistence, which is absolutely requisite to keep the laborer in bare existence as a laborer. What, therefore, the wage-laborer appropriates by means of his labor, merely suffices to prolong and reproduce a bare existence. We by no means intend to abolish this personal appropriation of the products of labor, an appropriation that is made for the maintenance and reproduction of human life and that leaves no surplus wherewith to command the labor of others. All that we want to do away with is the miserable character of this appropriation, under which the laborer lives merely to increase capital and is allowed to live only in so far as the interest of the ruling class requires it.

In bourgeois society, living labor is but a means to increase accumulated labor. In Communist society, accumulated labor is but a means to widen, to enrich, to promote the existence of the laborer.

In bourgeois society, therefore, the past dominates the present; in Communist society, the present dominates the past. In bourgeois society capital is independent and has individuality, while the living person is dependent and has no individuality.

And the abolition of this state of things is called by the bourgeois abolition of individuality and freedom! And rightly so. The abolition of bourgeois individuality, bourgeois independence, and bourgeois freedom is undoubtedly aimed at.

By freedom is meant, under the present bourgeois conditions of production, free trade, free selling and buying.

But if selling and buying disappears, free selling and buying disappears also. This talk about free selling and buying, and all the other "brave words" of our bourgeoisie about freedom in general, have a meaning, if any, only in contrast with restricted selling and buying, with the fettered traders of the Middle Ages, but have no meaning when opposed to the Communistic abolition of buying and selling, of the bourgeois conditions of production, and of the bourgeoisie itself.

You are horrified at our intending to do away with private property. But in your existing society, private property is already done away with for nine tenths of the population; its existence for the few is solely due to its nonexistence in the hands of those nine tenths. You reproach us, therefore, with intending to do away with a form of property, the necessary condition for whose existence is, the nonexistence of any property for the immense majority of society.

In one word, you reproach us with intending to do away with your property. Precisely so; that is just what we intend.

From the moment when labor can no longer be converted into capital, money, or rent, into a social power capable of being monopolized, *i.e.*, from the moment when individual property can no longer be transformed into bourgeois property, into capital, from that moment, you say, individuality vanishes.

You must, therefore, confess that by "individual" you mean no other person than the bourgeois, than the middle class owner of property. This person must, indeed, be swept out of the way, and made impossible.

Communism deprives no man of the power to appropriate the products of society; all that it does is to deprive him of the power to subjugate the labor of others by means of such appropriation.

It has been objected that upon the abolition of private property all work will cease, and universal laziness will overtake us.

According to this, bourgeois society ought long ago to have gone to the dogs through sheer idleness; for those of its members who work, acquire nothing, and those who acquire anything, do not work. The whole of this objection is but another expression of the tautology: that there can no longer be any wage labor when there is no longer any capital.

All objections urged against the Communistic mode of producing and appropriating material products, have, in the same way, been urged against the Communistic modes of producing and appropriating intellectual products. Just as, to the bourgeois, the disappearance of class property is the disappearance of production itself, so the disappearance of class culture is to him identical with the disappearance of all culture.

That culture, the loss of which he laments, is for the enormous majority a mere training to act as a machine.

III.
The Bourgeois Society Compared To The Communist State

But don't wrangle with us so long as you apply to our intended abolition of bourgeois property the standard of your bourgeois nations of freedom, culture, law, etc. Your very ideas are but the outgrowth of the conditions of your bourgeois production and bourgeois property, just as your jurisprudence is but the will of your class made into a law for all, a will, whose essential character and direction are determined by the economic conditions of existence of your class.

The selfish misconception that induces you to transform into eternal laws of nature and of reason, the social forms springing from your present mode of production and form of property—historical relations that rise and disappear in the progress of production—this misconception you share with every ruling class that has preceded you. What you see clearly in the case of ancient property, what you admit in the case of feudal property, you are of course forbidden to admit in the case of your own bourgeois form of property.

Abolition of the family! Even the most radical flare up at this infamous proposal of the Communists.

On what foundation is the present family, the bourgeois family based? On capital, on private gain. In its completely developed form this family exists only among the bourgeoisie. But this state of things finds its complement in the practical absence of the family among the proletarians and in public prostitution.

The bourgeois family will vanish as a matter of course when its complement vanishes, and both will vanish with the vanishing of capital.

Do you charge us with wanting to stop the exploitation of children by their parents? To this crime we plead guilty.

But, you will say, we destroy the most hallowed of relations when we replace home education by social.

And your education! Is not that also social and determined by the social conditions under which you educate, by the intervention, direct or indirect, of society, by means of schools, etc.? The Communists have not invented the intervention of society in education; they only seek to alter the character of that intervention and to rescue education from the influence of the ruling class.

The bourgeois claptrap about the family and education, about the hallowed relationship between parent and child, becomes all the more disgusting, the more that, as a result of modern industry, all family ties among the proletarians are torn asunder and their children transformed into simple articles of commerce and instruments of labor.

But you Communists would introduce community of women, screams the whole bourgeoisie in chorus.

The bourgeois sees in his wife a mere instrument of production. He hears that the instruments of production are to be exploited in common, and, naturally, can come to no other conclusion than that the lot of being common to all will likewise fall to the women.

He has not even a suspicion that the real point aimed at is to do away with the status of women as mere instruments of production.

For the rest, nothing is more ridiculous than the virtuous indignation of our bourgeois at the community of women which, they pretend, is to be openly and officially established by the Communists. The Communists have no need to introduce community of women; it has existed almost from time immemorial.

Our bourgeois, not content with having the wives and daughters of their proletarians at their disposal, not to speak of common prostitutes, take the greatest pleasure in seducing each others' wives.

Bourgeois marriage is in reality a system of wives in common and thus, at the most, what the Communists might possibly be reproached with is that they desire to introduce, in place of a hypocritically concealed community of women, an openly legalized one. For the rest, it is self-evident that the abolition of the present system of production must bring with it the abolition of the community of women springing from that system, *i.e.*, of prostitution both public and private.

The Communists are further reproached with desiring to abolish countries and nationality.

The working men have no country. We cannot take from them what they have not got. Since the proletariat must first of all acquire political supremacy, must rise to be the leading class of the nation, must constitute itself *the* nation, it is to this extent itself national, though not in the bourgeois sense of the word.

National differences and antagonisms between peoples are daily more and more vanishing, owing to the development of the bourgeoisie, to freedom of commerce, to the world market, to uniformity in the mode of production and in the conditions of life corresponding thereto.

The supremacy of the proletariat will cause them to vanish still faster. United action, at least of the leading civilized countries, is one of the first conditions for the emancipation of the proletariat.

To the extent that the exploitation of one individual by another is put to an end, the exploitation of one nation by another will also be put to an end. To the extent that the antagonism between classes within the nation vanishes, the hostility of one nation to another will come to an end.

The charges against Communism made from a religious, a philosophical, and, generally, from an ideological standpoint, are not deserving of serious examination.

Does it require deep intuition to comprehend that man's ideas, views and conceptions, in one word, man's consciousness, changes with every change in the conditions of his material existence, in his social relations and in his social life?

What else does the history of ideas prove than that intellectual production changes its character to the extent that material production is changed? The ruling ideas of each age have always been the ideas of its ruling class.

When people speak of ideas that revolutionize society, they only express the fact, that within the old society, the elements of a new one have been created, and that the dissolution of the old ideas keeps pace with the dissolution of the old conditions of existence.

When the ancient world was in its last throes, the ancient religions were overcome by Christianity. When Christian ideas succumbed in the eighteenth century to rationalist ideas, feudal society fought its death battle with the then revolutionary bourgeoisie. The ideas of religious liberty and freedom of conscience merely gave expression to the sway of free competition within the domain of knowledge.

"Undoubtedly," it will be said, "religious, moral, philosophical and juridical ideas have been modified in the course of historical development. But religion, morality, philosophy, political science, and law constantly survived this change."

"There are, besides, eternal truths, such as Freedom, Justice, etc., that are common to all states of society. But Communism abolishes eternal truths; it abolishes all religion, and all morality, instead of constituting them on a new basis; it therefore acts in contradiction to all past historical experience."

To what does this accusation reduce itself? The history of all past society has consisted in the development of class antagonisms, antagonisms that assumed different forms at different epochs.

But whatever form they may have taken, one fact is common to all past ages, *viz.*, the exploitation of one part of society by the other. No wonder, then, that the social consciousness of past ages, despite all the multiplicity and variety it displays, moves within certain common forms, or general ideas, which cannot completely vanish except with the total disappearance of class antagonisms.

The Communist revolution is the most radical rupture with traditional property relations; no wonder that its development involves the most radical rupture with traditional ideas.

But let us be done with the bourgeois objections to Communism.

We have seen above that the first step in the revolution by the working class is to raise the proletariat to the position of ruling class, to win the battle of democracy.

The proletariat will use its political supremacy to wrest, by degrees, all capital from the bourgeoisie, to centralize all instruments of production in the hands of the State (*i.e.*, the proletariat organized as the ruling class), and to increase the total of productive forces as rapidly as possible.

Of course, in the beginning, this cannot be effected except by means of despotic inroads on the rights of property and on the conditions of bourgeois production; by means of measures, therefore, which appear economically insufficient and untenable, but which, in the course of the movement, outstrip themselves, necessitate further inroads upon the old social order, and are unavoidable as a means of entirely revolutionizing the mode of production.

These measures will of course be different in different countries.

Nevertheless in the most advanced countries, the following will be pretty generally applicable.

1. Abolition of property in land and application of all rents of land to public purposes.
2. A heavy progressive or graduated income tax.
3. Abolition of all right of inheritance.
4. Confiscation of the property of all emigrants and rebels.
5. Centralization of credit in the hands of the State, by means of a national bank with State capital and an exclusive monopoly.
6. Centralization of the means of communication and transport in the hands of the State.
7. Extension of factories and instruments of production owned by the State; cultivation of waste-lands; and improvement of the soil generally in accordance with a common plan.
8. Equal liability of all to labor. Establishment of industrial armies, especially for agriculture.
9. Combination of agriculture with manufacturing industries; and gradual abolition of the distinction between town and country by a more equable distribution of the population over the country.
10. Free education for all children in public schools. Abolition of children's factory labor in its present form. Combination of education with industrial production, etc.

When, in the course of development, class distinctions have disappeared and all production has been concentrated in the hands of a vast association of the whole nation, the public power will lose its political character. Political power, properly so called, is merely the organized power of one class for oppressing another. If the proletariat during its contest with the bourgeoisie is compelled, by the force of circumstances, to organize itself as a class, if, by means of a revolution, it makes itself the ruling class and as such sweeps away by force the old conditions of production, then it will have swept away, along with these conditions, the conditions for the existence of class antagonisms and classes generally and will thereby have abolished its own supremacy as a class.

In place of the old bourgeois society, with its classes and class antagonisms, we shall have an association in which the free development of each is the condition for the free development of all.*

IV.
Conclusion

The Communists fight for the attainment of the immediate aims, for the enforcement of the momentary interests of the working class; but in the movement of the present, they also represent and take care of the future of that movement. In France the Communists ally themselves with the Social Democrats against the conservative and radical bourgeoisie, reserving, however, the right to take up a critical position in regard to phrases and illusions traditionally handed down from the great Revolution.

In Switzerland they support the Radicals, without losing sight of the fact that this party consists of antagonistic elements, partly of Democratic Socialists, in the French sense, partly of radical bourgeois.

In Poland they support the party that insists on an agrarian revolution as the prime condition for national emancipation, that party which fomented the insurrection of Cracow in 1846.

In Germany they fight with the bourgeoisie whenever it acts in a revolutionary way against the absolute monarchy, the feudal squirearchy, and the petty bourgeoisie.

But they never cease for a single instant to instill into the working class the clearest possible recognition of the hostile antagonism between bourgeoisie and proletariat, in order that the German workers may use as so many weapons against the bourgeoisie the social and political conditions that the bourgeoisie must necessarily introduce along with its supremacy, and in order that, after the fall of the reactionary classes in Germany, the fight against the bourgeoisie itself may immediately begin.

The Communists turn their attention chiefly to Germany, because that country is on the eve of a bourgeois revolution that is bound to be carried out under more advanced conditions of European civilization, and with a much more developed proletariat, than that of England was in the seventeenth, and of France in the eighteenth century, and because the bourgeois revolution in Germany will be but the prelude to an immediately following proletarian revolution.

In short, the Communists everywhere support every revolutionary movement against the existing social and political order of things.

In all these movements they bring to the fore, as the leading question in each, the property question, no matter what its degree of development at the time.

---

* Pp. 11-42.

Finally, they labor everywhere for the union and agreement of the democratic parties of all countries.

The Communists disdain to conceal their views and aims. They openly declare that their ends can be attained only by the forcible overthrow of all existing social conditions. Let the ruling classes tremble at a Communistic revolution. The proletarians have nothing to lose but their chains. They have a world to win.

WORKING MEN OF ALL COUNTRIES, UNITE!*

Friedrich Engels

I.
The Breakdown Of The Bourgeois State And The Rise Of Utopian Socialism

Modern socialism is, in its essence, the direct product of the recognition, on the one hand, of the class antagonisms existing in the society of today between proprietors and non-proprietors, between capitalists and wage-workers; on the other hand, of the anarchy existing in production. But, in its theoretical form, modern socialism originally appears ostensibly as a more logical extension of the principles laid down by the great French philosophers of the eighteenth century. Like every new theory, modern socialism at first had to connect itself with the intellectual stock-in-trade ready at hand, however deeply its roots lay in material economic facts.

The great men, who in France prepared men's minds for the coming revolution, were themselves extreme revolutionists. They recognized no external authority of any kind whatever. Religion, natural science, society, political institutions—everything was subjected to the most unsparing criticism: everything must justify its existence before the judgment of reason or give up existence. Reason became the sole measure of everything. It was the time when, as Hegel says, the world stood upon its head; first in the sense that the human head, and the principles arrived at by its thought, claimed to be the basis of all human action and association; but by and by, also, in the wider sense that the reality which was in contradiction to these principles had, in fact, to be turned upside down. Every form of society and government then existing, every old traditional notion was flung into the lumber-room as irrational; the world had hitherto allowed itself to be led solely by prejudices; everything in the past deserved only pity and contempt. Now, for the first time, appeared the light of day, the kingdom of reason; henceforth superstition, injustice, privilege, oppression, were to be superseded by eternal truth, eternal Right, equality based on Nature and the inalienable rights of man.

---

* Pp. 57-58.

Reprinted from Friedrich Engels, *Socialism: Utopian and Scientific* (New York: Charles Scribner's Sons, 1892), pp. 1-4, 7-10, 28, 36-87.

We know today that this kingdom of reason was nothing more than the idealized kingdom of the bourgeoisie; that this eternal Right found its realization in bourgeois justice; that this equality reduced itself to bourgeois equality before the law; that bourgeois property was proclaimed as one of the essential rights of man; and that the government of reason, the Social Contract of Rousseau, came into being, and only could come into being, as a democratic bourgeois republic. The great thinkers of the eighteenth century could, no more than their predecessors, go beyond the limits imposed upon them by their epoch.*

We saw how the French philosophers of the eighteenth century, the forerunners of the Revolution, appealed to reason as the sole judge of all that is. A rational government, rational society, were to be founded; everything that ran counter to eternal reason was to be remorselessly done away with. We saw also that this eternal reason was in reality nothing but the idealized understanding of the eighteenth century citizen, just then evolving into the bourgeois. The French Revolution had realized this rational society and government.

But the new order of things, rational enough as compared with earlier conditions, turned out to be by no means absolutely rational. The state based upon reason completely collapsed. Rousseau's Social Contract had found its realization in the Reign of Terror, from which the bourgeoisie, who had lost confidence in their own political capacity, had taken refuge first in the corruption of the Directorate, and, finally, under the wing of the Napoleonic despotism. The promised eternal peace was turned into an endless war of conquest. The society based upon reason had fared no better. The antagonism between rich and poor, instead of dissolving into general prosperity, had become intensified by the removal of the guild and other privileges, which had to some extent bridged it over, and by the removal of the charitable institutions of the Church. The "freedom of property" from feudal fetters, now veritably accomplished, turned out to be, for the small capitalists and small proprietors, the freedom to sell their small property, crushed under the overwhelming competition of the large capitalists and landlords, to these great lords, and thus, as far as the small capitalists and peasant proprietors were concerned, became "freedom *from* property." The development of industry upon a capitalistic basis brought poverty and misery to the working masses' conditions of social existence. Cash payment became more and more, in Carlyle's phrase, the sole nexus between man and man. The number of crimes increased from year to year. Formerly, the feudal vices had openly stalked about in broad daylight; though not eradicated, they were now at any rate thrust into the background. In their place, the bourgeois vices, hitherto practiced in secret, began to blossom all the more luxuriantly. Trade became to a greater and greater extent cheating. The "fraternity" of the revolutionary motto was realized in the chicanery and rivalries of the battle of competition. Oppression by force was replaced by corruption; the sword, as the first social lever, by gold. The right of the first night was transferred from the feudal lords to the bourgeois manufacturers. Prostitution increased to an unheard-of extent. Marriage itself remained, as before, the legally recognized form, the official cloak of prostitution, and, moreover, was supplemented by rich crops of adultery.

In a word, compared with the splendid promises of the philosophers, the social

---

* Pp. 1-4.

and political institutions born of the "triumph of reason" were bitterly disappointing caricatures.*

II. Hegelian Philosophy And The Dialectic View Of Industrial And Social Processes

In the meantime, along with and after the French philosophy of the eighteenth century there had arisen the new German philosophy, culminating in Hegel. Its greatest merit was the resumption of dialectics as the highest form of reasoning.†

In this system—and herein is its great merit—for the first time the whole world, natural, historical, intellectual, is represented as a process, *i.e.*, as in constant motion, change, transformation, development; and the attempt is made to trace out the internal connection that makes a continuous whole of all this movement and development. From this point of view the history of mankind no longer appeared as a wild whirl of senseless deeds of violence, all equally condemnable by the judgment of mature philosophic reason and best forgotten as quickly as possible, but as the process of evolution of man himself. It was now the task of the intellect to follow the gradual march of this process through all its devious ways, and to trace out the inner law running through all its apparently accidental phenomena. . . .

On the one hand, its essential proposition was the conception that human history is a process of evolution, which, by its very nature, cannot find its intellectual final term in the discovery of any so-called absolute truth. But, on the other hand, it laid claim to being the very essence of this absolute truth. A system of natural and historical knowledge, embracing everything, and final for all time, is a contradiction of the fundamental law of dialectic reasoning. This law, indeed, by no means excludes, but, on the contrary, includes the idea that the systematic knowledge of the external universe can make giant strides from age to age.

The perception of the fundamental contradiction in German idealism led necessarily back to materialism, but, *nota bene,* not to the simply metaphysical, exclusively mechanical materialism of the eighteenth century. Old materialism looked upon all previous history as a crude heap of irrationality and violence; modern materialism sees in it the process of evolution of humanity, and aims at discovering the laws thereof. With the French of the eighteenth century, and even with Hegel, the prevailing conception was one of Nature as a whole, moving in narrow circles, and for ever immutable, with its eternal celestial bodies, as Newton taught, and unalterable organic species, as Linnaeus taught. Modern materialism embraces the more recent discoveries of natural science, according to which Nature also has its history in time, the celestial bodies, like the organic species that, under favorable conditions, people them, being born and perishing. And even if Nature, as a whole, must still be said to move in recurrent cycles, these cycles assume infinitely larger dimensions. In both aspects, modern materialism is essentially dialectic, and no

---

* Pp. 7-10.

† P. 28.

longer requires the assistance of that sort of philosophy which, queenlike, pretended to rule the remaining mob of sciences. As soon as each special science makes clear its position in the great totality of things and our knowledge of things, a special science dealing with this totality is superfluous or unnecessary. That which still survives of all earlier philosophy is the science of thought and its laws—formal logic and dialectics. Everything else is subsumed in the positive science of Nature and history.

While, however, the revolution in the conception of Nature could only be made in proportion to the corresponding positive materials furnished by research, already much earlier certain historical facts had occurred which led to a decisive change in the conception of history. In 1831, the first working-class rising took place in Lyons; between 1838 and 1842, the first national working class movement, that of the English Chartists, reached its height. The class struggle between proletariat and bourgeoisie came to the fore in the history of the most advanced countries in Europe, in proportion to the development, on the one hand, of modern industry, and on the other, of the newly acquired political supremacy of the bourgeoisie. Facts more and more forcefully gave the lie to the teachings of bourgeois economy as to the identity of the interests of capital and labor, as to the universal harmony and universal prosperity that would be the consequence of unbridled competition. All these things could no longer be ignored, any more than the French and English socialism, which, though very imperfect, was their theoretical expression. But the old idealist conception of history, which was not yet dislodged, knew nothing of class struggles based upon economic interests, knew nothing of economic interests; production and all economic relations appeared in it only as incidental, subordinate elements in the "history of civilization."

The new facts made imperative a new examination of all past history. Then it was seen that *all* past history, with the exception of its primitive stages, was the history of class struggles; that these warring classes of society are always the products of the modes of production and of exchange—in a word, of the *economic* conditions of their time; that the economic structure of society always furnishes the real basis, starting from which we can alone work out the ultimate explanation of the whole superstructure of juridical and political institutions as well as of the religious, philosophical, and other ideas of a given historical period. Hegel had freed history from metaphysics—he had made it dialectic; but his conception of history was essentially idealistic. But now idealism was driven from its last refuge, the philosophy of history; now a materialistic treatment of history was propounded, and a method found of explaining man's "knowing" by his "being," instead of, as heretofore, his "being" by his "knowing."

From that time forward socialism was no longer an accidental discovery of this or that ingenious brain, but the necessary outcome of the struggle between two historically developed classes—the proletariat and the bourgeoisie. Its task was no longer to manufacture a system of society as perfect as possible, but to examine the historico-economic succession of events from which these classes and their antagonism had of necessity sprung, and to discover in the economic conditions thus created the means of ending the conflict. But the socialism of earlier days was as incompatible with this materialistic conception as the conception of Nature of the French materialists was with dialectics and modern natural science. The socialism of earlier days certainly criticized the existing capitalistic mode of production and its consequences. But it could not explain them, and, therefore, could not master them. It could only simply reject them as bad. The more strongly this earlier socialism denounced the exploitation of the working class, inevitable under capitalism, the less able was it clearly to show in what this exploitation consisted and how it arose. But for this it was necessary—(1) to present the capitalistic method of production in its historical connection and its inevitableness during a particular historical period, and therefore, also, to present its inevitable downfall; and (2) to lay bare its essential character, which was still a secret. This was done by the discovery of *surplus value.* It was shown that the appropriation of unpaid labor is the basis of the capitalist mode of production and of the exploitation of the worker that occurs under it; and even if the capitalist buys the labor power of his laborer at its full value as a commodity on the market, he yet extracts more value from it than he paid for; and that in the ultimate analysis this surplus value forms those sums of value from which are heaped up the constantly increasing masses of capital in the hands of the possessing classes. The genesis of capitalist production and the production of capital were both explained.

These two great discoveries, the materialistic conception of history and the revelation of the secret of capitalistic production through surplus value, we owe to Marx. With these discoveries socialism became a science. The next thing was to work out all its details and relations.*

III.
The Collapse Of Capitalism And The Emergence Of The Final Stage Of Social Development— Communism

The materialist conception of history starts from the proposition that the production of the means to support human life and, next to production, the exchange of things produced, is the basis of all social structure; that in every society that has appeared in history, the manner in which wealth is distributed and society divided into classes or orders is dependent upon what is produced, how it is produced, and how the products are exchanged. From this point of view the final causes of all social changes and political revolutions are to be sought, not in men's brains, not in man's better insight into eternal truth and justice, but in changes in the modes of production and exchange. They are to be sought not in the *philosophy,* but in the *economics* of each particular epoch. The growing perception that existing social institutions are unreasonable and unjust, that reason has become unreason and right wrong, is only proof that in the modes of production and exchange changes have silently taken place with which the social order, adapted to earlier economic conditions, is no longer in keeping. From this it also follows that the means of getting rid of the incongruities that have been brought to light must also be present, in a more or less developed condition, within the changed modes of production themselves. These means are not to be invented by deduction from fundamental princi-

* Pp. 36-44.

ples, but are to be discovered in the stubborn facts of the existing system of production.

What is, then, the position of modern socialism in this connection?

The present structure of society—this is now pretty generally conceded—is the creation of the ruling class of today, of the bourgeoisie. The mode of production peculiar to the bourgeoisie, known, since Marx, as the capitalist mode of production, was incompatible with the feudal system, with the privileges it conferred upon individuals, entire social ranks and local corporations, as well as with the hereditary ties of subordination which constituted the framework of its social organization. The bourgeoisie broke up the feudal system and built upon its ruins the capitalist order of society, the kingdom of free competition, personal liberty, the equality, before the law, of all commodity owners, and all the rest of the capitalist blessings. Thenceforth the capitalist mode of production could develop in freedom. Since steam, machinery, and the making of machines by machinery transformed the older manufacturing into modern industry, the productive forces evolved under the guidance of the bourgeoisie developed with a rapidity and to a degree unheard of before. But just as the older manufacturing, in its time, and handicraft, further developing under its influence, had come into collision with the feudal trammels of the guilds, so now modern industry, in its more complete development, comes into collision with the bounds within which the capitalistic mode of production confines it. The new productive forces have already outgrown the capitalistic mode of using them. And this conflict between productive forces and modes of production is not a conflict engendered in the mind of man, like that between original sin and divine justice. It exists, in fact, objectively, outside us, independently of the will and actions even of the men that have brought it on. Modern socialism is nothing but the reflex, in thought, of this conflict in fact; its ideal reflection in the minds, first, of the class directly suffering under it, the working class.

Now, in what does this conflict consist?

Before capitalistic production, *i.e.*, in the Middle Ages, the system of petty industry generally prevailed, based upon the private property of the laborers in their means of production; in the country, the agriculture of the small peasant, freeman or serf; in the towns, the handicrafts organized in guilds. The instruments of labor—land, agricultural implements, the workshop, the tool—were the instruments of labor of single individuals, adapted for the use of one worker, and, therefore, of necessity, small, dwarfish, circumscribed. But, for this very reason they belonged, as a rule, to the producer himself. To concentrate these scattered, limited means of production, to enlarge them, to turn them into the powerful levers of production of the present day—this was precisely the historic role of capitalist production and of its upholder, the bourgeoisie. In the fourth section of *Capital* Marx has explained in detail, how since the fifteenth century this has been historically worked out through the three phases of simple co-operation, manufacturing and modern industry. But the bourgeoisie, as is also shown there, could not transform these puny means of production into mighty productive forces without transforming them, at the same time, from means of production of the individual into *social* means of production only workable by a collectivity of men. The spinning-wheel, the hand-loom, the blacksmith's hammer were replaced by the spinning-machine, the power-loom, the steam-hammer; the individual workshop, by the factory involving the co-operation of hundreds and thousands of workmen. In like manner, production itself changed from a series of individual into a series of social acts, and the products from individual to social products. The yarn, the cloth, the metal articles that now came out of the factory, were the joint product of many workers, through whose hands they had successively to pass before they were ready. No one person could say of them: "I made that; this is *my* product."

But where, in a given society, the fundamental form of production is that spontaneous division of labor which creeps in gradually and not upon any preconceived plan, there the products take on the form of *commodities,* whose mutual exchange, buying and selling, enable the individual producers to satisfy their manifold wants. And this was the case in the Middle Ages. The peasant, *e.g.,* sold to the artisan agricultural products and bought from him the products of handicraft. Into this society of individual producers, of commodity producers, the new mode of production thrust itself. In the midst of the old division of labor, grown up spontaneously and upon *no definite plan,* which had governed the whole of society, now arose division of labor upon a *definite plan,* as organized in the factory; side by side with *individual* production appeared *social* production. The products of both were sold in the same market, and, therefore, at prices at least approximately equal. But organization upon a definite plan was stronger than spontaneous division of labor. The factories working with the combined social forces of a collectivity of individuals produced their commodities far more cheaply than the individual small producers. Individual production succumbed in one department after another. Socialized production revolutionized all the old methods of production. But its revolutionary character was, at the same time, so little recognized that it was, on the contrary, introduced as a means of increasing and developing the production of commodities. When it arose, it found ready-made, and made liberal use of, certain machinery for the production and exchange of commodities; merchants' capital, handicraft, wage-labor. Socialized production thus introducing itself as a new form of the production of commodities, it was a matter of course that under it the old forms of appropriation remained in full swing and were applied to its products as well.

In the medieval stage of the evolution of commodity production, the question as to the owner of the product of labor could not arise. The individual producer, as a rule, had, from raw material belonging to himself and generally his own handiwork, produced it with his own tools, by the labor of his own hands or of his family. There was no need for him to appropriate the new product. It belonged wholly to him, as a matter of course. His property in the product was, therefore, based *upon his own labor.* Even where external help was used, this was, as a rule, of little importance, and very generally was compensated by something other than wages. The apprentices and journeymen of the guilds worked less for board and wages than for education, in order that they might become master craftsmen themselves.

Then came the concentration of the means of production and of the producers in large workshops and manufactories, their transformation into actual socialized means of production and socialized producers. But the socialized producers and means of production and their products were still treated, after this change, just as they had been before, *i.e.,* as the means of production and the products of individuals. Hitherto, the owner of the instruments of labor had himself appropriated the product, because, as a rule, it was his own product and the assistance of others was the exception. Now the owner of the instruments of labor always appropriated to himself the product, although it was no longer *his* product but exclusively the product of the *labor of others.* Thus, the products now produced socially were not appropriated by those who had actually set in motion the means of production and actually produced the commodities, but by the *capitalists.* The means of production, and production itself, had become in essence socialized. But they were subjected to a form of appropriation which presupposes the private production of individuals, under which, therefore, everyone owns his own product and brings it to market. The mode of production is subjected to this form of appropriation, although it abolishes the conditions upon which the latter rests.

This contradiction, which gives to the new mode of production its capitalistic character, *contains the germ of all the social antagonisms of today.* The greater the mastery obtained by the new mode of production over all important fields of production and in all manufacturing countries, the more it reduced individual production to an insignificant residuum, *the more clearly was brought out the incompatibility of socialized production with capitalistic appropriation.*

The first capitalists found, as we have said, alongside other forms of labor, wage-labor ready-made for them on the market. But it was exceptional, complementary, accessory, transitory wage-labor. The agricultural laborer, though upon occasion hiring himself out by the day, had a few acres of his own land on which he could at all events live in a pinch. The guilds were so organized that the journeyman of today became the master of tomorrow. But all this changed, as soon as the means of production became socialized and concentrated in the hands of capitalists. The means of production, as well as the product, of the individual producer became more and more worthless; there was nothing left for him but to turn wage-worker under the capitalist. Wage-labor, heretofore the exception and accessory, now became the rule and basis of all production; heretofore complementary, it now became the sole remaining function of the worker. The wage-worker for a time became a wage-worker for life. The number of these permanent wage-workers was further enormously increased by the breaking-up of the feudal system that occurred at the same time, by the disbanding of the retainers of the feudal lords, the eviction of the peasants from their homesteads, etc. The separation was made complete between the means of production concentrated in the hands of the capitalists, on the one side, and the producers, possessing nothing but their labor-power, on the other. *The contradiction between socialized production and capitalistic appropriation manifested itself as the antagonism between proletariat and bourgeoisie.*

We have seen that the capitalistic mode of production thrust its way into a society of commodity producers, of individual producers, whose social bond was the exchange of their products. But every society based upon the production of commodities has this peculiarity: the producers have lost control over their own social interrelations. Each man produces for himself with such means of production as he may happen to have, and for such exchange as he may require to satisfy his remaining wants. No one knows how much of his particular article is coming on the market, nor how much of it will be wanted. No one knows whether his individual product will meet an actual demand, whether he will be able to make good his costs of production or even to sell his commodity at all. Anarchy reigns in socialized production.

But the production of commodities, like every other form of production, has its peculiar, inherent laws inseparable from it; and these laws work, despite anarchy, in and through anarchy. They reveal themselves in the only persistent form of social interrelations, *i.e.*, in exchange, and here they affect the individual producers as compulsory laws of competition. They are, at first, unknown to these producers themselves, and have to be discovered by them gradually and as the result of experience. They work themselves out, therefore, independently of the producers, and in antagonism to them, as inexorable natural laws of their particular form of production. The product governs the producers.

In medieval society, especially in the earlier centuries, production was essentially directed towards satisfying the wants of the individual. It satisfied, in the main, only the wants of the producer and his family. Where relations of personal dependence existed, as in the country, it also helped to satisfy the wants of the feudal lord. In all this there was, therefore, no exchange; the products, consequently, did not assume the character of commodities. The family of the peasant produced almost everything they wanted: clothes and furniture, as well as means of subsistence. Only when it began to produce more than was sufficient to supply its own wants and the payments in kind to the feudal lord, only then did it also produce commodities. This surplus, thrown into socialized exchange and offered for sale, became commodities.

The artisans of the towns, it is true, had from the first to produce for exchange. But they, also, themselves supplied the greatest part of their own individual wants. They had gardens and plots of land. They turned their cattle out into the communal forest, which also yielded them timber and firing. The women spun flax, wool, and so forth. Production for the purpose of exchange, production of commodities, was only in its infancy. Hence, exchange was restricted, the market narrow, the methods of production stable; there was local exclusiveness toward the outside, local unity within; the Mark in the country; in the town, the guild.

But with the extension of the production of commodities and especially with the introduction of the capitalist mode of production, the laws of commodity production, hitherto latent, came into action more openly and with greater force. The old bonds were loosened, the old exclusive limits broken through, the producers were more and more turned into independent, isolated producers of commodities. It became apparent that the production of society at large was ruled by absence of plan, by accident, by anarchy; and this anarchy grew to greater and greater height. But the chief means by aid of which the capitalist mode of production intensified this anarchy of socialized production was the exact opposite of anarchy. It was the increasing organization of production, upon a social basis, in every individual productive establishment. By this, the old, peaceful, stable condition of things was ended. Wherever this organization of production was introduced into a branch of industry, it brooked no other method of production by its side. The field of labor became a battleground. The great geographical discoveries and the colonization following upon them, multiplied markets and quickened the transformation of handicraft into manufacturing. The war did not simply break out between the individual producers of particular localities. The local struggles produced in their turn national conflicts, the commercial wars of the seventeenth and the eighteenth centuries.

Finally, modern industry and the opening of the world market made the struggle universal and at the same time gave it an unheard-of virulence. Advantages in natural or artificial conditions of production now decide the existence or nonexistence of individual capitalists, as well as of whole industries and countries. He that falls is remorselessly cast aside. It is the Darwinian struggle of the individual for existence transferred from Nature to society with intensified violence. The conditions of existence natural to the animal appear as the final term of human development. The contradiction between socialized production and capitalistic appropriation now presents itself as *an antagonism between the organization of production in the individual workshop and the anarchy of production in society generally.*

The capitalistic mode of production moves in these two forms of the antagonism immanent to it from its very origin. It is never able to get out of that "vicious circle" which Fourier had already discovered. What Fourier could not, indeed, see in his time is that this circle is gradually narrowing; that the movement becomes more and more a spiral and must come to an end, like the movement of the planets, by collision with the center. It is the compelling force of anarchy in the production of society at large that more and more completely turns the great majority of men into proletarians; and it is the masses of the proletariat again who will finally put an end to anarchy in production. It is the compelling force of anarchy in social production that turns the limitless perfectibility of machinery under modern industry into a compulsory law by which every individual industrial capitalist must perfect his machinery more and more, under penalty of ruin.

But the perfecting of machinery is making human labor superfluous. If the introduction and increase of machinery means the displacement of millions of manual workers by a few machine-workers, improvement in machinery means the displacement of more and more of the machine-workers themselves. It means, in the last analysis, the production of a number of available wage-workers in excess of the average needs of capital, the formation of a complete industrial reserve army, as I called it in 1845, available at the times when industry is working at high pressure, to be cast out on the street when the inevitable crash comes, a constant dead weight upon the limbs of the working class in its struggle for existence with capital, a regulator for keeping wages down to the low level that suits the interests of capital. Thus it comes about, to quote Marx, that machinery becomes the most powerful weapon in the war of capital against the working class; that the instruments of labor constantly tear the means of subsistence out of the hands of the laborer; that the very product of the worker is turned into an instrument for his subjugation. Thus it comes about that the economizing of the instruments of labor becomes at the same time, from the outset, the most reckless waste of labor power, and robbery based upon the normal conditions under which labor functions; that machinery, "the most powerful instrument for shortening labor time, becomes the most unfailing means for placing every moment of the laborer's time and that of his family at the disposal of the capitalist for the purpose of expanding the value of his capital." (*Capital,* English edition, p. 406.) Thus it comes about that the overwork of some becomes the preliminary condition for the idleness of others, and that modern industry, which hunts after new consumers over the whole world, forces the consumption of the masses at home down to a starvation minimum, and in doing this destroys its own home market. "The law that always equilibrates the relative surplus population, or industrial reserve army, to the extent and energy of accumulation, this law rivets the laborer to capital more firmly than the wedges of Vulcan did Prometheus to the rock. It establishes an accumulation of misery, corresponding to the accumulation of capital. Accumulation of wealth at one pole is, therefore, at the same time, accumulation of misery, agony of toil, slavery, ignorance, brutality, mental degradation, at the opposite pole, *i.e.*, on the side of the class that produces *its own product in the form of capital.*" (Marx's *Capital*, p. 661.) And to expect any other division of the products from the capitalistic mode of production is the same as expecting the electrodes of a battery not to decompose acidulated water, not to liberate oxygen at the positive, hydrogen at the negative pole, so long as they are connected with the battery.

We have seen that the ever-increasing perfectibility of modern machinery is, by the anarchy of social production, turned into a compulsory law that forces the individual industrial capitalist always to improve his machinery, always to increase its productive force. The bare possibility of extending the field of production is transformed for him into a similar compulsory law. The enormous expansive force of modern industry, compared with which that of gases is mere child's play, appears to us now as a *necessity* for expansion, both qualitative and quantitative, that laughs at all resistance. Such resistance is offered by consumption, by sales, by the markets for the products of modern industry. But the capacity for extension, extensive and intensive, of the markets is primarily governed by quite different laws that work much less energetically. The extension of the markets cannot keep pace with the extension of production. The collision becomes inevitable, and as this cannot produce any real solution so long as it does not break in pieces the capitalist mode of production, the collisions become periodic. Capitalist production has produced another "vicious circle."

As a matter of fact, since 1825, when the first general crisis broke out, the whole industrial and commercial world, production and exchange among all civilized peoples and their more or less barbaric hangers-on, are thrown out of joint about once every ten years. Commerce is at a standstill, the markets are glutted, products accumulate, as multitudinous as they are unsaleable, hard cash disappears, credit vanishes, factories are closed, the mass of the workers are in want of the means of subsistence, because they have produced too much of the means of subsistence; bankruptcy follows upon bankruptcy, execution follows execution. The stagnation lasts for years; productive forces and products are wasted and destroyed wholesale, until the accumulated mass of commodities finally filters off, more or less depreciated in value, until production and exchange gradually begin to move again. Little by little the pace quickens. It becomes a trot. The industrial trot breaks into a canter, the canter in turn grows into the headlong gallop of a perfect steeplechase of industry, commercial credit, and speculation which finally, after breakneck leaps, ends where it began—in the ditch of a crisis. And so over and over again. We have now, since the year 1825, gone through this five times, and at the present moment (1877) we are going through it for the sixth time. And the character of these crises is so clearly defined that Fourier hit all of them off when he described the first as "*crise pléthorique,*" a crisis from plethora.

In these crises, the contradiction between socialized production and capitalist appropriation ends in a violent explosion. The circulation of commodities is, for the time being, stopped. Money, the means of circulation, becomes a hindrance to circulation. All the laws of production and circulation of commodities are turned upside down. The economic collision has reached its apogee. *The mode of production is in rebellion against the mode of exchange.*

The fact that the socialized organization of production within the factory has developed so far that it has become incompatible with the anarchy of production in society, which exists side by side with and dominates it, is brought home to the capitalists themselves by the violent concentration of capital that occurs during crises, through the ruin of many large, and a still greater number of small, capitalists. The whole mechanism of the capitalist mode of production breaks down under the pressure of the productive forces, its own creations. It is no longer able to turn all this mass of means of production into capital. They lie fallow, and for that very reason the industrial reserve army must also lie fallow. Means of production, means of subsistence, available laborers, all the elements of production and of general wealth, are present in abundance. But "abundance becomes the source of distress and want" (Fourier), because it is the very thing that prevents the transformation of the means of production and subsistence into capital. For in capitalistic society the means of production can only function when they have undergone a preliminary transformation into capital, into the means of exploiting human labor power. The necessity of this transformation into capital of the means of production and subsistence stands like a ghost between these and the workers. It alone prevents the coming together of the material and personal levers of production; it alone forbids the means of production to function, the workers to work and live. On the one hand, therefore, the capitalistic mode of production stands convicted of its own incapacity to further direct these productive forces. On the other, these productive forces themselves, with increasing energy, press forward to the removal of the existing contradiction, to the abolition of their quality as capital, to the *practical recognition of their character as social productive forces.*

This rebellion of the productive forces, as they grow more and more powerful, against their quality as capital, this stronger and stronger command that their social character shall be recognized, forces the capitalist class itself to treat them more and more as social productive forces, so far as this is possible under capitalist conditions. The period of industrial high pressure, with its unbounded inflation of credit, not less than the crash itself, by the collapse of great capitalist establishments, tends to bring about that form of socialization of the great masses of means of production which we meet within the different kinds of joint-stock companies. Many of these means of production and distribution are, from the outset, so colossal that, like the railways, they exclude all other forms of capitalistic exploitation. At a further stage of evolution this form also becomes insufficient. The producers on a large scale in a particular branch of industry in a particular country unite in a trust, a union for the purpose of regulating production. They determine the total amount to be produced, parcel it out among themselves, and thus enforce the selling price fixed beforehand. But trusts of this kind, as soon as business becomes bad, are generally liable to break up, and on this very account compel a yet greater concentration of association. The whole of the particular industry is turned into one gigantic joint-stock company; internal competition gives place to the internal monopoly of this one company. This has happened in 1890 with the English alkali production, which is now, after the fusion of 48 large works, in the hands of one company, conducted upon a single plan, and with a capital of £6,000,000.

In the trusts, freedom of competition changes into its very opposite—into monopoly; and production without any definite plan of capitalistic society capitulates to production upon a definite plan of the invading socialistic society. Certainly this is so far still to the benefit and advantage of the capitalists. But in this case the exploitation is so palpable that it must break down. No nation will put up with production conducted by trusts, with so barefaced an exploitation of the community by a small band of dividend-mongers.

In any case, with trusts or without, the official representative of capitalist society—the state—will ultimately have to undertake the direction of production. This necessity for conversion into state property is felt first in the great institutions for intercourse and communication—the post office, the telegraphs, the railways.

If the crises demonstrate the incapacity of the bourgeoisie for managing any longer modern productive forces, the transformation of the great establishments for production and distribution into joint-stock companies, trusts and state property shows how unnecessary the bourgeoisie are for that purpose. All the social functions of the capitalist are now performed by salaried employees. The capitalist has no further social function than that of pocketing dividends, tearing off coupons, and gambling on the Stock Exchange, where the different capitalists despoil one another of their capital. At first the capitalistic mode of production forces out the workers. Now it forces out the capitalists, and reduces them, just as it reduced the workers, to the ranks of the surplus population, although not immediately into those of the industrial reserve army.

But the transformation, either into joint-stock companies and trusts, or into state ownership, does not do away with the capitalistic nature of the productive forces. In the joint-stock companies and trusts this is obvious. And the modern state, again, is only the organization that bourgeois society takes on in order to support the external conditions of the capitalist mode of production against encroachments as well of the workers as of individual capitalists. The modern state, no matter what its form, is essentially a capitalist machine, the state of the capitalists, the ideal personification of the total national capital. The more it proceeds to the taking over of productive forces, the more does it actually become the national capitalist, the more citizens does it exploit. The workers remain wage-workers—proletarians. The capitalist relation is not done away with. It is rather brought to a head. But, brought to a head, it topples over. State ownership of the productive forces is not the solution of the conflict, but concealed within it are the technical conditions that form the elements of that solution.

This solution can only consist in the practical recognition of the social nature of the modern forces of production, and therefore in harmonizing the modes of production, appropriation, and exchange with the socialized character of the means of production. And this can only come about by society openly and directly taking possession of the productive forces which have outgrown all control except that of society as a whole. The social character of the means of production and of the products today reacts against the producers, periodically disrupts all production and exchange, and acts only like a law of Nature, working blindly, forcibly, destructively. But with the assumption by society of the productive forces, the social character of the means of production and of the products will be utilized by the producers with a perfect understanding of its nature, and instead of being a source of disturbance and periodic collapse, will become the most powerful lever of production itself.

Active social forces work exactly like natural forces: blindly, forcibly, destructively, so long as we do not understand and reckon with them. But once we understand them, once we grasp their action, their direction, their effects, it depends only upon ourselves to subject them more and more to our own will, and by means of them to reach our own ends. And this holds especially for the mighty productive forces of today. As long as we obstinately refuse to understand the nature and the character of these social means of action—and this understanding goes against the grain of the capitalist mode of production and its defenders—so long will these forces work in spite of us, in opposition to us, so long will they master us, as we have shown above in detail.

But once their nature is understood, they can, in the hands of the producers working together, be transformed from master demons into willing servants. The difference is as that between the destructive force of electricty in the lightning of a storm, and electricity under command in a telegraph and a voltaic arc; the difference between a conflagration, and fire working in the service of man. With this recognition, at last, of the real nature of the productive forces of today, the social anarchy of production gives place to a social regulation of production upon a definite plan, according to the needs of the community and of each individual. Then the capitalist mode of appropriation, in which the product enslaves first the producer and then the appropriator, is replaced by the mode of appropriation of the products that is based upon the nature of the modern means of production: on the one hand, direct social appropriation, as means for the maintenance and extension of production; on the other, direct individual appropriation, as means of subsistence and enjoyment.

While the capitalist mode of production more and more completely transforms the great majority of the population into proletarians, it creates the power which, under penalty of its own destruction, is forced to accomplish this revolution. While it forces on more and more the transformation of the vast means of production, already socialized, into state property, it shows itself the way to accomplish this revolution. *The proletariat seizes political power and turns the means of production into state property.*

But, in doing this, it abolishes itself as proletariat, abolishes all class distinctions and class antagonisms, abolishes also the state as state. Society thus far, based upon class antagonisms, had need of the state; that is, of an organization of the particular class which was *pro tempore* the exploiting class, an organization for the purpose of preventing any interference with the existing conditions of production, and, therefore, especially, for the purpose of forcibly keeping the exploited classes in the condition of oppression corresponding with the given mode of production (slavery, serfdom, wage-labor). The state was the official representative of society as a whole, the gathering of it into a visible embodiment. But it was this only in so far as it was the state of that class which itself represented, for the time being, society as a whole: in ancient times, the state of slaveowning citizens; in the Middle Ages, the feudal lords; in our time, the bourgeoisie. When at last it becomes the real representative of the whole of society, it renders itself unnecessary. As soon as there is no longer any social class to be held in subjection; as soon as class rule, and the individual struggle for existence based upon our present anarchy in production, with the collisions and excesses arising from these, are removed, nothing more remains to be repressed, and a special repressive force, a state, is no longer necessary. The first act by virtue of which the state really constitutes itself the representative of the whole of society—the taking possession of the means of production in the name of society—this is, at the same time, its last independent act as a state. State interference in social relations becomes, in one domain after another, superfluous, and then dies out by itself; the government of persons is replaced by the administration of things and by the conduct of the processes of production. The state is not "abolished." *It dies out.* This gives the measure of the value of the phrase *"a free state,"* both as to its justifiable use at times by agitators and as to its ultimate scientific insufficiency; and also of the demands of the so-called anarchists for the abolition of the state out of hand.

Since the historical appearance of the capitalist mode of production, the appropriation by society of all the means of production has often been dreamed of, more or less vaguely, by individuals, as well as by sects, as the ideal of the future. But it could become possible, could become a historical necessity, only when the actual conditions for its realization were there. Like every other social advance, it becomes practicable, not by men understanding that the existence of classes is in contradiction to justice, equality, etc., not by the mere willingness to abolish these classes, but by virtue of certain new economic conditions. The separation of society into an exploiting and an exploited class, a ruling and an oppressed class, was the necessary consequence of the deficient and restricted development of production in former times. So long as the total social labor only yields a produce which but slightly exceeds that barely necessary for the existence of all; so long, therefore, as labor engages all or almost all the time of the great majority of the members of society—so long, of necessity, is this society divided into classes. Side by side with the great majority, exclusively bond slaves to labor, arises a class freed from direct productive labor, which looks after the general affairs of society: the direction of labor, state business, law, science, art, etc. It is, therefore, the law of division of labor that lies at the basis of the division into classes. But this does not prevent the division into classes from being carried out by means of violence and robbery, trickery and fraud. It does not prevent the ruling class, once having the upper hand, from consolidating its power at the expense of the working class, from turning its social leadership into an intensified exploitation of the masses.

But if, upon this showing, division into classes has a certain historical justification, it has this only for a given period, only under given social conditions. It was based upon the insufficiency of production. It will be swept away by the complete development of modern productive forces. And, in fact, the abolition of classes in society presupposes a degree of historical evolution at which the existence, not simply of this or that particular ruling class, but of any ruling class at all, and, therefore, the existence of class distinction itself has become an obsolete anachronism. It presupposes, therefore, the development of production carried out to a degree at which appropriation of the means of production and of the products, and, with this, of political domination, of the monopoly of culture, and of intellectual leadership by a particular class of society, has become not only superfluous but economically, politically and intellectually, a hindrance to development.

This point is now reached. Their political and intellectual bankruptcy is scarcely any longer a secret to the bourgeoisie themselves. Their economic bankruptcy recurs regularly every ten years. In every crisis, society is suffocated beneath the weight of its own productive forces and products, which it cannot use, and stands helpless, face to face with the absurd contradiction that the producers have nothing to consume, because consumers are wanting. The expansive force of the means of production bursts the bonds that the capitalist mode of production had imposed upon them. Their deliverance from these bonds is the one precondition for an unbroken, constantly accelerated development of the productive forces, and therewith for a practically unlimited increase of production itself. Nor is this all. The socialized appropriation of the means of production does away, not only with the present artificial restrictions upon production, but also with the positive waste and devastation of productive forces and products that are at the present time the inevitable concomitants of production and that reach their height in the crises. Further, it sets free for the community at large a mass of means of production and of products by doing away with the senseless extravangance of the ruling classes of today and their political representatives. The possibility of securing for every member of society, by means of socialized production, an existence not only sufficient materially, and becoming day by day more fully so, but an existence guaranteeing to all the free development and exercise of their physical and mental faculties—this possibility is now for the first time here, but *it is here.*

With the seizing of the means of production by society, production of commodities and, simultaneously, the mastery of the product over the producer are abolished. Anarchy in social production is replaced by systematic, definite organization. The struggle for individual existence disappears. Then for the first time man, in a certain sense, is finally marked off from the rest of the animal kingdom and emerges from mere animal conditions of existence into really human ones. The whole sphere of the conditions of life which surround man, and which have hitherto ruled man, now comes under the dominion and control of man, who for the first time becomes the real, conscious lord of Nature, because he has now become master of his own social organization. The laws of his own social action, hitherto standing face to face with man as laws of Nature foreign to and dominating him, will then be used with full understanding and thereby mastered by him. Man's own social organization, hitherto confronting him as a necessity imposed by Nature and history, now becomes the result of his own free action. The extraneous objective forces that have hitherto governed history pass under the control of man himself. Only from that time will man himself, more and more consciously, make his own history—only from that time will the social causes set in motion by him have, in the main and in a constantly growing measure, the results intended by him. It is the ascent of man from the kingdom of necessity to the kingdom of freedom.

Let us briefly sum up our sketch of historical evolution.

I. *Medieval Society*—Individual production on a small scale. Means of production adapted for individual use; hence primitive, ungainly, petty, dwarfed in action. Production for immediate consumption, either of the producer himself or of his feudal lord. Only where an excess of production over this comsumption occurs is such excess offered for sale, enters into exchange. Production of commodities, therefore, only in its infancy. But already it contains within itself, in embryo, *anarchy in the production of society at large.*

II. *Capitalist Revolution*—Transformation of industry, at first by means of simple co-operation and manufacturing. Concentration of the means of production, hitherto scattered, into great workshops. As a consequence, their transformation from individual to social means of production—a transformation which does not, on the whole, affect the form of exchange. The old forms of appropriation remain in force. The capitalist appears. In his capacity as owner of the means of production, he also appropriates the products and turns them into commodities. Production has become a *social act.* Exchange and appropriation continue to be *individual* acts, the acts of individuals. *The social product is appropriated by the individual capitalist.* Fundamental contradiction, whence arise all the contradictions in which our present-day society moves and which modern industry brings to light.

A. Severance of the producer from the means of production. Condemnation of the worker to wage-labor for life. *Antagonism between the proletariat and the bourgeoisie.*

B. Growing predominance and increasing effectiveness of the laws governing the production of commodities. Unbridled competition. *Contradiction between socialized organization in the individual factory and social anarchy in production as a whole.*

C. On the one hand, the perfecting of machinery made by competition compulsory for each individual manufacturer and complemented by a constantly growing displacement of laborers. *Industrial reserve army.* On the other hand, unlimited extension of production, also compulsory under competition for every manufacturer. On both sides, unheard-of development of productive forces, excess of supply over demand, overproduction, glutting of the markets, crises every ten years, the vicious circle: excess here, of means of production and products—excess there, of laborers, without employment and without means of existence. But these two levers of production and of social well-being are unable to work together, because the capitalist form of production prevents the productive forces from working and the products from circulating, unless they are first turned into capital—which their very superabundance prevents. The contradiction has grown into an absurdity. *The mode of production rises in rebellion against the form of exchange.* The bourgeoisie are convicted of incapacity further to manage their own social productive forces.

D. Partial recognition of the social character of the productive forces forced upon the capitalists themselves. Taking over of the great institutions for production and communication, first by joint-stock companies, later on by trusts, then by the state. The bourgeoisie demonstrated to be a superfluous class. All its social functions are now performed by salaried employees.

III. *Proletarian Revolution*—Solution of the contradictions. The proletariat seizes the public power, and by means of this transforms the socialized means of production, slipping from the hands of the bourgeoisie, into public property. By this act, the proletariat frees the means of production from the character of capital they have thus far borne, and gives their socialized character complete freedom to work itself out. Socialized production upon a predetermined plan becomes henceforth possible. The development of production makes the existence of different classes of society thenceforth an anachronism. In proportion as anarchy in social production vanishes, the political authority of the state dies out. Man, at last the master of his own form of social organization, becomes at the same time the lord over Nature, his own master—free.

To accomplish this act of universal emancipation is the historical mission of the modern proletariat. To comprehend thoroughly the historical conditions and thus the very nature of this act, to impart to the now oppressed proletarian class a full knowledge of the conditions and of the meaning of the momentous act it is called upon to accomplish, this is the task of the theoretical expression of the proletarian movement, scientific Socialism.*

---

* Pp. 45-87.

Part 4

REVOLUTION, WAR, AND CONTEMPORARY MAN

20th Century

COMMUNISM

Nicolai Lenin

Vladimir Ilyich Ulyanov, better known as Nicolai Lenin (1870–1924), was born into the middle class, the son of an educator in the Russian bureaucracy. Although Lenin was not a radical in his youth, he was suspected of revolutionary activities because his brother Alexander was convicted and executed in 1887 for his part in a plot to assassinate the Czar. After being expelled from Kazan university for alleged subversive behavior, Lenin moved to the country where, between 1889 and 1893, he studied the works of Marx. In 1893 Lenin moved to St. Petersburg to join a Marxist revolutionary group led by Georgi Plekanov. Two years later Lenin was arrested and exiled to Siberia where he remained until 1900. Permitted to have books and to write, he continued his study of Marx and produced *The Development of Capitalism in Russia.* This work affirmed that Russia was moving toward capitalism as the first step in the process toward Socialism.

Of Lenin, the man and revolutionary, Louis Fischer has written:

> Lenin was a man with iron will, self-enslaving self-discipline, scorn for opponents and obstacles, the cold determination of a zealot, the drive of a fanatic, and the ability to convince or browbeat weaker persons by his singleness of purpose, imposing intensity, impersonal approach, personal sacrifice, political astuteness, and complete conviction of the possession of the absolute truth. . . .[1] Unambitious as an individual, abstemious to the point of ascetic self-denial, he lived not for himself or his wife or friends or comrades but for an idea. He was a Marxist Monk.[2]

In August 1914, four months before the Bolsheviks seized power, Lenin's *State and Revolution* was published. Written as an attack upon those who deviated from Marxist doctrines, *State and Revolution* clarified doctrines on revolution and freedom laid down by Marx and Engels and added Lenin's principles which have become a significant part of communist ideology. Lenin asserted that where the state exists, man is oppressed. Therefore, freedom will become the condition for all men only when the state is abolished.

---

[1] Louis Fischer, *The Life of Lenin* (New York: Harper and Row, 1964), pp. 21-22.

[2] *Ibid.*, pp. 43-44.

I.
The "Withering Away" Of The State And Revolution

Engels' words regarding the "withering away" of the state are so widely known, so often quoted, and so clearly reveal the essence of the customary adulteration Marxism into opportunism that we must deal with them in detail. We shall quote the whole argument from which they are taken.

> The proletariat takes political powers and turns the means of production in the first instance into state property. But, in doing this, it abolishes itself as proletariat, abolishes all class distinctions and class antagonisms, and abolishes also the state as state. Society thus far, based upon class antagonisms, had need of the state, that is, of an organization of the exploiting class, for the maintenance of its external conditions of production; which means especially for the purpose of forcibly keeping the exploited classes in the condition of oppression corresponding with the given mode of production (slavery, serfdom, wage labor). The state was the official representative of society as a whole; the gathering of it together into a visible embodiment. But it was this only in so far as it was the state of that class which itself represented, for the time being, society as a whole: in ancient times, the state of slave-owning citizens; in the Middle Ages, the feudal lords; in our own time, the bourgeoisie. When at last it becomes the real representative of the whole of society, it renders itself unnecessary. As soon as there is no longer any social class to be held in subjection; as soon as class rule, and the individual struggle for existence based upon our present anarchy in production, with the collisions and excesses arising from these, are removed, nothing more remains to be repressed, and a special repressive force, a state, is no longer necessary. The first act by virtue of which the state really constitutes itself the representative of the whole of society—the taking possession of the means of production in the name of society—this is, at the same time, its last independent act as a state. State interference in social relations becomes, in one domain after another, superfluous, and then withers away of itself. The government of persons is replaced by the administration of things and by the management of the processes of production. The state is not "abolished." *It withers away.* This gives the measure of the value of the phrase "a free people's state," which can justifiably be used at times by agitators, but which is, in the final analysis, scientifically inadequate. It is on this basis that we should also evaluate the demands of the so-called anarchists for the immediate abolition of the state. *(Herr Eugen Dühring's Revolution in Science* [*Anti-Dühring*], pp. 301-03, third German edition.)

It may be said without fear of error that of this argument of Engels' which is so remarkably rich in ideas, only one point has become an integral part of socialist thought among modern socialist parties, namely, that according to Marx the state "withers away"—as distinct from the anarchist doctrine of the "abolition" of the state. To prune Marxism in such a manner is to reduce it to opportunism, for such an "interpretation" only leaves a vague notion of a slow, even, gradual change, of absence of leaps and storms, of absence of revolution. The current widespread,

---

Reprinted from Vladimir Lenin, "State and Revolution," *The Essential Works of Marxism*, ed. Arthur P. Mendel (New York; Bantam Books, 1965), pp. 111-17, 134-41, 143-45, 167-83, by permission of the publisher. Copyright © 1961 by Bantam Books, Inc.

mass, if one may say so, conception of the "withering away" of the state undoubtedly means toning down, if not repudiating, revolution.

Such an "interpretation," however, is the crudest distortion of Marxism, advantageous only to the bourgeoisie; in point of theory, it is based on a disregard for the most important circumstances and considerations indicated, even in Engels' "summary" argument we have just quoted in full.

In the first place, at the very outset of his argument Engels says that, in taking state power, the proletariat thereby "abolishes the state as state." It is not "good form" to ponder over the meaning of this. Generally, it is either ignored altogether, or is considered to be something in the nature of an "Hegelian weakness" on Engels' part. . . . As a matter of fact, Engels speaks here of the proletarian revolution "abolishing" the *bourgeois* state, while the words about the state withering away refer to the remnants of the *proletarian state after* the socialist revolution. According to Engels the bourgeois state does not "wither away," but is *"abolished"* by the proletariat in the course of the revolution. What withers away after this revolution is the proletarian state or semi-state.

Secondly, the state is a "special repressive force." Engels gives this splendid and extremely profound definition here with the utmost lucidity. And from it follows that the "special repressive force" for the suppression of the proletariat by the bourgeoisie, of millions of laborers by handfuls of the rich, must be replaced by a "special repressive force" for the suppression of the bourgeoisie by the proletariat (the dictatorship of the proletariat). This is precisely what is meant by "the abolition of the state as state." This is precisely the "act" of taking possession of the means of production in the name of society. And it is self-evident that *such* a replacement of one (bourgeois) "special force" by another (proletarian) "special force" cannot possibly take place in the form of "withering away."

Thirdly, in speaking of the state "withering away," and the even more graphic and colorful "ceasing of itself," Engels refers quite clearly and definitely to the period *after* "the state has taken possession of the means of production in the name of the whole of society," that is, *after* the socialist revolution. We all know that the political form of the "state" at that time is the most complete democracy. But it never enters the head of any of the opportunists who shamelessly distort Marxism that Engels is consequently speaking here of *democracy* "ceasing of itself," or "withering away." This seems very strange at first sight. But it is "incomprehensible" only to those who have not pondered over the fact that democracy is *also* a state and that, consequently, democracy will also disappear when the state disappears. Revolution alone can "abolish" the bourgeois state. The state in general, *i.e.*, the most complete democracy, can only "wither away."

Fourthly, after formulating his famous proposition, that "the state withers away," Engels at once explains specifically that this proposition is directed against both the opportunists and the anarchists. In doing this Engels puts in the forefront that conclusion drawn from the proposition that "the state withers away" which is directed against the opportunists.

One can wager that out of every 10,000 persons who have read or heard about the "withering away" of the state, 9,990 are completely unaware, or do not remember, that Engels directed his conclusions from this proposition *not only* against the anarchists. And of the remaining ten, probably nine do not know the meaning of "free people's state" or why an attack on this slogan means an attack on the opportunists. This is how history is written! This is how a great revolutionary teaching is imperceptibly falsified and adapted to prevailing philistinism! The conclusion directed against the anarchists has been repeated thousands of times, vulgarized, dinned into people's heads in the shallowest form and has acquired the strength of a prejudice. But the conclusion directed against the opportunists has been slurred over and "forgotten"!

The "free people's state" was a program demand and a widely current slogan of the German Social Democrats in the seventies. This slogan is devoid of all political content except for the fact that it describes the concept of democracy in the pompous philistine fashion. In so far as it hinted in a legally permissible manner at a democratic republic, Engels was prepared to "justify" its use "for a time" from an agitational point of view. But it was an opportunist slogan, for it expressed not only an embellishment of bourgeois democracy, but also failure to understand the socialist criticism of the state in general. We are in favor of a democratic republic as the best form of the state for the proletariat under capitalism; but we have no right to forget that wage slavery is the lot of the people even in the most democratic bourgeois republic. Furthermore, every state is a "special force for the suppression" of the oppressed class. Consequently, no state is *free* or is a *people's state.* Marx and Engels explained this repeatedly to their party comrades in the seventies.

Fifthly, this very same work of Engels', of which everyone remembers the argument about the withering away of the state, also contains an argument of the significance of violent revolution. Engels' historical analysis of its role becomes a veritable panegyric on violent revolution. This "no one remembers." It is not good form in modern socialist parties to talk or even think about the significance of this idea, and it plays no part whatever in their daily propaganda and agitation among the masses. And yet, it is inseparably bound with the "withering away" of the state into one harmonious whole.

Here is Engels' argument:

> . . . Force, however, plays also another role in history (other than that of a diabolical power), namely, a revolutionary role. In the words of Marx, it is the midwife of every old society which is pregnant with a new one; it is the instrument with the aid of which social movement forces its way through and shatters the dead, fossilized political forms—of this there is not a word in Herr Dühring. It is only with sighs and groans that he admits the possibility that force will perhaps be necessary for the overthrow of the economic system of exploitation—unfortunately, because all use of force, forsooth, demoralizes the person who uses it. And this in spite of the immense moral and spiritual impetus which has been given by every victorious revolution! And this in Germany, where a violent collision—which indeed may be forced on the people—would at least have the advantage of wiping out the servility which has permeated the national consciousness as a result of the humiliation of the Thirty Years' War. And this parson's mode of thought—lifeless, insipid and impotent—claims the right to impose itself on the most revolutionary party that history has known! (p. 193, third German edition, part II, end of chap. IV.)

How can this panegyric on violent revolution, which Engels insistently brought to the attention of the German Social Democrats between 1878 and 1894, *i.e.*, right up to the time of his death, be combined with the theory of the "withering away" of the state to form a single doctrine?

Usually the two are combined by means of eclecticism, by an unprincipled, or sophistic selection made arbitrarily (or to please the powers that be) of now one, now another argument, and in ninety-nine cases out of a hundred, if not more often, it is the idea of the "withering away" that is placed in the forefront. Dialectics are replaced by eclecticism—this is the most usual, the most widespread phenomenon to be met with in present-day official Social-Democratic literature in relation to Marxism. This sort of substitution is, of course, no new thing, it was observed even in the history of classic Greek philosophy. In falsifying Marxism in opportunist fashion, the substitution of eclecticism for dialectics is the easiest way of deceiving the masses; it gives an illusory satisfaction; it seems to take into account all sides of the process, all tendencies of development, all the conflicting influences, and so forth, whereas in reality it presents no integral and revolutionary conception of the process of social development at all.

We have already said above, and shall show more fully later, that the teaching of Marx and Engels concerning the inevitability of a violent revolution refers to the bourgeois state. The latter *cannot* be superseded by the proletarian state (the dictatorship of the proletariat) through the process of "withering away," but, as a general rule, only through a violent revolution. The panegyric Engels sang in its honor, and which fully corresponds to Marx's repeated declarations (recall the concluding passages of *The Poverty of Philosophy* and the *Communist Manifesto,* with their proud and open proclamation of the inevitability of a violent revolution; recall what Marx wrote nearly thirty years later, . . .—this panegyric is by no means a mere "impulse," a mere declamation or a polemical sally. The necessity of systematically imbuing the masses with *this* and precisely this view of violent revolution lies at the root of *all* the teachings of Marx and Engels. . . .

The replacement of the bourgeois state by the proletarian state is impossible without a violent revolution. The abolition of the proletarian state, *i.e.,* of the state in general, is impossible except through the process of "withering away."*

II.
The Commune

In 1847, in the *Communist Manifesto,* Marx's answer to this question [—what will replace the existing states—] was as yet a purely abstract one, or, to speak more correctly, it was an answer that indicated the tasks, but not the ways of accomplishing them. The answer given in the *Communist Manifesto* was that this machine was to be replaced by "the proletariat organized as the ruling class," by the "victory of democracy."

Not indulging in utopias, Marx expected the *experience* of the mass movement to provide the reply to the question as to what specific forms this organization of the proletariat as the ruling class will assume and as to the exact manner in

* Pp. 111-17.

which this organization will be combined with the most complete and consistent "victory of democracy."

Marx subjected the experience of the Commune, meager as it was, to the most careful analysis in *The Civil War in France.* Let us quote the most important passages of this work.

> Originating from the Middle Ages, there developed in the nineteenth century "the centralized state power, with its ubiquitous organs of standing army, police, bureaucracy, clergy, and judicature." With the development of class antagonisms between capital and labor, ". . . the state power assumed more and more the character of a public force for the oppression of labor, an engine of class rule. After every revolution marking a progressive phase in the class struggle, the purely repressive character of the state power stands out in bolder and bolder relief." After the Revolution of 1848-1849, the state power became "the national war weapon of capital against labor." The Second Empire consolidated this.
>
> The direct antithesis to the empire was the Commune. "It was the positive form" of "a republic that was not only to supersede the monarchical form of class-rule, but class-rule itself. . . ."

What was this "positive" form of the proletarian, the socialist republic? What was the state it began to create?

> . . . The first decree of the Commune . . . was the suppression of the standing army and its replacement by the armed people. . . .

This demand now figures in the program of every party claiming the name of socialist. . . .

> . . . The Commune was formed of the municipal councillors, chosen by universal suffrage in the various wards of the town, responsible and removable at any time. The majority of its members were naturally working men, or acknowledged representatives of the working class. . . .
>
> Instead of continuing to be the agent of the central government, the police was at once stripped of its political attributes, and turned into the responsible and at all times revocable organ of the Commune. The same was true for the officials of all other branches of the Administration. From the members of the Commune downwards, public service had to be done at *workmen's wages.* All privileges and the representation allowances of the high dignitaries of state disappeared along with the high dignitaries themselves. . . . Having once got rid of the standing army and the police, the instruments of physical force of the old government, the Commune was anxious to break the spiritual force of repression, the power of the priests. . . . The judicial functionaries were to be divested of that sham independence . . . they were to be elective, responsible, and revocable. . . .

Thus the Commune appears to have replaced the smashed state machine "only" by fuller democracy. The standing army was abolished, and all officials were to be elected and subject to recall. But as a matter of fact this "only" signifies a gigantic replacement of certain institutions by other institutions of a fundamentally different order. This is, in fact, a case of "the transformation of quantity into quality": democracy, introduced as fully and consistently as is at all conceivable, transformed from bourgeois democracy into proletarian democracy, from the state (= a special force for the suppression of a particular class) into something which is no longer really the state.

It is still necessary to suppress the bourgeoisie and crush its resistance. This was particularly necessary for the Commune, and one of the reasons for its defeat was that it did not do this with sufficient determination. But the organ of suppression is now the majority of the population, and not a minority, as was always the case under slavery, serfdom and wage slavery. And since the majority of the people *itself* suppresses its oppressors, a "special force" for suppression is *no longer necessary!* In this sense the state *begins to wither away*. Instead of the special institutions of a privileged minority (privileged officialdom, the chiefs of the standing army), the majority itself can directly fulfill all these functions, and the more the functions of state power devolve upon the people as a whole the less need is there for the existence of this power. . . .

The Commune substitutes for the venal and rotten parliamentarism of bourgeois society institutions in which freedom of opinion and of discussion does not degenerate into deception, for the parliamentarians themselves have to work, have to execute their own laws, have themselves to test their results in real life, and to render account directly to their constituents. Representative institutions remain, but there is *no* parliamentarism here as a special system, as the division of labor between the legislative and the executive, as a privileged position for the representatives. We cannot imagine democracy, even proletarian democracy, without representative institutions, but we can and *must* imagine democracy without parliamentarism, if criticism of bourgeois society is not mere empty words for us, if the desire to overthrow the rule of the bourgeoisie is our earnest and sincere aim, and not a mere "campaign issue" for catching workers' votes, as it is with the Mensheviks and Socialist-Revolutionaries. . . .

It is extremely instructive to note that, in speaking of the functions of *those* officials who are necessary for the Commune and for proletarian democracy, Marx compares them to the workers of "every other employer," that is, of the ordinary capitalist enterprise, with its "workers, foremen and bookkeepers."

There is no trace of utopianism in Marx, in the sense that he made up or invented a "new" society. No, he studied the *birth* of the new society *outof* the old, the forms of transition from the latter to the former as a natural-historical process. He examined the actual experience of a mass proletarian movement and tried to draw practical lessons from it. He "learned" from the Commune, just as all the great revolutionary thinkers were not afraid to learn from the experience of the great movements of the oppressed classes, and never addressed them with pedantic "homilies." . . .

There can be no thought of abolishing the bureaucracy at once, everywhere and completely. That is utopia. But *to smash* the old bureaucratic machine at once and to begin immediately to construct a new one that will permit the gradual abolition of all bureaucracy—this is *not* utopia, this is the experience of the Commune, this is the direct and immediate task of the revolutionary proletariat.

Capitalism simplifies the functions of "state" administration; it makes it possible to cast "bossing" aside and to confine the whole matter to the organization of the proletarians (as the ruling class), which will hire "workers, foremen and bookkeepers" in the name of the whole society.

We are not utopians, we do not indulge in "dreams" of dispensing *at once* with all administration, with all subordination. These anarchist dreams, based upon a lack of understanding of the tasks of the proletarian dictatorship, are totally alien to Marxism, and, as a matter of fact, serve only to postpone the socialist revolution until people are different. No, we want the socialist revolution with people as they are now, with people who cannot dispense with subordination, control and "foremen and bookkeepers."

But the subordination must be to the armed vanguard of all the exploited and laboring people, *i.e.*, to the proletariat. A beginning can and must be made at once, overnight, of replacing the specific "bossing" of state officials by the simple functions of "foremen and bookkeepers," functions which are already fully within the capacity of the average city dweller and can well be performed for "workmen's wages."

We ourselves, the workers, will organize large-scale production on the basis of what capitalism has already created, relying on our own experience as workers, establishing strict, iron discipline supported by the state power of the armed workers. We will reduce the role of the state officials to that of simply carrying out our instructions as responsible, revocable, modestly paid "foremen and bookkeepers" (of course, with the aid of technicians of all sorts, types and degrees). This is *our* proletarian task, this is what we can and must *start* with in accomplishing the proletarian revolution. Such a beginning, on the basis of large-scale production, will of itself lead to the gradual "withering away" of all bureaucracy, to the gradual creation of an order, an order without quotation marks, an order bearing no similarity to wage slavery, an order in which the functions of control and accounting—becoming more and more simple—will be performed by each in turn, will then become a habit and will finally die out as the *special* functions of a special section of the population.

A witty German Social Democrat of the seventies of the last century called the *postal service* an example of the socialist economic system. This is very true. At present the postal service is a business organized on the lines of a state-*capitalist* monopoly. Imperialism is gradually transforming all trusts into organizations of a similar type, in which, standing over the "common" laborers, who are overworked and starved, is the same bourgeois bureaucracy. But the mechanism of social management is here already at hand. We have but to overthrow the capitalists, to crush the resistance of these exploiters with the iron hand of the armed workers, to smash the bureaucratic machine of the modern state—and we shall have a splendidly equipped mechanism, freed from the "parasite," a mechanism which can very well be set going by the united workers themselves, who will hire technicians, foremen and bookkeepers, and pay them *all*, as, indeed *all* "state" officials in general, a workman's wage. Here is a concrete, practical task, immediately possible of fulfillment in relation to all trusts, a task that will rid the laborers of exploitation and take account of what the Commune had already begun to practice (particularly in building up the state).

To organize the *whole* national economy on the lines of the postal service, so that the technicians, foremen, bookkeepers, as well as *all* officials, shall receive salaries no higher than "a workman's wage," all under the control and leadership of the armed proletariat—this is our immediate aim. It is such a state, standing on such an economic foundation, that we need. This is what will bring about the abolition of parliamentarism and the preservation of representative institutions.

This is what will rid the laboring classes of the prostitution of these institutions by the bourgeoisie.

> ". . . In a rough sketch of national organization which the Commune had no time to develop, it states clearly that the Commune was to be . . . the political form of even the smallest country hamlet. . . ." The Communes were to elect the "National Delegation" in Paris.
>
> ". . . The few but important functions which still would remain for a central government were not to be suppressed, as has been intentionally misstated, but were to be discharged by Communal, and therefore strictly responsible, officials.
>
> ". . . The unity of the nation was not to be broken, but, on the contrary, to be organized by the Communal organization. It was to become a reality by the destruction of the state power which claimed to be the embodiment of that unity but which wanted to be independent of, and superior to, the nation itself. In fact, this state power was but a parasitic growth on the body of the nation. . . . While the merely repressive organs of the old governmental power were to be amputated, its legitimate functions were to be wrested from an authority claiming to stand over society and restored to the responsible servants of society."

. . . To confuse Marx's views on the "destruction of the state power—the parasite"—with Proudhon's federalism is positively monstrous! But it is no accident, for it never occurs to the opportunist that Marx does not speak here at all about federalism as opposed to centralism, but about smashing the old, bourgeois state machine which exists in all bourgeois countries.*

> Marx, as though foreseeing the possibility of his views being distorted, purposely emphasized the fact that the charge that the Commune wanted to destroy the unity of the nation, to abolish the central authority, was a deliberate fake. Marx purposely used the words: "The unity of the nation was . . . to be organized," so as to oppose conscious, democratic, proletarian centralism to bourgeois, military, bureaucratic centralism.
>
> But . . . there are none so deaf as those who will not hear. And the very thing the opportunists of present-day Social Democracy do not want to hear about is the destruction of the state power, the amputation of the parasite.

We have already quoted Marx's statements on this subject, and we must now supplement them.

> ". . . It is generally the fate of new historical creations," he wrote, "to be mistakenly considered as similar to older and even defunct forms of social life, to which they may bear a certain likeness. Thus, this new Commune, which breaks the modern state power, has been mistaken for a reproduction of the mediaeval Communes . . . for a federation of small states . . . for an exaggerated form of the ancient struggle against overcentralization. . . .
>
> "The Communal organization would have restored to the social body all the forces hitherto absorbed by the state parasite feeding upon and hampering the free movement of society. By this one act it would have promoted the regeneration of France. . . .
>
> "The Communal organization would have brought the rural producers under the

* Pp. 134-41.

intellectual lead of the central towns of their districts, and there secured to them, in the working men, the natural trustees of their interests. The very existence of the Commune involved, as a matter of course, local municipal liberty, but no longer as a check upon state power, which would then have become superfluous."

"The destruction of the state power," which was a "parasitic growth"; its amputation," its "smashing"; "the state power, which would then have become superfluous"—these are the expressions Marx used in regard to the state when appraising and analyzing the experience of the Commune.

All this was written a little less than half a century ago, and now one has to engage in excavations, as it were, in order to bring undistorted Marxism to the knowledge of the masses. The conclusions drawn from the observation of the last great revolution which Marx lived through were forgotten just at the moment when the time for the next great proletarian revolutions had arrived.

> . . . The multiplicity of interpretations to which the Commune has been subjected and the multiplicity of interests which construed it in their favor, show that it was a thoroughly expansive political form, while all previous forms of government had been emphatically repressive. Its true secret was this. It was essentially *a working-class government,* the result of the struggle of the producing against the appropriating class, the political form, at last discovered, by which the economic emancipation of labor could be achieved.
>
> Except on this last condition, the Communal organization would have been an impossibility and a delusion. . . .

The utopians busied themselves with "discovering" political forms under which the socialist transformation of society was to take place. The anarchists waived the question of political forms altogether. The opportunists of present-day Social Democracy accepted the bourgeois political forms of the parliamentary democratic state as the limit which should not be overstepped. They battered their foreheads praying before this "sacred image" and denounced as anarchism all desire to *smash* these forms.

Marx deduced from the whole history of socialism and the political struggle that the state was bound to disappear, and that the transitional form of its disappearance (the transition from state to non-state) would be the "proletariat organized as the ruling class." But Marx did not set out to *discover* the political *forms* of this future stage. He limited himself to observing precisely French history, to analyzing it, and to drawing the conclusion to which the year 1851 had led, *viz.,* that matters were moving towards the *smashing* of the bourgeois state machine.

And when the mass revolutionary movement of the proletariat burst forth, Marx, in spite of the failure of that movement, in spite of its short life and its patent weakness, began to study what forms it had *discovered.*

The Commune is the form "at last discovered" by the proletarian revolution, under which the economic emancipation of labor can take place.

The Commune is the first attempt of a proletarian revolution to *smash* the bourgeois state machine; and it is the political form "at last discovered," by which the smashed state machine can and must be *replaced.**

---

* Pp. 143-45.

III.
Freedom And The Emergence Of Communism

Clearly there can be no question of defining the exact moment of the *future* "withering away"—the more so since it will obviously be a lengthy process. . . .

The whole theory of Marx is the application of the theory of development—in its most consistent, complete, considered and pithy form—to modern capitalism. Naturally, Marx was faced with the problem of applying this theory both to the *forthcoming* collapse of capitalism and to the *future* development of *future* communism.

On the basis of what *data,* then, can the question of the future development of future communism be dealt with?

On the basis of the fact that *it has its origin* in capitalism, that it develops historically from capitalism, that it is the result of the action of a social force to which capitalism *gave birth.* There is no trace of an attempt on Marx's part to conjure up a utopia, to make idle guesses about what cannot be known. Marx treats the question of communism in the same way as a naturalist would treat the question of the development, say, of a new biological variety, once he knew that such and such was its origin and such and such the definite direction in which it was changing.

Marx, first of all, brushes aside the confusion . . . of the relation between state and society. He writes:

> . . . Present-day society is capitalist society, which exists in all civilized countries, more or less free from medieval admixture, more or less modified by the special historical development of each country, more or less developed. On the other hand, the "present-day state" changes with a country's frontier. It is completely different in the Prusso-German Empire from what it is in Switzerland; it is completely different in England from what it is in the United States. The "present-day state" is, therefore, a fiction.
>
> Nevertheless, the different states of the different civilized countries, in spite of their manifold diversity of form, all have this in common, that they are based on modern bourgeois society, more or less capitalistically developed. They have, therefore, also certain essential features in common. In this sense it is possible to speak of the "present-day state," in contrast with that of the future, when its present root, bourgeois society, will have died off.
>
> The question then arises: what transformation will the state undergo in communist society? In other words, what social functions will then remain in existence that are analogous to the present functions of the state? This question can only be answered scientifically, and one does not get a flea-hop nearer to a solution by a thousandfold combination of the word "people" with the word "state". . . .

Having thus ridiculed all talk about a "people's state," Marx formulates the question and warns us, as it were, that a scientific answer to it can be secured only by using firmly established scientific data.

The first fact that has been established with complete exactitude by the whole theory of development, by science as a whole—a fact that was forgotten by the utopians and is forgotten by present-day opportunists, fearful of the socialist revolution—is that, historically, there must undoubtedly be a special stage or a special phase of *transition* from capitalism to communism.

Marx continues:

> . . . Between capitalist and communist society lies the period of the revolutionary transformation of the one into the other. There corresponds to this also a political transition period in which the state can be nothing but *the revolutionary dictatorship of the proletariat. . . .*

Marx bases this conclusion on an analysis of the role played by the proletariat in modern capitalist society, on data concerning the development of this society, and on the irreconcilability of the antagonistic interests of the proletariat and the bourgeoisie.

Previously the question was put in this way: in order to achieve its emancipation, the proletariat must overthrow the bourgeoisie, win political power and establish its revolutionary dictatorship.

Now the question is put somewhat differently: the transition from capitalist society—which is developing towards communism—to a communist society is impossible without a "political transition period," and the state in this period can only be the revolutionary dictatorship of the proletariat.

What, then, is the relation of this dictatorship to democracy?

We have seen that the *Communist Manifesto* simply places side by side the two concepts: "to raise the proletariat to the position of the ruling class" and "to win the battle of democracy." On the basis of all that has been said above, it is possible to determine more precisely how democracy changes in the transition from capitalism to communism.

In capitalist society, providing it develops under the most favorable conditions, we have a more or less complete democracy in the democratic republic. But this democracy is always hemmed in by the narrow limits set by capitalist exploitation and, consequently, always remains, in essence, a democracy for the minority, only for the propertied classes, only for the rich. Freedom in capitalist society always remains about the same as it was in the ancient Greek republics: freedom for the slaveowners. Owing to the conditions of capitalist exploitation the modern wage slaves are so crushed by want and poverty that "they cannot be bothered with democracy," "they cannot be bothered with politics." In the ordinary peaceful course of events the majority of the population is debarred from participation in public and political life.

The correctness of this statement is perhaps most clearly confirmed by Germany, precisely because in that country constitutional legality steadily endured for a remarkably long time (1871-1914), and during this period Social Democracy in Germany was able to achieve far more than in other countries in the way of "utilizing legality," organizing a larger proportion of the workers into a political party than anywhere else in the world.

What is this largest proportion of politically conscious and active wage slaves that has so far been observed in capitalist society? One million members of the Social Democratic Party—out of fifteen million wage-workers! Three million organized in trade unions—out of fifteen million!

Democracy for an insignificant minority, democracy for the rich—that is the democracy of capitalist society. If we look more closely into the machinery of capitalist democracy, we shall see everywhere, in the "petty"—supposedly petty—details of the suffrage (residential qualification, exclusion of women, etc.), in the technique of the representative institutions, in the actual obstacles to the right of assembly (public buildings are not for "beggars"!), in the purely capitalist organization of the daily press, etc., etc.—we shall see restriction after restriction upon democracy. These restrictions, exceptions, exclusions, obstacles for the poor, seem slight, especially in the eyes of one who has never known want himself and has never been in close contact with the oppressed classes in their mass life (and nine tenths, if not ninety-nine hundredths, of the bourgeois publicists and politicians are of this category). But in their sum total these restrictions exclude and squeeze out the poor from politics, from active participation in democracy.

Marx grasped this *essence* of capitalist democracy splendidly, when, in analyzing the experience of the Commune, he said that the oppressed are allowed once every few years to decide which particular representatives of the oppressing class shall represent and repress them in parliament!

But from this capitalist democracy—that is inevitably narrow, stealthily pushes aside the poor, and is therefore hypocritical and false to the core—forward development does not proceed simply, directly and smoothly towards "greater and greater democracy," as the liberal professors and petty-bourgeois opportunists would have us believe. No, forward development, *i.e.*, towards communism, proceeds through the dictatorship of the proletariat. It cannot be otherwise, for the *resistance* of the capitalist exploiters cannot be *broken* by anyone else or in any other way.

And the dictatorship of the proletariat, *i.e.*, the organization of the vanguard of the oppressed as the ruling class for the purpose of suppressing the oppressors, cannot result merely in an expansion of democracy. *Simultaneously* with an immense expansion of democracy, which *for the first time*, becomes democracy for the poor, democracy for the people, and not democracy for the moneybags, the dictatorship of the proletariat imposes a series of restrictions on the freedom of the oppressors, the exploiters, the capitalists. We must suppress them in order to free humanity from wage slavery. Their resistance must be crushed by force; and it is clear that where there is suppression, where there is violence, there is no freedom and no democracy.

Engels expressed this splendidly in his letter to Bebel when he said, as the reader will remember, that "the proletariat uses the state not in the interests of freedom but in order to hold down its adversaries, and as soon as it becomes possible to speak of freedom the state as such ceases to exist."

Democracy for the vast majority of the people and suppression by force, *i.e.*, exclusion from democracy, of the exploiters and oppressors of the people—this is the change democracy undergoes during the *transition* from capitalism to communism.

Only in communist society, when the resistance of the capitalists has been completely crushed, when the capitalists have disappeared, when there are no classes (*i.e.*, when there is no difference between the members of society as regards their relation to the social means of production), *only* then "the state . . . ceases to exist," and it "*becomes possible to speak of freedom.*" Only then will there become possible and be realized a truly complete democracy, democracy without any restrictions whatever. And only then will democracy begin to *wither away*, owing to the simple fact that, freed from capitalist slavery, from the untold horrors, savagery, absurdities and infamies of capitalist exploitation, people will gradually *become accustomed* to observing the elementary rules of social intercourse that have been known for centuries and repeated for thousands of years in all copybook maxims. They will become accustomed to observing them without force, without compulsion, without subordination, *without the special apparatus* for compulsion which is called the state.

The expression "the state *withers away*" is very well chosen, for it indicates both the gradual and the spontaneous nature of the process. Only habit can, and undoubtedly will, have such an effect; for we see around us on millions of occasions how readily people become accustomed to observing the necessary rules of social intercourse when there is no exploitation, when there is nothing that arouses indignation, nothing that evokes protest and revolt and creates the need for *suppression.*

Thus, in capitalist society we have a democracy that is curtailed, wretched, false; a democracy only for the rich, for the minority. The dictatorship of the proletariat, the period of transition to communism, will for the first time create democracy for the people, for the majority, along with the necessary suppression of the minority—the exploiters. Communism alone is capable of giving really complete democracy, and the more complete it is the more quickly will it become unnecessary and wither away of itself.

In other words, under capitalism we have the state in the proper sense of the word, that is, a special machine for the suppression of one class by another, and, what is more, of the majority by the minority. Naturally, to be successful, such an undertaking as the systematic suppression of the exploited majority by the exploiting minority calls for the utmost ferocity and savagery in the work of suppressing; it calls for seas of blood through which mankind has to wade in slavery, serfdom and wage labor.

Furthermore, during the *transition* from capitalism to communism suppression is *still* necessary; but it is now the suppression of the exploiting minority by the exploited majority. A special apparatus, a special machine for suppression, the "state," is *still* necessary. But this is now a transitional state and no longer a state in the proper sense of the word; for the suppression of the minority of exploiters by the majority of *yesterday's* wage slaves is comparatively so easy, simple and natural a task that it will entail far less bloodshed than the suppression of the risings of slaves, serfs or wage laborers, and it will cost mankind far less. Moreover, it is compatible with the extension of democracy to such an overwhelming majority of the population that the need for a *special machine* of suppression will begin to disappear. The exploiters are naturally unable to suppress the people without a highly complex machine for performing this task: but *the people* can suppress the exploiters with even a very simple "machine," almost without a "machine," without a special apparatus, by the simple *organization of the armed masses* (such as the Soviets of Workers' and Soldiers' Deputies, we may note, anticipating somewhat).

Finally, only communism makes the state absolutely unnecessary, for there is *nobody* to be suppressed—"nobody" in the sense of a *class,* in the sense of a systematic struggle against a definite section of the population. We are not utopians and do not in the least deny the possibility and inevitability of excesses on the part of *individual persons* or the need to suppress *such* excesses. But, in the first place, no special machine, no special apparatus of suppression is needed for this: this will be done by the armed people itself, as simply and as readily as any crowd of civilized people, even in modern society, interferes to stop a scuffle or to prevent a woman from being assaulted. And, secondly, we know that the fundamental social cause of excesses, involving violations of the basic rules of social intercourse, is the exploitation of the masses, their want and their poverty. With the removal of this chief cause, excesses will inevitably begin to "*wither away.*" We do not know how quickly and in what succession, but we know that they will wither away. With their withering away the state will also *wither away.*

Without indulging in utopias, Marx defined more fully what can be defined *now* regarding this future; namely, the difference between the lower and higher phases (levels, stages) of communist society. . . .

Marx [also] shows that from the whole of the social labor of society there must be deducted a reserve fund, a fund for the expansion of production, for the replacement of the "wear and tear" of machinery, and so on. In addition, from the means of consumption there must be deducted a fund for the expenses of administration, schools, hospitals, homes for the aged, and so on.

. . . Marx makes a sober estimate of exactly how socialist society will have to manage its economy. Marx proceeds to make a *concrete* analysis of the conditions of life of a society in which there will be no capitalism, and says:

> What we have to deal with here (in analyzing the program of the workers' party) is not a communist society that has *developed* on its own foundations, but, on the contrary, that has just *emerged* from capitalist society and that is thus in every respect, economically, morally and intellectually, still stamped with the birthmarks of the old society from whose womb it emerges.

And it is this communist society—a society which has just emerged into the light of day out of the womb of capitalism and which, in every respect, bears the birthmarks of the old society—that Marx terms the "first," or lower phase of communist society.

The means of production are no longer the private property of individuals. The means of production belong to the whole of society. Every member of society, performing a certain part of the socially necessary work, receives a certificate from society to the effect that he has done such and such an amount of work. With this certificate he receives from the public store of consumers' goods a corresponding quantity of products. After a deduction is made of the amount of labor which goes to the public fund, every worker, therefore, receives from society as much as he has given to it.

"Equality" apparently reigns supreme.

But when Lassalle,[1] having in view such a social order (usually called socialism, but termed by Marx the first phase of communism), says that this is "equitable distribution," that this is "the equal right of all members of society to an equal product of labor," Lassalle is mistaken and Marx exposes his error.

"Equal right," says Marx, we indeed have here; but it is *still* a "bourgeois right," which, like every right, *presupposes inequality.* Every right is an application of an *equal* measure to *different* people who in fact are not alike, are not equal to one another. That is why "equal right" is really a violation of equality and an injustice. Indeed, every man, having performed as much social labor as another, receives

---

[1] Lassalle, Ferdinand (1825-1864), a leading German socialist. Next to Marx, Lassalle is probably the most famous nineteenth-century German socialist. Although it was partly under the influence of Marx's writings that he turned to socialism, his stress on the role of the State as an instrument for social reform differentiates him from Marx. His active participation in German political life laid the foundations for what was to become the German Social Democratic Party, but the differences between his views and Marx's continued to breed dissension in the party.

an equal share of the social product (after the above-mentioned deductions).

But people are not alike: one is strong, another is weak; one is married, another is not; one has more children, another has less, and so on. And the conclusion Marx draws is:

> . . . with an equal performance of labor and, hence, an equal share in the social consumption fund, one will in fact receive more than another, one will be richer than another, and so on. To avoid all these defects, right instead of being equal would have to be unequal. . . .

Consequently, the first phase of communism cannot yet produce justice and equality: differences, and unjust differences, in wealth will still exist, but the *exploitation* of man by man will have become impossible, because it will be impossible to seize the *means of production,* the factories, machines, land, etc., as private property. While smashing . . . petty-bourgeois, confused phrases about "equality" and "justice" *in general,* Marx shows the *course of development* of communist society, which is *compelled* to abolish at first *only* the "injustice" of the means of production having been seized by individuals, and which is *unable* at once to eliminate the other injustice, which consists in the distribution of articles of consumption "according to the amount of labor performed" (and not according to needs).

The vulgar economists, including the bourgeois professors . . . constantly reproach the socialists with forgetting the inequality of people and with "dreaming" of eliminating this inequality. Such a reproach, as we see, only proves the extreme ignorance of the bourgeois ideologists.

Marx not only most scrupulously takes account of the inevitable inequality of men, but he also takes into account the fact that the mere conversion of the means of production into the common property of the whole of society (commonly called "socialism") *does not remove* the defects of distribution and the inequality of "bourgeois right," which *continues to prevail* as long as products are divided "according to the amount of labor performed." Continuing, Marx says:

> . . . But these defects are inevitable in the first phase of communist society when it has just emerged after prolonged birth pangs from capitalist society. Right can never be higher than the economic structure of society and its cultural development conditioned thereby. . . .

And so, in the first phase of communist society (usually called socialism) "bourgeois right" is *not* abolished in its entirety, but only in part, only in proportion to the economic revolution so far attained, *i.e.,* only in respect of the means of production. "Bourgeois right" recognizes them as the private property of individuals. Socialism converts them into *common* property. *To that extent*—and to that extent alone—"bourgeois right" disappears.

However, it continues to exist as far as its other part is concerned: it continues to exist as a regulator (determining factor) in the distribution of products and the allotment of labor among the members of society. The socialist principle: "He who does not work, neither shall he eat," is *already* realized. The other socialist principle: "An equal amount of products for an equal amount of labor," is also *already* realized. But this is not yet communism, and it does not yet abolish "bourgeois right," which gives to unequal individuals, in return for unequal (really unequal) amounts of labor, equal amounts of products.

This is a "defect," says Marx, but it is unavoidable in the first phase of communism; for if we are not to indulge in utopianism, we must not think that having overthrown capitalism people will at once learn to work for society *without any standard of right;* and indeed the abolition of capitalism *does not immediately create* the economic premises for *such* a change.

And there is no other standard than that of "bourgeois right." To this extent, therefore, there still remains the need for a state, which, while safeguarding the public ownership of the means of production, would safeguard equality in labor and equality in the distribution of products.

The state withers away in so far as there are no longer any capitalists; there are no longer any classes, therefore, to be suppressed.

But the state has not yet completely withered away, since there still remains the safeguarding of "bourgeois right," which sanctifies actual inequality. For the state to wither away completely complete communism is necessary.

Marx continues:

> . . . In the higher phase of communist society, after the enslaving subordination of the individual to the division of labor and, therewith, also the antithesis between mental and physical labor, has vanished; after labor has become not only a means of life but life's prime need; after the productive forces have increased together with the advance of the individual's all-round development, and all the springs of co-operative wealth flow abundantly—only then can the narrow horizon of bourgeois right be crossed completely and society inscribe on its banners: "From each according to his ability, to each according to his needs!"

Only now can we appreciate to the full the correctness of Engels' remarks in which he mercilessly ridiculed the absurdity of combining the words "freedom" and "state." So long as the state exists there is no freedom. When there will be freedom, there will be no state.

The economic basis for the complete withering away of the state is that high stage of development of communism when the antithesis between mental and physical labor disappears, when there disappears consequently one of the principal sources of modern *social* inequality—a source, moreover, which cannot on any account be removed immediately by the mere conversion of the means of production into public property, by the mere expropriation of the capitalists.

This expropriation will create *the possibility* of an enormous development of the productive forces. And when we see how incredibly capitalism is already *retarding* this development, when we see how much progress could be achieved on the basis of the level of technique now already attained, we are entitled to say with the fullest confidence that the expropriation of the capitalists will inevitably result in an enormous development of the productive forces of human society. But how rapidly this development will proceed, how soon it will reach the point of breaking away from the division of labor, of doing away with the antithesis between mental and physical labor, of transforming labor into "the prime necessity of life"—we do not and *cannot* know.

That is why we are entitled to speak only of the inevitable withering away of the state, emphasizing the protracted nature of this process and its dependence upon the rapidity of development of the *higher phase* of communism, and leaving completely open the question of the time required for, or the concrete forms of, the withering away, because there is *no* material for answering these questions.

It will become possible for the state to wither away completely when society adopts the rule: "From each according to his ability, to each according to his needs," *i.e.*, when people have become so accustomed to observing the fundamental rules of social intercourse and when their labor becomes so productive that they will voluntarily work *according to their ability*. "The narrow horizon of bourgeois right," which compels one to calculate with the coldheartedness of a Shylock whether one has not worked half an hour more than somebody else, whether one is not getting less pay than somebody else—this narrow horizon will then be crossed. There will then be no need for society to regulate the quantity of products to be received by each: each will take freely "according to his needs."

From the bourgeois point of view, it is easy to declare that such a social order is "sheer utopia" and to sneer at the socialists for promising everyone the right to receive from society, without any control over the labor of the individual citizen, any quantity of truffles, automobiles, pianos, etc. Even to this day, most bourgeois "savants" confine themselves to sneering in this way, thereby displaying both their ignorance and their mercenary defense of capitalism.

Ignorance—for it has never entered the head of any socialist to "promise" that the higher phase of the development of communism will arrive; whereas the great socialists, in *foreseeing* that it will arrive presuppose not the present productivity of labor *and not the present* ordinary run of people, who, like the seminary students in Pomyalovsky's stories, are capable of damaging the stocks of public wealth "just for fun" and of demanding the impossible.

Until the "higher" phase of communism arrives, the socialists demand the *strictest* control by society *and by the state* of the measure of labor and the measure of consumption; but this control must *start* with the expropriation of the capitalists and with the establishment of workers' control over the capitalists, and it must be exercised not by a state of bureaucrats, but by a state of *armed workers*.

The mercenary defense of capitalism by the bourgeois ideologists . . . consists precisely in that they *substitute* controversies and discussions about the distant future for the vital and burning question of *present-day* politics, *viz.*, the expropriation of the capitalists, the conversion of *all* citizens into workers and employees of *one* huge "syndicate"—the whole state—and the complete subordination of the entire work of this syndicate to a genuinely democratic state, to *the state of the Soviets of Workers' and Soldiers' Deputies*.

Actually, when a learned professor, followed by the philistine . . . talks about unreasonable utopias, the demagogic promises of the Bolsheviks, and the impossibility of "introducing" socialism, it is the higher stage or phase of communism they have in mind, which no one has ever promised or even thought to "introduce," because it generally cannot be "introduced."

And this brings us to the question of the scientific difference between socialism and communism, which Engels touched on in his above-quoted argument about the incorrectness of the name "Social Democrat." Politically the difference between the first, or lower, and the higher phase of communism will in time, probably, be tremendous; but it would be ridiculous to take cognizance of this difference now, under capitalism, and only individual anarchists, perhaps, could invest it with primary importance. . . .

But the scientific difference between socialism and communism is clear. What is usually called socialism was termed by Marx the "first" or lower phase of communist society. In so far as the means of production become *common* property, the word "communism" is also applicable here, providing we do not forget that this is *not* complete communism. The great significance of Marx's explanations is that here, too, he consistently applies materialist dialectics, the theory of development, regarding communism as something which develops *out of* capitalism. Instead of scholastically invented, "concocted" definitions and fruitless disputes about words (what is socialism? what is communism?), Marx gives an analysis of what might be called the stages of the economic ripeness of communism.

In its first phase, or first stage, communism *cannot* as yet be fully ripe economically and entirely free from traditions or remnants of capitalism. Hence, the interesting phenomenon that communism in its first phase retains "the narrow horizon of *bourgeois* right." Of course, bourgeois right in regard to the distribution of articles of *consumption* inevitably presupposes the existence of the *bourgeois state,* for right is nothing without an apparatus capable of *enforcing* the observance of the standards of right.

It follows that under communism there remains for a time not only bourgeois right, but even the bourgeois state without the bourgeoisie!

This may sound like a paradox or simply a dialectical conundrum, of which Marxism is often accused by people who do not take the slightest trouble to study its extraordinarily profound content.

But as a matter of fact, remnants of the old surviving in the new confront us in life at every step, both in nature and in society. And Marx did not arbitrarily insert a scrap of "bourgeois" right into communism, but indicated what is economically and politically inevitable in a society emerging *out of the womb* of capitalism.

Democracy is of enormous importance to the working class in its struggle against the capitalists for its emancipation. But democracy is by no means a boundary not to be crossed: it is only one of the stages on the road from feudalism to capitalism and from capitalism to communism.

Democracy means equality. The great significance of the proletariat's struggle for equality and of equality as a slogan will be clear if we correctly interpret it as meaning the abolition of *classes.* But democracy means only *formal* equality. And as soon as equality is achieved for all members of society *in relation* to ownership of the means of production, that is, equality of labor and equality of wages, humanity will inevitably be confronted with the question of advancing farther, from formal equality to actual equality, *i.e.,* to the realization of the rule, "from each according to his ability, to each according to his needs." By what stages, by means of what practical measures humanity will proceed to this supreme aim—we do not and cannot know. But it is important to realize how infinitely mendacious is the ordinary bourgeois conception of socialism as something lifeless, petrified, fixed once for all, whereas in reality *only* under socialism will there begin in all spheres of public and personal life a rapid, genuine, really mass forward movement, embracing first the *majority* and then the whole of the population.

Democracy is a form of the state, one of its varieties. Consequently, like every state, it represents the organized, systematic use of violence against persons. But it also signifies the formal recognition of the equality of citizens, the equal right of all to determine the structure of the state and to administer it. This, in turn, results in the fact that, at a certain stage in the development of democracy, it first welds together the class that wages a revolutionary struggle against capitalism—the proletariat, and enables it to crush, to smash to bits, to wipe off the face of the earth the bourgeois, even the republican bourgeois, the state machine, the standing army, the police and the bureaucracy, and to substitute for them a *more* democratic state machine, but a state machine nevertheless, in the shape of the armed masses of workers who develop into a militia in which the entire population takes part.

Here "quantity turns into quality": *such* a degree of democracy involves leaving the boundaries of bourgeois society and beginning its socialist reconstruction. If really *all* take part in the administration of the state, capitalism cannot retain its hold. And the development of capitalism itself creates, in turn, the *premises* that *enable* "all" to take part in the administration of the state. Some of these premises are universal literacy, which has already been achieved in a number of the most advanced capitalist countries, and the "training and disciplining" of millions of workers by the huge, complex, socialized apparatus of the postal service, railways, big factories, large-scale commerce, banking, etc., etc.

Given these *economic* premises it is quite possible, after the overthrow of the capitalists and the bureaucrats, to proceed immediately, overnight, to replace them in the *control* of production and distribution, in the work of *keeping account* of labor and products by the armed workers, by the whole of the armed population. (The question of control and accounting should not be confused with the question of the scientifically trained staff of engineers, agronomists and so on. These gentlemen, working today in obedience to the wishes of the capitalists, will work even better tomorrow in obedience to the wishes of the armed workers.)

Accounting and control—that is the *main* thing required for "arranging" the smooth working, the correct functioning of the *first phase* of communist society. *All* citizens are transformed here into hired employees of the state, which consists of the armed workers. *All* citizens become employees and workers of a *single* nationwide state "syndicate." All that is required is that they should work equally, do their proper share of work, and get equally paid. The accounting and control necessary for this have been *simplified* by capitalism to the extreme and reduced to the extraordinarily simple operations—which any literate person who knows arithmetic can perform—of supervising, recording, and issuing appropriate receipts.

When the *majority* of the people begin independently and everywhere to keep such accounts and maintain such control over the capitalists (now converted into employees) and over the gentry intellectuals who preserve their capitalist habits, this control will really become universal, general, popular. And there will be no way of getting away from it; there will be "nowhere to go."

The whole of society will have become a single office and a single factory, with equality of labor and equality of pay.

But this "factory" discipline, which the proletariat, after defeating the capitalists and overthrowing the exploiters, will extend to the whole of society, is by no means our ideal, or our ultimate goal. It is but a necessary *step* for the purpose of thoroughly purging society of all the infamies and abominations of capitalist exploitation *and for further* progress.

From the moment all members of society, or even only the vast majority, have learned to administer the state *themselves,* have taken this work into their own hands, have "arranged" control over the insignificant minority of capitalists, the gentry who wish to preserve their capitalist habits and the workers who have been profoundly corrupted by capitalism—from this moment the need for government of any kind begins to disappear altogether. The more complete the democracy, the nearer the moment approaches when it becomes unnecessary. The more democratic the "state," consisting of the armed workers and "no longer a state in the proper sense of the word," the more rapidly does *every form* of state begin to wither away.

For when *all* have learned to administer and actually do administer independently social production, independently keep accounts and exercise control over the idlers, gentlefolk, swindlers and other such "guardians of capitalist traditions," the escape from this popular accounting and control will inevitably become so incredibly difficult, such a rare exception, and will probably be accompanied by such swift and severe punishment (for the armed workers are practical men and not sentimental intellectuals, and they will scarcely allow anyone to trifle with them), that the *necessity* of observing the simple, fundamental rules of human intercourse will very soon become a *habit.*

And then the door will be wide open for the transition from the first phase of communist society to its higher phase, and with it, to the complete withering away of the state.*

---

* Pp. 167-83.

FASCISM

Benito Mussolini

During the 1920s and 1930s Fascists in Italy and Germany renounced Western humanist and liberal traditions. In the *Political and Social Doctrines of Fascism* (1933), Benito Mussolini (1883–1945), dictator of Italy and a prophet of fascism, conceived government as a meaningless form which was subordinate to a pattern of pathless *action.* He saw the state as the embodiment of the will and spirit of the people. Mussolini argued that a society built on individual liberty was incompatible with Nature, "in whose workings the race alone seems to be taken into consideration, and the individual sacrificed to it. . . . The state, as conceived of and as created by Fascism, is a spiritual and moral fact in itself." Clearly the Fascists believed that the individual was insignificant and liberty irrelevant in the absolute and living state.

I.
The Rise Of Fascism To Power

When in the now distant March of 1919, I summoned a meeting at Milan through the columns of the *Popolo d'Italia* of the surviving members of the Interventionist Party who had themselves been in action, and who had followed me since the creation of the Fascist Revolutionary Party (which took place in the January of 1915), I had no specific doctrinal attitude in my mind. I had a living experience of one doctrine only—that of Socialism, from 1903-4 to the winter of 1914—that is to say, about a decade: and from Socialism itself, even though I had taken part in the movement first as a member of the rank and file and then later as a leader, yet I had no experience of its doctrine in practice. My own doctrine, even in this period, had always been a doctrine of action. A unanimous, universally-accepted theory of Socialism did not exist after 1905, when the revisionist movement began in Germany under the leadership of Bernstein, while under pressure of the tendencies

Reprinted from Benito Mussolini, *The Political and Social Doctrine of Fascism* (London: Hogarth Press, 1933), by permission of the publisher.

of the time, a Left Revolutionary movement also appeared, which though never getting further than talk in Italy, in Russian Socialistic circles laid the foundations of Bolshevism. . . . Already the echoes of these terms are spent—while in the great stream of Fascism are to be found ideas which began with Sorel, Peguy, with Lagerdelle in the "Mouvement Socialiste," and with the Italian trades-union movement which throughout the period 1904-14 was sounding a new note in Italian Socialist circles (already weakened by the betrayal of Giolitti) through Olivetti's *Pagine Libre,* Orano's *La Lupa,* and Enrico Leone's *Divenire Sociale.*

After the War, in 1919, Socialism was already dead as a doctrine: it existed only as a hatred. There remained to it only one possibility of action, especially in Italy, reprisals against those who had desired the War and who must now be made to "expiate" its results. The *Popolo d'Italia* was then given the sub-title of "The newspaper of ex-service men and producers," and the word producers was already the expression of a mental attitude. Fascism was not the nursling of a doctrine worked out beforehand with detailed elaboration; it was born of the need for action and it was itself from the beginning practical rather than theoretical; it was not merely another political party but, even in the first two years, in opposition to all political parties as such, and itself a living movement. The name which I then gave to the organization fixed its character. And yet, if one were to re-read, in the now dusty columns of that date, the report of the meeting in which the *Fasci Italiana di combattimento* were constituted, one would there find no ordered expression of doctrine, but a series of aphorisms, anticipations and aspirations which, when refined by time from the original one, were destined after some years to develop into an ordered series of doctrinal concepts, forming the Fascist political doctrine—different from all others either of the past or the present day.

"If the bourgeoisie," I said then, "think that they will find lightning-conductors in us, they are the more deceived; we must start work at once. . . . We want to accustom the working-class to real and effectual leadership, and also to convince them that it is no easy thing to direct an industry or a commercial enterprise successfully. . . . We shall combat every retrograde idea, technical or spiritual. . . . When the succession to the seat of government is open, we must not be unwilling to fight for it. We must make haste; when the present regime breaks down, we must be ready at once to take its place. It is we who have the right to the succession, because it was we who forced the country into the War, and led her to victory. The present method of political representation cannot suffice, we must have a representation direct from the individuals concerned. It may be objected against this programme that it is a return to the conception of the corporation, but that is no matter. . . . Therefore, I desire that this assembly shall accept the revindication of national trades-unionism from the economic point of view. . . ."

Now is it not a singular thing that even on this first day in the Piazza San Sepolcro that word "corporation" arose, which later, in the course of the Revolution, came to express one of the creations of social legislation at the very foundation of the regime?

The years which preceded the march to Rome were years of great difficulty, during which the necessity for action did not permit of research or any complete elaboration of doctrine. The battle had to be fought in the towns and villages. There was much discussion, but—what was more important and more sacred—men died. They knew how to die. Doctrine, beautifully defined and carefully elucidated, with headlines and paragraphs, might be lacking; but there was to take its place something more decisive—Faith. Even so, anyone who can recall the events of the time through the aid of books, articles, votes of congresses and speeches of great and minor importance—anyone who knows how to research and weigh evidence—will find that the fundamentals of doctrine were cast during the years of conflict. It was precisely in those years that Fascist thought armed itself, was refined, and began the great task of organization. The problem of the relation between the individual citizen and the State; the allied problems of authority and liberty; political and social problems as well as those specifically national—a solution was being sought for all these while at the same time the struggle against Liberalism, Democracy, Socialism and the Masonic bodies was being carried on, contemporaneously with the "punitive expedition." But, since there was inevitably some lack of system, the adversaries of Fascism have disingenuously denied that it had any capacity to produce a doctrine of its own, though that doctrine was growing and taking shape under their very eyes, even though tumultuously; first, as happens to all ideas in their beginnings, in the aspect of a violent and dogmatic negation, and then in the aspect of positive construction which has found its realization in the laws and institutions of the regime as enacted successively in the years 1926, 1927, and 1928.

II.
The Doctrines Of Fascism

Fascism is now a completely individual thing, not only as a regime but as a doctrine. And this means that to-day Fascism, exercising its critical sense upon itself and upon others, has formed its own distinct and peculiar point of view, to which it can refer and upon which, therefore, it can act in the face of all problems, practical or intellectual, which confront the world.

And above all, Fascism, the more it considers and observes the future and the development of humanity quite apart from political considerations of the moment, believes neither in the possibility nor the utility of perpetual peace. It thus repudiates the doctrine of Pacifism—born of a renunciation of the struggle and an act of cowardice in the face of sacrifice. War alone brings up to its highest tension all human energy and puts the stamp of nobility upon the peoples who have the courage to meet it. All other trials are substitutes, which never really put men into the position where they have to make the great decision—the alternative of life or death. Thus a doctrine which is founded upon this harmful postulate of peace is hostile to Fascism. And thus hostile to the spirit of Fascism, though accepted for what use they can be in dealing with particular political situations, are all the international leagues and societies which, as history will show, can be scattered to the winds when once strong national feeling is aroused by any motive—sentimental, ideal, or practical. This anti-Pacifist spirit is carried by Fascism even into the life of the individual; the proud motto of the *Squadrista,* "Me ne frego," written on the bandage of the wound, is an act of philosophy not only stoic, the summary of a doctrine not only political—it is the education to combat, the acceptation of the risks which combat implies, and a new way of life for Italy. Thus the Fascist accepts life and loves it, knowing nothing of and despising suicide: he rather conceives of life as duty and struggle and conquest, life which should be high and full, lived for oneself, but above all for others—those who are at hand and those who are far distant, contemporaries, and those who will come after.

This "demographic" policy of the regime is the result of the above premise. Thus the Fascist loves in actual fact his neighbour, but this "neighbour" is not merely a vague and undefined concept, this love for one's neighbour puts no obstacle in the way of necessary educational severity, and still less to differentiation of status and to physical distance. Fascism repudiates any universal embrace, and in order to live worthily in the community of civilized peoples watches its contemporaries with vigilant eyes, takes good note of their state of mind and, in the changing trend of their interests, does not allow itself to be deceived by temporary and fallacious appearances.

Such a conception of life makes Fascism the complete opposite of that doctrine, the base of so-called scientific and Marxian Socialism, the materialist conception of history; according to which the history of human civilization can be explained simply through the conflict of interests among the various social groups and by the change and development in the means and instruments of production. That the changes in the economic field—new discoveries of raw materials, new methods of working them, and the inventions of science—have their importance no one can deny; but that these factors are sufficient to explain the history of humanity excluding all others is an absurd delusion. Fascism, now and always, believes in holiness and in heroism; that is to say, in actions influenced by no economic motive, direct or indirect. And if the economic conception of history be denied, according to which theory men are no more than puppets, carried to and fro by the waves of chance, while the real directing forces are quite out of their control, it follows that the existence of an unchangeable and unchanging class-war is also denied—the natural progeny of the economic conception of history. And above all Fascism denies that class-war can be the preponderant force in the transformation of society. These two fundamental concepts of Socialism being thus refuted, nothing is left of it but the sentimental aspiration—as old as humanity itself—towards a social convention in which the sorrows and sufferings of the humblest shall be alleviated. But here again Fascism repudiates the conception of "economic" happiness, to be realized by Socialism and, as it were, at a given moment in economic evolution to assure to everyone the maximum of well-being. Fascism denies the materialist conception of happiness as a possibility, and abandons it to its inventors, the economists of the first half of the nineteenth century: that is to say, Fascism denies the validity of the equation, well-being-happiness, which would reduce men to the level of animals, caring for one thing only—to be fat and well-fed—and would thus degrade humanity to a purely physical existence.

After Socialism, Fascism combats the whole complex system of democratic ideology, and repudiates it, whether in its theoretical premises or in its practical application. Fascism denies that the majority, by the simple fact that it is a majority, can direct human society; it denies that numbers alone can govern by means of a periodical consultation, and it affirms the immutable, beneficial and fruitful inequality of mankind, which can never be permanently levelled through the mere operation of a mechanical process such as universal suffrage. The democratic regime may be defined as from time to time giving the people the illusion of sovereignty, while the real effective sovereignty lies in the hands of other concealed and irresponsible forces. Democracy is a regime nominally without a king, but it is ruled by many kings—more absolute, tyrannical and ruinous than one sole king, even though a tyrant. This explains why Fascism, having first in 1922 (for reasons of expediency) assumed an attitude tending towards republicanism, renounced this point of view before the march to Rome; being convinced that the question of political form is not to-day of prime importance, and after having studied the examples of monarchies and republics past and present reached the conclusion that monarchy or republicanism are not to be judged, as it were, by an absolute standard; but that they represent forms in which the evolution—political, historical, traditional or psychological—of a particular country has expressed itself. Fascism supersedes the antithesis monarchy or republicanism, while democracy still tarries beneath the domination of this idea, for ever pointing out the insufficiency of the first and for ever the praising of the second as the perfect regime. To-day, it can be seen that there are republics innately reactionary and absolutist, and also monarchies which incorporate the most ardent social and political hopes of the future.

"Reason and science," says Renan (one of the inspired pre-Fascists) in his philosophical meditations, "are products of humanity, but to expect reason as a direct product of the people and a direct result of their action is to deceive oneself by a chimera. It is not necessary for the existence of reason that everybody should understand it. And in any case, if such a decimation of truth were necessary, it could not be achieved in a low-class democracy, which seems as though it must of its very nature extinguish any kind of noble training. The principle that society exists solely through the well-being and the personal liberty of all the individuals of which it is composed does not appear to be conformable to the plans of nature, in whose workings the race alone seems to be taken into consideration, and the individual sacrificed to it. It is greatly to be feared that the last stage of such a conception of democracy (though I must hasten to point out that the term 'democracy' may be interpreted in various ways) would end in a condition of society in which a degenerate herd would have no other preoccupation but the satisfaction of the lowest desires of common men." Thus Renan. Fascism denies, in democracy, the absurd conventional untruth of political equality dressed out in the garb of collective irresponsibility, and the myth of "happiness" and indefinite progress. But, if democracy may be conceived in diverse forms—that is to say, taking democracy to mean a state of society in which the populace are not reduced to impotence in the State—Fascism may write itself down as "an organized, centralized and authoritative democracy."

Fascism has taken up an attitude of complete opposition to the doctrines of Liberalism, both in the political field and the field of economics. There should be no undue exaggeration (simply with the object of immediate success in controversy) of the importance of Liberalism in the last century, nor should what was but one among many theories which appeared in that period be put forward as a religion for humanity for all time, present and to come. Liberalism only flourished for half a century. It was born in 1830 in reaction against the Holy Alliance, which had been formed with the object of diverting the destinies of Europe back to the period before 1789, and the highest point of its success was the year 1848, when even Pius IX was a Liberal. Immediately after that date it began to decay, for if the year 1848 was a year of light and hope, the following year, 1849, was a year of darkness and tragedy. The Republic of Rome was dealt a mortal blow by a sister-republic—that of France—and in the same year Marx launched the gospel of the Socialist religion, the famous Communist Manifesto. In 1851 Napoleon III carried out his far from Liberal *coup d'etat* and reigned in France until 1870, when he was deposed by a popular movement as the consequence of a military defeat which must be counted as one of the most decisive in history. The victor was Bismarck, who knew nothing of the religion of liberty, or the prophets by which that faith was revealed. And it is symptomatic that such a highly civilized people as the Germans were completely ignorant of the religion of liberty during the whole of the nineteenth century. It was nothing but a parenthesis, represented by that body which has been called "The ridiculous Parliament of Frankfort," which lasted only for a short period. Germany attained her national unity quite outside the doctrines of Liberalism—a doctrine which seems entirely foreign to the German mind, a mind essentially monarchic—while Liberalism is the logical and, indeed, historical forerunner of anarchy. The stages in the achievement of German unity are the three wars of '64, '66, and '70, which were guided by such "Liberals" as Von Moltke and Bismarck. As for Italian unity, its debt to Liberalism is completely inferior in contrast to that which it owes to the work of Mazzini and Garibaldi, who were not Liberals. Had it not been for the intervention of the anti-Liberal Napoleon, we should not have gained Lombardy; and without the help of the again anti-Liberal Bismarck at Sadowa and Sedan it is very probable that we should never have gained the province of Venice in '66, or been able to enter Rome in '70. From 1870 to 1914 a period began during which even the very high priests of the religion themselves had to recognize the gathering twilight of their faith—defeated as it was by the decadence of literature and atavism in practice—that is to say, Nationalism, Futurism, Fascism. The era of Liberalism, after having accumulated an infinity of Gordian knots, tried to untie them in the slaughter of the World War—and never has any religion demanded of its votaries such a monstrous sacrifice. Perhaps the Liberal Gods were athirst for blood? But now, to-day, the Liberal faith must shut the doors of its deserted temples, deserted because the peoples of the world realize that its worship—agnostic in the field of economics and indifferent in the field of politics and morals—will lead, as it has already led, to certain ruin. In addition to this, let it be pointed out that all the political hopes of the present day are anti-Liberal, and it is therefore supremely ridiculous to try to classify this sole creed as outside the judgment of history, as though history were a hunting ground reserved for the professors of Liberalism alone—as though Liberalism were the final unalterable verdict of civilization.

But the Fascist negation of Socialism, Democracy and Liberalism must not be taken to mean that Fascism desires to lead the world back to the state of affairs before 1789, the date which seems to be indicated as the opening years of the succeeding semi-Liberal century: we do not desire to turn back; Fascism has not chosen De Maistre for its high-priest. Absolute monarchy has been and can never return, any more than blind acceptance of ecclesiastical authority.

So, too, the privileges of the feudal system "have been," and the division of society into castes impenetrable from outside, and with no intercommunication among themselves: the Fascist conception of authority has nothing to do with such a polity. A party which entirely governs a nation is a fact entirely new to history, there are no possible references or parallels. Fascism uses in its construction whatever elements in the Liberal, Social or Democratic doctrines still have a living value; it maintains what may be called the certainties which we owe to history, but it rejects all the rest—that is to say the conception that there can be any doctrine of unquestioned efficacy for all times and all peoples. Given that the nineteenth century was the century of Socialism, of Liberalism, and of Democracy, it does not necessarily follow that the twentieth century must also be a century of Socialism, Liberalism and Democracy: political doctrines pass, but humanity remains; and it may rather be expected that this will be a century of authority, a century of the Left, a century of Fascism. For if the nineteenth century was a century of individualism (Liberalism always signifying individualism) it may be expected that this will be the century of collectivism, and hence the century of the State. It is a perfectly logical deduction that a new doctrine can utilize all the still vital elements of previous doctrines.

No doctrine has ever been born completely new, completely defined and owing nothing to the past; no doctrine can boast a character of complete originality; it must always derive, if only historically, from the doctrines which have preceded it and develop into further doctrines which will follow. Thus the scientific Socialism of Marx is the heir of the Utopian Socialism of Fourier, of the Owens and of Saint-Simon; thus again the Liberalism of the eighteenth century is linked with all the advanced thought of the seventeenth century, and thus the doctrines of Democracy are the heirs of the Encyclopedists. Every doctrine tends to direct human activity towards a determined objective; but the action of men also reacts upon the doctrine, transforms it, adapts it to new needs, or supersedes it with something else. A doctrine then must be no mere exercise in words, but a living act; and thus the value of Fascism lies in the fact that it is veined with pragmatism, but at the same time has a will to exist and a will to power, a firm front in face of the reality of "violence."

III.
The Fascist State Versus The Individual

The foundation of Fascism is the conception of the State, its character, its duty, and its aim. Fascism conceives of the State as an absolute, in comparison with which all individuals or groups are relative, only to be conceived of in their relation to the State. The conception of the Liberal State is not that of a directing force, guiding the play and development, both material and spiritual, of a collective body, but merely a force limited to the function of recording results: on the other hand, the Fascist State is itself conscious, and has itself a will and a personality—thus it may be called the "ethic" State. In 1929, at the first five-yearly assembly of the Fascist regime, I said:

"For us Fascists, the State is not merely a guardian, preoccupied solely with the duty of assuring the personal safety of the citizens; nor is it an organization with purely material aims, such as to guarantee a certain level of well-being and peaceful conditions of life; for a mere council of administration would be sufficient to realize such objects. Nor is it a purely political creation, divorced from all contact with the complex material reality which makes up the life of the individual and the life of the people as a whole. The State, as conceived of and as created by Fascism, is a spiritual and moral fact in itself, since its political, juridical and economic organization of the nation is a concrete thing: and such an organization must be in its origins and development a manifestation of the spirit. The State is the guarantor of security both internal and external, but it is also the custodian and transmitter of the spirit of the people, as it has grown up through the centuries in language, in customs and in faith. And the State is not only a living reality of the present, it is also linked with the past and above all with the future, and thus transcending the brief limits of individual life, it represents the immanent spirit of the nation. The forms in which States express themselves may change, but the necessity for such forms is eternal. It is the State which educates its citizens in civic virtue, gives them a consciousness of their mission and welds them into unity; harmonizing their various interests through justice, and transmitting to future generations the mental conquests of science, of art, of law and the solidarity of humanity. It leads men from primitive tribal life to that highest expression of human power which is Empire: it links up through the centuries the names of those of its members who have died for its existence and in obedience to its laws, it holds up the memory of the leaders who have increased its territory and the geniuses who have illumined it with glory as an example to be followed by future generations. When the conception of the State declines, and disunifying and centrifugal tendencies prevail, whether of individuals or of particular groups, the nations where such phenomena appear are in their decline."

From 1929 until to-day, evolution, both political and economic, has everywhere gone to prove the validity of these doctrinal premises. Of such gigantic importance is the State. It is the force which alone can provide a solution to the dramatic contradictions of capitalism, and that state of affairs which we call the crisis can only be dealt with by the State, as between other States. Where is the shade of Jules Simon, who in the dawn of Liberalism proclaimed that, "The State must labour to make itself unnecessary, and prepare the way for its own dismissal"? Or of McCulloch, who, in the second half of the last century, affirmed that the State must guard against the danger of governing too much? What would the Englishman, Bentham, say to-day to the continual and inevitably-invoked intervention of the State in the sphere of economics, while according to his theories industry should ask no more of the State than to be left in peace? Or the German Humboldt, according to whom the "lazy" State should be considered the best? It is true that the second wave of Liberal economists were less extreme than the first, and Adam Smith himself opened the door—if only very cautiously—which leads to State intervention in the economic field: but whoever says Liberalism implies individualism, and whoever says Fascism implies the State. Yet the Fascist State is unique, and an original creation. It is not reactionary, but revolutionary, in that it anticipates the solution of the universal political problems which elsewhere have to be settled in the political field by the rivalry of parties, the excessive power of the Parliamentary regime and the irresponsibility of political assemblies; while it meets the problems of the economic field by a system of syndicalism which is continually increasing in importance, as much in the sphere of labour as of industry: and in the moral field enforces order, discipline, and obedience to that which is the determined moral code of the country. Fascism desires the State to be a strong and organic body, at the same time reposing upon broad and popular support. The Fascist State has drawn into itself even the economic activities of the nation, and, through the corporative social and educational institutions created by it, its influence reaches every aspect of the national life and includes, framed in their respective organizations, all the political, economic and spiritual forces of the nation. A State which reposes upon the support of millions of individuals who recognize its authority, are continually conscious of its power and are ready at once to serve it, is not the old tyrannical State of the medieval lord nor has it anything in common with the absolute governments either before or after 1789. The individual in the Fascist State is not annulled but rather multiplied, just in the same way that a soldier in a regiment is not diminished but rather increased by the number of his comrades. The Fascist State organizes the nation, but leaves a sufficient margin of liberty to the individual; the latter is deprived of all useless and possibly harmful freedom, but retains what is essential; the deciding power in this question cannot be the individual, but the State alone.

The Fascist State is not indifferent to the fact of religion in general, or to that particular and positive faith which is Italian Catholicism. The State professes no theology, but a morality, and in the Fascist State religion is considered as one of the deepest manifestations of the spirit of man, thus it is not only respected but defended and protected. The Fascist State has never tried to create its own God, as at one moment Robespierre and the wildest extremists of the Convention tried to do; nor does it vainly seek to obliterate religion from the hearts of men as does Bolshevism: Fascism respects the God of the ascetics, the saints and heroes, and equally, God as He is perceived and worshipped by simple people.

The Fascist State is an embodied will to power and government: the Roman tradition is here an ideal of force in action. According to Fascism, government is not so much a thing to be expressed in territorial or military terms as in terms of morality and the spirit. It must be thought of as an Empire—that is to say, a nation which directly or indirectly rules other nations, without the need for conquering a single square yard of territory. For Fascism, the growth of Empire, that is to say the expansion of the nation, is an essential manifestation of vitality, and its opposite a sign of decadence. Peoples which are rising, or rising again after a period of decadence, are always imperialist; any renunciation is a sign of decay and of death. Fascism is the doctrine best adapted to represent the tendencies and the aspirations of a people, like the people of Italy, who are rising again after many centuries of abasement and foreign servitude. But Empire demands discipline, the co-ordination of all forces and a deeply-felt sense of duty and sacrifice: this fact explains many aspects of the practical working of the regime, the character of many forces in the State, and the necessarily severe measures which must be taken against those who would oppose this spontaneous and inevitable movement of Italy in the twentieth century, and would oppose it by recalling the outworn ideology of the nineteenth century—repudiated wheresoever there has been the courage to undertake great experiments of social and political transformation: for never before has the nation stood more in need of authority, of direction and of order. If every age has its own characteristic doctrine, there are a thousand signs which point to Fascism as the characteristic doctrine of our time. For if a doctrine must be a living thing, this is proved by the fact that Fascism has created a living faith; and that this faith is very powerful in the minds of men, is demonstrated by those who have suffered and died for it.

Fascism has henceforth in the world the universality of all those doctrines which, in realizing themselves, have represented a stage in the history of the human spirit.

ESCAPE FROM FREEDOM

Erich Fromm

While most of the disastrous effects of fascism in Italy and Germany have faded into history, the question of how such a political monstrosity could occur remains unanswered. Erich Fromm (1900–), a social psychologist who left Germany after Hitler seized power, thought the answer could be found in the basic nature of man. In *Escape From Freedom* (1941) Fromm probed the meaning of man, his role in society, and the inclination of man to surrender his freedom. Fromm stated that man was partly a biological, psychological, and spiritual being who needed security and freedom. While passing through the process of self-actualization the individual was susceptible to a sense of growing aloneness and anxiety which could be overwhelming, lead to submission, and result in a loss of freedom.

Although Fromm used this analysis of man to explain the rise of fascism in Germany, he also warned that persons living in democracies, especially the United States, could easily lose their freedom, not by external conquest, but by an internal surrender of their spontaneity and individuality to "anonymous authority." Since the Second World War Dr. Fromm has developed many of the themes found in *Escape From Freedom* in a series of articles and books, including *The Art of Loving, The Sane Society, Man for Himself,* and recently *The Revolution of Hope.*

I.
Introduction

Modern European and American history is centered around the effort to gain freedom from the political, economic, and spiritual shackles that have bound men. The battles for freedom were fought by the oppressed, those who wanted new

Reprinted from Erich Fromm, *Escape From Freedom* (New York; Rinehart, 1941) pp. 2-6, 22-37, 206-18, 240-41, 253-71, by permission of Holt, Rinehart and Winston, Inc. Copyright 1941, © 1969 by Erich Fromm.

liberties, against those who had privileges to defend. While a class was fighting for its own liberation from domination, it believed itself to be fighting for human freedom as such and thus was able to appeal to an ideal, to the longing for freedom rooted in all who are oppressed. In the long and virtually continuous battle for freedom, however, classes that were fighting against oppression at one stage sided with the enemies of freedom when victory was won and new privileges were to be defended.

Despite many reverses, freedom has won battles. Many died in those battles in the conviction that to die in the struggle against oppression was better than to live without freedom. Such a death was the utmost assertion of their individuality. History seemed to be proving that it was possible for man to govern himself, to make decisions for himself, and to think and feel as he saw fit. The full expression of man's potentialities seemed to be the goal toward which social development was rapidly approaching. The principles of economic liberalism, political democracy, religious autonomy, and individualism in personal life, gave expression to the longing for freedom, and at the same time seemed to bring mankind nearer to its realization. One tie after another was severed. Man had overthrown the domination of nature and made himself her master; he had overthrown the domination of the Church and the domination of the absolutist state. The *abolition of external domination* seemed to be not only a necessary but also a sufficient condition to attain the cherished goal: freedom of the individual.

The First World War was regarded by many as the final struggle and its conclusion the ultimate victory for freedom. Existing democracies appeared strengthened, and new ones replaced old monarchies. But only a few years elapsed before new systems emerged which denied everything that men believed they had won in centuries of struggle. For the essence of these new systems, which effectively took command of man's entire social and personal life, was the submission of all but a handful of men to an authority over which they had no control.

At first many found comfort in the thought that the victory of the authoritarian system was due to the madness of a few individuals and that their madness would lead to their downfall in due time. Others smugly believed that the Italian people, or the Germans, were lacking in a sufficiently long period of training in democracy, and that therefore one could wait complacently until they had reached the political maturity of the Western democracies. Another common illusion, perhaps the most dangerous of all, was that men like Hitler had gained power over the vast apparatus of the state through nothing but cunning and trickery, that they and their satellites ruled merely by sheer force; that the whole population was only the willess object of betrayal and terror.

In the years that have elapsed since, the fallacy of these arguments has become apparent. We have been compelled to recognize that millions in Germany were as eager to surrender their freedom as their fathers were to fight for it; that instead of wanting freedom, they sought for ways of escape from it; that other millions were indifferent and did not believe the defense of freedom to be worth fighting and dying for. We also recognize that the crisis of democracy is not a peculiarly Italian or German problem, but one confronting every modern state. Nor does it matter which symbols the enemies of human freedom choose: freedom is not less endangered if attacked in the name of anti-Fascism than in that of outright

Fascism.[1] This truth has been so forcefully formulated by John Dewey that I express the thought in his words: "The serious threat to our democracy," he says, "is not the existence of foreign totalitarian states. It is the existence within our own personal attitudes and within our own institutions of conditions which have given a victory to external authority, discipline, uniformity and dependence upon The Leader in foreign countries. The battlefield is also accordingly here—within ourselves and our institutions."[2]

If we want to fight Fascism we must understand it. Wishful thinking will not help us. And reciting optimistic formulae will prove to be as inadequate and useless as the ritual of an Indian rain dance.

In addition to the problem of the economic and social conditions which have given rise to Fascism, there is a human problem which needs to be understood. It is the purpose of this book to analyze those dynamic factors in the character structure of modern man, which made him want to give up freedom in Fascist countries and which so widely prevail in millions of our own people.*

Before we proceed, it may be helpful to sum up our general approach to the problems of social psychology. Human nature is neither a biologically fixed and innate sum total of drives nor is it a lifeless shadow of cultural patterns to which it adapts itself smoothly; it is the product of human evolution, but it also has certain inherent mechanisms and laws. There are certain factors in man's nature which are fixed and unchangeable: the necessity to satisfy the physiologically conditioned drives and the necessity to avoid isolation and moral aloneness. We have seen that the individual has to accept the mode of life rooted in the system of production and distribution peculiar for any given society. In the process of dynamic adaptation to culture, a number of powerful drives develop which motivate the actions and feelings of the individual. The individual may or may not be conscious of these drives, but in any case they are forceful and demand satisfaction once they have developed. They become powerful forces which in their turn become effective in molding the social process. How economic, psychological, and ideological factors interact and what further general conclusion concerning this interaction one can make will be discussed later in the course of our analysis of the Reformation and of Fascism. This discussion will always be centered around the main theme of this book: that man, the more he gains freedom in the sense of emerging from the original oneness with man and nature and the more he becomes an "individual," has no choice but to unite himself with the world in the spontaneity of love and productive work or else to seek a kind of security by such ties with the world as destroy his freedom and the integrity of his individual self.†

---

* Pp. 2-6.

† Pp. 22-23.

[1] I use the term Fascism or authoritarianism to denote a dictatorial system of the type of the German or Italian one. If I mean the German system in particular, I shall call it Nazism.

[2] John Dewey, *Freedom and Culture*, G. P. Putnam's Sons, New York, 1939.

II.
The Nature Of Man And "The Emergence Of The Individual And The Ambiguity Of Freedom"

Before we come to our main topic—the question of what freedom means to modern man, and why and how he tries to escape from it—we must first discuss a concept which may seem to be somewhat removed from actuality. It is, however, a premise necessary for the understanding of the analysis of freedom in modern society. I mean the concept that freedom characterizes human existence as such, and furthermore that its meaning changes according to the degree of man's awareness and conception of himself as an independent and separate being.

The social history of man started with his emerging from a state of oneness with the natural world to an awareness of himself as an entity separate from surrounding nature and men. Yet this awareness remained very dim over long periods of history. The individual continued to be closely tied to the natural and social world from which he emerged; while being partly aware of himself as a separate entity, he felt also part of the world around him. The growing process of the emergence of the individual from his original ties, a process which we may call "individuation," seems to have reached its peak in modern history in the centuries between the Reformation and the present.

In the life history of an individual we find the same process. A child is born when it is no longer one with its mother and becomes a biological entity separate from her. Yet, while this biological separation is the beginning of individual human existence, the child remains functionally one with its mother for a considerable period.

To the degree to which the individual, figuratively speaking, has not yet completely severed the umbilical cord which fastens him to the outside world, he lacks freedom; but these ties give him security and a feeling of belonging and of being rooted somewhere. I wish to call these ties that exist before the process of individuation has resulted in the complete emergence of an individual "primary ties." They are organic in the sense that they are a part of normal human development; they imply a lack of individuality, but they also give security and orientation to the individual. They are the ties that connect the child with its mother, the member of a primitive community with his clan and nature, or the medieval man with the Church and his social caste. Once the stage of complete individuation is reached and the individual is free from these primary ties, he is confronted with a new task: to orient and root himself in the world and to find security in other ways than those which were characteristic of his preindividualistic existence. Freedom then has a different meaning from the one it had before this stage of evolution is reached. It is necessary to stop here and to clarify these concepts by discussing them more concretely in connection with individual and social development.

The comparatively sudden change from foetal into human existence and the cutting off of the umbilical cord mark the independence of the infant from the mother's body. But this independence is only real in the crude sense of the separation of the two bodies. In a functional sense, the infant remains part of the mother. It is fed, carried, and taken care of in every vital respect by the mother. Slowly the child comes to regard the mother and other objects as entities apart from itself.

One factor in this process is the neurological and the general physical development of the child, its ability to grasp objects—physically and mentally—and to master them. Through its own activity it experiences a world outside of itself. The process of individuation is furthered by that of education. This process entails a number of frustrations and prohibitions, which change the role of the mother into that of a person with different aims which conflict with the child's wishes, and often into that of a hostile and dangerous person. This antagonism, which is one part of the educational process though by no means the whole, is an important factor in sharpening the distinction between the "I" and the "thou."

A few months elapse after birth before the child even recognizes another person as such and is able to react with a smile, and it is years before the child ceases to confuse itself with the universe. Until then it shows the particular kind of egocentricity typical of children, an egocentricity which does not exclude tenderness for and interest in others, since "others" are not yet definitely experienced as really separate from itself. For the same reason the child's leaning on authority in these first years has also a different meaning from the leaning on authority later on. The parents, or whoever the authority may be, are not yet regarded as being a fundamentally separate entity; they are part of the child's universe, and this universe is still part of the child; submission to them, therefore, has a different quality from the kind of submission that exists once two individuals have become really separate. . . .

The more the child grows and to the extent to which primary ties are cut off, the more it develops a quest for freedom and independence. But the fate of this quest can only be fully understood if we realize the dialectic quality in this process of growing individuation.

This process has two aspects: one is that the child grows stronger physically, emotionally, and mentally. In each of these spheres intensity and activity grow. At the same time, these spheres become more and more integrated. An organized structure guided by the individual's will and reason develops. If we call this organized and integrated whole of the personality the self, we can also say that the *one side of the growing process of individuation is the growth of self-strength.* The limits of the growth of individuation and the self are set, partly by individual conditions, but essentially by social conditions. For although the differences between individuals in this respect appear to be great, every society is characterized by a certain level of individuation beyond which the normal individual cannot go.

The other aspect of the process of individuation is *growing aloneness.* The primary ties offer security and basic unity with the world outside of oneself. To the extent to which the child emerges from that world it becomes aware of being alone, of being an entity separate from all others. This separation from a world, which in comparison with one's own individual existence is overwhelmingly strong and powerful, and often threatening and dangerous, creates a feeling of powerlessness and anxiety. As long as one was an integral part of that world, unaware of the possibilities and responsibilities of individual action, one did not need to be afraid of it. When one has become an individual, one stands alone and faces the world in all its perilous and overpowering aspects.

Impulses arise to give up one's individuality, to overcome the feeling of aloneness and powerlessness by completely submerging oneself in the world outside. These impulses, however, and the new ties arising from them, are not identical with the primary ties which have been cut off in the process of growth itself. Just as a child can never return to the mother's womb physically, so it can never reverse, psychically, the process of individuation. Attempts to do so necessarily assume the character of submission, in which the basic contradiction between the authority and the child who submits to it is never eliminated. Consciously the child may feel secure and satisfied, but unconsciously it realizes that the price it pays is giving up strength and the integrity of its self. Thus the result of submission is the very opposite of what it was to be: submission increases the child's insecurity and at the same time creates hostility and rebelliousness, which is the more frightening since it is directed against the very persons on whom the child has remained—or become—dependent.

However, submission is not the only way of avoiding aloneness and anxiety. The other way, the only one which is productive and does not end in an insoluble conflict, is that of *spontaneous relationship to man and nature,* a relationship that connects the individual with the world without eliminating his individuality. This kind of relationship—the foremost expressions of which are love and productive work—are rooted in the integration and strength of the total personality and are therefore subject to the very limits that exist for the growth of the self.

The problem of submission and of spontaneous activity as two possible results of growing individuation will be discussed later on in great detail; here I only wish to point to the general principle, the dialectic process which results from growing individuation and from growing freedom of the individual. The child becomes more free to develop and express its own individual self unhampered by those ties which were limiting it. But the child also becomes more free *from* a world which gave it security and reassurance. The process of individuation is one of growing strength and integration of its individual personality, but it is at the same time a process in which the original identity with others is lost and in which the child becomes more separate from them. This growing separation may result in an isolation that has the quality of desolation and creates intense anxiety and insecurity; it may result in a new kind of closeness and a solidarity with others if the child has been able to develop the inner strength and productivity which are the premise of this new kind of relatedness to the world.

If every step in the direction of separation and individuation were matched by corresponding growth of the self, the development of the child would be harmonious. This does not occur, however. While the process of individuation takes place automatically, the growth of the self is hampered for a number of individual and social reasons. The lag between these two trends results in an unbearable feeling of isolation and powerlessness, and this in its turn leads to psychic mechanisms . . . *of escape.*

Phylogenetically, too, the history of man can be characterized as a process of growing individuation and growing freedom. Man emerges from the prehuman stage by the first steps in the direction of becoming free from coercive instincts. If we understand by instinct a specific action pattern which is determined by inherited neurological structures, a clear-cut trend can be observed in the animal kingdom. The lower an animal is in the scale of development, the more are its adaptation to nature and all its activities controlled by instinctive and reflex action mechanisms. The famous social organizations of some insects are created entirely by instincts. On the other hand, the higher an animal is in the scale of development, the more flexibility of action pattern and the less completeness of structural adjustment do we find at birth. This development reaches its peak with man. He is the most helpless of all animals at birth. His adaptation to nature is based essentially on the process of learning, not on instinctual determination. "Instinct . . . is a diminishing if not a disappearing category in higher animal forms, especially in the human."[3]

Human existence begins when the lack of fixation of action by instincts exceeds a certain point; when the adaptation to nature loses its coercive character; when the way to act is no longer fixed by hereditarily given mechanisms. In other words, *human existence and freedom are from the beginning inseparable.* Freedom is here used not in its positive sense of "freedom to" but in its negative sense of "freedom from," namely freedom from instinctual determination of his actions.

Freedom in the sense just discussed is an ambiguous gift. Man is born without the equipment for appropriate action which the animal possesses; he is dependent on his parents for a longer time than any animal, and his reactions to his surroundings are less quick and less effective than the automatically regulated instinctive actions are. He goes through all the dangers and fears which this lack of instinctive equipment implies. Yet this very helplessness of man is the basis from which human development springs; *man's biological weakness is the condition of human culture.*

From the beginning of his existence man is confronted with the choice between different courses of action. In the animal there is an uninterrupted chain of reactions starting with a stimulus, like hunger, and ending with a more or less strictly determined course of action, which does away with the tension created by the stimulus. In man that chain is interrupted. The stimulus is there but the kind of satisfaction is "open," that is, he must choose between different courses of action. Instead of a predetermined instinctive action, man has to weigh possible courses of action in his mind; he starts to think. He changes his role toward nature from that of purely passive adaptation to an active one: he produces. He invents tools and, while thus mastering nature, he separates himself from it more and more. He becomes dimly aware of himself—or rather of his group—as not being identical with nature. It dawns upon him that his is a tragic fate: to be part of nature, and yet to transcend it. He becomes aware of death as his ultimate fate even if he tries to deny it in manifold phantasies.

One particularly telling representation of the fundamental relation between man and freedom is offered in the biblical myth of man's expulsion from paradise.

The myth identifies the beginning of human history with an act of choice, but it puts all emphasis on the sinfulness of this first act of freedom and the suffering resulting from it. Man and woman live in the Garden of Eden in complete harmony with each other and with nature. There is peace and no necessity to work; there is no choice, no freedom, no thinking either. Man is forbidden to eat from the tree of knowledge of good and evil. He acts against God's command, he breaks through the state of harmony with nature of which he is a part without transcending it. From the standpoint of the Church which represented authority, this is essentially sin. From the standpoint of man, however, this is the beginning of human freedom. Acting against God's orders means freeing himself from coercion, emerging from the unconscious existence of prehuman life to the level of man. Acting against the command of authority, committing a sin, is in its positive human aspect the first act of freedom, that is, the first *human* act. In the myth the sin in its formal

[3] L. Bernard, *Instinct,* Holt & Co., New York, 1924, p. 509.

aspect is the eating of the tree of knowledge. The act of disobedience as an act of freedom is the beginning of reason. The myth speaks of other consequences of the first act of freedom. The original harmony between man and nature is broken. God proclaims war between man and woman, and war between nature and man. Man has become separate from nature, he has taken the first step toward becoming human by becoming an "individual." He has committed the first act of freedom. The myth emphasizes the suffering resulting from this act. To transcend nature, to be alienated from nature and from another human being, finds man naked, ashamed. He is alone and free, yet powerless and afraid. The newly won freedom appears as a curse; he is free *from* the sweet bondage of paradise, but he is not free to govern himself, to realize his individuality.

"Freedom from" is not identical with positive freedom with "freedom to." The emergence of man from nature is a long-drawn-out process; to a large extent he remains tied to the world from which he emerged; he remains part of nature—the soil he lives on, the sun and moon and stars, the trees and flowers, the animals, and the group of people with whom he is connected by the ties of blood. Primitive religions bear testimony to man's feeling of oneness with nature. Animate and inanimate nature are part of his human world or, as one may also put it, he is still part of the natural world.

The primary ties block his full human development; they stand in the way of the development of his reason and his critical capacities; they let him recognize himself and others only through the medium of his, or their, participation in a clan, a social or religious community, and not as human beings; in other words, they block his development as a free, self-determining, productive individual. But although this is one aspect, there is another one. This identity with nature, clan, religion, gives the individual security. He belongs to, he is rooted in, a structuralized whole in which he has an unquestionable place. He may suffer from hunger or suppression, but he does not suffer from the worst of all pains—complete aloneness and doubt.

We see that the process of growing human freedom has the same dialectic character that we have noticed in the process of individual growth. On the one hand it is a process of growing strength and integration, mastery of nature, growing power of human reason, and growing solidarity with other human beings. But on the other hand this growing individuation means growing isolation, insecurity, and thereby growing doubt concerning one's own role in the universe, the meaning of one's life, and with all that a growing feeling of one's own powerlessness and insignificance as an individual.

If the process of the development of mankind had been harmonious, if it had followed a certain plan, then both sides of the development—the growing strength and the growing individuation—would have been exactly balanced. As it is, the history of mankind is one of conflict and strife. Each step in the direction of growing individuation threatened people with new insecurities. Primary bonds once severed cannot be mended; once paradise is lost, man cannot return to it. There is only one possible, productive solution for the relationship of individualized man with the world: his active solidarity with all men and his spontaneous activity, love and work, which unite him again with the world, not by primary ties but as a free and independent individual.

However, if the economic, social and political conditions on which the whole process of human individuation depends, do not offer a basis for the realization of individuality in the sense just mentioned, while at the same time people have lost those ties which gave them security, this lag makes freedom an unbearable burden. It then becomes identical with doubt, with a kind of life which lacks meaning and direction. Powerful tendencies arise to escape from this kind of freedom into submission or some kind of relationship to man and the world which promises relief from uncertainty, even if it deprives the indiviudal of his freedom.

European and American history since the end of the Middle Ages is the history of the full emergence of the individual. It is a process which started in Italy, in the Renaissance, and which only now seems to have come to a climax. It took over four hundred years to break down the medieval world and to free people from the most apparent restraints. But while in many respects the individual has grown, has developed mentally and emotionally, and participates in cultural achievements in a degree unheard-of before, the lag between "freedom from" and "freedom to" has grown too. The result of this disproportion between freedom *from* any tie and the lack of possibilities for the positive realization of freedom and individuality has led, in Europe, to a panicky flight from freedom into new ties or at least into complete indifference.*

The automatization of the individual in modern society has increased the helplessness and insecurity of the average individual. Thus, he is ready to submit to new authorities which offer him security and relief from doubt. The following chapter will discuss the special conditions that were necessary to make this offer accepted in Germany; it will show that for the nucleus—the lower middle class—of the Nazi movement, the authoritarian mechanism was most characteristic. In the last chapter of this book we shall continue the discussion of the automaton with regard to the cultural scene in our own democracy.†

III.
The Rise Of Nazism And The Escape From Freedom To Authoritarianism

In discussing the psychology of Nazism we have first to consider a preliminary question—the relevance of psychological factors in the understanding of Nazism. In the scientific and still more so in the popular discussion of Nazism, two opposite views are frequently presented: the first, that psychology offers no explanation of an economic and political phenomenon like Fascism, the second, that Fascism is wholly a psychological problem.

The first view looks upon Nazism either as the outcome of an exclusively economic dynamism—of the expansive tendencies of German imperialism, or as an essentially political phenomenon—the conquest of the state by one political party backed by industrialists and Junkers; in short, the victory of Nazism is looked upon as the result of a minority's trickery and coercion of the majority of the population.

The second view, on the other hand, maintains that Nazism can be explained only in terms of psychology, or rather in those of psychopathology. Hitler is looked

---

* Pp. 23-37.
† P. 6.

upon as a madman or as a "neurotic," and his followers as equally mad and mentally unbalanced. According to this explanation, as expounded by L. Mumford, the true sources of Fascism are to be found "in the human soul, *not in economics.*" He goes on: "In overwhelming pride, delight in cruelty, neurotic disintegration—in this and not in the Treaty of Versailles or in the incompetence of the German Republic lies the explanation of Fascism." [4]

In our opinion none of these explanations which emphasize political and economic factors to the exclusion of psychological ones—or vice versa—is correct. Nazism is a psychological problem, but the psychological factors themselves have to be understood as being molded by socio-economic factors; Nazism is an economic and political problem, but the hold it has over a whole people has to be understood on psychological grounds. What we are concerned with in this chapter is this psychological aspect of Nazism, its human basis. This suggests two problems: the character structure of those people to whom it appealed, and the psychological characteristics of the ideology that made it such an effective instrument with regard to those very people.

In considering the psychological basis for the success of Nazism this differentiation has to be made at the outset: one part of the population bowed to the Nazi regime without any strong resistance, but also without becoming admirers of the Nazi ideology and political practice. Another part was deeply attracted to the new ideology and fanatically attached to those who proclaimed it. The first group consisted mainly of the working class and the liberal and Catholic bourgeoisie. In spite of an excellent organization, especially among the working class, these groups, although continuously hostile to Nazism from its beginning up to 1933, did not show the inner resistance one might have expected as the outcome of their political convictions. Their will to resist collapsed quickly and since then they have caused little difficulty for the regime (excepting, of course, the small minority which has fought heroically against Nazism during all these years). Psychologically, this readiness to submit to the Nazi regime seems to be due mainly to a state of inner tiredness and resignation, which, as will be indicated in the next chapter, is characteristic of the individual in the present era even in democratic countries. In Germany one additional condition was present as far as the working class was concerned: the defeat it suffered after the first victories in the revolution of 1918. The working class had entered the postwar period with strong hopes for the realization of socialism or at least for a definite rise in its political, economic, and social position; but, whatever the reasons, it had witnessed an unbroken succession of defeats, which brought about the complete disappointments of all its hopes. By the beginning of 1930 the fruits of its initial victories were almost completely destroyed and the result was a deep feeling of resignation, of disbelief in their leaders, of doubt about the value of any kind of political organization and political activity. They still remained members of their respective parties and, consciously, continued to believe in their political doctrines; but deep within themselves many had given up any hope in the effectiveness of political action.

An additional incentive for the loyalty of the majority of the population to the Nazi government became effective after Hitler came into power. For millions of people Hitler's government then became identical with "Germany." Once he held

---

[4] L. Mumford, *Faith for Living,* Harcourt, Brace & Co., New York, 1940, p. 118.

the power of government, fighting him implied shutting oneself out of the community of Germans; when other political parties were abolished and the Nazi party "was" Germany, opposition to it meant opposition to Germany. It seems that nothing is more difficult for the average man to bear than the feeling of not being identified with a larger group. However much a German citizen may be opposed to the principles of Nazism, if he has to choose between being alone and feeling that he belongs to Germany, most persons will choose the latter. It can be observed in many instances that persons who are not Nazis nevertheless defend Nazism against criticism of foreigners because they feel that an attack on Nazis is an attack on Germany. The fear of isolation and the relative weakness of moral principles help any party to win the loyalty of a large sector of the population once that party has captured the power of the state.

This consideration results in an axiom which is important for the problems of political propaganda: any attack on Germany as such, any defamatory propaganda concerning "the Germans" (such as the "Hun" symbol of the last war), only increases the loyalty of those who are not wholly identified with the Nazi system. This problem, however, cannot be solved basically by skillful propaganda but only by the victory in all countries of one fundamental truth: that ethical principles stand above the existence of the nation and that by adhering to these principles an individual belongs to the community of all those who share, who have shared, and who will share this belief.

In contrast to the negative or resigned attitude of the working class and of the liberal and Catholic bourgeoisie, the Nazi ideology was ardently greeted by the lower strata of the middle class, composed of small shopkeepers, artisans, and white-collar workers.

Members of the older generation among this class formed the more passive mass basis; their sons and daughters were the more active fighters. For them the Nazi ideology—its spirit of blind obedience to a leader and of hatred against racial and political minorities, its craving for conquest and domination, its exaltation of the German people and the "Nordic Race"—had a tremendous emotional appeal and it was this appeal which won them over and made them into ardent believers in and fighters for the Nazi cause. The answer to the question why the Nazi ideology was so appealing to the lower class has to be sought for in the social character of the lower middle class. Their social character was markedly different from that of the working class, of the higher strata of the middle class, and of the nobility and the upper classes. As a matter of fact, certain features were characteristic for this part of the middle class throughout its history: their love of the strong, hatred of the weak, their pettiness, hostility, thriftiness with feelings as well as with money, and essentially their asceticism. Their outlook on life was narrow, they suspected and hated the stranger, and they were curious and envious of their acquaintances, rationalizing their envy as moral indignation; their whole life was based on the principle of scarcity—economically as well as psychologically.

To say that the social character of the lower middle class differed from that of the working class does not imply that this character structure was not present in the working class also. But it was *typical* for the lower middle class, while only a minority of the working class exhibited the same character structure in a similarly clear-cut fashion; the one or the other trait, however, in a less intense form, like enhanced respect of authority or thrift, was to be found in most members of the working class too. On the other hand it seems that a great part of the white-collar workers—probably the majority—more closely resembled the character structure of the manual workers (especially those in big factories) than that of the "old middle class," which did not participate in the rise of monopolistic capitalism but was essentially threatened by it.

Although it is true that the social character of the lower middle class had been the same long before the war of 1914, it is also true that the events after the war intensified the very traits to which the Nazi ideology had its strong appeal: its craving for submission and its lust for power.

In the period before the German Revolution of 1918, the economic position of the lower strata of the old middle class, the small independent businessman and artisan, was already on the decline; but it was not desperate and there were a number of factors which made for its stability.

The authority of the monarchy was undisputed, and by leaning on it and identifying with it the member of the lower middle class acquired a feeling of security and narcissistic pride. Also, the authority of religion and traditional morality was still firmly rooted. The family was still unshaken and a safe refuge in a hostile world. The individual felt that he belonged to a stable social and cultural system in which he had his definite place. His submission and loyalty to existing authorities were a satisfactory solution of his masochistic strivings; yet he did not go to the extreme of self-surrender and he retained a sense of the importance of his own personality. What he was lacking in security and aggressiveness as an individual, he was compensated for by the strength of the authorities to whom he submitted himself. In brief his economic position was still solid enough to give him a feeling of self-pride and of relative security, and the authorities on whom he leaned were strong enough to give him the additional security which his own individual position could not provide.

The postwar period changed this situation considerably. In the first place, the economic decline of the old middle class went at a faster pace; this decline was accelerated by the inflation, culminating in 1923, which wiped out almost completely the savings of many years' work.

While the years between 1924 and 1928 brought economic improvement and new hopes to the lower middle class, these gains were wiped out by the depression after 1929. As in the period of inflation, the middle class, squeezed in between the workers and the upper classes, was the most defenseless group and therefore the hardest hit.

But besides these economic factors there were psychological considerations that aggravated the situation. The defeat in the war and the downfall of the monarchy was one. While the monarchy and the state had been the solid rock on which, psychologically speaking, the petty bourgeois had built his existence, their failure and defeat shattered the basis of his own life. If the Kaiser could be publicly ridiculed, if officers could be attacked, if the state had to change its form and to accept "red agitators" as cabinet ministers and a saddlemaker as president, what could the little man put his trust in? He had identified himself in his subaltern manner with all these institutions; now, since they had gone, where was he to go?

The inflation too, played both an economic and a psychological role. It was a deadly blow against the principle of thrift as well as against the authority of the state. If the savings of many years, for which one had sacrificed so many little pleasures, could be lost through no fault of one's own, what was the point in saving anyway? If the state could break its promises printed on its bank notes and loans, whose promises could one trust any longer?

It was not only the economic position of the lower middle class that declined more rapidly after the war, but its social prestige as well. Before the war one could feel himself as something better than a worker. After the revolution the social prestige of the working class rose considerably and in consequence the prestige of the lower middle class fell in relative terms. There was nobody to look down upon any more, a privilege that had always been one of the strongest assets in the life of small shopkeepers and their like.

In addition to these factors the last stronghold of middle-class security had been shattered too: the family. The postwar development, in Germany perhaps more than in other countries, had shaken the authority of the father and the old middle-class morality. The younger generation acted as they pleased and cared no longer whether their actions were approved by their parents or not.

The reasons for this development are too manifold and complex to discuss here in detail. I shall mention only a few. The decline of the old social symbols of authority like monarchy and state affected the role of the individual authorities, the parents. If these authorities, which the younger generation had been taught by the parents to respect, proved to be weak, then the parents lost prestige and authority too. Another factor was that, under the changed conditions, especially the inflation, the older generation was bewildered and puzzled and much less adapted to the new conditions than the smarter, younger generation. Thus the younger generation felt superior to their elders and could not take them, and their teachings, quite seriously any more. Furthermore, the economic decline of the middle class deprived the parents of their economic role as backers of the economic future of their children.

The older generation of the lower middle class grew more bitter and resentful, but in a passive way; the younger generation was aggravated by the fact that the basis for an independent economic existence, such as their parents had had, was lost; the professional market was saturated, and the chances of making a living as a physician or lawyer were slight. Those who had fought in the war felt that they had a claim for a better deal than they were actually getting. Especially the many young officers, who for years had been accustomed to command and to exercise power quite naturally, could not reconcile themselves to becoming clerks or traveling salesmen.

The increasing social frustration led to a projection which became an important source for National Socialism: instead of being aware of the economic and social fate of the old middle class, its members consciously thought of their fate in terms of the nation. The national defeat and the Treaty of Versailles became the symbols to which the actual frustration—the social one—was shifted.

It has often been said that the treatment of Germany by the victors in 1918 was one of the chief reasons for the rise of Nazism. This statement needs qualification. The majority of Germans felt that the peace treaty was unjust; but while the middle class reacted with intense bitterness, there was much less bitterness at the Versailles Treaty among the working class. They had been opposed to the old regime and the loss of the war for them meant defeat of that regime. They felt that they had fought bravely and that they had no reason to be ashamed of themselves. On the other hand the victory of the revolution which had only been possible by the defeat of the monarchy had brought them economic, political, and human gains. The resentment against Versailles had its basis in the lower middle class; the nationalistic resentment was a rationalization, projecting social inferiority to national inferiority.

This projection is quite apparent in Hitler's personal development. He was the typical representative of the lower middle class, a nobody with no chances or future. He felt very intensely the role of being an outcast. He often speaks in *Mein Kampf* of himself as the "nobody," the "unknown man" he was in his youth. But although this was due essentially to his own social position, he could rationalize it in national symbols. Being born outside of the Reich he felt excluded not so much socially as nationally, and the great German Reich to which all her sons could return became for him the symbol of social prestige and security.

The old middle class's feeling of powerlessness, anxiety, and isolation from the social whole and the destructiveness springing from this situation was not the only psychological source of Nazism. The peasants felt resentful against the urban creditors to whom they were in debt, while the workers felt deeply disappointed and discouraged by the constant political retreat after their first victories in 1918 under a leadership which had lost all strategic initiative. The vast majority of the population was seized with the feeling of individual insignificance and powerlessness which we have described as typical for monopolistic capitalism in general.

Those psychological conditions were not the "cause" of Nazism. They constituted its human basis without which it could not have developed. . . .*

IV.
The Illusion Of Individuality And Freedom In A Democracy

. . . I have tried to show that certain factors in the modern industrial system in general and in its monopolistic phase in particular make for the development of a personality which feels powerless and alone, anxious and insecure. I have discussed the specific conditions in Germany which make part of her population fertile soil for an ideology and political practice that appeal to what I have described as the authoritarian character.

But what about ourselves? Is our own democracy threatened only by Fascism beyond the Atlantic or by the "fifth column" in our own ranks? If that were the case, the situation would be serious but not critical. But although foreign and internal threats of Fascism must be taken seriously, there is no greater mistake and no graver danger than not to see that in our own society we are faced with the same phenomenon that is fertile soil for the rise of Fascism anywhere: the insignificance and powerlessness of the individual.

---

* Pp. 206-18.

This statement challenges the conventional belief that by freeing the individual from all external restraints modern democracy has achieved true individualism. We are proud that we are not subject to any external authority, that we are free to express our thoughts and feelings, and we take it for granted that this freedom almost automatically guarantees our individuality. *The right to express our thoughts,* however, *means something only if we are able to have thoughts of our own;* freedom from external authority is a lasting gain only if the inner psychological conditions are such that we are able to establish our own individuality. Have we achieved that aim, or are we at least approaching it? This book deals with the human factor; its task, therefore, is to analyze this very question critically. In doing so we take up threads that were dropped in earlier chapters. In discussing the two aspects of freedom for modern man, we have pointed out the economic conditions that make for increasing isolation and powerlessness of the individual in our era; in discussing the psychological results we have shown that this powerlessness leads either to the kind of escape that we find in the authoritarian character, or else to a compulsive conforming in the process of which the isolated individual becomes an automaton, loses his self, and yet at the same time consciously conceives of himself as free and subject only to himself.*

The particular difficulty in recognizing to what extent our wishes—and our thoughts and feelings as well—are not really our own but put into us from the outside, is closely linked up with the problem of authority and freedom. In the course of modern history the authority of the Church has been replaced by that of the State, that of the State by that of conscience, and in our era, the latter has been replaced by the anonymous authority of common sense and public opinion as instruments of conformity. Because we have freed ourselves of the older overt forms of authority, we do not see that we have become the prey of a new kind of authority. We have become automatons who live under the illusion of being self-willing individuals. This illusion helps the individual to remain unaware of his insecurity, but this is all the help such an illusion can give. Basically the self of the individual is weakened, so that he feels powerless and extremely insecure. He lives in a world to which he has lost genuine relatedness and in which everybody and everything has become instrumentalized, where he has become a part of the machine that his hands have built. He thinks, feels, and wills what he believes he is supposed to think, feel, and will; in this very process he loses his self upon which all genuine security of a free individual must be built.

The loss of the self has increased the necessity to conform, for it results in a profound doubt of one's own identity. If I am nothing but what I believe I am supposed to be—who am "I"? We have seen how the doubt about one's own self started with the breakdown of the medieval order in which the individual had had an unquestionable place in a fixed order. The identity of the individual has been a major problem of modern philosophy since Descartes. Today we take for granted that we are we. Yet the doubt about ourselves still exists, or has even grown. In his plays Pirandello has given expression to this feeling of modern man. He starts with the question: Who am I? What proof have I for my own identity other than the continuation of my physical self? His answer is not like Descartes'—the affirmation of the individual self—but its denial: I have no identity, there is no

* Pp. 240-41.

self excepting the one which is the reflex of what others expect me to be: I am "as you desire me."

This loss of identity then makes it still more imperative to conform; it means that one can be sure of oneself only if one lives up to the expectations of others. If we do not live up to this picture we not only risk disapproval and increased isolation, but we risk losing the identity of our personality, which means jeopardizing sanity.

By conforming with the expectations of others, by not being different, these doubts about one's own identity are silenced and a certain security is gained. However, the price paid is high. Giving up spontaneity and individuality results in a thwarting of life. Psychologically the automaton, while being alive biologically, is dead emotionally and mentally. While he goes through the motions of living, his life runs through his hands like sand. Behind a front of satisfaction and optimism modern man is deeply unhappy; as a matter of fact, he is on the verge of desperation. He desperately clings to the notion of individuality; he wants to be "different," and he has no greater recommendation of anything than that "it is different." We are informed of the individual name of the railroad clerk we buy our tickets from; handbags, playing cards, and portable radios are "personalized," by having the initials of the owner put on them. All this indicates the hunger for "difference" and yet these are almost the last vestiges of individuality that are left. Modern man is starved for life. But since, being an automaton, he cannot experience life in the sense of spontaneous activity he takes as surrogate any kind of excitement and thrill: the thrill of drinking, of sports, of vicariously living the excitements of fictitious persons on the screen.

What then is the meaning of freedom for modern man?

He has become free from the external bonds that would prevent him from doing and thinking as he sees fit. He would be free to act according to his own will, if he knew what he wanted, thought, and felt. But he does not know. He conforms to anonymous authorities and adopts a self which is not his. The more he does this, the more powerless he feels, the more he is forced to conform. In spite of a veneer of optimism and initiative, modern man is overcome by a profound feeling of powerlessness which makes him gaze toward approaching catastrophes as though he were paralyzed.

Looked at superficially, people appear to function well enough in economic and social life; yet it would be dangerous to overlook the deep-seated unhappiness behind that comforting veneer. If life loses its meaning because it is not lived, man becomes desperate. People do not die quietly from physical starvation; they do not die quietly from psychic starvation either. If we look only at the economic needs as far as the "normal" person is concerned, if we do not see the unconscious suffering of the average automatized person, then we fail to see the danger that threatens our culture from its human basis: the readiness to accept any ideology and any leader, if only he promises excitement and offers a political structure and symbols which allegedly give meaning and order to an individual's life. The despair of the human automaton is fertile soil for the political purposes of Fascism.*

---

* Pp. 253-56.

V.
Conclusion: Love, Spontaneity And Freedom

Does our analysis lend itself to the conclusion that there is an inevitable circle that leads from freedom into new dependence? Does freedom from all primary ties make the individual so alone and isolated that inevitably he must escape into new bondage? Are *independence* and freedom identical with *isolation* and fear? Or is there a state of positive freedom in which the individual exists as an independent self and yet is not isolated but united with the world, with other men, and nature?

We believe that there is a positive answer, that the process of growing freedom does not constitute a vicious circle, and that man can be free and yet not alone, critical and yet not filled with doubts, independent and yet an integral part of mankind. This freedom man can attain by the realization of his self, by being himself. What is realization of the self? Idealistic philosophers have believed that self-realization can be achieved by intellectual insight alone. They have insisted upon splitting human personality, so that man's nature may be suppressed and guarded by his reason. The result of this split, however, has been that not only the emotional life of man but also his intellectual faculties have been crippled. Reason, by becoming a guard set to watch its prisoner, nature, has become a prisoner itself; and thus both sides of human personality, reason and emotion, were crippled. We believe that the realization of the self is accomplished not only by an act of thinking but also by the realization of man's total personality, by the active expression of his emotional and intellectual potentialities. These potentialities are present in everybody, they become real only to the extent to which they are expressed. In other words, *positive freedom consists in the spontaneous activity of the total, integrated personality.*

We approach here one of the most difficult problems of psychology: the problem of spontaneity. An attempt to discuss this problem adequately would require another volume. However, on the basis of what we have said so far, it is possible to arrive at an understanding of the essential quality of spontaneous activity by means of contrast. Spontaneous activity is not compulsive activity, to which the individual is driven by his isolation and powerlessness; it is not the activity of the automaton, which is the uncritical adoption of patterns suggested from the outside. Spontaneous activity is free activity of the self and implies, psychologically, what the Latin root of the word, *sponte,* means literally: of one's free will. By activity we do not mean "doing something," but the quality of creative activity that can operate in one's emotional, intellectual, and sensuous experiences and in one's will as well. One premise for this spontaneity is the acceptance of the total personality and the elimination of the split between "reason" and "nature"; for only if man does not repress essential parts of his self, only if he has become transparent to himself, and only if the different spheres of life have reached a fundamental integration, is spontaneous activity possible.

Why is spontaneous activity the answer to the problem of freedom? We have said that negative freedom by itself makes the individual an isolated being, whose relationship to the world is distant and distrustful and whose self is weak and constantly threatened. Spontaneous activity is the one way in which man can overcome the terror of aloneness without sacrificing the integrity of his self; for in the spontaneous realization of the self man unites himself anew with the world—with man, nature, and himself. Love is the foremost component of such spontaneity; not love as the dissolution of the self in another person, not love as the possession of another person, but love as spontaneous affirmation of others, as the union of the individual with others on the basis of the preservation of the individual self. The dynamic quality of love lies in this very polarity: that it springs from the need of overcoming separateness, that it leads to oneness—and yet that individuality is not eliminated. Work is the other component; not work as a compulsive activity in order to escape aloneness, not work as a relationship to nature which is partly one of dominating her, partly one of worship of and enslavement by the very products of man's hands, but work as creation in which man becomes one with nature in the act of creation. What holds true of love and work holds true of all spontaneous action, whether it be the realization of sensuous pleasure or participation in the political life of the community. It affirms the individuality of the self and at the same time it unites the self with man and nature. The basic dichotomy that is inherent in freedom—the birth of individuality and the pain of aloneness—is dissolved on a higher plane by man's spontaneous action.

In all spontaneous activity the individual embraces the world. Not only does his individual self remain intact; it becomes stronger and more solidified. *For the self is as strong as it is active.* There is no genuine strength in possession as such, neither of material property nor of mental qualities like emotions or thoughts. There is also no strength in use and manipulation of objects; what we use is not ours simply because we use it. Ours is only that to which we are genuinely related by our creative activity, be it a person or an inanimate object. Only those qualities that result from our spontaneous activity give strength to the self and thereby form the basis of its integrity. The inability to act spontaneously, to express what one genuinely feels and thinks, and the resulting necessity to present a pseudo self to others and oneself, are the root of the feeling of inferiority and weakness. Whether or not we are aware of it, there is nothing of which we are more ashamed than of not being ourselves, and there is nothing that gives us greater pride and happiness than to think, to feel, and to say what is ours.

This implies that what matters is the activity as such, the process and not the result. In our culture the emphasis is just the reverse. We produce not for a concrete satisfaction but for the abstract purpose of selling our commodity; we feel that we can acquire everything material or immaterial by buying it, and thus things become ours independently of any creative effort of our own in relation to them. In the same way we regard our personal qualities and the result of our efforts as commodities that can be sold for money, prestige, and power. The emphasis thus shifts from the present satisfaction of creative activity to the value of the finished product. Thereby man misses the only satisfaction that can give him real happiness—the experience of the activity of the present moment—and chases after a phantom that leaves him disappointed as soon as he believes he has caught it—the illusory happiness called success.

If the individual realizes his self by spontaneous activity and thus relates himself to the world, he ceases to be an isolated atom; he and the world become part of one structuralized whole; he has his rightful place, and thereby his doubt concerning himself and the meaning of life disappears. This doubt sprang from his separateness and from the thwarting of life; when he can live, neither compulsively nor automatically but spontaneously, the doubt disappears. He is aware of himself as an active and creative individual and recognizes that *there is only one meaning of life: the act of living itself.*

If the individual overcomes the basic doubt concerning himself and his place in life, if he is related to the world by embracing it in the act of spontaneous living, he gains strength as an individual and he gains security. This security, however, differs from the security that characterizes the preindividualist state in the same way in which the new relatedness to the world differs from that of the primary ties. The new security is not rooted in the protection which the individual has from a higher power outside of himself; neither is it a security in which the tragic quality of life is eliminated. The new security is dynamic; it is not based on protection, but on man's spontaneous activity. It is the security acquired each moment by man's spontaneous activity. It is the security that only freedom can give, that needs no illusions because it has eliminated those conditions that necessitate illusions.

Positive freedom as the realization of the self implies the full affirmation of the uniqueness of the individual. Men are born equal but they are also born different. The basis of this difference is the inherited equipment, physiological and mental, with which they start life, to which is added the particular constellation of circumstances and experiences that they meet with. This individual basis of the personality is as little identical with any other as two organisms are ever identical physically. The genuine growth of the self is always a growth on this particular basis; it is an organic growth, the unfolding of a nucleus that is peculiar for this one person and only for him. The development of the automaton, in contrast, is not an organic growth. The growth of the basis of the self is blocked and a pseudo self is superimposed upon this self, which is—as we have seen—essentially the incorporation of extraneous patterns of thinking and feeling. Organic growth is possible only under the condition of supreme respect for the peculiarity of the self of other persons as well as of our own self. This respect for and cultivation of the uniqueness of the self is the most valuable achievement of human culture and it is this very achievement that is in danger today.

The uniqueness of the self in no way contradicts the principle of equality. The thesis that men are born equal implies that they all share the same fundamental human qualities, that they share the basic fate of human beings, that they all have the same inalienable claim on freedom and happiness. It furthermore means that their relationship is one of solidarity, not one of domination-submission. What the concept of equality does not mean is that all men are alike. Such a concept of equality is derived from the role that the individual plays in his economic activities today. In the relation between the man who buys and the one who sells, the concrete differences of personality are eliminated. In this situation only one thing matters, that the one has something to sell and the other has money to buy it. In economic life one man is not different from another; as real persons they are, and the cultivation of their uniqueness is the essence of individuality.

Positive freedom also implies the principle that there is no higher power than this unique individual self, that man is the center and purpose of his life; that the growth and realization of man's individuality is an end that can never be subordinated to purposes which are supposed to have greater dignity. This interpretation may arouse serious objections. Does it not postulate unbridled egotism? Is it not the negation of the idea of sacrifice for an ideal? Would its acceptance not lead to anarchy? These questions have actually already been answered, partly explicitly, partly implicitly, during our previous discussion. However, they are too important for us not to make another attempt to clarify the answers and to avoid misunderstanding.

To say that man should not be subject to anything higher than himself does not deny the dignity of ideals. On the contrary, it is the strongest affirmation of ideals. It forces us, however, to a critical analysis of what an ideal is. One is generally apt today to assume that an ideal is any aim whose achievement does not imply material gain, anything for which a person is ready to sacrifice egotistical ends. This is a purely psychological—and for that matter relativistic—concept of an ideal. From this subjectivist viewpoint a Fascist, who is driven by the desire to subordinate himself to a higher power and at the same time to overpower other people, has an ideal just as much as the man who fights for human equality and freedom. On this basis the problem of ideals can never be solved.

We must recognize the difference between genuine and fictitious ideals, which is just as fundamental a difference as that between truth and falsehood. All genuine ideals have one thing in common: they express the desire for something which is not yet accomplished but which is desirable for the purposes of the growth and happiness of the individual. We may not always know what serves this end, we may disagree about the function of this or that ideal in terms of human development, but this is no reason for a relativism which says that we cannot know what furthers life or what blocks it. We are not always sure which food is healthy and which is not, yet we do not conclude that we have no way whatsoever of recognizing poison. In the same way we can know, if we want to, what is poisonous for mental life. We know that poverty, intimidation, isolation, are directed *against* life; that everything that serves freedom and furthers the courage and strength to be oneself is *for* life. What is good or bad for man is not a metaphysical question, but an empirical one that can be answered on the basis of an analysis of man's nature and the effect which certain conditions have on him.

But what about "ideals" like those of the Fascists which are definitely directed against life? How can we understand the fact that men are following these false ideals as fervently as others are following true ideals? The answer to this question is provided by certain psychological considerations. The phenomenon of masochism shows us that men can be drawn to the experiencing of suffering or submission. There is no doubt that suffering, submission, or suicide is the antithesis of positive aims of living. Yet these aims can be subjectively experienced as gratifying and attractive. This attraction to what is harmful in life is the phenomenon which more than any other deserves the name of a pathological perversion. Many psychologists have assumed that the experience of pleasure and the avoidance of pain is the only legitimate principle guiding human action; but dynamic psychology can show that the subjective experience of pleasure is not a sufficient criterion for the value of certain behavior in terms of human happiness. The analysis of masochistic phenomena is a case in point. Such analysis shows that the sensation of pleasure can be the result of a pathological perversion and proves as little about the objective meaning of the experience as the sweet taste of a poison would prove about its function for the organism. We thus come to define a genuine ideal as any aim which furthers the growth, freedom, and happiness of the self, and to define as fictitious ideals those compulsive and irrational aims which subjectively are attractive experiences (like the drive for submission), but which actually are harmful to life. Once we accept this definition, it follows that a genuine ideal is not some veiled force superior to the individual, but that it is the articulate expression of utmost affirmation of the self. Any ideal which is in contrast to such affirmation proves by this very fact that it is not an ideal but a pathological aim.

From here we come to another question, that of sacrifice. Does our definition of freedom as nonsubmission to any *higher* power exclude sacrifices, including the sacrifice of one's life?

This is a particularly important question today, when Fascism proclaims self-sacrifice as the highest virtue and impresses many people with its idealistic character. The answer to this question follows logically from what has been said so far. There are two entirely different types of sacrifice. It is one of the tragic facts of life that the demands of our physical self and the aims of our mental self can conflict; that actually we may have to sacrifice our physical self in order to assert the integrity of our spiritual self. This sacrifice will never lose its tragic quality. Death is never sweet, not even if it is suffered for the highest ideal. It remains unspeakably bitter, and still it can be the utmost assertion of our individuality. Such sacrifice is fundamentally different from the "sacrifice" which Fascism preaches. There, sacrifice is not the highest price man may have to pay to assert his self, but it is an aim in itself. This masochistic sacrifice sees the fulfillment of life in its very negation, in the annihilation of the self. It is only the supreme expression of what Fascism aims at in all its ramifications—the annihilation of the individual self and its utter submission to a higher power. It is the perversion of true sacrifice as much as suicide is the utmost perversion of life. True sacrifice presupposes an uncompromising wish for spiritual integrity. The sacrifice of those who have lost it only covers up their moral bankruptcy.

One last objection is to be met: If individuals are allowed to act freely in the sense of spontaneity, if they acknowledge no higher authority than themselves, will anarchy be the inevitable result? In so far as the word anarchy stands for heedless egotism and destructiveness, the determining factor depends upon one's understanding of human nature. I can only refer to what has been pointed out in the chapter dealing with mechanisms of escape: that man is neither good nor bad; that life has an inherent tendency to grow, to expand, to express potentialities; that if life is thwarted, if the individual is isolated and overcome by doubt or a feeling of aloneness and powerlessness, then he is driven to destructiveness and craving for power or submission. If human freedom is established as *freedom to*, if man can realize his self fully and uncompromisingly, the fundamental cause for his asocial drives will have disappeared and only a sick and abnormal individual will be dangerous. This freedom has never been realized in the history of mankind, yet it has been an ideal to which mankind has stuck even if it was often expressed in abstruse and irrational forms. There is no reason to wonder why the record of history shows so much cruelty and destructiveness. If there is anything to be surprised at—and encouraged by—I believe it is the fact that the human race, in spite of all that has happened to men, has retained—and actually developed—such qualities of dignity, courage, decency, and kindness as we find them throughout history and in countless individuals today.

If by anarchy one means that the individual does not acknowledge any kind of authority, the answer is to be found in what has been said about the difference between rational and irrational authority. Rational authority—like a genuine ideal—represents the aims of growth and expansion of the individual. It is, therefore, in principle never in conflict with the individual and his real, and not his pathological, aims.

It has been the thesis of this book that freedom has a twofold meaning for modern man: that he has been freed from traditional authorities and has become an "individual," but that at the same time he has become isolated, powerless, and an instrument of purposes outside of himself, alienated from himself and others; furthermore, that this state undermines his self, weakens and frightens him, and makes him ready for submission to new kinds of bondage. Positive freedom on the other hand is identical with the full realization of the individual's potentialities, together with his ability to live actively and spontaneously. Freedom has reached a critical point where, driven by the logic of its own dynamism, it threatens to change into its opposite. The future of democracy depends on the realization of the individualism that has been the ideological aim of modern thought since the Renaissance. The cultural and political crisis of our day is not due to the fact that there is too much individualism but that what we believe to be individualism has become an empty shell. The victory of freedom is possible only if democracy develops into a society in which the individual, his growth and happiness, is the aim and purpose of culture, in which life does not need any justification in success or anything else, and in which the individual is not subordinated to or manipulated by any power outside of himself, be it the State or the economic machine; finally, a society in which his conscience and ideals are not the internalization of external demands, but are really *his* and express the aims that result from the peculiarity of his self. These aims could not be fully realized in any previous period of modern history; they had to remain largely ideological aims, because the material basis for the development of genuine individualism was lacking. Capitalism has created this premise. The problem of production is solved—in principle at least—and we can visualize a future of abundance, in which the fight for economic privileges is no longer necessitated by economic scarcity. The problem we are confronted with today is that of the organization of social and economic forces, so that man—as a member of organized society—may become the master of these forces and cease to be their slave.*

---

* Pp. 257-71.

Part 5

MAN IN TODAY'S SOCIETY

1945-present

EXISTENTIALISM

Jean-Paul Sartre

The anxiety and insecurity characterizing contemporary Western man resulted in part from the trauma of recent wars and the incredible acts of cruelty by men toward their fellow man. The spectre of millions of people killed in World Wars I and II, mass extermination at concentration camps like Auschwitz, and indiscriminate annihilation in Dresden and Hiroshima made a sham of conventional doctrines of morality and progress. Optimism toward the future of mankind was eroded further by the reality of potential total destruction from a nuclear holocaust. These conditions generated a formidable challenge to traditional philosophies, values, and ethics by an alienated generation seeking meaning in their lives. Existentialism provided a timely alternative to conventional attitudes and an appealing view of the nature of society and meaning of man.

The roots of existentialism can be clearly seen in the nineteenth century. Fyodor Dostoevsky (1821–81), Soren Kierkegaard (1813–85), and Friedrich Nietzsche (1844–1900) displayed insight into the loneliness of man and a perception of life's absurdity. Existentialism, however, "is not a philosophy but a label for several widely different revolts against traditional philosophy . . . it is not a school of thought nor is it reducible to any set of tenets. . . ." Existentialism repudiates "the adequacy of any body of beliefs whatever," and considers "traditional philosophy as superficial, academic and remote from life." [1] In the twentieth century the works of Franz Kafka (1883–1924), Karl Jaspers (1883–1969), Martin Heidegger (1905–   ), Gabriel Marcel (1884–   ), Albert Camus (1913–60), and Jean-Paul Sartre have added their motifs to the search for a new morality to fill the spiritual vacuum of modern man.

Jean-Paul Sartre (1905–   ) was born in Paris and raised by his grandfather, an uncle of the famous humanitarian Albert Schweitzer. Sartre was trained at the Ecole Normale Superieure and the Institut Francais in Berlin where he studied under Martin Heidegger. Sartre's first novel, *Nausea* (1938), which many critics claim as his best work, portrayed a sense of "nothingness" through Sartre's character Antoine Roquentin. In a mystic scene in a garden Roquentin discovered a kind

[1] Walter Kaufmann, *Existentialism from Dostoevsky to Sartre* (Cleveland: World Publishing Co., 1956), pp. 11-12.

of salvation through self-realization of his existence, uniqueness, and freedom. Sartre further elaborated, expressed and developed his views toward man and society in scores of later novels, plays, and his massive volume, *Being and Nothingness* (1943). In a lecture published in 1946 as *Existentialism and Humanism,* Sartre applied his theories of existential phenomenology to man. Sartre argued that man does not have a fixed character of something called human nature. Man "is what he wills, and as he conceives himself after already existing." He is "nothing else but that which he makes of himself." Sartre concluded that society was irrelevant to the individual and that freedom, meaning the achievement of the "total being," was all that mattered.

I.
The Meaning Of Existentialism; And, The Existential View Of The Nature Of Man And Freedom

. . . we can begin by saying that existentialism, in our sense of the word, is a doctrine that does render human life possible; a doctrine, also, which affirms that every truth and every action imply both an environment and a human subjectivity. The essential charge laid against us is, of course, that of over-emphasis upon the evil side of human life. I have lately been told of a lady who, whenever she lets slip a vulgar expression in a moment of nervousness, excuses herself by exclaiming, "I believe I am becoming an existentialist." So it appears that ugliness is being identified with existentialism. That is why some people say we are "naturalistic," and if we are, it is strange to see how much we scandalise and horrify them, for no one seems to be much frightened or humiliated nowadays by what is properly called naturalism. Those who can quite well keep down a novel by Zola such as *La Terre* are sickened as soon as they read an existentialist novel. Those who appeal to the wisdom of the people—which is a sad wisdom—find ours sadder still. And yet, what could be more disillusioned than such sayings as "Charity begins at home" or "Promote a rogue and he'll sue you for damage, knock him down and he'll do you homage"? We all know how many common sayings can be quoted to this effect, and they all mean much the same—that you must not oppose the powers-that-be; that you must not fight against superior force; must not meddle in matters that are above your station. Or that any action not in accordance with some tradition is mere romanticism; or that any undertaking which has not the support of proven experience is foredoomed to frustration; and that since experience has shown men to be invariably inclined to evil, there must be firm rules to restrain them, otherwise we shall have anarchy. It is, however, the people who are forever mouthing these dismal proverbs and, whenever they are told of some more or less repulsive action, say "How like human nature!"—it is these very people, always harping upon realism, who complain that existentialism is too gloomy a view of things. Indeed their excessive protests make me suspect that what is annoying them is not so much our pessimism, but, much more likely,

Reprinted from Jean-Paul Sartre, *Existentialism and Humanism,* trans. Philip Mairet (London: Methuen & Co., 1948), pp. 24-34, 38-53, 55-56.

our optimism. For at bottom, what is alarming in the doctrine that I am about to try to explain to you is—is it not?—that it confronts man with a possibility of choice. To verify this, let us review the whole question upon the strictly philosophic level. What, then, is this that we call existentialism? . . .

The question is only complicated because there are two kinds of existentialists. There are, on the one hand, the Christians, amongst whom I shall name Jaspers and Gabriel Marcel, both professed Catholics; and on the other the existential atheists, amongst whom we must place Heidegger as well as the French existentialists and myself. What they have in common is simply the fact that they believe that *existence* comes before *essence*—or, if you will, that we must begin from the subjective. What exactly do we mean by that?

If one considers an article of manufacture—as, for example, a book or a paper-knife—one sees that it has been made by an artisan who had a conception of it; and he has paid attention, equally, to the conception of a paper-knife and to the pre-existent technique of production which is a part of that conception and is, at bottom, a formula. Thus the paper-knife is at the same time an article producible in a certain manner and one which, on the other hand, serves a definite purpose, for one cannot suppose that a man would produce a paper-knife without knowing what it was for. Let us say, then, of the paper-knife that its essence—that is to say the sum of the formulae and the qualities which made its production and its definition possible—precedes its existence. The presence of such-and-such a paper-knife or book is thus determined before my eyes. Here, then, we are viewing the world from a technical standpoint, and we can say that production precedes existence.

When we think of God as the creator, we are thinking of him, most of the time, as a supernal artisan. Whatever doctrine we may be considering, whether it be a doctrine like that of Descartes, or of Leibnitz himself, we always imply that the will follows, more or less, from the understanding or at least accompanies it, so that when God creates he knows precisely what he is creating. Thus, the conception of man in the mind of God is comparable to that of the paper-knife in the mind of the artisan: God makes man according to a procedure and a conception, exactly as the artisan manufactures a paper-knife, following a definition and a formula. Thus each individual man is the realisation of a certain conception which dwells in the divine understanding. In the philosophic atheism of the eighteenth century, the notion of God is suppressed, but not, for all that, the idea that essence is prior to existence; something of that idea we still find everywhere, in Diderot, in Voltaire and even in Kant. Man possesses a human nature; that "human nature," which is the conception of human being, is found in every man; which means that each man is a particular example of an universal conception, the conception of Man. In Kant, this universality goes so far that the wild man of the woods, man in the state of nature and the bourgeois are all contained in the same definition and have the same fundamental qualities. Here again, the essence of man precedes that historic existence which we confront in experience.

Atheistic existentialism, of which I am a representative, declares with greater consistency that if God does not exist there is at least one being whose existence comes before its essence, a being which exists before it can be defined by any conception of it. That being is man or, as Heidegger has it, the human reality.

What do we mean by saying that existence precedes essence? We mean that man first of all exists, encounters himself, surges up in the world—and defines himself afterwards. If man as the existentialist sees him is not definable, it is because to begin with he is nothing. He will not be anything until later, and then he will be what he makes of himself. Thus, there is no human nature, because there is no God to have a conception of it. Man simply is. Not that he is simply what he conceives himself to be, but he is what he wills, and as he conceives himself after already existing—as he wills to be after that leap towards existence. Man is nothing else but that which he makes of himself. That is the first principle of existentialism. And this is what people call its "subjectivity," using the word as a reproach against us. But what do we mean to say by this, but that man is of a greater dignity than a stone or a table? For we mean to say that man primarily exists—that man is, before all else, something which propels itself towards a future and is aware that it is doing so. Man is, indeed, a project which possesses a subjective life, instead of being a kind of moss, or a fungus or a cauliflower. Before that projection of the self nothing exists; not even in the heaven of intelligence: man will only attain existence when he is what he purposes to be. Not, however, what he may wish to be. For what we usually understand by wishing or willing is a conscious decision taken—much more often than not—after we have made ourselves what we are. I may wish to join a party, to write a book or to marry—but in such a case what is usually called my will is probably a manifestation of a prior and more spontaneous decision. If, however, it is true that existence is prior to essence, man is responsible for what he is. Thus, the first effect of existentialism is that it puts every man in possession of himself as he is, and places the entire responsibility for his existence squarely upon his own shoulders. And, when we say that man is responsible for himself, we do not mean that he is responsible only for his own individuality, but that he is responsible for all men. The word "subjectivism" is to be understood in two senses, and our adversaries play upon only one of them. Subjectivism means, on the one hand, the freedom of the individual subject and, on the other, that man cannot pass beyond human subjectivity. It is the latter which is the deeper meaning of existentialism. When we say that man chooses himself, we do mean that every one of us must choose himself; but by that we also mean that in choosing for himself he chooses for all men. For in effect, of all the actions a man may take in order to create himself as he wills to be, there is not one which is not creative, at the same time, of an image of man such as he believes he ought to be. To choose between this or that is at the same time to affirm the value of that which is chosen; for we are unable ever to choose the worse. What we choose is always the better; and nothing can be better for us unless it is better for all. If, moreover, existence precedes essence and we will to exist at the same time as we fashion our image, that image is valid for all and for the entire epoch in which we find ourselves. Our responsibility is thus much greater than we had supposed, for it concerns mankind as a whole. If I am a worker, for instance, I may choose to join a Christian rather than a Communist trade union. And if, by that membership, I choose to signify that resignation is, after all, the attitude that best becomes a man, that man's kingdom is not upon this earth, I do not commit myself alone to that view. Resignation is my will for everyone, and my action is, in consequence, a commitment on behalf of all mankind. Or if, to take a more personal case, I decide to marry and to have children, even though this decision proceeds simply from my situation, from my passion or my desire, I am thereby committing not only myself, but humanity as a whole, to the practice of monogamy. I am thus responsible for myself and for all men, and I am creating a certain image of man as I would have him to be. In fashioning myself I fashion man.

This may enable us to understand what is meant by such terms—perhaps a little grandiloquent—as anguish, abandonment and despair. As you will soon see, it is very simple. First, what do we mean by anguish? The existentialist frankly states that man is in anguish. His meaning is as follows—When a man commits himself to anything, fully realising that he is not only choosing what he will be, but is thereby at the same time a legislator deciding for the whole of mankind—in such a moment a man cannot escape from the sense of complete and profound responsibility. There are many, indeed, who show no such anxiety. But we affirm that they are merely disguising their anguish or are in flight from it. Certainly, many people think that in what they are doing they commit no one but themselves to anything: and if you ask them, "What would happen if everyone did so?" they shrug their shoulders and reply, "Everyone does not do so." But in truth, one ought always to ask oneself what would happen if everyone did as one is doing; nor can one escape from that disturbing thought except by a kind of self-deception. The man who lies in self-excuse, by saying "Everyone will not do it" must be ill at ease in his conscience, for the act of lying implies the universal value which it denies. By its very disguise his anguish reveals itself. . . . Everything happens to every man as though the whole human race had its eyes fixed upon what he is doing and regulated its conduct accordingly. So every man ought to say, "Am I really a man who has the right to act in such a manner that humanity regulates itself by what I do." If a man does not say that, he is dissembling his anguish. Clearly, the anguish with which we are concerned here is not one that could lead to quietism or inaction. It is anguish pure and simple, of the kind well known to all those who have borne responsibilities. When, for instance, a military leader takes upon himself the responsibility for an attack and sends a number of men to their death, he chooses to do it and at bottom he alone chooses. No doubt he acts under a higher command, but its orders, which are more general, require interpretation by him and upon that interpretation depends the life of ten, fourteen or twenty men. In making the decision, he cannot but feel a certain anguish. All leaders know that anguish. It does not prevent their acting, on the contrary it is the very condition of their action, for the action presupposes that there is a plurality of possibilities, and in choosing one of these, they realise that it has value only because it is chosen. Now it is anguish of that kind which existentialism describes, and moreover, as we shall see, makes explicit through direct responsibility towards other men who are concerned. Far from being a screen which could separate us from action, it is a condition of action itself.

And when we speak of "abandonment"—a favourite word of Heidegger—we only mean to say that God does not exist, and that it is necessary to draw the consequences of his absence right to the end. The existentialist is strongly opposed to a certain type of secular moralism which seeks to suppress God at the least possible expense. Towards 1880, when the French professors endeavoured to formulate a secular morality, they said something like this:—God is a useless and costly hypothesis, so we will do without it. However, if we are to have morality, a society and a law-abiding world, it is essential that certain values should be taken seriously; they must have an *a priori* existence ascribed to them. It must be considered obligatory *a priori* to be honest, not to lie, not to beat one's wife, to bring up children and so forth; so we are going to do a little work on this subject, which will enable us to show that these values exist all the same, inscribed in an intelligible heaven although, of course, there is no God. In other words—and this is, I believe, the purport of all that we in France call radicalism—nothing will be changed if God does not exist; we shall re-discover the same norms of honesty, progress and humanity, and we shall have disposed of God as an out-of-date hypothesis which will die away quietly of itself. The existentialist, on the contrary, finds it extremely embarrassing that God does not exist, for there disappears with Him all possibility of finding values in an intelligible heaven. There can no longer be any good *a priori,* since there is no infinite and perfect consciousness to think it. It is nowhere written that "the good" exists, that one must be honest or must not lie, since we are now upon the plane where there are only men. Dostoievsky once wrote "If God did not exist, everything would be permitted"; and that, for existentialism, is the starting point. Everything is indeed permitted if God does not exist, and man is in consequence forlorn, for he cannot find anything to depend upon either within or outside himself. He discovers forthwith, that he is without excuse. For if indeed existence precedes essence, one will never be able to explain one's action by reference to a given and specific human nature; in other words, there is no determinism—man is free, man *is* freedom. Nor, on the other hand, if God does not exist, are we provided with any values or commands that could legitimise our behaviour. Thus we have neither behind us, nor before us in a luminous realm of values, any means of justification or excuse. We are left alone, without excuse. That is what I mean when I say that man is condemned to be free. Condemned, because he did not create himself, yet is nevertheless at liberty, and from the moment that he is thrown into this world he is responsible for everything he does. The existentialist does not believe in the power of passion. He will never regard a grand passion as a destructive torrent upon which a man is swept into certain actions as by fate, and which, therefore, is an excuse for them. He thinks that man is responsible for his passion. Neither will an existentialist think that a man can find help through some sign being vouchsafed upon earth for his orientation: for he thinks that the man himself interprets the sign as he chooses. He thinks that every man, without any support or help whatever, is condemned at every instant to invent man.*

You are free, therefore choose—that is to say, invent. No rule of general morality can show you what you ought to do: no signs are vouchsafed in this world. The Catholics will reply, "Oh, but they are!" Very well; still, it is myself, in every case, who have to interpret the signs. Whilst I was imprisoned, I made the acquaintance of a somewhat remarkable man, a Jesuit, who had become a member of that order in the following manner. In his life he had suffered a succession of rather severe setbacks. His father had died when he was a child, leaving him in poverty, and he had been awarded a free scholarship in a religious institution, where he had been made continually to feel that he was accepted for charity's sake, and, in consequence, he had been denied several of those distinctions and honours which gratify children. Later, about the age of eighteen, he came to grief

---

* Pp. 24-34.

in a sentimental affair; and finally, at twenty-two—this was a trifle in itself, but it was the last drop that overflowed his cup—he failed in his military examination. This young man, then, could regard himself as a total failure: it was a sign—but a sign of what? He might have taken refuge in bitterness or despair. But he took it—very cleverly for him—as a sign that he was not intended for secular successes, and that only the attainments of religion, those of sanctity and of faith, were accessible to him. He interpreted his record as a message from God, and became a member of the Order. Who can doubt but that this decision as to the meaning of the sign was his, and his alone? One could have drawn quite different conclusions from such a series of reverses—as, for example, that he had better become a carpenter or a revolutionary. For the decipherment of the sign, however, he bears the entire responsibility. That is what "abandonment" implies, that we ourselves decide our being. And with this abandonment goes anguish.

As for "despair," the meaning of this expression is extremely simple. It merely means that we limit ourselves to a reliance upon that which is within our wills, or within the sum of the probabilities which render our action feasible. Whenever one wills anything, there are always these elements of probability. If I am counting upon a visit from a friend, who may be coming by train or by tram, I presuppose that the train will arrive at the appointed time, or that the tram will not be derailed. I remain in the realm of possibilities; but one does not rely upon any possibilities beyond those that are strictly concerned in one's action. Beyond the point at which the possibilities under consideration cease to affect my action, I ought to disinterest myself. For there is no God—and no prevenient design, which can adapt the world and all its possibilities to my will. When Descartes said, "Conquer yourself rather than the world," what he meant was, at bottom, the same—that we should act without hope.

Marxists, to whom I have said this, have answered: "Your action is limited, obviously, by your death; but you can rely upon the help of others. That is, you can count both upon what the others are doing to help you elsewhere, as in China and in Russia, and upon what they will do later, after your death, to take up your action and carry it forward to its final accomplishment which will be the revolution. Moreover you must rely upon this; not to do so is immoral." To this I rejoin, first, that I shall always count upon my comrades-in-arms in the struggle, in so far as they are committed, as I am, to a definite, common cause; and in the unity of a party or a group which I can more or less control—that is, in which I an enrolled as a militant and whose movements at every moment are known to me. In that respect, to rely upon the unity and the will of the party is exactly like my reckoning that the train will run to time or that the tram will not be derailed. But I cannot count upon men whom I do not know, I cannot base my confidence upon human goodness or upon man's interest in the good of society, seeing that man is free and that there is no human nature which I can take as foundational. I do not know whither the Russian revolution will lead. I can admire it and take it as an example in so far as it is evident, to-day, that the proletariat plays a part in Russia which it has attained in no other nation. But I cannot affirm that this will necessarily lead to the triumph of the proletariat: I must confine myself to what I can see. Nor can I be sure that comrades-in-arms will take up my work after my death and carry it to the maximum perfection, seeing that those men are free agents and will freely decide, to-morrow, what man is then to be.

To-morrow, after my death, some men may decide to establish Fascism, and the others may be so cowardly or so slack as to let them do so. If so, Fascism will then be the truth of man, and so much the worse for us. In reality, things will be such as men have decided they shall be. Does that mean that I should abandon myself to quietism? No. First I ought to commit myself and then act my commitment, according to the time-honoured formula that "one need not hope in order to undertake one's work." Nor does this mean that I should not belong to a party, but only that I should be without illusion and that I should do what I can. For instance, if I ask myself "Will the social ideal as such, ever become a reality?" I cannot tell, I only know that whatever may be in my power to make it so, I shall do; beyond that, I can count upon nothing.

Quietism is the attitude of people who say, "let others do what I cannot do." The doctrine I am presenting before you is precisely the opposite of this, since it declares that there is no reality except in action. It goes further, indeed, and adds, "Man is nothing else but what he purposes, he exists only in so far as he realises himself, he is therefore nothing else but the sum of his actions, nothing else but what his life is." Hence we can well understand why some people are horrified by our teaching. For many have but one resource to sustain them in their misery, and that is to think, "Circumstances have been against me, I was worthy to be something much better than I have been. I admit I have never had a great love or a great friendship; but that is because I never met a man or a woman who were worthy of it; if I have not written any very good books, it is because I had not the leisure to do so; or, if I have had no children to whom I could devote myself it is because I did not find the man I could have lived with. So there remains within me a wide range of abilities, inclinations and potentialities, unused but perfectly viable, which endow me with a worthiness that could never be inferred from the mere history of my actions." But in reality and for the existentialist, there is no love apart from the deeds of love; no potentiality of love other than that which is manifested in loving; there is no genius other than that which is expressed in works of art. . . .

In life, a man commits himself, draws his own portrait and there is nothing but that portrait. No doubt this thought may seem comfortless to one who has not made a success of his life. On the other hand, it puts everyone in a position to understand that reality alone is reliable; that dreams, expectations and hopes serve to define a man only as deceptive dreams, abortive hopes, expectations unfulfilled; that is to say, they define him negatively, not positively. Nevertheless, when one says, "You are nothing else but what you live," it does not imply that an artist is to be judged solely by his works of art, for a thousand other things contribute no less to his definition as a man. What we mean to say is that a man is no other than a series of undertakings, that he is the sum, the organisation, the set of relations that constitute the undertakings.

In the light of all this, what people reproach us with is not, after all, our pessimism, but the sternness of our optimism. If people condemn our works of fiction, in which we describe characters that are base, weak, cowardly and sometimes even frankly evil, it is not only because those characters are base, weak, cowardly or evil. For suppose that, like Zola, we showed that the behaviour of these characters was caused by their heredity, or by the action of their environment upon them, or by determining factors, psychic or organic. People would be reassured, they would say, "You see, that is what we are like, no one can do anything about it." But the existentialist, when he portrays a coward, shows him as responsible for his cowardice. He is not like that on account of a cowardly heart or lungs or cerebrum, he has not become like that through his physiological organism; he is like that because he has made himself into a coward by his actions. There is no such thing as a cowardly temperament. There are nervous temperaments; there is what is called impoverished blood, and there are also rich temperaments. But the man whose blood is poor is not a coward for all that, for what produces cowardice is the act of giving up or giving way; and a temperament is not an action. A coward is defined by the deed that he has done. What people feel obscurely, and with horror, is that the coward as we present him is guilty of being a coward. What people would prefer would be to be born either a coward or a hero. One of the charges most often laid against the *Chemins de la Liberté* is something like this—"But, after all, these people being so base, how can you make them into heroes?" That objection is really rather comic, for it implies that people are born heroes: and that is, at bottom, what such people would like to think. If you are born cowards, you can be quite content, you can do nothing about it and you will be cowards all your lives whatever you do; and if you are born heroes you can again be quite content; you will be heroes all your lives, eating and drinking heroically. Whereas the existentialist says that the coward makes himself cowardly, the hero makes himself heroic; and that there is always a possibility for the coward to give up cowardice and for the hero to stop being a hero. What counts is the total commitment, and it is not by a particular case or particular action that you are committed altogether.

We have now, I think, dealt with a certain number of the reproaches against existentialism. You have seen that it cannot be regarded as a philosophy of quietism since it defines man by his action; nor as a pessimistic description of man, for no doctrine is more optimistic, the destiny of man is placed within himself. Nor is it an attempt to discourage man from action since it tells him that there is no hope except in his action and that the one thing which permits him to have life is the deed. Upon this level therefore, what we are considering is an ethic of action and self-commitment. However, we are still reproached, upon these few data, for confining man within his individual subjectivity. There again people badly misunderstand us.

Our point of departure is, indeed, the subjectivity of the individual, and that for strictly philosophic reasons. It is not because we are bourgeois, but because we seek to base our teaching upon the truth, and not upon a collection of fine theories, full of hope but lacking real foundations. And at the point of departure there cannot be any other truth than this, *I think, therefore I am,* which is the absolute truth of consciousness as it attains to itself. Every theory which begins with man, outside of this moment of self-attainment, is a theory which thereby suppresses the truth, for outside of the Cartesian *cogito,* all objects are no more than probable, and any doctrine of probabilities which is not attached to a truth will crumble into nothing. In order to define the probable one must possess the true. Before there can be any truth whatever, then, there must be an absolute truth, and there is such a truth which is simple, easily attained and within the reach of everybody; it consists in one's immediate sense of one's self.

In the second place, this theory alone is compatible with the dignity of man, it is the only one which does not make man into an object. All kinds of materialism lead one to treat every man including oneself as an object—that is, as a set of pre-determined reactions, in no way different from the patterns of qualities and phenomena which constitute a table, or a chair or a stone. Our aim is precisely to establish the human kingdom as a pattern of values in distinction from the material world. But the subjectivity which we thus postulate as the standard of truth is no narrowly individual subjectivism, for as we have demonstrated, it is not only one's own self that one discovers in the *cogito,* but those of others too. . .

Thus the man who discovers himself directly in the *cogito* also discovers all the others, and discovers them as the condition of his own existence. He recognises that he cannot be anything (in the sense in which one says one is spiritual, or that one is wicked or jealous) unless others recognise him as such. I cannot obtain any truth whatsoever about myself, except through the mediation of another. The other is indispensable to my existence, and equally so to any knowledge I can have of myself. Under these conditions, the intimate discovery of myself is at the same time the revelation of the other as a freedom which confronts mine, and which cannot think or will without doing so either for or against me. Thus, at once, we find ourselves in a world which is, let us say, that of "inter-subjectivity." It is in this world that man has to decide what he is and what others are. . . .

What is at the very heart and centre of existentialism, is the absolute character of the free commitment, by which every man realises himself in realising a type of humanity—a commitment always understandable, to no matter whom in no matter what epoch—and its bearing upon the relativity of the cultural pattern which may result from such absolute commitment. One must observe equally the relativity of Cartesianism and the absolute character of the Cartesian commitment. In this sense you may say, if you like, that every one of us makes the absolute by breathing, by eating, by sleeping or by behaving in any fashion whatsoever. There is no difference between free being—being as self-committal, as existence choosing its essence—and absolute being. And there is no difference whatever between being as an absolute, temporarily localised—that is, localised in history—and universally intelligible being.

This does not completely refute the charge of subjectivism. Indeed that objection appears in several other forms, of which the first is as follows. People say to us, "Then it does not matter what you do," and they say this in various ways. First they tax us with anarchy; then they say, "You cannot judge others, for there is no reason for preferring one purpose to another"; finally, they may say, "Everything being merely voluntary in this choice of yours, you give away with one hand what you pretend to gain with the other." These three are not very serious objections. As to the first, to say that it matters not what you choose is not correct. In one sense choice is possible, but what is not possible is not to choose. I can always choose, but I must know that if I do not choose, that is still a choice. This, although it may appear merely formal, is of great importance as a limit to fantasy and caprice. For, when I confront a real situation—for example, that I am a sexual being, able to have relations with a being of the other sex and able to have children—I am obliged to choose my attitude to it, and in every respect I bear the responsibility of the choice which, in commiting myself, also commits the whole of humanity. Even if my choice is determined by no *á priori* value whatever, it can have nothing to do with caprice: and if anyone thinks that this is only Gide's theory of the *acte gratuit* over again, he has failed to see the enormous difference between this theory and that of Gide. Gide does not know what a situation is, his "act" is one of pure caprice. In our view, on the contrary, man finds himself in an organised situation in which he is himself involved: his choice involves mankind in its entirety, and he cannot avoid choosing. Either he must remain single, or he must marry without having children, or he must marry and have children. In any case, and whichever he may choose, it is impossible for him, in respect of this situation, not to take complete responsibility. Doubtless he chooses without reference to any pre-established values, but it is unjust to tax him with caprice. Rather let us say that the moral choice is comparable to the construction of a work of art. . . .

There is this in common between art and morality, that in both we have to do with creation and invention. We cannot decide *á priori* what it is that should be done. . . . Man makes himself; he is not found ready-made; he makes himself by the choice of his morality, and he cannot but choose a morality, such is the pressure of circumstances upon him. We define man only in relation to his commitments; it is therefore absurd to reproach us for irresponsibility in our choice.

In the second place, people say to us, "You are unable to judge others." This is true in one sense and false in another. It is true in this sense, that whenever a man chooses his purpose and his commitment in all clearness and in all sincerity, whatever that purpose may be it is impossible to prefer another for him. It is true in the sense that we do not believe in progress. Progress implies amelioration; but man is always the same, facing a situation which is always changing, and choice remains always a choice in the situation. The moral problem has not changed since the time when it was a choice between slavery and anti-slavery—from the time of the war of Secession, for example, until the present moment when one chooses between the M.R.P.[1] and the Communists.

We can judge, nevertheless, for, as I have said, one chooses in view of others, and in view of others one chooses himself. One can judge, first—and perhaps this is not a judgment of value, but it is a logical judgment—that in certain cases choice is founded upon an error, and in others upon the truth. One can judge a man by saying that he deceives himself. Since we have defined the situation of man as one of free choice, without excuse and without help, any man who takes refuge behind the excuse of his passions, or by inventing some deterministic doctrine, is a self-deceiver. One may object: "But why should he not choose to deceive himself?" I reply that it is not for me to judge him morally, but I define his self-deception as an error. Here one cannot avoid pronouncing a judgment of truth. The self-deception is evidently a falsehood, because it is a dissimulation of man's complete liberty of commitment. Upon this same level, I say that it is also a self-deception if I choose to declare that certain values are incumbent upon me; I am in contradiction with myself if I will these values and at the same time say that they impose themselves upon me. If anyone says to me, "And what if I wish to deceive myself?" I answer, "There is no reason why you should not, but I declare that you are doing so, and that the attitude of strict consistency alone is that of good faith. Furthermore, I can pronounce a moral judgment. For I declare that freedom, in respect of concrete circumstances, can have no other end and aim

---

[1] Mouvement Rèpublicain Populaire.

but itself; and when once a man has seen that values depend upon himself, in that state of forsakenness he can will only one thing, and that is freedom as the foundation of all values. That does not mean that he wills it in the abstract: it simply means that the actions of men of good faith have, as their ultimate significance, the quest of freedom itself as such. A man who belongs to some communist or revolutionary society wills certain concrete ends, which imply the will to freedom, but that freedom is willed in community. We will freedom for freedom's sake, and in and through particular circumstances. And in thus willing freedom, we discover that it depends entirely upon the freedom of others and that the freedom of others depends upon our own. Obviously, freedom as the definition of a man does not depend upon others, but as soon as there is a commitment, I am obliged to will the liberty of others at the same time as mine. I cannot make liberty my aim unless I make that of others equally my aim. Consequently, when I recognise, as entirely authentic, that man is a being whose existence precedes his essence, and that he is a free being who cannot, in any circumstances, but will his freedom, at the same time I realise that I cannot not will the freedom of others. Thus, in the name of that will to freedom which is implied in freedom itself, I can form judgments upon those who seek to hide from themselves the wholly voluntary nature of their existence and its complete freedom. Those who hide from this total freedom, in a guise of solemnity or with deterministic excuses, I shall call cowards. Others, who try to show that their existence is necessary, when it is merely an accident of the appearance of the human race on earth,—I shall call scum. But neither cowards nor scum can be identified except upon the plane of strict authenticity. Thus, although the content of morality is variable, a certain form of this morality is universal. Kant declared that freedom is a will both to itself and to the freedom of others. Agreed: but he thinks that the formal and the universal suffice for the constitution of a morality. We think, on the contrary, that principles that are too abstract break down when we come to defining action*

Man is all the time outside of himself: it is in projecting and losing himself beyond himself that he makes man to exist; and, on the other hand, it is by pursuing transcendent aims that he himself is able to exist. Since man is thus self-surpassing, and can grasp objects only in relation to his self-surpassing, he is himself the heart and centre of his transcendence. There is no other universe except the human universe, the universe of human subjectivity. This relation of transcendence as constitutive of man (not in the sense that God is transcendent, but in the sense of self-surpassing) with subjectivity (in such a sense that man is not shut up in himself but forever present in a human universe)—it is this that we call existential humanism. This is humanism, because we remind man that there is no legislator but himself; that he himself, thus abandoned, must decide for himself; also because we show that it is not by turning back upon himself, but always by seeking, beyond himself, an aim which is one of liberation or of some particular realisation, that man can realise himself as truly human.†

---

* Pp. 38-53.

† Pp. 55-56.

TECHNOCRACY

Herbert Marcuse

The year following Hitler's take-over of power in Germany, Herbert Marcuse (1898-) immigrated to the United States. From 1934 until 1940 he was associated with the Institute of Social Research at Columbia University. After becoming a United States citizen in 1940 Marcuse worked in the federal government, serving with the OSS and the State Department. After leaving the government in 1950 he returned to teaching and writing. Among his works are *Reason and Revolution* (1941), *Eros and Civilization* (1954), and *Soviet Marxism* (1958). He is now a professor of philosophy at the University of California, San Diego.

Professor Marcuse has become a controversial person because of his belief in Marxism, his opposition to the technocratic state and his forecast—and indeed encouragement—of revolution by the clusters of alienated persons in this society. He developed these views in *One Dimensional Man* (1964). Marcuse agreed with Fromm that man achieved "freedom from" many material and natural deprivations and has failed to realize "freedom to" by extending his rational powers and fulfilling his self. Marcuse explained that man's positive freedom was being suffocated by "technocratic totalitarianism" and his liberty repressed by economic forces, political machines, and the grip of mass opinion. The reestablishment of liberty "depends on the consciousness of servitude" among a small group of alienated people. He argued that their opposition to technocratic totalitarianism is revolutionary and their violence is an expression of an attempt—often apparently mindless—to restore liberty and humanity to society.

I.
The Technocratic State And The Repression Of Freedom

A comfortable, smooth, reasonable, democratic unfreedom prevails in advanced industrial civilization, a token of technical progress. Indeed, what could be more rational than the suppression of individuality in the mechanization of socially

Reprinted from Herbert Marcuse, *One Dimensional Man* (Boston: Beacon Press, 1964), pp. 1-18, 247-57, by permission of the publisher. Copyright © 1964 by Herbert Marcuse.

necessary but painful performances; the concentration of individual enterprises in more effective, more productive corporations; the regulation of free competition among unequally equipped economic subjects; the curtailment of prerogatives and national sovereignties which impede the international organization of resources. That this technological order also involves a political and intellectual coordination may be a regrettable and yet promising development.

The rights and liberties which were such vital factors in the origins and earlier stages of industrial society yield to a higher stage of this society: they are losing their traditional rationale and content. Freedom of thought, speech, and conscience were—just as free enterprise, which they served to promote and protect—essentially *critical* ideas, designed to replace an obsolescent material and intellectual culture by a more productive and rational one. Once institutionalized, these rights and liberties shared the fate of the society of which they had become an integral part. The achievement cancels the premises.

To the degree to which freedom from want, the concrete substance of all freedom, is becoming a real possibility, the liberties which pertain to a state of lower productivity are losing their former content. Independence of thought, autonomy, and the right to political opposition are being deprived of their basic critical function in a society which seems increasingly capable of satisfying the needs of the individuals through the way in which it is organized. Such a society may justly demand acceptance of its principles and institutions, and reduce the opposition to the discussion and promotion of alternative policies *within* the status quo. In this respect, it seems to make little difference whether the increasing satisfaction of needs is accomplished by an authoritarian or a non-authoritarian system. Under the conditions of a rising standard of living, non-conformity with the system itself appears to be socially useless, and the more so when it entails tangible economic and political disadvantages and threatens the smooth operation of the whole. Indeed, at least in so far as the necessities of life are involved, there seems to be no reason why the production and distribution of goods and services should proceed through the competitive concurrence of individual liberties.

Freedom of enterprise was from the beginning not altogether a blessing. As the liberty to work or to starve, it spelled toil, insecurity, and fear for the vast majority of the population. If the individual were no longer compelled to prove himself on the market, as a free economic subject, the disappearance of this kind of freedom would be one of the greatest achievements of civilization. The technological processes of mechanization and standardization might release individual energy into a yet uncharted realm of freedom beyond necessity. The very structure of human existence would be altered; the individual would be liberated from the work world's imposing upon him alien needs and alien possibilities. The individual would be free to exert autonomy over a life that would be his own. If the productive apparatus could be organized and directed toward the satisfaction of the vital needs, its control might well be centralized; such control would not prevent individual autonomy, but render it possible.

This is a goal within the capabilities of advanced industrial civilization, the "end" of technological rationality. In actual fact, however, the contrary trend operates: the apparatus imposes its economic and political requirements for defense and expansion on labor time and free time, on the material and intellectual culture.

By virtue of the way it has organized its technological base, contemporary industrial society tends to be totalitarian. For "totalitarian" is not only a terroristic political coordination of society, but also a nonterroristic economic-technical coordination which operates through the manipulation of needs by vested interests. It thus precludes the emergence of an effective opposition against the whole. Not only a specific form of government or party rule makes for totalitarianism, but also a specific system of production and distribution which may well be compatible with a "pluralism" of parties, newspapers, "countervailing powers," etc.

Today political power asserts itself through its power over the machine process and over the technical organization of the apparatus. The government of advanced and advancing industrial societies can maintain and secure itself only when it succeeds in mobilizing, organizing, and exploiting the technical, scientific, and mechanical productivity available to industrial civilization. And this productivity mobilizes society as a whole, above and beyond any particular individual or group interests. The brute fact that the machine's physical (only physical?) power surpasses that of the individual, and of any particular group of individuals, makes the machine the most effective political instrument in any society whose basic organization is that of the machine process. But the political trend may be reversed; essentially the power of the machine is only the stored-up and projected powers of man. To the extent to which the work world is conceived of as a machine and mechanized accordingly, it becomes the *potential* basis of a new freedom for man.

Contemporary industrial civilization demonstrates that it has reached the stage at which "the free society" can no longer be adequately defined in the traditional terms of economic, political, and intellectual liberties, not because these liberties have become insignificant, but because they are too significant to be confined within the traditional forms. New modes of realization are needed, corresponding to the new capabilities of society.

Such new modes can be indicated only in negative terms because they would amount to the negation of the prevailing modes. Thus economic freedom would mean freedom *from* the economy—from being controlled by economic forces and relationships; freedom from the daily struggle for existence, from earning a living. Political freedom would mean liberation of the individuals *from* politics over which they have no effective control. Similarly, intellectual freedom would mean the restoration of individual thought now absorbed by mass communication and indoctrination, abolition of "public opinion" together with its makers. The unrealistic sound of these propositions is indicative, not of their utopian character, but of the strength of the forces which prevent their realization. The most effective and enduring form of warfare against liberation is the implanting of material and intellectual needs that perpetuate obsolete forms of the struggle for existence.

The intensity, the satisfaction and even the character of human needs, beyond the biological level, have always been preconditioned. Whether or not the possibility of doing or leaving, enjoying or destroying, possessing or rejecting something is seized as a *need* depends on whether or not it can be seen as desirable and necessary for the prevailing societal institutions and interests. In this sense, human needs are historical needs and, to the extent to which the society demands the repressive development of the individual, his needs themselves and their claim for satisfaction are subject to overriding critical standards.

We may distinguish both true and false needs. "False" are those which are superimposed upon the individual by particular social interests in his repression: the needs which perpetuate toil, aggressiveness, misery, and injustice. Their satisfaction might be most gratifying to the individual, but this happiness is not a condition which has to be maintained and protected if it serves to arrest the development of the ability (his own and others) to recognize the disease of the whole and grasp the chances of curing the disease. The result then is euphorian unhappiness. Most of the prevailing needs to relax, to have fun, to behave and consume in accordance with the advertisements, to love and hate what others love and hate, belong to this category of false needs.

Such needs have a societal content and function which are determined by external powers over which the individual has no control; the development and satisfaction of these needs is heteronomous. No matter how much such needs may have become the individual's own, reproduced and fortified by the conditions of his existence: no matter how much he identifies himself with them and finds himself in their satisfaction, they continue to be what they were from the beginning—products of a society whose dominant interest demands repression.

The prevalence of repressive needs is an accomplished fact, accepted in ignorance and defeat, but a fact that must be undone in the interest of the happy individual as well as all those whose misery is the price of his satisfaction. The only needs that have an unqualified claim for satisfaction are the vital ones—nourishment, clothing, lodging at the attainable level of culture. The satisfaction of these needs is the prerequisite for the realization of *all* needs, of the unsublimated as well as the sublimated ones.

For any consciousness and conscience, for any experience which does not accept the prevailing societal interest as the supreme law of thought and behavior, the established universe of needs and satisfactions is a fact to be questioned—questioned in terms of truth and falsehood. These terms are historical throughout, and their objectivity is historical. The judgment of needs and their satisfaction, under the given conditions, involves standards of *priority*—standards which refer to the optimal development of the individual, of all individuals, under the optimal utilization of the material and intellectual resources available to man. The resources are calculable. "Truth" and "falsehood' of needs designate objective conditions to the extent to which the universal satisfaction of vital needs and, beyond it, the progressive alleviation of toil and poverty, are universally valid standards. But as historical standards, they do not only vary according to area and stage of development, they also can be defined only in (greater or lesser) *contradiction* to the prevailing ones. What tribunal can possibly claim the authority of decision?

In the last analysis, the question of what are true and false needs must be answered by the individuals themselves, but only in the last analysis; that is, if and when they are free to give their own answer. As long as they are kept incapable of being autonomous, as long as they are indoctrinated and manipulated (down to their very instincts), their answer to this question cannot be taken as their own. By the same token, however, no tribunal can justly arrogate to itself the right to decide which needs should be developed and satisfied. Any such tribunal is reprehensible, although our revulsion does not do away with the question: how can the people who have been the object of effective and productive domination by themselves create the conditions of freedom?

The more rational, productive, technical, and total the repressive administration of society becomes, the more unimaginable the means and ways by which the administered individuals might break their servitude and seize their own liberation. To be sure, to impose Reason upon an entire society is a paradoxical and scandalous idea—although one might dispute the righteousness of a society which ridicules this idea while making its own population into objects of total administration. All liberation depends on the consciousness of servitude, and the emergence of this consciousness is always hampered by the predominance of needs and satisfactions which, to a great extent, have become the individual's own. The process always replaces one system of preconditioning by another; the optimal goal is the replacement of false needs by true ones, the abandonment of repressive satisfaction.

The distinguishing feature of advanced industrial society is its effective suffocation of those needs which demand liberation—liberation also from that which is tolerable and rewarding and comfortable—while it sustains and absolves the destructive power and repressive function of the affluent society. Here, the social controls exact the overwhelming need for the production and consumption of waste; the need for stupefying work where it is no longer a real necessity; the need for modes of relaxation which soothe and prolong this stupefaction; the need for maintaining such deceptive liberties as free competition at administered prices, a free press which censors itself, free choice between brands and gadgets.

Under the rule of a repressive whole, liberty can be made into a powerful instrument of domination. The range of choice open to the individual is not the decisive factor in determining the degree of human freedom, but *what* can be chosen and what *is* chosen by the individual. The criterion for free choice can never be an absolute one, but neither is it entirely relative. Free election of masters does not abolish the masters or the slaves. Free choice among a wide variety of goods and services does not signify freedom if these goods and services sustain social controls over a life of toil and fear—that is, if they sustain alienation. And the spontaneous reproduction of superimposed needs by the individual does not establish autonomy; it only testifies to the efficacy of the controls.

Our insistence on the depth and efficacy of these controls is open to the objection that we overrate greatly the indoctrinating power of the "media," and that by themselves the people would feel and satisfy the needs which are now imposed upon them. The objection misses the point. The preconditioning does not start with the mass production of radio and television and with the centralization of their control. The people enter this stage as preconditioned receptacles of long standing; the decisive difference is in the flattening out of the contrast (or conflict) between the given and the possible, between the satisfied and the unsatisfied needs. Here, the so-called equalization of class distinctions reveals its ideological function. If the worker and his boss enjoy the same television program and visit the same resort places, if the typist is as attractively made up as the daughter of her employer, if the Negro owns a Cadillac, if they all read the same newspaper, then this assimilation indicates not the disappearance of classes, but the extent to which the needs and satisfactions that serve the preservation of the Establishment are shared by the underlying population.

Indeed, in the most highly developed areas of contemporary society, the transplantation of social into individual needs is so effective that the difference between them seems to be purely theoretical. Can one really distinguish between the mass media as instruments of information and entertainment, and as agents of manipulation and indoctrination? Between the automobile as nuisance and as convenience? Between the horrors and the comforts of functional architecture? Between the work for national defense and the work for corporate gain? Between the private pleasure and the commercial and political utility involved in increasing the birth rate?

We are again confronted with one of the most vexing aspects of advanced industrial civilization: the rational character of its irrationality. Its productivity and efficiency, its capacity to increase and spread comforts, to turn waste into need, and destruction into construction, the extent to which this civilization transforms the object world into an extension of man's mind and body makes the very notion of alienation questionable. The people recognize themselves in their commodities; they find their soul in their automobile, hi-fi set, split-level home, kitchen equipment. The very mechanism which ties the individual to his society has changed, and social control is anchored in the new needs which it has produced.

The prevailing forms of social control are technological in a new sense. To be sure, the technical structure and efficacy of the productive and destructive apparatus has been a major instrumentality for subjecting the population to the established social division of labor throughout the modern period. Moreover, such integration has always been accompanied by more obvious forms of compulsion: loss of livelihood, the administration of justice, the police, the armed forces. It still is. But in the contemporary period, the technological controls appear to be the very embodiment of Reason for the benefit of all social groups and interests—to such an extent that all contradiction seems irrational and all counteraction impossible.

No wonder then that, in the most advanced areas of this civilization, the social controls have been introjected to the point where even individual protest is affected at its roots. The intellectual and emotional refusal "to go along" appears neurotic and impotent. This is the socio-psychological aspect of the political event that marks the contemporary period: the passing of the historical forces which, at the preceding stage of industrial society, seemed to represent the possibility of new forms of existence.

But the term "introjection" perhaps no longer describes the way in which the individual by himself reproduces and perpetuates the external controls exercised by his society. Introjection suggests a variety of relatively spontaneous processes by which a Self (Ego) transposes the "outer" into the "inner." Thus introjection implies the existence of an inner dimension distinguished from and even antagonistic to the external exigencies—an individual consciousness and an individual unconscious *apart from* public opinion and behavior. The idea of "inner freedom" here has its reality: it designates the private space in which man may become and remain "himself."

Today this private space has been invaded and whittled down by technological reality. Mass production and mass distribution claim the *entire* individual, and industrial psychology has long since ceased to be confined to the factory. The manifold processes of introjection seem to be ossified in almost mechanical reactions. The result is, not adjustment but *mimesis:* an immediate identification of the individual with *his* society and, through it, with the society as a whole.

This immediate, automatic identification (which may have been characteristic of primitive forms of association) reappears in high industrial civilization; its new "immediacy," however, is the product of a sophisticated, scientific management and organization. In this process, the "inner" dimension of the mind in which opposition to the status quo can take root is whittled down. The loss of this dimension, in which the power of negative thinking—the critical power of Reason—is at home, is the ideological counterpart to the very material process in which advanced industrial society silences and reconciles the opposition. The impact of progress turns Reason into submission to the facts of life, and to the dynamic capability of producing more and bigger facts of the same sort of life. The efficiency of the system blunts the individuals' recognition that it contains no facts which do not communicate the repressive power of the whole. If the individuals find themselves in the things which shape their life, they do so, not by giving, but by accepting the law of things—not the law of physics but the law of their society.

I have just suggested that the concept of alienation seems to become questionable when the individuals identify themselves with the existence which is imposed upon them and have in it their own development and satisfaction. This identification is not illusion but reality. However, the reality constitutes a more progressive stage of alienation. The latter has become entirely objective; the subject which is alienated is swallowed up by its alienated existence. There is only one dimension, and it is everywhere and in all forms. The achievements of progress defy ideological indictment as well as justification; before their tribunal, the "false consciousness" of their rationality becomes the true consciousness.

This absorption of ideology into reality does not, however, signify the "end of ideology." On the contrary, in a specific sense advanced industrial culture is *more* ideological than its predecessor, inasmuch as today the ideology is in the process of production itself.[1] In a provocative form, this proposition reveals the political aspects of the prevailing technological rationality. The productive apparatus and the goods and services which it produces "sell" or impose the social system as a whole. The means of mass transportation and communication, the commodities of lodging, food, and clothing, the irresistible output of the entertainment and information industry carry with them prescribed attitudes and habits, certain intellectual and emotional reactions which bind the consumers more or less pleasantly to the producers and, through the latter, to the whole. The products indoctrinate and manipulate; they promote a false consciousness which is immune against its falsehood. And as these beneficial products become available to more individuals in more social classes, the indoctrination they carry ceases to be publicity; it becomes a way of life. It is a good way of life—much better than before—and as a good way of life, it militates against qualitative change. Thus emerges a pattern of *one-dimensional thought and behavior* in which ideas, aspirations, and objectives that, by their content, transcend the established universe of discourse and action are either repelled or reduced to terms of this universe. They are redefined by the rationality of the given system and of its quantitative extension.

The trend may be related to a development in scientific method: operationalism in the physical, behaviorism in the social sciences. The common feature is a total empiricism in the treatment of concepts; their meaning is restricted to the representation of particular operations and behavior. The operational point of view is well illustrated by P. W. Bridgman's analysis of the concept of length:

---

[1] Theodor W. Adorno, *Prismen, Kulturkritik und Gesellschaft* (Frankfurt: Suhrkamp, 1955), p. 24.

> We evidently know what we mean by length if we can tell what the length of any and every object is, and for the physicist nothing more is required. To find the length of an object, we have to perform certain physical operations. The concept of length is therefore fixed when the operations by which length is measured are fixed: that is, the concept of length involves as much and nothing more than the set of operations by which length is determined. In general, we mean by any concept nothing more than a set of operations; *the concept is synonymous with the corresponding set of operations.*[2]

Bridgman has seen the wide implications of this mode of thought for the society at large:

> To adopt the operational point of view involves much more than a mere restriction of the sense in which we understand "concept," but means a far-reaching change in all our habits of thought, in that we shall no longer permit ourselves to use as tools in our thinking concepts of which we cannot give an adequate account in terms of operations.[3]

Bridgman's prediction has come true. The new mode of thought is today the predominant tendency in philosophy, psychology, sociology, and other fields. Many of the most seriously troublesome concepts are being "eliminated" by showing that no adequate account of them in terms of operations or behavior can be given. The radical empiricist onslaught thus provides the methodological justification for the debunking of the mind by the intellectuals—a positivism which, in its denial of the transcending elements of Reason, forms the academic counterpart of the socially required behavior.

Outside the academic establishment, the "far-reaching change in all our habits of thought" is more serious. It serves to coordinate ideas and goals with those exacted by the prevailing system, to enclose them in the system, and to repel those which are irreconcilable with the system. The reign of such a one-dimensional reality does not mean that materialism rules, and that the spiritual, metaphysical, and bohemian occupations are petering out. On the contrary, there is a great deal of "Worship together this week," "Why not try God," Zen, existentialism, and beat ways of life, etc. But such modes of protest and transcendence are no longer contradictory to the status quo and no longer negative. They are rather the ceremonial part of practical behaviorism, its harmless negation, and are quickly digested by the status quo as part of its healthy diet.

One-dimensional thought is systematically promoted by the makers of politics and their purveyors of mass information. Their universe of discourse is populated by self-validating hypotheses which, incessantly and monopolistically repeated, become hypnotic definitions or dictations. For example, "free" are the institutions which operate (and are operated on) in the countries of the Free World; other transcending modes of freedom are by definition either anarchism, communism, or propaganda. "Socialistic" are all encroachments on private enterprises not undertaken by private enterprise itself (or by government contracts), such as universal and comprehensive health insurance, or the protection of nature from all too sweep-

[2] P. W. Bridgman, *The Logic of Modern Physics* (New York: Macmillan, 1928), p. 5.
[3] *Ibid.*, p. 31.

ing commercialization, or the establishment of public services which may hurt private profit. This totalitarian logic of accomplished facts has its Eastern counterpart. There, freedom is the way of life instituted by a communist regime, and all other transcending modes of freedom are either capitalistic, or revisionist, or leftist sectarianism. In both camps, non-operational ideas are non-behavioral and subversive. The movement of thought is stopped at barriers which appear as the limits of Reason itself.

Such limitation of thought is certainly not new. Ascending modern rationalism, in its speculative as well as empirical form, shows a striking contrast between extreme critical radicalism in scientific and philosophic method on the one hand, and an uncritical quietism in the attitude toward established and functioning social institutions. Thus Descartes' *ego cognitans* was to leave the "great public bodies" untouched, and Hobbes held that "the present ought always to be preferred, maintained, and accounted best." Kant agreed with Locke in justifying revolution *if and when* it has succeeded in organizing the whole and in preventing subversion.

However, these accommodating concepts of Reason were always contradicted by the evident misery and injustice of the "great public bodies" and the effective, more or less conscious rebellion against them. Societal conditions existed which provoked and permitted real dissociation from the established state of affairs; a private as well as political dimension was present in which dissociation could develop into effective opposition, testing its strength and the validity of its objectives.

With the gradual closing of this dimension by the society, the self-limitation of thought assumes a larger significance. The interrelation between scientific-philosophical and societal processes, between theoretical and practical Reason, asserts itself "behind the back" of the scientists and philosophers. The society bars a whole type of oppositional operations and behavior; consequently, the concepts pertaining to them are rendered illusory or meaningless. Historical transcendence appears as metaphysical transcendence, not acceptable to science and scientific thought. The operational and behavioral point of view, practiced as a "habit of thought" at large, becomes the view of the established universe of discourse and action, needs and aspirations. The "cunning of Reason" works, as it so often did, in the interest of the powers that be. The insistence on operational and behavioral concepts turns against the efforts to free thought and behavior *from* the given reality and *for* the suppressed alternatives. Theoretical and practical Reason, academic and social behaviorism meet on common ground: that of an advanced society which makes scientific and technical progress into an instrument of domination.

"Progress" is not a neutral term; it moves toward specific ends, and these ends are defined by the possibilities of ameliorating the human condition. Advanced industrial society is approaching the stage where continued progress would demand the radical subversion of the prevailing direction and organization of progress. This stage would be reached when material production (including the necessary services) becomes automated to the extent that all vital needs can be satisfied while necessary labor time is reduced to marginal time. From this point on, technical progress would transcend the realm of necessity, where it served as the instrument of domination and exploitation which thereby limited its rationality; technology would become subject to the free play of faculties in the struggle for the pacification of nature and of society.

Such a state is envisioned in Marx's notion of the "abolition of labor." The term "pacification of existence" seems better suited to designate the historical alternative of a world which—through an international conflict which transforms and suspends the contradictions within the established societies—advances on the brink of a global war. "Pacification of existence" means the development of man's struggle with man and with nature, under conditions where the competing needs, desires, and aspirations are no longer organized by vested interests in domination and scarcity—an organization which perpetuates the destructive forms of this struggle.

Today's fight against this historical alternative finds a firm mass basis in the underlying population, and finds its ideology in the rigid orientation of thought and behavior to the given universe of facts. Validated by the accomplishments of science and technology, justified by its growing productivity, the status quo defies all transcendence. Faced with the possibility of pacification on the grounds of its technical and intellectual achievements, the mature industrial society closes itself against this alternative. Operationalism, in theory and practice, becomes the theory and practice of *containment*. Underneath its obvious dynamics, this society is a thoroughly static system of life: self-propelling in its oppressive productivity and in its beneficial coordination. Containment of technical progress goes hand in hand with its growth in the established direction. In spite of the political fetters imposed by the status quo, the more technology appears capable of creating the conditions for pacification, the more are the minds and bodies of man organized against this alternative.

The most advanced areas of industrial society exhibit throughout these two features: a trend toward consummation of technological rationality, and intensive efforts to contain this trend within the established institutions. Here is the internal contradiction of this civilization: the irrational element in its rationality. It is the token of its achievements. The industrial society which makes technology and science its own is organized for the ever-more-effective domination of man and nature, for the ever-more-effective utilization of its resources. It becomes irrational when the success of these efforts opens new dimensions of human realization. Organization for peace is different from organization for war; the institutions which served the struggle for existence cannot serve the pacification of existence. Life as an end is qualitatively different from life as a means.

Such a qualitatively new mode of existence can never be envisaged as the mere by-product of economic and political changes, as the more or less spontaneous effect of the new institutions which constitute the necessary prerequisite. Qualitative change also involves a change in the *technical* basis on which this society rests—one which sustains the economic and political institutions through which the "second nature" of man as an aggressive object of administration is stabilized. The techniques of industrialization are political techniques; as such, they prejudge the possibilities of Reason and Freedom.

To be sure, labor must precede the reduction of labor, and industrialization must precede the development of human needs and satisfactions. But as all freedom depends on the conquest of alien necessity, the realization of freedom depends on the *techniques* of this conquest. The highest productivity of labor can be used for the perpetuation of labor, and the most efficient industrialization can serve the restriction and manipulation of needs.

When this point is reached, domination—in the guise of affluence and liberty—extends to all spheres of private and public existence, integrates all authentic opposition, absorbs all alternatives. Technological rationality reveals its political character as it becomes the great vehicle of better domination, creating a truly totalitarian universe in which society and nature, mind and body are kept in a state of permanent mobilization for the defense of this universe.*

II.
Conclusion: The Increasing Irrationality Of Man And Society; Alienation And Forces Of Revolution

The advancing one-dimensional society alters the relation between the rational and the irrational. Contrasted with the fantastic and insane aspects of its rationality, the realm of the irrational becomes the home of the really rational—of the ideas which may "promote the art of life." If the established society manages all normal communication, validating or invalidating it in accordance with social requirements, then the values alien to these requirements may perhaps have no other medium of communication than the abnormal one of fiction. The aesthetic dimension still retains a freedom of expression which enables the writer and artist to call men and things by their name—to name the otherwise unnameable.

The real face of our time shows in Samuel Beckett's novels; its real history is written in Rolf Hochhut's play *Der Stellvertreter.* It is no longer imagination which speaks here, but Reason, in a reality which justifies everything and absolves everything—except the sin against its spirit. Imagination is abdicating to this reality, which is catching up with and overtaking imagination. Auschwitz continues to haunt, not the memory but the accomplishments of man—the space flights; the rockets and missiles; the "labyrinthine basement under the Snack Bar"; the pretty electronic plants, clean, hygienic and with flower beds; the poison gas which is not really harmful to people; the secrecy in which we all participate. This is the setting in which the great human achievements of science, medicine, technology take place; the efforts to save and ameliorate life are the sole promise in the disaster. The willful play with fantastic possibilities, the ability to act with good conscience, *contra naturam,* to experiment with men and things, to convert illusion into reality and fiction into truth, testify to the extent to which Imagination has become an instrument of progress. And it is one which, like others in the established societies, is methodically abused. Setting the pace and style of politics, the power of imagination far exceeds Alice in wonderland in the manipulation of words, turning sense into nonsense and nonsense into sense.

The formerly antagonistic realms merge on technical and political grounds—magic and science, life and death, joy and misery. Beauty reveals its terror as highly classified nuclear plants and laboratories become "Industrial Parks" in pleasing surroundings; Civil Defense Headquarters display a "deluxe fallout-shelter" with wall-to-wall carpeting ("soft"), lounge chairs, television, and Scrabble, "designed as a combination family room during peacetime (sic!) and family fallout shelter should war break out."[4] If the horror of such realizations does not penetrate into

---

* Pp. 1-18.

[4] According to *The New York Times,* November 11, 1960, displayed at the New York City Civil Defense Headquarters, Lexington Ave. and Fifty-fifth Street.

consciousness, if it is readily taken for granted, it is because these achievements are (a) perfectly rational in terms of the existing order, (b) tokens of human ingenuity and power beyond the traditional limits of imagination.

The obscene merger of aesthetics and reality refutes the philosophies which oppose "poetic" imagination to scientific and empirical Reason. Technological progress is accompanied by a progressive rationalization and even realization of the imaginary. The archetypes of horror as well as of joy, of war as well as of peace lose their catastrophic character. Their appearance in the daily life of the individuals is no longer that of irrational forces—their modern avatars are elements of technological domination, and subject to it.

In reducing and even canceling the romantic space of imagination, society has forced the imagination to prove itself on new grounds, on which the images are translated into historical capabilities and projects. The translation will be as bad and distorted as the society which undertakes it. Separated from the realm of material production and material needs, imagination was mere play, invalid in the realm of necessity, and committed only to a fantastic logic and a fantastic truth. When technical progress cancels this separation, it invests the images with its own logic and its own truth; it reduces the free faculty of the mind. But it also reduces the gap between imagination and Reason. The two antagonistic faculties become interdependent on common ground. In the light of the capabilities of advanced industrial civilization, is not all play of the imagination playing with technical possibilities, which can be tested as to their chances of realization? The romantic idea of a "science of the Imagination" seems to assume an ever-more-empirical aspect.

The scientific, rational character of Imagination has long since been recognized in mathematics, in the hypotheses and experiments of the physical sciences. It is likewise recognized in psychoanalysis, which is in theory based on the acceptance of the specific rationality of the irrational; the comprehended imagination becomes, redirected, a therapeutic force. But this therapeutic force may go much further than in the cure of neuroses. It was not a poet but a scientist who has outlined this prospect:

> Toute une psychanalyse matérielle peut . . . nous aider à guérir de nos images, ou du moins nous aider á limiter l'emprise de nos images. On peut alors espérer . . . *pouvoir rendre l'imagination heureuse,* autrement dit, pouvoir donner bonne conscience à l'imagination, en lui accordant pleinement tous ses moyens d'expression, toutes les images matérielles qui se produisent dans les *rêves naturels,* dans l'activité onorique normale. Rendre heureuse l'imagination, lui accorder toute son exubérance, c'est précisément donner à l'imagination sa véritable fonction d'entrainement psychique.[5]

Imagination has not remained immune to the process of reification. We are possessed by our images, suffer our own images. Psychoanalysis knew it well, and knew the consequences. However, "to give to the imagination all the means of expression" would be regression. The mutilated individuals (mutilated also in their

[5] "An entire psychoanalysis of matter can help us to cure us of our images or at least help us to limit the hold of our images on us. One may then hope *to be able to render imagination happy,* to give it good conscience in allowing it fully all its means of expression, all material images which emerge in *natural dreams,* in normal dream activity. To render imagination happy, to allow it all its exuberance, means precisely to grant imagination its true function as psychological impulse and force." Gaston Bachelard, *Le Matérialisme rationnel* (Paris, Presses Universitaires, 1953), p. 18 (Bachelard's emphasis).

faculty of imagination) would organize and destroy even more than they are now permitted to do. Such release would be the unmitigated horror—not the catastrophe of culture, but the free sweep of its most repressive tendencies. Rational is the imagination which can become the *a priori* of the reconstruction and redirection of the productive apparatus toward a pacified existence, a life without fear. And this can never be the imagination of those who are possessed by the images of domination and death.

To liberate the imagination so that it can be given all its means of expression presupposes the repression of much that is now free and that perpetuates a repressive society. And such reversal is not a matter of psychology or ethics but of politics, in the sense in which this term has here been used throughout: the practice in which the basic societal institutions are developed, defined, sustained, and changed. It is the practice of individuals, no matter how organized they may be. Thus the question once again must be faced: how can the administered individuals—who have made their mutilation into their own liberties and satisfactions, and thus reproduce it on an enlarged scale—liberate themselves from themselves as well as from their masters? How is it even thinkable that the vicious circle be broken?

Paradoxically, it seems that it is not the notion of the new societal *institutions* which presents the greatest difficulty in the attempt to answer this question. The established societies themselves are changing, or have already changed the basic institutions in the direction of increased planning. Since the development and utilization of all available resources for the universal satisfaction of vital needs is the prerequisite of pacification, it is incompatible with the prevalence of particular interests which stand in the way of attaining this goal. Qualitative change is conditional upon planning for the whole against these interests, and a free and rational society can emerge only on this basis.

The institutions within which pacification can be envisaged thus defy the traditional classification into authoritarian and democratic, centralized and liberal administration. Today, the opposition to central planning in the name of a liberal democracy which is denied in reality serves as an ideological prop for repressive interests. The goal of authentic self-determination by the individuals depends on effective social control over the production and distribution of the necessities (in terms of the achieved level of culture, material and intellectual).

Here, technological rationality, stripped of its exploitative features, is the sole standard and guide in planning and developing the available resources for all. Self-determination in the production and distribution of vital goods and services would be wasteful. The job is a technical one, and as a truly technical job, it makes for the reduction of physical and mental toil. In this realm, centralized control is rational if it establishes the preconditions for meaningful self-determination. The latter can then become effective in its own realm—in the decisions which involve the production and distribution of the economic surplus, and in the individual existence.

In any case, the combination of centralized authority and direct democracy is subject to infinite variations, according to the degree of development. Self-determination will be real to the extent to which the masses have been dissolved into individuals liberated from all propaganda, indoctrination, and manipulation, capable of knowing and comprehending the facts and of evaluating the alternatives. In other words, society would be rational and free to the extent to which it is organized, sustained, and reproduced by an essentially new historical Subject.

At the present stage of development of the advanced industrial societies, the material as well as the cultural system denies this exigency. The power and efficiency of this system, the thorough assimilation of mind with fact, of thought with required behavior, of aspirations with reality, militate against the emergence of a new Subject. They also militate against the notion that the replacement of the prevailing control over the productive process by "control from below" would mean the advent of qualitative change. This notion was valid, and still is valid, where the laborers were, and still are, the living denial and indictment of the established society. However, where these classes have become a prop of the established way of life, their ascent to control would prolong this way in a different setting.

And yet, the facts are all there which validate the critical theory of this society and of its fatal development: the increasing irrationality of the whole; waste and restriction of productivity; the need for aggressive expansion; the constant threat of war; intensified exploitation; dehumanization. And they all point to the historical alternative: the planned utilization of resources for the satisfaction of vital needs with a minimum of toil, the transformation of leisure into free time, the pacification of the struggle for existence.

But the facts and the alternatives are there like fragments which do not connect, or like a world of mute objects without a subject, without the practice which would move these objects in the new direction. Dialectical theory is not refuted, but it cannot offer the remedy. It cannot be positive. To be sure, the dialectical concept, in comprehending the given facts, transcends the given facts. This is the very token of its truth. It defines the historical possibilities, even necessities; but their realization can only be in the practice which responds to the theory, and, at present, the practice gives no such response.

On theoretical as well as empirical grounds, the dialectical concept pronounces its own hopelessness. The human reality is its history and, in it, contradictions do not explode by themselves. The conflict between streamlined, rewarding domination on the one hand, and its achievements that make for self-determination and pacification on the other, may become blatant beyond any possible denial, but it may well continue to be a manageable and even productive conflict, for with the growth in the technological conquest of nature grows the conquest of man by man. And this conquest reduces the freedom which is a necessary *a priori* of liberation. This is freedom of thought in the only sense in which thought can be free in the administered world—as the consciousness of its repressive productivity, and as the absolute need for breaking out of this whole. But precisely this absolute need does not prevail where it could become the driving force of a historical practice, the effective cause of qualitative change. Without this material force, even the most acute consciousness remains powerless.

No matter how obvious the irrational character of the whole may manifest itself and, with it, the necessity of change, insight into necessity has never sufficed for seizing the possible alternatives. Confronted with the omnipresent efficiency of the given system of life, its alternatives have always appeared utopian. And insight into necessity, the consciousness of the evil state, will not suffice even at the stage where the accomplishments of science and the level of productivity have eliminated the utopian features of the alternatives—where the established reality rather than its opposite is utopian.

Does this mean that the critical theory of society abdicates and leaves the field to an empirical sociology which, freed from all theoretical guidance except a methodological one, succumbs to the fallacies of misplaced concreteness, thus performing an ideological service while proclaiming the elimination of value judgments? Or do the dialectical concepts once again testify to their truth—by comprehending their own situation as that of the society which they analyze? A response might suggest itself if one considers the critical theory precisely at the point of its greatest weakness—its inability to demonstrate the liberating tendencies *within* the established society.

The critical theory of society, was, at the time of its origin, confronted with the presence of real forces (objective and subjective) *in* the established society which moved (or could be guided to move) toward more rational and freer institutions by abolishing the existing ones which had become obstacles to progress. These were the empirical grounds on which the theory was erected, and from these empirical grounds derived the idea of the liberation of *inherent* possibilities—the development, otherwise blocked and distorted of material and intellectual productivity, faculties, and needs. Without the demonstration of such forces, the critique of society would still be valid and rational, but it would be incapable of translating its rationality into terms of historical practice. The conclusion? "Liberation of inherent possibilities" no longer adequately expresses the historical alternative.

The enchained possibilities of advanced industrial societies are: development of the productive forces on an enlarged scale, extension of the conquest of nature, growing satisfaction of needs for a growing number of people, creation of new needs and faculties. But these possibilities are gradually being realized through means and institutions which cancel their liberating potential, and this process affects not only the means but also the ends. The instruments of productivity and progress, organized into a totalitarian system, determine not only the actual but also the possible utilizations.

At its most advanced stage, domination functions as administration, and in the overdeveloped areas of mass consumption, the administered life becomes the good life of the whole, in the defense of which the opposites are united. This is the pure form of domination. Conversely, its negation appears to be the pure form of negation. All content seems reduced to the one abstract demand for the end of domination—the only truly revolutionary exigency, and the event that would validate the achievements of industrial civilization. In the face of its efficient denial by the established system, this negation appears in the politically impotent form of the "absolute refusal"—a refusal which seems the more unreasonable the more the established system develops its productivity and alleviates the burden of life. In the words of Maurice Blanchot:

> "Ce que nous refusons n'est pas sans valeur ni sans importance. C'est bien à cause de cela que le refus est nécessaire. Il y a une raison que nous n'accepterons plus, il y a une apparence de sagesse qui nous fait horreur, il y a une offre d'accord et de conciliation que nous n'entendrons pas. Une rupture s'est produite. Nous avons été ramenés à cette franchise qui ne tolére plus la complicité."[6]

---

[6] "What we refuse is not without value or importance. Precisely because of that, the refusal is necessary. There is a reason which we no longer accept, there is an appearance of wisdom which horrifies us, there is a plea for agreement and conciliation which we will no longer heed. A break has occurred. We have been reduced to that frankness which no longer tolerates complicity." "Le Refus," in *le 14 Juillet*, no. 2, Paris, Octobre 1958.

But if the abstract character of the refusal is the result of total reification, then the concrete ground for refusal must still exist, for reification is an illusion. By the same token, the unification of opposites in the medium of technological rationality must be, *in all its reality*, an illusory unification, which eliminates neither the contradiction between the growing productivity and its repressive use, nor the vital need for solving the contradiction.

But the struggle for the solution has outgrown the traditional forms. The totalitarian tendencies of the one-dimensional society render the traditional ways and means of protest ineffective—perhaps even dangerous because they preserve the illusion of popular sovereignty. This illusion contains some truth: "the people," previously the ferment of social change, have "moved up" to become the ferment of social cohesion. Here rather than in the redistribution of wealth and equalization of classes is the new stratification characteristic of advanced industrial society.

However, underneath the conservative popular base is the substratum of the outcasts and outsiders, the exploited and persecuted of other races and other colors, the unemployed and the unemployable. They exist outside the democratic process; their life is the most immediate and the most real need for ending intolerable conditions and institutions. Thus their opposition is revolutionary even if their consciousness is not. Their opposition hits the system from without and is therefore not deflected by the system; it is an elementary force which violates the rules of the game and, in doing so, reveals it as a rigged game. When they get together and go out into the streets, without arms, without protection, in order to ask for the most primitive civil rights, they know that they face dogs, stones, and bombs, jail, concentration camps, even death. Their force is behind every political demonstration for the victims of law and order. The fact that they start refusing to play the game may be the fact which marks the beginning of the end of a period.

Nothing indicates that it will be a good end. The economic and technical capabilities of the established societies are sufficiently vast to allow for adjustments and concessions to the underdog, and their armed forces sufficiently trained and equipped to take care of emergency situations. However, the spectre is there again, inside and outside the frontiers of the advanced societies. The facile historical parallel with the barbarians threatening the empire of civilization prejudges the issue; the second period of barbarism may well be the continued empire of civilization itself. But the chance is that, in this period, the historical extremes may meet again: the most advanced consciousness of humanity, and its most exploited force. It is nothing but a chance. The critical theory of society possesses no concepts which could bridge the gap between the present and its future; holding no promise and showing no success, it remains negative. Thus it wants to remain loyal to those who, without hope, have given and give their life to the Great Refusal.

At the beginning of the fascist era, Walter Benjamin wrote:

> *Nur um der Hoffnungslosen willeno ist uns die Hoffnung gegeben.*
>
> It is only for the sake of those without hope that hope is given to us.*

* Pp. 247-57.

Peter Drucker

Peter Drucker (1909–   ) was raised in Vienna, Austria, and trained as a lawyer, but his first position was with the Frankfurt *General-Anzeiger* as the paper's foreign and financial editor. In 1933 Drucker left Germany for England where he worked at an international banking house. In 1937 he immigrated to the United States where he became a citizen in 1943. In 1942 Drucker joined the faculty at Bennington College and since 1950 he has been professor of management at New York University, a consultant to many corporations, a frequent contributor to magazines, and the author of numerous books focusing on the dilemmas facing man in the industrial-technological society.

Professor Drucker's first book, *The End of Economic Man* (1939), reflected his disillusionment with capitalism and his rejection of Marxism-Socialism because these dogmas could not, in practice, guarantee freedom and liberty. He detested totalitarianism because it extinguished freedom and individuality by making man a cog in the vast machinery of the state. Concluding his analysis of *The End of Economic Man,* Drucker appealed to the democratic states to lay a new social and economic framework based on a concept—which he left undeveloped—of the "Free and Equal Man."

Through successive works such as *The New Society* (1950), *The Age of Discontinuity* (1968), and the recent edition of his essays *Technology, Management and Society* (1970), Drucker has penetrated further into the nature of society, the role of the individual, and the quality of freedom in contemporary technological society. While many critics of technological society promote a gloom-doom attitude toward the future of man's freedom and individuality, Drucker stressed the potential for human freedom in a world where technology is the servant of man instead of his master. Rather than seeing inevitable catastrophy Drucker emphasized that man is faced with a choice of either fulfilling human potential and creating a society promoting freedom and liberty, or experiencing the Armaggedon prophesied by modern Jeremiahs.

I.
The Nature Of Modern Society

Historians two hundred years hence may see as central to the twentieth century what we ourselves have been paying almost no attention to: the emergence of a society of organizations in which every single social task of importance is entrusted to a large institution. To us, the contemporaries, one of these institutions—government or big business, the university or the labor union—often looks like the institution. To the future historian, however, the most impressive fact may be the emergence of a new and distinct pluralism, that is, of a society of institutional diversity and diffusion of power. He may report for the closing decades of the twentieth century an upsurge of creative thought in the social and political spheres as great as that of the seventeenth century, when Bodin, Locke, and Hobbes gave us what we still call "modern social theory."

To most of us today, the power of central government seems to be unchallenged—whether we applaud or deplore it. Tomorrow's historian may come to call our era "the twilight of central government." Impotence rather than omnipotence may well appear to him the most remarkable feature of government in the closing decades of the twentieth century. And new political theory regarding the structure, organization, and limitations of power and government, both domestically and internationally, may play a prominent part in his narrative. Sixty years ago, before World War I, the social scene everywhere looked much like the Kansas prairie: the largest thing on the horizon was the individual. Most social tasks were accomplished in and through family-sized units. Even government, no matter how formidable it looked, was really small and cozy. The government of Imperial Germany looked like a colossus to its contemporaries, but an official in the middle ranks could still know personally everyone of importance in every single ministry and department.

The scaling-up in size since then is striking. There is no country in the world today where the entire government establishment of 1910 could not comfortably be housed in the smallest of the new government buildings now going up, with room to spare for a grand opera house and a skating rink.

This is true of the United States, where all the government agencies of Teddy Roosevelt's time—federal, state, and local—would find ample office space in a single one of the regional buildings of the federal service that are now going up in Denver or Boise. It is just as true of Japan. Even the smallest Japanese prefecture has a brand-new office building that rivals the Tokyo ministry buildings that sufficed Imperial Japan when it challenged the West for world leadership twenty-five years ago.

Shortly before World War I, the citizens of Zurich in Switzerland built a new city hall. At the time it was strongly criticized as an extravaganza grandiose beyond anything that would ever be needed. Zurich has grown little in the half-century

Reprinted from Peter F. Drucker, *The Age of Discontinuity* (New York: Harper and Row, 1968), pp. 171-78, 243-60; Copyright © 1968, 1969 by Peter F. Drucker, and Peter F. Drucker, "Technology and Society in the Twentieth Century," in *Technology in Western Civilization*, ed. Melvin Kranzberg and Carroll W. Pursell, Jr. (New York: Oxford University Press, 1967), 2: 31-33, Copyright © 1967 by The Regents of the University of Wisconsin. Reprinted by permission of the publishers.

since. And the Swiss rightly pride themselves on the simplicity and modesty of their local governments. Yet Zurich has long outgrown the city hall of 1910; most of the local government is now in office skyscrapers all over town.

The army of little Israel that clobbered the Arabs in June 1967 had less than one-tenth of the manpower of the army that Imperial Germany launched against France and Russia in 1914. But each Israeli soldier had at his disposal about two hundred times the firepower of his 1914 Prussian counterpart. Indeed the Vietcong soldiers in Vietnam, for all that they are "guerrillas" and "live off the land," have many times the firepower per soldier of the most highly powered army prior to the closing years of World War II.

The hospital of 1914 was a place for the poor to die. Fewer than three out of every hundred babies born in this country (or any place else in the West) were born in hospitals at that time. Today all but one or two out of every hundred babies are born in hospitals—and most of the exceptions are born in the ambulance on the way. For each hundred patients, the hospital fifty years ago had thirty employees, most of them washerwomen and cooks. Now for every hundred patients it has three hundred employees, most of them highly trained "health-care professionals" (such as medical and X-ray technicians, dieticians, psychiatric and social case workers, physical therapists, and so on). The doctor of 1900 could easily practice medicine without access to a hospital. If he spent any time there, he did so to tend charity patients, out of the kindness of his heart. Today the doctor is increasingly dependent on the hospital. Twenty years hence, doctors may well have their offices in the hospital. The hospital rather than the doctor's office is rapidly becoming the center of modern health care.

No university in the Western world had more than 5,000 students before 1914. Even so the largest of them—Berlin—had become too big to be manageable; the Germans, in the years before World War I, had to split out research in the sciences and set it up in separate institutes. Today universities of 20,000 students are "medium-sized." And the research laboratory has grown just as fast. The first of the early German institutes for pure research, which numbered such giants as Planck and Einstein among its members, had a total employment of twenty or thirty scientists. Today, the Menninger Foundation in Topeka, Kansas—a specialized center for research in psychiatry and mental health and by no means a very large one—has nine hundred employees of whom two hundred are professionals: psychiatrists, psychologists, neurologists, and so on.

In the days before World War I, the one "large" organization around was business. But the "big business" of 1910 would strike us today as a veritable minnow. The "octopus" that gave our grandparents nightmares, John D. Rockefeller's Standard Oil Trust, was cut into fourteen pieces by the Supreme Court in 1911. Less than thirty years later, by 1940, every one of these successor companies was larger than Rockefeller's Standard Oil Trust had been—by every measurement: employees, sales, capital invested, and so on. Yet only three of these fourteen Standard Oil daughter companies (Jersey Standard, Socony Mobil, and Standard of California) were "major" international oil companies. The rest ranked from "small" to "middling" by 1940 yardsticks and would be "small business" today, another thirty years later.

We cannot hope to understand this society of ours unless we accept that *all* institutions have become giants. Businesses today are a good deal bigger than the biggest company was in John D. Rockefeller's time. But universities are relatively a good deal bigger still than Rockefeller's other creation: the University of Chicago, which he founded, around the turn of the century, as perhaps the first modern university in America. Hospitals are relatively bigger still and a great deal more complex than any of the other institutions.

Even voluntary or charitable associations have become giants. The Young Men's Christian Association (YMCA) of the United States now has a budget in excess of $200 million—more than even large states in this country spent before World War II. The YMCA employs thousands of people, and has its own internal staff concerned with management and organization.

The Carnegie Corporation—our oldest philanthropic foundation—was a veritable giant only a generation ago. But the new giant, the Ford Foundation, in one recent year (1966) outspent Carnegie twenty-five times. Indeed the Ford Foundation's disbursements that year—$350 million—were larger than Carnegie's total assets. And the Ford Foundation staff is so huge that it has its own big office buildings not only in New York City but also in many capitals throughout the world where Ford has larger missions than any but the Great Powers.

The problem of the "concentration" of power is no longer peculiar to the economy. Business concentration has not increased in the last sixty years or so, and "small" business (which is also a good deal bigger than it used to be) is holding its own, apparently without difficulty. But the three or four largest labor unions hold relatively much more industrial power than the ten or twenty or thirty largest businesses. And we have a "concentration of brain power" in a few large universities such as has never been seen in any other area of social life—and such as would not have been tolerated earlier. The great majority of all doctorates in the United States are given by some twenty universities—one-tenth of one per cent of all institutions of higher learning in the country. And nothing resembling the concentration of military might in the arsenals of the "superpowers," the United States and Russia, has been known in international society since the Roman Empire at the peak of its power in the first century A.D.

But the scaling-up in size and budget is not the most important change. What makes the real difference is that all our major social functions are today being discharged in and through these large, organized institutions. Every single social task of major impact—defense and education, government and the production and distribution of goods, health care and the search for knowledge—is increasingly entrusted to institutions which are organized for perpetuity and which are managed by professionals, whether they are called "managers," "administrators," or "executives."

Government looks like the most powerful of these institutions—it is certainly the one that spends the most. But each of the others discharges a function that is essential to society and has to be discharged in its own right. Each has its own autonomous management. Each has its own job to do and therefore its own objectives, its own values, and its own rationale. If government is still the "lord," it can no longer be the "master." Increasingly, whatever the theory of a government or its constitutional law, government functions as a "coordinator," a "chairman," or at most a "leader." Yet, paradoxically, government suffers from doing too much and too many things. Government, to be effective and strong, may have to learn to "decentralize" to the other institutions, to *do* less in order to *achieve* more.

What has emerged in this half-century is *a new pluralism.* There is little left of the structure that our seventeenth-century political theory still preaches, a structure in which government is the only organized power center. It is totally inadequate, however, to see just one of these new institutions—business, for instance, or the labor union, or the university—and proclaim it *the* new institution.* Social theory, to be meaningful at all, must start out with the reality of a pluralism of institutions—a galaxy of suns rather than one big center surrounded by moons that shine only by reflected light.

Pluralist power centers of yesterday—the duke, the count, the abbot, even the yeoman—differed from each other only in titles and revenues. One was the superior and overlord of the other. Each center was limited in territory, but each was a total community and embraced whatever organized social activity and political life there was. Each center was concerned with the same basic activity, above all, wresting a livelihood from the land. The federalism of the American system still assumes this traditional pluralism. The federal government, state governments, and municipalities all have their own distinct geographic limitations and stand to each other in a position of higher and lower. But each has essentially the same function. Each is a territorial government with police powers and tax powers, charged with traditional governmental tasks, whether defense or justice or public order.

This is simply not true of the new institutions. Each of them is a special-purpose institution. The hospital exists for the sake of health care, the business to produce economic goods and services, the university for the advancement and teaching of knowledge, each government agency for its own specific purpose, the armed services for defense, and so on. Not one of them can be considered "superior" or "inferior" to the other, for only a fool would consider the advancement of knowledge superior to health care or to the provision of economic goods and services. But at the same time, not one of them can be defined territorially. Each, in other words, is "universal" in a way that none of the old institutions (excepting only the medieval church) ever claimed to be. And yet each of them is limited to a small fragment of human existence, to a single facet of human community.

The problems of this new pluralism are quite different from the problems of both the pluralisms of our past and the unitary society of our political theory and constitutional law. In earlier pluralisms every member of the system, from the yeoman up to the most powerful king, understood exactly the positions of the other members of the hierarchy, their tasks and their problems. Indeed, everyone had exactly the same tasks and the same problems; only the scale varied. In the new pluralism each institution has different tasks. It takes different things for granted. It considers different things to be important. While the vice president of a big business, the division chief in the government agency, and the department chairman in the university may operate on a very similar scale and have managerial

* I must plead guilty to having done this myself—twenty-odd years ago. In *Concept of the Corporation* (New York: John Day, 1946) I called big business the "determining" institution of our time. However, the other institutions were then barely visible; the crystalline structure of our society had not yet become apparent. There is little excuse today, however, for such oversimplification as that in John Kenneth Galbraith's latest book, *The New Industrial State* (Boston: Houghton Mifflin, 1967), which fails to notice any institution except business.

problems of comparable magnitude, they do not easily understand each other's roles, tasks, and decisions. The members of earlier pluralisms were forever worried about their "precedence" and their place in the hierarchy relative to each other. This is not a major concern in today's pluralism. The hospital administrator is not particularly concerned as to whether he ranks the corporation president or the union leader or the air force general. But they all worry about "communications." It takes a great deal of experience—or, at the least, a great deal of imagination—for one of the executives in today's pluralism to have any idea what the other ones are up to and why.

These organizations have to live together and to work together. They are interdependent. Not one of them could exist by itself. Not one of them is by itself viable, let alone a total community, as were the components of earlier pluralist society.

A theory of the society of organizations would have to be built on organizational interdependence. The modern armed services depend fully on the civilian apparatus of government. They depend equally on the economic institutions. Most of all, perhaps, do they depend on the universities. Dwight Eisenhower in his farewell message as President in 1961 warned of the "military-industrial complex," formed by the symbiosis of a powerful and permanent military establishment and a powerful and permanent defense industry. But actually, even at the height of the Vietnam war, the United States economy was not particularly dependent on defense business. If all the defense business had been eliminated with one stroke, there would have been no great crisis except in a few spots such as Southern California. The large universities of the country are, however, increasingly dependent on the military—and the military, in turn, on them. To speak of the "military-university complex" makes a good deal of sense. And government depends on the economic fruits of business and the taxes they generate. The labor union is dependent on management; it is equally dependent on government. Indeed, of all our major institutions, the union is the most nearly derivative. It requires both business management to produce the economic results which sustain the union and satisfy its demands, and government to provide the political support without which no union movement would last long.

Never having known anything remotely like the society of organizations we now have, we have yet to learn to understand our pluralist society and to make policy for it. What is required is a clear view of its structure, realization that every single major task has become institutionalized and that we will have to deal with the problems this creates as generic problems of our society and as its norm.

This is a big change in perception. The first to make it were the hippies. Where the liberal and the conservative alike still singled out this or that institution as either the "villain" or the "hero" of society, the hippies these last ten years have seen clearly that all society is one of organizations. While very few young people are hippies, the perception of our society as one of organizations is shared by the entire generation that is now reaching adulthood. It is the most visible characteristic of the "generation gap." The young are as alienated from the university as they are from the armed services or the government agency.

We will not be granted the luxury of the hippies' rejection of all organizations. This is a luxury only the very young can afford, a luxury that presumes that the adults are taking care of things. But the adults will have to concern themselves with the reality that the hippies would like to make go away—the reality of a society of organizations.*

In this different world, technology itself is seen differently; we are aware of it as a major element in our lives, indeed, in human life throughout history. We are becoming aware that the major questions regarding technology are not technical but human questions, and are coming to understand that a knowledge of the history and evolution of technology is essential to an understanding of human history. Furthermore, we are rapidly learning that we must understand the history, the development, and the dynamics of technology in order to master our contemporary technological civilization, and that, unless we do so, we will have to submit to technology as our master.

The naive optimism of 1900, which expected technology somehow to create paradise on earth, would be shared by few people today. Most would also ask: What does technology do *to* man as well as for him? For it is only too obvious that technology brings problems, disturbances, and dangers as well as benefits. First, economic development based on technology carries the promise of abolishing want over large parts of the earth. But there is also the danger of total war leading to total destruction; and the only way we now know to control this danger is by maintaining in peacetime a higher level of armaments in all major industrial countries than any nation has ever maintained. This hardly seems a fitting answer to the problem, let alone a permanent one. Also, modern public-health technology—insecticides above all—has everywhere greatly increased man's life span. But since birth rates in the underdeveloped countries remain at their former high level while the death rates have declined, the world's poor nations are threatened by a population explosion which not only eats up all the fruits of economic development but threatens world famine and new pestilence. In government, modern technology and the modern economy founded on it have outmoded the national state as a viable unit. Even Great Britain, with fifty million inhabitants, has been proven in recent decades to have too small a productive base and market for independent economic survival and success. Nationalism is still the most potent political force, as developments in the new nations of Asia and Africa clearly show; yet the revolution in transportation and communication has made national borders an anachronism, respected by neither airplanes nor electronic waves.

The metropolis has become the habitat of modern man. Yet paradoxically we do not know how to make it habitable. We have no effective political institutions to govern it. Urban decay and traffic jams, overcrowding and urban crime, juvenile delinquency and loneliness are endemic in all modern great cities. No one looking at any of the world's big cities would maintain that they offer an aesthetically satisfying environment. The divorce from direct contact with nature in work with soil and materials has permitted us to live much better; yet technological change itself seems to have speeded up so much as to deprive us of the psychological and cultural bearings we need.

The critics of technology and dissenters from technological optimism in 1900 were lonely voices. Disenchantment with technology did not set in until after World War I and the coming of the Great Depression. The new note was first fully struck in the novel *Brave New World* by the English writer Aldous Huxley (1894–1964),

* *The Age of Discontinuity*, pp. 171-78.

published in 1932, at the very bottom of the Depression. In this book Huxley portrayed the society of the near future as one in which technology had become the master, and man, its abject slave, was kept in bodily comfort without knowledge of want or pain but also without freedom, beauty, or creativity, indeed, without a personal existence. Five years later the most popular actor of the period, the great Charlie Chaplin (1889-), drove home the same idea in his movie *Modern Times,* which depicted the common man as the hapless and helpless victim of a dehumanized technology. These two artists have set the tone: only by renouncing modern civilization altogether can man survive as man. This theme has since been struck with increasing frequency, and certainly with increasing loudness. The pessimists of today, however, suffer from a bad case of romantic delusion; the "happier society of the preindustrial past" they invoke never existed. In the late thirteenth century, Genghis Khan and his Mongols, whose raids covered an area from China to central Europe, killed as many people—and a much larger proportion of a much smaller population—as two twentieth-century world wars and Hitler put together, yet their technology was the bow and arrow.

However much justice there may be in Huxley's and Charlie Chaplin's thesis, it is sterile. The repudiation of technology they advocate is clearly not the answer. The only positive alternative to destruction by technology is to make technology work as our servant. In the final analysis this surely means mastery by man over himself, for if anyone is to blame, it is not the tool but the human maker and user. "It is a poor carpenter who blames his tools," says an old proverb. It was naive of the nineteenth-century optimist to expect paradise from tools and it is equally naive of the twentieth-century pessimists to make the new tools the scapegoat for such old shortcomings as man's blindness, cruelty, immaturity, greed, and sinful pride.

It is also true that better tools demand a better, more highly skilled, and more careful carpenter. As its ultimate impact on man and his society, twentieth-century technology, by its very mastery of nature, may thus have brought man face to face again with his oldest and greatest challenge: himself.*

II.
How Can The Individual Maintain Freedom And Liberty In Modern Society

Student unrest is nothing new. But the present alienation of the most privileged of today's society, the college youth, is something very new indeed.

All earlier outbreaks were local, and directed at specific institutions of an individual country or society. This was true in the major previous epoch of student unrest in the West, the rebellion of the students of continental Europe against absolutist government after the Napoleonic Wars. It ushered in long, bitter struggles in Russia,

* "Technology and Society," pp. 31-33.

Germany, and Italy, but it evoked only a faint echo west of the Rhine, and England was not touched by it at all.

Similarly the massive Chinese student unrest in the early years of the century, while eventually leading to the downfall of the Manchu Dynasty and to a half-century of civil war (which may not be over yet), was confined to one country. Even the large Chinese populations outside of mainland China were hardly affected by it.

Today, however, there is a true "student international." There is, of course, no central command, no common creed; but there is a common enemy. It is organization. Today's student "activists" are against organization and its authority in any form or shape. Above all, they oppose what used to be considered the "good guys" among organizations, university, and government. The young priests and religious of the Catholic Church are equally opposed to the authority and organization of the Roman Curia. And that traditional symbol of rebellion, the Communist party, was one of the main targets of the French students and of the young among the French workers in the uprising against all authority in May 1968.

The war in Vietnam and the racial troubles of the black ghetto may explain the rebellion of the young people of America. But they hardly explain why the Italian students storm their university buildings, or why the students of Poland and Yugoslavia battle with their respective regimes and their police. Nor do they explain the outbreaks of student rebellion in India and Indonesia, let alone the organized anarchism of the Chinese students who enrolled by the hundreds of thousands in Mao's "Cultural Revolution" against school, government, and Communist party authority. Clearly the "causes" only trigger the rebellion. They do not "cause" it.

The perception of the young that society has become a society of organizations, and that this is in striking contrast to the society of our textbooks, our political rhetoric, and our conventions is sound and realistic insight. The response, however, is futile. There is no sign that our society has decided to do without the services that only the organization can supply. We are not willing to do without defense or without education, without economic goods and services, or without health care. The organizations will not go away. Repudiating them is not going to make them disappear. It will not even reduce their power.

Indeed, scorning power only makes it more oppressive. Power has to be used. It is a reality. If the decent and idealistic toss power in the gutter, the guttersnipes pick it up. If the able and educated refuse to exercise power responsibly, irresponsible and incompetent people take over the seats of the mighty and the levers of power. Power not being used for social purposes passes to people who use it for their own ends. At best, it is taken over by the careerists who are led by their own timidity into becoming arbitrary, autocratic, and bureaucratic.

Anarchism is a valid philosophical position and perhaps the only "pure" political theory. The only trouble with it is that it does not work. In practice it inevitably leads to oppression, the first victims of which are the philosophical anarchists themselves.

But there is even greater danger in the rebellion against organization by the young people of today: their vulnerability to false leaders. It is not true that young people repudiate leadership. They seek leadership. They need leadership. If they cannot find it in the "establishment"—not even within the "loyal opposition"—they become easy prey to the demagogues. If one "cannot trust anyone over thirty," one trusts, in the end, someone who acts the juvenile. For one has to trust someone.

There is a frightening resemblance between the student "activists" of today, with their slogans of "idealism" and "sincerity," and the German youth movement just before and just after World War I. The resemblance even extends to externals, to long hair, to folk songs, and to such slogans as "Make love, not war." Yet the idealistic, antiauthoritarian *Wandervoegel* of the German youth movement—who also did not trust "anyone over thirty"—became in short order fanatical, dedicated, unquestioning Nazis and idolators of Hitler. The young want and need faith. And the demagogue is the specialist in "sincerity."

The "activists" represent a tiny fraction of the youth of today. The "lunatic fringe," the "hippies," the "beats," and so on, are a smaller fraction still. The great majority of today's students will, as their predecessors did, settle speedily into the deep ruts of convention. They will soon enough conform to middle age as they now conform to "flaming youth." Maybe they will keep on complaining about the "organization man." But the young engineers, scientists and—above all—the young college professors who so desperately want to be "accepted" by the kids, are the ones who impose conformity on organization. No one is more conformist than the "conventionally unconventional."

Students have always tended to be restless. Suddenly the number of students everywhere has tremendously increased. To a large extent, the present student unrest is but a symptom of the "educational explosion" as a result of which we now keep in school very large numbers of young people who, in earlier days, would have been at work.

That the great bulk of today's college students come from homes without tradition of higher education is in itself a major reason for student unrest. In that respect, today's student rebellion can be compared to the traditional rebellion of the second generation American against the immigrant background of his parents. And just as these rebels from the Irish, Swedish, Jewish, or Italian homes soon settled down as comfortable members of American middle-class society, the students of today can be expected to settle down soon as middle-class members of educated society.

The generation gap is particularly wide today. Societies are younger in their average age than they have been for a long time. Yet, because lifespan—and especially working lifespan—has been greatly extended, a far larger number of older men is living much longer, and holding on much longer to positions of leadership and power. Never before in modern history have there been so many young educated people; yet never before has leadership been so old. Leadership in every institution and in every country is still held largely by a generation that has its roots in the era preceding World War I. Indeed, only in the last ten years have leadership positions passed into the hands of people even born in this century.

In few eras was the gap in experience between generations greater than the one that divides those for whom World War I, the twenties, and the Great Depression were the formative experiences from those who were still children when World War II came to an end but who are today in their mid-thirties and well into middle age. For those who were born after World War II, the world of their elders, the world of the thirties and early forties, is almost unimaginable. Action and behavior based on these earlier experiences, that is, the action and behavior natural to the older generation, must seem to the young irrational, meaningless, and totally irrelevant.

The alienation of the young could therefore be explained away—as confined to a small fraction; as nothing more than a fashionable pose and the current expression of the short-lived *Weltschmerz,* that common, but rarely fatal, disease of adolescence; or as an accident of demography that will rapidly straighten itself out. But as a symptom, the alienation of the young needs to be taken seriously. Underlying it is the realization that the society of organizations poses problems to the individual that social and political theory does not yet see, let alone answer.

The "student activists" are certainly not going to answer the question of the fate and role of the individual in this pluralist society of organizations. Indeed they do not even address themselves to it. Yet their rebellion establishes that the question is central and will have to be tackled. . . .

Erich Fromm's first book, *Escape from Freedom* (1940), was written just before World War II to explain the attraction of totalitarianism—of the Right or of the Left—for the young after World War I. A similar book today, trying to explain the alienation of the young, might well be entitled *Escape from Decision.*

It is, above all, the burden of decision imposed by the society of organizations which the young find frightening and against which they rebel. Suddenly there are career choices; the great majority only yesterday had their careers determined from birth on. Suddenly there are decisions on the direction and purpose of knowledge. Suddenly we have to have new economic policies; we can no longer trust either the automatic operation of Adam Smith's "complementary trade," or the "inevitability of history" of the Marxian schema. Suddenly we have acquired enough knowledge in medicine to have to make decisions—on heart transplants or artificial kidneys, for instance—about whom to keep alive and whom to let die.

The rhetoric of the young complains bitterly about being "manipulated." But their actions make it clear that it is the burden of decision that frightens them. They want to "drop out" so that there are no decisions, no choices, no responsibility.

To sidestep decision is also a decision—and as the young will find out, the one least likely to be right. The students, for instance, who stay on in graduate school (or who join the Peace Corps) to avoid having to decide, are likely to find, a few years later, that they have indeed made the wrong decision. They are lucky if all they have lost is time.

But the reaction of the young, while futile, again reflects true insight. The society of organizations demands of the individual decisions regarding himself. At first sight, the decision may appear only to concern career and livelihood. "What shall I do?" is the form in which the question is usually asked. But actually it reflects a demand that the individual take responsibility for society and its institutions. "What cause do I want to serve?" is implied. And underlying this question is the demand that the individual take responsibility for himself. "What shall I do *with myself?"* rather than "What shall I do?" is really being asked of the young by the multitude of choices around them. The society of organizations forces the individual to ask of himself: "Who am I?" "What do I want to be?" "What do I want to put into life and what do I want to get out of it?"

These are existential questions for all that they are couched in secular form and appear as choices between a job in government, in business, or in college teaching. They have not been asked—at least not by Western man—for several centuries. The Protestant Reformation four hundred years ago last posed them as general questions to be answered by everyone. Where medieval Catholicism had given an "automatic" answer of salvation through observance, the Reformation demanded of the individual that he ask himself: "Who do I *want* to be in order to be saved?"

Ever since Descartes in the mid-seventeenth century brushed aside man's spiritual existence as irrelevant, the West has concerned itself with what goes on outside of man—nature and society. Of all the major thinkers of the nineteenth century, only Kierkegaard even asked, "How is human existence possible?" To all the others this was a meaningless and unfashionable question. They all asked: "How is society possible?" Rousseau asked it, Hegel asked it, the classical economists asked it. Marx answered it in one way, liberal Protestantism in another. The concern all through the last two centuries of Western history was the society, its rights, its functions, its performance.*

Now for the first time, we are again face to face with the age-old question of individual meaning, individual purpose, and individual freedom. Narcotic drugs and avoidance of soap are not particularly relevant answers. But at least the alienation of the young throughout the world today ensures that the questions will have to be considered. For the society of organizations offers choices, and therefore imposes on the individual the burden of decisions. It demands of him the price of freedom: responsibility. . . .

Totalitarianism differs from all tyrannies of the past in that it aims at total control of society rather than at control of government alone. Therein lies its danger; in a society where every social task is discharged in and through a large organization, total control seems both attractive and possible.

But at the same time, in such a society the danger of traditional, purely political tyranny is remote. As long as no one organization is permitted to become *the* organization—as a Communist or a Nazi party strives to be—a pluralist society guarantees freedom from domination by any single group. Pluralist society is an organization of "countervailing powers," as J. Kenneth Galbraith pointed out almost twenty years ago.† In fact, the danger in pluralism, as history teaches, is not domination by this or that interest group; it is collapse into indecision and into a stalemate of competing "countervailing powers."

But the individual may still be oppressed, even though the powerful institutions fight each other to a stalemate. Galbraith held out the promise of freedom in the interstices between powers. But this is precarious living. Little Black Sambo did indeed survive because "the tigers ate each other up." But I doubt that Little Black Sambo greatly enjoyed the experience or that he would wish to go through it again, let alone to spend his life between those snapping and snarling jaws.

The sociologist of the New Left, the late C. Wright Mills, was on shaky ground in his talk of a new "power-elite" based on a conspiracy of the managers—of business, of the military, of the labor union, of the big universities, and so on. Conspiracies are rare, and successful conspiracies are exceedingly rare. And this particular conspiracy was a figment of Mills' imagination. Yet the fact that the New Left believes in it should give us pause. Even though these "elites" see

* This paragraph is from my essay, "The Unfashionable Kierkegaard," which first appeared in the Autumn, 1949, issue of the *Sewanee Review*.

† In his book *American Capitalism* (Boston: Houghton Mifflin, 1952).

themselves in sharp and bitter competition with each other, they may well appear to the individual as the tigers appeared to Little Black Sambo. There is no guarantee that they will not, at any one moment, make common cause against the individual. And that, ten minutes later, they will fight each other again is scant comfort to the individual whom they have devoured in the meantime.

There is only one dependable safeguard of freedom in such a pluralist society: to confine each institution to its task and mission. The demand that each institution concentrate on its task is a political demand in addition to being a managerial and a social demand. The slightest attempt on the part of any one institution to claim "responsibility" beyond its narrow sphere should be considered usurpation. It may be meant well. It may, in the short run, appear to be in the social interest. It may indeed be the only way to get an urgent job done and done well. But it is incompatible with a free society. It is a threat to freedom.

This needs to be stressed for the government agency. The government agency is not part of the sovereign. It is not a necessary part of the decision making, the governing, the directing intelligence of society. It is an organ of society for the discharge of a specific, a particular, a partial task. That its ownership is public and its management appointed by the political authority is irrelevant. To make the agency a part of the "sovereign" is, in effect, to usurp power.

The public knows this. It feels the need for a line between "government agency" and "government." When judges go on strike, the public is upset, if not outraged. But when subway workers go out, the citizen treats it as just another fight between labor and management, even though it inconveniences and indeed endangers him more than a strike by the judges. To dispense justice is a function of the sovereign. Transportation is an "industry," albeit a vital one. To inject economic warfare into a sovereign function is inappropriate, is indeed outrage. To use it in an industry, while a nuisance, is appropriate. The first to strike and the last to go back in the French general strike in May 1968 were the men in the government-owned French industries, especially in the automotive and aircraft plants.

We are, in other words, approaching the point where the distinction we make between various kinds of strikes is not a formal and legal one, but one of substance. Whether a government agency is involved or not is no longer relevant. We have come to look upon a number of areas as essential to the functioning and survival of modern society. Disruptions of such services are threats to the public. Whether they should be allowed and under what conditions is a hotly disputed and a difficult question. The solution will be the same, however, whether the service is performed by government or not. And "nationalizing" a service is no substitute for a solution.

This distinction is, however, quite incompatible with the positions still maintained by political theory and public law. Both still follow John Austin's nineteenth-century doctrine of "formal sovereignty." Both still hold that anything is an act or a sphere of the "sovereign" that can be traced back through formal, logical analysis to a legally valid "sovereign" act, a law, an ordinance, or a verdict. The most extreme Austinians in their legal doctrine (if not in their political theory) are the orthodox Communists, to whom every institution, including the chess club, is an organ of the government, and every organ of the government an embodiment of the ultimate sovereign, "the working class," and as such, infallible and absolute.

In the pluralist society of organizations, the rule will have to be the opposite: every organization, no matter what its legal position or ownership, is a special-purpose tool. Only insofar as its actions are necessary for the discharge of its special purpose are they legitimate. Otherwise they are null and void. Function rather than form determines what is lawful for an organization.

This also means, however, that regardless of legal form, institutions doing different tasks must be autonomous. The freedom of the individual in a pluralist society demands autonomy of institutions.

Practice may have moved further in this direction than our theory or our rhetoric might indicate. To convert the Post Office into a "public corporation" may not bring about the great increases in efficiency promised by advocates of this step. But that we can even discuss such a move seriously—when postal communications have been considered an "attribute of sovereignty" since Roman times—indicates clearly that we are already considering function rather than form. Indeed no one (except the postal workers' union) would be terribly shocked any more by the idea that the postal service might eventually be "reprivatized." Few would even be terribly surprised at the suggestion that, twenty years hence, we might abandon postal service altogether as no longer capable of competing with new and different forms of telecommunications, no matter how deeply entrenched as an "attribute of sovereignty" it might once have been.

Similar developments are going on in Communist countries; in large measure, they explain the institutional crisis in the developed Communist countries, i.e., Russia and her European satellites.

Traditionally European jurisprudence, since the days of Justinian, divided law into "public" and "private." We may have to add a third category: "organizational law." It would be "private" law, even if the organization were government owned and government run. But it would be "public" law even if the organization were totally owned by private investors and run by their representatives. Every institution would be considered as limited to the specific service to the members of society which it is intended to perform, and as such, "private." Yet, since every institution has power within its sphere, it would be, as such (in the elegant phrase of the American lawyer), "affected with the public interest."

Such a new view of all organizations as being autonomous *and* limited is needed both to make organization perform and to safegaurd the individual's freedom.

A similar approach might have to be thought through with respect to the internal powers of organization, the power over what have been called its "members." The very term "member" is impermissible. There are only "employees," as regards the rights and powers of organizations over people. "Member" implies that the institution controls, indeed that the bond is indissoluble. To cut off a member is to destroy it (or him). An arm is not capable of sustained existence without being a "member" of the body. Employment, however, is a specific and limited contract in which both parties retain their identity and their freedom. And the employment contract can always be terminated. This may seem like semantic quibbling. But the ultimate safeguard of freedom for the individual, Rousseau taught two hundred years ago, is the right to emigrate.

We need safeguards against arbitrary cancellation of the employment contract by the employer. The law has a duty to protect the weaker in a contractual relationship and to constrain the more powerful from abuse of his advantage. Limitations on the right to terminate employment arbitrarily are therefore legitimate (though not without dangers to the capacity of a society to adapt to change). But restrictions on the mobility of the employee are quite illegitimate and must not be allowed if the pluralist society of organizations is to have a meaningful sphere of individual freedom.

This is going to be particularly important for the central employees of the society: the knowledge workers. Where this freedom does not exist today, we already see them demanding it.

The young educated Japanese, for instance, would be most unhappy were Japanese employers to abandon the tradition of "lifetime employment." They strongly resist all attempts to give the employer power to discharge any but top management people. But they increasingly demand for themselves the right to leave and go elsewhere, even though it is contrary to tradition. One Japanese company, Sony, the electronics manufacturer, has been highly successful in attracting unusually able people to its employ. This success is largely traced by Sony managers to their practice of offering senior jobs to able people who work for other companies and of helping employees who want to leave to find better jobs elsewhere—both in violation of Japanese custom. At the same time, every Sony employee has all the "rights" of "lifetime employment." Once he has joined he can stay on the payroll until he retires if he so desires.

The other Japanese employers are still afraid of such mobility. They fear that knowledge workers—engineers, accountants, or computer experts—will become migratory. But, of course, there are never many who "emigrate" in any society.* What matters is that the escape route remain open. This requires both that employees can quit and that they can go to work elsewhere. Both must be possible without paying an exorbitant legal or economic price. The fear of losing people is the best incentive to respecting them.

The most dangerous restrictions on mobility are not police stockades. They are restrictions that present themselves as benefits. The greatest obstacles to organizational mobility today are the "golden fetters," such as pension plans, stock option plans, delayed compensation schemes, and so on, with which we tie managers, professionals, and skilled people to a particular employer. These benefits are to be looked at with grave suspicion. They are eagerly sought by the employees themselves. They offer a means to escape the crushing burden of taxation. They are, in turn, favored, if not subsidized, by government and by the tax authorities. But they are antisocial. It is, of course, the government rather than the employer—whether a business or a university—that is antisocial by offering tax inducements that make these benefits all but irresistible, thus indicating that they are what public policy desires.

The serfdom of medieval Europe was originally an "employee benefit" which was sought eagerly by the peasants. It guaranteed to a weak man the protection of a powerful lord, and especially of the holy men of a monastery. It guaranteed a poor man the enjoyment of his meager holding of land. It shielded against greedy gatherers of tax and tribute. Yet within one generation it turned into loss of freedom

* The Japanese, as well as the Europeans, grotesquely exaggerate the extent of actual "job-hopping" in American industry. After the first five years, the great majority of knowledge workers in America become as settled as the Europeans and almost as immobile as the Japanese.

and subjection. The worst fetters are those that make our self-interest enslave us. They are the ones against which we have to be especially on guard.

In addition to legal safeguard against oppressive power, we need administrative safeguard against oppressive rule. In organization small men have a good deal of power. The postal clerk behind the counter of a substation is a nobody in the post office and probably in his home as well. But he can, and will unless sharply restrained, "throw his weight around" and act the *fonctionnaire,* abusing the public, keeping it waiting, and so on. If he could be reformed by reminding him that he is being paid to serve the public, the French or Austrian postal clerk would be the most considerate and friendliest servant of the public instead of being the surliest of petty tyrants. That postal clerks in the United States are, by contrast, normally considerate and helpful is the result of a system of "postal inspectors" who secretly monitor the clerk's behavior and take disciplinary action against *fonctionnaire*-like arrogance.

With organization the pervasive reality of society, defense of the individual against administrative sloth, arrogance, and petty tyranny becomes an essential safeguard of the individual.

This is the idea behind the Swedish invention of the ombudsman, whose job it is to protect the citizen against bureaucracy. What the ombudsman (or the postal inspector) does is not nearly so important as his existence. The knowledge that such a person exists, that he is independent, and that to be found remiss by him is likely to be painful, is a powerful deterrent. He cannot prevent the subversion of freedom by dictatorship. But he can curb the erosion of liberty through thoughtlessness, laziness, carelessness, and arrogance. He forces officialdom to think before it callously treats the individual as a "case." He will not make rude men polite. But he may make thoughtless men a little considerate.

One of the rights of the individual the ombudsman needs to guard the most jealously—and against all organizations—is the right to privacy. To be sure, no such right ever existed. In the communities of yesterday, the tribe, the village, the small town, privacy was unknown. A hermit in his cave was the only man who ever enjoyed privacy. Everybody else was public in all his actions and in all his circumstances—his thoughts, at best, were private. Even the greatest men of earlier times had no privacy. Indeed nothing less private could possibly be imagined than the life of the king of yesterday. Compared to the total lack of privacy Louis XIV had to put up with, even the glare of television cameras in which the modern ruler lives seems private.

Privacy is a boon of the Industrial Revolution and of a middle-class society. The number of people who really want privacy is probably small. Yet in a world of powerful organizations, it is a necessary safeguard of freedom. Protection of the citizens' privacy is one of the important political innovations we need. The question should always be asked: "Is the knowledge about the individual necessary?" If the answer is "no," it should be denied—even if the individual is perfectly willing to grant it. Privacy is not an individual privilege but a social need. There should therefore be a way to stop the gathering of information about individuals unless the social need can be shown to be paramount.

That we can put all the information—and misinformation—about people on computer memories is not the reason for our concern with privacy. The computer memory is only the mechanical expression of the organizational fact. Organizations operate on information, and therefore always try to gather as much as they can. The line between the information the organization truly needs, which therefore is justly "affected with the public interest," and the citizen's privacy, which is essential to his freedom, needs to be established, and reaffirmed again and again.

In a pluralist society there are neither "good guys" nor "bad guys" among organizations. All are needed, yet all are capable of degeneration. All are threatened by the bureaucratic disease that subordinates the true rationale of the institution—the satisfaction of an individual need or want—to the procedure, inertia, and convenience of its bureaucracy. The ombudsman is therefore needed in and against all organizations. He is needed to champion the individual against management in the business corporation, but also against the labor union, whatever the latter's claim to "represent the workers." He is needed in and against the government agency, but also in and against the university. The ombudsman is, so to speak, the hygiene of organizations—or at least their toothbrush.

All this is really implied in the general proposition that each organization, the government agency included, must be held to its own specific task and must be forced to keep its authority, as well as its responsibility, within the narrow and strictly interpreted limits of the task. For a pluralist society, strict adherence to specific purpose and narrow boundaries is the first law of liberty.

Businesses, no matter who owns them, should stick to providing economic goods and services in the expectation of economic returns. Universities should stick to advancing and teaching knowledge and to making it effective. The military should stick to the defense of the nation. No doubt it is tempting to have business take on "social responsibilities"—and gratifying to the businessmen to be invited to do so. It is tempting for the Department of Defense to apply its fantastic purchasing power to the reform of education (as Mr. McNamara proposed while Secretary of Defense), and especially tempting for the university to play universal aunt to every community need. But no matter how well meant, it is irresponsibility. It is usurpation. It goes beyond the authority for which the institution exists. It goes beyond the task whose fulfillment is the sole reason for its authority.

Pluralist societies do not degenerate into tyranny because of the power lust of the barons. This is easily curbed by other barons. The Europe of Charlemagne degenerated because abbots and bishops, i.e., the good, saintly men in a violent and wicked society, took upon themselves "social responsibilities" that were none of their business, to wit, the administration of justice. This only meant that the mighty and wicked, the great barons, had no opposition when they took the prerogative of justice by force from the abbots.

The rise of England to greatness, historians have long agreed, rested in large degree on the control of justice by the Crown. Governing England by right of conquest, the Plantagenet kings—otherwise no models of virtue or effectiveness—never allowed anyone else to take over the administration of justice. The difference between England and the European continent did not lie in the assertion of judicial autonomy by archbishops. The difference was that Thomas à Becket's claim to "social responsibility" for justice was put down—brutally, cravenly, by assassination, but effectively. What the kings of England knew was that one cannot grant authority to one power within pluralist society without granting it to others. One cannot grant it to archbishops in respect to their flock without having barons grab it without any pretense to "social responsibility."

We will have to learn again that power we grant to one pluralist body, e.g., the government agency, will in the end be demanded by all the others as well. If we do not want this to happen, we had better deny the power to any of them, including the government agency, the university, or any other "good guy" of political folklore. We will have to learn that all organizations are tools of society, each "good" for a specific purpose, each a menace beyond it.

So far, we have been talking about what the Germans used to call the *Rechtsstaat:* a political society in which the individual is protected against abuse of power on the part of authority. We have been talking of providing for the individual a preserve on which he will not be hunted down by organization, a "national park" outside of organization, so to speak, in which he will be undisturbed in his "natural habitat."

But this *freedom from* the abuse of power is not enough for a free society. A free society rests on the *freedom to* make responsible decisions.

Modern organization frees the individual to move out of the narrow and tightly restricted environment of tribe, village, and small town. It is the modern organization that is creating the opportunities for educated people to put knowledge to work and to get paid for it—and paid very well. But these benefits impose on the individual the burden of decision. They impose on him responsibility for what he wants to be and what he wants to become.

They also impose on him responsibility for what the organization should be and should become. What then should the individual demand of organization? And what must he do himself to make organization serve his ends? We will have to learn to demand of organization that it provide status and function to the individual.* But of ourselves we will have to demand that we learn how to use organization as opportunity for our own accomplishments and achievements.

The young are right when they protest against the tendency of organization to look upon an individual as a tool. But they are wrong when they blame organization for this. They have never asked themselves: "How can I make this or that organization serve *my* end and *my* needs?" "How can I make it enable *me* to perform, to achieve, to contribute?"

That the young rebel against being "inputs" to the computer is understandable. But the clever demonstrations in which they dress up as punch cards and parade with the slogan, "Don't fold, don't mutilate, don't spindle" miss the point. That's what cards are for. The question is: "How can we use the computer and its cards as tools for individual ends?" For to do this one has to understand a little bit about the computer—though not much more than that one can always pull out the plug and stop it (something the fanciful myths about computers taking over the world tend to overlook). Then one sees right away that the computer, for those who understand anything about it, is emancipation for the individual. The purpose of the computer is to enable us not to spend time on "controls," but to use the time for tasks that require perception, imagination, human relations, and creativity—the tasks in which the young rebels profess to believe.

---

* On this see my book *The New Society* (New York: Harper & Row, 1950).

This is only one illustration. Modern organization makes demands on the individual to learn something he has never been able to do before: to use organization intelligently, purposefully, deliberately, responsibly. If he runs away from this task and its decisions, organization will indeed become the master. If the individual accepts this responsibility, he will be free and in control.

Organizations themselves see this only dimly. Yet we talk today increasingly about the "free-form" organization as alone appropriate to knowledge work—in business, as well as in the military, the university, and government service. This is an organization in which discipline shifts to the individual. What controls is not rank but the task. For people who believe that true love consists of being promiscuous (as the very young have always tended to believe), this is, of course, still "restraint." What it really is, however, is responsibility.

To make the society of organizations a free society requires acceptance of responsibility by the individual, above all, acceptance of responsibility for contribution—his own, as well as those of organization. This is frightening, and not only to the young. But it is not particularly new. We have known all along that freedom is responsibility, and not license.

Young people in the society of organizations need systematic information how to make organization serve their own purposes, values, and aspirations. They will have to learn organization as their forefathers learned farming. It is the mark of a mature person to ask: "What do I want to get out of life?"—and to know that one gets out only as much as one puts in. Tomorrow it will be the mark of a free person to ask: "What do I get out of organizations?"—and to know that he gets out only as much as he puts in.

To make our society function requires that we know how to manage, i.e., how to obtain organizational performance through the work of the individual. To make our society free will also require that the individual learn how to manage organization—how to make organization and his job in it serve his ends, his values, his desire to achieve.

A society needs to be able to allow the individual to opt out and lead a "private life." But this is not freedom. This is indifference. In a free society, the citizen takes responsibility, above all, for his society and its institutions. In the society of organizations, the pluralist society of our time, this is a different task from that of the eighteenth century. Indeed the political tradition of the eighteenth century, the tradition of Locke, is clearly at its end. But the society of organizations may offer greater opportunities for meaningful, effective, responsible freedom than earlier society. Whether they will be realized depends on what *we* do rather than on what "they," the institutions do.

We face a period of hard new thinking on the political structure of society and on the position and role of the individual in it. What we have so far is a new pluralism, a new society of organizations. What we need is a new individualism, a new responsibility.*

---

* *The Age of Discontinuity*, pp. 243-60.

Part 6

A SHORT STORY: AN ALLEGORY OF MAN AND FREEDOM

William Sansom

William Sansom (1912–   ) was born in England and has spent the bulk of his life traveling and writing. Much of his work is surrealistic and creates a mood where reality is difficult to separate from illusion. In "The Long Sheet" captives are placed in four steel rooms and told that they can gain their freedom when a long wet sheet in each cell has been wrung dry. Within this apparently simple motif Sansom analyzed the variety of reactions of the inmates to the challenge of freedom. The reader will find a partial reflection of himself in the attitudes and actions of the captives. In a startling conclusion Sansom projects yet another view of the meaning of freedom.

The Long Sheet

Have you ever wrung dry a wet cloth; wrung it bone-white dry—with only the grip of your fingers and the muscles of your arms? If you have done this, you will understand better the situation of the captives at Device Z when the warders set them the task of the long sheet.

You will remember how, having stretched the cloth between your hands, you begin by twisting one end—holding the other firmly so that the water is corkscrewed from its hiding place. At first the water spurts out easily, but later you will find yourself screwing with both hands in different directions, whitening your knuckles, straining every fiber of your diaphragm—and all to extract the smallest drop of moisture! The muscle of your arm swells like an egg—yet the wet drop remains a pinhead! As you work, the cloth will gradually change from a gray color to the whiteness of dried bone, yet even then the cloth will be wet! Still you will knot your muscles, still you will wrench away at the furtive damp. Then—at last!—you

Reprinted from William Sansom, "The Long Sheet," *Fireman Flower* (New York: Vanguard Press, 1945), pp. 125-37, by permission of The Hogarth Press, London, and Elaine Greene Ltd.

will believe the cloth to be dry . . . but in the next second the tip of a finger will quiver tragically as it touches some cold, hidden veil of damp clinging deep down in the interlaced threads.

Such, then, was the task of the captives. They were placed in a long steel box of a room with no windows and no doors. The room was some six feet wide and six feet high, but it ran one hundred feet in length. It resembled thus a rectangular tunnel with no entrance and no exit, yet the sensation inside was not really that of a tunnel. For instance, a quantity of light flowed through thick glass panels set at intervals along the ceiling; these were the skylights, and through these the captives had been dropped into the box. Again, the impression of living in a tunnel was offset by a system of cubicle walls that separated the captive into groups. These cubicle walls were made from the same riveted steel as the main walls: there was no communication from cubicle to cubicle except through a half-foot of space left between the top of the wall and the ceiling. Thus each group of captives occupied, as it were, a small room. There were twenty-two captives. They were grouped in unequal number within four cubicles.

Through the entire length of this system, raised three feet from the ground, passing through the very center of each room, ran a long wound sheet. It was made from coarse white linen bundled into a loose cylinder of cloth some six inches in diameter.

When the captives were first thrown into their cubicles, the long sheet was heavy with water. The warders had soaked the material so thoroughly that in the folds the water had gathered into lakes. The warders then issued their instructions. The captives were to wring the sheet dry. It would not do to wring the sheet to what we would normally call a "dry" state—as of clothes ready for airing. On the contrary—this sheet must be purged of every moisture. It must be wrung as dry as a bone. This, the warders concluded, might take a long time. It might even take months of hard work. In fact, they had taken special care to treat the linen so that it would be durable over a lengthy period. But when the task was finally completed, then the men and women would be granted their freedom. They would be released.

As the grave faces of the warders disappeared and the glass skylights slid shut, the captives smiled for the first time. For months they had lived with the fear of death, they had shrunk in ceaseless apprehension of the terrible devices that awaited them. And now that future had devolved into the wringing of a simple sheet! A long sheet, it was true, but child's play in comparison with what they had expected. Thus they sank to the steel floor in relief. Few laid a hand on the sheet that day.

But after three months the captives began to realize the true extent of their task. By this time each group in each cubicle had wrung the worst water from their section of the sheet. Yet with all their sweating and straining they could not rid the cloth of its last dampness.

It was apparent that the warders had no intention of presenting them with a simple task. For through vents near the roof, hot steam was injected mechanically into the cubicles as long as daylight lasted. This steam naturally moistened the sheet afresh. The steam was so regulated that it hindered rather than prevented the fulfillment of the wringing. Thus there was always less steam entering than moisture wrung from the sheet at a normal rate of working. The steam injection merely meant that for every ten drops of water wrung seven new drops would settle upon the sheet, so that eventually the captives would still be able to wring the sheet dry. The device of the warders was introduced solely to complicate the task. It seemed that the warders were acting in two ways; daily they encouraged the efforts of the captives with promises of release, but daily they turned on the steam cocks.

In the cubicles the air was thick with steam. It was the air of a laundry, where steam catches in the throat, where it is sometimes difficult to breathe, where the smell of hot, wet cloth sickens the heart. The steel walls sweated. Condensed water trickled in winding trails down the gray plate. Beads of moisture clustered at the rivet heads. The long sheet spattered a few drops into the central gutter in the floor as the captives twisted against time. Both men and women worked half-naked. Since the sheet was positioned three feet from the ground, they were forced to stoop. If they sat at their work, then their arms grew numb in the raised attitude at which they had to be maintained. There was nothing for it but to stoop. In the hot air they sweated, yet they dared not lean over the sheet for fear their sweat should fall on the hungry cloth. Their muscles knotted, their backs cried out as they twisted. The end was far, but there was an end. That meant that there was hope. This knowledge lent fire to the struggling ambition that lived in their human hearts. They worked.

Yet some were not always equal to the task.

ROOM THREE—
THOSE WHO SOUGHT OUTSIDE

There were four rooms. Take Room Three. This housed five people—two married couples and a young Serbian grocer. All five of them wanted freedom. They worked earnestly at their task. That the task was in essence unproductive did not worry them. At least, it would produce their freedom. It was thus artificially productive. These five people set about the problem in a normal businesslike way. Previously, they had been used to habitual hours, a life of steady formula. This was now applied to the new business of wringing. Set hours were allotted to each person. It was as if they commuted regularly from their suburbia (the steel sleeping corner) to the office (the long sheet). They worked in relays, in four-hour stretches throughout the day and night.

However, as I have said, they were not equal to the task. The framework of habit overcame them. Like so many who live within a steady, comfortable routine, they allowed the routine around the work to predominate in importance above the work itself. They arrived at the long sheet punctually, and with consciences thus satisfied, they put insufficient effort into the actual work. Furthermore, when they had fulfilled the routine assiduously for a period, one or the other would congratulate his conscience and really believe that he deserved a "little relaxation", and he would take the afternoon off. Such was the force of his emphasis on obedience to the letter that he was convinced the law would not suffer. Thus the real work of wringing suffered. New moisture crept in where his hands were weak. These people had set about the quest for freedom in the right way, but they were unhappily convinced of their righteousness.

. . . One of the women became pregnant. Her child was born in the steam box, but, under the influence of Room Three's routine, that child could never be free.

The influence, the constriction, and the hopeless task of the parents would keep the child in the steam box for life. The child would never have the chance to learn to wring with effect.

ROOM TWO— THOSE WHO SOUGHT IN AND OUT AND AROUND

In another of the rooms—Room Two—there were five men. Their names and their professions do not matter. It is how they attacked the long sheet that matters. They attacked it in five different ways.

Here were five individuals, five who were forced by the set of their minds to approach their problems in various ways of their own. Day after day they labored in the hot, damp steel cubicle, each twisting the long cylinder of cloth with different reasonings.

One man had been frightened by a sheet when he was young. On some indefinite day of his childhood, a new nurse had appeared. Her black eyes had burned with a powerful scorn; her small lascivious teeth and huge drooping cheeks had threatened him in the candlelight. On her first day the new nurse had made a little white monster from a white sheet. It had two little heads and a shapeless flowing body. The little heads were sharp, and always bobbing. The nurse had come silently into the night nursery when it was dark. Lighting a candle on the floor behind the end of the bed, she had quietly raised her little white monster so that the boy could just see it above his toes. Then she had begun a strident sing-song crowing, like the harsh crowing of Punch.[1] The boy had awaked to this sound, and had seen the sharp bobbing heads of the little monster.

Now, some thirty years later, the man has forgotten the scene, but somehow his hands cannot touch the long sheet without a great sensation of uneasiness. Consequently, he is forever making excuses to avoid working on the sheet. He feigns illness . . . He has mutilated his hands . . . Oh, there is no end to the devices the fellow had invented from his sadness! But whatever he does cannot eradicate the awful uneasiness that clouds the far reaches of his mind. At the moment of writing, this man is still in the steel cubicle. He will never be free.

Another of the men in Room Two was a simple quiet fellow. The others took no interest in him, he was too simple a fellow. Yet a most amazing thing—his section of the sheet was white and quite dry. There was a good reason for this. Without any conscious knowledge, without planning and scheming, he had naturally gone at his wringing the good way. He was accustomed to wring sitting astride the cloth. In this position, his legs squeezed at the cloth too. Thus, without questioning, he surrendered his *whole* body to the task. His heart, too, for he was such a simple fellow. This man's sheet was dry. But the others never even noticed. He was such a simple fellow.

There was one man in Room Two whose *métier* in life had always been the short cut. As previously in business, in love, in all relationships, he attempted to apply the short cut system to the most important task of all—the wringing of the long sheet. He tried out a great many tricks and petty deceptions. He blocked up the pipe through which the guards pumped the steam. The next morning, like a mushroom, another pipe had grown at the side of the first. He tried feigning

[1] *Punch,* a common character in English Punch-and-Judy or puppet shows.

madness. The warders threw buckets of cold water down through the skylight. Some of this water splashed on to the sheet, destroying a whole month's work. The other men nearly killed him for this. Once he bribed one of the warders to send him a pot of white enamel. With this he painted the sheet white. The enamel dried hard. The sheet seemed dry! But the next day the warders came to chip the enamel off. They punished him with a traveling hose jet. This jet traveled inconsequently about the room. To save the water hitting the sheet, the man had to intercept the jet with his body. He was kept running and jumping and squatting for a whole day—until toward evening he dropped exhausted and rolled into the central gutter. The warders, of course, can never be bribed.

Then there was another man who can best be described as a fumbler. He worked hard and earnestly. He was up at the wringing well before the others, he seldom lay down till long after the skylights were dark and the air cleared of steam. But he fumbled. His mind co-ordinated imperfectly with his body. Although he felt that he concentrated his whole effort, psychic and physical, on the job of wringing—his mind would wander to other things. He never knew that this happened, but his hands did. They stopped wringing, they wrung the wrong way—and the fatal drops of moisture accumulated. He could never understand this. He thought his mind was always on the job. But instead his mind settled too often on matters only near to the job, not the job in essence. For a small instance—his mind might wander to the muscle on his left forearm. He might see that it bulges at a downward screw of the wet linen. He watches this bulge as he works. The bulge then absorbs his interest to such an extent that he makes greater play with this left arm to stimulate further the bulge of muscle. In compensation the right arm slackens its effort. The wringing becomes uneven and inefficient. Yet all this time he himself in honesty believes that he is concentrating upon his job. The muscle is, in fact, part of the job. Yet it is only a facet, not the full perspective. He fumbles because he does not see clearly: and to wring dry the long sheet a man must give his whole thought in calm and complete clarity.

The fifth man in Room Two was a good worker: that is, he had found the way to wring effectively, and at times his portion of the sheet was almost dry. But he was perverted. This man liked to wring the sheet almost dry—then stand by and watch the steam settle into the folds once more! He liked to watch the fruits of his labor rot. In this way he freed himself from the task. He freed himself by attaining his object, and then treating it with the scorn he imagined it deserved. He felt himself master of the work—but in reality he never became the master of his true freedom. There was no purity in this man. His freedom was false.

ROOM FOUR—
THOSE WHO NEVER SOUGHT AT ALL

Room Number Four housed more captives than the others. Seven people were crowded into this one cell of steam and steel. There were three women, one girl of twelve, and three men. These people seldom did much work. They were a source of great disappointment to the warders. To these people the effort was not worth eventual freedom. The immensity of the task had long ago disheartened them. Their minds were not big enough to envisage the better future. They had enough. They had their breeding and their food. The state of life held no interest for them.

Vaguely, they would have preferred better conditions. But at the cost of toil and thought—no. These people were squalid and small. Their desire for freedom had been killed by a dull acceptance of their impotence. This also became true of the little girl of twelve. She had no alternative but to follow the others.

The warders never played their favorite trick on Room Four, for the simple reason that the trick would have had no effect. The trick was to release into the cells small squadrons of saturated birds. The birds flew into the cells and scattered water from their wings everywhere. The birds flew in all directions and the captives ran wildly here and there in hysterical efforts to trap them before they splashed water onto the sacred sheet. The warders considered that the element of chance implicit in these birds was a healthy innovation. Otherwise, life for the captives would have been too ordered. There must be risk, said the warders. And so from time to time, with no warning, they injected these little wet birds and the captives hastened to protect the purity of their work against the interference of fate. If they could not catch the birds in time, they learnt in this manner how to accept misfortune: and in patience they redoubled their efforts to retrieve the former level of their work.

But into Room Four the birds never flew. The trick would never have affected the inhabitants, who lived at the low ebb of misfortune already. Perhaps the real tragedy of these dispirited people was not their own misfortune, to which they had grown accustomed, but that their slackness had its effect on those whose ambitions were pure and strong. The sheet was so wet in Room Four that the water seeped through into Room One. And in Room One lived the most successful of all the captives.

ROOM ONE—
THOSE WHO SOUGHT INSIDE

There were five of them in cubicle One. Four men and one woman. They were successful no more for their method of wringing than for their attitude toward wringing. At first, when they had been dropped through the skylight, when they saw the long sheet, when they slowly accustomed themselves to the idea of what lay before them, they were profoundly shocked. Unlike the others, they thought death preferable to such senseless and unproductive labor. But they were good people. Soon they had passed through and rejected the various phases experienced and retained by the other rooms. They had known the defeat of Room Four, the individual terrors and escapes of Room Two, the veneer of virtue beneath which the inhabitants of Room Three purred with such alarming satisfaction. No, it was not so very long before these good people saw beyond the apparent and thenceforth set themselves to work with body and soul, gently but with strength, humbly yet fearlessly, towards the only end of value—freedom.

First these people said "Unproductive? The long sheet of senseless drudgery? Yes—but why not? In whatever other sphere of labor could we ever have produced ultimately anything? It is not the production that counts, but the life lived in the spirit during production. Production, the tightening of the muscles, the weaving of the hands, the pouring forth of shaped materials—this is only an employment for the nervous body, the dying legacy of the hunter's will to movement. Let the hands weave, but at the same time let the spirit search. Give the long sheet its rightful place—and concentrate on a better understanding of the freedom that is our real object?"

At that time, they saw to it that the sheet was wrung efficiently. They arranged a successful rota system. They tried various methods and positions with their hands. Examining every detail, they selected in every way the best approach. They did not overtax themselves. They did not hurry themselves. They worked with a rhythmic resilience, conserving this energy for the exertion of that. They allowed no extremes. They applied themselves with sincerity and a good will.

Above all they had faith. Their attitude was broad—but led in one direction. Their endeavor was freedom. They learned neither work nor weakness. These things did not exist for them; their existence was a material through which they could achieve, by calm and sensitive understanding, the goal of perfect freedom.

Gradually these people achieved their end. In spite of the steam, in spite of the saturated birds, in spite of the vaporous contagion seeping through from the room of the defeated, in spite of the long hours and the heat and the squared horizon of rusting steel—their spirit prevailed and they achieved the purity they sought. One day, seven years later, the wet gray sheet dawned a bright white—dry as desert ivory, dry as marble dust.

They called up through the skylight to the warders. The grave faces appeared. Coldly the warders regarded the white sheet. There were nods of approbation.

"Freedom?" said the captives.

The guards brought out their great hoses and doused the white sheet sodden gray with a huge pressure of water.

"You already have it," they answered. "Freedom lies in an attitude of the spirit. There is no other freedom." And the skylights silently closed.